The New Testament

The New Testament

A Student's Introduction

THIRD EDITION

Stephen L. Harris

California State University, Sacramento

MAYFIELD PUBLISHING COMPANY

Mountain View, California

London · Toronto

Library of Congress Cataloging-in-Publication Data

Harris, Stephen L.
    The New Testament: a student's introduction / Stephen L. Harris.
    —3rd ed.
        p.   cm.
    Includes bibliographical references and index.
    ISBN 0–7674–0014–3
    1. Bible. N.T.—Introductions. 2. Bible. N.T.—Textbooks.
    I. Title.
    BS2330.2.H326   1998
    225.6′1—dc21   97–51733
                                                                    CIP

Manufactured in the United States of America

10   9   8   7   6   5   4   3

Mayfield Publishing Company
1280 Villa Street
Mountain View, CA 94041

Sponsoring editor, Kenneth King; production editor, Julianna Scott Fein; manuscript editor, Thomas
L. Briggs; design manager, Susan Breitbard; text and cover designer, Claire Seng-Niemoeller; cover
art, *Annunciation,* Fra Angelico, © Erich Lessing/Art Resource, NY; art manager, Amy Folden;
illustrators, Alice and Will Thiede, Carto-Graphics, and Judith Ogus; photo researcher, Brian Pecko;
manufacturing manager, Randy Hurst. The text was set in 10/12 ACaslon Regular by ColorType and
printed on acid-free 45# Chromatone Matte, PMS 647, by Banta Book Group.

Excerpt from "Hymn of Isis" from M. Eugene Boring, Klaus Berger, Carsten Colpe, eds., *Hellenistic
Commentary to the New Testament,* Abingdon Press, 1995, pp. 272–273. Used with permission of the
publisher.   Excerpts from James H. Charlesworth, *The Old Testament Pseudepigrapha.* Copyright
© 1983, 1985 by James H. Charlesworth. Used with permission of Doubleday, a division of Bantam
Doubleday Dell Publishing Group, Inc.   Excerpts from the *Revised Standard Version of the Bible.*
Copyright © 1946, 1952, 1971 by the Division of Christian Education of the National Council of
the Churches of Christ in the USA. Used by permission.   Excerpts from the *New English Bible.*
Copyright © 1961, 1970 Oxford University Press and Cambridge University Press. Used with
permission of the publishers.   Excerpts from Robert J. Miller, *The Complete Gospels: Annotated
Scholars Version,* Second Edition, HarperSanFrancisco, 1994. Used with permission of Polebridge
Press, Santa Rosa, CA.

To Geoffrey Edwin and Jason Marc

Preface

Like its predecessors, the third edition of this introductory text is designed for students undertaking their first systematic study of the New Testament. The purpose of this revision is twofold: to familiarize readers with the content and major themes of each book of the New Testament and to acquaint them with the goals and methods of important biblical scholarship.

In general, this text's organization reflects the canonical order of the New Testament's twenty-seven books. After introducing material essential to understanding the historical and religious milieu in which Christianity originated, the text examines each New Testament document on a book-by-book basis, beginning with the four Gospels and their four diverse portraits of Jesus. Because the early Christian community placed the stories of Jesus first in its collection of sacred writings, New Testament editors accorded Jesus' teachings and deeds a centrality and preeminence that exerts an implicit control over the books that follow in the canon, from Acts' picture of the early church, to Paul's letters, to Revelation's vision of Jesus' climactic return. Honoring the New Testament sequence, this text emphasizes the Gospel accounts, adding to them an expanded chapter on modern scholarship's ongoing attempts to distinguish the Jesus of history from later theological interpretations of him.

As a guiding principle, this text allows each New Testament writer to speak for himself. The text makes no attempt to force the viewpoints of one writer to conform to those of another, nor does it advocate any denominational or sectarian program. In studying the different Gospel presentations of Jesus, students are encouraged to listen to the individual Gospel author's distinctive voice, to recognize that each Evangelist portrays Jesus according to his characteristic theology. Thus, Mark's "hidden" Messiah, revealed only in suffering and death, differs qualitatively from John's portrayal of Jesus as a virtually omniscient embodiment of divine Wisdom. Similarly, Matthew's picture of Jesus as a teacher of Torah righteousness sent "only to the house of Israel" is balanced by Luke's depiction of an Elijah-like prophet who becomes a universal "savior" and a model of service for Gentile (non-Jewish) nations.

Although united in their conviction that Jesus' life and death are crucial to humanity's relationship to God, the various New Testament authors reveal a rich diversity and range of thought in elucidating the theological meaning of the Christ event. Exploring the various canonical writers' personal expression of their faith offers a liberating approach to investigating the New Testament.

Because biblical scholarship continues to illuminate the cultural, social, and religious environment in which Christianity originated, the third edition incorporates fresh material in almost every section. Chapters 3, 4, and 5 have been revised to illustrate more clearly the multiplicity of Jewish beliefs in

Jesus' day, the struggle the Jewish community under-went to preserve its religious integrity in a sometimes hostile world, and the Hellenistic religious ideas that anticipated some Christian doctrines.

To help readers better comprehend the Greco-Roman context of first-century Christianity, the discussion has been expanded to include new material on the Olympian gods; on parallels in traditions about such heroes or deities as Asclepius, Dionysus, and Jesus; and on the growth of the Hellenistic ruler cult, a practice promoting the posthumous de-ification of historical figures such as Alexander the Great and some Roman emperors. A new section underscores different New Testament writers' con-trasting attitudes toward the Roman government, further illustrating the evolving interaction of social-political forces and religious responses.

Introducing students to the variety of scholarly methods used to analyze the Gospels' origin and de-velopment, chapter 6 now examines the role that oral tradition played in shaping traditions about Jesus, as well as recent studies of Q (the hypothetical Sayings Gospel), which many scholars believe was the first written collection of Jesus' words. A new chart shows the theoretical stages by which the four canonical Gospels gradually evolved into their present form. Although discussions of the Gospels (chapters 7–10) have been partly revised to incorporate recent schol-arship, the author's principle of allowing each indi-vidual Gospel author to speak for himself remains in place. In a new box comparing the last words of Jesus ascribed to him by all four Evangelists, it becomes evident that each Gospel writer presents Jesus' final speech as a summation of that writer's distinctive theological understanding of his subject.

Attracting an ever-growing public interest, mod-ern scholars' quest to recover the historical Jesus is covered in chapter 11, which provides a historical overview of the process, including recent critical re-sponses, both pro and con, to the controversial work of the Jesus Seminar. Illustrating some posi-tive results of current research, a new compilation of Jesus' teachings that scholars believe represents his authentic voice has been added.

The discussions of Paul, including his role in Acts, his crucial assumptions about cosmic duality,

and his lasting influence on Christian thought, have been partly revised. Paul's eschatology, which helped motivate both his theology and his mission-ary activities, is further clarified in an expanded coverage of 1 Thessalonians, the oldest surviving Christian document. There is also fuller coverage of the problem of pseudonymity in the New Testa-ment, with discussions of 2 Thessalonians and Colossians transferred to chapter 17, "Continuing the Pauline Tradition."

To facilitate student learning about significant is-sues in New Testament study, more than a dozen new boxes have been added containing mini-essays on selected topics, including the thematic organi-zation and structure of the New Testament; the transmission of New Testament manuscripts; the probable contents of Q; Mark's identification of Jesus as "Son of God" (paralleling the "Son of Man" box); additional examples of Matthew's edit-ing of Markan material; Matthew's use of "Hell" (Gehenna); a comparison of the "Great Feast" par-able in Matthew, Luke, and Thomas; the "I am" statements of Isis; and representative passages from noncanonical writings, such as the Gospel of Peter and the Infancy Gospel (Protoevangelium) of James.

In preparing this third edition, every care has been taken to make the book a more useful study re-source. A new and simplified time line, revised chronological charts, completely redesigned maps, and a new table of contents for maps and figures will help orient students to historical causes and effects, providing valuable historical perspective. Additional important terms have been set in boldface type and incorporated in the Glossary; bibliographies have been updated with the latest scholarly publica-tions; many of the "Key Theme" summaries have been revised, and the end-of-chapter questions have been largely reorganized and partly rewritten, dis-tinguishing factual "Questions for Review" from "Questions for Discussion and Reflection."

Students wishing to pursue a particular subject may consult a list of major reference works in the "Recommended Readings" appearing at the end of each chapter. Available at most college and univer-sity libraries, these references include the work of leading scholars whose research has illuminated the field of New Testament study. The author's indebtedness to these scholars is gratefully acknowledged by their inclusion in the bibliographies.

Acknowledgments   I am grateful to the colleagues who have used earlier editions of this text and generously offered commentary and advice for improving its quality and usefulness in the classroom: David T. Landry, University of St. Thomas; Robert J. Miller, Midway College; Mikeal C. Parsons, Baylor University; Richard L. Schebera, St. Louis University; and Ronald L. Tyler, Pepperdine University.

I am also grateful to Jim Bull, the original sponsoring editor, and his successor at Mayfield Publishing Company, Ken King, for his oversight of the project. I would also like to thank Julianna Scott Fein, the production editor, for her expertise, good nature, and encouragement, and Tom Briggs for his unusually skillful copyediting of the manuscript.

Finally, I would like to express my appreciation to my friend and colleague Brad Nystrom for his expert and readable translation of Cleanthes' "Hymn to Zeus."

Contents

Chapter 7

Mark's Portrait of Jesus:
The Hidden Messiah and Eschatological Judge   101

Chapter 8

Matthew's Portrait of Jesus:
The Great Teacher   129

PART V   GENERAL LETTERS AND A VISION OF END TIME   321

Chapter 18   *General Letters on Faith and Behavior:*
Hebrews and the Catholic Epistles   *321*

Chapter 19   *Continuing the Apocalyptic Hope:*
The Book of Revelation   *339*

Illustrations

CHAPTER 1

An Overview of the New Testament

Here begins the Gospel of Jesus Christ. Mark 1:1

Key Themes The New Testament consists of twenty-seven Greek documents — Gospels, a church history, letters, and an apocalypse (revelation) — which the early Christian community added to the Hebrew Scriptures (Old Testament). Although the New Testament books were composed between about 50 and 150 C.E., many were not generally accepted as part of the **canon** (official list of church-approved writings) for several centuries. The first list that corresponds exactly to the present New Testament appeared in 367 C.E.

People read the New Testament for an almost infinite variety of reasons. Some read to satisfy their curiosity about the origins of one of the great world religions. They seek to learn more about the social and historical roots of Christianity, a faith that began in the early days of the Roman Empire and that today commands the allegiance of nearly 2 billion people, approximately a third of the global population. Because Christianity bases its most characteristic beliefs on the New Testament writings, it is to this source that the historian and social scientist must turn for information about the religion's birth and early development.

Most people, however, probably read the New Testament for more personal reasons. Many readers search its pages for answers to some of life's important ethical and religious questions. For hundreds of millions of Christians, the New Testament sets the only acceptable standards of personal belief and behavior (see box 1.1). Readers attempt to discover authoritative counsel on issues that modern science or speculative philosophy cannot resolve, such as the nature of God, the survival of the soul after death, and the ultimate destiny of humankind.

Jesus of Nazareth, the central character of the New Testament, provides many people with the most compelling reason to read the book. As presented by the Gospel writers, he is like no other figure in history. His teachings and pronouncements have an unequaled power and authority. As an itinerant Jewish prophet, healer, and teacher in early first-century Palestine, the historical Jesus — in terms of the larger Greco-Roman world around him — lived a relatively obscure life and died a criminal's death at the hands of Roman executioners. His followers' conviction that he subsequently rose from the grave and appeared to them launched a vital new faith that eventually swept the Roman Empire. In little more than three centuries after Jesus' death, Christianity became Rome's official state religion.

Clearly, the New Testament authors present Jesus as much more than an ordinary man. The Gospel of John pictures him as the human expression of divine wisdom, the **Word** of God made flesh. Jesus' teaching about the eternal world of spirit is thus definitive, for he is depicted as having descended from heaven to earth to reveal ultimate truth. About 300 years after Jesus' crucifixion, Christian leaders assembled at

1

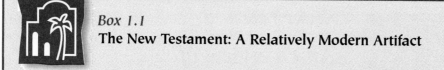

Box 1.1
The New Testament: A Relatively Modern Artifact

A printed, bound copy of the New Testament that readers can hold in their hands is a relatively modern development. Until the fourth century C.E., the New Testament did not even exist as a coherent entity—a single volume containing the twenty-seven books in its now-familiar table of contents. Before then, believers, and even church leaders, had access to individual Gospels or subcollections, such as compilations of Paul's letters, but not to a comprehensive edition of the entire text.

Even after Rome made Christianity the state religion and imperial patronage encouraged the production of an official Christian scripture, New Testaments were extremely rare. Not only were manuscript copies prohibitively expensive, the vast majority of people in the Roman Empire could neither read nor write. It was not until the printing press was invented in the fifteenth century C.E., permitting the eventual mass production of Bibles, that the New Testament as we know it came into being.

the town of Nicaea in Asia Minor to decree that Jesus is not only the Son of God but God himself.

Given the uniquely high status that orthodox Christianity accords the person of Jesus, the New Testament accounts of his life have extraordinary value. Jesus' words recorded in the Gospels are seen not merely as the utterances of a preeminently wise teacher but also as the declarations of the Being who created and sustains the universe. The hope of encountering "God's thoughts," of discovering otherwise unattainable knowledge of unseen realities, gives many believers a powerful incentive for studying the New Testament.

What Is the New Testament?

When asked to define the New Testament, many students respond with such traditional phrases as "the Word of God" or "Holy Scripture." These responses are really confessions of faith that the Christian writings are qualitatively different from ordinary books. Some students express surprise that non-Christian religions also have **scriptures**—documents that these groups consider sacred and authoritative (having the power to command belief and prescribe behavior). In fact, many other world religions possess holy books that their adherents believe to represent a divine revelation to humankind. Hindus cherish the Vedas, the Upan-

ishads, and the Bhagavadgita; Buddhists venerate the recorded teachings of Buddha, the "enlightened one"; and followers of Islam (meaning "submission to the will of Allah") revere the Qur'an (Koran) as transmitting the one true faith. Ideally, we approach all sacred writings with a willingness to appreciate the religious insights they offer and to recognize their connection with the cultural and historical context out of which they grew.

Given the historical fact that the New Testament is a book written by and for believers in Jesus' divinity, in practice many readers tend to approach it as they do no other work of ancient literature. Whether or not they are practicing Christians, students commonly bring to the New Testament attitudes and assumptions very different from those they employ when reading other works of antiquity. The student usually has little trouble bringing an open or neutral mind to exploring stories about the Greek and Roman gods. One can read Homer's *Iliad,* an epic poem celebrating the Greek heroes of the Trojan War, without any particular emotional involvement with the Homeric gods. However, this objective attitude toward supernatural beings is rare among persons studying the New Testament.

To be fair to the New Testament, we will want to study it with the same open-mindedness we grant to the writings of any world religion. This call for objectivity is a challenge to all of us, for we live in a culture that defines its highest values largely in terms of the Judeo-Christian tradition. We can most fully appreciate the New Testament if we begin by recognizing that it developed in, and partly in reaction to, a society profoundly different from our own. It will help, too, if we remember that reading the Bible in church as part of an act of worship is necessarily a different experience from studying it analytically in a classroom. Each situation requires an appropriate mode of appreciation. By examining the New Testament in the complex social environment in which it originated and by attempting to discover the historical concerns and purposes of its authors, we can free ourselves to hear the voices of early Christianity speaking as meaningfully to us today as they did to their first audience almost 1900 years ago.

The New Testament and the Hebrew Bible

If someone from another planet asked us to define the New Testament, describing it as a divine revelation would not be a very enlightening response. The extraterrestrial might point out that the scriptures of virtually all the world's principal religions make that claim. It is more useful to begin by stating exactly what the book itself is. Although sometimes published as a separate book, the New Testament typically is printed as the second part of a larger volume containing both the Hebrew and Christian Scriptures and known as the Bible. Derived from the term *biblia* (meaning "little books"), the word **Bible** is an appropriate title because this volume is really a collection of many different books. An anthology of religious documents composed over a time span exceeding 1000 years, the first section of the Christian Bible is much longer and more diverse than the New Testament. Often called the Old Testament, this part is properly known as the **Hebrew Bible** (see figure 1.1). Written largely in the Hebrew language (some late books were composed in a related tongue called **Aramaic**), the Hebrew Bible records the history of the Jewish people's relationship with their God. Also called the **Tanak**, the Hebrew Bible contains many different types of literature, ranging from lyric poetry to legal material to historical narrative to prophecy (see boxes 1.2 and 1.3).

At the time of Jesus and the first several generations of his followers, this collection was the only written authority for both Jews and Christians. When the New Testament writers refer to "Scripture" or "the Law and the Prophets," they mean the Hebrew Bible, although they commonly use a Greek translation of the Hebrew text known as the **Septuagint (LXX).**

TESTAMENT AND COVENANT

The term *New Testament* is intimately connected with the Hebrew Scriptures. In biblical terms, **testament** is a synonym for **covenant,** which means an agreement, contract, or bond. To appreciate the New Testament concept of the bond between God and humanity, we must review briefly the older Hebrew tradition. The Hebrew Bible is largely a meditation on the consequences of God's making a covenant with the nation of Israel, whom the Deity chose to be his representative people on earth. Exodus, the second book of the Hebrew Bible, recounts the solemn ceremony in which the Israelites conclude their central covenant with **Yahweh** (the sacred personal name of Israel's God) (Exod. 19–20; 24). Under the terms of the **Mosaic Covenant** (so called because the Israelite leader **Moses** acts as the covenant mediator between Yahweh and the people), Israel swears to uphold all the laws and commandments that Yahweh enjoins upon them. These legal injunctions are contained in the Books of Exodus, Leviticus, Numbers, and Deuteronomy. Together with the Book of Genesis, which serves as a general introduction to the giving of the Mosaic Covenant, this section of the Hebrew Bible is known as the **Torah** (see figure 1.2). Meaning "law," "teaching," or "instruction," the Torah is also referred to as the **Pentateuch** (meaning "five scrolls" or books).

In the Torah, Yahweh's protection of Israel was made contingent upon the people's faithfulness in keeping Yahweh's Law as handed down through Moses (Deut. 28–29). Some of Israel's prophets concluded that the people had been so unfaithful to the Mosaic Covenant that eventually Yahweh regarded it as broken. Writing about 600 years before the time of Jesus, the prophet Jeremiah promised that Yahweh would replace the old Mosaic

Figure 1.1 A page from Genesis. This exquisitely decorated manuscript of the Hebrew Bible was produced in Provence, probably Avignon, about 1422. (© The Pierpont Morgan Library/Art Resource, NY)

Box 1.2
Hebrew Bible Canon and Apocrypha

TORAH

Genesis

Exodus

Leviticus

Numbers

Deuteronomy

PROPHETS

Former Prophets

    Joshua

    Judges

    Samuel (1 and 2)

    Kings (1 and 2)

Latter Prophets

    Isaiah

    Jeremiah

    Ezekiel

The Twelve (Minor Prophets)

    Hosea

    Joel

    Amos

    Obadiah

    Jonah

    Micah

    Nahum

    Habakkuk

    Zephaniah

    Haggai

    Zechariah

    Malachi

WRITINGS

Psalms

Job

Proverbs

Ruth

Song of Solomon

Ecclesiastes

Lamentations

Esther

Daniel

Ezra-Nehemiah

Chronicles (1 and 2)

DEUTEROCANONICAL BOOKS (APOCRYPHA)

1 Esdras

2 Esdras

Tobit

Judith

The Rest of the Chapters of the Book of Esther

The Wisdom of Solomon

Ecclesiasticus, or the Wisdom of Jesus Son of Sirah

Baruch

A Letter of Jeremiah

The Song of the Three

Daniel and Susanna

Daniel, Bel, and the Snake

The Prayer of Manasseh

1 Maccabees

2 Maccabees

agreement with a "new covenant [testament]" (Jer. 31:31).

The Gospel writers believed that Jesus instituted the promised New Covenant at the **Last Supper** he held with his disciples. "And he took the cup, and gave thanks, and gave it to them, saying Drink ye all of it: For this is my blood of the new testament..."

(Matt. 26:27–28, King James Version). The adjective *new*, not present in the earliest manuscripts, was added later to emphasize the change in God's relationship with humankind. (Most modern translations, including the Revised Standard Version, the Jerusalem Bible, and the New English Bible, omit the interpolated "new" and use "covenant"

> ### Box 1.3
> ## Organization of the Hebrew and Christian Greek Scriptures
>
> The contents of the New Testament are arranged in a way that approximates the order of the Hebrew Bible, which is also called the Tanak, a term whose consonants represent the three principal divisions of the Hebrew Scriptures: the *Torah* (Mosaic Law or instruction), the *Nevi'im* (Prophets), and the *Kethuvim* (Writings).
>
> | OLD COVENANT (TESTAMENT) | NEW COVENANT (TESTAMENT) |
> |---|---|
> | *T* *Torah* (five books of Moses) | Four Gospels (story of Jesus) |
> | *A* | |
> | *N* *Nevi'im* (Prophets) | |
> | Histories of Joshua–Kings | Book of Acts (church history) |
> | Books of the Prophets | Letters of Paul and other church leaders |
> | *A* | |
> | *K* *Kethuvim* (Writings) | Book of Hebrews, catholic epistles, and an |
> | Books of poetry, wisdom, and an | apocalypse (Revelation) |
> | apocalypse (Daniel) | |

instead of "testament" in this passage.) Believing themselves to be the people of the New Covenant with God, Christians eventually called their Gospels and other sacred writings the New Testament. The Hebrew Bible, which dealt with the older Mosaic Covenant, became known as the Old Testament. The Christian community, however, regarded both parts of the Bible as authoritative and suitable for religious instruction.

The Septuagint

Although the New Testament writers regarded the Hebrew Bible as their chief written authority, they did not quote from the original Hebrew text. Instead, they used a popular Greek translation of the Hebrew Bible that had been published in Alexandria, Egypt, during the last two and a half centuries B.C.E. (B.C.E. means "before the common era," a religiously neutral calendar that can be used by Jews, Christians, Muslims, and others. As a chronological symbol, it is the same as B.C., "before Christ." C.E., the "common era," is synonymous with A.D., "*anno domini*," Latin for "in the year of the Lord.")

According to one tradition, the Septuagint translation was the work of seventy-two Hebrew scholars who labored seventy-two days to produce seventy-two identical translations. Popularly known as the work of "the seventy" and called the Septuagint, this version became the standard biblical text for Greek-speaking Jews scattered throughout the Greco-Roman world. It was then adopted by Christians as their favored version of the Hebrew Scriptures and is the version cited most often in the New Testament.

Language and Literature of the New Testament

KOINĒ GREEK

The New Testament was written in the same kind of *koinē* (common) Greek as the Septuagint. The most widely spoken language of the early Christian era, *koinē* became the dominant tongue of the eastern Mediterranean region after the conquests of Alexander the Great (356–323 B.C.E.). Although less polished and elegant than the classical Greek of the great Athenian poets and philosophers, *koinē*

Figure 1.2 A Torah scroll. Copies of the Mosaic Torah are kept in every Jewish temple or synagogue. This elegant manuscript is approximately one-third the size of the standard Torah scroll. (© Jewish Museum, London)

was then spoken by so large a percentage of the population that it communicated far more effectively than Hebrew or Latin.

Most of the twenty-seven books of the New Testament were composed during the half century between about 50 and 100 C.E., although a few were written as late as the mid-second century C.E. The oldest surviving Christian writings are the letters of **Paul,** a Greek-educated Jew from **Tarsus,** a prosperous city in an eastern province of the Roman Empire (now southeast Turkey). Paul's letters span the dozen years between about 50 and 62 C.E. Most of the remaining books, including the four Gospels and the Book of Acts, were written somewhat later, between about 66 and 100 C.E. A few letters ascribed to some of Jesus' most eminent disciples and known collectively as the **catholic** (general) **epistles** appeared several decades after the turn of the first century.

NEW TESTAMENT LITERARY FORMS

The New Testament contains several different genres (categories) of literature, although it has considerably less variety than the Hebrew Bible. The contents are arranged not in the chronological order of their dates of composition, but according to their literary classification, beginning with the Gospels and ending with the Book of Revelation.

Gospels   The first four books are called **Gospels,** a term that translates the Greek word *euangelion* (good news). Designed to proclaim the "good news" about Jesus, the Gospels tell the story of Jesus' ministry, death, and resurrection. The term **Evangelist** refers to the writer of an *euangelion* (Gospel).

In the Greek-speaking world of New Testament times, *euangelion* commonly was used to denote public proclamations about the Roman emperor. The "good news" of the emperor's military victories, welfare policies, or elevation to the status of a god were typical examples of Roman political "evangelizing." Paul uses *euangelion* to describe his message about salvation through Jesus Christ. Matthew also employs it to denote Jesus' oral teaching (Matt. 4:23; 9:35; 24:14; 26:13). Mark, however, is apparently the first to use *euangelion* to describe a written work about Jesus' life. To distinguish *gospel,* an oral message, from *Gospel,* a literary work, we will capitalize the term when it refers to the written Gospel form.

The only literary genre the early Christians invented, the Gospel is a narrative—a story—about Jesus' deeds and teachings. Although the Gospels recount the actions and sayings of Jesus in ostensibly chronological order, they are not real biographies in the modern sense. They do not attempt to present a complete life of Jesus or to explain what forces—social, psychological, cultural, historical, or political—caused him to become the kind of man he was. Only two of the Gospels—Matthew and Luke—include traditions about Jesus' birth and infancy. None gives even a scrap of information about his formative years, education, associations, or other experiences that modern historians would regard as essential. Luke records a single incident of Jesus' youth, a pilgrimage from his hometown of Nazareth to Jerusalem, Judaism's holy city (Luke 2:22–40). But the Gospels tell us nothing about what happened to Jesus between the ages of twelve and "about thirty" (Luke 3:23). All four concentrate exclusively on the last phase of Jesus' life, the period of his public ministry when his teachings both attracted devoted followers and created bitter enemies.

In all four Gospel accounts, only the final week of Jesus' human existence is related in detail—the events leading up to and including his arrest, trial, and execution by the Romans. The significance of Jesus' suffering and death (known as the **Passion**) is the central concern of each Evangelist. Even the **Fourth Gospel** (John), which includes a longer version of Jesus' public career than any other, devotes nearly half of its narrative to retelling the story of Jesus' last few days on earth. Observing this emphasis of the Evangelists, New Testament scholars have described the Gospel form as a Passion narrative with a long introduction. All incidents in Jesus' life leading up to his crucifixion are rigorously subordinated to the climactic circumstances of his death. The Gospels' form and content are shaped not by purely historical or biographical considerations but by their respective authors' theological viewpoints. Combining the Greek *theos* (God) with *logos* ("word" or "logical analysis"), **theology** means "a study of God." It is a religious discipline involving the study of God's nature, will, and activity among humankind. The theologian typically defines and interprets systems of belief that express a

religion's essential worldview. The Gospel writers are theologians, and, like all New Testament authors, the Evangelists write primarily to voice their individual understanding of Jesus' religious or theological significance.

A History of the Early Church   The second literary form in the New Testament is a historical narrative celebrating the deeds of a few early Christian leaders. Written by the author of **Luke**'s Gospel, the Book of Acts continues the story of Christianity's origins. Beginning with an account of Jesus' ascension to heaven and ending with the apostle Paul's preaching activity in Rome, Acts narrates a series of crucial episodes in Christianity's early development, covering the thirty years from about 30 to 60 C.E.

Letters, or Epistles   Whereas the first five books of the New Testament are all narratives that relate the activities of Jesus and his first disciples, the following section consists of another distinct literary type. After the Gospel and history forms comes a collection of twenty-one letters, or **epistles,** all of which are ascribed to famous leaders of the early church. The first set of letters is by Paul, the most influential of all Christian missionaries, and by Pauline disciples who later wrote in his name and spirit. In addition, seven epistles (a more formal version of the letter) are attributed to other leaders associated with the original Jerusalem church, such as **Peter, James, Jude,** and **John.**

An Apocalypse   The Book of Revelation represents the fourth and final literary category in the Christian Scriptures. The title *Revelation* translates the Greek noun *apokalypsis,* which means an "uncovering" or "unveiling." Like other **apocalyptic literature,** Revelation features visions of an unseen world inhabited by spirit creatures both good and evil. It highlights the cosmic struggle between God and Satan, a conflict involving both heaven and earth that ultimately sees evil defeated, God's kingdom triumphant, and the creation of a new earth and heaven (Rev. 12; 16; 20–21). Revelation's message is urgent, demanding that believers hold firm in the faith because, like all apocalyptic writers, the author believes that the universal war he visualizes is about to begin (Rev. 1:1, 3; 12:12; 22:7, 11, 12).

Apocalyptic ideas played an extremely important role in early Christian thought and dominate many passages in the New Testament. As we study the Gospel accounts of Jesus' preaching, we will find numerous apocalyptic concepts, commonly involving **eschatology.** Derived from combining two Greek phrases — *to eschaton* (referring to the world's end) and *ho logos* (meaning "study of") — eschatology refers to beliefs about events occurring at the End of time. On a personal level, eschatology involves momentous events at the end of an individual's life: death, posthumous judgment, heaven, hell, and **resurrection.** On a more general level, it relates to developments that culminate in the End of human society and history as we know them.

Although the twenty-seven documents comprising the New Testament generally fit into one of four broad literary genres, most also contain a number of subgenres. The Gospels, for example, include not only biographical narrations about Jesus but also such disparate forms as genealogies, parables, aphorisms, confrontation stories, prayers, reconstructions of conversations, and, in the case of John's Gospel, long metaphysical discourses. The Book of Acts similarly incorporates public speeches, private dialogs, anecdotes about individual figures, and perhaps even excerpts from a diary or travel journal.

Some documents grouped in the third section — the Pauline letters and catholic epistles — are technically not forms of correspondence. Except for its opening phrases, the Book of James is more like a collection of traditional wisdom sayings than a letter. The Book of Hebrews is actually an elaborate sermon, whereas 1 John and Jude resemble tracts directed against opponents who are (or had been) part of their respective authors' religious communities.

DIVERSITY AND UNITY IN THE NEW TESTAMENT DOCUMENTS

The New Testament's variety of literary genres is paralleled by the diversity of its authors' thoughts. Whereas all canonical writers are unified in their conviction of Jesus' supreme value, they respond to his life and teachings in significantly different ways. Modern scholarship has increasingly come to realize that not only were early Christians an ethnically and theologically diverse group but also they produced a literature — including the New Testament books — reflecting that diversity. Scholars such as Raymond E. Brown, James D. G. Dunn, and John Reumann (see "Recommended Reading") have explored the intellectual, social, and theological forces operating in — and in some cases dividing — different early Christian communities.

Paul's genuine letters, written to largely **Gentile** (non-Jewish) congregations between about 50 and 62 C.E., advocate a Christian's total freedom from the "bondage" of Mosaic Law. By contrast, the Gospel of Matthew, probably composed in Antioch for Jews converted to Christianity, promotes continuing obedience to the Mosaic heritage. A third group, which emphasized the unique divinity of Jesus, issued the Gospel of John as its foundation document. That community, based on the teachings of "the disciple whom Jesus loved," later split into factions debating the question of Jesus' physical humanity, a division reflected in the letters of 1 and 2 John (see chapters 10 and 18).

After Paul's death, a variety of writers claimed his authority for their particular group. While one Pauline school created the Book of Ephesians, updating Paul's thought to deal with new issues and situations, another composed the Letters to Timothy and Titus, promulgating church structure, administrative authority, and the power of received tradition (see chapter 17). Whereas these pseudo-Pauline works were eventually accepted into the New Testament, others also attributed to the apostle, such as the apocryphal Acts of Paul, were not.

After Roman armies destroyed Jerusalem in 70 C.E. — and along with it Christianity's mother church (see chapter 4) — New Testament writers differ strikingly in their attitude toward the secular government. The author of Luke-Acts adopts a policy of quiet cooperation with Roman authorities (as Paul had done in Romans 13), whereas the fiery visionary who wrote Revelation denounces the empire and predicts its imminent destruction (see chapter 19).

Formation of the New Testament Canon

The process by which the twenty-seven books of the New Testament became recognized as Christian Scripture took place gradually over a long span of time. For the first four centuries C.E., visitors attending services at different churches located in different parts of the Roman Empire likely would find a startling variety of writings that individual churches considered sacred. Whereas collections of Paul's letters and one or more of the four canonical Gospels were widely used, many churches rejected such familiar books as Revelation, James, and 2 Peter, while, at least tentatively, accepting works that would be totally unfamiliar to modern readers, such as the Epistle of Barnabas, the Apocalypse of Peter, and the Shepherd of Hermas.

Although most of the documents eventually included in the New Testament were composed between about 50 and 140 C.E., it was not until late in the fourth century C.E. that a list of books appeared that corresponds exactly to the twenty-seven we know today (see box 1.4). In 367 C.E., Athanasius, then bishop of Alexandria, made this list part of his Easter Letter. Even after Athanasius issued his definitive tally, however, numerous churches continued to use New Testament collections that differed significantly from one another.

The diversity of writings accepted in different Christian communities reflects the diverse historical origins of New Testament books. Each book first appeared as a separate document independent of the others and circulated by itself in different geographical areas. Paul's genuine letters, the oldest extant Christian works, were sent individually to disparate small congregations scattered throughout Asia Minor, Greece, and Italy. Similarly, the four Gospels—Mark, Matthew, Luke, and John—were created for distinct Christian groups living in a particular city or region. Matthew, for example, seems to have been directed to a congregation at Antioch in Syria, where it probably served as a foundation document for that group. Many scholars believe that the last Gospel written, that ascribed to John, served to define the distinctive ideas of a religious community based on the teachings of a "disciple whom Jesus loved." Neither the name of the beloved disciple nor the original location of his group is known (see chapter 10).

THE PROCESS OF GROWTH

Perhaps the first step in creating the New Testament occurred toward the end of the first century C.E., when one or more of Paul's admirers searched the archives of the various Pauline churches for surviving copies of his correspondence, gathering them together in a single unit. This anonymous Pauline disciple began an anthology of early Christian literature to which the Gospels, Acts, and other documents gradually were added, forming a New Testament canon.

A word derived from the Greek *kanon*, canon refers to a standard or measurement, the norm by which something is evaluated or judged acceptable. In religious usage, a canon is the official inventory of books, like that of Athanasius, that a religious community regards as its authoritative source of doctrinal and ethical belief.

By the mid-second century C.E., when 2 Peter (thought to be the last-written canonical work) was published, Paul's letters had been recognized as Scripture—at least in some circles (2 Pet. 3:15–16). In the meantime, a large number of Gospels, all purporting to represent Jesus' authentic teachings, had also been composed. Well into the second century, most churches apparently recognized only the one Gospel known to their local group. The earliest surviving reference to the four canonical Gospels occurs in a book called 2 Clement, written in the name of Clement, a famous early bishop of Rome. Dating from the early second century C.E., this work quotes a passage from Matthew as "Scripture." Perhaps a few decades later, Justin Martyr, a church leader executed in Rome in the 160s C.E., cited the "memoirs of the Apostles" or "Gospels" as though they had attained an authority equal to that of the Hebrew Bible.

The titles by which we now know the Gospels ascribed to Matthew, Mark, Luke, and John, how-

Box 1.4
New Testament Books: Approximate Order of Composition

APPROX. DATE (C.E.)	TITLE OF BOOK	AUTHOR
c. 50	1 Thessalonians	Paul
	2 Thess. (if by Paul)	
c. 54–55	1 and 2 Corinthians	Paul
c. 56	Galatians	Paul
c. 56–57	Romans	Paul
c. 61	Colossians (if by Paul)	Paul
c. 61	Philippians	Paul
c. 62	Philemon	Paul
c. 66–70	Gospel of Mark	Anonymous
66–73	*Jewish War Against Rome: Destruction of Jerusalem and Temple*	
c. 80–85	Gospel of Matthew	Anonymous
c. 85–90	Gospel of Luke, Book of Acts	Anonymous
c. 85–95	Hebrews, 1 Peter, Ephesians, James	Anonymous
c. 90–95	Gospel of John	Anonymous
c. 95	Revelation (the Apocalypse)	John of Patmos
c. 95–100	Letters of John	The Elder
c. 110–130	1 and 2 Timothy, Titus	Anonymous
c. 130–150	Jude, 2 Peter	Anonymous

ever, did not become part of the New Testament tradition until more than a century after they were written. Until late in the second century C.E., the Gospels apparently circulated anonymously among Christian congregations. Slowly, they came to be regarded as the work of Jesus' initial **apostles**—men whom Jesus himself had called to be his close followers—or of later companions of the apostles, such as Mark and Luke, who were not eyewitnesses to Jesus' ministry.

By the end of the second century C.E., the international church reached a compromise between the single Gospel championed by some of the oldest individual churches and the many different Gospels then in circulation. In accepting the present four, the Christian communities rejected numerous others, such as the Gospel attributed to Peter and the Gospel of Thomas, consigning them to disuse and ultimate oblivion. In 1945, a complete copy of the Thomas Gospel, containing 114 sayings ascribed to Jesus, was found in an Egyptian cemetery. Except for this "Fifth Gospel," all the others survive only in small fragments (see chapter 20).

The notion that a single, consistent Gospel—rather than four diverse and sometimes contradictory accounts—should be the church norm was expressed in the *Diatessaron* of Tatian, compiled about 170 C.E. and now lost. This composite version, which for centuries prevailed in the East, particularly Syria, ingeniously wove together the contents of Matthew, Mark, Luke, and John, as well as elements from oral tradition, into a unified narrative.

The Muratorian Canon   Whereas a compilation of Paul's letters, four Gospels, and Acts was widely accepted by the end of the second century, many other New Testament books—notably Hebrews, Revelation, and the seven brief documents known as the Catholic Epistles—took an additional two or three hundred years to find general recognition. The Muratorian Canon, which scholars once dated to the late second or early third century C.E. but now think was probably assembled in the fourth century, is typical of the mixed bag of canonical and apocryphal books found in different church catalogs. Listing twenty-four books, the Muratorian Canon includes the four Gospels, Acts, thirteen letters ascribed to Paul (but not Hebrews), Jude, 1 and 2 (but not 3) John, the Wisdom of Solomon, Revelation, and the Apocalypse of Peter. The Muratorian list excludes five books that finally achieved canonical status, but it includes a Greek Wisdom book that was ultimately assigned to the Old Testament Apocrypha and an "apostolic" vision of hell that was not included in any canon.

The Codex Claromontanus is a sixth-century Greek-Latin manuscript that contains a list also thought to derive ultimately from the fourth century C.E. Besides enumerating most of the (ultimately) canonical works, this codex includes the Epistle of Barnabas, the Shepherd of Hermas, the Acts of Paul, and the Apocalypse of Peter—all four of which were finally omitted from the canon. Even the Codex Sinaiticus, one of the oldest (fourth century) and most important manuscripts containing all twenty-seven New Testament books, also includes the Epistle of Barnabas and the Shepherd of Hermas. As late as the fifth century, a Greek manuscript known as the Codex Alexandrinus included both 1 and 2 Clement as part of the Christian testament. Whereas 1 Clement is a letter written around 96 C.E. by a bishop of Rome, 2 Clement is pseudonymous (composed by an unknown writer in the name of a famous person). The practice of **pseudonymity** was common among many Greco-Roman, as well as Jewish and Christian, authors in the Hellenistic world. (See chapters 17 and 18 for a discussion of pseudonymous letters attributed to Paul, Peter, and other leaders of the early Christian movement.)

Writing in the fourth century C.E., the church historian Eusebius observed that even after Christianity had become legally validated by the Roman government, the New Testament canon was not yet fixed. In describing the church's current opinion of a given book's authenticity, Eusebius divided

contenders for official canonization into three categories. The universally "acknowledged" works number twenty-one, including the Gospels, Acts, Paul's letters, and some of the Catholic Epistles. The "disputed" books, accepted by some churches but not others, include six that eventually entered the canon: Revelation, James, Jude, 2 Peter, and 2 and 3 John. Five other candidates for official inclusion failed to make the cut: the Acts of Paul, the Shepherd of Hermas, the Apocalypse of Peter, the Epistle of Barnabas, and the Didache, a fascinating compendium of primitive Christian rituals and moral teachings. Eusebius's "rejected" books are the Gospels ascribed to Peter, Thomas, and Matthias and the Acts of Andrew, John, and other works judged spurious.

Whereas some Christian groups endorsed books later barred from the canon, others repudiated works that were eventually canonized. Such well-known writings as Revelation and the Gospel of John (thought in some circles to be Gnostic compositions) fail to appear in many New Testament lists. Several important churches, including those at **Alexandria** and **Antioch,** resisted accepting Revelation, partly because it was not believed to be the work of John the Apostle. Although eventually canonized, among Eastern churches Revelation did not attain the same authority as most other New Testament books. The Syrian churches consistently denied it canonical honors. (Box 1.5 gives an overview of the New Testament canonical structure.)

MARCION AND GNOSTICISM

Marcion's Disputed Role   At no time did a single church authority or council of church leaders formally decide on the contents of the Christian Scriptures. The long, hotly debated process by which the present New Testament slowly assumed its final form involved several historical controversies and other developments. Many scholars formerly thought that the concept of fashioning a Christian scripture distinct from the Old Testament received its initial stimulus from the radical proposals of Marcion. A Roman Christian who advocated Gnosticism, Marcion (c. 140 C.E.) insisted that Christians should repudiate the entire Hebrew

Box 1.5
Structure of the Canonical New Testament: An Overview

The order in which fourth- and fifth-century Christian editors arranged the twenty-seven separate books comprising the New Testament roughly parallels the organization of the Hebrew Bible, with the Gospels corresponding to the Books of Moses; Acts to the historical narratives of Joshua through Kings; Paul's letters to the prophetic books; and Hebrews, the catholic epistles, and Revelation to the Tanak's third major division, the Writings. The New Testament's present order also reflects the historical process by which the official canon evolved, with the books that were first accepted as sacred—the Gospels, Acts, and Paul's letters—standing first in the canon. The others, including most of the catholic epistles and Revelation, the authority of which was disputed for centuries, were placed literally at the back of the collection.

Despite the historical accident of their placement and the theological diversity of their contents, the canonical arrangement of the New Testament's twenty-seven different books manifests a high degree of thematic unity. When readers study the individual books in their canonical sequence—from Gospels to Revelation—they may perceive an overriding design that gives this anthology of early Christian literature a particularly effective structure.

Perusing the New Testament book by book, from start to finish, readers travel from the alpha of Jesus'

obscure arrival on earth to the omega of his universal triumph. Two astronomical images in the first and last books of the canon impart a cosmic frame to the rest of the collection. In Matthew's nativity story, a mysterious star leads foreign astrologers to Jesus' birthplace, inadvertently inciting King Herod's attempts to kill the child (Matt. 2:1–12). In Revelation's description of the risen Jesus, the once vulnerable infant has become a gigantic figure dominating the sky and holding an entire constellation of stars in one hand (Rev. 1:8–2:1). Editors thus gave the New Testament a linear narrative structure that begins with Matthew's genealogy linking Jesus with heroes from Israel's distant past and ends with visions of a future new creation ruled by that same Jesus, now transformed into the cosmic Christ.

Bracketed between Matthew's story of Jesus' origins and Revelation's Big Bang account of his global conquest are a disparate assortment of three additional Gospels, a church history, and twenty-one letters, sermons, and tracts. For all the theological variety encountered in these books, they exhibit one overriding concern: the absolute centrality of Jesus' role in God's plan for human salvation. By placing four different versions of Jesus' biography at the head of the canon, Christian editors not only illustrated the divergent ways in which the Christ event could be

(continued)

Bible and replace it with a carefully edited version of Luke's Gospel and Paul's letters, the sole Christian writings he deemed worthy of belief. According to this older view, church leaders began to see the importance of defining a New Testament canon only after Marcion had proposed his severely abbreviated list of authoritative writings.

In Marcion's day, the Bible used by Christians consisted primarily of the Septuagint version of the Hebrew Scriptures (which included the **Apocrypha,** approximately fourteen books or parts of books not accepted in the official Jewish canon) and—at least in some locations—one or more of the Gospels and the anthologized Pauline letters.

When Marcion demanded that Christians must dispense with the entire Old Testament, which, he asserted, presented a violent and savage image of God, the church responded by affirming the indispensable authority of the Hebrew Bible, thereby assuring that Christianity would be firmly rooted in the religion of ancient Israel. It also began to emphasize the importance of writings other than a single Gospel and Paul's letters.

Gnosticism Marcion belonged to a movement then widespread within the early church called **Gnosticism.** Taking its name from the Greek word *gnosis* (knowledge), Gnosticism is a general label

Box 1.5 *(continued)*

interpreted acceptably by four different Christian groups but also affirmed the supreme importance of Jesus' ministry, death, and resurrection. The canonical order thus emphasizes the primacy of Jesus' story, the four Gospels together forming a composite foundation document for the Christian religion. No matter how influential the writings that appear later, such as Paul's letters with their radical declaration that salvation comes to Jew and Gentile alike through faith, they must always be weighed against the initial presentations of what Jesus said and did.

To a large extent, the books that follow the Gospels either explore the consequences of Jesus' redemptive career or offer interpretative meditations on it. The New Testament's second part, the Book of Acts, is a sequel to Luke's Gospel, showing how an idealized early church grew and prospered because it was led by the same Spirit that inspired Jesus. According to the author of Luke-Acts, Jesus' later disciples imitate their master's example of service by perpetuating his activities throughout the Greco-Roman world.

Whereas Acts gives a theological overview of Christianity's rapid expansion in the Roman Empire, the New Testament's twenty-one letters (some of which are actually sermons or tracts) offer close-up views of individual Christian communities and their difficulties in trying to follow Jesus in a sometimes hostile world. Letters by (or attributed to) Paul form the New Testament's third major division. Written

before the Gospels appeared, the authentic Pauline letters vividly reflect the struggle for unity of thought and purpose taking place in the Greek-speaking congregations Paul served.

The miscellaneous documents comprising the final part of the New Testament echo the hopes and troubles of widely scattered churches in the late first and early second centuries C.E., a period well after that of Paul's missionary activities. Whereas Hebrews is anonymous, the collection of seven short works known as the Catholic Epistles are ascribed to early leaders of the original Jerusalem church, the apostles Peter and John and two of Jesus' kinsmen, James and Jude. Although their real authors are unknown and several of the epistles were not accorded scriptural status until very late in the canonization process, they express the postapostolic church's ongoing concerns, particularly the problems raised by heretical teachers and the inexplicable delay in Jesus' promised return (see chapter 18). The last book in the canon conveys little of the compassion and forgiveness the Gospels attribute to Jesus, but Revelation's powerful image of Christ as cosmic warrior assures readers that he remains in full control of human history. As victorious conqueror, he permanently defeats Evil, compensates the faithful for their suffering, and gloriously renews all creation, thus completing the divine plan for humanity initiated in Genesis.

---

applied to an extremely diverse set of beliefs and practices. Because the church later declared the Gnostic view of Christianity heretical (guilty of false teaching), most of our information about the movement derives from churchly attacks against it.

In general, Gnosticism expresses a strongly mystical attitude toward human existence, emphasizing that an enlightened believer achieves salvation through attaining a spiritual "knowledge" of heavenly truths denied the average person. Following Plato's duality of body and soul, Gnostics taught that reality consists of two distinct modes of being: an invisible realm of pure spirit that is intrinsically good and to which the human soul belongs, and an inferior physical world to which the desire-filled

and corruptible body belongs. A "higher God" is the source of ultimate reality, the unseen generator of the spirit realm who sent Jesus Christ into the material world to impart a saving awareness of an immortal divine nature dwelling in human beings. By contrast, Yahweh, the Old Testament Deity, was an inferior power responsible for making the inherently corrupt world of matter.

Focusing on the insights of a spiritual elite, Gnosticism became a major source of dissension within the Christian community during the first three centuries of its existence. The Gnostics produced numerous influential writings, including several Gospels interpreting the teachings of Christ, all of which were eventually condemned by official church decrees. (For possible Gnostic elements in John's Gospel and the letters of John, see chapters 10 and 18.)

Although Marcion's challenge to define a uniquely Christian scripture undoubtedly had its effect, most scholars now believe that the evolution of the New Testament canon resulted from a broader set of social and historical circumstances. Noting that Paul's letters had already been collected before Marcion, scholars also point out that by 140 C.E. individual Gospels were already being employed in various churches, although few, if any, groups were then familiar with all four. These documents were regularly and extensively used in worship services and in teaching converts. Read aloud in churches from Syria to Gaul (France), some books proved their long-term usefulness in maintaining a connection with Christianity's beginnings.

In general, it seems that the New Testament canon evolved to serve two related purposes. First, canonization of certain texts clarified within the Christian community what beliefs church leaders considered true and acceptable. Questioners like Marcion and his Gnostic followers could thus be confronted with an officially sanctioned list of books that largely defined the faith. Second, the canon provided a unifying force for churches dispersed throughout the empire, imparting a firm written authority for universal belief and practice.

The Latin Vulgate Although canons at individual churches differed even after Athanasius's Easter list, a major development at the end of the fourth century C.E. was perhaps conclusive in permanently establishing the New Testament canon—Jerome's translation of the Bible, both Old and New Testaments, into Latin. Known as the **Vulgate** because it renders Scripture into the "vulgar" (common) Latin of the western Roman Empire, this landmark work remains the official Bible of the Roman Catholic Church. Its translator, Jerome, one of the great scholars and theologians of the period, followed Athanasius's canon and included all seven catholic epistles, as well as the controversial Hebrews and Revelation. Jerome's translation excluded other "disputed" Christian writings, however, including the Epistle of Barnabas and the Apocalypse of Peter; once regarded as virtually equal to what we think of as "genuine" New Testament works, these texts were henceforth relegated to obscurity.

As time went on and the age of Jesus and the apostles receded ever further, it was no longer possible to draw on the orally transmitted memories of persons who had heard the teachings of first- or second-generation Christians. Believers had to rely on written documents thought to be derived from persons who had witnessed the origins of Christianity. By the close of the second century C.E., a movement within the international Church authenticated certain writings by assigning their authorship to particular apostles or their associates. This process of identifying previously anonymous Gospels and other works with specific "founding fathers" helped to ensure that Christianity's roots— and doctrines—would be firmly planted in apostolic soil.

Summary

One among many of the sacred books produced by various world religions, the New Testament is a small library of Greek documents written by (mostly) anonymous members of the early Christian community. It forms the second part of the Christian Bible, the larger first section of which is the Hebrew Bible, a diverse collection of writings produced by the Jewish community of faith. Each of the twenty-seven canonical New Testament books originated separately and at first circulated independently of the others. Only gradually were these writings gathered together into a single collection. Nearly three centuries elapsed between the time of the books' composition and the formation of the canonical list we know today.

QUESTIONS FOR REVIEW

1. Define the term *testament* and explain the relationship of the Old Testament (the Hebrew Bible) to the New Testament.

2. What version of the Hebrew Bible did early Christians use? In what common language are the Septuagint and New Testament written?

3. Define and describe the major literary forms (genres) contained in the New Testament.

4. Which part of the New Testament was written first? Who was the author, and when did he write?

5. Describe the overall structure of the New Testament. In what specific ways does the figure of Jesus dominate the entire collection of books?

6. What is an apocalypse? Define the terms *apocalyptic* (adjective) and *eschatology* (noun), and explain their application to the early Christian worldview.

7. Briefly summarize the formation of the New Testament canon. Why did the early church decide that it needed a Scripture comparable to the Hebrew Bible? Discuss the role of Marcion and Gnosticism in this process.

8. How do some of the early New Testament canons (lists of accepted New Testament books) differ from the present New Testament? Which books were almost always included in most lists, and which books were commonly omitted? Why do you think that certain books were widely recognized as authoritative (possessing the authority to express correct teaching) while others were not?

9. In determining the books accepted as part of the New Testament canon, what forces or needs of early Christianity were at work? When did the first list of New Testament contents identical to today's canon appear?

QUESTIONS FOR DISCUSSION AND REFLECTION

1. Try to define and describe the New Testament to someone who has never before heard of it. In what ways does this collection of early Christian documents resemble the scriptures of other world religions? In what ways does the New Testament differ from other sacred books?

2. The literary form or category in which writers choose to convey their ideas always influences the way in which those ideas are expressed. Why do you suppose early Christian writers invented the Gospel form to express their views about Jesus? Why do you think that all four Gospel authors focused on the last week of Jesus' life?

3. Only one Gospel writer also wrote a history of the early Church, continuing his story of the Jesus movement with additional stories about a few of Jesus' followers. Given that the New Testament contains *four* different accounts of Jesus' ministry, why do you think there is only *one* narrative about the church?

4. Of the twenty-seven New Testament books, twenty-one are letters or epistles. Why do you suppose the letter form was so popular among early Christians? In a church scattered throughout the Roman Empire, what advantage did letter writing have over other literary forms?

TERMS AND CONCEPTS TO REMEMBER *

Hebrew Bible (Old Testament)	apocalyptic literature
Tanak	eschatology
Septuagint	canon
covenant (testament)	Marcion
Torah	Gnosticism
Gospel	Muratorian Canon
	Vulgate

RECOMMENDED READING

Bailey, James L., and Vander Broek, Lyle. *Literary Forms in the New Testament: A Handbook.* Louisville, Ky.: Westminster/John Knox Press, 1992. An excellent discussion of literary categories found in the New Testament.

Brown, Raymond E. *The Churches the Apostles Left Behind.* New York: Paulist Press, 1984. A brief but authoritative survey of seven different Christian communities — and their distinctive theologies — that produced major parts of the New Testament literature.

Dunn, James D. G. *Unity and Diversity in the New Testament: An Inquiry into the Character of Earliest Christianity,* 2nd ed. London/Philadelphia: SCM Press/Trinity Press International, 1990. Contains a detailed examination of theological differences manifested in different New Testament books, as well as a summary of nine themes contributing to theological unity of canonical authors.

Farmer, William R., and Farkasfalvy, D. M. *The Formation of the New Testament Canon: An Ecumenical Approach.* New York: Paulist Press, 1983.

---

*Most of these terms appear in both the main text and in the glossary at the end of the book. The reader may find it helpful to define new terms introduced in each chapter and to check them in the glossary.

Gamble, Harry Y. *Books and Readers in the Early Church: A History of Early Christian Texts.* New Haven, Conn.: Yale University Press, 1995. Explores such topics as the extent of literacy in the Greco-Roman world, the interaction of oral and written materials in the early Christian community, and the community's production and circulation of books.

Gneuse, Robert. *The Authority of the Bible: Theories of Inspiration, Revelation and the Canon of Scripture.* New York: Paulist Press, 1985. A brief but thoughtful review of biblical authority and the nature of divine inspiration.

Metzger, Bruce M. *The Canon of the New Testament.* New York: Oxford University Press, 1987.

Reumann, John. *Variety and Unity in the New Testament.* New York: Oxford University Press, 1989.

von Campenhausen, Hans. *The Formation of the Christian Bible.* Translated by J. A. Baker. Philadelphia: Fortress Press, 1972.

CHAPTER 2

How the New Testament Was Handed Down to Us

The use of books is endless.   Ecclesiastes 12:12

Key Themes The oldest complete manuscripts of the New Testament date from the fourth century C.E., when Christianity was first officially recognized by the Roman emperor. Although the first translators of the Bible into English, Wycliffe and Tyndale, were condemned by the church of their day, we now have many excellent versions of the Christian Scriptures in modern English.

Originally composed for Greek-speaking audiences, the New Testament is now available in hundreds of different languages, including dozens of recent English translations. The process by which this ancient Greek work has been transmitted to us in English makes a fascinating story.

Transmitting the New Testament Texts

No original author's copies of any New Testament texts have yet come to light. Our oldest transcriptions are fragmentary copies dating from about 200 C.E., about a century to a century and a half after the original texts were composed. The earliest surviving manuscript is a tiny scrap of the Gospel of John containing four verses from chapter 18. On the basis of its calligraphy (form of handwriting), historians date

it at about 125 C.E., a mere twenty-five to thirty years after the Gospel was written (see figure 2.1).

Most of these early manuscripts survive only in small fragments, and all were found in Egypt, where the dry climate aids preservation of the papyrus on which they were written. The oldest copies of the New Testament as a whole, the Codex Sinaiticus and Codex Vaticanus, were made in the fourth century C.E. These famous texts are written on parchment, an expensive writing material made from sheepskin or goatskin, and much more durable than papyrus.

The fourth-century parchment editions reflect the newfound prosperity of the Christian church. They appeared shortly after Christianity became the favored religion of the Roman emperors. The literary productivity encouraged by Constantine I, the first Christian emperor (306–337 C.E.), contrasts sharply with conditions a few years earlier under the emperor Diocletian. During the "Great

Figure 2.1 The oldest surviving manuscript of a New Testament book, this fragment of the Gospel of John dates from about 125 C.E. Preserved for 1800 years in the dry sands of an Egyptian grave, the tiny scrap of papyrus contains four verses from John 18. (Reproduced by courtesy of the Director and University Librarian, the John Rylands University Library of Manchester)

Persecution" (303–305 C.E.), Diocletian attempted to exterminate Christianity, ordering the imprisonment or execution of its adherents and the burning of their books. Diocletian's savage attacks on the church help explain why we have no complete New Testament texts dating prior to Constantine's time.

PROBLEMS IN TRANSMISSION

The uncomfortably large gap between the time that most of the New Testament was composed (roughly 50–100 C.E.) and the age of the oldest complete manuscript copies (fourth century C.E.) creates a problem for textual scholars. Questions about whether surviving copies accurately represent the authors' original work are compounded by the

fact that no two extant manuscripts or manuscript fragments are precisely alike (see box 2.1). Although scholars have reconstructed what most believe to be a reliable version of the New Testament Greek text, it is impossible to confirm that we possess exact copies of the letters that Paul dictated or the Gospels as they first circulated in their respective authors' communities. Some scholars suggest that, besides making relatively minor errors of transmission, generations of Christian scribes who copied New Testament books may have edited various passages to make them conform more closely to evolving doctrines of the church. A number of scribal additions have long been recognized and omitted in modern translations—such as interpolated trinitarian passages in 1 John—but, in the absence of first- or second-century manuscripts, scholars can only speculate about the nature and degree of scribal modifications.

In preserving their sacred writings, Christians pioneered the use of the **codex**. Rather than continue recording texts on scrolls—long sheets of papyrus or parchment rolled around a stick—Christian scribes assembled page-sized manuscript sheets bound together in the manner of a modern book (see figure 2.2).

Manuscript Types   The great fourth-century codex editions of the New Testament are written in uncial characters. Also called "majuscules," uncials are large or capital letters written in continuous script without spaces between words and usually without accents. Later manuscripts, called "minuscules," are written in small cursive letters, with individual letters connected to form groups and syllables.

ASSEMBLING A COMPOSITE NEW TESTAMENT TEXT

The uncial codices are the most important basis of the text from which modern translations into English or other languages are made. The most valuable is the Codex Sinaiticus, a mid-fourth-century manuscript discovered during the mid-1800s in the monastery of St. Catherine at the foot of Mount Sinai. Besides the entire New Testament

Box 2.1

Copyists' Modifications of New Testament Manuscripts

No two ancient Greek manuscripts of New Testament books are precisely alike. Although most differences in the texts were probably caused by unintentional errors in copying, some textual variations seem to result from deliberate changes, many of which may have been motivated by theological considerations. A few of the oldest manuscripts, including the Codex Sinaiticus, do not contain the phrase "son of God" in Mark 1:1, leading some scholars to think that the phrase was inserted at the beginning of the Gospel to refute a belief that Jesus became God's adopted son at his baptism (see chapter 7). Another possibly intentional change, made for the same purpose, may appear in Luke's account of Jesus' baptism, where some early manuscripts have God declare: "You are my son; *this day* I have begotten you," a quotation from Psalm 2 (Luke 3:22; italics added). Most modern translations use an alternative phrasing that avoids the adoption issue, having God say, "in you I am well pleased" or "in you I delight" (New English Bible).

Similar concerns about an orthodox understanding of Jesus' origins apparently influenced manuscript changes in Luke's story of the youthful Jesus' being left behind in the Temple. Mary's reprimand to the child, "your father and I have been anxiously searching for you," was, in some manuscripts, changed to "*we* have been searching for you" (Luke 2:48; italics added), ostensibly to avoid any implication that Joseph was Jesus' real father. A theological belief in Jesus' omniscience may have prompted deletion of references to "the Son" from some copies of Matthew's statement that "about that day and hour [of the End] no one knows, . . . not even the Son; no one but the Father alone" (Matt. 24:36).

Perhaps the most striking New Testament interpolation appears in very late manuscripts of 1 John 5:7–8, where a scribe inserted the Bible's only explicit reference to the Christian doctrine of the Trinity, asserting that God exists in three persons and that "these three are one." This trinitarian statement occurs in no manuscript dating prior to the fourteenth century.

Some scholars argue that theological controversies over such issues as Christ's eternally divine nature and equality with God prompted some scribes to emend manuscripts so that they conformed to the orthodox position (see Ehrman in "Recommended Reading").

(including the Epistle of Barnabas and the Shepherd of Hermas), the Sinaiticus also contains most of the Greek Old Testament.

Even older is the Codex Vaticanus (early fourth century), but it lacks part of Hebrews, several Pauline letters, and Revelation. Together with the slightly later uncial editions — the Codex Alexandrinus, which incorporates 1 and 2 Clement and a book of Jewish poetry called the Psalms of Solomon, and the Codex Bezae, which includes a Latin translation of the Greek text — these landmark editions provide scholars with the foundation on which to construct a relatively authoritative New Testament text.

The fourth-century codices represent only the beginning of the laborious process of textual reconstruction. Scholars must consult many hundreds of manuscript fragments; abundant quotations from church writers of the second, third, and fourth centuries; various minuscule editions; and scores of translations made in Latin, Syriac, Coptic, and other languages spoken throughout the Greco-Roman world. With no fewer than 5000 ancient manuscript copies of the New Testament, most in fragmentary form, we have an abundance of texts from which to deduce a "standard text." The problem is that no two of these 5000 texts are identical. Some contain passages that other equally authoritative texts do not; some manifest remarkable differences in the wording or the arrangement of material.

The Standard Greek Text   Beginning in the early sixteenth century, European scholars like Desiderius Erasmus, one of the most brilliant leaders of the northern Renaissance, attempted to establish a reliable Greek text from which translations could be

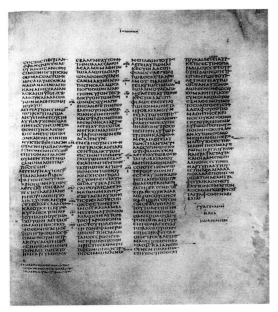

Figure 2.2 Christians pioneered the use of the codex, manuscript pages bound together like a modern book. This Greek text from the Gospel of John contrasts with older copies of New Testament books, which typically survive only in fragmentary form. After Constantine recognized Christianity as a legal religion in the early fourth century, New Testament manuscripts increased in number and quality. (Courtesy of the British Library, no. 4445 *f* 85r)

made. After several centuries of labor by scholars in almost every Western nation, a seemingly definitive Greek text was established. In 1881–1882, B. F. Westcott and F. J. Hort published *New Testament in the Original Greek,* an exhaustively researched critical text that is now the basis for virtually all contemporary work on the Greek Scriptures.

Thanks to Westcott and Hort and their successors, it is possible today to produce a much more accurate translation than ever before. Where modern translations differ from the long-familiar readings in the King James, or "Authorized Version," of the Bible, it is commonly because contemporary translators work from a far better Greek text than was available to the King James editors when their version was first published in 1611.

Since the Westcott and Hort text appeared over a century ago, the scholarly process of refining and improving the text has continued. Although no single new edition threatens to replace Westcott and Hort, new discoveries of ancient manuscripts (an additional dozen pages of the Codex Sinaiticus were found in 1975), and a more expert understanding of the *koinē* Greek permit increasingly precise modifications of Westcott and Hort's basic work.

English Translations

The New Testament continued to circulate in its original *koinē* Greek throughout the eastern half of the Roman Empire (later known as the Byzantine Empire). In the West, however, where Latin was the dominant tongue, Latin translations of the Septuagint and New Testament began to appear during the early centuries C.E. This movement culminated in Jerome's masterful translation of the Vulgate, a monumental work of biblical scholarship. After barbarian invasions triggered the collapse of the western empire in the late fifth century C.E., both education and literacy declined precipitously. During the Dark Ages of the early Medieval period, new European languages gradually developed among the politically fractured regions and states of Europe. Latin remained the official language of the Roman Catholic Church, however, and for nearly 1000 years no major new translations of the Bible appeared (see figure 2.3).

Isolated scholars occasionally undertook to translate selected books of Scripture into one of the new European languages. The first person credited with doing so was the Venerable Bede, a Benedictine monk and historian of Anglo-Saxon England, who translated the Bible into his native English. In the 730s, Bede rendered part of Jerome's Latin Vulgate into Old English. During the tenth and eleventh centuries, a few other Bible books, including the Psalms and Gospels, also appeared in English. Not until the fourteenth century, however, did the entire Bible become available in English. This pioneering translation was the work of an English priest named John Wycliffe, who wished to make Scripture accessible to Christian laypeople who did not understand Latin. Wycliffe finished his task of translating both

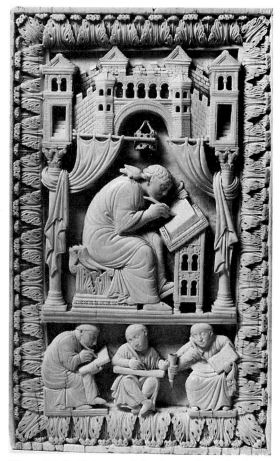

Figure 2.3 St. Gregory and the three scribes, a book cover of the ninth century. Scholarly priests copied and transmitted the New Testament texts. (© Kunsthistoriches Museum, Vienna)

Old and New Testaments by about 1384. The national church, however, fearing the consequences of the Bible's being read and interpreted by laypersons, condemned Wycliffe's version in 1408 and forbade any future translations.

THE INVENTION OF PRINTING

Two historical events ensured that the Bible would find a large reading public in English. The first was Johannes Gutenberg's invention of movable type in

1455, a revolutionary advance that made it possible to print books relatively quickly rather than copying them laboriously by hand. The second was a strong religious movement known as the Protestant Reformation, begun in Germany in 1517. In that year, a German priest named Martin Luther vigorously protested administrative corruption and other practices within the Roman Catholic Church. Luther's German translation of the Bible (1522–1534) was the first version in a modern European language based not on the Latin Vulgate but on the original Hebrew and Greek.

The first English translator to work directly from Hebrew and Greek manuscripts was William Tyndale; under the threat of church persecution, he fled to Germany, where his translation of the New Testament was published in 1525 (revised 1534). Official hostility to his work prevented him from completing his translation of the Old Testament, and in 1535–1536, he was betrayed, tried for **heresy,** and burned at the stake. Tyndale's superb English phrasing of the New Testament has influenced almost every other English translation since.

Although the church forbade the reading of Wycliffe's or Tyndale's translations, it nevertheless permitted free distribution of the first printed English Bible — the Coverdale Bible (1535), which relied heavily on Tyndale's work. Matthew's Bible (1537), containing additional sections of Tyndale's Old Testament, was revised by Coverdale, and the result was called the Great Bible (1539). The Bishop's Bible (1568) was a revision of the Great Bible, and the King James Version was commissioned as a scholarly revision of the Bishop's Bible. The Geneva Bible (1560), which the English Puritans had produced in Switzerland, also significantly influenced the King James Bible.

THE KING JAMES BIBLE (AUTHORIZED VERSION)

By far the most popular English Bible of all time, the King James translation was authorized by James I, son of Mary, Queen of Scots, who appointed fifty-four scholars to make a new version of the Bishop's Bible for official use in the English

Box 2.2
Comparative Translations of Selected New Testament Passages

JOHN 1:1

KING JAMES VERSION

In the beginning was the Word, and the Word was with God, and the Word was God.

NEW REVISED STANDARD VERSION

In the beginning was the Word, and the Word was with God, and the Word was God.

REVISED ENGLISH BIBLE

In the beginning the Word already was. The Word was in God's presence, and what God was, the Word was.

THE FIVE GOSPELS (SCHOLAR'S VERSION)

In the beginning there was the divine word and wisdom. The divine word and wisdom was there with God, and it was what God was.

FOUR TRANSLATIONS OF THE LORD'S PRAYER

KING JAMES VERSION

Our Father who art in heaven,
Hallowed be thy name,
Thy kingdom come,
Thy will be done,
   On earth as it is in heaven.
Give us this day our daily bread,
And forgive us our debts,
   As we have forgiven our debtors;
And lead us not into temptation,
   But deliver us from evil.

NEW REVISED STANDARD VERSION

Our Father in heaven,
   hallowed be your name.
Your kingdom come.
Your will be done,
   on earth as in heaven.
Give us this day our
   daily bread.
And forgive us our debts,
   as we have also forgiven our debtors.
And do not bring us to the time of trial,
   but rescue us from the evil one.

REVISED ENGLISH BIBLE

Our Father in heaven,
May your name be hallowed;
Your kingdom come,
Your will be done,
on earth as in heaven.
Give us today our daily bread.
Forgive us the wrong we have done,
as we have forgiven those who have wronged us.
And do not put us to the test,
but save us from the evil one.

THE FIVE GOSPELS (SCHOLAR'S VERSION)

Our Father in the heavens,
your name be revered.
Impose your imperial rule,
enact your will on earth as you have in heaven.

Provide us with the bread we need for the day.

Forgive our debts
to the extent that we have forgiven those in debt to us.
And please don't subject us to test after test,
but rescue us from the evil one.

(Anglican) church. After seven years' labor, during which the oldest manuscripts then available were diligently consulted, the king's scholars produced in 1611 the Authorized, or King James, Version. One of the masterpieces of English literature, it was created at a time when the language was at its richest and most vivid. In the beauty of its rhythmic prose and colorful imagery, the King James Version remains unsurpassed in literary excellence. Later translations may be more accurate and have the

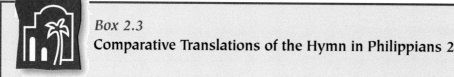

Box 2.3

Comparative Translations of the Hymn in Philippians 2

Unlike the two other great monotheistic religions, Judaism and Islam, Christianity traditionally expresses its ideas and insights in formal doctrines. During the first three or four centuries C.E., Christian teachers were bitterly divided on the precise way to define Jesus' divine nature and his relationship to God. Whereas some Christians argued that Jesus was subordinate to the Father, others insisted that he was coequal and coeternal with God. The view that Jesus and God were the same Being eventually prevailed and was formulated in the concept of the Trinity, a doctrine articulated in the famous Nicene Creed.

Throughout the long controversy, both sides cited Paul's letter to the church at Philippi to support their conflicting arguments. In the second chapter of Philippians, Paul apparently quotes a pre-Pauline Christian hymn praising Jesus' example of humble obedience to the Father, a willing submission to the divine will that led to his ultimate exaltation. Understanding exactly what the hymn states about Jesus' relation to God — whether in a prehuman heavenly existence he was "equal to God" — depends largely on how one interprets a crucial Greek verb, which translators render in a variety of ways, giving different theological meanings to the text. The King James Version provides a traditional wording consistent with the orthodox belief that Jesus is the Second Person of the Trinity, whereas most modern translations reflect the ambiguity of the passage. The Living Bible, which offers a loose paraphrase of the Greek text rather than a real translation, illustrates the dangers inherent in doctrinally biased editions of the New Testament. The key phrase (in verse 6) is highlighted in italics in the eight representative translations given here. (For a discussion of this hymn in the context of Paul's thought about the Adam–Jesus parallel, see chapter 16.)

PHILIPPIANS 2:5–11

KING JAMES VERSION

Let this mind be in you, which was also in Christ Jesus: *who, being in the form of God, thought it not robbery to be equal with God:* but made himself of no reputation, and took upon him the form of a servant, and was made in the likeness of men: and being found in fashion as a man, he humbled himself, and became obedient unto death, even the death of the cross. Wherefore God also hath highly exalted him, and given him a name which is above every name: that at

the name of Jesus every knee should bow, of *things* in heaven, and *things* in earth, and *things* under the earth; and *that* every tongue should confess that Jesus Christ *is* Lord, to the glory of God the Father.

NEW AMERICAN BIBLE

Your attitude must be that of Christ.
Though he was in the form of God,
  he did not deem equality with God
  something to be grasped at.
Rather, he emptied himself
  and took the form of a slave,
  being born in the likeness of men.

He was known to be of human estate,
  and it was thus that he humbled himself,
  obediently accepting even death,
  death on a cross!

Because of this,
  God highly exalted him
  and bestowed on him the name
  above every other name,

So that at Jesus' name
  every knee must bend
  in the heavens, on the earth,
  and under the earth,
  and every tongue proclaim
  to the glory of God the Father:
Jesus Christ Is Lord!

NEW REVISED STANDARD VERSION

Let the same mind be in you that was in Christ Jesus,
  who, *though he was in the form of God,*
  did not regard equality with God
  as something to be exploited,
but emptied himself, taking the form of a slave,
  being born in human likeness.
And being found in human form,
  he humbled himself
  and became obedient to the point of death —
  even death on a cross.
Therefore God also highly exalted him
  and gave him the name
  that is above every name,
so that at the name of Jesus
  every knee should bend,
  in heaven and on earth and under the earth,

and every tongue should confess
that Jesus Christ is Lord,
to the glory of God the Father.

REVISED ENGLISH BIBLE

Take to heart among yourselves what you find in Christ Jesus: *He was in the form of God; yet he laid no claim to equality with God,* but made himself nothing, assuming the form of a slave. Bearing the human likeness, sharing the human lot, he humbled himself, and was obedient, even to the point of death, death on a cross! Therefore God raised him to the heights and bestowed on him the name above all names, that at the name of Jesus every knee should bow—in heaven, on earth, and in the depths—and every tongue acclaim, "Jesus Christ is Lord," to the glory of God the Father.

NEW INTERNATIONAL VERSION

Your attitude should be the same as that of Christ Jesus:
*Who, being in very nature God,
did not consider equality with God something to be grasped,*
but made himself nothing,
taking the very nature of a servant,
being made in human likeness.
And being found in appearance as a man,
he humbled himself
and became obedient to death—even death on a cross!
Therefore God exalted him to the highest place
and gave him the name that is above every name,
that at the name of Jesus every knee should bow,
in heaven and on earth and under the earth,
and every tongue confess that Jesus Christ is Lord,
to the glory of God the Father.

NEW JERUSALEM BIBLE

Make your own the mind of Christ Jesus:
*Who, being in the form of God,
did not count equality with God
something to be grasped.*

But he emptied himself,
taking the form of a slave,
becoming as human beings are;

and being in every way like a human being,
he was humbler yet,
even to accepting death, death on a cross.

NEW JERUSALEM BIBLE *(cont.)*

And for this God raised him high,
and gave him the name
which is above all other names;

so that *all beings*
in the heavens, on earth and in the underworld,
should bend the knee at the name of Jesus
and that *every tongue should acknowledge*
Jesus Christ as Lord,
to the glory of God the Father.

GOOD NEWS FOR MODERN MAN

The attitude you should have is the one that Christ Jesus had:
He always had *the very nature of God,*
But *he did not think that by force he should try to become equal with God.*
Instead, of his own free will he gave it all up,
And took the nature of a servant.
He became like man, he appeared in human likeness;
He was humble and walked the path of obedience to death—his death on the cross.
For this reason God raised him to the highest place above,
And gave him the name that is greater than any other name,
So that, in honor of the name of Jesus,
All beings in heaven, and on the earth, and in the world below
Will fall on their knees,
And all will openly proclaim that Jesus Christ is the Lord,
To the glory of God the Father.

THE LIVING BIBLE

Your attitude should be the kind that was shown us by Jesus Christ, who, *though he was God, did not demand and cling to his rights as God, but laid aside his mighty power and glory,* taking the disguise of a slave and becoming like men. And he humbled himself even further, going so far as actually to die a criminal's death on a cross.

Yet it was because of this that God raised him up to the heights of heaven and gave him a name which is above every other name, that at the name of Jesus every knee shall bow in heaven and on earth and under the earth, and every tongue shall confess that Jesus Christ is Lord, to the glory of God the Father.

advantage of being based on older and more authoritative Hebrew and Greek manuscripts, but none has phrased the Scriptures in so memorable or quotable a fashion.

Despite its wonderful poetic qualities, however, the King James Version has grave disadvantages as a text for studying the Bible. The very attributes that contribute to its linguistic elegance — the archaic diction, poetic rhythms, and Renaissance vocabulary — tend to obscure the explicit meaning of the text for many readers. Translated by scholars who grew up on the then-contemporary poetry of Edmund Spenser and William Shakespeare, the King James text presents real problems of comprehensibility to the average American student. Students who have difficulty undertaking *Hamlet* cannot expect to follow Paul's sometimes complex arguments when they are couched in terms that have been largely obsolete for centuries.

MODERN ENGLISH AND AMERICAN TRANSLATIONS

Realizing that language changes over the years and that words lose their original meanings and take on new connotations, Bible scholars have repeatedly updated and reedited the King James text. The first Revised Version of the King James was published in England between 1881 and 1885; a slightly modified text of this edition, the American Standard Revised Version, was issued in 1901. Using the (then) latest studies in archaeology and linguistics, the Revised Standard Version (RSV) appeared between 1946 and 1952. Because modern scholarship continues to advance in understanding of biblical languages and textual history, an updated edition, the New Revised Standard, with the Apocrypha, was published in 1991.

Readers can now choose from a wide selection of modern translations, most of which incorporate the benefits of expert scholarship that draws on interdisciplinary fields of linguistic, historical, and literary studies (see boxes 2.2 and 2.3). These include the Jerusalem Bible (JB) (1966), which transliterates several Hebrew terms for God — notably the personal name Yahweh and the title El Shaddai — into the English text. An updated edition, the New

Jerusalem Bible, appeared in 1989. The New English Bible (NEB) (1970, 1976), the product of an international body of Roman Catholic, Jewish, and Protestant scholars, was recently further refined and reissued as The Revised English Bible (1989). Unless otherwise indicated, all biblical citations in this textbook are from the NEB.

The widely used New International Version (NIV), completed in the 1970s, reflects a generally conservative Protestant viewpoint. A popular Roman Catholic translation, the New American Bible (NAB) (1970), is also highly readable. Like the Jerusalem Bible and the New (and Revised) English Bible, it includes fresh renderings of the deuterocanonical books (the Apocrypha). Most of these new translations are available in paperback editions, which contain extensive annotations, maps, and scholarly commentary. (See box 2.4.)

Some translations favored by many students need to be used with caution. Whereas the Good News Bible offers a fluent paraphrase of the original languages in informal English, many scholars think that the Living Bible strays so far from the original texts that it is unreliable and misleading. Some doctrinally oriented versions, such as the New World Translation published by the Watchtower Society (Jehovah's Witnesses), consistently tend to render controversial passages in a way that supports their distinctive beliefs.

The multivolume Doubleday Anchor Bible is an excellent study aid. A cooperative effort by Protestant, Roman Catholic, and Jewish scholars, each volume in the series is the work of an individual translator, who provides extensive interpretative commentary. The Scholars Version (SV) is another in-progress multivolume translation with extensive annotation. Intended as an aid in discovering the historical Jesus, the Scholars Version of *The Five Gospels* (1993) (including the Gospel of Thomas) uses a color code to indicate the relative authenticity of sayings ascribed to Jesus. Sayings considered most likely to be accurate memories of Jesus' actual words are printed in red or pink, doubtful sayings in gray, and those deemed not to represent his authentic voice in black (see chapter 11). Adopting an idiomatic, conversational style, the SV translators have also issued *The Complete Gospels,* which com-

Box 2.4
Useful Abbreviations

ABBREVIATIONS OF NEW TESTAMENT BOOKS

Acts	Acts of the Apostles
Col.	Colossians
1 Cor.	1 Corinthians
2 Cor.	2 Corinthians
Eph.	Ephesians
Gal.	Galatians
Heb.	Hebrews
James	James
John	John (Gospel)
1 John	1 John (Epistle)
2 John	2 John (Epistle)
3 John	3 John (Epistle)
Jude	Jude
Luke	Luke (Gospel)
Mark	Mark (Gospel)
Matt.	Matthew (Gospel)
1 Pet.	1 Peter
2 Pet.	2 Peter
Phil.	Philippians
Philem.	Philemon
Rev.	Revelation (the Apocalypse)
Rom.	Romans

1 Thess.	1 Thessalonians
2 Thess.	2 Thessalonians
1 Tim.	1 Timothy
2 Tim.	2 Timothy
Titus	Titus

OTHER ABBREVIATIONS

B.C.E.	Before the common era. Dates correspond to dates B.C.
C.E.	Common era. Dates correspond to dates A.D.
KJV	The King James Version of the Bible, also called the Authorized Version (AV)
NAB	New American Bible
NEB	The New English Bible
NIV	The New International Version of the Bible
NJB	New Jerusalem Bible
NKJV	The New King James Version of the Bible
NT	The New Testament
OT	The Old Testament
RSV	The Revised Standard Version of the Bible
SV	The Scholars Version of the Bible

piles all known canonical and noncanonical Gospel material from the first three centuries of Christianity, including the fragmentary Secret Mark and Gospel of Peter (see chapter 20).

Summary

Written first on a highly perishable substance called papyrus, the oldest copies of the New Testament survive only as generally small fragments. Following Constantine's adoption of Christianity, however, more expensive editions written on parchment appeared, such as the Codex Sinaiticus and Codex Vaticanus.

Of the approximately 5000 surviving manuscript copies of all or part of the New Testament, no two are precisely alike. It was thus the task of scholars to compile a standard Greek text by consulting and comparing the (apparently) most reliable of extant manuscripts. In the late nineteenth century, Westcott and Hort produced a critically established text that is still the version that most modern translators use.

Based on the pioneering labors of Wycliffe and Tyndale, the King James Bible (Authorized Version, 1611) became the most popular translation in the English-speaking world. More modern translations, however, such as the Revised Standard Version and the New English Bible, offer closer and more careful approximations of the original Greek text.

QUESTIONS FOR REVIEW

1. In what manuscript forms was the New Testament preserved during the first three centuries C.E.? What is the oldest surviving fragment of a New Testament book, and where was it found? Why do we have more complete textual copies after the time of the emperor Constantine?

2. Given that no two copies of the New Testament texts are identical, how did Bible scholars compile a relatively reliable version of the Greek text? What is the standard Greek text today?

3. Discuss Jerome's role in providing a standard Latin edition of the Old and New Testaments. What is Jerome's translation called, and when was it produced?

4. Summarize the historical events that stimulated the translation of the New Testament into modern languages like English. Discuss the roles of Wycliffe, Luther, and Tyndale.

5. Describe the strengths and weaknesses of the King James (Authorized Version) Bible for the modern reader.

QUESTIONS FOR DISCUSSION AND REFLECTION

1. Point out some of the problems scholars face in trying to compile a reliable Greek text of the New Testament. Can you cite specific passages that some Christian scribes may have intentionally changed? What do many scholars think motivated copyists to make these changes?

2. Discuss the advantages for classroom study of modern English translations like the New American Bible, the Revised Standard Version, the Scholars Version, and the New English Bible (the version used in this textbook).

TERMS AND CONCEPTS TO REMEMBER

manuscript
codex
the Great Persecution
Constantine
Codex Sinaiticus
Codex Vaticanus
Westcott and Hort (the standard Greek text)

John Wycliffe
Protestant Reformation
William Tyndale
King James Bible (Authorized Version)

RECOMMENDED READING

Bruce, F. F. *History of the Bible in English,* 3rd ed. New York: Oxford University Press, 1978. A concise history and critical evaluation of all major English translations from Anglo-Saxon times to the present.

Ehrman, Bart D. *The Orthodox Corruption of Scripture: The Effect of Early Christological Controversies on the Text of the New Testament.* New York: Oxford University Press, 1993. Provides detailed analysis of variations in ancient manuscripts, demonstrating that copyists' intentional changes are typically motivated by theological concerns.

Lewis, Jack P. *The English Bible from KJV to NIV: A History and Evaluation.* Grand Rapids, Mich.: Baker Book House, 1982. A scholarly review of major English translations from the King James to the New International Version.

Metzger, Bruce M. *The Text of the New Testament, Its Transmission, Corruption, and Restoration,* 3rd ed. New York: Oxford University Press, 1992. A scholarly investigation of the process of textual transmission.

Vaganay, Leon, and Amphoux, Christian-Bernard. *An Introduction to New Testament Textual Criticism,* 2nd ed. Cambridge, Eng./New York: Cambridge University Press, 1991.

CHAPTER 3

Alexander and the Hellenistic World

The Greeks look for wisdom. 1 Corinthians 1:23

Key Themes The military conquests of Alexander the Great (reigned 336–323 B.C.E.) radically transformed the eastern Mediterranean world, creating a new international culture, the Hellenistic. Combining Greek and older Oriental traditions, Hellenistic society, in which early Christianity first evolved, offered a rich diversity of religious and philosophical ideas and practices.

According to the Gospels of Matthew and Luke, before Jesus began his public ministry, he was first tempted to imitate Greek and Roman leaders who had succeeded in conquering the world. The Gospel authors present the temptation to become another Alexander the Great or **Caesar** Augustus as if it originated with Evil incarnate—the **devil** (Greek, *diabolos*). Offered "all the kingdoms of the world and their splendor," Jesus is pictured as vigorously rejecting a "devilish" goal that would inevitably involve military violence (Matt. 4:1–9; Luke 4:3–13).

To appreciate the Gospel writers' view that a single individual could achieve global rulership, one must realize that recent Greco-Roman history had provided people in Jesus' era with outstanding examples of men who had gained control of enormous empires (see figure 3.1; also see figures 4.3, 4.5, and 4.7). The first-century social and political environment was largely shaped by the exploits of several extraordinary conquerors, beginning with Alexander the Great and ending with Augustus, the emperor ruling when Jesus was born (Matt. 1:5;

Luke 2:1). Shortly before Jesus' birth, a devastating series of power struggles in the Mediterranean world had been resolved in favor of Augustus's one-man rule of the vast **Roman Empire,** which included the Judean homeland.

The possibility that a new charismatic leader, such as Jesus, could reverse the status quo and seize power for himself was, in some minds at least, still conceivable (Luke 24:21; John 6:15; Acts 1:6–8). Many of Jesus' compatriots, in fact, eagerly anticipated a God-sent ruler who would forcibly evict occupying Roman forces from Palestine and restore the Israelite kingdom of David (see chapter 5).

Alexander and His Successors

The most spectacular, and in many ways the most influential, of all ancient leaders was **Alexander the Great** (ruled 336–323 B.C.E.) (see figure 3.2). The son of **Philip II**, king of **Macedonia** (a region in

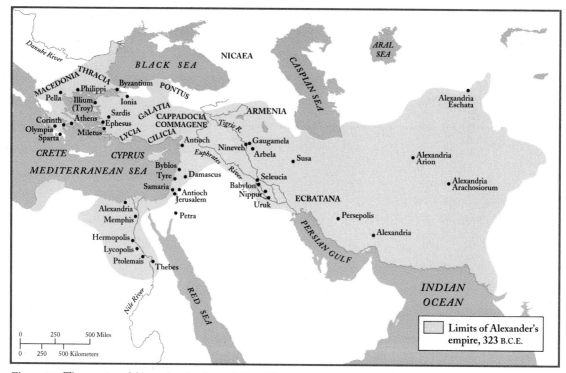

Figure 3.1 The empire of Alexander the Great (336–323 B.C.E.). Alexander's rapid conquest of the older Persian Empire created a new Greek-speaking empire that included all of the ancient centers of civilization from Greece eastward to India. Influenced by Greek language, ideas, and customs, the resultant new international culture is known as Hellenistic.

northern Greece), Alexander came to the throne at age twenty. A brilliant military strategist and magnetic commander who won and held the devotion of his troops, Alexander embodied some of the most admired virtues of his age. Tutored by the philosopher-scientist Aristotle, he was both a practical man of action and a passionate disciple of Greek thought. Viewing himself as a new Achilles, the warrior-hero of Homer's *Iliad,* he was said to have kept a copy of the poem under his pillow, as if determined even in sleep to absorb its message of valor and personal honor. By the time he was age thirty, Alexander had led his Macedonian armies on an unprecedented series of military victories that created the largest empire the world had yet known. Extending from Greece eastward through the ancient realms of Egypt, Babylonia, Persia, and Af-

ghanistan into western India, Alexander's empire included most of the (then-recognized) civilized world (figure 3.1). At age thirty-two, stricken by a sudden fever, Alexander died in **Babylon** (323 B.C.E.). He did not live long enough to consolidate his far-flung conquests and achieve his presumed goal of a single world government united under the flag of Greek civilization.

After Alexander's death, his empire slowly disintegrated, but large sections remained under the control of his successors, known collectively as the Diadochi (see box 3.1). By about 300 B.C.E., three distinct powers had emerged to dominate the eastern Mediterranean basin. One of Alexander's ablest generals, **Ptolemy I,** founded a dynasty that ruled Egypt for nearly three centuries. Another of Alexander's successors was **Seleucus,** who established the Seleucid Empire that controlled Syria, then a large territory that stretched from western Asia Minor (now Turkey) to Mesopotamia (modern Iraq). Eventually, the son of a third successor, Antigonus, governed Macedonia and parts of Greece. Sporadic efforts to reunite Alexander's empire failed, but the descendants of his commanders continued to rule Greece and the Near East until their various kingdoms were gradually incorporated into the Roman Empire (see figure 3.3).

Hellenistic Thought and Culture

Alexander's conquests did not achieve his vision of a permanently united world, but they did create a lasting result in the form of a new international culture known as Hellenistic. A mixture of the classical Greek (Hellenic) culture with the older civilizations of the Near East, the **Hellenistic** synthesis produced a creative flowering of Greek and Oriental motifs in art, architecture, philosophy, literature, and religion. Arbitrarily dated as beginning with Alexander's death in 323 B.C.E., the Hellenistic period chronologically overlaps the period of Roman expansion and continues into the early Christian centuries.

Along with a new form of the Greek language, the *koinē* spoken by Alexander's soldiers, Hellenistic culture introduced new ways of thought and expression into the eastern Mediterranean region where Christianity first took root. It also produced, among educated classes at least, a more open worldview in which Hellenistic peoples saw themselves as citizens not merely of a particular city-state (the *polis*) but of the world (*cosmos*) as a whole. This *cosmopolitan* outlook helped break down barriers between different traditions, allowing an integration of Greek with other ethnic customs, a process by which even Judaism became partly Hellenized (see chapter 4).

Under Alexander and his successors, Greek attitudes and ideas dominated the education of youths everywhere. Among leading thinkers and writers, the Greek influence was all-pervasive. The Greek love of learning, intense intellectual curiosity, and

Figure 3.2 Portrait bust of Alexander the Great. Although he managed to conquer most of the known world before his death at age thirty-two, Alexander's dream of unifying east and west under a single government was never achieved. (© British Museum)

confidence in the power of reason to discover truth became near-universal standards in the educational experience. (The phenomenon of **Hellenization,** however, seems to have been restricted largely to the middle and upper classes in urban centers. The inhabitants of rural areas and villages, such as those in Galilee, were perhaps little touched by the Hellenistic innovations.)

As a Greek book, the New Testament profoundly reflects the Hellenistic environment in which it grew. In many important ways, the New Testament writers combine their Jewish heritage of biblical traditions

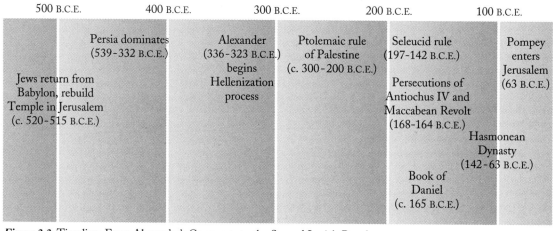

Figure 3.3 Timeline: From Alexander's Conquests to the Second Jewish Revolt.

with Greek philosophical concepts. To understand the dual legacy that the Christian Greek Scriptures transmit to us, we must review briefly some major aspects of Hellenistic philosophy and religion.

Greek Philosophy

A term meaning "love of wisdom," *philosophy* is an attempt to understand human life and its place in the universe by applying rational analysis to a body of observable facts. At first indistinguishable from primitive science, Greek philosophy began in the late seventh century B.C.E. in Miletus and other Greek cities along the coast of western Asia Minor. By the fifth century B.C.E., the center of intellectual activity had shifted to the mainland city of Athens. There, it rapidly developed into numerous schools of thought that endeavored to define the nature of reality and to offer meaningful advice on ethical questions, such as how one may discover and lead the "good" or worthy life.

SOCRATES, PLATO, AND THE IMMORTAL SOUL

The most famous philosopher was the Athenian Socrates (c. 469–399 B.C.E.) (see figure 3.4). A bril-

liant and humorous "lover of wisdom," Socrates made his life an unending quest for truth. Rather than offer final answers to people's questions about life's ultimate meaning, Socrates questioned every belief that his fellow Athenians cherished as "obviously" true. Good-naturedly cross-examining tradesmen, teachers, and politicians alike—demanding to know how they could be so sure their beliefs were valid—Socrates attracted a small circle of devoted followers.

He also irritated many of Athens' influential citizens, some of whom regarded this "gadfly" with his stinging questions as dangerous to conventional morality. As a result, Socrates was eventually tried and executed for criticizing the ethical inadequacy of his opponents' beliefs and practices, the only thinker in Athens' history to be put to death for expressing his ideas.

Socrates left nothing in writing, but his disciple Plato made him the hero of a series of philosophical dialogs in which a saintly and impish Socrates always outargues and outwits his opponents. Because all of Plato's compositions feature Socrates as the chief speaker, it is difficult to separate the writer's ideas from those of his master. (Scholars face a similar problem in trying to distinguish Jesus' sayings from the Gospel writers' added commentary.)

During his eighty years, Plato developed a coherent worldview that has directly or indirectly

1 C.E.	50 C.E.	100 C.E.

Herod appointed king (40 B.C.E.)	Pontius Pilate procurator (26-36 C.E.)	Jewish revolt against Rome (66-73 C.E.)	Academy of Jamnia (c. 90 C.E.)	Second Jewish revolt (132-135 C.E.)
Temple rebuilt	Ministry of Jesus (c. 27-30 C.E.)	Destruction		Gospel of John
Birth of Jesus (c. 6-4 B.C.E.)		Letters of Paul (50-c. 62 C.E.)	of Jerusalem (70 C.E.)	
Death of Herod (4 B.C.E.)		Oral traditions about Jesus		
		Gospel of Mark (c. 66-70 C.E.)		

influenced all subsequent thought about ethical behavior, government, human psychology, and the nature of both physical and spiritual reality. Plato's philosophy is dualistic—it posits the coexistence of two separate worlds, one the familiar physical environment of matter and sense impressions, the other an invisible realm of perfect, eternal ideas. In this philosophy, our bodies belong to the material world and are chained to the physical processes of change, decay, and death. Our souls, however, originate in the unseen spirit world and after death return to it for reward or punishment. Education involves recognizing the superiority of the soul to the body and cultivating those virtues that prepare the soul for its immortal destiny. Hence, the person who truly loves Wisdom, the genuine philosopher, will seek the knowledge of eternal Truths that make real goodness possible, helping others along the way to realize that ambitions for worldly power or riches are unworthy goals. The wise seek the perfect justice of the unseen world and find eternal life.

Over the centuries, Plato's ideas were modified and widely disseminated until, in one form or another, they became common knowledge during the Hellenistic era. Some New Testament writers, such as the author of Hebrews, use Platonic concepts to illustrate parallels and correspondences between the spiritual and physical worlds (Heb. 1:1-4; 9:1-14).

Hebrews' famous definition of faith is primarily a confession of belief in the reality of the invisible realm (Heb. 11:1-2).

STOICISM AND STOIC ENDURANCE

Another Greek philosophy that became extremely popular among the educated classes during Roman times was Stoicism. Founded in Athens by Zeno (c. 336-263 B.C.E.), the Stoic school emphasizes the order and moral purpose of the universe. In the Stoic view, Reason is the divine principle that gives coherence and meaning to our universe. Identified as **Logos** (a Greek term for "word" or "cosmic wisdom"), this universal mind unifies the world and makes it intelligible to the human intellect. Human souls are sparks from the divine Logos, which is symbolized by cosmic fire and sometimes associated with a supreme god.

Stoic teaching urges the individual to listen to the divine element within, to discipline both body and mind to attain a state of harmony with nature and the universe. Stoics must practice severe self-control, learning self-sufficiency and noble indifference to both pleasure and pain. The Stoic ideal is to endure either personal gain or loss with equal serenity, without any show of emotion.

Many celebrated Romans pursued the Stoic way, including the philosopher Seneca (Nero's tutor),

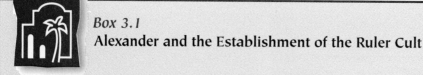

Box 3.1
Alexander and the Establishment of the Ruler Cult

Besides the dissemination of Greek art, science, philosophy, language, and social organization throughout the known world, Alexander's legacy included a more problematic innovation—the Greco-Roman ruler cult. Regarded as godlike for his masterful leadership and achievement of absolute and undisputed power, in 331 B.C.E. Alexander is said to have received confirmation of his superhuman status from a priest of the god Ammon at Siwa in the Libyan desert. The priest reportedly hailed Alexander, who had just been crowned king of Egypt, as the son of Amon-Ra (the chief Egyptian deity, whom the Greeks identified with Zeus), a conventional form of address traditionally accorded Egypt's pharaohs. Because the oracle of Ammon enjoyed enormous prestige, however, many Greeks, including Alexander himself, seem to have taken the priest's words more literally, indicating the conqueror's divine nature and justifying the establishment of a cult in his honor.

Alexander's successors, particularly the Ptolemaic and Seleucid dynasties, also found it politically useful to elicit divine honors from their subjects. Many Hellenistic cities vied with one another in acknowledging the king as their divinely empowered benefactor, offering sacrifices and practicing other rites modeled on those granted the Olympian gods. Although many Greeks opposed treating human beings as if they were gods, the practice was widely accepted and eventually adopted by the Romans.

By the fourth century B.C.E., Romulus, the legendary founder of Rome, was given posthumous deification and identified with a minor Italian deity, Quirinus. After his assassination, the Roman Senate formally declared Julius Caesar (c. 100–44 B.C.E.) henceforth a god, an honor they also granted the emperor Augustus following his death in 14 C.E. Whereas Augustus and other "good" emperors did not accept divine honors during their lifetimes, a few, such as Gaius Caligula and Commodus, demanded to be worshiped while still alive, a requirement that sometimes brought Christians, who held that Christ alone combined the human and divine, into conflict with the state.

As Christian missionaries carried their proclamation of Jesus' death and resurrection to heavenly power from its original, monotheistic context in Judea into the Hellenistic world, they encountered a Greco-Roman audience long familiar with the concept of great persons being posthumously transformed into gods. In his *Metamorphoses of the Gods,* composed at about the turn of the Christian era, Ovid had vividly described the martyred Julius Caesar's soul ascending—like a blazing comet—to celestial glory. Jupiter (Zeus), Ovid states, guaranteed Caesar's entry into heaven "as a god," who will also "have his temples on earth."

Some emperors retained a wry sense of humor about receiving postmortem honors. When, on his deathbed, Vespasian was asked how he felt, he is said to have replied, "I fear I am becoming a god."

---

the Greek slave Epictetus, and the emperor Marcus Aurelius (161–180 C.E.). The hero of Virgil's epic poem *The Aeneid,* with his rigid concept of duty toward the gods and unselfish service to the state, is intended to represent the Stoic virtues. When Paul discusses self-discipline or the ability to endure want or plenty, he echoes Stoic values that were commonplace in Greco-Roman society (Phil. 4:11–14).

EPICUREANISM

A strikingly different philosophical outlook appears in the teachings of Epicurus (c. 342–270 B.C.E.).

Whereas the Stoics believe in the soul's immortality and a future world of rewards or penalties, Epicurus asserts that everything is completely physical or material, including the soul, which after death dissolves into nothingness along with the body. The gods may exist, but they have no contact with or interest in human beings. Without a cosmic intelligence to guide them, people must create their own individual purposes in life. A major goal is the avoidance of pain, which means that the shrewd individual will avoid public service or politics, where rivals may destroy one. Cultivating a private garden, the wise forgo sensual indulgences that weaken physically and mentally. Using reason not to discover ultimate

Truth but to live well, the enlightened mind seeks intellectual pleasures because mental enjoyments outlast those of the body.

Epicurus's stress on the material, perishable nature of both body and soul found support in the philosopher Democritus's atomic theory. Democritus (born about 460 B.C.E.) taught that all things are formed of tiny invisible particles called atoms. It is the nature of atoms to move and collide, temporarily forming objects, including sentient ones like animals and human beings, and then to disintegrate and re-form as other objects elsewhere. Wise or foolish, all persons are merely chance collections of atoms destined to dissolve without a trace.

CYNICISM

A school of philosophy deriving from Antisthenes, one of Socrates' disciples, Cynicism included several famous teachers, particularly Diogenes of Sinope (c. 404–323 B.C.E.) and his student Crates of Thebes (died about 270 B.C.E.). Teaching that virtue is the greatest goal in life, Cynics emphasized strict self-discipline and opposition to prevailing social custom and values, such as respect for money or political power. Demonstrating their antimaterialistic beliefs by their actions, Cynics were famous for scorning all creature comforts and traveling about thinly clad and barefoot, earning a meager subsistence by teaching and/or begging. Some scholars find elements of Cynic principles in Jesus' injunctions to his disciples, who were to wander barefoot throughout Israel, preaching the kingdom and relying on handouts to survive (Mark 10; Luke 10:1–10).

According to the Book of Acts, early Christian missionaries and Greek philosophers had their first significant encounter in the university city of Athens about 50 C.E. Acts reports that the apostle Paul debated Stoic and Epicurean philosophers, to whom he presented the novel idea of Jesus' resurrection. Living up to their reputation as champions of intellectual freedom, the Athenians invited Paul to speak at the Areopagus (a public forum). Acts states that Paul's audience listened politely until he preached about Jesus rising from the dead, a notion foreign to Greek thought, which conceived of

Figure 3.4 Statue of Socrates (c. 469–399 B.C.E.). Condemned to death for challenging the religious assumptions of his fellow Athenians, Socrates lives on in the dialogs of his great disciple, the philosopher Plato. (© British Museum)

posthumous survival in the form of an immaterial soul. Paul apparently did not succeed in establishing a new congregation of believers in Athens as he did in some other Greek cities; tension between the conflicting claims of Greek reason and Judeo-Christian revelation would characterize the church for many centuries.

Greco-Roman Religion

THE TWELVE OLYMPIANS

In contrast to Jewish **monotheism** (belief in a single, all-powerful God), Greco-Roman religion was characterized by **polytheism** (belief in many gods). Although the Greeks and Romans accepted the existence of innumerable deities, the highest gods were only twelve in number. Because they dwelt on Mount Olympus, the loftiest peak in northern Greece, they were known as the Olympians. **Zeus,** whom the Romans called **Jupiter** or Jove, ruled as king of the Olympian gods, all of whom were part of a divine family consisting of Zeus's brothers, sisters, and children. The champion of justice, lawful order, and cosmic harmony, Zeus was a sky-god associated with both daylight and storm, a patriarchal deity who enforced his rule by obliterating opponents with his thunderbolt (see figure 3.5).

Wiser than the older generations of gods whom he had overthrown to assume universal sovereignty, Zeus willingly shared power with the other Olympians, each of whom had a distinctive function or sphere of influence. Zeus's hot-tempered brother Poseidon (the Roman Neptune) was lord of the sea and earthquakes, while his other brother **Hades** (Pluto), known as the "Zeus of the Underworld," presided over a subterranean realm that housed the dead. Representing a sinister aspect of divinity, Hades lent his name to the gloomy kingdom he ruled, a name that New Testament writers also used to designate the soul's posthumous abode (Rev. 20).

Zeus's sister-wife Hera (Juno) was queen of heaven and guardian of marriage and domesticity; his sister Demeter promoted the fertility of earth's soil that yielded life-sustaining grain; and his sister Hestia (Vesta) embodied the fixity and stability of the hearth and home. An important temple to Vesta stood near the Roman forum, where a sacred flame was kept burning, symbol of the eternal city's vital force.

Zeus's eldest child was Athene, goddess of wisdom, who—like a divine thought—had emerged fully formed from her father's head. Zeus also fathered Apollo, god of self-discipline, health, manly beauty, prophecy, and the creative arts; and Apollo's twin sister Artemis (Diana), virgin patron of wildlife and the hunt. Zeus's other Olympian children were Hermes (Mercury), messenger of the gods and guide of souls to the Underworld; Ares (Mars), god of war and aggression; Aphrodite, personification of feminine beauty and sexual allure; and Dionysus, god of wine and ecstasy. (When Zeus's son Dionysus ascended to Mount Olympus, Hestia was customarily demoted to keep the total number of Olympians at twelve.)

THE HYMN TO ZEUS

Although the Olympian religion has long since been supplanted by Christianity, nonetheless it was once capable of inspiring some worshipers with a deep sense of spiritual feeling. In his "Hymn to Zeus," the Stoic poet Cleanthes shows a profound reverence for the king of heaven, praising him in terms not unlike those found in the biblical psalms.

> O Zeus, most glorious of immortals,
> many-named, almighty and eternal,
> lord of nature who guides all things
> in accordance with law,
> it is fitting that all mortals
> should call upon you,
> *for we are your children.* . . .
> Obedient to your direction
> as it rolls around the earth,
> all the universe submits willingly to your rule.
> Your invincible hands hold nothing less
> than the eternal thunderbolt—two-edged,
>   flaming—
> whose stroke causes all nature to shudder. . . .
> Apart from you, lord, nothing is done on earth,
> in the sacred heights of heaven, or in the sea,
> except those things the wicked do in their folly.
> Indeed, you are able to make wrong things right
> and to create order out of chaos.
> In your sight even worthless things are worthy,
> for you have so fitted together
> all things good and evil
> that supreme Reason reigns forever over all.
>   (Translated by Brad Nystrom)

Figure 3.5 Zeus holding a (vanished) thunderbolt. King of the Olympian gods, Zeus was both a personification of storm and lightning and the heavenly enforcer of justice, lawful order, and cosmic harmony. Unlike the Judeo-Christian God, who is eternal, Zeus is the descendant of older generations of gods who ruled the universe before him. This larger-than-life bronze statue dates from the fifth century B.C.E. (© Foto Marburg/Art Resource, NY)

Cleanthes's reference to the fatherhood of God— "we are all your children"—expressed the Stoic belief in the universal brotherhood of all humanity. Another Stoic writer, Aratus, who voiced the same idea, is quoted in Acts 17, thus becoming part of Christian Scripture (Acts 17:28).

GODS OFFERING WORSHIPERS A PERSONAL RELATIONSHIP

By the time Augustus assumed imperial leadership of Rome in the first century B.C.E., the Olympian gods were still honored in the public sacrifices and rituals of the state-supported religion, but to many people, they seemed increasingly remote from ordinary human concerns. Only a few deities associated with the Olympian cult apparently offered a satisfying personal relationship with their worshipers. Two of the most accessible figures were Asclepius and Dionysus, both of whom were born mortal and underwent suffering and death before achieving immortality, experiences that allowed them to bridge the gulf between humanity and divinity.

Asclepius, the most humane and compassionate of Greek heroes, was the mortal son of Apollo and Coronis, daughter of a king in Thessaly (see figure 3.6). Inheriting from his divine father the gift of miraculous healing, Asclepius became the archetypal physician, devoting his abilities to curing the sick and maimed. When his skill became so great

Figure 3.6 Asclepius and suppliant. The son of Apollo and a mortal woman, Asclepius, the first physician, is patron of the healing arts. A wise, compassionate god who was concerned about the welfare of individual human beings, Asclepius was worshiped throughout the Greco-Roman world. Ministering to both mind and body, the god invited patients to sleep overnight at his shrine, where he appeared in their dreams to prescribe remedies and, sometimes, to perform miraculous cures. (© Archaeological Receipts Fund)

bined faith healing with the practice of scientific medicine. To create a direct relationship with the god, patients usually began their cure by spending several nights sleeping at his temple, during which time Asclepius was said to appear in their dreams, asking questions about their health and giving advice. Attending physicians then prescribed a variety of therapies, ranging from changes in diet and exercise to surgical procedures. Grateful patients commemorated their restoration to health by dedicating inscriptions and plaster replicas of the body parts that the kindly god had healed. Although Asclepius demanded strict ethical behavior of those he helped, he was also acclaimed for welcoming the poor and disadvantaged to his sanctuaries.

DIONYSUS OF THEBES AND JESUS OF NAZARETH

Whereas Asclepius's compassionate nature and benevolent works anticipate aspects of Jesus' ministry, **Dionysus** has a life story that foreshadows theologically important events in Jesus' biography (see figure 3.7). Like Asclepius, Heracles, Perseus, and other heroes of the Greco-Roman era, Dionysus has a divine father and human mother. The only Olympian born to a mortal woman, he is also the only major deity to endure rejection, suffering, and death before ascending to heaven to join his immortal parent. The son of Zeus and Semele, a princess of Thebes, Dionysus was known as the "twice-born." Motivated by jealousy of her husband's human mistress, Hera deceived Semele, then pregnant with Dionysus, into compelling Zeus to reveal himself in his true form. The resulting blaze of lightning incinerated Semele, but Zeus snatched the unborn child from her womb and placed it in his own body, from which the infant Dionysus had a second birth. In one version of the myth, Hera released the Titans, ancient gods whom Zeus had chained in Tartarus (the dark abyss below Hades), who attacked the young Dionysus, dismembered his body, and ate it (see the section "Dionysus and Orphism"). In another tradition, the risen Dionysus descended to the netherworld to retrieve his mother, Semele, and install her on the celestial Olympus. Having experienced an agonizing

that he was able to raise the dead, however, Zeus killed him with a thunderbolt for disrupting the natural order. After attaining posthumous divinity, Asclepius, as the supreme patron of medicine, extended his benevolence throughout the Greco-Roman world. Professional healers, known as the Sons of Asclepius, officiated at hundreds of sanctuaries, such as Epidaurus in Greece, where patients flocked to be relieved of their afflictions. Reports of miraculous cures abounded, causing Asclepius to be hailed as the "savior" and friend of human beings.

People seeking divine help at Asclepius's many shrines commonly underwent treatment that com-

Figure 3.7 Dionysus pictured as a young man. A god who inspires both joy and terror, Dionysus, also called Bacchus, embodies the principles of mutability and transformation in both external nature and the human psyche. The inventor of wine, his chief gift to humanity, he offers an escape from life's burdens, bringing intoxication, spiritual ecstasy, and, in his mystery cult, the promise of immortal life. As the son of Zeus and the mortal Semele, Dionysus experienced death, a descent to the Underworld, and ascension to heaven. This bas-relief was found in Herculaneum, a Roman city buried by an eruption of Mount Vesuvius in 79 C.E. (© Alinari/Art Resource, NY)

Figure 3.8 Dionysus riding a panther. This mosaic from Delos pictures Dionysus mounted on a wild beast, symbol of the wine god's potential violence and affinity with unpredictable, savage nature. As the patron of Greek drama, he presided over both tragedy and comedy, two seemingly contradictory aspects of human existence. (© École Française d'Archéologie, Délos, Maison des Mosques, #5044)

death and journey to Hades' realm, Dionysus, alone among Olympians, personally knew what it is to suffer and die.

Wine, the Beverage of Communion Between Gods and Humans

As the inventor of wine making, Dionysus bestowed upon humanity a beverage that is a two-edged sword: It can liberate people from their cares, temporarily giving them the freedom of a god, but its potentially negative aftereffects can also deliver a painful reminder of human limitations, the inability to assimilate a divine gift with impunity (see figure 3.8). Most authors of the Hebrew Bible similarly regard wine as a mixed blessing, overindulgence in which can bring misery but which, in general, represents God's benefaction, one that produces a "merry heart" (Ps. 104:15) and "gives joy to life" (Eccles. 10:19). Sacrificed to Yahweh in Israelite worship (Lev. 23:13; Num. 28:14), wine was also the drink to be served at the future messianic banquet celebrating God's ultimate dominion over the earth (Isa. 25:6).

Long before Jesus linked wine and bread as part of the Christian liturgy (Mark 14:22–25; Luke 22:17–20), the two tokens of divine favor were associated in the Dionysian tradition. In the *Bacchae* (worshipers of Bacchus, another name for Dionysus), the Athenian playwright Euripides (c. 485–406 B.C.E.) has the prophet Tiresias observe that Demeter and Dionysus, respectively, had given humanity two indispensable gifts: grain or bread to sustain life and wine to make life bearable. Emblematic of divine generosity, bread and wine were tangible evidence of the gods' care for humankind. In this context, the Gospel tradition frames Jesus' public ministry with momentous feasts involving bread and/or wine. In John's Gospel, Jesus' first miraculous act is to change water into vintage wine at a Jewish wedding, a "sign" of his divinity that seems to mimic the wine-making magic of some Dionysian priests. In the Gospels of Mark, Matthew, and Luke (but, strangely, not in John), Jesus hosts a final Passover dinner with his friends at which he announces that the bread he disburses

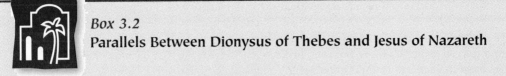

Box 3.2
Parallels Between Dionysus of Thebes and Jesus of Nazareth

Scholars of world religion and mythology detect numerous parallels between the stories of heroes and gods from widely different cultures and periods. Tales of mortal heroes who ultimately become gods characterize the ancient traditions of Egypt, Mesopotamia, India, Greece, and Rome, as well as the native cultures of Mesoamerica and North America. In comparing the common elements found in the world's heroic myths, scholars discern a number of repeated motifs that form a distinctive pattern. Although Jesus is a historical figure and Dionysus a mythic being, their received life stories reveal components of an archetypal pattern, including the hero's birth to a divine parent; his narrow escape from attempts to kill him as an infant; his "missing" formative years; his sudden appearance as a young adult manifesting miraculous gifts; his struggle with evil forces; his return to his place of origin, commonly resulting in rejection; his betrayal, suffering, and death; and his resurrection to divine status, followed by the establishment of a new cult honoring his name.

DIONYSUS	JESUS
Is son of Zeus, king of the Greek gods	Is Son of God (Mark 15:39)
Is son of Semele, a virgin princess of Thebes	Is son of Mary, a virgin of Nazareth (Luke 2)
Survives attempt by Hera to kill him as an infant	Survives attempt by King Herod to kill him as an infant (Matt. 2)
Performs miracles to inspire faith in his divinity	Performs healings and other miracles (Mark 1–2)
Battles supernatural evil in the form of Titans	Resists Satan; exorcizes demons (Mark 1–3; Matt. 4; Luke 4)
Returns to birthplace, where he is denied and rejected by family and former neighbors	Returns to hometown, where he is rejected and threatened with death (Mark 6; Luke 4)
Invents wine; promotes his gift to humanity throughout the world	Transforms water into wine (John 2); makes wine the sacred beverage in communion (Mark 14)
Suffers wounding and death at the hands of the Titans	Suffers wounding and crucifixion at the hands of the Romans (Mark 15; John 19)
Descends into the Underworld	Descends into the Underworld (1 Peter 3:19; 4:6)
Rises to divine immortality, joining his father Zeus on Olympus	Resurrected to glory; reigns in heaven at God's right hand (Phil. 2; Acts 7:55–57)
Evangelizes the world, establishing his universal cult	Directs followers to evangelize the world (Matt. 28:19–20)
Punishes opponents who denied his divinity	Will return to effect judgment on nonbelievers (Matt. 24–25; Rev. 19–20)

is his "body" and the wine he shares is his "blood" (Mark 14). The next day, Roman soldiers execute him; his wounding and crucifixion represent a form of *sparagmos,* the ritual tearing asunder of a male sacrificial victim, a fate reminiscent of Dionysus's at the hands of the Titans.

In interpreting the theological meaning of Jesus' life to a Greco-Roman audience, New Testament authors did not present their hero as a new version of Dionysus, but nonetheless they told his story in ways that strikingly parallel the Dionysian tradition (see box 3.2). The Gospel accounts of Jesus' return to Nazareth, the Galilean town where he had grown up, strongly resemble the myth of Dionysus's return to Thebes, his birthplace. In both cases, family and former neighbors fail to recognize the hero's divinity—that he is God's son—and reject him, even threatening him with death (Mark 6:1–6; Luke 4:16–30). In Euripides' *Bacchae,* the unvalued god exacts a fearful revenge on those who are blind to his divine nature, whereas in the Gospel tradition, Jesus emphasizes forgiveness of those who reject and kill him (Luke 23:34). The author of Revelation, however, portrays the glorified Christ as behaving with Dionysian vindictiveness when he returns to punish nonbelievers (Rev. 19–20).

The Mystery Religions

Alongside the public state rituals honoring the principal Olympians, Greco-Roman society also fostered a number of "underground religions" that exerted a wide influence. Known as the **mysteries** (Greek, *mysteria*) because their adherents took oaths never to reveal their secrets, these cults initiated members into the sacred rites of gods who were thought to welcome human devotees, becoming their spiritual guardians and protectors. Because Greco-Roman deities did not demand exclusive devotion, people commonly were initiated into more than one mystery religion, simultaneously cultivating a mystic bond with such diverse gods as Dionysus, Demeter, Persephone, Isis, Osiris, and Mithras. Although scholars question the extent to which these esoteric cults anticipated Christian rites, in some cases participants shared a communal meal in which their god was invisibly present, perhaps allowing them to absorb the divine body into themselves and thus partake of the diety's immortality.

DIONYSUS AND ORPHISM

Although Dionysus was the most widely celebrated Greco-Roman example of the dying and rising god, other cults centered around such figures as Orpheus, a mortal poet and musician whose music delighted both gods and humans, exerting a power to calm even savage beasts. When Orpheus bravely descended into Hades' realm to rescue his deceased wife, Eurydice, he reputedly learned the mysteries of the next world. The poetry later written in Orpheus's name supposedly contained instructions for purifying the soul to attain a happy afterlife and magic formulae that deceased souls could recite to guarantee their safe journey through netherworld darkness. *Orphism,* based on a body of occult literature ascribed to Orpheus, may not have been a unified cult, but its arcane teachings significantly influenced many Greco-Roman ideas about the soul and its fate after death.

Orphic teachers promoted a distinctive version of Dionysus's story that emphasized both the wine god's triumph over death and his intimate connection with human nature. According to Orphic tradition, Dionysus was originally the son of Zeus and Persephone, a daughter of Demeter (goddess of the soil's fertility) and queen of the Underworld. Because his son combined heavenly power with earth's secret wisdom, Zeus planned to enthrone Dionysus as king of the universe. When the Titans attacked and killed Dionysus, Athene managed to save the young god's heart, carrying it to her father, Zeus. After Zeus swallowed the heart, integrating it into himself, he fathered his son anew by Semele, who gave the child a second birth as *Dionysus Zagreus.*

Zeus punished the Titans by incinerating them with his lightning bolts. Orphic religion taught that the human race sprang from the Titans' ashes, which accounts for humanity's dual nature: Human beings are rebels against the gods, but they also contain elements of the divine, the flesh of Zeus's son, which the Titans had consumed. Although flawed by destructive impulses (the Titan heritage), humanity is partly redeemed by an inherent spark of divinity (Zeus's son, Dionysus).

Because they house a "god within," humans can be awakened to their divine potential. Through ritual purification and ethical behavior, initiates could, in the next world, eventually share their god's eternal life. The material body (Greek, *soma*), meanwhile, was the soul's prison (*sema*); death was merely the freeing of the soul to attain its ultimate home, the celestial realm above.

In Orphic doctrine, the Underworld became a place of regeneration and eventual rebirth, commonly through the soul's reincarnation into new

Figure 3.9 Mithras slaying a sacred bull. The principal rival to Christianity during the first three centuries C.E., the cult of Mithras was extremely popular with soldiers, merchants, and traders throughout the Roman Empire. Men (women were excluded) initiated into the god's mysteries received a cleansing baptism with the blood of a sacrificial animal and participated in a ritual meal. As with the religions of Isis and Dionysus, Mithraism offered adherents glimpses of the spirit realm and assurances of the soul's future life. (© Giraudon/Art Resource, NY)

bodies until a state of spiritual purity and salvation was reached.

Because Orphism foreshadows some of the themes and symbols of Christianity, it is not surprising that early Christian artists commonly used the figure of Orpheus—or even Dionysus—to depict Christ.

MITHRAS AND MITHRAISM

Perhaps the most rigorously organized and politically effective mystery cult in the Roman Empire was that of **Mithras,** which became Rome's official state religion in the third century C.E. Although Mithras, whose name means "covenant," was originally a Persian god embodying the divine power of light, his mysteries did not appear in the Greco-Roman world until the first century C.E. Scholars believe that although *Mithraism* uses names taken from ancient Persian mythology, it developed as a new cult in the west under the influence of Hellenistic astrology. Pictorial carvings decorating the caves in which Mithraic rituals were performed show that Mithras was a solar diety who presided over the stars, planets, and other astronomical features of the celestial zodiac. He is born from a rock on December 25, then calculated as the winter solstice, the crucial turning point of the solar year when hours of daylight begin to lengthen. After his birthplace is visited by shepherds, Mithras goes forth to slay a bull (the zodiacal sign of Taurus), from whose blood and semen new life appears (see figure 3.9).

His sacred myth identifies Mithras with the invisible forces ruling the universe, his sacrifice of the

Figure 3.10 A priestess of Isis. Originally an Egyptian mother goddess, Isis was worshiped throughout the Roman Empire as the embodiment of wisdom who offered worldly success and protection to persons initiated into her cult. (© Alinari/Art Resource, NY)

tual rebirth, making the worshiper a soldier of his god, committed to the principles of light and life that Mithras personified. Enormously popular among ordinary soldiers and merchants, Mithraism established sanctuaries in virtually every part of the Roman world, from Britain and Germany to Mesopotamia and Egypt.

Christianity's leading competitor during the first three centuries C.E., Mithraism featured some rituals paralleling those of the church, including baptism, sharing a communal meal, and administering oaths of celibacy. As Christians were figuratively washed in the "blood of the Lamb" (Rev. 7:14), Mithraic initiates were sprinkled and purified with the blood flowing from a sacrificed bull. Despite the fact that it apparently fulfilled its members' emotional and spiritual needs, Mithraism had a fatal flaw: Women could not be admitted to the god's service. When the Christian church, which baptized women as well as men, overcame its chief rival, however, it retained one of Mithraism's most potent symbols, the natal day of its lord. Because the solstice appropriately signifies the birth of God's Son, "the light of the world" (as well as the rebirth of the Mithraic sun), the church eventually chose Mithras's birthday to celebrate as that of Jesus.

THE MOTHER GODDESSES

Other mystery religions stress the importance of a female figure, a mother goddess who can offer help in this life and intervene for one in the next world. Demeter, who gave the world grain—the bread of life—and her daughter Persephone were worshiped at Eleusis and elsewhere in the eastern Mediterranean. Originally concerned with agricultural fertility and the cycle of the seasons, the Eleusinian Mysteries developed into a mystical celebration of death and rebirth.

Isis Even more popular in Roman times was Isis, an Egyptian mother goddess whom artists typically depicted as a madonna holding her infant son Horus (see figure 3.10). Representing motherly compassion allied with divine power, Isis was the center of a mystery cult that promised initiates per-

cosmic bull a manifestation of his omnipotence. Although we do not know how Mithras's story relates to the rites practiced in the small underground chambers where men were initiated into his mysteries, the initiation ceremony represented a spiri-

sonal help in resolving life's problems, as well as the assurance of a happy existence after death. As an embodiment of creative intelligence and cosmic wisdom, Isis was known as the goddess of "a thousand names," a deity whom the whole world honored in one form or another. Offering the individual worshiper far more comfort than the official state religions of Greece or Rome, the Isis cult found dedicated adherents throughout the Roman Empire.

In his novel *The Golden Ass*, the Roman author Apuleius (second century C.E.) reveals more about the mystical effects of initiation into a mystery cult than any other ancient writer, describing his visionary experience in which the goddess Isis became his personal savior. Like countless others before and after him, Apuleius seems to have undergone a religious awakening that transcended normal reality and bound him to a beneficent and caring deity who redeemed him from his animal nature, unveiled heavenly secrets, and imparted new meaning to his life.

The myth of Isis involved her male consort Osiris, originally a mortal ruler of ancient Egypt. Like Dionysus, Osiris suffered death by being torn in pieces but was restored to new life as god of the Underworld. Osiris owed his postmortem existence to his sister-wife Isis, who had searched throughout the world to find and reassemble the pieces of his dismembered corpse. By Greco-Roman times, the cults of Isis and Osiris, king and judge of the dead, had developed mystical rituals that promised worshipers a posthumous union with the divine.

Summary

The world of Jesus' day offered people a wide variety of religious options. This multiplicity of philosophies and religions, both public and secret, suggests that many persons in Hellenistic society felt a need to find spiritual direction and purpose in their lives. Offering practical help in this world and immortality in the next, many mystery cults focused on the promise inherent in myths dramatizing the death of a young male figure who is reborn to eternal life. Others stressed the wisdom and compassion of a mother goddess. Virtually all such cults involved a ritual or sacred meal in which worshipers were initiated into the mysteries of spiritual regeneration.

During the century following Jesus' death, Christianity developed and spread in competition with these older philosophies and religions. Addressing persons familiar with the symbols, rites, and concepts of the Hellenistic world, New Testament writers commonly phrased their message about Jesus in terms their Greek readers will understand. In a cosmopolitan environment that offered so many different answers to important religious questions, Paul, the Gospel authors, and others strove to articulate Christianity's distinctive vision of life's purpose.

QUESTIONS FOR REVIEW

1. Summarize the exploits of Alexander and the historical developments that caused the New Testament writers to use the Greek language and employ Greek concepts.

2. Define the term *philosophy*, and summarize Plato's teaching about the immortality of the soul and eternal spirit world.

3. How do the Stoics and Epicureans differ in their views of reality? How did ideas expressed in Cleanthes's *Hymn to Zeus* become part of the New Testament?

4. Identify the major Olympian gods and their principal attributes. In what ways does the Greek myth of Dionysus anticipate elements in Jesus' story? Name some parallels between the two "sons of God" who suffered, died, and attained posthumous immortality.

5. What were the "mystery religions"? What benefits did initiation into the cults of Dionysus, Demeter, Mithras, Isis, and Osiris confer on the worshiper? Enumerate some of the resemblances between some mystery cults, such as that of Mithras, and early Christianity.

QUESTIONS FOR DISCUSSION AND REFLECTION

1. Religion was an important part of life in the Greco-Roman world. How can we explain the parallels between some pre-Christian cults, such as those of Asclepius, Dionysus, and Mithras, and early Christianity? Why do you suppose the idea of a hero with a divine father and mortal mother, one who underwent

pain, death, and a descent into the Underworld, had such appeal to the Hellenistic imagination? Why did humans tend to regard their heroes and saviors as possessing the qualities of both god and man?

2. Discuss the practice of posthumously according divine honors to Greek and Roman rulers. With whom did the custom begin, and how do you think it may have prepared the way for people in the Roman Empire to accept the idea of a crucified Jewish prophet as the resurrected Son of God? Do you think that it was easier in the Hellenistic world to accept supernatural interventions than it is today?

TERMS AND CONCEPTS TO REMEMBER

monotheism and
  polytheism
philosophy
Socrates, the "gadfly"
Platonism
Stoicism and
  Epicureanism
Cynicism

Olympian religion
mystery religion
Dionysus and Orpheus
Isis and Osiris
Mithras
December 25 and the
  rebirth of the sun

RECOMMENDED READING

Boring, M. Eugene; Berger, Klaus; and Colpe, Carsten. *Hellenistic Commentary to the New Testament.* Nashville, Tenn.: Abingdon Press, 1995. An invaluable resource that provides extensive parallels between ideas in the New Testament and concepts appearing in Hellenistic literature.

Eusebius. *The History of the Church.* Translated by G. A. Williamson. Baltimore: Penguin Books, 1965. A valuable early history of Christian origins.

Fox, R. L. *Pagans and Christians.* New York: Knopf, 1987. A comprehensive and insightful investigation of Greco-Roman religious life from the second to the fourth century C.E.

Grant, F. C., ed. *Hellenistic Religions: The Age of Syncretism.* Indianapolis, Ind.: Bobbs-Merrill, 1953. A collection of Greco-Roman religious studies.

Kee, H. C. *The New Testament in Context: Sources and Documents.* Englewood Cliffs, N.J.: Prentice-Hall, 1984. An important collection of Greco-Roman documents containing parallels to New Testament ideas and teachings.

Koester, Helmut. *Introduction to the New Testament.* Vol. 1, *History, Culture, and Religion of the Hellenistic Age,* 2nd ed. Philadelphia: Fortress Press, 1995. An informative and scholarly study.

Martin, Luther H. *Hellenistic Religions: An Introduction.* New York: Oxford University Press, 1987. A solid introduction to the principal of Greco-Roman religious movements and cults.

Turcan, Robert. *The Cults of the Roman Empire.* Translated by Antonia Nevill. Cambridge, Mass.: Blackwell, 1996. Provides a lucid survey of the major cults and mystery religions that rivaled early Christianity.

CHAPTER 4

The Jewish Covenant Community

Keeping God's Law in a Gentile-Ruled World

You yourselves [the Jewish people] are my witnesses — it is Yahweh who speaks — my servants whom I have chosen, that men may know and believe that it is I . . . I am Yahweh, there is no other savior but me.   Isaiah 43:10–11, *Jerusalem Bible*

Key Themes Despite countless differences, the Hellenistic Jewish community was bound together by its collective allegiance to Yahweh, his law covenant, his promise of a national homeland, and his sacrificial cult at the Jerusalem Temple. Struggling to maintain their distinctive religious identity amid the rising tide of Hellenism, the Jewish people successfully resisted attempts by Antiochus IV, king of Syria, to eradicate the Mosaic tradition. Led by the Maccabees, Torah loyalists and guerrilla fighters drove out occupying Syrian forces and established an independent Jewish state ruled by the Hasmonean dynasty (142–63 B.C.E.).

Under control of the Roman Empire after 63 B.C.E., the covenant people were successively ruled by Roman-appointed Herodian kings and exploitative governors, such as Pontius Pilate and his successors. Widespread political discontent climaxed in a massive rebellion against Rome (66–73 C.E.), which resulted in the destruction of Jerusalem and the Jewish state.

Early Christianity expanded and developed in the Hellenistic soil of the Greco-Roman world, where teachings about Jesus' theological significance often reflected previously existing Greek concepts of divinity, but it first took root in Palestine, the heartland of the Jewish religion. Both Jesus and his original disciples were all children of Israel, born and raised in the Jewish faith. Jesus' message is explainable only in terms of Judaism, the parent religion of Christianity.

The One God, Yahweh

Although Hellenistic Judaism was extremely diverse, encompassing many conflicting groups or sects, virtually all practicing Jews held certain tenets in common that set them apart as a distinctive religious community. Many of these shared beliefs were based on the Hebrew Bible, particularly the Torah and the **Prophets.** Foremost was the **Shema,** which proclaimed the oneness of the national God, Yahweh:

> Listen, Israel: Yahweh your God is the one Yahweh. (Deut. 6:4, Jerusalem Bible)

Alone among the religions of the ancient world, Judaism, in all its manifestations, was absolutely monotheistic, accepting the existence of a single Supreme Being, Creator and Judge of heaven and earth (Isa. 40–43). According to Exodus 3:13–16, this Deity revealed himself to Moses as Yahweh, a personal name apparently based on the Hebrew verb "to be." Speaking in the first person, Yahweh declared that he is the eternal "I Am," the One who brings all into existence, including his chosen nation Israel. Because of the prohibition against taking Yahweh's name "in vain" (Exod. 20:7), after about the fourth century B.C.E. most Jews began to substitute the title *Adonai* (commonly translated "Lord") when referring to Yahweh, whose sacred name was too holy to be pronounced by unworthy persons.

Yahweh's character was qualitatively different from that of many other gods worshiped in the ancient world. A pure and holy Being who created and ruled the universe, he demanded absolute allegiance from his people. The many gods of Greece, Rome, and other polytheistic societies did not object to sharing with other deities the sacrifices and rituals of human worship. By contrast, Yahweh described himself as a "jealous God," demanding exclusive devotion and refusing to accept a worshiper who acknowledged any other deity (Exod. 20). This exclusivism, and a profound conviction that there is only one correct way to please the One God, Judaism passed on to Christianity (1 Cor. 8:5) and later to Islam, which is also strictly monotheistic.

The Torah

A second cohesive force in Judaism was the Torah (meaning instruction, law, or teaching), the first five books of the Hebrew Bible—Genesis, Exodus, Leviticus, Numbers, and Deuteronomy. Whereas Genesis presents colorful narratives extending from the world's creation to the origin of Israel's twelve tribes and their migration to Egypt, the other four books largely focus on Yahweh's making a **covenant**—a sacred agreement or pact—with the entire people of Israel, who assemble at Mount Sinai (also called Horeb) to receive the legal directives that will distinguish them as a unique worshiping community. Acting as Yahweh's agent, Moses, who had led Israel from slavery in Egypt, conducts a solemn covenant ratification, at which the people swear to obey not only the Ten Commandments but also more than 600 other laws, statutes, and ordinances. These include far more than the pledge to worship Yahweh alone, to abstain from fashioning images of him, to observe a code of ethical conduct toward one's fellow human beings, and to keep an official day of rest (the **Sabbath**). All Israel must also adhere to a host of complex dietary restrictions; perform elaborate rites involving animal, fruit, and grain sacrifices; and follow purity laws that define the concept of holiness, rigorously separating "clean" objects and activities from those deemed "unclean." The priestly Book of Leviticus specifies long lists of actions or conditions that disqualify one from participating in the nation's religious functions, including contact with corpses, menstruating women, mothers of newborn children, or objects contaminated by them.

In a farewell speech given as Israel is poised to enter the Promised Land of Canaan, Moses emphasizes that the divinely revealed Torah obligations lie well within the people's capacity to observe and are binding not merely on those gathered at Sinai but on all future Israelite generations as well (Deut. 29:13–15; 30:11–14). Even more crucial, Israel's future success as a nation—including the blessings of abundant crops, material prosperity, and victory in war—is exclusively dependent on its strict obedience to the Mosaic Torah. By contrast, disobedience will bring national disaster, including plagues, crop failures, famines, military defeats, and, eventually, exile and domination by Gentiles (Deut. 28–30).

Many Bible writers, including the prophet Jeremiah and the authors of historical narratives such as the books of Kings, blamed all of Israel's national disasters on the people's collective failure to honor their covenant obligations. Jeremiah viewed Babylon's destruction of Jerusalem in 587 B.C.E. and the subsequent Babylonian captivity (587–538 B.C.E.) as the direct result of covenant breaking. Although successive waves of Jewish leaders returned from Babylon to Jerusalem during the late sixth and fifth centuries B.C.E., the Jewish people did not regain political independence, remaining under the successive domination of Persia, Greece, and Rome. With its ancient monarchy and national autonomy gone, the covenant community was increasingly led by priests and scribes who were also the official editors, caretakers, and interpreters of the Torah.

Constantly pressured by the dominant Gentile powers that controlled their political and economic environment, the priests and Torah instructors struggled to maintain Jewish identity, creatively reinterpreting the Mosaic heritage to fit the people's changing circumstances. Because keeping Torah commands was seen as a covenant member's primary duty, the Mosaic Law and its correct implementation assumed an overwhelming importance in Jewish daily life, a trend reflected in Hellenistic Jewish literature. The noncanonical Book of Jubilees, for example, which is a Pharisee writer's retelling of Genesis and part of Exodus, presents the Torah as not only supreme but also eternal: It existed before God created the universe. Because it was delivered through Moses as a perfect and infallible expression of the divine will, the Torah could never be abrogated. Significantly, Jubilees also makes the oral law—orally transmitted commentaries about how the Torah is to be applied in specific situations—equally binding (see chapter 5).

Readers will find that individual New Testament authors express differing attitudes toward Torah-keeping. Whereas the writer of Matthew's Gospel insists that the entire Torah will remain in force until "heaven and earth disappear" (Matt. 5:17–19, Jerusalem Bible), Paul's letters argue that the Law's power ended with Jesus' sacrificial death (Gal. 3–5). The Gospels typically show Jesus disputing with Pharisees and other opponents over legal issues, including Sabbath observance (Mark 2:23–28), fasting (Mark 2:18–22), dietary prohibitions (Mark

7:14–23), and divorce (Mark 10:1–12). As Gentiles joined the originally Jewish Christian community in increasing numbers, however, questions about such Torah-mandated rules as circumcision generated heated controversy and bitterly divided Torah-observant Jewish Christians from other believers who were influenced by Paul's radical "gospel" of breaking with Mosaic tradition (Gal. 3–6; Acts 15). After a vast influx of Gentile converts overwhelmed the early churches and eventually made the Torah problem largely irrelevant within the Christian fold, the Torah remained a divisive factor in the churches' relationship to Judaism, a situation that persists to this day.

The Promised Land of Canaan

Another biblical concept that bound many Palestinian Jews together was the conviction that Yahweh had given them the land of Canaan (Palestine) forever. As descendants of the patriarch (tribal father) **Abraham,** Jesus' countrymen saw themselves as Abraham's "children," permanent heirs to the "promised land" (Gen. 12:1–3; 17:1–8; John 8:33, 39). According to the Abrahamic Covenant, the Jewish people were to become a mighty and populous nation with a dynasty of kings (Gen. 17:1–9; 22:15–18).

Only briefly in their history, however, were all the Jewish tribes united under a single monarchy. During the reigns of King **David** (c. 1000–961 B.C.E.) and his son **Solomon** (c. 961–922 B.C.E.), the nation of Israel exercised control over the entire territory described in the Abrahamic pact. After Solomon's death, the Davidic empire was divided into the competing smaller states of Israel and Judah, which, in turn, were swept away by the greater Near Eastern powers of Assyria and Babylon. By Jesus' lifetime, the Holy Land had been successively occupied by Persians, Greeks, Syrians, and Romans. Free control of their own land was only a memory to most Jews, many of whom lived outside Palestine in the **Diaspora** ("scattering" of Jews among foreign lands). To some patriotic Jews,

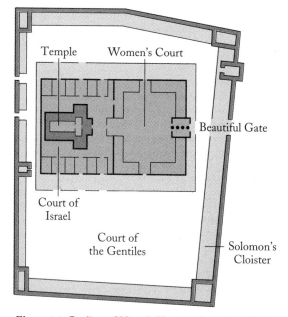

Figure 4.1 Outline of Herod's Temple, Jerusalem. With its great courtyards and porticoes, the Temple covered many acres. The main sanctuary, however, was a simple rectangular building with an outer porch, a long inner room, and an innermost chamber known as the Holy of Holies. A heavily bejeweled curtain separated the two inner chambers.

Figure 4.2 King Herod I's extensive renovations of the Jerusalem Temple, begun about 20 B.C.E., had been completed only a few years before the Romans destroyed it in 70 C.E. According to Josephus, the bejeweled curtain veiling the Sanctuary's innermost room, the Holy of Holies, depicted a panorama of heaven. Visible through the main entrance (shown here in a modern scale model), the curtain is said to have been "torn in two from top to bottom" at the moment of Jesus' death (Mark 15:38). In Mark's Gospel, this event corresponds to the heavens being "torn open" at the time of Jesus' baptism (Mark 1:10). (© Zev Radovan, Jerusalem)

however, driving foreign idolaters from their native soil was a sacred duty. To such "Zealots," as they were later called, Judaism and political nationalism were inseparable.

The Jerusalem Temple

A more tangible unifying symbol for many in the Jewish faith was the great **Temple** of Yahweh in Jerusalem. According to Deuteronomy 12, Yahweh recognized only one site on earth as the place where the animal sacrifices required by the Torah were acceptable to him. King Solomon, famous for his wisdom, wealth, and building projects, had first erected a monumental sanctuary on Zion's hill in Jerusalem. Solomon's Temple had housed the **ark of the covenant,** the sacred chest containing the imple-

ments of the Mosaic faith. It was believed that Yahweh's **kavod,** or "glory," dwelt in the innermost room, called the **Holy of Holies.** After the Babylonians destroyed Solomon's magnificent sanctuary in 587 B.C.E., a smaller building was constructed on the site and rededicated about 515 B.C.E. Extensively restored and enlarged by Herod the Great, this second Temple was commonly known in New Testament times as Herod's Temple (see figures 4.1 and 4.2).

Devout Jews, whenever possible, made annual pilgrimages to the Jerusalem sanctuary, for only there would Yahweh accept their obligatory offerings of grain, firstfruits, and unblemished sacrificial animals. According to Luke's Gospel, Jesus' family is especially scrupulous about Temple observances. Mary journeys there from Bethlehem to undergo the purification rites necessary after childbirth, and her infant son is presented there as required by Law (Luke 2:22–39; Exod. 13:2; Lev. 5:7). The Temple is where the twelve-year-old Jesus first manifests an

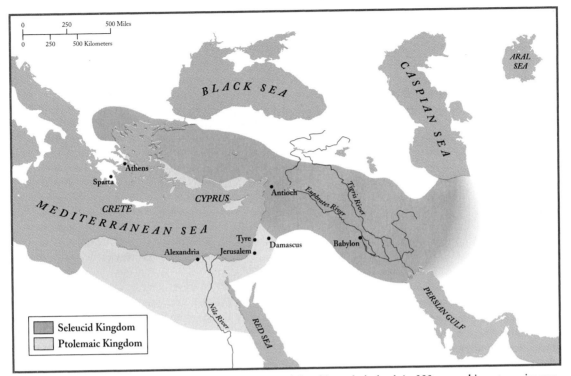

Figure 4.3 Map of the Seleucid and Ptolemaic kingdoms. After Alexander's death in 323 B.C.E., his vast empire was divided among his military successors. General Ptolemy assumed control of Egypt, while another general, Seleucus, ruled Syria and Mesopotamia. The Ptolemaic and Seleucid dynasties repeatedly fought each other for control of Palestine.

awareness of his special calling (Luke 2:41–50) and where Jesus' family goes to observe the holy days of the Jewish religious calendar (John 7:2–10).

Jesus' family repeatedly traveled to Jerusalem from Galilee, but many pious Jews made arduous pilgrimages to the Temple from distant parts of the Roman Empire. Members of the large Jewish colonies established in Alexandria, Damascus, Antioch, and Rome itself journeyed to the Temple to offer sacrifices and participate in the ceremonies of such solemn occasions as the **Day of Atonement (Yom Kippur).** Held in the fall of the year, the atonement ritual required Israel's High Priest to present sin offerings for the people so that their God could absolve them both individually and collectively for their wrongdoing. On this special day alone, the High Priest entered into the Temple's Holy of Holies to present a sacrifice on

the people's behalf and to utter the sacred name of Yahweh.

Antiochus's Persecution and the Maccabean Revolt

PALESTINE AND THE HELLENISTIC KINGDOMS

From the biblical perspective, the two most important nations derived from Alexander's empire are Ptolemaic Egypt and Seleucid Syria (see figure 4.3). When Ptolemy took control of Egypt, he also acquired Palestine, the Jewish homeland. We know little about events during this period (c. 300–200 B.C.E.), but it appears that under the **Ptolemaic**

dynasty, the Jews inhabiting **Judea**—the territory surrounding Jerusalem—enjoyed relative peace and prosperity. Shortly after 200 B.C.E., however, the Ptolemaic forces were driven out of Palestine, and the Seleucid kings of Syria assumed control. Conflict between the Syrian monarchs and the Jews reached a climax during the reign of Antiochus IV (175–163 B.C.E.).

Antiochus, who called himself *Epiphanes* (God Manifest) (see figure 4.4), attempted to unify the many diverse religious and ethnic groups in his empire by actively promoting Hellenization, forcing on his subjects the adoption of Greek culture, customs, and religion. Attracted by Greek ideas and social institutions, many Jews voluntarily abandoned their ancestral traditions to embrace the Greek way of life. Eager to become members of the gymnasium, the equivalent of a municipal athletic club, many Jewish youths underwent surgery to disguise the marks of **circumcision** (the ritual removal of the male's foreskin prescribed by Mosaic Law) so that they could not be identified as Jews when exercising nude. Mass adoption of Hellenistic practices, particularly among the Jewish upper classes, threatened to destroy Jewish ethnic distinctiveness.

Whereas many Jews willingly joined Hellenistic society, others firmly resisted the process. Aware that some Jews publicly opposed his policy of cultural and political assimilation, Antiochus determined to outlaw the ancient rituals and practices that made the Jews so different from other peoples in his empire. Departing from the usual Greek attitude of tolerance toward non-Greek religions, Antiochus attempted to eradicate the ancient Jewish faith. He forbade reading or teaching the Mosaic Law, ordered copies of the Hebrew Bible burned, executed women who had their sons circumcised, and ordered the infants' bodies tied around their mothers' necks. Keeping the Sabbath was also declared a crime punishable by death.

Besides making traditional Jewish religious observances a capital offense, Antiochus also directed an attack on the Jerusalem Temple, where Yahweh's "glory" dwelt invisibly. After stripping the Temple of its treasures to pay for his wars against Egypt, Antiochus erected a statue of the Olympian Zeus in the sanctuary courtyard and polluted Yahweh's

Figure 4.4 Shown in profile on this Greek coin, Antiochus IV Epiphanes (175–163 B.C.E.) was the Seleucid ruler of Hellenistic Syria who profaned the Jerusalem Temple by erecting a statue of Olympian Zeus there, an "abomination" that resounds through the books of Daniel and 1 Maccabees and resurfaces as a sign of End time in the Gospels of Mark and Matthew (Mark 13:14; Matt. 24:15–16). (© Hirmer Fotoarchiv)

altar by sacrificing pigs there. (This desecration is the "abomination" described in the Book of Daniel and echoed in the gospel predictions of the Roman destruction of the Temple [Dan. 9:27; 12:11; Mark 13:14; Matt. 24:15–16].) Devout Jews who refused to eat swine's flesh, an act prohibited by their Law, or who refused otherwise to compromise their ancestral religion were slaughtered by royal command. These "pious ones" who preferred death to giving up cherished traditions became known as the **Hasidim,** religious loyalists from whom the Pharisees and other Jewish denominations of Jesus' day were descended.

TORAH LOYALISM, MARTYRDOM, AND THE REWARD OF FUTURE LIFE

The persecutions of Antiochus mark the first time in biblical history that Jews died not for defending their country militarily against foreign invaders, but merely for practicing their faith. The Book of 2 Maccabees paints horrific pictures of faithful Jews paying for their integrity with torture, mutilation, and death. When Eleazar, a ninety-year-old Torah instructor, spits out the pig's flesh that Antiochus's soldiers had forced on him, he is viciously bludgeoned to death. Even worse were the agonies endured by seven young brothers who similarly refused to pass the king's test of religious conformity by eating what the Torah forbade. One by one, before their mother's eyes, they are scalped, their heads flayed, their tongues cut out, their hands and feet lopped off, and then, still conscious, they are thrust into huge pans and slowly fried alive (2 Macc. 7).

As martyrs who willingly died in a religious cause, the anonymous seven brothers not only served as models for other Jews forced to choose between life and Torah loyalty but also voiced a belief that their unspeakable sufferings would be compensated for in a future life. Expressing a conviction that God will resurrect the faithful dead—a view that enters the biblical record only with the Hellenistic Book of Daniel (Dan. 12:1–3)—the second brother places his martyrdom in the light of eternity: "The King of the world will raise us up, since it is for his laws that we die, to live again for ever" (2 Macc. 7:9). Appearing initially in the crisis ignited by enforced Hellenization, the concept that enduring a painful but holy death would lead to immortality ultimately exerted a pervasive influence on the early Christian community.

THE MACCABEAN REVOLT

To some Jewish thinkers, Antiochus's savage attacks on the Hasidim seemed to represent the "great tribulation" heralding the end of the world. The apocalyptic parts of Daniel (chs. 7–12), with their eschatological visions of God's overthrow of Antiochus's tyranny, are believed to have been written at this time.

For the Hasidim, the situation was desperate, but help came from an unexpected quarter. When Syrian commissioners tried to compel an aged village priest named **Mattathias** to sacrifice to the state-imposed cult, the old man killed first a fellow Jew who had sacrificed and then the king's representative. The author of 1 Maccabees places this defiant speech on Mattathias's lips:

> Although all the nations within the king's dominions obey him and forsake their ancestral worship, . . . yet I and my sons and brothers will follow the covenant of our fathers, . . . nor will we deviate one step from our forms of worship.
> (1 Macc. 2:19–22)

Fleeing with his five sons to the hills, Mattathias organized a band of guerrilla fighters that proved surprisingly effective against the Syrian army. After Mattathias's death, his most capable son, **Judas Maccabeus** ([God's] Hammer), carried on the revolt. In December 164 B.C.E., Judas's followers recaptured and purified the Jerusalem Temple, an event later commemorated annually as the **Feast of Dedication** (1 Macc. 4) and known today as **Hanukkah.**

Following Judas's death, leadership of the Jewish war for religious freedom passed to various Maccabean brothers, who eventually succeeded in forcing the Syrians to grant Israel national independence (142 B.C.E.). Despite protests from other Jewish groups, including many of the Hasidim, the **Maccabees** made themselves kings, establishing the **Hasmonean** dynasty (named after a Maccabean ancestor, Hasmoneas).

THE DOMINATION OF ROME

The Maccabean political and social legacy was less effective than its military accomplishments. The Hasmonean period (142–40 B.C.E.) is largely a record of intrigue, ambition, and treachery—a series of tragically missed opportunities for achieving Jewish unity and peace. Eventually, rivalry among the Hasmonean rulers led to a decision fatal to Jewish national autonomy: an invitation to involve Rome militarily in Jewish affairs. In 63 B.C.E., a claimant to the Hasmonean throne, John Hyrcanus II, asked Rome for help in ousting his younger brother, Aristobulus II, who had made himself both High Priest and king. In response, Rome dispatched Pompey, whose troops overthrew Aristobulus and installed John Hyrcanus as High Priest and "eth-narch" (63–40 B.C.E.) over a Jewish state much reduced in size and prestige. The change in title from "king" to "ethnarch" (provincial governor) is significant, for after 63 B.C.E. Jewish rulers were mere puppets of Rome, and the Holy Land merely another province in the Empire.

THE HEROD FAMILY

Herod the Great, the monarch ruling Palestine for the Romans when Jesus was born (Matt. 2:1; Luke 1:5), was appointed king by the Roman Senate in 40 B.C.E. Although ostensibly Jewish in religion, Herod was a native of **Idumea** (ancient Edom, a traditional enemy of Israel) and had to overcome armed resistance to take the territory the Romans had assigned him. By 37 B.C.E. Herod had captured Jerusalem and begun a reign marked by a strange combination of administrative skill, cruelty, and bloodshed. Politically, Herod was remarkably successful. Enjoying Roman support, he extended the boundaries of his kingdom almost to the limits of David's biblical empire. Under Herod, the Jewish state expanded to include the districts of Samaria and Galilee (where Jesus grew up) and territories east of the Jordan River (see figure 4.5).

Herod's building program matched his political ambitions. He constructed monumental fortresses, the best known of which is **Masada** on the west shore of the Dead Sea. He also founded the port city **Caesarea,** which later became the Roman administrative capital. Herod's most famous project, however, was rebuilding the Temple in Jerusalem, transforming it into one of the most magnificent sanctuaries in the ancient world (see figure 4.6). This was the Temple where Jesus and the disciples worshiped (Mark 11:27–13:2; Luke 2:22–38, 41–50; 19:47–48; 20:1–21:7; Acts 2:46; 3:1–10; 21:18–30). Begun in 20 B.C.E., the Temple was not completed until about 62 C.E., only eight years before the Romans destroyed it.

Despite his grandiose achievements, Herod's treachery and violence made him hated by most of his Jewish subjects. He murdered his Hasmonean wife Mariamne and their two sons, Alexander and Aristobulus, as well as other family members. His

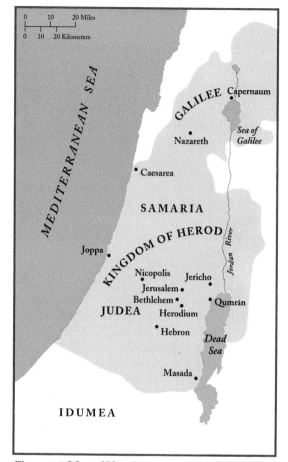

Figure 4.5 Map of Herod's kingdom. Appointed ruler by the Romans, Herod the Great (40–4 B.C.E.) expanded the boundaries of the Jewish state to include most of the land once held by King David (1000 B.C.E.). At his death, Herod's kingdom was divided among his three sons.

fear that some conspiracy would rob him of his throne and his ruthless elimination of any potential rival provide the background for the Gospel story that Herod massacred Bethlehem's children (Matt. 2:16–17).

HEROD'S SUCCESSORS

When Herod died in 4 B.C.E. (according to modern calendars, Jesus was probably born a few years B.C.E.), his kingdom was divided among his three

Figure 4.6 In this scale model of Jerusalem (first century C.E.), the simple flat-roofed tenements housing the general population contrast with the monumental public buildings that Herod I (40–4 B.C.E.) erected. The heavily fortified Temple area appears in the top right. (© Erich Lessing/PhotoEdit)

Rome. The most celebrated of these local governors was the procurator **Pontius Pilate** (26–36 C.E.), the man who sentenced Jesus to death.

The Roman Emperors

Although Pilate and representatives of the Herod family are the most prominent political figures in the Gospel accounts, the real center of political power in Jesus' world lay in the person of the Roman emperor. At Jesus' birth, the emperor **Augustus** (originally named Gaius Octavius, 27 B.C.E.–14 C.E.) ruled over an empire even larger and more diverse than Alexander's (see figure 4.7). Rome controlled not only the Near East but also all of North Africa and most of Europe. Military conquests had reduced the Mediterranean Sea to the status of a Roman lake. Located at the eastern margin of the empire, the Jewish homeland was only an insignificant, although politically troublesome, part of an international colossus. As a further insult to Jewish sensibilities, the Romans adopted the Greek name for this area, calling it **Palestine** after the Philistines, a sea people who had once been Israel's chief enemy (Judges; 1 Sam.).

THE BEGINNING OF IMPERIAL RULE

Rule of the empire by a single man who could wield almost unlimited power had been instituted only a short time before Jesus' birth. The grandnephew of Julius Caesar, Gaius Octavius (the future Augustus), joined with Mark Antony to defeat Brutus and Cassius, Caesar's assassins, at the Battle of Philippi (42 B.C.E.). With Lepidus, another of Caesar's supporters, Octavius and Mark Antony formed the Second Triumvirate (the first had been an unofficial alliance between Julius Caesar, Pompey, and Crassus) and shared the governing of Rome. The real power was divided between Mark Antony, who took control of the east, and Octavius, who administered Italy and the western dominions. Competition between the two men culminated in the Battle of Actium (31 B.C.E.), a naval engagement in which Octavius's forces defeated those of Antony and his paramour,

surviving sons. **Philip** (4 B.C.E.–34 C.E.) became tetrarch of the areas north and east of the Lake of Galilee. He seems to have been a competent ruler, and we hear little of him. His brother, **Herod Antipas** (4 B.C.E.–39 C.E.), was given the territories of Galilee and Perea, a region east of the Jordan River. This is the Herod who beheaded John the Baptist (Mark 6:14–29; Matt. 14:1–12) and whom Jesus characterized as "that fox" (Luke 13:31–32). As ruler of Galilee, Jesus' homeland, Herod examined Jesus at Pilate's request (Luke 23:6–12). A third brother, **Herod Archelaus,** inherited the southwestern portion of Herod the Great's realm (Judea, Samaria, and Idumea) but proved a vicious and incompetent ruler. The Romans removed him in 6 C.E. and in his place appointed a series of prefects (later **procurators**) to govern the region directly for

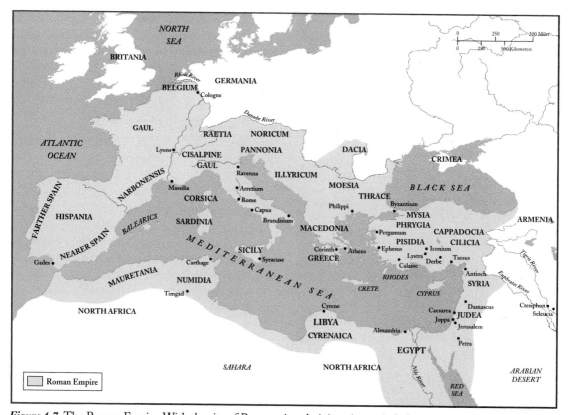

Figure 4.7 The Roman Empire. With the city of Rome as its administrative capital, the empire governed most of the known world. Its subjects included people of virtually every race, language group, and ethnic background.

Cleopatra VII, a descendant of Alexander's general Ptolemy, who then ruled Egypt. Antony's death and Cleopatra's suicide (30 B.C.E.) allowed Egypt to be incorporated into the empire and left Octavius the sole ruler of the Roman state.

After decades of civil war, Rome was finally at peace. A grateful Senate voted Octavius the title of "princeps" (27 B.C.E.), recognizing him as the undisputed head of state. The ascension of Octavius (henceforth called Augustus) to imperial dignity marked the end of the ancient Roman Republic and cost the citizens of Rome many of their traditional political rights. The Romans, however, seemed willing to exchange civil freedom for the restoration of public order, political stability, and economic prosperity that Augustus's reign brought (see figure 4.8).

Augustus was succeeded by his stepson **Tiberius** (14–37 C.E.), the emperor reigning during Jesus' ministry (Luke 3:1). It was Tiberius's governmental appointee Pontius Pilate who found Jesus guilty of treason against Rome (Matt. 27:11–44; Mark 15:2–32; Luke 22:66–23:38; John 18:28–19:22). Box 4.1 chronicles some key events that helped shape Jesus' world.

NEW TESTAMENT ATTITUDES TOWARD ROME

Rome's military presence in Judea pervades the Gospel accounts of Jesus' life, as it did the lives of most first-century Jews. To some, Rome was "the evil empire," and its occupying armies no better than a horde of demons afflicting the land. This

Figure 4.8 Head of Augustus (Gaius Octavius), first emperor of Rome (27 B.C.E.–14 C.E.). Defeating all rivals for control of the Roman Empire, Augustus ended centuries of civil war and introduced a new era of peace and political stability. (© The Metropolitan Museum of Art, Rogers Fund, 1980. (08.258.47))

negative view seems to echo in Mark's story of Jesus exorcising the Gerasene demoniac, a man possessed by "unclean spirits" who announce that their name is "legion"—the term designating a Roman military unit of about 5400 soldiers—"because there are so many of us." (Mark 5:1–13). The sensitive issue of paying taxes to support an idolatrous Gentile government, which troubled many Jews, is addressed in Jesus' famous directive to "pay Caesar [the Roman emperor] what belongs to Caesar, and God what belongs to God," a pronouncement that reaffirms the covenant people's primary allegiance to Yahweh (Mark 12:17). Jesus also repudiates the Roman custom of economic and social patronage—an almost ubiquitous sys-

tem in which a rich "benefactor" distributed favors to his dependent "clients" (Luke 22:24–27). As Jesus presents it, the "kingdom of God," a concept that he makes central to his teaching, is both an implicit criticism of and an exciting alternative to Roman rule.

Although Jesus is a political victim of Rome's determination to eliminate any potential leader who might oppose its absolutism, the Gospel authors depict individual Roman soldiers as playing key roles in Jesus' story. Luke pictures a group of Jewish leaders identifying a Roman centurion as a "friend of our nation . . . who built us our synagogue" (meeting place), adding that he deserves to have Jesus heal a favorite servant. Impressed by the Roman officer's trust in his curative powers, Jesus exclaims that "not even in Israel have I found such faith" (Luke 7:1–10; Matt. 8:5–13). Another centurion in effect returns the compliment at Jesus' crucifixion, recognizing him as "a son of God" (Mark 15:39) or, in Luke's version, pronouncing him "innocent" of sedition against Rome (Luke 23:47).

By placing favorable judgments of Jesus on the lips of Roman soldiers, the Gospel writers anticipate the historical fact that Jesus' followers achieved far greater success among Greeks and Romans than among their fellow Jews (see chapters 9 and 12). As a result, most New Testament writers actively promote an accommodation with Roman power. In his letter to the church at Rome, Paul urges Christians to submit to Roman law and institutions (Rom. 13), while the author of Luke-Acts emphasizes that from its inception Christianity was a law-abiding movement that merited governmental protection and support (see chapter 12). A glaring exception is the mystic who wrote Revelation, which paints Rome as a persecutor of the godly, an obscenely rich "harlot" who draws her imperial power from the "great dragon," Satan (Rev. 17–18).

The Jewish Revolt Against Rome

Although most Jews living in cities scattered throughout the Roman Empire probably held a wide variety of views about their Gentile rulers,

Box 4.1
Some Representative Events That Shaped the World of Jesus' Day

c. 334–323 B.C.E. Alexander's conquests create a new international culture, the Hellenistic, bringing Greek language, literature, ideas, and customs to the entire Near Eastern world, including Palestine. This broad diffusion of Greek philosophic and religious thought plays a major role in the development of both Judaism and Christianity.

323–197 B.C.E. The Ptolemaic dynasty, established by Ptolemy I, general and one of Alexander's successors, controls Palestine. Many Jews are attracted to Greek learning and the Hellenistic way of life.

200–197 B.C.E. The Seleucid dynasty of Syria, descendants of Alexander's general Seleucus, drive the Ptolemys from Palestine and become the new masters of the Jews (197–142 B.C.E.).

168–164 B.C.E. The Seleucid ruler Antiochus IV, "Epiphanes," attempts to eradicate the Jewish religion. He forbids circumcision, Sabbath observance, reading of the Torah, and so on. Antiochus erects a statue of the Olympian Zeus in the Temple precincts ("the abomination" of Daniel 9:27). The Hasidim (pious ones) refuse to compromise their religion; many are tortured and murdered. Mattathias, a religious loyalist, and his five sons initiate the Maccabean Revolt.

164 B.C.E. Led by Judas Maccabeus, a Jewish guerrilla army recaptures, purifies, and rededicates the Temple, an event later commemorated in the festival of Hanukkah.

142–63 B.C.E. By 142 B.C.E. the Jews have expelled the Syrian armies and established an independent state governed by Hasmonean (Maccabean) rulers. Internal strife and intrigue fatally weaken the Hasmonean kingdom.

63 B.C.E. Pompey's legions occupy Palestine, annexing it as part of the Roman Empire.

40 B.C.E. The Roman Senate appoints Herod (Herod the Great), a nobleman of Idumea (the ancient Edom), king of Judea.

37–4 B.C.E. After laying siege to Jerusalem, Herod takes the city by force; his long reign is marked by ambitious building programs (including a massive renovation of the Jerusalem Temple) and acts of cruelty and violence.

27 B.C.E.–14 C.E. Gaius Octavius, having defeated his rival Mark Antony at the Battle of Actium (31 B.C.E.), becomes undisputed ruler of the entire Roman Empire. Renamed Augustus by the Roman Senate, Octavius ends the civil wars that had divided Rome for generations and establishes a long period of civil order called the *Pax Romana* (Roman Peace).

c. 6–4 B.C.E. Jesus is born to Mary and Joseph, citizens of Nazareth.

4 B.C.E. After Herod the Great's death, his kingdom is divided among his three sons. Herod Antipas (4 B.C.E.–39 C.E.) rules Galilee and Perea; Herod Philip (4 B.C.E.–34 C.E.) rules territories north and east of Galilee; Herod Archelaus (4 B.C.E.–6 C.E.) rules Judea, Samaria, and Idumea but is deposed. His territories henceforth are administered directly by Roman officials.

14–37 C.E. Tiberius, stepson of Augustus, rules Rome.

26–36 C.E. Pontius Pilate, appointed by Rome, governs as procurator of Judea (26–36 C.E.). Pilate tries and condemns Jesus of Nazareth (c. 30 or 33 C.E.).

c. 27–29 C.E. John the Baptist conducts an apocalyptic campaign of repentance, baptizing the penitent in the Jordan River.

c. 27–30 or 29–33 C.E. Jesus' public ministry: Jesus and a small band of disciples tour villages and cities in and around Galilee, including forays into Phoenicia and the Decapolis (league of Greek cities east of Galilee). A final journey to Jerusalem results in Jesus' rejection by religious authorities and his execution by Pilate on charges of treason.

---

most seem to have accepted the political realities of imperial domination. The case was fatally different in the Jewish homeland.

About thirty years after Jesus' crucifixion, the Palestinian Jews rose in armed revolt against Rome. Led by passionate Jewish nationalists, many of whom believed it sinful even to allow idol-worshiping Gentiles to occupy the Holy Land, the Jewish War against Rome (66–73 C.E.) proved an overwhelming disaster for the Jewish people.

Figure 4.9 Portrait bust of the Emperor Vespasian (69–79 C.E.). Appointed by Nero to crush the Jewish revolt (66–73 C.E.), Vespasian conquered Galilee but withdrew from the war after Nero's suicide. A year later, he became emperor. He then appointed his son Titus to carry on the siege of Jerusalem. (© British Museum)

Figure 4.10 Portrait bust of the Emperor Titus (79–81 C.E.). When his father, Vespasian, left him in charge of putting down the Jewish revolt, Titus laid siege to Jerusalem, capturing the city and burning its Temple in August 70 C.E. He succeeded his father as emperor in 79 C.E., but died after a brief reign. (© British Museum)

When the revolt broke out in 66 C.E., the emperor **Nero** sent a veteran military commander, **Vespasian,** to crush the rebellion (see figure 4.9). Galilee fell easily to the Roman army, but before Vespasian could occupy Judea, the territory in southern Palestine of which Jerusalem was the capital, Nero was driven from the throne and committed suicide (June 68 C.E.). Following a year of political chaos, Vespasian was acclaimed emperor by the Roman legions and confirmed by the Senate. Leaving his son **Titus** in charge of the Jewish War, Vespasian returned to Rome (see figure 4.10). After a siege of six months, Titus captured and destroyed Jerusalem, burning Herod's splendidly rebuilt Temple in August 70 C.E. (see figure 4.11).

Our main source of information about the war is **Flavius Josephus,** a first-century Jewish historian who first participated in the rebellion but later became an ally of the Romans. An eyewitness to many of the events he describes, Josephus wrote to explain and defend his countrymen's action in revolting against Roman oppression. In *The Jewish War,* he vividly recounts the Roman capture of Jerusalem and the slaughter of many thousands of men, women, and children. While attempting to evoke sympathy for his people and to make their religion comprehensible to his Greek and Roman readers, Josephus also blames a small minority of political fanatics for their refusal to negotiate a compromise settlement with the Roman forces.

Figure 4.11 Detail from the Arch of Titus, which the Roman Senate erected in the Forum of Rome about 100 C.E. Created in honor of Titus's victories in the Jewish War, this frieze depicts Roman soldiers carrying off loot from the Jerusalem Temple, including the Menorah—the seven-branched candelabrum formerly housed in the sanctuary. (© Alinari/Art Resource, NY)

According to Josephus, the extreme revolutionary party, the **Zealots,** virtually forced General Titus to destroy the holy city and its Temple by their obstinate refusal to accept the Roman terms of peace. Many historians doubt Josephus's sometimes self-serving interpretation of events, but his surviving works, including a history of Israel called *Antiquities of the Jews,* are an invaluable record of this turbulent period.

A second Jewish revolt against Rome (132–135 C.E.) was led by a young man named **bar Kochba** (Son of the Star), whom many Palestinian Jews believed to be the Messiah who would restore David's kingdom. Brutally suppressed by the em-

peror Hadrian, the bar Kochba rebellion resulted in a second Roman destruction of Jerusalem (135 C.E.). A Roman shrine was then constructed on the site of Herod's Temple, and Jews were forbidden to enter their city on pain of death. (Box 4.2 lists the Roman emperors of the New Testament period.)

Summary

The period of Jesus' life is thus chronologically framed by two Jewish wars for religious and political independence. The first, led by the Maccabees,

Box 4.2
Roman Emperors of the New Testament Period

The imperial form of government, in which a single man ruled the entire Roman Empire, was established by Augustus a generation before the birth of Jesus and continued until the collapse of the western empire in 476 C.E. Emperors reigning during the rise of early Christianity, and some of the principal events that affected the Christian community, are given here.

THE JULIO-CLAUDIAN DYNASTY

Augustus (30 B.C.E.–14 C.E.) Establishment of *Pax Romana;* Jesus' birth, c. 6–4 B.C.E.; Jesus' youth in Nazareth, Galilee

Tiberius (14–37 C.E.) John the Baptist's revival campaign; Jesus' ministry in Galilee and Judea; the Crucifixion c. 30 or 33 C.E.; the conversion of Paul

Gaius (Caligula) (37–41) Threatened installation of the emperor's statue in the Jerusalem Temple; Paul's early missionary journeys

Claudius (41–54) Expelled some Jews from Rome (c. 49)

Nero (54–68) Persecution of Christians in Rome; outbreak of the Jewish War; Vespasian's suppression of the Galilean revolt; executions of James (Jesus' kinsman), Peter, and Paul

YEAR OF THE FOUR EMPERORS AND THE FLAVIAN DYNASTY

Galba (68–69); Otho (69); Vitellius (69)

Vespasian (69–79) Destruction of Jerusalem (70) and Masada (73); Mark written

Titus (79–81)

Domitian (81–96) Luke-Acts' positive view of Rome; sporadic persecutions; Revelation's visions of Rome's fall; community of the Beloved Disciple's production of the Fourth Gospel

THE ADOPTIVE AND ANTONINE EMPERORS

Nerva (96–98)

Trajan (98–117) Letter of Pliny the Younger describing the persecution of Christians in Asia Minor

Hadrian (117–138) Second Jewish revolt, led by bar Kochba (132–135); Jews barred from Jerusalem

Antoninus Pius (138–161) Marcion's excommunication in Rome; composition of 2 Peter, the last canonical document written

Marcus Aurelius (161–180)

Commodus (180–192)

---

created an autonomous Jewish state. The second, a generation after Jesus' death, resulted in national annihilation. Bar Kochba's later attempt to restore Jewish fortunes met a similar defeat. From this time until 1948, when the modern nation of Israel was established, the Jews were to be a people without a country.

QUESTIONS FOR REVIEW

1. Describe the concepts or beliefs common to most groups of first-century Judaisms. How was the ideal of Jewish monotheism related to Torah practice and the Temple cult?

2. What did the Greek-Syrian King Antiochus IV attempt to accomplish in his policy toward his Jewish

subjects? How did the Hasidim oppose Antiochus's enforced Hellenization, and what part did the Maccabees play in Jewish resistance to assimilation?

3. After the Romans conquered Palestine, what role did Herod and his successors play in Jewish history? Describe the functions of Roman governors such as Pontius Pilate.

QUESTIONS FOR DISCUSSION AND REFLECTION

1. How did belief in a single holy God who requires exclusive devotion affect Jewish behavior during the persecutions of Antiochus IV? Why were Jews willing to suffer torture and death rather than disobey Torah commands? How is the concept of

martyrdom related to notions about compensation in the afterlife?

2. Discuss Jewish relations with Rome. What led to the great revolt of 66–73 C.E., and what were its consequences for the Jewish people? In what different ways did New Testament authors regard Rome?

TERMS AND CONCEPTS TO REMEMBER

Yahweh
Torah
Abrahamic Covenant
Yom Kippur
   (Day of Atonement)
Antiochus IV
Maccabean revolt

Hasmonean dynasty
Herod the Great
Herod Antipas
Augustus
Jewish revolts against
   Rome
Flavius Josephus

RECOMMENDED READING

Boardman, John; Griffin, Jasper; and Murray, Oswyn. *The Oxford History of the Classical World.* New York: Oxford University Press, 1986. An authoritative collection of informative essays by leading scholars.

Boren, H. C. *The Ancient World: An Historical Perspective,* 2nd ed. Englewood Cliffs, N.J.: Prentice-Hall, 1986. A readable history surveying the world from ancient Sumer to the fall of Rome.

Green, Peter. *Alexander to Actium: The Historical Evolution of the Hellenistic Age.* Berkeley: University of California Press, 1990. Includes an evaluation of Antiochus's policies and the Maccabean revolt in the general context of Hellenistic culture.

Josephus, Flavius. *The Jewish War,* rev. ed. Translated by G. A. Williamson. Edited by E. M. Smallwood. New York: Penguin Books, 1981. The most important contemporary source for conditions in Palestine during the first century C.E.

Peters, F. E. *The Harvest of Hellenism: A History of the Near East from Alexander the Great to the Triumph of Christianity.* New York: Simon & Schuster, 1970. A comprehensive presentation of Greek and Roman history affecting Palestine.

CHAPTER 5

The Diverse World of First-Century Judaisms

For you [Israel] are a people consecrated to Yahweh your God; it is you that Yahweh our God has chosen to be his very own people out of all the peoples of the earth. Deuteronomy 7:6, *Jerusalem Bible*

Key Themes In Jesus' day, the Jewish faith was extremely diverse, split into numerous parties and factions, the most prominent of which included the Sadducees, Pharisees, Essenes, Samaritans, and Zealots. Although the majority of Jews did not then belong to any particular party, many held eschatological convictions (beliefs about the imminent end of the world) and hoped that God's Messiah would soon arrive to deliver them from their enemies. As Jewish writings of this period demonstrate, even in Palestine Judaism was thoroughly saturated with Hellenistic ideas.

Reverence for the Mosaic Torah, the land, the Jerusalem Temple, and the transcendent Being whose invisible presence sanctified it were unifying aspects of first-century Judaisms. Nevertheless, the Jews of Jesus' time were so deeply divided on so many different issues, both religious and political, that it is impossible to describe the Jewish religion as a coherent whole. The more scholars learn about the period before 70 C.E., the more diverse Judaisms appear to have been.

First-Century Jewish Diversity

The Gospel writers and Josephus mention several distinct Jewish groups — the **Sadducees**, Pharisees, Herodians, Samaritans, and Zealots — but these sects or parties represent only a fraction of first-century Judaism's bewildering variety. Keeping in mind that the groups discussed here constitute a mere sample of Jewish pluralism, we will survey four of the best-known denominations (or "philosophies" as Josephus calls them).

THE SADDUCEES

Because none of their writings survive, we know the Sadducees only through brief references in the New Testament and in other secondary sources, such as Josephus. Represented as among Jesus' chief opponents, the Sadducees were typically members of the Jewish upper class, wealthy landowning aristocrats who largely controlled the priesthood and the Temple. Their name (Greek *Saddoukaioi*, from the Hebrew *Zaddukim* or *tsaddiqim*) means "righteous ones" and may be descriptive, or it may reflect their claim to be the spiritual heirs of Zadok, the High Priest under David and Solomon (1 Kings 1:26). Because the prophet Ezekiel had stated that only the "sons of Zadok" could "approach Yahweh" in the Temple service (Ezek. 40:46), the Sadducees, the officiating priests at the Jerusalem sanctuary, emphasized their inherited right to this role. High Priests like **Caiaphas** (who condemned Jesus) were apparently always of their number. Along with their opponents the Pharisees, the Sadducees dominated the Great Council (Sanhedrin), Judaism's highest court of religious law.

The Sadducees and the Romans Although the New Testament and Josephus give us an incomplete picture of the group, the Sadducees seem to have acted as chief mediators between the Jewish people and the occupying Roman forces. As beneficiaries of the Roman-maintained political order, the Sadducees had the most to lose from civil disorder and typically opposed a Jewish nationalism that might attempt to overthrow the status quo. Their adoption of Hellenistic customs and their friendship with Rome made it possible for them to manipulate some Palestinian political affairs. The Sadducees' determination to preserve the uneasy accommodation with Rome is revealed in their eagerness to get rid of Jesus, whom they apparently regarded as a potential revolutionary and a threat to Judea's political security. Their view that rebellion against Rome would lead to total annihilation of the Jewish nation was vindicated during the Jewish revolt (66–73 C.E.), when Roman troops decimated Jerusalem and Judea.

As conservative religiously as they were politically, the Sadducees practiced a literal reading of the Torah, rejecting the Pharisees' "oral law" and other interpretations of the biblical text. It is uncertain how much of the Prophets or Writings they accepted, but they did not share Pharisaic beliefs about a coming judgment, resurrection, angels, or demons (Mark 12:18; Acts 23:8). As a group, the Sadducees did not survive the first century C.E. Their close association with Rome; their refusal to accept developing ideas based on the Prophets, the Writings, and the Apocrypha; and their narrow focus on Temple ritual—all spelled their doom. After the Temple's destruction (70 C.E.), the Sadducees disappear from history. The Pharisees, emphasizing education and progressive reinterpretation

of Scripture, became the leaders in formulating post-70s Judaism.

THE PHARISEES

The Gospels' bitter attacks on the **Pharisees,** who are shown as Jesus' leading opponents, have made Pharisee synonymous with hypocrisy and heartless legalism (Matt. 23). To the Gospel writers, the Pharisees and their associates the **scribes** are "blind guides" who perversely reject Jesus' message and thereby doom their people to divine punishment (Matt. 21:33–46; 22:1–14; 23:37–39; Luke 19: 41–44). Modern historians recognize, however, that the Gospels' picture of the Pharisees is biased and unfair. According to most scholars, the Evangelists' antagonism toward the group stems not so much from the historical Jesus' debates with the Pharisees as from the historical situation at the time the Gospels were composed. Written several decades after Jesus' death, the Gospels reflect a period of intense ill feeling between the early Christian community and the Jewish leadership.

Hostility between the church and **synagogue** climaxed following the Roman destruction of Jerusalem in 70 C.E. In the years immediately after Jerusalem's fall, the Pharisees became the dominant force within Judaism and the chief spokesmen for the position that Jesus of Nazareth was not the expected Jewish Messiah. Although Jews and Christians had previously worshiped side-by-side in the Temple, following the failure of the Jewish War against Rome, Jewish-Christian relations deteriorated rapidly. After about 90 C.E. some Jewish Christians were expelled from the synagogues and condemned as perverters of the Jewish heritage (see John 9). The Gospels preserve the Christian response in their rancorous denunciations of the Pharisees.

Whatever their quarrel with the historical Jesus may have been, as a group the Pharisees were completely devoted to the Mosaic Torah and its application to all the concerns of daily life. The meaning of their name is obscure, although it seems to have been derived from the Hebrew verb "to separate." As spiritual descendants of the Hasidim, who separated themselves from what they saw as the corrupting influence of Hellenistic culture, the Pharisees rigorously observed a code of ritual purity. They scrupulously segregated themselves from contaminating contact with anything the Law forbade.

Strict Torah Observance Many Pharisees were deeply learned in the Torah and skilled at its interpretation. Josephus states that the common people regarded them as the most authoritative interpreters of the Law. Unlike their rivals the Sadducees, the Pharisees accepted not only the written Law contained in the Mosaic Torah but also a parallel oral law. Pharisaic oral teachings, which the Gospel of Mark calls the "tradition of the elders" (Mark 7:3), were intended to extend the laws of Temple purity to virtually every aspect of daily life, including Sabbath observance, dietary regulations, alms giving, and prayer. After many generations of oral transmission — the effect of which was to "build a fence around the Torah" — this vast body of commentary and case law was codified in the Mishnah. The **Mishnah,** compiled about 200 C.E. by Rabbi Judah ha-Nasi, is the first document of rabbinic Judaism. An informal term meaning "master" or "teacher" in Jesus' day, after the two Jewish wars against Rome, **rabbi** became a title designating scholars ordained or officially recognized as authoritative in their practice and exposition of Jewish law. In time, the Mishnah ("that which is learned by repetition") became the basis of further commentary, resulting in the **Gemara** (completion), which was added to the Mishnah to form the **Talmud** (teaching), an immense compendium of rabbinic scholarship containing about 2.5 million words. Two Talmuds developed, one in Palestine (also known as the Jerusalem Talmud) about 400 C.E. and one in Babylon about 550 C.E. The Babylonian Talmud, in thirty-six tractates or books, became the supreme guidebook of **Judaism,** and its case laws the regulators of Jewish life.

Although many scholars believe that Pharisaism evolved into the rabbinic Judaism that eventually produced the Talmud — and hence modern Judaism — the rabbinic compilers never refer to themselves as Pharisees and seem to avoid the term. After the Temple's destruction, however, it was Pharisaic emphasis on reapplication of the Torah to the Jewish people's radically changed circumstances that helped make possible the survival of their religion and distinctive way of life.

Hillel and Shammai Two influential Pharisaic leaders whose teachings are remembered in the rabbinic commentaries are Hillel and Shammai, who lived into the first decades of the first century C.E. A famous anecdote illustrates the striking differences in temperament of these two eminent Pharisees. It was said that a Gentile persistently besought Shammai, known for his aloof personality and strict interpretation of the Law, to explain the essential meaning of the Law while the Gentile stood on one foot. Appalled that anyone could be simple enough to imagine that the profundities of the Mosaic revelation could be articulated so tersely, Shammai sent the Gentile packing. Undaunted, the Gentile then went to Hillel with the same question. Taking the man's inquiry as sincere, Hillel is said to have replied: "Do not do to your neighbor what is hateful to yourself. That is the entire Torah. All the rest is commentary." Although expressed negatively, Hillel's concise summary of the Law's human significance anticipates Jesus' expression of the golden rule (Matt. 7:12).

Despite his remembered disagreements with Pharisees on how the Law should be practiced, Jesus is known to have been on good terms with some of their number, dining at their homes and even benefiting from a friendly warning about a plot on his life (Luke 7:36–50; 13:31–32). Matthew's Gospel depicts Jesus as sharing the Pharisees' view that the Law is eternally binding (Matt. 5:17–19) and that they interpret it correctly (Matt. 23:2–3). On numerous matters of belief, Jesus and the Pharisees see eye-to-eye (Mark 11:18–26). Unlike the Sadducees, they believe in a coming judgment day, resurrection of the dead, a future life of rewards and penalties based on deeds in this life, and the existence of angels, demons, and other inhabitants of the invisible world. By devotedly studying the Hebrew Bible and flexibly adapting its principles to the constantly changing situation in which Jews found themselves, the Pharisees depended on the possession of neither the Temple nor the Promised Land to perpetuate the Jewish faith. Some may have been rigid or overly ingenious in their application of the Torah's requirements, perhaps making the Law impossible for the poor or ignorant to keep (Matt. 23:6–23). As a group, however, they pursued a standard of religious commitment and personal righteousness that was virtually unique in the ancient world.

Gamaliel According to the Book of Acts, it was Rabbi **Gamaliel,** a leading first-century Pharisee, who protected the early Jesus movement from excessive repression by the Jerusalem authorities (Acts 5:34–42). Depicted in Acts as the apostle Paul's teacher and an advocate of religious tolerance, Gamaliel is rarely mentioned in the Mishnah, although it observes that "when he died the glory of the Torah ended." Acts portrays Paul, even after his conversion to Christianity, as remaining proud of his Pharisaic background and appealing for support from his fellow Pharisees when he stood trial before the Jerusalem religious council (Acts 23:6–9; Phil. 3:4–7).

THE ACADEMY OF JAMNIA (YAVNEH)

After Rome's destruction of the Jewish state in 70 C.E., Roman authorities apparently wished to show their goodwill toward prominent Jews who had not advocated violent revolt against the empire. The leading force behind this Roman-endorsed movement to reorganize the postwar Jewish faith was Yohanan ben Zakkai (c. 1–80 C.E.), an eminent Pharisee. According to one tradition, during the Roman siege of Jerusalem, ben Zakkai—who favored a peaceful settlement with Rome—escaped from the city by feigning death and being carried in a coffin outside Jerusalem's walls for burial. Like the historian Josephus, who also went over to the Romans, ben Zakkai won the favor of Vespasian, the general (and later emperor) whom Nero had dispatched to quell the insurrection. Ben Zakkai received Vespasian's permission to travel to Jamnia (also called Javneh or Jabneh), a city west of Jerusalem on the Mediterranean coast that had not participated in the Jewish revolt.

At Jamnia, ben Zakkai gathered other Pharisaic teachers together and presided over an already-existing Jewish council there, the *Bet Din* (House of Judgment). During the years following 70 C.E., the

pronouncements and interpretations of ben Zakkai and other sages of the **Academy of Jamnia** exercised tremendous influence over Judaism, which thus entered into a new stage of development known as formative Judaism. The Jamnia rabbis successfully confronted the challenge of enabling Judaism to survive without the Temple, an officiating priesthood, or even a homeland. It is said that when ben Zakkai visited the ruins of Jerusalem with another rabbi, his companion lamented the fact that with the Temple gone, their religion had no means of making the atonement sacrifices necessary to cleanse the people from sin. Ben Zakkai reportedly answered that henceforth "deeds of love"—humanitarian service—would replace the old system of animal sacrifice. He then quoted the Scripture in which God declares, "I require mercy, not sacrifice" (Hos. 6:6), a passage that Jesus is also said to have emphasized (Matt. 9:13).

After his retirement or death, ben Zakkai was succeeded by Gamaliel's grandson, Gamaliel the Younger (c. 30–100 C.E.). Along with debating the official contents of the Hebrew Bible, the Jamnia scholars also sought to define the essential requirements—and limits—of Judaism. According to a Talmudic tradition, the benediction against the *Minim* (heretics) was formulated during this period (about 90 C.E.). Many scholars believe that this interdiction was aimed at the Christians, whose beliefs about Jesus' superiority to Moses, transmitter of God's Torah, increasingly separated them from Jamnia's views of acceptable Judaism. It seems probable that after 85 or 90 C.E., Jewish Christians were sporadically expelled from the synagogues, causing a bitter division between the Christian and Jewish communities. The Gospel of John appears to reflect this exclusion of Jesus' followers (John 9:22, 34), as does the Gospel of Matthew, which vehemently denounces Pharisaic policies while simultaneously commending their general teachings (Matt. 23).

THE SAMARITANS

Named for the capital city, Samaria, of the ancient Northern Kingdom of Israel, the Samaritans were a distinctive Jewish group who occupied the territory lying between Judea and Galilee. Although 2 Kings 17 depicts Samaritans as the descendants of Mesopotamians whom Assyrian conquerors settled in the area during the late eighth century B.C.E.—and therefore not "authentic" Jews—this picture is historically inaccurate. By the time of the Roman occupation of Palestine, Jews in Judea regarded the Samaritans as an alien people who practiced a false version of the Jewish religion.

Whereas Jews worshiped at the Jerusalem Temple on Mount Zion, Samaritans viewed Mount Gerizim, near the ancient Israelite sanctuary of Shechem, as God's approved holy place (John 4:20). When the Hasmonean king John Hyrcanus invaded Samaria in 108 B.C.E., however, he destroyed the Samaritan temple erected on Mount Gerizim. For most observant Jews, the Samaritan branch of Hellenistic Judaism—which recognized only the Mosaic Torah, but not the prophets or other biblical writings, as binding Scripture—was little better than a Gentile cult.

By contrast, New Testament writers generally portray the Samaritans favorably, offering them none of the blistering denunciations they heap upon the Sadducees and Pharisees. The author of Luke-Acts not only shows Jesus conducting a brief ministry in Samaria (Luke 17:11–19) and making a Samaritan the hero of a famous parable (Luke 10:33–36) but also presents Samaria as the first step beyond Judea on the church's worldwide mission (Acts 1:8; 8:1–40). In John's Gospel, after Jesus holds a long discussion with a Samaritan woman about the differences between her people and the Jews of Jerusalem, she perceives that he is the Messiah and, acting as one of his first missionaries, persuades her fellow villagers to become Jesus' disciples (John 4). Some of Jesus' adversaries even label him a Samaritan (John 8:48)!

Although these Gospel anecdotes suggest that early Christianity found a more friendly reception among some Samaritans than among many adherents of mainstream Judaism, most Samaritans did not become Christians. Among the various Jewish parties cited in Josephus and the New Testament, the Samaritans are unique in being the only group—apart from what became rabbinical Judaism—that survives to the present day. A Samaritan community continues to practice its ancient rites at Mount Gerizim, near the modern city of Nablus.

THE ESSENES AND THE DEAD SEA SCROLLS

In 1947 began a series of sensational discoveries that have revolutionized scholars' understanding of Judaism's complexities during the early New Testament period. According to one version of the story, in that year a Bedouin shepherd boy, who had been idly throwing stones into the mouth of a cave near the Dead Sea, heard a sound like shattering pottery. When he climbed into the cave to investigate, he found pottery jars full of ancient manuscripts, now world famous as the **Dead Sea Scrolls** (see figure 5.1).

Before the young shepherd made his astonishing find, scholars had almost no Jewish literature dating from the centuries immediately before or during the formative period of Christianity. Books of the Hebrew Bible are considerably older than the time of Jesus, and the Mishnah was compiled almost two centuries after his death. With the unexpected discovery of the Dead Sea Scrolls, however, scholars now have an entire religious library that was composed or transcribed between the mid-second century B.C.E. and late first century C.E. The scrolls not only encompass the chronological period when Christianity first developed but also originated in a place near the Jewish wilderness where John the Baptist held his revival campaign—the locale in which Jesus began his ministry (see figure 5.2).

A large majority of scholars are convinced that the scrolls were produced by the **Essenes,** an ascetic Jewish sect that flourished in Palestine from about 140 B.C.E. until 68 C.E., when it was destroyed or dispersed by Roman armies. First-century Jewish authors, such as **Philo Judaeus** of Alexandria and Josephus, had described some of the Essene beliefs and practices. But only after 1947 did their own extensive writings—found in eleven different caves—gradually become available. When some of the Dead Sea Scrolls were first published in English, a few scholars theorized that the Essene group was an early form of Christianity. More recently, some commentators have speculated that the "Teacher of Righteousness"—the sect's founder and early leader—was

Figure 5.1 An apocalyptic sect that awaited Yahweh's call to battle the Romans, the Essenes maintained a monastic colony at Qumran near the northwest shores of the Dead Sea. After the Essenes had hidden their library—the Dead Sea Scrolls—in nearby caves, the Roman army destroyed Qumran (68 C.E.), the ruins of which have since been excavated. (© Jacques Benbassat/Leo de Wys)

none other than Jesus of Nazareth or perhaps his brother (kinsman) **James,** who was known as "James the Righteous." Other critics have claimed that Paul, who rejects Torah keeping in favor of divine grace, is the "wicked priest" whom the scrolls condemn. One commentator has even assigned the "wicked priest" role to Jesus!

Despite a few extreme—and almost universally repudiated—claims, the scholarly consensus holds that the primary value of the scrolls in studying Christian origins is the evidence they provide for the Palestinian roots of earliest Christianity. Many ideas, terms, and phrases previously thought to have arisen in a non-Palestinian Hellenistic environment were actually present in Jesus' homeland during his lifetime. Documents outlining the Essenes' mode of worship, communal meals, purification rites involving immersion in water, and conviction that they alone formed a "New Covenant" community representing true Israel demonstrate abundant parallels to Christian teachings.

Rather than prove that the Jesus movement developed out of Essene beliefs, however, the scrolls generally show that a marginal Jewish religious group anticipated a number of Christian practices. Certain rituals, such as a shared meal of bread and wine or water baptism of initiates, are not unique to Christianity but are paralleled in earlier Essene rituals, just as Greco-Roman myths about a dying and rising savior deity foreshadow theological interpretations of Jesus' life and death.

Qumran Although many Essenes lived in cities, one particularly rigorous group settled in **Qumran,** located near the northwest corner of the Dead Sea. The Qumran group apparently pursued a monastic existence, renouncing marriage, holding all possessions in common, and unquestioningly obeying their priestly superiors. The Qumran community may have been founded shortly after the Maccabean revolt when Hasmonean rulers assumed the office of High Priest, a practice the Essenes abhorred as an

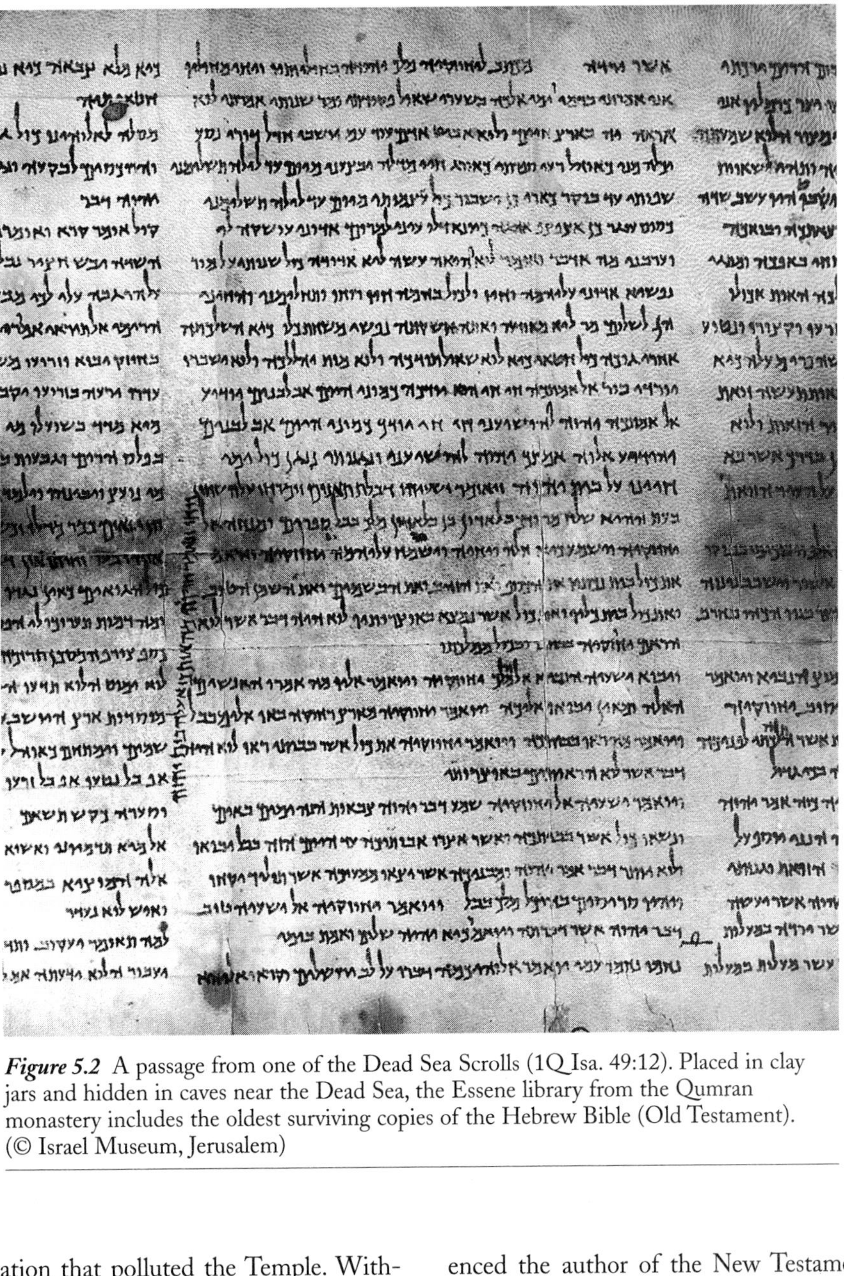

Figure 5.2 A passage from one of the Dead Sea Scrolls (1Q Isa. 49:12). Placed in clay jars and hidden in caves near the Dead Sea, the Essene library from the Qumran monastery includes the oldest surviving copies of the Hebrew Bible (Old Testament). (© Israel Museum, Jerusalem)

illegal usurpation that polluted the Temple. Withdrawn from the world in their isolated desert community, the Essenes patiently awaited the arrival of two Messiahs—a priestly Messiah descended from **Aaron,** Moses' brother and Israel's first High Priest, and a second "Messiah of Israel," a leader descended from King David. The only Jewish sect known to expect two such leaders, the Essenes may have influenced the author of the New Testament Book of Hebrews, which is unique in presenting the risen Christ as both a Davidic and a high priestly Messiah. Essene interest in **Melchizedek,** a mysterious king-priest mentioned briefly in the books of Genesis and Psalms, is similarly reflected in Hebrews' comparison of Christ to Melchizedek, the only canonical writing to do so (see chapter 18).

Figure 5.3 Masada. Built as a fortress retreat by King Herod, during the Jewish revolt Masada served as the rebels' last holdout against Roman troops. According to Josephus, in 73 C.E. Masada's occupying force of 1000, including some women and children, committed mass suicide rather than become Roman slaves. (© Richard T. Nowitz)

Contents of the Qumran Library   The Dead Sea documents, which the Essenes may have hidden in caves shortly before the Roman armies razed Qumran, are enormously important for biblical research. First, the manuscripts contain the oldest surviving copies of the Hebrew Bible, some fragments of which date back to the second century B.C.E. The complete **scroll** of Isaiah, which is perhaps 900 years older than any other previously known Isaiah manuscript, shows few variations from the Hebrew **Masoretic Text** (MT), the medieval edition of the Hebrew Bible from which most translations are made. Other Qumran copies of Scripture differ significantly from the "standard" Masoretic edition. Extensive variations between some of the Qumran biblical texts and later copies of the Hebrew Bible

suggest that by the first century C.E. Jewish scholars had not yet adopted a universally recognized version of their sacred writings.

Second, the Qumran scrolls include copies and fragments of apocryphal and pseudepigraphal works, such as Tobit, 1 Enoch, and the Book of Jubilees. Generally written later than the canonical books of the Hebrew Bible, **Pseudepigrapha** (literally, "false writings") are typically ascribed to eminent figures of the distant past such as Enoch (mentioned in Genesis 5:21–24). Enoch reputedly was carried up to heaven where he witnessed sacred mysteries and then returned to disclose esoteric knowledge to a select few. The presence of 1 Enoch (fragments were also found at the nearby fortress of Masada; see figure 5.3) interspersed among canonical books indicates that the Essenes may have accepted a larger canon than that eventually promulgated at Jamnia (Yavneh). Whether the Essenes regarded works like Enoch or the Book of Jubilees (a retelling of Genesis and part of Exodus) as part of the Bible is open to question, but numerous fragments of these and similar compositions among the Dead Sea Scrolls reveal that they were carefully preserved and studied. Like the Essenes, some New Testament writers apparently accepted the authority of Enoch, which is quoted repeatedly in the Book of Jude (see chapter 18).

Third, some of the most notable documents are Essene commentaries on canonical books, such as those on the prophets Habakkuk, Isaiah, Hosea, and Micah. The Habakkuk commentary is particularly illuminating because it shows that the Essenes used the same methods of interpreting biblical texts later employed by many New Testament writers. Gospel authors such as Matthew regard the Hebrew Bible as a repository of prophetic texts foretelling events fulfilled in his own day among his own community. This approach was also adopted by the Habakkuk commentator, who interprets Habakkuk's words as predictions about recent Essene leaders and experiences. Both Essene and New Testament writers characteristically view their own group as God's only loyal worshipers and hence the culmination of the divine plan for humanity.

Finally, besides preserving the earliest extant copies of canonical and noncanonical biblical texts and commentaries typical of Christian **exegesis,** the scrolls include numerous compositions produced entirely by and for the Essene community. Containing numerous works whose existence had not been previously suspected, this fourth group includes the following:

1. A "Manual of Discipline" giving requirements and regulations for life in the Qumran monastery. Also called "The Community Rule," this document features a declaration that all humanity is divided into two mutually exclusive categories: (a) the "children of light," who are guided by a "spirit of truth" and are ruled by the "Prince of Light," and (b) the "children of falsehood," who walk in darkness under an "Angel of Darkness."

This truth–error and light–dark dichotomy also typifies the language of John's Gospel.

2. A compendium of messianic rules designating qualities of age, physical condition, ritual purity, and doctrinal orthodoxy for members of the community—especially relevant to Christians for its description of a solemn meal of bread and wine that strikingly resembles Gospel accounts of Jesus' Last Supper.

3. An extensive collection of Essene hymns that were probably sung during Qumran worship services. Because the Essenes rejected the Jerusalem Temple as contaminated by its (to them) illegitimate Sadducean priests, they attempted to duplicate certain rituals and ceremonies in their own settlement.

4. Liturgical fragments containing blessings for the obedient and cursings for the wicked.

5. The "Zadokite Document" (a version of which had been discovered in a Cairo synagogue in the 1890s), which outlines the "New Covenant" made in the "land of Damascus" (presumably a code word for the Qumran establishment) under which the Essene group lived.

6. Passages of biblical interpretation on such topics as the Blessing of Jacob, the Admonition of Moses, a prayer attributed to the Babylonian king Nabonidus, an exposition of signs marking the last days, and an anthology of messianic predictions.

7. A scroll entitled the "War of the Sons of Light Against the Sons of Darkness," a surprisingly mundane battle plan for the cosmic war that would culminate in the defeat of the ungodly and the establishment of God's kingdom.

The New Testament is silent on the Essenes, their desert monastery, and their austere lives of pious scholarship. The absence of references to the Essenes may reflect the fact that by the time the Gospels were written, the sect had ceased to exist as an identifiable group. Some historians, however, suggest that the Gospels' silence may reflect their authors' consciousness that Jesus and his first disciples may have been influenced by Essene teachings.

Although a few scholars argue that Jesus spent the "lost years" between ages twelve and thirty as a member of the Essene community, the suggestion has not been widely accepted. By contrast, **John the Baptist**—whom the Gospels paint as a desert ascetic condemning Jewish religious and political leadership and preaching a doctrine of repentance before an impending holocaust—seems to echo some of the Essenes' characteristic views. What relationship John might have had to the Essene movement, however, remains conjectural.

THE ZEALOTS

Known for their passionate commitment to Jewish religious and political freedom, the Zealots formed a party dedicated to evicting the Romans from Palestine. Opposition to the Roman occupation that began in 63 B.C.E. flared repeatedly during the first century C.E., climaxing in the Jewish War against Rome (66–73 C.E.). In 6 C.E. a Jewish patriot known as **Judas the Galilean** led an armed rebellion that fueled nationalistic hopes but which the Romans crushed easily. **Simon,** one of Jesus' disciples, is called a "zealot" (Luke 6:15; Acts 1:13), and in Acts a parallel is drawn between Jesus' activity and that of Judas (Acts 5:37–39), causing some historians to suspect that Jesus may also have been involved in some form of rebellion against Rome. Most scholars, however, believe that Simon's designation as a "zealot" probably refers to his zeal or enthusiasm for the Law and that Jesus firmly refused to become involved in any political schemes (Mark 8:33; 10:38–39; Luke 24:21; Acts 1:6).

Although many Jews had fought against foreign oppression since the time of the Maccabees, the Zealots did not constitute an identifiable political party until shortly after the revolt against Rome began in 66 C.E. According to Josephus, the Zealots' blind nationalism forced the Palestinian Jews on a suicidal course. In his history of the Jewish War, Josephus argues that it was the Zealots' refusal to surrender, even after Jerusalem had been captured, and their occupation of the Temple precincts that compelled the Romans to destroy the sanctuary. According to Josephus, General Titus, the

Roman commander-in-chief, had not originally intended to commit this desecration. This catastrophe and the later bar Kochba rebellion of 132–135 C.E. discredited both the Zealot party and its **apocalyptic** hope of divine intervention in achieving national liberation. Thanks to the Zealot failures, both armed revolution and end-of-the-world predictions were henceforth repudiated by mainstream Judaism.

The Messiah: First-Century Expectations

Given the vast diversity of first-century Judaisms, we should not expect to find general agreement among different Jewish groups about the nature and function of the **messiah.** It seems that many Jews did not make expectation of a coming Messiah a major part of their religious hope. The Sadducees apparently denied that there would be one, while the Essenes anticipated two separate figures who would, respectively, fill either a priestly or a political role. The Christian view that Jesus of Nazareth was the Messiah was not accepted by mainstream Judaism for a variety of reasons that will become clearer as we study the Gospels (see chapters 6–10). Among other things, it appears that many Jews questioned the biblical correctness of Jesus' teaching and the "shameful" manner of his death. The Hebrew prophets did not foresee that Israel's deliverer would be executed as a criminal by Gentiles (John 7:12, 27, 31, 40–44), making the crucifixion "a stumbling block" to scripturally literate Jews (1 Cor. 1:23). Mark's Gospel reflects these objections and emphasizes the unexpected or "hidden" quality of Jesus' messiahship.

THE ROYAL COVENANT OF KING DAVID

Despite the heated debates between Jewish and Christian viewpoints preserved in the Gospels, it is possible to draw a general picture of Israel's concept of the Messiah by tracing its development in the Hebrew Bible. Derived from the Hebrew word *mashiah,* Messiah means "anointed one" and refers to the ceremony in which priests anointed (poured oil on) the heads of persons singled out or commissioned by God for some special undertaking. In the Hebrew Bible, *mashiah* is most frequently applied to the kings of ancient Israel, particularly those descended from King David (Ps. 18:50; 89:20, 38, 51; 132:10, 17). Because of his outstanding success in establishing a powerful Israelite state, David was regarded as the prototype of the divinely favored ruler, and his kingdom a foreshadowing of the reign of God on earth. According to 2 Samuel 7, Yahweh concluded an "everlasting covenant" or treaty with David's "house" (dynasty). The covenant terms specified Yahweh's unconditional promise to maintain an unending line of Davidic kings on the throne of Israel. If certain of David's royal descendants misbehaved, Yahweh would punish them, but he vowed never to remove them from the throne (2 Sam. 7:8–17; 23:1–5). Perhaps as a result of this "royal covenant theology," David's heirs ruled uninterrupted over the land of Judah for nearly 400 years (961–587 B.C.E.). (By contrast, the northern kingdom of Israel, separated from Judah in 922 B.C.E., saw many changes of ruling families before its destruction by the Assyrians in 721 B.C.E.)

Historical End of the Davidic Dynasty   David's line of reigning kings came to an abrupt end in 587 B.C.E., when Nebuchadnezzar of Babylon destroyed Jerusalem, burned King Solomon's Temple, and removed the last Davidic monarch, Zedekiah, from the throne. Nebuchadnezzar also deported much of Jerusalem's upper class to his imperial capital. When a devoted remnant of Judah's former leadership returned to Jerusalem from Babylon in 538 B.C.E., the Davidic monarchy was not restored. The land of Judah was placed under the administration of the Persian Empire, which installed local governors rather than kings over its Jewish subjects. The first of these Persian-appointed governors was Zerubbabel, a descendant of the Davidic family. Zerubbabel was apparently the focus of national hopes for a restoration of the Davidic kingdom and was hailed in messianic terms by the prophets Haggai and Zechariah (Hag. 2:20–23; Zech. 2:10; 6:12). Hopes for a renewed Davidic state failed to materialize, however, and the figure of Zerubbabel

disappeared from history. Israel was never again to have a Davidic king, the "anointed of God."

During the long years of Persian rule, the Jewish people looked mainly to the spiritual leadership of their High Priest (who was also anointed with holy oil when installed in office [Lev. 4:3, 5]). The High Priest and his many priestly assistants administered the rebuilt Temple and provided a focus of communal religious identity. Without a king or political autonomy, Judah became increasingly a theocratic (God-ruled) community, guided by a priestly class that supervised the Temple sacrifices and interpreted the Mosaic Torah.

ISRAEL'S HOPES FOR A NEW DAVIDIC KING

Even after many centuries of foreign domination, as Judah was successively ruled by Babylonians, Persians, Greeks, Syrians, and Romans, Israel's collective memory of the Davidic Covenant did not fade. Yahweh's sworn oath that his people would have a Davidic heir to rule them forever (2 Sam. 7; 23:1–5; Ps. 89:19–31) was reinforced by Israel's **prophets,** who envisioned a future golden age when a man like David, "anointed of God," would rise to liberate Israel, defeat its enemies, and help bring God's kingdom to earth.

The prophet Isaiah of Jerusalem, who was a staunch supporter of the Davidic monarchy during the late eighth century B.C.E., had delivered unforgettable oracles (prophetic words) from Yahweh:

> For a boy has been born for us, a son given to us to
>   bear the symbol of dominion on his shoulder;
> and he shall be called
> in purpose wonderful, in battle
> God-like,
> Father for all time, Prince of peace.
> Great shall the dominion be and boundless the
>   peace
>   bestowed on David's throne and on his kingdom,
> to establish it and sustain it with justice and
> righteousness from now and for evermore.
> The zeal of the LORD [Yahweh] of Hosts shall
>   do this.   (Isa. 9:6–7)

Isaiah's further allusions to a righteous king "from the stock of Jesse [David's father]" (Isa. 11:1–9) and visions of a Davidic Jerusalem to which the

Gentile nations would flock (Isa. 2:1–4) not only enhanced the prestige of the Davidic royal family but also associated it irrefutably with the coming earthwide reign of Yahweh.

The Messiah as a Political Leader   All of Israel's Davidic kings were literally "messiahs," "anointed ones." They ruled as Yahweh's "sons," adopted as such at the time of their consecration or coronation (Ps. 2:7). Because the prophets had conceived of the Messiah as a warrior-king like David, a hero whom Yahweh chose to act as his agent in establishing a dominion of universal peace, the messianic leader was typically regarded as primarily a political figure. His function was to demonstrate the omnipotence of Israel's God by setting up an earthly kingdom whose righteous government would compel the nations' respect for both Yahweh and his chosen people (Isa. 11; Dan. 2:44).

Messianic Claimants Before and After Jesus

Judea's troubled relationship with Rome inspired a series of prophets, revolutionaries, or other leaders who typically promised the Jewish people relief from Roman economic and social oppression. Some rebel leaders reputedly claimed the title of Jewish king, the crime for which Pontius Pilate executed Jesus. Most of those aspiring to royal status did not claim to be a "*son* [descendant] of David" but merely to be "*like* David," a previously obscure youth who was raised from among the common people to become Israel's champion against a foreign military threat. It could be said of these popular national leaders what the psalmist's God said of David: "I have conferred the crown on a hero, and promoted one chosen from my people" (Ps. 89:19).

In his accounts of peasant uprisings against the Romans or their **Herodian** puppets, the Jewish historian Flavius Josephus reports that several prominent rebels were also messianic pretenders (i.e., they assumed the function of Israel's *anointed* kings). Most of these popular kings appeared either during the turmoil following the death of Herod the Great (4 B.C.E.) or during the greater upheaval of the Jewish War against Rome (66–73 C.E.). After Herod's death, a rebel named Judas, son of a brigand or terrorist named Hezekiah, led Galilee in a revolt against Roman occupational forces. According to Josephus, this Judas was motivated by an ambition to achieve "royal rank" (*Antiquities*, 17:271–272). Simon of Perea, the territory east of Galilee, similarly donned "the diadem," symbol of kingly status, and plundered Herod's palace in Jericho. After leading a band of unruly followers, Simon was captured by the Romans and beheaded, a fate anticipating that of John the Baptist. A third would-be king, Athronges, resembled David in beginning his career as a shepherd, after which he also wore a royal diadem and, supported by his brothers and their armed followers, attacked both Roman and Herodian armies. Roman retaliation against such popular uprisings was swift and severe: In 4 B.C.E. the Galilean town of Sepphoris, which had aided the rebels, was burned and its inhabitants sold into slavery. Located only a few miles from Nazareth, Sepphoris was lavishly rebuilt during Jesus' early years, a project on which it is remotely possible that he and his "carpenter [artisan]" father may have worked.

Early in the first Jewish revolt against Rome (about 67–68 C.E.), several large groups of bandits or guerrilla fighters who had been plundering the countryside infiltrated Jerusalem and occupied the Temple area, which they made their headquarters. This impromptu coalition formed a party of radical nationalists—the Zealots. Composed largely of peasants, the Zealots appear to have been as dedicated to overthrowing the Jerusalem ruling class—which they accused of exploiting the poor and collaborating with Rome—as they were to freeing their land from foreign domination.

Whereas the Zealots derived from the rural poor, the Sicarii (from the Latin *sicarius*, meaning "dagger") were a group of urban terrorists and assassins. Well-organized, the Sicarii carried out a carefully plotted series of murders, eliminating priests and other Jerusalem authorities who favored compromise with Rome. According to Josephus, one of the Sicarii leaders, Menachem—the son or grandson of the rebel Judas—assumed the trappings of kingship. Menachem ostentatiously entered Jerusalem as the people's king, a warrior-monarch in the tradition of David.

Another Sicarii pretender, Simon **bar** (son of) Giora, who also had messianic pretensions, led the largest and most powerful force resisting the Roman reconquest of Jerusalem. Josephus states that after Titus's soldiers had captured and demolished the Temple, Simon, arrayed in royal robes, suddenly appeared among the ruins. If he hoped for a last-minute divine intervention to vindicate his kingly aspirations, he was disappointed: The Romans took him as a prisoner to Rome, where he was executed.

The most famous messianic claimant was Simon bar Kochba, who led the second Jewish revolt against Rome in 132–135 C.E. Akiba, a prominent rabbi, proclaimed that bar Kochba fulfilled the promise in Numbers 24:17 that "a star shall go forth from Jacob." While Rabbi Akiba and other supporters called Simon "bar Kochba," which means "son of the star," his detractors derisively labeled the revolutionary "bar Koziba"—"son of the lie." His attempt to liberate Judea and restore a theocratic state was doomed by Roman might, which again annihilated Jewish armies and brought a terrible end to Jewish political messianic hopes.

PSALM OF SOLOMON 17

The most striking description of Israel's expected Messiah was written only about five or six decades before Jesus' birth. Ascribed to Solomon, the progenitor of Israel's wisdom tradition, a collection of prophetic poems known as the Psalms of Solomon envisions a righteous king who would drive the hated foreigners (Roman occupational forces) from Jerusalem and establish a just sovereignty over both Gentiles and Jews. Psalm of Solomon 17 is the first known work of Jewish literature to use the terms *son of David* and *Lord Messiah* (Christ), distinctive titles that New Testament writers apply to Jesus.

Although Psalm of Solomon 17 sees the Messiah as sinless and powerful, he is clearly a human rather than a supernatural figure, God's agent but

not a divine being. His promised activities include gathering together "a holy people" who will be "children of their God," cleansing Jerusalem (presumably including its Temple) and ruling compassionately over the Gentiles. Although a Davidic heir, this "Lord Messiah" achieves his dominion without military conquest because he is "powerful in the holy spirit" and strengthened by "wisdom and understanding." This vision of a peaceful Messiah subduing opponents through "the word of his mouth [his teaching]" is much closer to that adopted by the Gospel authors than the traditional expectation of a warrior-king like the historical David (see box 5.1).

A CHRISTIAN VIEW OF THE MESSIAH

As presented in the Gospels, Jesus of Nazareth takes a view of the Messiah's role and the kingdom of God that was disappointing or perplexing to many. Despite some modern commentators' attempts to associate him with the Zealot or revolutionary party, Jesus (as portrayed by the Evangelists) does not present himself as a military or political savior of Israel. As John's Gospel concludes, his "kingdom does not belong to this world" (John 18:36).

Jesus' Multiple Role   Despite Jesus' reluctance to assert his right to rule Israel, the Gospel writers nonetheless are convinced that he is the same Messiah whose life Isaiah and the other Hebrew prophets foresaw. In identifying Jesus as Israel's Messiah, however, the New Testament authors broaden his role beyond that of the largely political nature of the prophesied Davidic ruler. To defend Jesus against charges that he "failed" to reestablish David's kingdom, early Christians point to certain passages in the Hebrew Bible that seemed to them to illustrate the nature of Jesus' unexpected messiahship. In Christian interpretations of the Messiah, he became the "prophet like Moses" described in Deuteronomy (18:15–20) and the mysterious "suffering servant" in Isaiah (52:13–53:12). In the original texts, neither the Mosaic prophet nor the anonymous servant is associated with the Messiah,

Box 5.1
Psalm of Solomon 17

See, Lord, and raise up for them [Israel] their king,
    the *son of David* [italics added] to rule over your servant Israel
    in the time known to you, O God.
Undergird him with the strength to destroy the unrighteous rulers,
    to purge Jerusalem from gentiles
    who trample her to destruction;
    in wisdom and righteousness to drive out
    the sinners from the inheritance; . . .
To destroy the unlawful nations with the word of his mouth;
At his warning the nations will flee from his presence,
    and he will condemn sinners by the thoughts of their hearts.
He will gather a holy people
    whom he will lead in righteousness. . . .
For he shall know them
    that they are all children of their God. . . .
He will judge peoples and nations in the wisdom of his righteousness.
And he will have gentile nations serving him under his yoke
    and he will glorify the Lord in (a place) prominent (above)
    the whole earth.
And he will purge Jerusalem
    (and make it) holy as it was even from the beginning,
    (for) nations to come from the ends of the earth to see his glory,
    to bring as gifts the children who had been driven out, . . .
And he will be a righteous king over them, taught by God.
There will be no unrighteousness among them in his days,
    for all shall be holy,
    and their king shall be the *Lord Messiah* [italics added].

(*continued*)

and we do not know whether these two unidentified figures were given a messianic emphasis before the Christian period. Isaiah's "Song of the Suffering Servant," dramatizing the unjust punishment of a righteous man who suffers for the sins of others and thereby somehow redeems them, became a crucial text for explaining the theological significance of Jesus' death (Mark 10:45). Psalm 22, which records the lament of a man tormented by Gentile enemies, was also used to reinforce the Christian view that the true Messiah was destined to suffer. The Christian concept of the Messiah is a paradox: a God-anointed king who is rejected and dies, but whose voluntary death is a triumph over forces of darkness and evil and a source of hope for mortal humanity.

Summary

As New Testament documents reveal, their authors present Jesus as far more than a Davidic king. Taken together, the canonical writings present Jesus as a composite figure, one who represents the sum of all Israel's heritage. He is not only the anointed

(For) he will not rely on horse and rider and bow,
   nor will he collect gold and silver for war.
Nor will he build up hope in a multitude for a day of war.
The Lord himself is his king,
   the hope of the one who has a strong hope in God.
He shall be compassionate to all the nations
   (who) reverently stand before him. . . .
And he himself (will be) free from sin, (in order) to rule
   a great people.
He will expose officials and drive out sinners
   by the strength of his word.
And he will not weaken in his days, (relying) on his God,
   for God made him powerful in the holy spirit
   and wise in the counsel of understanding,
   with strength and righteousness. . . .
Faithfully and righteously shepherding the Lord's flock,
   he will not let any of them stumble in their pasture.
He will lead them all in holiness
   and there will be no arrogance among them,
   that any should be oppressed.
This is the beauty of the king of Israel
   which God knew,
   to raise him over the house of Israel
   to discipline it. . . .
Blessed are those born in those days
   to see the good fortune of Israel
   which God will bring to pass in the assembly of the tribes.

monarch whom David foreshadowed; he is also a lawgiver and prophet like Moses, a blameless and humble servant who suffers for others, a heavenly sacrifice and eternal priest, a teacher of supreme wisdom, and the icon or "image of the invisible God" by, through, and for whom the universe was created.

Translating the Hebrew *mashiah* as the Greek *Christos*, the New Testament writers commonly speak as if Christ were not a title but part of Jesus' proper name. Composed in a Hellenistic context and for a Greek-thinking audience, the New Testament books present Jesus almost exclusively in his function as Christ, a universal savior whose role goes far beyond that of the Davidic ruler. In interpreting Jesus' religious meaning, the New Testament authors apply to their hero many different concepts borrowed from the rich lore of Hellenistic Jewish ideas about the Messiah.

QUESTIONS FOR REVIEW

1. Define some essential differences between the Sadducees and Pharisees. Which party controlled the Jerusalem Temple and was apparently on better terms with the Romans?

2. Discuss some of the beliefs that Pharisees, Essenes, and Christians held in common. What connection did the Essenes have to the Dead Sea Scrolls and possibly to John the Baptist?

3. Discuss the role that the Zealots played in the Jewish revolt against Rome. What happened to the Jewish state and religion as a result of the revolt? How does Josephus contribute to our understanding of the Jewish War for independence?

4. Summarize the concept of the Messiah found in the Hebrew Bible. To what degree is the biblical Messiah a political figure related to the restoration of King David's royal dynasty? How do New Testament writers modify the concept of the Davidic Messiah?

QUESTIONS FOR DISCUSSION AND REFLECTION

1. How do you account for the extreme diversity of first-century Jewish religious groups, all of whom believed they were following the Mosaic Torah? Why do you think that the Essenes regarded themselves the only "true" Israel, the single group loyal to its covenant obligations? Discuss the similarities between the Essene conviction that they alone served God's plan and the later Christian belief that their community uniquely represented the "new Israel."

2. Most passages in the Hebrew Bible present the future Messiah as a descendant of King David who, as a God-empowered conqueror, would restore Israel to its former political independence and prosperity. Because Jesus did not deliver the covenant people from their oppressors, the Romans, nor restore David's throne, how can he be accepted as the Messiah whom Israel's prophets envisioned?

TERMS AND CONCEPTS TO REMEMBER

Sadducees	Essenes
Pharisees	Dead Sea Scrolls
oral law (traditions of the fathers)	Zealots
	apocalyptic
Mishnah and Talmud	Messiah
Jews and rabbinic Judaism	Psalm of Solomon
Jamnia (Yavneh)	

RECOMMENDED READING

Cohen, Shaye J. D. *From the Maccabees to the Mishnah.* Philadelphia: Westminster Press, 1987. A readable survey of evolving Jewish religious ideas that gave birth to both rabbinic Judaism and Christianity.

Cross, Frank M. *Qumran and the History of the Biblical Text.* Cambridge, Mass.: Harvard University Press, 1975.

————. *The Ancient Library of Qumran,* 2nd ed. Grand Rapids, Mich.: Baker, 1980.

Finkelstein, Louis. *The Pharisees,* Vols. 1 and 2. Philadelphia: Jewish Publication Society of America, 1962. Provides reliable information.

Gaster, Theodor H. *The Dead Sea Scriptures in English Translation.* Garden City, N.Y.: Doubleday, 1976.

Hengel, Martin. *Judaism and Hellenism,* Vols. 1 and 2. Philadelphia: Fortress Press, 1974. A thorough and detailed analysis of Hellenistic influences on Jewish thought during the last three centuries B.C.E.

————. *Jews, Greeks, and Barbarians: Aspects of the Hellenism of Judaism in the Pre-Christian Period.* Philadelphia: Fortress Press, 1980.

Horsley, Richard A. "Messianic Movements in Judaism." In D. N. Freedman, ed., *Anchor Bible Dictionary,* Vol. 4, pp. 791–797. New York: Doubleday, 1992. An excellent introduction to political messianic claimants at the time of Jesus.

Horsley, Richard A., and Hanson, John S. *Bandits, Prophets, and Messiahs: Popular Movements at the Time of Jesus.* Minneapolis/Chicago/New York: Winston Press, 1985.

Josephus, Flavius. *Josephus: Complete Works.* Translated by W. Whiston. Grand Rapids, Mich.: Kregel Publications, 1960. A dated translation but contains the complete texts of *The Antiquities of the Jews* and *The Jewish War,* as well as the "Discourse on Hades."

————. *The Jewish War,* rev. ed. Translated by G. A. Williamson. Edited by E. M. Smallwood. New York: Penguin Books, 1981. The most important contemporary source for conditions in Palestine during the first century C.E.

Murphy, Frederick J. *The Religious World of Jesus: An Introduction to Second Temple Palestinian Judaism.* Nashville, Tenn.: Abingdon Press, 1991. A recent survey of pertinent cultural and religious groups at the time of Jesus.

Neusner, Jacob. *From Politics to Piety: The Emergence of Pharisaic Judaism.* Englewood Cliffs, N.J.: Prentice-Hall, 1973.

Newsome, James D. *Greeks, Romans, Jews: Currents of Culture and Belief in the New Testament World.* Philadelphia: Trinity Press International, 1992. A superbly researched compendium of historical documents relevant to Jewish religious thought and practice during the era of Christianity's inception.

Sandmel, Samuel. *Judaism and Christian Beginnings.* New York: Oxford University Press, 1978.

Shanks, Hershel, ed. *Christianity and Rabbinic Judaism.* Washington, D.C.: Biblical Archaeological Society, 1992. A collection of scholarly essays profiling the parallel development of Christianity and formative Judaism.

———. *Understanding the Dead Sea Scrolls.* New York: Random House, 1992. A collection of popular essays from the *Biblical Archaeology Review.*

Stone, M. E. *Scriptures, Sects, and Visions: A Profile of Judaism from Ezra to the Jewish Revolts.* Philadelphia: Fortress Press, 1980. A readable introduction to the period.

Talmon, Shemaryahu, ed. *Jewish Civilization in the Hellenistic Period.* Philadelphia: Trinity Press International, 1991. A collection of scholarly essays about the fusion of Hebraic and Hellenistic culture that gave birth to rabbinic Judaism and Christianity.

Vermes, Geza. *The Dead Sea Scrolls: Qumran in Perspective.* London: Collins, 1977.

CHAPTER 6

The Gospels

Form and Purpose

Many writers have undertaken to draw up an account of the events that have happened among us [the early Christian community] following the traditions handed down to us by the original eyewitnesses and servants of the Gospel.

Luke 1:1–2

Key Themes Three of the Gospels—narratives about Jesus' life and teachings—are so similar that they can be placed side-by-side and viewed horizontally, their authors having arranged events in almost exactly the same order. Known as the Synoptic Gospels because they can be "seen together," Matthew, Mark, and Luke clearly have a close literary relationship, the resolution of which is called the Synoptic Problem. By contrast, the Gospel of John presents Jesus' story in a different order; its contents cannot be paralleled with the Synoptic texts.

The first section of the New Testament contains four separate and distinct accounts of Jesus' life. The early Christian community produced many other **Gospels**—narratives about Jesus or collections of his sayings—but only these four were generally recognized among early Christian churches as authoritative and suitable for teaching.

Despite significant differences in theme and emphasis, the first three **canonical Gospels**— Matthew, Mark, and Luke—bear a striking resemblance to each other. So similar are these three that one can arrange their contents in parallel columns and compare their three versions of the same saying or incident in Jesus' life at a single glance (see box 6.1). In general, all three follow the same order or sequence of events. Because they present Jesus' biography from essentially the same viewpoint, they are called the **Synoptic Gospels** (seeing the whole together).

In contrast to the Synoptic Gospels stands the narrative "according to John." Whereas the first three contain a large amount of material in common, the Fourth Gospel consists mostly of strikingly different accounts of Jesus' deeds and speeches. The general story is the same—a public ministry of healing and teaching followed by rejection and death in Jerusalem—but 90 percent of John's version is unique. In John the order of events, the geographical location of Jesus' ministry, and the manner in which Jesus speaks and refers to

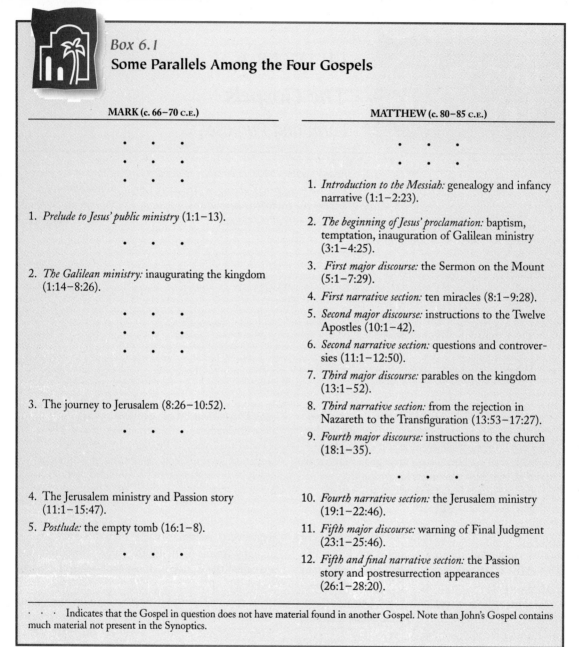

Box 6.1
Some Parallels Among the Four Gospels

MARK (c. 66–70 C.E.)	MATTHEW (c. 80–85 C.E.)
· · ·	· · ·
· · ·	· · ·
· · ·	1. *Introduction to the Messiah:* genealogy and infancy narrative (1:1–2:23).
1. *Prelude to Jesus' public ministry* (1:1–13).	2. *The beginning of Jesus' proclamation:* baptism, temptation, inauguration of Galilean ministry (3:1–4:25).
· · ·	
	3. *First major discourse:* the Sermon on the Mount (5:1–7:29).
2. *The Galilean ministry:* inaugurating the kingdom (1:14–8:26).	4. *First narrative section:* ten miracles (8:1–9:28).
	5. *Second major discourse:* instructions to the Twelve Apostles (10:1–42).
· · ·	6. *Second narrative section:* questions and controversies (11:1–12:50).
· · ·	7. *Third major discourse:* parables on the kingdom (13:1–52).
· · ·	8. *Third narrative section:* from the rejection in Nazareth to the Transfiguration (13:53–17:27).
3. The journey to Jerusalem (8:26–10:52).	9. *Fourth major discourse:* instructions to the church (18:1–35).
· · ·	
	· · ·
4. The Jerusalem ministry and Passion story (11:1–15:47).	10. *Fourth narrative section:* the Jerusalem ministry (19:1–22:46).
5. *Postlude:* the empty tomb (16:1–8).	11. *Fifth major discourse:* warning of Final Judgment (23:1–25:46).
· · ·	12. *Fifth and final narrative section:* the Passion story and postresurrection appearances (26:1–28:20).

· · · Indicates that the Gospel in question does not have material found in another Gospel. Note than John's Gospel contains much material not present in the Synoptics.

himself reflect a portrait of Christ profoundly different from that painted in the Synoptics.

Because it contains almost nothing not found in Matthew and/or Luke, Mark is perhaps the least

read of the Gospels. According to one ancient tradition, it is only a summary of Matthew, trimmed to meet the tastes of a Roman audience. Since the beginning of this century, however, scholars have

LUKE (c. 85–90 c.e.)	**JOHN (c. 90–100 c.e.)**

* * *

1. Formal preface
2. Infancy narratives of the Baptist and Jesus (1:5–2:52).
3. *Prelude to Jesus' ministry:* baptism, genealogy, and temptation (3:1–4:13).

* * *

4. Jesus' Galilean ministry and Luke's "lesser interpolation" (4:14–9:50).

* * *

* * *

5. Jesus' teachings on the journey to Jerusalem, Luke's "greater interpolation" (9:51–18:14).
6. *The Jerusalem ministry:* Jesus' challenge to the holy city (18:31–21:38).
7. The final conflict and Passion story (22:1–23:56).
8. *Epilog:* postresurrection appearances in the vicinity of Jerusalem (24:1–53).

* * *

JOHN (c. 90–100 c.e.)

1. *Prolog:* Hymn to the Logos (Word); testimony of the Baptist (1:1–51).

* * *

2. The Book of Signs (2:1–11:57).
   a. The miracle at Cana
   b. The assault on the Temple (compare Mark 11)
   c. Dialog with Nicodemus
   d. Conversations with a Samaritan woman and a woman taken in adultery
   e. Five more miraculous signs in Jerusalem and Galilee; Jesus' discourses witnessing to his divine nature.

   f. The resurrection of Lazarus (the seventh sign)
3. The book of Glory (12:1–20:31).
   a. The plot against Jesus
   b. The Last Supper and farewell discourses
   c. The Passion story
   d. The empty tomb and postresurrection appearances in Jerusalem
4. *Epilog:* postresurrection appearances in Galilee; parting words to Peter and the Beloved Disciple (21:1–25).

accorded Mark a crucial importance. Although a few still argue that Matthew was written first, most New Testament scholars now believe that Mark is our earliest Gospel, the first attempt to record the life of Jesus. If the scholars are right, then the similarities of the three **Synoptics** can be explained by the assumption that Matthew and Luke both used Mark as a major source of their own Gospels.

The Gospels
and Modern Scholarship

ASSUMPTIONS AND APPROACHES

How we undertake a study of the Gospels depends largely on our preconceptions about the nature and kind of religious authority they represent. Approaches range from an uncritical acceptance of every Gospel statement at face value to an intense skepticism that denies the works any historical credibility. Between these two extremes lie a great variety of viewpoints, each with its characteristic assumptions—standards of evidence or attitudes about historical plausibility that are taken for granted. These sometimes-unconscious assumptions can profoundly influence the reader's understanding of the Gospel text, predetermining its meaning.

This author believes that the Gospels are best understood when studied in the context of the Greek-speaking Jewish-Christian community that produced them. This historical–critical approach assumes that the more we know about first-century Jewish and Hellenistic language, literary forms, ideas, and religious beliefs, the better equipped we are to appreciate the original meaning and purpose of the New Testament.

SCHOLARSHIP AND CRITICISM

An international community of scholars—Roman Catholic, Protestant, Jewish, and others—use a wide variety of methods to illuminate the nature and growth of the New Testament documents. This cosmopolitan body of scholars, historians, textual experts, literary critics, archaeologists, sociologists, and theologians includes thousands of university faculty, clergy, seminary instructors, and academic researchers from many disciplines. Collectively, their efforts have provided us with an increasingly precise and well-documented study of the New Testament literature and the environment out of which it grew.

Before briefly describing the principal fields or branches of biblical scholarship, we should clarify the term *biblical criticism.* The word *criticism* may awaken negative feelings in some people, perhaps implying fault finding or an unfavorable judgment. But in biblical study, it is a positive means of understanding scriptural texts more accurately and objectively. *Criticism* derives from the Greek word *krino,* which means "to judge" or "to discern," to exercise rational analysis in evaluating something. In the fields of art and literature, it involves the ability to recognize artistic worth and to distinguish among the relative merits or defects of a given work. In New Testament studies, various critical methods are used, ranging from techniques for investigating the oral traditions that preceded the written Gospels to literary analysis of their final form, content, and structure.

Like much recent New Testament criticism, this book approaches the Gospels employing a combination of critical methods to illuminate both the historical process by which they were created and the end product of that evolution, the literary texts themselves. **Historical criticism** involves the analysis of documents that purport to record historical events, a methodology that attempts to discover what actually happened. Using standards of evaluation developed in the physical sciences, historical critics test a given account against several criteria, including such standards as factual accuracy, logical plausibility, historical probability, and authorial objectivity. Historical critics investigate such matters as a document's authorship, date, place of composition, intended audience, and the social and cultural setting in which it was first composed.

The Gospels represent almost insurmountable challenges for historical critics. Because the Gospels are the only extant first-century accounts of Jesus' life and were written by believers in his divinity, their representations of his words and miraculous actions cannot be checked against (theoretically) more objective non-Christian accounts. Scholarly recognition that the Evangelists were more concerned with interpreting Jesus' theological significance than with recording a balanced biographical account means that historians must approach the Gospels carefully, endeavoring to distinguish between theological claims and (probable) historical fact. One major problem in applying scientific

Figure 6.1 A typical example of early Christian art in the catacombs of Rome, this wall painting shows communicants celebrating the Eucharist, or communal meal. The fish and the baskets recall Jesus' twin miracles of feeding 4000 and 5000 in Mark's Gospel. (© Alinari/Art Resource, NY)

methodology—which demands a rigorously logical analysis of any claim—to the Gospels is that the Gospel authors portray Jesus as possessing supernatural powers. Ordinary historical characters do not expel demons, walk on water, feed thousands with a few fish, or rise from the dead—yet the Gospel writers attribute all these extraordinary deeds to their hero, making claims that oppose both the norms of human experience and the scientific worldview (see figure 6.1).

Historical critics can find no way to validate the Gospel accounts of Jesus' supernatural acts; they can only examine the Evangelists' reports in their contemporary historical context. Rather than look for arguments to rationalize seemingly inexplicable events, such as proposing that Jesus' cures were not physical miracles but examples of psychological healing, modern historians look to beliefs about supernatural forces that were prevalent in Jesus' time. Investigating what most Palestinian Jews believed about evil spirits and divine intervention during the first century C.E. helps historians understand the supernaturalism pervading Gospel accounts.

In the following discussion, we will define the problems facing modern scholars as they attempt to discover the Gospels' complex interrelationship and the evolutionary development the Gospels underwent before reaching their present form. Awareness of the historical, theological, and literary forces at work in producing the Gospel texts will help us to understand the reasons for both their similarities and their differences.

The Synoptic Problem

In contrast to John, the three Synoptic Gospels are so similar in content and narrative order that they appear to have a close literary relationship. One of the Synoptic writers must have used at least one of the others as a source. Scholarly attempts to unravel the literary dependence or connection among the three is known as the **Synoptic Problem.** For reasons described here, the overwhelming majority of scholars now believe that Mark was the first Gospel written and that Matthew and Luke, independently of each other, drew on Mark as their basic narrative source.

In analyzing the Synoptic accounts, scholars discovered a number of facts that point to Markan priority. All three Synoptics generally follow the same sequence of events, narrating Jesus' life in suggestively similar fashion. This shared narrative (and some teaching) material is known as the *triple tradition*. In addition, Matthew and Luke include a large quantity of teaching material that does not appear in Mark but that is remarkably comparable in form. This mysterious *double tradition* includes some of Jesus' best-known sayings, such as the Lord's Prayer, the golden rule, and the Beatitudes (blessings that Jesus pronounces on the poor, the meek, and the helpless). In many cases, there is almost verbatim agreement on the passages, absent from Mark, that Matthew and Luke share.

In scrutinizing the order of events in the Synoptic triple tradition, scholars also noticed that either Matthew or Luke may sometimes differ from Mark's order, but almost never do they differ from Mark in the same place and in the same way. When Matthew departs from the Markan order, Luke does not; when Luke disagrees with Mark, Matthew does not. This pattern strongly suggests that Mark is the determining factor in the Synoptics' version of the principal events in Jesus' story, that his Gospel is the source of the other two.

Although Mark is the shortest Gospel, his version of an episode reported in all three Synoptics is commonly longer than those of Matthew or Luke. Most scholars think it likely that Matthew and Luke, both of which contain much more teaching material than Mark and are considerably longer, edited and abbreviated many of Mark's narrative passages.

THE TWO-DOCUMENT THEORY

Source criticism, the analysis of a document to discover and identify its written sources, has been particularly helpful in resolving the Synoptic Problem. After recognizing that Mark was the source for the chronological framework in Matthew and Luke, source critics also identified a second major

document to account for the extensive teaching material that does not appear in Mark but that Matthew and Luke have in common. According to the two-document theory, Matthew and Luke not only used Mark but also drew on a written collection of Jesus' sayings, including many of his parables. This hypothetical collection is known as the **Q** document (from *Quelle*, the German term for "source") (see figure 6.2).

FROM ORAL PREACHING TO WRITTEN GOSPEL

The Oral Period   In the view of most New Testament scholars, the two-document theory not only most satisfactorily resolves the Synoptic Problem but also allows us to trace several distinct stages of the Gospels' development over time (see box 6.2). The first stage was entirely oral, represented initially by Jesus' spoken teachings and then by his earliest followers' preachings about him. For approximately forty years—between the time of the Crucifixion (about 30–33 C.E.) and the appearance of Mark (about 66–70 C.E.)—the Christian *kerygma* (proclamation about Jesus) was almost entirely by word of mouth. Paul's letters were composed during this period (between about 50–62 C.E.), but Paul rarely mentions events in Jesus' life or quotes his teachings. (For exceptions, see Jesus' words of institution at the Last Supper [1 Cor. 11:23–26] and the received tradition about the postresurrection appearances [1 Cor. 15:3–7].)

The oral *kerygma* began in Judea, Galilee, and adjoining regions where Aramaic was spoken. When Christian missionaries carried their message into Greek-speaking territories, however, important changes had to be made. Not only were Jesus' sayings necessarily translated into koinē, they had to be explained, reinterpreted, and applied to urban conditions very different from those in rural Palestine where they originated. Busy merchants in the crowded Hellenistic marketplaces might require an explanation of Jesus' parables, initially designed for poor villagers and peasants in an agricultural economy, that perhaps challenged missionaries' ingenuity. Similarly, Christian preachers themselves eventually needed reinterpretations of some teach-

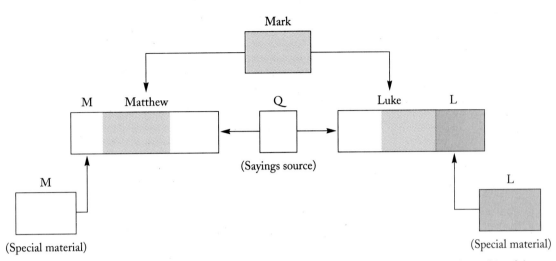

Figure 6.2 This drawing illustrates the two-document theory, an attempt to explain the literary relationship of the three Synoptic Gospels. Note that this theory takes Mark's Gospel as a major source for Matthew and Luke. In addition, both Matthew and Luke incorporate teaching material from Q (*Quelle*, a hypothetical collection of Jesus' sayings). Matthew also uses special material unique to his Gospel, here designated M; Luke similarly includes material found only in his account, here labeled L.

ings. Jesus' homely parable of the laborer sowing seeds was ultimately transformed into an allegory illustrating Christians' diverse experience as preachers in the Hellenistic world, where they were sometimes welcomed, often rejected, and occasionally persecuted. (See chapter 7, where Mark 4, with its elaborate application of the sower parable to conditions in the early church, is discussed.)

As scholars have learned from studying the growth of oral traditions in different cultures around the globe, transmitting stories orally to new audiences inevitably produces variations in phrasing and emphasis as the speaker adapts the tale to different hearers and situations. Until a tradition is finally fixed in writing, it is characterized by extreme fluidity, changing with each fresh recitation. In the case of Jesus' sayings, which presumably were venerated even at the earliest stages of transmission, Christians probably made every effort to repeat them verbatim. Even so, the Gospels contain a wide range of variation in what appear to have been the same sayings. To cite only one example among many, in Mark, Jesus states that "he who is not against us is for us," whereas in Matthew he says

the opposite: "He who is not with me is against me, and he who does not gather with me scatters" (cf. Mark 9:40 and Matt. 12:30). To complicate the matter further, Luke preserves both forms of the saying (Luke 7:50; 11:23). The degree of variation in some traditions is so great that the meanings become mutually exclusive, as in the strikingly different versions of the wedding feast parable, which appears in two canonical Gospels, Matthew (22:2–13) and Luke (14:16–23), as well as the apocryphal Gospel of Thomas (64) (see box 9.5).

Divergent oral renditions of Jesus' sayings and parables multiplied in widely separated geographical areas, including important Christian centers at Jerusalem, Antioch in Syria, Ephesus in Asia Minor, and Corinth in Greece. Each center undoubtedly cultivated distinct traditions closely associated with the earliest missionaries, teachers, and prophets in their respective communities. Given the multiplicity of variations that developed, it is difficult, if not impossible, to recover the original form of a given saying. Inheritors of a complex process of oral transmission, the Gospel writers compiled not necessarily

Box 6.2

From Oral *Kerygma* to Written Gospel: Hypothetical Stages in the Gospels' Historical Development

New Testament scholars employ a variety of critical methods to discover the processes by which originally oral traditions about Jesus gradually evolved into written form. Historical and literary analysis of the Gospels suggests that they developed over a relatively long period (about 30–100 C.E.), undergoing several discrete stages of growth. The following list provides a hypothetical reconstruction of events and movements leading to the Gospels' creation.

DATE	EVENT OR DEVELOPMENT

I. Period of Exclusively Oral Traditions

30 C.E.	Oral preaching by Jesus in Galilee, Samaria, and Judea
30–33 C.E.	Crucifixion
30–50 C.E.	Oral preaching about Jesus by Aramaic-speaking disciples in Galilee, Samaria, Judea, and neighboring regions; formation of first Christian community at Jerusalem, led by Peter, John, and James; formation of additional Aramaic-speaking communities throughout Palestine; development of a second major Christian center at Antioch in Syria
40–60 C.E.	Missionary tours of Paul and associates; establishment of new, larger Gentile, Greek-speaking churches in Asia Minor and Greece

II. Period of Earliest Written Documents

50–70 C.E.	Oldest surviving Christian documents (Paul's letters to Gentile congregations) composed; collection of Jesus' sayings, in Greek (the Q document), compiled; possible collection of Jesus' miraculous works, the Signs Gospel (later incorporated into the Gospel of John); possible first edition of the Gospel of Thomas (like Q, a Sayings Gospel)

III. The Jewish Revolt Against Rome and the Appearance of the First Canonical Gospel

66 C.E.	Outbreak of Jewish War
66–70 C.E.	Mark's "wartime" Gospel composed, relating Jesus' suffering to that of his persecuted followers
70 C.E.	Roman destruction of Jerusalem, the Temple, and the original Christian center

IV. Production of New, Enlarged Editions of Mark

80–90 C.E.	Composition of Matthew and Luke, who use Mark and Q as their primary sources (plus their individual special sources, respectively M and L)

V. Production of New Gospels Promoting an Independent (Non-Synoptic) Tradition

90–100 C.E.	Composition of the Gospel of John, incorporating the older Signs Gospel; second edition of the Gospel of Thomas, incorporating the older Thomas sayings collection

what Jesus exactly said or did, but what the believing community collectively understood to be the tenor of his actions and sayings.

Form Criticism   Recognizing that originally Palestinian oral traditions about Jesus had been modified to accommodate a new, ethnically and religiously diverse Gentile audience, German scholars early in this century began to emphasize the implications of such adaptations. The critical method that attempts to identify the oldest oral forms underlying the Gospels' written texts is called **form criticism**. Form critics discovered that the Gospels are made up of many individual units—brief narrative episodes, discrete conflict stories, pronouncements, parables, and sayings—that circulated orally and independently of one another before the Gospel authors assembled them in written form.

Mark's Gospel, for instance, seems to consist of a string of incidents, anecdotes, and sayings that are very loosely connected to one another. The individual units, such as the account of Jesus exorcizing demons or performing miraculous cures, are generally brief, self-contained narrative episodes that have clear-cut beginnings and endings and can stand alone. During the oral period, they were autonomous, existing free of a narrative framework. Jesus' pithy statements comparing God's kingdom to a mustard seed or a priceless pearl, for example, do not depend on the larger Gospel context to convey their message. Such detachable units are called **pericopes**. Derived from the Greek *peri* (about) and *koptein* (to cut), the term denotes the individual, orally transmitted building blocks from which the longer Gospel account is constructed.

The form critic searches for the *Sitz im leben*, the probable "life-setting" or social circumstances from which stories about Jesus originated and were orally transmitted by the early church. The first Christians spoke about Jesus in many different situations and for many different purposes—preaching to fellow Jews, defending their beliefs to Greek or Roman officials, instructing new converts, settling disputes among themselves, and conducting worship services. By establishing the probable pre-written form of a particular saying or incident, the form critic enables us to see how the Gospel writers edited these previously free-floating units to express their respective views about Jesus.

THE Q (SOURCE) DOCUMENT

At an unknown date, Christians began to make brief compilations of Jesus' sayings, such as the cluster of kingdom parables underlying Mark 4 and Matthew 13. A much more comprehensive written collection of Jesus' teachings, the Q document, is thought to have been assembled between about 50 and 70 C.E. Because it does not survive as a separate document, scholars must reconstruct its contents from passages that Matthew and Luke have in common but that did not derive from Mark (see box 6.3).

These shared passages, totaling about 250 verses, contain some of Jesus' most celebrated teachings, including much of the material in Matthew's Sermon on the Mount (Matt. 5–7) and Luke's parallel Sermon on the Plain (Luke 6). An increasing number of scholars ascribe enormous importance to Q, for this Sayings Gospel, at least in its first edition, may preserve one of the earliest forms of Christianity. It appears to have been written, in Greek, by a community of itinerant preachers living in Galilee or western Syria who regarded Jesus as both prophet and wisdom teacher. Containing virtually no narrative, Q presents Jesus as one "greater than Solomon" (the traditional founder of Israel's wisdom school) who is the last in a long line of God's prophets and sages, a martyr rejected and killed by an unappreciative people. Q thus includes no theology interpreting Jesus' death as a saving act, focusing almost exclusively on the living man's moral exhortations, parables, and spiritual insights. Before being assimilated into Matthew and Luke, Q was apparently a Gospel in its own right, providing the first written witness to Jesus' primary teachings. A scholarly reconstruction of Q appears in Robert Miller's *The Complete Gospels*; a detailed analysis of the text is available in A. D. Jacobson's *The First Gospel: An Introduction to Q* (see "Recommended Reading").

Some scholars also posit the existence of another pre-Gospel narrative source, a primitive account of Jesus' miraculous deeds or "signs," that was later incorporated into the Gospel of John (see chapter 10). Some also believe that at least parts of the Gospel of Thomas, the only noncanonical Gospel to survive intact, predated the composition of the canonical Gospels. Like the hypothetical Q, Thomas consists entirely of sayings, evidence that early Christians did create Gospels without either a Passion story or other narrative component.

COMPOSITION OF THE CANONICAL GOSPELS

The author of Mark is generally credited with inventing the Gospel genre, reshaping previously fluid oral traditions about Jesus into the fixed written form of a popular Greek biography designed for a Hellenistic audience. Transforming the oral

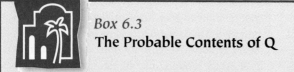

Box 6.3
The Probable Contents of Q

Although we lack absolute proof that Q, a hypothetical collection of Jesus' sayings, ever existed, many scholars believe that it is possible to reconstruct its contents. By carefully isolating teaching material contained in both Luke and Matthew but absent from Mark, scholars have compiled a list of almost 250 verses they believe were originally part of Q. These passages include some of Jesus' most characteristic teachings, including the Beatitudes, his command to love one's enemies, his commissioning of the disciples, and his renunciation of material possessions.

Because Luke seems to have preserved Q's original order better than Matthew, Q sayings are customarily cited by Lukan chapter and verse. Although in many cases the two Gospel writers show an almost verbatim agreement on Q's wording, in places where they disagree scholars can typically reconstruct the original phrasing by taking the two Evangelists' editorializing tendencies into account. The saying about having a rafter lodged in one's eye (Luke 6:41–2/Matt. 7:3–5),

for example, reveals Luke and Matthew in total agreement. In the Beatitudes, however, Matthew appears to modify Jesus' original commendations of the literally poor and hungry, making them "poor in spirit" and hungry for "justice" or "righteousness," a characteristic Matthean term.

Because it contains little narrative and few references to Jesus' martyrdom, Q appears to have originated in a community that remembered Jesus primarily as a wisdom teacher and prophet whose death resembled those of Israel's earlier prophets. Mark, however, made Jesus' death of paramount importance, God's means of redeeming humanity. By combining Q's wisdom teachings with Mark's theology of the cross, Matthew and Luke demonstrated that the two ways of regarding Jesus' significance were not necessarily mutually exclusive.

The following summary of some representative Q material lists parallel verses in Luke and Matthew.

Q MATERIAL	LUKE	MATTHEW
The ministry of John the Baptist	3:7–9, 16–17	3:7–12
The testing of Jesus by Satan	4:1–4, 9–12, 5–8, 13	4:1–11
The Beatitudes	6:20–26	5:3, 4, 6, 11–12
The admonition to love one's enemies and abide by the golden rule	6:27–36	5:44, 39–42; 7:12; 5:46–47, 45, 48
The construction of houses on sand or rock	6:46–49	7:21, 24–27
The healing of a Roman officer's slave	7:1–10	7:28; 8:5–10, 13
Praise by Jesus for John the Baptist	7:24–28	11:7–11
The differences between Jesus and John	7:31–35	11:16–19
The commissioning of the disciples	10:2–12	9:37–38; 10:7–16
The Lord's Prayer	11:2–4	6:9–13
The sign of Jonah	11:16, 29–32	12:38–42
The rejection of God's wisdom	11:49–51	23:34–36
The avoidance of anxieties and reliance on God	12:22–31	6:25–33
The great feast	14:16–24	22:1–10
The rejection of family ties	14:26–27	10:37–39
The parable of invested money	19:12–26	25:14–30

For a complete reconstruction of Q's probable contents, see "The Sayings Gospel Q," pp. 249–300 in Robert J. Miller, ed., *The Complete Gospels*, 3rd ed. (San Francisco: HarperSanFrancisco, 1994).

Figure 6.3 *Christ with the Crown of Thorns.* In this wooden carving of Jesus crowned with thorns, an anonymous twentieth-century African sculptor beautifully captures both the sorrow and the mystery of Mark's suffering Son of Man. (© Boltin Picture Library)

kerygma into a sequential narrative about Jesus' public career, Mark concluded with a long, remarkably detailed account of Jesus' arrest, trial, and execution (see figure 6.3). Because it emphasizes Jesus' suffering and death as the most important aspect of his biography, Mark's Gospel has been called a Passion narrative with a long introduction (see chapter 7). Certainly, Mark's strong emphasis on the cross clearly distinguished its viewpoint from that of the Q community, which apparently did not give great theological weight to the manner of Jesus' demise. Even if Mark's author was aware of this Sayings Gospel, it is not surprising that he does not make use of it.

Authorial Intent in Gospel Writing   Other than an opening declaration to present Jesus' story as a gospel — "good news" — Mark's author says nothing explicit about his purpose in writing. Nor does he identify himself, his intended readers, his place of composition, or the date on which he writes. Mark's anonymity characterizes all four of the canonical Gospels, none of which gives the name of its author. The traditional Gospel titles — "The Gospel According to Mark," or "Matthew," or "Luke," or "John" — appear nowhere in the main texts and seem to be headings added late in the second century C.E., long after the Gospels themselves were written. Careful study of the Gospel texts does not confirm either the traditional authorship or the belief that the writers were eyewitnesses to the events they described. For convenience, we continue to refer to the authors by their traditional names, but it is a disappointing fact that scholarship as yet has found no way to identify the four Evangelists (see box 6.4).

Matthew's Gospel   Incorporating about 90 percent of Mark into his narrative, the author of Matthew produced a new, enlarged edition of Mark that also included extensive teaching material drawn from Q. In addition, the unknown author also used a source unique to his Gospel, which scholars designate as **M** (special Matthean material). Writing about 85 C.E. to answer Jewish criticism of Christian claims about Jesus and to emphasize Jesus' adherence to the Mosaic Torah, Matthew portrays Jesus as a greater Moses who demands a "higher righteousness" than that practiced by the Pharisees. Into Mark's narrative outline, he inserts five clusters of sayings and parables — mostly borrowed from Q and M — arranging them as five separate speeches corresponding to the five books of Torah.

Matthew frames Mark's narrative with accounts of Jesus' infancy and postresurrection appearances. Most distinctively, he represents Jesus' birth and ministry as fulfilling prophecies from the Hebrew Bible, which Matthew cites in Greek translation (see box 8.1). He cites about 130 scriptural passages to refute Jewish arguments that Jesus had not lived up to prophetic expectations of the Messiah. So

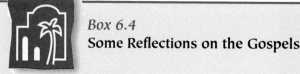

Box 6.4
Some Reflections on the Gospels

In studying the Gospels, it is helpful to remember some basic facts about their composition and purpose.

Authorship: None of the Gospel authors reveals his name, his background, or the place or date of composition. No Gospel writer claims to be an eyewitness to the events he narrates (although John implies that his account of Jesus' death draws on the testimony of an anonymous disciple [John 19:35]). None claims to be inerrant or inspired; such claims were made for them by later generations of Christians.

Date: The earliest canonical Gospel—Mark—was not written until approximately forty years after the Crucifixion. The other three were composed even later, between about 80 and 95 C.E.

Place of composition: Despite traditions that Mark was written in Rome and John in Ephesus, scholars are unable to verify their place of composition. Matthew may have originated somewhere in Syria, perhaps in Antioch, where Peter and other Torah-observant Jewish Christians predominated (compare Paul's encounter with Peter in Antioch [Gal. 2:11–14] with Matt. 16:13–20).

Influence of Jewish Scriptures: Beginning with Mark, all Gospel writers present events in Jesus' life as the unfolding and continuation of the same prophetic force that created the Hebrew Bible. For every important milestone—particularly Jesus' birth, baptism, healing ministry, public rejection, arrest, and execution—the authors cite a biblical precedent or parallel. Matthew most fully exploits this tendency to view almost every aspect of Jesus' biography as the fulfillment of ancient prophecy. Quoting selected passages from the Septuagint (Greek translation of the Hebrew Bible), Matthew shapes his portrait of Jesus to demonstrate that he was the long-awaited Messiah, embodiment of the covenant promises made to Abraham and David (see chapter 8). As a result of Gospel writers' compiling Jesus' story with ready-made phrases from Scripture, information about Jesus that did not clearly illustrate the prophecy-fulfillment pattern was likely to be ignored or excluded from the written account.

Absence of non-Christian documents about Jesus: Because the Gospels are the only first-century sources of information about Jesus, it is impossible to check their representation of him against contemporary accounts that might provide a more objective report.

Completely lacking any non-Christian verification of the Gospels' theological claims about Jesus, we must rely almost exclusively on testimonies composed by people who believed in his divinity.

Theological orientation: Committed to interpreting Jesus' life and death as manifestations of the same God who had prompted Israel's ancient prophets, Gospel authors were more interested in emphasizing Jesus' theological significance than in preserving biographical facts. By carefully examining the different ways in which individual writers present the same incident or saying, scholars can discover how each author modifies the tradition to emphasize his particular theological concerns (see chapters 7–10). Whereas Mark shows Jesus experiencing almost unbearable agony and near-despair during his final hours, John paints a serene and confident Jesus who seems to rise above mere human suffering. The differences result not from either writer's historical concern with reporting exactly how Jesus felt or behaved, but from their differing theological perspectives. Mark sees Jesus as a model of human suffering and self-sacrifice, one that his disciples can imitate. In contrast, John depicts him as God's heavenly Wisdom incarnated in a human body, a divine being immune to doubt or despair (see figure 10.2).

Jesus' uniqueness: Most world religions honor a founder who effectively mediated between the human sphere and the divine. In Jewish tradition, Moses acted as mediator between Yahweh and Israel, bringing down from Mount Sinai the Torah that bound the covenant people to their God. Zoroaster, an eschatological prophet in ancient Persia, revealed the ongoing struggle between invisible forces of Good and Evil that shapes human experience, urging his listeners to resist Ahriman (the Persian devil) and side with Ahura Mazda, god of light and life. In India, a young Hindu prince became Buddha (the enlightened one) by rejecting the illusory quality of ordinary existence and perceiving the nature of ultimate reality. Seven centuries after Jesus, an Arab prophet, Mohammed, founded the last of the great world religions, preaching Islam (submission) to the only God, Allah. By contrast, New Testament writers portray Jesus as divine himself. He is not merely a servant of God, like Moses or Mohammed, but in his own being a unique manifestation of the eternal God.

successful was Matthew's integration of Jesus' teachings, biblical proof texts, and Mark's older narrative that Matthew's Gospel—with its directives for regulating the Christian community—soon became the most popular, ranking first among the four (see chapter 8).

Luke's Gospel   During the 90s C.E., perhaps only five or ten years after the appearance of Matthew, Luke's Gospel, the most literate and formally correct of the Synoptic accounts, was written. Luke's narrative reproduces about half of Mark, along with generous portions of Q and the author's own special source, known as **L**, which comprises about a third of his Gospel. The only Evangelist to provide a sequel to his version of Jesus' life, Luke also wrote the Book of Acts, which continues the story of Christian origins, tracing the expansion of the new religion from Jerusalem, to Greece, to Rome. In Luke's two-volume set, Jesus' career is presented as the turning point in Israel's history, the beginning of an innovative religious movement that brings salvation to Greeks as well as Jews. In Luke-Acts, Jesus is the model of service to others whose example is followed by many generations of disciples, including not only the apostles who founded the first church at Jerusalem but also an unlimited number of Gentiles who form a multiethnic, international community throughout the Roman Empire. According to Luke, the abiding presence of the Holy Spirit, which inspired Jesus' ministry, ensures that the Church functions as a successor and extension of Jesus himself, perpetuating his activity in the world.

Luke and Oral Tradition   The only Gospel writer to offer a direct statement about his intent and methodology, Luke opens his account with a formal preface explaining his indebtedness to secondary sources, both oral traditions and previously existing Gospels:

> The author to Theophilus: Many writers have undertaken to draw up an account of the events that have happened among us, following the traditions handed down to us by the original eyewitnesses and servants of the Gospel. And so I in my turn, your Excellency, as one who has gone over the whole course of these events in detail, have decided to write a connected narrative for you, so as to give you authentic knowledge about the matters of which you have been informed. (Luke 1:1–4)

Luke's brief introduction reveals his understanding of the connection between the oral teaching that characterized the Christian community—spoken reports of "the events that have happened among us"—and his authorial purpose. He wishes to create "a connected narrative" (according to accepted Hellenistic literary standards) so that his readers can receive "authentic knowledge" to supplant the oral traditions on which believers had formerly depended. Luke is also aware that "many writers" had earlier compiled Gospels that drew on oral tradition—testimony "handed down" from previous generations, "the original eyewitnesses," and other "servants of the Gospel" (see chapter 9).

The Griesbach Theory   Although most scholars think that the two-source theory most satisfactorily explains the literary relationship of the Synoptic Gospels, a small minority deny Markan priority. According to this view, Mark is a conflation (blending together) and abridgment of the other two Synoptics. Known as the Griesbach theory, after Johann Griesbach (1745–1812), who first published this solution to the Synoptic Problem, this hypothesis has been recently revived by several conservative scholars, notably William Farmer. These dissenting scholars emphasize the fact that a few short passages in the triple tradition (material occurring in all three Synoptics) show Matthew and Luke agreeing *against* Mark. Proponents of the two-source theory, however, argue that such "minor agreements" merely suggest that both Mark and Q had some limited material in common, that in a few instances they overlapped. Other defenders of the theory suggest that the "minor agreements" are the result of early scribal attempts to make the Synoptic texts more consistent. Despite some objections, most scholars think that the two-source hypothesis most adequately explains both the similarities and the differences in the Synoptic Gospels.

The Gospel of John

Shortly before the end of the first century C.E., the Fourth Gospel, that ascribed to John, was composed, apparently both the last canonical Gospel written and the last to attain canonical status. (Numerous apocryphal Gospels also circulated in the early church, but only Thomas survives complete; the others exist only in fragments; see chapter 20). This document differs so extremely from the three Synoptic accounts that scholars regard it as a special case. John's narrative presents a radically different picture of Jesus' character and teaching. Instead of speaking in earthy images and parables drawn from the experience of his peasant listeners, John's Jesus delivers long, philosophical monologues about his unique relationship to the Father and his imminent ascension to heaven. Rather than focusing on the in-breaking kingdom of God and a reinterpretation of the Jewish Torah, the Johannine Jesus dwells primarily on his divine nature and his significance to the believer. Whereas Mark, Matthew, and Luke show Jesus promulgating a modified form of traditional Judaism, John is less interested in preserving Jesus' own religion than he is in promoting a religion *about* Jesus, an approach in which the teacher, rather than his historical message, becomes the object of veneration. John's insistence on Jesus as a divinity walking the earth in human form—and the almost total absence of topics that characterized Jesus' Synoptic teachings—make scholars doubt the Fourth Gospel's historical value. Because both the Synoptics and John cannot be right about the form and content of Jesus' message—and John's version is outvoted three to one—scholars generally focus on the Synoptic accounts in their search for the historical Jesus, regarding John as essentially a theological meditation on Jesus' life.

Literary Analysis of the Gospels

Possessing the complete written texts of five Gospels (including the apocryphal Thomas), scholars can compare these documents using the tools of **literary criticism.** Rather than analyzing a text to determine its historical background and oral or written sources, literary critics study the finished product, a skill that many careful students have already acquired. Every experienced reader practices literary criticism to some extent, studying a text not only to gain information but also to detect its principal concerns and themes. Like all literary narratives, the Gospel stories have the basic elements of setting, character, dialog, plot, style, and rhetorical techniques, such as the use of irony. Readers automatically assimilate clues—characteristic words, images, and repeated phrases—that indicate how the author intends them to react toward a character's particular statements or behavior.

REDACTION CRITICISM

In recent decades, scholars have increasingly focused on the role of the individual Gospel writer in editing, revising, and reshaping the oral and written traditions he inherited. A form of literary analysis, **redaction criticism** (from the German *Redaktionsgeschite*) emphasizes the redactor's (author-editor's) importance in assembling, rearranging, and reinterpreting his sources. Matthew and Luke do not slavishly follow their primary sources—Mark and Q—but freely adapt them to express their individual theological viewpoints. The recognition that the Gospel writers were not mere compilers of older material but active interpreters of it, creatively modifying traditions to make a theological point, deepens our understanding of differences in the three Synoptic accounts. By scrutinizing the way Matthew and Luke edit Mark's narrative and the changes they make in rendering the same saying or parable, scholars can discover their particular theological orientation. When either Matthew or Luke revises Mark or gives a different version of a shared saying, they invariably do it for theological reasons.

As readers become familiar with an Evangelist's distinctive views, they will eventually be able to explain why Matthew's rendition of the wedding feast parable, for example, differs from that of Luke or Thomas. In each case, the author edits the parable to fit his religious perspective (see box 9.5). At crucial moments in his narrative, such as Jesus' crucifixion, each Evangelist emphasizes his particular understanding of the event by ascribing different last words to Jesus. Whereas Mark and Matthew agree that the dying Jesus utters a single despairing cry, the other two Gospel authors present final statements that reflect a totally different mood and meaning, with Luke and John highlighting their hero's serene confidence and control of the situation (see box 10.8). In their distinctive death scenes, the four authors ascribe to Jesus a climactic utterance consistent with the distinctive theological picture of Jesus depicted throughout their respective Gospels.

NARRATIVE CRITICISM

A method of literary interpretation that is increasingly applied to studying the Gospels, **narrative criticism** emphasizes such factors as the manner in which a story is constructed, the point of view from which it is told, the author's implied attitude toward his subject or characters, and even the use of geographical settings to convey authorial intent. The Gospel authors do not tell their stories in the first person, nor do they present themselves as eyewitnesses to the incidents they describe. Instead of introducing themselves to readers and citing their personal credentials as historians of Christian origins, the Gospel writers all assume the role of an anonymous but omniscient narrator—fully but inexplicably aware of everything that occurs. They presume to know Jesus' private thoughts, his opponents' secret motives, and even words spoken when there are no witnesses present to overhear, as when Jesus prays alone in Gethsemane while all his disciples sleep (Mark 14). The Gospel authors almost never intrude directly into their stories—the chief exception being the narrator of John's Gospel in his description of the Crucifixion and his statement of authorial purpose (John 20–21). The effect of the omniscient storyteller, who reports the speeches of heavenly voices, exorcized demons, and angelic visitors in exactly the same way that he records ordinary human conversations, is to impress on readers the narrator's comprehensive authority.

Gospel authors also use geographical locations to express value judgments. In Mark's Gospel, the author presents Jesus' career in terms of two opposing territories. In the first half of Mark's story, Jesus recruits disciples and enjoys considerable success in his native Galilee, the largely rural area of peasant farmers north of Samaria and Judea. Mark sets the final part of his Gospel in Jerusalem, where his hero performs no miracles and is betrayed, tried for treason, and crucified. When a tiny group of women find Jesus' tomb empty on the first Easter morning, Mark has an angel tell them *not* to look for their risen Lord there—in Jerusalem—but back "in Galilee."

Mark's negative attitude toward Jerusalem (and its original church?) contrasts with Luke's positive view of the Jewish capital. In Luke's account, all of Jesus' postresurrection appearances take place in or around Jerusalem. Luke reports that Jesus explicitly commands his followers to *remain* in Jerusalem and wait for an outpouring of the Spirit. He also devotes the first part of Acts, the sequel to his Gospel, to describing the flowering of the Jerusalem community, which he presents as the Spirit-guided nucleus of Christianity's expansion into the larger world (Acts 1:8). Readers influenced by Mark are likely to differ significantly from Luke's readers in their opinions of Jerusalem's desirability or importance in the Christian scheme of things.

In his presentation of Jesus' opponents—scribes (scholars) and Pharisees—Luke guides readers to a relatively sympathetic attitude toward Jews rejecting the Christian message. The Lukan author describes those who played a part in instigating Jesus' execution as more to be pitied than condemned, picturing them as acting in ignorance. By contrast, Matthew portrays Jesus' religious opponents as vicious hypocrites, threatening them with the fires of **Gehenna,** a symbol of posthumous torment (Matt. 23). Unfortunately for the history of relations between Judaism and Christianity, Matthew has thus far proven the more persuasive narrator, his negative picture of Jewish leaders helping to inspire two millennia of Christian persecution of Jews.

A COMPOSITE PORTRAIT OF JESUS

The fact that the early Christian community generally did not promote a single, uniform edition of Jesus' life or adopt one "official" version free of seeming contradictions is significant. Instead of an

Box 6.5
The Gospels' Cast of Characters

Because the four Gospel writers present four distinctive ways of telling Jesus' story, they do not all include the same cast of characters. Although a few personages, such as John the Baptist, Peter, and Pontius Pilate, appear in all four accounts, the three New Testament lists of Jesus' twelve chief disciples differ significantly. John introduces a number of figures, such as Nicodemus and Lazarus, who are not mentioned in the Synoptics. The major players in each of the four narratives, along with representative passages in which they appear, are given here.

	MARK	MATTHEW	LUKE	JOHN
1. Jesus' mother, Mary	3:20–21, 31–35; 6:3	1:18–25; 2:11, 21	1:26–56; 2:5–7, 16–19, 33–34, 48; 51	2:2–5; 19:25–27
2. Jesus' putative father, Joseph		1:16, 18–25; 2:13–14	1:27; 2:4–5, 16, 48; 3:23	1:45; 6:42
3. Jesus' "brothers" (close kinsmen):	3:31–35			7:1–9
James, Joseph, Judas, and Simon	6:3 (named)	13:55		
4. Jesus' unnamed "sisters"	6:3	13:56		
5. *Characters in the Bethlehem birth story:*				
Herod the Great		2:1–8, 13–19	1:5	
The Magi (foreign astrologers)		2:1–2, 7–12		
Shepherds			2:8–20	
Elizabeth and Zechariah, parents of the future Baptist			1:5–25, 40–45, 57–80	
Gabriel, angel of the annunciation			1:26–38	
Simeon, Temple prophet			2:25–35	
Anna, an aged prophetess			2:36–38	
6. *John the Baptist:*				
Baptism of Jesus	1:4–11, 14	3:1–17	1:15–17, 21	1:15–36
Comparison between John and Jesus		11:7–19	7:24–35	
Inquiry about Jesus' identity		11:2–6	7:18–23	
Execution by Herod Antipas	6:14–29	14:1–12	3:19–20; 9:7–9	
7. *Jesus' inner circle of disciples:*				
Simon Peter and Andrew (brothers)	1:16–18; 9:2–6	4:18; 17:1	9:28	
Peter's confession	8:27–33	16:13–25	9:18–22	
Peter's denial of Jesus	14:26–31, 66–72	26:33–35, 69–75	22:31–34, 54–61	18:15–18, 25–27
James and John, sons of Zebedee	1:19–20	4:21–22; 17:1		
Wish to be first in the kingdom	10:35–45	20:20–28	(22:24–27)	

	MARK	MATTHEW	LUKE	JOHN
8. *Other disciples (in speaking roles):*				
Andrew, Peter's brother				1:40–42, 44; 6:8–9; 12:20–22
Philip, one of the Twelve				1:43–49; 6:5–7; 12:20–22
Nathaniel, one of the Twelve				1:45–51
Thomas, one of the Twelve				20:24–28
The unidentified Beloved Disciple				13:23–26; 18:15–16; 19:26–27; 20:2–10; 21:7, 20–24
9. List of the Twelve	3:13–19	10:1–4	6:12–16	
10. *Persons whom Jesus heals:*				
The Gerasene demoniac	5:1–20	8:28–34	8:26–39	
Jairus and his daughter	5:22–24, 35–43	9:18–19, 23–26	8:40–42, 49–56	
Woman with hemorrhages	5:25–34	9:20–22	8:43–48	
Syrophoenician (Canaanite) woman	7:14–30	15:21–28		
Deaf man	7:32–37			
Blind man (or men)	8:22–26	20:29–34	18:35–43	
Epileptic boy	9:15–29	17:14–20	9:37–43a	
Centurion's slave (or son)		8:5–13	7:2–10	
The widow of Nain and her son			7:11–17	
A man born blind				9:1–38
Lazarus, brother of Mary and Martha				11:1–44; 12:1–11
11. *Women disciples or women whom Jesus befriends:*				
Galilean women who support Jesus			8:1–3	
Woman who anoints Jesus	14:3–9	26:6–13	7:36–50	12:1–8
A Samaritan woman				4:7–42
Women at the cross and/or tomb:				
Mary of Magdala	15:40–41, 47; 16:1–8	27:55–56; 28:1–11	8:2; 23:49; 24: 10–11	19:25; 20:1–10
Mary, mother of James and Joseph	15:40–41, 47; 16:1–8	20:1–18	24: 10–11	
Salome	15:40–41, 47; 16:1–8	27:56; 28:1	24: 10–11	
The sisters, Mary and Martha			10:38–39	11:19–36, 39, 45; 12:1–8
12. *Other friends or acquaintances of Jesus:*				
A rich young man	10:17–22	19:16–26	18:18–27	
Zacchaeus, a wealthy tax collector			19:1–10	

(continued)

Box 6.5 *(continued)*

	MARK	MATTHEW	LUKE	JOHN
12. *Other friends or acquaintances of Jesus (continued):*				
Simon the leper (perhaps the same as Simon the Pharisee)	14:3		7:36–46	
Man carrying a water jar	14:13–16	26:17–19	22:7–13	
Nicodemus				3:1–12; 7:50–52; 19:39
13. *Figures in the Passion narrative:*				
Judas Iscariot	14:10–11, 43–46	26:14–16, 21–25, 47–50; 27:1–5	22:3–6, 47–48	13:21–30; 18:2–3
Caiaphas, the High Priest	14:53–64	26:57–66	22:54, 66–71	11:47–53; 18:13–14
Annas, father-in-law of Caiaphas				18:13, 19–24
Pontius Pilate, Roman procurator	15:1–15, 43–44	27:1, 11–26, 58	23:1–7, 11–25, 52	18:26–19:16, 19–22
Herod Antipas			23:6–12	
Barabbas, the terrorist	15:6–15	27:15–26	23:18–25	18:38–40
Simon of Cyrene, impressed to carry the cross	15:21	27:32	23:26	
Two unnamed crucified criminals	15:27	27:38	23:32–33, 39–43	
The Roman centurion who praises Jesus	15:39	27:54	23:47	
Joseph of Arimathaea, who buries Jesus	15:42–46	27:57–60	23:50–54	19:38–42
Resurrected saints in Jerusalem		27:52–53		
Angels at Jesus' tomb	16:5–8	28:2–7	24:4–7	20:12–14

"authorized" biography, the church accepted the four canonical Gospels, perhaps recognizing that different Christian groups scattered throughout the Roman Empire had already adopted one or more different Gospels as foundation documents of their particular communities. Although individual churches, such as Antioch, where Matthew was probably written, would not relinquish *their* Evangelist's work in favor of another, by the late second century C.E. many seem to have accepted two or three of the Synoptics. John, which some early church leaders condemned as a Gnostic fabrication, took longer to be accepted by the church at large.

Its position as the Fourth Gospel may reflect its relatively late inclusion in the canon. Box 6.5 summarizes the extensive cast of characters appearing in the Gospels—many shared but some unique.

As Jesus elicited widely different responses during his lifetime, so he inspired the Evangelists to represent him in significantly different guises, ranging from the Galilean carpenter-prophet in Mark to the incarnate heavenly Word of God in John. This composite portrait, with all its attendant problems and unanswered questions, is the one deemed appropriate to reflect early Christianity's diverse community of faith.

Summary

This book respects the integrity of each individual Gospel text. The author believes that each Gospel is best understood when studied as an independent work, embodying the distinctive thought of its particular writer. Each Gospel will be examined on its own terms and in the context of its author's individual theology without any attempt to make it conform to ideas expressed in any other New Testament book. By allowing each Evangelist to speak for himself, we can recognize the rich diversity of New Testament Christianity, as well as its thematic unity—the unparalleled significance of the Christ event. In studying the Gospels, Paul's letters, and the other canonical writings, we benefit from all the scholarly research and methodologies that help illuminate the historical origins, the literary development, and the theological insights contained in the twenty-seven documents that collectively became the standard-bearers of the Christian faith.

QUESTIONS FOR REVIEW

1. Explain the relationship between the oral preaching (*kerygma*) of the first Christians and the composition of written Gospels. What does the gap of forty to sixty years between the time of Jesus' death and the dates of the Gospels' compositions suggest? Review some of the circumstances that may have caused early Christian communities to produce several different versions of Jesus' life and teachings.

2. Define the Synoptic Problem. Why do scholars believe that the first three canonical Gospels (Matthew, Mark, and Luke) have a literary relationship? In contrast to John (the Fourth Gospel), what factors indicate that the Synoptics depend on a common tradition?

3. Describe some of the scholarly methods used to study the Gospels. Define these scholarly terms and explain how each functions in analyzing a document: *historical criticism, source criticism, form criticism, literary criticism, and narrative criticism.*

4. Define and explain the two-source hypothesis. How does this thesis account for the kinship among the Synoptic Gospels? In what ways do scholars believe that Matthew and Luke are related to Mark? Explain scholars' reasons for postulating the existence of the Q document. What kind of material did this hypothetical source contain? What do the abbreviations M and L stand for?

5. Define and explain the Griesbach theory. How does it differ from the two-source theory? Which of these two hypotheses do you think best explains the similarities and differences among the three Synoptic Gospels?

QUESTION FOR DISCUSSION AND REFLECTION

1. Scholars recognize that the Gospel authors are not historians or biographers in the modern sense. As you read the Gospel accounts carefully, consider whether the writers are interested primarily in preserving historical facts about Jesus or in explaining and interpreting his life in religious terms. Relate the Evangelists' theological concerns to redaction criticism.

TERMS AND CONCEPTS TO REMEMBER

Synoptic Gospels
kerygma
relation of Aramaic to Greek in the Gospel traditions
Luke's method of composition
historical criticism
source criticism
relation of the scientific method to belief in the supernatural

Synoptic Problem
two-document (source) theory
the Q (*Quelle*) document
M and L
Griesbach theory
form criticism
pericopes
redaction criticism
literary criticism
narrative criticism

RECOMMENDED READING

Bultmann, Rudolf. *The History of the Synoptic Tradition.* Translated by J. Marsh. New York: Harper & Row, 1963. A masterful, if somewhat technical, study by the great German scholar.

Farmer, W. R. *The Synoptic Problem.* New York: Macmillan, 1964. Argues for the priority of Matthew.

Funk, Robert W., ed. *New Gospel Parallels.* Vol. 1, *The Synoptic Gospels*; Vol. 2, *John and the Other Gospels.* Philadelphia: Fortress Press, 1985. The most valuable scholarly tool for comparing the Gospel texts.

Funk, Robert W.; Hoover, Roy W.; and the Jesus Seminar. *The Five Gospels: The Search for the Authentic Words of Jesus.* New York: Macmillan, 1993. The New Scholars

Version of the Gospels, with Jesus' sayings printed in red, pink, gray, or black, depending on the scholars' view of their probable authenticity.

Green, Joel, ed. *Hearing the New Testament: Strategies for Interpretation.* Grand Rapids, Mich.: Eerdmans, 1995. Lists methodologies and goals of critical interpretations.

Jacobson, Arland D. *The First Gospel, An Introduction to Q.* Sonoma, Calif.: Polebridge Press, 1992. A study of Q's development and theology.

Kloppenborg, John S. *The Formation of Q: Trajectories in Ancient Wisdom Collections.* Studies in Antiquity and Christianity. Philadelphia: Fortress Press, 1987. A scholarly study of the presumed Q text that finds two layers of traditions, the first presenting Jesus as a wisdom teacher and the second, later addition picturing Jesus as an apocalyptic judge.

Kloppenborg, John S.; Meyer, Marvin W.; Patterson, Stephen J.; and Steinhauser, Michael G. *Q Thomas Reader.* Sonoma, Calif.: Polebridge Press, 1990. Includes an annotated reconstruction of the presumed sayings source.

Koester, Helmut. *Introduction to the New Testament.* Vol. 2, *History and Literature of Early Christianity.* Philadelphia: Fortress Press, 1982. Translated from the original German, this is a major and incisive study of New Testament origins.

Miller, Robert J., ed. *The Complete Gospels,* 3rd ed. San Francisco: HarperSanFrancisco, 1994. Contains the complete texts of all known canonical and noncanonical Gospels, including a reconstruction of Q.

Neirynck, Frans. "Synoptic Problem." In R. E. Brown et al., eds., *The New Jerome Biblical Commentary,* pp. 587–595. Englewood Cliffs, N.J.: Prentice-Hall, 1990. A detailed examination of the literary kinship of the Synoptics.

Streeter, B. H. *The Four Gospels.* London: Macmillan, 1924. A landmark scholarly study arguing that Mark is the earliest Gospel.

Tuckett, C. M. "Q (Gospel Source)." In D. H. Freedman, ed., *The Anchor Bible Dictionary,* Vol. 5, pp. 567–572. New York: Doubleday, 1992. "Synoptic Problem." In D. N. Freedman, ed., *The Anchor Bible Dictionary,* Vol. 6, pp. 263–270. New York: Doubleday, 1992. A lucid introduction to theories about the interdependence of Matthew, Mark, and Luke.

CHAPTER 7

Mark's Portrait of Jesus

The Hidden Messiah and Eschatological Judge

For even the Son of Man did not come to be served but to serve and to give up his life as a ransom for many.   Mark 10:45

Key Themes Between about 64 C.E., when Nero began Rome's first official persecution of Christians, and 70 C.E., when the Romans destroyed Jerusalem (along with its Temple and the original apostolic church), the Christian community faced a series of crises that threatened its survival. Responding to the wars, revolts, and persecutions that afflicted his group, Mark composed what appears to be the earliest narrative account of Jesus' public career, presenting Jesus' story in a way that was strikingly relevant to the precarious circumstances of Mark's intended readers. Mark's Gospel thus portrays a Jesus who faces attack on three crucial fronts: from Jewish religious leaders, local (Herodian) rulers, and Roman officials. Painting Jesus as a "hidden Messiah" who was misunderstood and devalued by his contemporaries, Mark emphasizes that Jesus came to serve, to suffer, and to die—but also ultimately to triumph by submitting fully to the divine will.

Although he seems to have been the first author to transform oral traditions about Jesus into a biographical narrative, Mark was not the first Christian writer. About twenty years before Mark created his Gospel, Paul, Christianity's most successful missionary to the Gentiles, began composing a series of letters (c. 50–62 C.E.) in which he makes the risen Jesus his central focus. Except for the essential facts of Jesus' crucifixion and resurrection, however, Paul shows little interest in Jesus' earthly life or teachings. Paul's only extended quotation from Jesus is taken from a **tradition** passed on to him about Jesus' final meal with his disciples, the Last Supper (1 Cor. 11:23–26). One or two written collections of Jesus' sayings—Q and perhaps the first edition of Thomas—were probably also circulating among some Christian communities when Mark wrote, but if he was aware of their existence, he chose not to use them. Mark, in fact, cites relatively few of Jesus' teachings, instead emphasizing Jesus' actions, particularly his miraculous healings and willingness to sacrifice himself for others.

Mark's Historical Setting

Several critical methods are helpful in studying **Mark,** beginning with historical investigation of the Gospel's authorship, date, place of composition, possible sources, and social and religious environment. The earliest reference to Mark's Gospel comes from

---

THE GOSPEL ACCORDING TO MARK

Author: Traditionally John Mark, traveling companion of Paul and "interpreter" for Peter in Rome. The writer does not identify himself in the Gospel text, and scholars, unable to verify the late second-century tradition of Markan authorship, regard the work as anonymous.

Date: About 66–70 C.E., during the Jewish revolt against Rome.

Place of composition: Rome or Syria-Palestine.

Audience: Gentile Christians suffering persecution.

Papias, an early Christian writer who was bishop of Hierapolis in Asia Minor about 130–140 C.E. (see box 7.1). As quoted by Eusebius, Papias states that Mark had been a disciple of the apostle Peter in Rome and based his account on Peter's reminiscences of Jesus. Papias notes that Mark "had not heard the Lord or been one of his followers" so that his Gospel lacked "a systematic arrangement of the Lord's sayings" (Eusebius, *History* 3.39).

Besides Papias's intention to link Mark's Gospel to apostolic testimony, a consistent trend among church leaders during the second century C.E., he makes two important historical observations: (1) The author of Mark was *not an eyewitness* but depended on secondhand oral preaching, and (2) Mark's version of Jesus' activities is "not in [proper chronological] order." Careful scrutiny of Mark's Gospel has convinced most New Testament scholars that it does not derive from a single apostolic source, such as Peter, but is based on a general body of oral teachings about Jesus preserved in the author's community.

Mark's author offers few hints about where or for whom he wrote, except for his insistence that following Jesus demands a willingness to suffer for one's faith. Mark's near-equation of discipleship with suffering suggests that he directed his work to a group that was then undergoing severe testing and needed encouragement to remain steadfast (see Mark 8:34–38; 10:38–40). This theme of "carrying one's cross" may derive from the effects of Nero's persecution (c. 64–65), when numerous Roman Christians were crucified or burned alive. Papias and Iranaeus, another early church leader, agree that Mark wrote shortly after Peter's martyrdom, which, according to tradition, occurred during Nero's attack on Rome's Christian community.

Although Rome is the traditional place of composition, a growing number of scholars think it more likely that Mark wrote for an audience in Syria or Palestine. Critics favoring a Palestinian origin point to Mark's emphasis on the Jewish revolt (66–73 C.E.) and concurrent warnings to believers who were affected by the uprising (Mark 13; see box 7.6). In Mark's view, the "tribulation" climaxing in Jerusalem's destruction is the sign heralding Jesus' **Parousia,** or return in heavenly glory. The association of wars and national revolts with persecution of believers and Jesus' **Second Coming** gives an eschatological urgency to Mark's account.

Even though Papias and other second-century writers ascribe the Gospel to John Mark, a companion of Peter and Paul (Philem. 24; Col. 4:10; Acts 12:12–25; 14:36–40), the author does not identify himself in the text. The superscription—"The Gospel According to Mark"—is a later church embellishment, for second-century churchmen tried to connect extant writings about Jesus with apostles or their immediate disciples. The Gospel is anonymous; for convenience, we refer to the author as Mark.

MARK'S PUZZLING ATTITUDE TOWARD JESUS' CLOSE ASSOCIATES

Historical Sources   If scholars are right about assigning the Gospel to a time when the Jewish War against Rome had already begun and the Temple was expected to fall, most of the adult generation that had known Jesus was no longer alive. Even forty years after Jesus' death, however, there must have been some persons who had heard the disciples preach or who had known members of Jesus' family. James, whom Paul calls "the Lord's brother" (Gal. 1:9), was head of the Jerusalem church until his martyrdom in about 62 C.E. (Josephus, *Antiquities,* 20.9; Acts 12:17; 15:13–21; 21:16), making him a contemporary of Mark. Through his surviv-

Box 7.1
Papias on the Origin of Mark's Gospel

The oldest surviving reference to Mark's authorship of the Gospel bearing his name comes from Papias, who was a bishop of Hierapolis about 130 or 140 C.E. An early church historian, Eusebius of Caesarea, quotes Papias as writing that an unnamed *presbyter* (church elder) was his source:

> This, too, the presbyter used to say. "Mark, who had been Peter's interpreter, wrote down carefully, but not in order, all that he remembered of the Lord's sayings and doings. For he had not heard the Lord or been one of his followers, but later, as I said, one of Peter's. Peter used to adapt his teachings to the occasion, without making a systematic arrangement of the Lord's sayings, so that Mark was quite justified in writing down some things just as he remembered them. For he had one purpose only—to leave out nothing that he had heard, and to make no misstatement about it."
> (Eusebius, *The History of the Church*, 3.39)

Eusebius also quotes Papias's declaration that he preferred to learn Christian traditions from the testimony of persons who had known Jesus' companions rather than from written documents, such as the Gospels.

> And whenever anyone came who had been a follower of the presbyters, I inquired into the words of the presbyters, what Andrew or Peter had said, or Philip or Thomas or James or John or Matthew, or any other disciple of the Lord, and what Aristion and the presbyter John, disciples of the Lord, were still saying. For I did not imagine that things out of books would help me as much as the utterances of a living and abiding voice. (Eusebius, *The History of the Church*, 3.39)

Although Papias is a relatively early witness to the Christian tradition, scholars caution that we have no means of verifying the historicity of his claims.

---

ing associates, James would presumably have been an invaluable source of information when Mark began compiling data for a biography of Jesus.

Strangely, Mark does not seem to have regarded Jesus' relatives—or any other ordinary source a modern biographer would consult—as worthy informants. One of the author's prevailing themes is his negative presentation of virtually everyone associated with the historical Jesus (see box 7.2, which lists Mark's leading characters). From "his mother and brothers" (3:31) to his most intimate followers, Mark portrays all of Jesus' companions as oblivious to his real nature and/or obstacles to his work. Mark's Gospel consistently renders all Jesus' Palestinian associates as incredibly obtuse, unable to grasp his teachings, and blind to his value.

The Markan picture of Jesus' family implies that they, too, failed to appreciate or support him. "When his relatives heard of this [his drawing large crowds around him], they set out to take charge of him, convinced he was out of his mind" (3:21, Jerusalem Bible). When "his mother and his brothers" send a message asking for him, apparently demanding that he cease making a public spectacle of himself, Mark has Jesus declare "whoever does the will of God is my brother, my sister, my mother." This is a startling repudiation of his blood ties and an implication that in the Markan Jesus' view, his relatives were not doing the divine will (3:31–35). The force of this antifamily episode is intensified because Mark uses it to frame a controversy in which Jesus' opponents accuse him of expelling demons by the power of Beelzebub, another name for the Devil. Jesus countercharges that those who oppose his work are defying the **Holy Spirit,** an "unforgivable sin" (3:22–30). At this point in the narrative, Mark shows Jesus' family attempting to interrupt his ministry, thus subtly associating them with his adversaries (see also John 7:1–9).

Mark also depicts Jesus' acquaintances in **Nazareth** as hostile to a local carpenter's unexpected career as prophet and healer, questioning his credentials as sage and teacher. " 'Where does he get it from?' " his neighbors ask. " 'What wisdom is this

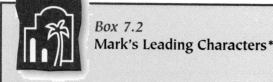

Box 7.2
Mark's Leading Characters*

John the Baptist (1:4–9); executed (6:17–29)

Jesus introduced (1:9); final words (15:34)

Simon Peter and his brother Andrew (1:16–18); Peter's imperfect discipleship (8:27–33; 9:2–6; 14:26–31, 66–72)

James and John, the fishermen sons of Zebedee (1:19–20); wish to be first in the kingdom (10:35–45)

Levi (Matthew), a tax collector (2:13–17)

The Twelve (3:13–19)

Judas Iscariot, Jesus' betrayer (3:19; 14:17–21, 43–46)

Mary, Jesus' mother, and other family members (3:20–21, 31–35; 6:3)

The Gerasene demoniac (5:1–20)

Herod Antipas, ruler of Galilee (4 B.C.E.–39 C.E.) (6:17–29; 8:15)

The Syrophoenician (Canaanite) woman (7:14–30)

A rich young man (10:17–22)

The woman who anoints Jesus at Bethany (14:3–9)

The High Priest Caiaphas (14:53–64)

Pontius Pilate, procurator of Judea (26–36 C.E.) (15:1–15, 43–44)

Barabbas, the terrorist released in place of Jesus (15:6–15)

Simon of Cyrene, the man impressed to carry Jesus' cross (15:21)

Joseph of Arimathaea, the Sanhedrin member who buries Jesus (15:42–46)

Mary of Magdala (in Galilee) (15:40–41, 47; 16:1)

Mary, mother of James and Joseph (15:40, 47; 16:1)

---

*Characters are listed in general order of appearance, along with the chief quality or event that distinguishes them in Mark's narrative.

---

that has been given him?' and 'How does he work such miracles? Is not this the carpenter, the son of Mary, the brother of James and Joseph and Judas and Simon? And are not his sisters here with us?' So they [turned against] him" (6:2–3). In this incident of Jesus' revisiting his home turf, Mark argues that those who thought they knew Jesus best doubted not only his right to be a religious leader but also his legitimacy—note Mark's reference to "the son of Mary," a contrast to the biblical custom of identifying a son through his male parentage even if his father were dead. The Nazarenes' refusal to see any merit in him results in a troubling diminution of Jesus' power: "He *could work no miracle there...*" except for some routine healings (6:6; italics added). Mark thus seems to dismiss both family and hometown citizens as acceptable channels of biographical tradition: They all fail to trust, comprehend, or cooperate with his hero.

Mark's allusion to Jesus' "brothers" and "sisters" (see also Matt. 13:54–56) may disturb some readers. Because his Gospel does not include a tradition

of Jesus' virginal conception or birth, the existence of siblings may not have been an issue with the Markan community (as it apparently was not for the Pauline churches; none of Paul's letters allude to a virgin birth). Matthew, however, explicitly affirms that Jesus was virginally conceived (Matt. 1:18–25), and Luke strongly implies it (Luke 1:26–38). Some Protestant Christians believe that following Jesus' delivery, his mother may have borne other children in the ordinary way. According to Roman Catholic doctrine, however, Mary remains perpetually virgin. Jesus' "brothers" (translating the Greek *adelphoi*) are to be understood as close male relatives, perhaps cousins or stepbrothers (sons of Mary's husband Joseph by a previous marriage). (An apocryphal infancy Gospel, the Protoevangelium of James, which probably dates from the second century C.E., depicts James as Jesus' older stepbrother and Mary as eternally virgin; see chapter 20.)

The Disciples   Mark's opinion of the Galilean **disciples** whom Jesus calls to follow him (3:13–19) is distinctly unsympathetic, although these are the Twelve Apostles on whose testimony the Christian faith is traditionally founded. Almost without exception, Mark paints the Twelve as dull-witted, inept, unreliable, cowardly, and, in at least one case, treacherous. When Jesus stills a storm, the disciples are impressed but unaware of the act's significance (4:35–41). After his feeding of the multitudes, the disciples "had not understood the intent of the loaves" because "their minds were closed" (6:52). The harshness of Mark's judgment is better rendered in the phrase "their hearts were hardened" (as given in the Revised Standard Version). This is the same phrase used to describe the Egyptian pharaoh when he arrogantly "hardened his heart" and refused to obey Yahweh's commands (Exod. 7:14–10:27). After listening for months to Jesus' teaching, the disciples are such slow learners that they are still ignorant of "what [Jesus' reference to] 'rising from the dead' could mean" (9:9–10). Not only do they fail to grasp the concept of sharing in Jesus' glory (10:35–41), but also even the simplest, most obvious parables escape their comprehension (4:10–13). As Jesus asks, "You do not understand this parable? How then will you understand any parable?" (4:13).

Although he has "explained everything" (4:33–34; see also 8:31–32) and the disciples have presumably recognized him as the Messiah (8:27–32), they desert him after his arrest (14:30). Peter, who had earlier confessed Jesus to be the Messiah, three times denies knowing him (14:66–72). Almost the only character in Mark shown as recognizing the significance of Jesus' death is an unnamed Roman soldier who perceives that "truly this man was a son of God!" (15:39).

Mark's recurring motif that all Jesus' original associates, including family, former neighbors, and followers, were almost preternaturally blind to his true identity and purpose carries through to the end of his Gospel. At the empty tomb, an unnamed youth in white directs a handful of women disciples not to linger in Jerusalem but to seek their Lord in Galilee, but they are too frightened to obey (16:1–8). The Gospel thus ends with the only disciples who had followed Jesus to the cross—a few Galilean women—inarticulate with terror, unable to cope with the news of his resurrection!

Mark's view that the resurrected Jesus will not be found near his burial site—Jerusalem—contrasts with the Lukan tradition that Jesus instructed his followers to remain in Jerusalem awaiting the Holy Spirit (Luke 24:47–53; Acts 1–2). Whereas Luke makes Jerusalem the center of Christian growth and expansion, the Spirit-empowered mother church led by Peter and James, Jesus' "brother" (Acts 1:4–3:34; 15:13–21; 21:16), Mark paints it as a hotbed of conniving hypocrites who scheme to murder the Son of God.

Mark's antipathy toward the historical Jesus' closest associates and the original Jerusalem church is puzzling. Does this apparent hostility mean that the group for which Mark wrote wished to distance itself from the Jerusalem community, whose founders included Jesus' closest family members, Mary and James (Acts 1:14; 12:17, etc.)? Does Mark's negative attitude represent a power struggle between his branch of Gentile Christianity and the Jewish-Christians who (until 70 C.E.) headed the original church? Most scholars caution that one should not necessarily postulate a historical tension between the Markan community and Palestinian Jewish Christians. Ancient historians and biographers commonly portray their heroes as enormously superior to their peers, depicting a subject's followers or disciples as constitutionally incapable of rising to his level of thought or achievement. Writing in this literary tradition, Mark may have emphasized the deficiencies of Jesus' contemporaries to underscore his hero's unique status: By magnifying Jesus' image, Mark demonstrates that Jesus alone does God's work and declares God's will.

Mark as a Literary Narrative

ORGANIZATION AND BIPOLAR STRUCTURE

Whatever the historicity of Mark's version of Jesus' career, it eventually exerted a tremendous influence on the Christian community at large, primarily through the enlarged and revised editions of Mark produced by Matthew and Luke. Because the two other Synoptic Gospels generally follow Mark's order of events in Jesus' life, it is important to understand the significance of Mark's bipolar organization. Mark arranges his narrative around a geographical north–south polarity. The first half of his narrative takes place in **Galilee** and adjacent areas of northern Palestine, a largely rural area of peasant farmers where Jesus recruits his followers, performs numerous miracles, and—despite some opposition—enjoys considerable success. The second half (after chapter 8) relates Jesus' fatal journey southward to Judea and Jerusalem, where he is rejected and killed (see figure 7.1). Besides dividing Jesus' career into two distinct geographical areas, Mark's Gospel presents two contrasting aspects of Jesus' story. In Galilee, Jesus is a figure of power, using his supernatural gifts to expel demons, heal the sick, control natural forces, and raise the dead. Representing the Hellenistic concept of an awe-inspiring divine man *(theios aner),* the Galilean Jesus speaks and acts with tremendous authority, effortlessly refutes his detractors, and affirms or invalidates the Mosaic Torah at will. Before leaving **Caesarea Philippi,** however, Jesus makes the first of three Passion predictions, warning his uncomprehending disciples that he will go to Jerusalem only to suffer humiliation and death (8:30–38; 9:31–32; 10:33–34).

By using the Passion predictions as a device to link the indomitable miracle worker in Galilee with the helpless figure on the cross in Judea, Mark reconciles the two seemingly irreconcilable components in his portrait of Jesus. The powerful Son of God who astonishes vast crowds with his mighty works is also the vulnerable Son of Man who, in weakness and apparent defeat, sacrifices his life "as a ransom for many" (10:45). Thus, the author balances older Christian traditions of his hero's phenomenal deeds with a bleak picture of Jesus' sufferings, devoting the last six chapters to a detailed account of the Passion. Although Matthew and Luke follow Mark in his north–south, power–weakness dichotomy, John's Gospel shows that there were other ways to arrange events in Jesus' story. In John, Jesus repeatedly travels back and forth between Galilee and Judea, performing miracles in both regions. As Papias's remark about the Gospel's lack of historical order warned, the Markan sequence of events (see box 7.3), with its emphasis on a single, final visit to Jerusalem, appears to express the writer's theological vision of Jesus' life rather than a literal reconstruction of his subject's actual movements.

Mark's Gospel can be divided into five parts:

1. Prelude to Jesus' public ministry (1:1–13)
2. The Galilean ministry; inaugurating the kingdom (1:14–8:26)
3. The journey to Jerusalem (8:27–10:52)
4. The Jerusalem ministry (11:1–15:47)
5. Postlude: the empty tomb (16:1–8)

PRELUDE TO JESUS' PUBLIC MINISTRY

Like the writer of a classical epic, Mark plunges into the middle of the action, providing no background about his hero but introducing him with apocalyptic suddenness. The opening line, "Here begins the gospel [good news] of Jesus Christ" (1:1), simultaneously announces his epic theme and echoes Genesis 1, alerting readers to see that in Jesus, God has begun a new creative activity. Jesus is the **Christ** (Greek translation of the Hebrew *mashiah*) and "the Son of God," titles that Mark seldom uses in his narrative, for one of his purposes is to demonstrate that in his lifetime the majority of people did not recognize Jesus' divine sonship. No person calls Jesus "a son of God" until almost the very end of Mark's Gospel (see box 7.4). Significantly, at that point Jesus is already dead, and the speaker is neither a Jew nor a disciple but a Roman centurion (15:39).

By citing a blend of passages from Isaiah (40:3) and Malachi (3:1)—that a divinely appointed "herald" and a "voice crying aloud in the wilderness" are preparing a path for the Lord—Mark immediately places Jesus' story in the context of the Hebrew Bible. Mark identifies the "herald" with John the Baptist, a desert ascetic then conducting a religious campaign in the Jordan River, where John baptizes converts "in token of repentance, for the forgiveness of sins" (1:4). Jesus, implicitly included among the repentant, appears for **baptism,** perhaps as John's disciple. Mark has John predict a "mightier" successor, although he does not show the Baptist as explicitly identifying Jesus as such.

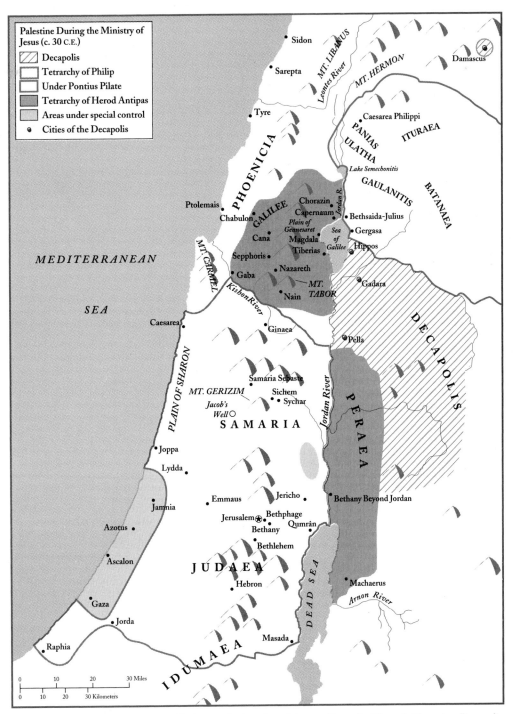

Figure 7.1 The political divisions of Palestine during the ministry of Jesus (c. 30 C.E.). Note that Rome directly administered Judea and Samaria through its procurator Pontius Pilate; Herod Antipas ruled Galilee (Jesus' home district) and Peraea; another son of Herod the Great, Philip, ruled an area to the northeast. The Decapolis was a league of ten Greek-speaking cities on the east side of the Jordan River.

Box 7.3
Mark's Order of Events in Jesus' Life

BEGINNING OF JESUS' MINISTRY (c. 27 or 29 C.E.)

Jesus is baptized by John at the Jordan River (1:9–11).

Jesus withdraws alone into the Judean desert (1:12–13).

Jesus begins preaching in Galilee (1:14–15).

Jesus recruits Peter, Andrew, James, and John to be his first disciples (1:16–20).

Jesus performs miraculous cures and exorcisms in Capernaum and throughout Galilee (1:21–3:12).

Jesus appoints twelve chief disciples from among his many followers; he explains the meaning of parables to this inner circle (3:13–34).

Jesus repeatedly crosses the Lake of Galilee, healing Jews on the western side and non-Jews on the eastern side (4:35–5:43).

Jesus returns to Nazareth, where his neighbors reject him (6:1–6).

Jesus sends the Twelve out on a mission to heal the sick and exorcise demons (6:7–13).

Herod Antipas beheads John the Baptist (6:14–29).

Jesus miraculously feeds a Jewish crowd of 5000 (6:30–44).

END OF JESUS' MINISTRY (c. 30 or 33 C.E.)

Jesus debates Torah rules with the Pharisees, who increasingly oppose his teaching (7:1–23).

Jesus leaves Galilee and travels through non-Jewish territories in Phoenicia and the Decapolis (7:24–37).

Jesus miraculously feeds a second crowd, this time of Gentiles (8:1–10, 14–21).

Jesus cures a blind man, and, near the town of Caesarea Philippi, Peter's eyes are opened to Jesus' true identity as the Messiah; Jesus rebukes Peter for failing to understand that the Messiah must suffer and die (8:22–9:1).

Jesus is gloriously transfigured before Peter, James, and John (9:1–13).

Jesus travels with the Twelve through Galilee to Capernaum, instructing them privately (9:30–50).

Jesus travels south to Judea, teaching the crowds and debating with Pharisees (10:1–33).

On the road to Jerusalem, Jesus for the third time predicts his imminent suffering and death (the Passion predictions) (8:31–33; 9:30–32; 10:32–34).

Approaching Jerusalem via Jericho, Jesus performs his last public miracle, curing a blind man (10:46–52).

EVENTS OF THE LAST WEEK OF JESUS' LIFE

On Palm Sunday, Jesus arranges his public entry into Jerusalem; his followers hail him in terms of the Davidic kingdom (11:1–11).

After a night at the Jerusalem suburb of Bethany, Jesus returns to Jerusalem and drives the money-changers out of the Temple (11:15–19).

Jesus debates the "chief priests," Sadducees, Pharisees, and other Jewish religious leaders in the Temple (11:27–12:40).

Seated on the Mount of Olives opposite Jerusalem, Jesus predicts the imminent destruction of the Temple (13:1–37).

Jesus' enemies conspire to kill him; Judas betrays Jesus (14:1–11).

Jesus holds a final Passover meal with the Twelve (14:12–31).

After the Last Supper, Jesus is arrested at Gethsemane on the Mount of Olives outside Jerusalem (14:32–52).

Jesus is tried on charges of blasphemy before the High Priest Caiaphas and the Sanhedrin (14:53–65).

After all of Jesus' followers have abandoned him, Peter denies even having known him (14:66–72).

On Good Friday, Jewish leaders accuse Jesus before Pontius Pilate; Jesus is declared guilty of treason, flogged, and condemned to crucifixion (15:1–20).

A passerby, Simon of Cyrene, is impressed to carry Jesus' cross to Golgotha, where Jesus is crucified (15:21–39).

A group of Galilean women witness the Crucifixion; Joseph of Arimathaea provides a tomb for Jesus (15:40–47).

On Easter Sunday, Mary of Magdala and other women discover that Jesus' tomb is empty; a young man instructs them to look for Jesus in Galilee, but the women are too frightened to tell anyone of their experience (16:1–8).

Box 7.4
Mark's Identification of Jesus as "Son of God"

Although Mark's preferred designation of Jesus is "Son of Man," he also identifies Jesus as "Son of God" at strategic places in his narrative. In most editions of Mark, the first reference to Jesus' divine parentage occurs in the opening verse and is addressed directly to readers, who must be aware of Jesus' supernatural identity if Mark's way of telling his hero's story — an ironic contrast between who Jesus really is and who people mistake him for — is to succeed. Because some early manuscripts omit the phrase "Son of God" in Mark 1:1, however, it is possible that the author originally intended readers to learn of Jesus' special relationship to the Father in the same manner that Jesus did, at his baptism, when a heavenly voice privately confides, "You are my beloved Son; in you I take delight" (Mark 1:11).

The "voice from heaven" paraphrases Psalm 2, a poem sung at the coronation of Israel's monarchs, a royal ceremony at which Yahweh is represented as adopting the newly consecrated king: "You are my son, . . . this day I become your father" (Ps. 2:7). Because Mark contains no reference to Jesus' virginal conception, many scholars think that he regards Jesus as becoming God's son by adoption, his baptism and visitation by the Holy Spirit the equivalent of Davidic kings' being anointed with holy oil.

In an ironic counterpoint to God's voice, Mark next uses the speech of a demon to reveal Jesus' hidden identity. When driven from a man he had possessed, the demon angrily declares: "*I* know who you are — the Holy One of God" (1:25). Whereas Mark's human characters fail to recognize Jesus' true nature until after his death, supernatural entities, including

"unclean spirits," know and fear him. In a typically Markan paradox, human opponents accuse Jesus of being an agent of Beelzebub, "the prince of demons" — allegedly the source of his supernatural power — while the demons themselves testify that Jesus is "the Son of God" (Mark 3:11, 22–28). Mark draws further on the questionable testimony of evil spirits when describing the Gerasene demoniac: The satanic "Legion" boldly announces that Jesus is "son of the Most High God" (Mark 5:1–13).

By contrast, when Peter finally perceives that Jesus is "the Christ," he apparently does not also intuit Jesus' divinity, confining his witness to his leader's messianic (political) role. In Mark's narrative, Jesus' closest disciples lack the perceptiveness of Beelzebub's imps! (Compare Mark's account of Peter's "confession" with Matthew's version, where the author has Peter employ a major Christological title, "Son of the living God," absent in Mark [Matt. 16:13–16].) Even after Jesus is miraculously transfigured before their eyes and the celestial voice again affirms that he is God's son (9:8), the Galilean disciples remain oblivious.

At Jesus' trial before the Sanhedrin, Mark presents a darkly paradoxical glimpse of his hero's real identity. When the High Priest asks if his prisoner is indeed the "Son of the Blessed One" (a pious circumlocution for God), Jesus, for the first time in Mark's account, admits that he is — a confession of divinity that condemns him to death. Only when Jesus hangs lifeless on the cross does a human figure — a Roman centurion — belatedly speak of Jesus as "a son of God," a Hellenistic Gentile's recognition that Jesus had died a heroic death worthy of divine honor.

The biographer's decision to introduce Jesus at the Jordan River is significant, for the Jordan was the gateway by which the Israelite tribes originally entered Palestine, their Promised Land. Mark may also have expected his readers to remember that Jesus is the Greek version of Joshua, the name of Moses' successor who led Israel across Jordan into its homeland. Mark's brief reference to Jesus' being tested for forty days in the Jewish wilderness also has biblical connotations. As the Israelites wan-

dered for forty years through the Sinai wilderness, undergoing trials and temptations, so Jesus is tempted by **Satan** in the desert, the untamed haunt of hostile entities. Jesus vanquishes Satan, just as Joshua conquered the Canaanite nations that opposed Israel (Josh. 1–6).

Mark's allusion to Jesus' overcoming the Evil One introduces another of the author's principal themes: God's Son will break the devil's hold on humanity. Jesus' **exorcisms** — the casting out of demons who have possessed human beings—are an important part of Jesus' ministry and are given proportionately greater space in Mark than in any other Gospel. (By contrast, John's Gospel does not contain a single reference to Jesus' performing exorcisms.)

Mark's Eschatological Urgency: Inaugurating the Kingdom

Mark launches Jesus' career with a startlingly eschatological message: "The time has come, the kingdom of God is upon you; repent and believe the Gospel" (1:15). Mark's sense of eschatological urgency permeates his entire Gospel, profoundly affecting his portrayal of Jesus' life and teaching. With the tradition that Jesus had prophesied the Temple's fall about to be fulfilled, Mark, writing about 70 C.E., sees the *eschaton*—the end of history as we know it—about to take place (13:1–4, 7–8, 14–20, 24–27, 30, 35–37). He therefore paints Jesus as an eschatological figure whose words are reinterpreted as specific warnings to Mark's generation. In the thought world Mark creates, the apocalyptic Son of Man who is about to appear in glory (13:24–31) is the same as the Son of Man who came forty years earlier to die on the cross (8:31, 38; 9:9–13, 31). The splendor of the One to come casts its radiance over Mark's portrait of the human Jesus (9:1–9).

Mark's style conveys his urgency: He uses the present tense throughout his Gospel and repeatedly connects the brief episodes (pericopes) of his narrative with the transition word *immediately.* Jesus scarcely finishes conducting a healing or exorcism in one Galilean village before he "immediately" rushes off to the next town to perform another miracle. In Mark's breathless presentation, the world faces an unprecedented crisis. Jesus' activity proclaims that history has reached its climactic moment. Hence, Mark measures time in mere days (during the Galilean ministry) and hours (during the Jerusalem episodes). Reduced to tiny increments, time is literally running out.

Mark represents Jesus as promising his original hearers that they will experience the *eschaton*—"the

present generation will live to see it all" (13:30). The kingdom, God's active rule, is so close that some of Jesus' contemporaries "will not taste death before they have seen the kingdom of God already come in power" (9:1). The long-awaited figure of Elijah, the ancient prophet whose reappearance is to be an infallible sign of the last days (Mal. 4:5), has already materialized in the person of John the Baptist (9:12–13). Such passages indicate that Mark's community anticipated the imminent consummation of all things, but many scholars question whether Mark's depiction of Jesus as a fervent apocalyptist accurately represents the historical Jesus (see chapter 11).

MARK AS APOCALYPSE

So pervasive is Mark's eschatology that some scholars regard the entire Gospel as a modified **apocalypse** *(apokalypsis),* a revelation of unseen realities and a disclosure of events destined soon to climax in God's final intervention in human affairs. Mark's use of apocalyptic devices is particularly evident at the beginning and ending of his Gospel. God speaks directly as a disembodied voice (a phenomenon Hellenistic Jews called the *bath qol*) at Jesus' baptism and again at the **Transfiguration,** an **epiphany** (manifestation of divine presence) in which the disciples see Jesus transformed into a luminous being seated beside the ancient figures of Moses and Elijah (1:11; 9:2–9). In this apocalyptic scene, Jesus appears with Moses and Elijah (who represent, respectively, the Torah and the prophets) to demonstrate his continuity with Israel's biblical tradition and his role as the one who embodies God's ultimate revelation to humanity. Mark's declaration that at Jesus' baptism the heavens are "torn apart," creating an opening to the spirit realm above, anticipates a later apocalyptic vision in the Book of Revelation. Revelation's author similarly describes "a door opened in heaven" and hears a voice inviting him to "come up here" and receive a preview of future history (Rev. 4:1–2).

At the most important event in his Gospel, Jesus' crucifixion, Mark repeats his image of the heavens being "torn" asunder. He states that at the instant of Jesus' death, "the curtain of the temple was torn in two from top to bottom," a phenomenon that inspires a Gentile soldier to recognize Jesus' divinity (15:37–39). In describing this incident, Mark apparently assumes that his readers will understand the symbolism of the Temple curtain. According to Josephus, the outer room of the Temple was separated from the innermost sanctuary — the Holy of Holies where God's "glory" was believed to dwell invisibly — by a huge curtain that was embroidered with astronomical designs, images of the visible heavens that hid God's celestial throne from mortal eyes. In Mark's view, Jesus' redemptive death "tore apart" the curtain, opening the way to a heavenly reality that the earthly Temple had symbolized. For Mark, this rending of the sacred veil functions as an apocalypse or revelation of Jesus' supreme significance.

Jesus as Son of Man   The author presents virtually all events during Jesus' final hours as revelatory of God's unfolding purpose. At the Last Supper, Jesus emphasizes that the eschatological "Son of Man is going the way appointed for him" and that he will "never again" drink wine with his disciples until he will "drink it new in the kingdom of God" (14:21, 25). At his trial before the **Sanhedrin,** the Jewish leaders' highest judicial council, Jesus reveals his true identity for the first time: He confesses that he *is* the Messiah and that the officiating High Priest "will see the Son of Man seated at the right hand of God and coming with the clouds of heaven" (14:62–63).

This disclosure — found only in Mark — associates Jesus' suffering and death with his ultimate revelation as the eschatological Son of Man. A designation that appears almost exclusively in the Gospels and then always on the lips of Jesus, **Son of Man** is Mark's favored expression to denote Jesus' three essential roles: as an earthly figure who teaches with authority, a servant who embraces suffering, and a future eschatological judge (see box 7.5). Although many scholars question whether the historical Jesus ever used this title, many others regard it as Jesus' preferred means of self-identification. Still other scholars postulate that Jesus may have used the title Son of Man to designate another, future-coming figure who would vindicate Jesus' own ministry and that the later church, because of its faith in Jesus' resurrection, retrojected that title back into the account of Jesus' life at points where it originally did not appear. In Mark's view, however, Jesus himself is clearly the eschatological Son of Man.

Son of Man in Hellenistic Jewish Literature   The Hebrew Bible offers few clues to what Jesus may have meant if he employed this term. The phrase appears frequently in the Book of Ezekiel, where "son of man" is typically synonymous with "mortal" or "human being," commonly the prophet himself. In the Book of Daniel, however, "one like a [son of] man" appears as a celestial figure who receives divine authority (Dan. 7:14). Most scholars think that this manlike figure (contrasting with the mystic "beasts" in Daniel's vision) originally symbolized a collective entity, Israel's faithful. By Jesus' time, Daniel's Son of Man apparently had assumed another identity, that of a supernatural individual who will come to judge the world.

The composite Book of 1 Enoch, which belongs to noncanonical Hellenistic Jewish writings known as the Pseudepigrapha, contains a long section (called the Similitudes or Parables) that prominently features the Son of Man as the one who, at the consummation of history, passes judgment on humanity (1 Enoch 37–71). Although some scholars dispute this claim, many believe that this section of 1 Enoch was written by the first century C.E. Fragments of Enoch (but not yet the Similitudes) have been found among the Dead Sea Scrolls, and the canonical Epistle of Jude cites Enoch as if it were Scripture (Jude 14–15). It seems likely that ideas about Enoch's Son of Man were current in Jesus' day and that he — or his immediate followers — applied them to his role in history.

The major element that Mark's Jesus adds to the Son of Man concept is that he is a servant who must suffer and die before attaining the kind of heavenly glory that Daniel 7 and 1 Enoch attribute to him (cf. Mark 8:30–31; 10:45; 13:26–27; 14:62).

"The Son of Man Has the Right on Earth . . ."   It is as the earthly Son of Man that Mark's Jesus claims the right to wield immense religious power

Box 7.5
The Synoptic Gospels' Use of the Term "Son of Man"

The authors of the Synoptic Gospels use the expression "Son of Man" in three distinct ways, all of which they place on the lips of Jesus to denote three important aspects of his ministry. The three categories identify Jesus as the Son of Man who serves on earth, the Son of Man who must suffer and die, and the Son of Man who will be revealed in eschatological judgment. Representative examples of these three categories appear below:

THE EARTHLY SON OF MAN

Mark 2:10 (Matt. 9:6; Luke 5:24): Has authority to forgive sins.

Mark 2:27 (Matt. 12:8; Luke 6:5): Is Lord of the Sabbath.

Matthew 11:19 (Luke 7:34): Son of Man comes eating and drinking.

Matthew 8:20 (Luke 9:58): Son of Man has nowhere to lie his head.

Luke 19:20: Son of Man came to seek and save the lost.

THE SUFFERING SON OF MAN

Mark 8:31 (Luke 9:22): Son of Man must suffer.

Mark 9:12 (Matt. 17:12): Son of Man will suffer.

Mark 9:31 (Matt. 17:22; Luke 9:44): Son of Man is delivered into hands of men.

Mark 10:33 (Matt. 20:18; Luke 18:31): Son of Man is delivered to chief priests, condemned to death.

Mark 10:45 (Matt. 20:28): Son of Man came to serve and give his life.

Mark 14:41 (Matt. 26:45): Son of Man is betrayed to sinners.

Matthew 12:40 (Luke 11:30): Son of Man will be three days in the earth.

THE ESCHATOLOGICAL SON OF MAN

Mark 8:38 (Matt. 16:27; Luke 9:26): Comes in glory of the Father and holy angels.

Mark 14:26 (Matt. 24:30; Luke 21:27): They will see Son of Man coming with clouds and glory.

Mark 14:62 (Matt. 26:64; Luke 22:69): You will see Son of Man sitting at the right hand of power.

Luke 12:40 (Matt. 24:44): Son of Man is coming at an hour you do not expect.

Luke 17:26 (Matt. 24:27): As it was in days of Noah, so in days of Son of Man.

Matthew 24:30: Then will appear the sign of the Son of Man.

Luke 17:30: So it will be on the day when the Son of Man is revealed.

For a fuller discussion of the Son of Man concept and its use by the Synoptic authors, see George Eldon Ladd, *A Theology of the New Testament* (Grand Rapids, Mich.: Eerdmans, 1974), pp. 145–158.

(see box 7.5). As Son of Man, the Markan Jesus assumes the authority to prescribe revolutionary changes in Jewish Law and custom (2:10). Behaving as if he already reigns as cosmic judge, Jesus forgives a paralytic's sins (2:1–12) and permits certain kinds of work on the Sabbath (3:1–5). In both instances, Jesus' pronouncements outrage Jewish leaders. Who but God can forgive sins? And who has the audacity to change Moses' inspired command to forbid all labor on God's day of rest? (Exod. 20:8–10; Deut. 5:12–15).

In the eyes of Jews scrupulously observing Torah regulations, Jesus dishonors the **Sabbath** by healing a man's withered arm on that holy day. The Pharisees interpreted the Torah to permit saving a life or to deal with other comparable emergencies on the Sabbath, but in this case (2:23–28) Jesus seems to have violated the Torah for no compelling reason.

As Mark describes the situation, it is Jesus' flexible attitude toward Sabbath-keeping that incites some Pharisees and supporters of Herod Antipas to hatch a murder plot against the Nazarene healer (3:5–6). To most readers, Jesus' opponents overreact inexplicably. To many law-abiding Jews, however, Jesus' Sabbath-breaking miracles and declaration that the Sabbath was created for humanity's benefit

(2:27–28) seem to strike at the heart of Jewish faith. Many devout Jews believed that the Torah was infallible and eternal. According to the Book of Jubilees, the Torah existed before God created the universe, and people *were* made to keep the Sabbath. Jesus' assertion that the Sabbath law is not absolute but relative to human needs appears to deny the Torah's unchanging validity and to question its status as God's final and complete revelation.

TEACHING THE MYSTERIES OF THE KINGDOM

Jesus' Parables   Many of Israel's prophets, and virtually all its apocalyptic writers, use highly symbolic language to convey their visions of the divine will. In depicting Jesus as the eschatological Son of Man, it is not surprising that Mark states categorically that Jesus never taught publicly without using parables (or other figures of speech) (4:34). The root meaning of the word **parable** is "a comparison," the discernment of similarities between one thing and another. Jesus' simplest parables are typically **similes,** comparisons using *as* or *like* to express unexpected resemblances between ostensibly unrelated objects, actions, or ideas. Thus, Jesus compares God's kingdom—which he never explicitly defines—to a number of items, including a mustard seed. Like the tiny seed, God's rule begins in an extremely small way, but eventually, like the mustard plant, it grows to an unexpectedly large size (4:30–32). (Jesus' intent in this parable may have been ironic, for farmers do not want wild mustard plants taking over their fields any more than most people wanted the kind of divine rule that Jesus promoted.) Like the parable of the growing seed (4:26–29), which occurs in Mark alone, the mustard plant analogy stresses the unnoticed evolution of divine sovereignty rather than explaining its nature or form. Most parables are open-ended: They do not provide a fixed conclusion, but invite the hearer to speculate about many possibilities inherent in the comparison. According to Mark, understanding parables involving germination and growth suggests the "secret" of God's kingdom, a glimpse into the mysterious principles by which God rules.

Other parables take the form of brief stories that exploit familiar situations or customs to illustrate a previously unrecognized truth. In the parable of the sower, a farmer plants seeds on different kinds of ground with distinctly different results (4:2–9). The lengthy interpretation that Mark attaches to the image of sowing seeds (4:13–20) transforms what was originally a simple parable into an allegory. An **allegory** is a complex literary form in which each element of the narrative—persons, places, actions, even objects—has a symbolic value. Because every item in the allegory functions as a symbol of something else, the allegory's meaning can be puzzled out only by identifying what each individual component in the story represents.

Almost all scholars believe that Mark's elaborate allegorical interpretations, equating different kinds of soil with the different responses people make when they receive the "seed" (gospel message), do not represent Jesus' original meaning. By the time Mark incorporated the sower pericope into his Gospel, the Christian community had already used it to explain people's contrasting reactions to their preaching. Jesus' pithy tale based on everyday agricultural practices was reinterpreted to fit the later experience of Christian missionaries. The reference to "persecution" (4:17) places the allegorical factor in Mark's time rather than in the context of Jesus' personal experience in Galilee.

In one of his most controversial passages, Mark states that Jesus uses parables to *prevent* the public from understanding his message (4:11–12). To many readers, it seems incredible that Jesus deliberately teaches in a way intended to confuse or alienate his audience. Mark justifies his hero's alleged practice by quoting from Isaiah (6:9–10), which pictures Yahweh telling the prophet that his preaching will be useless because Yahweh has already made it impossible for the Israelites to comprehend Isaiah's meaning. Mark's attempt to explain why most people did not follow Jesus seems contrary to the gracious goodwill that the Gospel writers normally associate with him and probably does not express the policy of the historical Jesus. In the historical experience of Mark's community, however, it appears that the kingdom's secrets were reserved for a few chosen disciples, such as those whom Mark says privately received Jesus' esoteric teaching (4:11). (In Luke's edition of Mark, he removes Isaiah's pessimistic declaration from Jesus' lips and places it in Paul's mouth to explain why the Apostle gave up trying to convert fellow Jews and concentrated instead on the more receptive Gentiles; cf. Mark 4:11–12; Luke 8:10; Acts 28:25–28.)

Jesus and the Demons   Eschatological beliefs are concerned not only with the end of the world but also with visions of invisible spirit beings, both good and evil (see chapter 19). Apocalyptic literature, such as Daniel and 1 Enoch, typically presents God's defeat of spiritual Evil as the ultimate victory that completes God's sovereignty over all components of the universe. Given Mark's strongly eschatological point of view, it is not surprising that he makes a battle between supernatural forces — God's Son versus Satan's demons — an integral part of his apocalyptic Gospel. After noting Jesus' resistance to Satan (1:12–13), Mark reinforces the theme of cosmic struggle by making Jesus' first miracle an exorcism. Remarkably, the demon that Jesus expels from a human victim is the first character in the Markan narrative to recognize Jesus as "the Holy One of God" — who has come "to destroy" the agents of Evil (1:23–26). In this episode, Mark also closely links Jesus' authority over "unclean spirits" with his teaching authority: For Mark, Jesus is the divine agent who demonstrates the power to command obedience from both visible and invisible dimensions of existence.

Following his exorcisms at **Capernaum,** Jesus performs similar feats in Gentile territory, "the country of the Gerasenes." Driving a whole army of devils from a Gerasene madman, Jesus casts them into a herd of pigs — the religiously unclean animals becoming a fit home for spirits who drive people to commit unclean acts (5:1–20). The demons' name — "legion" — is an unflattering reference to the Roman legions (large military units) then occupying Palestine (and in Mark's day assaulting Jerusalem). (Note that in Capernaum, a Galilean Jewish city, Jesus commands the demons to remain silent, whereas in the Gerasene case he orders the dispossessed Gentile to tell others about his cure.)

Mark arranges his material to show that Jesus does not choose to battle Evil in isolation. At the outset of his campaign through Galilee, Jesus gathers followers who will form the nucleus of a new society, one presumably free from demonic influence. Recruiting a band of Galilean fishermen and peasants, Jesus selects two sets of brothers, **Simon Peter** (also called **Cephas**) and **Andrew,** and James and John — sons of **Zebedee** also known as "**sons of thunder (Boanerges)**" — to form his inner circle (1:16–20). Later he adds another eight disciples to complete the Twelve, a number probably representing the twelve tribes of Israel: **Philip; Bartholomew; Matthew; Thomas; James,** son of Alphaeus; **Thaddeus;** Simon the Canaanite; and **Judas Iscariot** (3:16–19; cf. the different list in Acts 1). Mark states that when Jesus commissions the Twelve to perform exorcisms (6:7–13), they fail miserably (9:14–18, 28–29), a sad contrast to the success enjoyed by some exorcists who are *not* Jesus' followers (9:38–41).

Jesus Accused of Sorcery   In another incident involving demonic possession (3:22–30), Mark dramatizes a head-on collision between Jesus as God's agent for overthrowing Evil and persons who see Jesus as a tool of the devil. The clash occurs when "doctors of the law" (teachers and interpreters of the Torah) from Jerusalem accuse Jesus of using black magic to perform exorcisms. Denying that Evil can produce good, Jesus countercharges that persons who attribute good works to Satan "slander the Holy Spirit," the divine force manifested in Jesus' actions.

Matthew's version of the incident explicitly links Jesus' defeat of evil spirits with the arrival of the **kingdom of God.** The Matthean Jesus declares, "If it is by the Spirit of God that I drive out the devils, then be sure the kingdom of God has already come upon you" (Matt. 22–28). To both Evangelists, Jesus' successful attack on demonic control is a revelation that through his presence God now rules. Willful refusal to accept Jesus' healings as evidence of divine power is to resist the Spirit, an obstinacy that prevents spiritual insight.

The Existence of Demons   Mark's emphasis on exorcisms to illustrate Jesus' war on Satan's "kingdom" provokes a real crisis of credibility for most students today. Modern readers are likely to be troubled by the writer's uncritical acceptance of invisible malignant spirits that hold conversations with his hero. To many people, the notion of demonic possession is a superstition unworthy of a higher religion. This concept does not fit easily into the scientific worldview, which promotes a strictly rational approach to understanding reality. Many nineteenth-century scholars attempted to explain away the Gospel accounts of exorcisms by labeling them metaphors of mental derangement or nervous disorders, to which Jesus applied psychological healing.

Mark, like other New Testament authors, reflects a common Hellenistic belief in the existence of unseen entities that influence human lives for Good or Evil. Numerous Hellenistic documents record charms to ward off demons or free one from their control. In Judaism, works like the apocryphal Book of Tobit reveal a belief that demons could be driven out by the correct use of magical formulas (Tob. 6:1–8; 8:1–3). Josephus, who was Mark's contemporary, relates a story about Eleazar, who allegedly exorcised a demon in the presence of the emperor Vespasian (69–79 C.E.), drawing the malign spirit out through its victim's nose (*Antiquities*, 8.46–49).

Zoroastrianism   A belief in devils and demonic possession appears in Jewish literature primarily after the period of Persian domination (539–330 B.C.E.), when Persian religious ideas seem to have influenced Jewish thought. According to the Persian religion **Zoroastrianism,** the whole universe, visible and invisible, is divided into two contending powers of light and darkness, Good and Evil. Only after historical contact with Zoroastrian dualism does the figure of Satan emerge as humanity's adversary in biblical literature (Job 1–2; Zech. 3). **Angels** and demons thereafter populate Hellenistic Jewish writings, such as the Books of Daniel and 1 Enoch.

Belief in Supernatural Evil   Although Hellenistic Greek and Judean-Christian writers may express their beliefs about supernatural Evil in terms considered naive or irrational to today's scientifically disciplined mind, they reflect a viewpoint with important implications for contemporary society. Surrounded by threats of terrorism, lethal diseases such as cancer and AIDS, and frightening disregard for human life, people may wonder if the forces of cruelty and suffering are not greater than the sum of their human agents. Does Evil exist as a power independent of human volition? Such diverse works as the Synoptic Gospels, Ephesians (6:10–17), and Revelation show a keen awareness of Evil so pervasive and so profound that it cannot be explained solely in terms of human acts, individual or collective. Whatever philosophical view we choose to interpret the human predicament, the Gospel portrayal of Jesus' struggle to impart wholeness and health to others expresses the Evangelists' conviction that humanity cannot save itself without divine aid.

Jesus the Healer   Physical cures, as well as exorcisms, characterize Jesus' assault on Evil. In Mark's portrayal, one of Jesus' most important functions is to bring relief to the afflicted (see figure 7.2). He drives a fever from Simon Peter's mother-in-law (1:29–31), cleanses a leper (1:40–42), enables a paralyzed man to walk (2:1–12), restores a man's withered hand (3:1–6), stops a woman's chronic hemorrhaging (5:25–34), and resuscitates the comatose daughter of **Jairus,** a synagogue official (5:21–24, 35–43).

Presenting Jesus' healing campaign as a triumphant procession through Galilee, Mark summarizes the effect Jesus' actions had on the Galilean public: "Wherever he went, to farms . . . villages, or towns, they laid out the sick in the market-places and begged to let them simply touch the edge of his cloak; and all who touched him were cured" (6:56). To Mark, Jesus' restoration of physical health to suffering humanity is an indispensable component of divine rule, tangible confirmation that God's kingdom is about to dawn.

MARK'S USE OF LITERARY TECHNIQUES

In assembling from various oral sources a series of brief anecdotes about Jesus' ability to cure the sick, Mark stitches the miracle stories together like pearls on a string. Weaving these originally independent pericopes into the fabric of his narrative, Mark re-creates them with exciting vividness and immediacy. Besides using a wealth of concrete detail to help readers visualize the scene or feel its

Figure 7.2 *Christ with the Sick Around Him, Receiving Little Children* by Rembrandt (1606–1669). In this painting, healing light radiates from the central figure of Jesus and creates a protective circle of illumination around those whom he cures. (© The Metropolitan Museum of Art. Bequest of Mrs. H. O. Havemeyer, 1929. The H. O. Havemeyer Collection (29.107.35))

emotional impact, Mark commonly employs the technique of *intercalation,* inserting one story inside another. This sandwiching device typically serves to make the story placed inside another story function as interpretative commentary on the framing story. In telling of Jesus' family's attempt to impede his ministry (3:21, 31–35), for example, Mark inserts a seemingly unrelated anecdote about Jesus' opponents accusing him of sorcery (3:22–30), implicitly associating his "mother and brothers" with his adversaries.

Mark uses the same device of intercalation in his story about resuscitating Jairus's daughter, interrupting the Jairus narrative to incorporate the anecdote about a hemorrhaging woman into the middle of the story. Pushing through the crowds surrounding him, Jesus is on his way to help Jairus's seriously

ill daughter (5:22–24) when a woman—who Mark says had suffered for twelve years from unstoppable bleeding (and was therefore ritually unclean)—suddenly grabs his cloak and, as if by force of desperate need, draws into her ailing body Jesus' curative energy. This incident is doubly unique: It is the only Gospel healing to occur without Jesus' conscious will and the Evangelists' only hint about the physical nature of Jesus' ability to heal. Mark states that Jesus can *feel* his power flow out when the woman touches him, as if he were a dynamo being drained of electrical energy (5:25–34).

Mark then resumes the Jairus narrative: Although a messenger reports that the girl has already died, Jesus insists that she is only "asleep." Taking his three closest disciples into the girl's room, he commands her to "get up"—"*Talitha cum,*" an

Figure 7.3 A fishing boat returns to Capernaum on the Sea of Galilee. The village of Capernaum, home to Peter and his brother Andrew, served as a center for Jesus' early Galilean ministry. (© Erich Lessing/PhotoEdit)

Aramaic phrase that Mark's community probably revered for its association with Jesus' power over death (5:35–43). The author links the two stories by a simple numerical device — the mature woman had been afflicted for a dozen years and the young girl is twelve years old — and by the assertion that it is the participants' *faith* that cures them. The woman demonstrates unconditional trust in Jesus' power, and Jairus presumably accepts Jesus' advice to replace fear for his daughter's safety with "faith."

When Mark tells stories of Jesus' healings, he typically connects a person's willingness to trust Jesus — manifested by unusually assertive, even bizarre behavior — with a successful cure. The friends of a paralyzed man are so eager for Jesus to help him that they carry his cot to the top of a house where Jesus is staying, rip open the roof, and lower the paralytic through the hole to force him on Jesus' attention (2:1–12). The hemorrhaging woman — despite her religiously unacceptable status — is similarly aggressive in pressing her need, while Jairus forgets his dignity as president of a synagogue and takes the initiative in running out to find Jesus and persuade him to visit his house.

Whereas strangers violate norms of behavior to compel Jesus' help, Mark states that those who

ostensibly know him well fail to trust him. In Nazareth, where family and neighbors — familiar with the former carpenter's human background — are skeptical of his abilities, he is a prophet without honor. Marveling at their lack of trust, Jesus, as Mark reports it, "*could* work no miracle there . . ." (6:4–6; italics added).

MARK'S IRONIC VISION

In the Nazareth episode, Mark invites his readers to share Jesus' astonishment that people who should know better reject a golden opportunity to benefit from Jesus' presence. As Mark presents Jesus' story — which is largely a tale of humanity's self-defeating rejection of God's attempt to redeem it — such disparities abound. Demons steeped in evil instantly recognize who Jesus is, but most *people* — including his peasant neighbors and the educated religious elite — do not. The wind and waves obey him during a storm on the **Sea of Galilee** (4:35–41) (see figure 7.3), but his disciples ultimately prove disloyal. He miraculously feeds hungry multitudes (an incident Mark records in two different versions [6:30–44; 8:1–10]) and can suspend the laws of physics by striding across Galilee's waters (6:30–52;

8:1–10), but Jesus' closest followers are unable to grasp the meaning of his control over nature. Among the very few who respond positively to him, the majority are social outcasts or nobodies such as lepers, blind mendicants, ritually unclean women, and the diseased. This *irony*, or logical incongruity between normal expectation and what actually happens in the narrative, determines both Mark's structuring of his Gospel and his characterization of Jesus' messiahship.

The Journey to Jerusalem: Jesus' Predestined Suffering

Mark brackets the central section of his Gospel (8:27–10:45) with two parallel stories of Jesus' restoring sight to two different blind men (8:22–26; 10:46–52). In the first episode, a blind man at Bethsaida regains his vision gradually and is told not to tell anyone of his cure. In the second pericope, a blind beggar near Jericho, who addresses Jesus as "son of David" (a messianic title), not only instantly sees again but also decides to follow Jesus on the road to Jerusalem. These incidents function as ironic commentary on the spiritual blindness of persons failing to recognize Jesus' identity and, in the second case at least, as a model of correct response when seeing the "light" of Jesus' revelation.

MARK'S CENTRAL IRONY

In chapter 8, which forms the central pivot on which the entire Gospel turns, Mark ties together several themes that convey his essential vision of Jesus' ministry and what Jesus requires of those who would follow him. Beginning on a joyous note with his account of Jesus feeding a large crowd (8:1–10), this section continues through a crisis of misunderstanding between Jesus, Peter, and the other disciples (8:11–21, 27–33) and ends with Jesus' warning (to Mark's community) that he will disown unfaithful followers (8:38). The narrative movement from elation to gloom involves the disciples' failure to comprehend either the significance of Jesus' miracles or the purpose of his life and death.

Besides repeating the theme of the disciples' obtuseness, chapter 8 also sounds Mark's concurrent themes of the hidden or unexpected quality of Jesus' messiahship—especially the necessity of his suffering—and the requirement that all believers must be prepared to embrace a comparably painful fate. In contrast to John's Gospel, in which Jesus' identity is publicly affirmed at the outset of his career, Mark has no one even hint that Jesus is the Messiah until almost the close of the Galilean campaign when Peter—in a flash of insight—recognizes him as such (8:29). The Markan Jesus then swears the disciples to secrecy, as he had earlier ordered other witnesses of his deeds to keep silent (1:23–24, 34; 3:11–12; 5:7; 7:36; 8:30; see also 9:9). Jesus' reluctance to have news of his miracles spread abroad is known as the **messianic secret,** a term coined by the German scholar William Wrede (1901).

Some commentators have suggested that Mark's picture of Jesus' forbidding others to discuss him merely reflects historical fact: that during Jesus' lifetime most of his contemporaries did not regard him as God's special agent and that he himself made no public claims to be Israel's Messiah. Most scholars, however, believe that Mark's theme of the messianic secret represents the author's theological purpose. For Mark, people could not know Jesus' identity until *after* he had completed his mission. Jesus had to be unappreciated in order to be rejected and killed—to fulfill God's will that he "give up his life as a ransom for many" (10:45).

A conviction that Jesus must suffer an unjust death—an atonement offering for others—to confirm and complete his messiahship is the heart of Mark's **Christology** (concepts about the nature and function of Christ). Hence, Peter's confession at Caesarea Philippi that Jesus is the Christ (Messiah) is immediately followed by Jesus' first prediction that he will go to Jerusalem only to die (8:29–32). When Peter objects to this notion of a rejected and defeated Messiah, Jesus calls his chief disciple a "Satan." Derived from a Hebrew term meaning "obstacle," the epithet Satan labels Peter's attitude an obstacle or roadblock on Jesus' predestined path to the cross. Peter understands Jesus no better than outsiders, regarding the Messiah as a God-empowered hero who conquers his enemies, not as a submissive victim of their brutality.

At the end of chapter 8, Mark introduces a third idea: True disciples must expect to suffer as Jesus does. In two of the three Passion predictions, Jesus emphasizes that "anyone who wishes to be a follower of mine must leave self behind; he must take up his cross, and come with me" (8:27–34; 10:32–45). Irony permeates the third instance when James and John, sons of Zebedee, presumptuously ask to rule with Jesus, occupying places of honor on his right and left. As Jesus explains that reigning with him means imitating his sacrifice, Mark's readers are intended to remember that when Jesus reaches Jerusalem, the positions on his right and left will be taken by the two brigands crucified next to him (15:27).

In reiterating the necessity of suffering, Mark addresses a problem that undoubtedly troubled members of his own community: how to explain the contrast between the high expectations of reigning with Christ in glory (10:35–37) and the believers' actual circumstances. Instead of being vindicated publicly as God's chosen faithful, Christians of the late 60s C.E. were being treated like outcasts or traitors by Jewish Zealots and like criminals by the Roman emperor. Mark offers fellow believers the consolation that their hardships are foreshadowed by Jesus' experience; Christians must expect to be treated no more justly than their Master.

Mark's device of having a delegation of Jewish leaders conspire against Jesus in Galilee (3:6) and having Jesus repeatedly prophesy his death serves to cast the shadow of the cross backward in time over the Galilean ministry. These foreshadowing techniques help unify the polar opposites of Mark's narrative: They not only connect the powerful healer of Galilee with the sacrificial victim in Jerusalem but also link Jesus' experience with that of Mark's implied readers.

The Jerusalem Ministry: A Week of Sacred Time

In the third section of his Gospel, Mark focuses exclusively on the last week of Jesus' life, from the Sunday on which Jesus enters Jerusalem to the following Sunday's dawn when some Galilean women find his tomb empty (11:1–16:8). To Mark, this is a sacred period during which Jesus accomplishes his life's purpose, sacrificing himself for humanity's redemption. Mark's Christian Holy Week also corresponds to Passover week, when thousands of Jews from throughout the Greco-Roman world gather in Jerusalem to celebrate Israel's deliverance from slavery in Egypt. As he narrates Jesus' rejection by Jewish leaders and execution by Roman officials, Mark celebrates the irony of events: Blind to Jesus' value, no one recognizes Jesus as a deliverer greater than Moses and a sacrifice that epitomizes the essential meaning of Passover.

THE TRIUMPHAL ENTRY

If Mark was aware of Jesus' other visits to Jerusalem (narrated in John's Gospel), he dismisses them as unimportant compared with his last. In bold strokes, the author contrasts Jesus' joyous reception in the holy city with the tragedy of his crucifixion five days later. A crowd, probably of Galilean supporters, enthusiastically welcomes Jesus to Jerusalem, hailing him as restorer of "the coming kingdom of our father David" (11:9–10). As Mark reports it, Jesus had carefully arranged his entry to fulfill Zechariah's prophecy that the Messiah would appear in humble guise, riding on a beast of burden (Zech. 9:9). Mark thus portrays Jesus suddenly making a radical change in policy: Instead of hiding his messianic identity, Jesus now seems to "go public"—challenging Jerusalem to accept him as God's Anointed. Jesus' appearance as a messianic claimant also challenges Roman authority. Because the Messiah was commonly expected to reestablish David's monarchy, the Roman procurator Pontius Pilate was likely to interpret Jesus' actions as a political claim to Judean kingship and hence, to Rome, an act of treason (15:2–3).

FOCUS ON THE TEMPLE

Once in Jerusalem, Jesus' activities center around the Temple: His entrance into the city is not complete until he enters the Temple courts (11:1–10). During his brief time in the Judean capital, Jesus behaves in a manner that alienates both Roman and Jewish authorities, arousing the hostility of almost every religious party and institution in the Judean capital. On Monday following his arrival, he creates a riot in the **sanctuary,** overturning moneychangers' tables and disrupting the sale of sacrificial animals (11:15–19). This assault on the Sadducean administration brands him as a threat to public order and probably seals his fate with the chief priests and Temple police.

As Mark describes his actions, Jesus visits the Temple not to worship, but to pronounce eschatological judgment: Jesus' last teaching is a prophecy of the sanctuary's imminent destruction (ch. 13)—a prediction that may lie behind later charges that Jesus conspired to destroy the center of Jewish religion (14:56). Jesus' negative verdict on the Temple begins to take effect at his death, when the jeweled curtain veiling its inner sanctum is split apart (15:38), exposing its interior to public gaze and foreshadowing its imminent desecration by Gentiles.

Besides condemning the Temple **cult** and the Sadducean priests who control it, Mark uses other devices to indicate that Jesus' Jerusalem ministry is fundamentally an adverse judgment on the city. Jesus' cursing an unproductive fig tree—the curse (11:12–14) and its fulfillment (11:20–24) bracketing the story of his attack on Temple practices— represents Mark's intent to condemn the Jerusalem leaders who, in his opinion, do not bear "good fruit" and are destined to wither and die.

The parable of the wicked tenants who kill their landlord's son (12:1–11) has the same function: to discredit Jesus' enemies. In Mark's view, the landlord (God) has now given his vineyard, traditionally a symbol for Israel, to "others"—the author's Christian community.

CONFRONTATION AT THE TEMPLE

Even in Galilee, Mark had depicted Jesus as constantly under attack from religious opponents, typically identified as Jewish Pharisees and scribes. His adversaries accuse Jesus of blasphemy in daring to forgive sins (2:5); associating with degraded people—"tax collectors and sinners" (2:15–17); breaking Sabbath laws (2:23–28); allegedly working for Satan (3:22–27); and profaning tradition by neglecting to wash ritually before a meal (7:1–8). Most of Mark's conflict stories end with Jesus issu-

ing a pronouncement on some aspect of Torah observance: declaring all foods "clean"—an important point for Mark's Gentile church (7:14–23); making the Sabbath relevant to human needs (2:23–36); and revoking Moses' permission for men to divorce their wives (10:2–12). In each case, Jesus assumes the right to approve or invalidate both written and oral Torah.

In Jerusalem, clashes between Jesus and Jewish leaders intensify, becoming a matter of life and death. As Jesus moves through the Temple precincts, thronged with Passover pilgrims, Mark pictures him scoring success after success in a series of hostile encounters with representatives of leading religious parties. The Pharisees and Herod Antipas's supporters attempt to trap Jesus on the controversial issue of paying taxes to Rome, a snare he eludes by suggesting that people return government coins to their source while reserving for God the rest of one's life.

The Sadducees also suffer defeat when they try to force Jesus into an untenable position they hope will illustrate the illogic of a belief in resurrection to future life. When asked to which husband a woman who has been widowed six times would be married when all the former spouses are raised, Jesus states that there will be no ethical problem because resurrected persons escape the limits of human sexuality and become "like the angels in heaven" (12:18–25). Citing the Torah, apparently the only part of the Hebrew Bible that the Sadducees accept, he quotes Yahweh's words to Moses at the burning bush— that Yahweh is the God of Abraham, Isaac, and Jacob (Exod. 3:6)—arguing that because Yahweh is "not God of the dead but of the living," the ancient patriarchs must still be alive from the Deity's perspective (12:26–27).

Interestingly, Mark closes Jesus' Temple debates with a friendly encounter in which the Galilean and a Torah expert agree on the essence of true religion. Answering a "lawyer's" question about the Bible's most important requirement, Jesus cites the Shema, or Jewish declaration of monotheism: There is only one God, and Israel must love him with all its force and being (Deut. 6:4–5). To this he adds a second Torah command: to love one's neighbor as oneself (Lev. 19:18). In agreement,

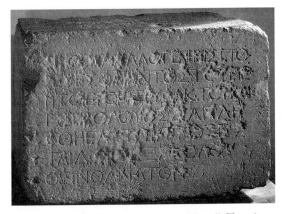

Figure 7.4 Warning inscription from Herod's Temple. Illustrating the barrier erected between Jews and Gentiles, this inscription warned Temple visitors that no Gentile could enter the inner sanctum except on pain of death. (© Erich Lessing/Art Resource)

the "lawyer" and Jesus exchange compliments. Although not a follower, the Jerusalem leader sees that active love is the essence of divine rule, a perception that Jesus says makes him "not far from the kingdom of God"—a more favorable verdict than Jesus ever passes on the Twelve (12:28–34).

JESUS' PROPHECY OF THE TEMPLE'S FALL

In chapter 13, Mark speaks plainly of his eschatological concerns. In answer to the disciples' question about when his prediction of Jerusalem's destruction will take place, Jesus is made to deliver his longest speech, associating the Temple's fall with an era of catastrophes that culminate in the Son of Man returning as eschatological judge (see figure 7.4). The author seems to have composed this discourse from a variety of sources, combining Jesus' words with older Jewish apocalyptic literature and perhaps with prophetic **oracles** from his own community as well. A considerably expanded version of the speech is preserved in Matthew 24, and a significantly modified version of Mark's eschatological expectations appears in Luke 21. John's Gospel contains no parallel to the Synoptic prophecies about the *eschaton*.

Readers will notice that Mark incorporates two somewhat contradictory views of the End. He states that a swarm of disasters and frightening astronomical phenomena will provide unmistakable "signs" that the Parousia is near, just as the budding fig tree heralds the arrival of spring (13:8, 14–20, 24–31). Conversely, neither the Son nor his followers can surmise the time of Final Judgment, so one must keep constant watch because the End will occur without previous warning (13:32–37).

Mark's strong emphasis on political and social upheavals as portents of the End may be explained by the turbulent era in which he composed his "war-time" Gospel. If, as historians believe, Mark wrote during the Jewish revolt when battles and insurrections were daily occurrences, he seems to have viewed these events as a turning point in history, an unprecedented crisis leading to the final apocalypse. Along with witnessing the intense suffering of Palestinian Jews, the Markan community was undoubtedly aware of recent persecutions in Rome that resulted in numerous deaths, including the executions of Christianity's two chief apostles, Peter and Paul (mid-60s C.E.). Between about 67 and 70 C.E., Zealots may also have attacked Palestinian Christians who accepted Gentiles into their communities, for extreme revolutionaries regarded virtually all Gentiles as enemies of the Jewish nation. These ordeals may well account for Mark's references to "persecutions" and assertions that unless this period of testing were "cut short," no believers could survive (13:9–13).

The 60s C.E. were also a decade of natural cataclysms, with great earthquakes (13:8) shaking the eastern Mediterranean, as well as central Italy, where Pompeii, Herculaneum, and Naples suffered heavy damage—the latter temblor a precursor of Vesuvius's catastrophic eruption in 79 C.E. In addition to military and geologic dangers, Mark also expresses concern about internal troubles in his church, with Christians being misled by rumors of new messiahs or imposters claiming to be Jesus returned. Mark's anxiety about false prophets suggests that some in his community may have been attracted to the prophets or popular kings associated with the Zealot movement (see ch. 5). Christian visionaries may also have issued predictions about Jesus' reappearance that were disproved when they failed to materialize (13:5–6, 21–23).

The "Abomination" Mark incorporates a cryptic passage from the Book of Daniel into his eschatological discourse. When believers see " 'the abomination of desolation' usurping a place which is not his," they are to abandon their homes in Judea and take refuge in nearby hills (13:14–20; cf. Daniel 9:27; 11:31; 12:11). Directly addressing his readers, the author alerts them to the importance of understanding this reference (13:14). Some scholars believe that Mark here refers to the Zealots' violent occupation of the Temple in 67–68 C.E. and their polluting its sacred precincts with the blood of their victims, which may have included some Christians (see box 7.6).

This tribulation, which threatens the people of God, will be concluded by the Son of Man's appearing with his angels to gather the faithful. Mark shows Jesus warning disciples that all these horrors and wonders will occur in the lifetime of his hearers, although no one knows the precise day or hour (13:24–32). Mark's eschatological fervor, which Matthew and Luke subsequently mute in their respective versions of the Markan apocalypse (cf. Matt. 24–25 and Luke 21), vividly conveys both the fears and hopes of the author's Christian generation. Mark's eschatology, in fact, closely resembles that of Paul, who—a few years earlier—wrote the church in Corinth that "the time we live in will not last long" (1 Cor. 7:29). As his first letter to the Thessalonians makes clear, Paul fully expected to be alive at the Parousia (1 Thess. 4:13–18; see chs. 13 and 14).

THE LAST SUPPER AND JESUS' BETRAYAL

Following the eschatological discourse, Jesus withdraws with his disciples to a private "upper room" in Jerusalem. On Thursday evening, he presides over a **Passover** feast of unleavened bread, an observance that solemnly recalls Israel's last night in Egypt when the Angel of Death "passed over" their houses to slay the Egyptian firstborn (Exod. 11:1–13:16). In a ritual at the close of their meal, Jesus gives the Passover a new significance, stating that the bread he distributes is his "body" and the wine his "blood of the [New] Covenant, shed for many" (14:22–25), liturgical symbols of his crucifixion. Mark's account of this Last Supper, the origin of

the Christian celebration of the **Eucharist,** or Holy Communion, closely resembles Paul's earlier description of the ceremony (1 Cor. 11:23–26).

Mark's Passion Narrative: Jesus' Trial and Crucifixion

In describing Jesus' Passion—his final suffering and death—Mark's narrative irony reaches its height. Although the author emphasizes many grim details of Jesus' excruciatingly painful execution, he means his readers to see the enormous disparity between the *appearance* of Jesus' vulnerability to the world's evil and the actual reality of his spiritual triumph. Jesus' enemies, who believe they are ridding Judea of a dangerous radical, are in fact making possible his saving death—all according to God's design.

Even so, Mark's hero is tested fully—treated with savage cruelty (14:65; 15:15–20), deserted by all his friends (14:50), and even (in human eyes) abandoned by God (15:34). The agony begins in **Gethsemane,** a grove or vineyard on the **Mount of Olives** opposite Jerusalem to which Jesus and the disciples retreat after the Last Supper. In the Gethsemane episode (14:28–52), Mark places a dual emphasis on Jesus' fulfilling predictions in the Hebrew Bible (14:26–31, 39) and on his personal anguish. By juxtaposing these two elements, Mark demonstrates that while the Crucifixion will take place as God long ago planned (and revealed in Scripture), Jesus' part in the drama of salvation demands heroic effort. While the disciples mindlessly sleep, Jesus faces the hard reality of his impending torture, experiencing "grief" and "horror and dismay." To Mark, his hero—emotionally ravaged and physically defenseless—provides the model for all believers whose loyalty is tested. Although Jesus prays that God will spare him the humiliation and pain he dreads, he forces his own will into harmony with God's. Mark reports that even during this cruel testing of the heavenly Father/Son of Man relationship, Jesus addresses the Deity as *Abba,* an Aramaic term expressing a child's trusting intimacy with the parent (14:32–41).

Box 7.6
The Desecrating "Abomination" and Mark's Eschatological Community

The longest speech that Mark assigns to Jesus is his prediction of Jerusalem's imminent destruction (Mark 13), suggesting that for Mark's intended audience this event was of great importance, a warning that the Parousia (Jesus' return in glory) was near. Mark's cryptic reference to the "abomination of desolation," an apocalyptic image borrowed from Daniel (Dan. 9:27; 11:31; 12:11), signifies a Gentile pollution of the Jerusalem Temple. Mark pointedly advises his readers to take careful note of this profanation of the sanctuary and, when they see it occurring, abandon their homes in Judea and take refuge in the surrounding hills.

In Daniel, the "abomination" was Antiochus IV's defilement of the Temple by sacrificing swine on its altar and erecting a statue of Zeus, king of the Hellenic gods, in its courtyard. Some scholars think that Mark regarded the Roman emperor Caligula's threat to install a statue of himself in Herod's Temple (about 40 C.E.) as the latter-day counterpart of Daniel's "abomination." Others believe that Caligula's threat, which never materialized, occurred too long before Roman armies surrounded Jerusalem and that it was the Roman troops' demolition of the Temple after Jerusalem's fall in 70 C.E. that was the desecration Mark had in mind.

Mark, however, explicitly cites the "abomination" as a visible warning to flee the doomed city. The presence of Gentile soldiers in the sanctuary (in late August 70 C.E.) would not serve this warning purpose because by that time Jerusalem already lay in ruins and much of its population had been slaughtered. Recently, some scholars have argued that the "abomination" to which Mark referred—and which was to alert Jerusalem's Christian inhabitants that the hour of tribulation had arrived—was the occupation of the Temple area by brigands shortly before the Roman siege began.

According to Josephus, in the winter of 67–68 C.E., a mixed band of Jewish guerrilla fighters moved into Jerusalem from the countryside and seized control of the Temple. Led by Eleazar, son of Simon (see chapter 5), this revolutionary group formed the Zealot party, which resolved not only to expel the Romans but also to purge the city of any Jewish leaders who cooperated with them. Adopting a policy of radical egalitarianism, the Zealots fiercely attacked Jerusalem's wealthy aristocracy and the Temple's priestly administration, which they condemned as traitors to the Jewish nation for having collaborated with the Romans. The Zealots assassinated many of the Jewish landowners and priests, staining the Temple pavements with the blood of Jerusalem's leadership, acts that outraged Josephus and may have been regarded as a polluting "abomination" by other Jews.

The Zealots also held illegal trials for and executions of those they suspected of not sharing their total commitment to the war against Rome. It is possible that Jerusalem's Christian community, which by then included Gentiles (an anathema to the Zealots), suffered Zealot persecution and that the shedding of Christian blood, both Jewish and Gentile, also contaminated the holy place, an "abominable" guarantee of its impending fall.

The church historian Eusebius records that shortly before Jerusalem was obliterated, Christians there received an "oracle" inciting them to escape from the city and settle in **Pella,** a mostly Gentile town in the Decapolis, a territory east of the Jordan dominated by a league of ten Hellenistic cities (*Eccl. Hist.* 3.5.3). Scholars still debate the historicity of this episode, but Josephus reveals that such "inspired" predictions about Jerusalem's dire fate were circulating among Jews during the war with Rome. He states that some Jews prophesied that the Temple would be destroyed "when sedition and native hands [the Zealots] should be the first to defile God's sacred precincts" (*The Jewish War* 4.6.3; see also 4.3.10 and 4.3.12). In Christian circles, oral traditions about Jesus' pronouncement on Jerusalem may have been the source of Mark's declaration to flee the city when the "abomination" (Zealot defilement of the sanctuary?) occurred.

For a detailed analysis of the Jewish revolt's influence on Mark 13, see Joel Marcus, "The Jewish War and the *Sitz im Leben* of Mark," *Journal of Biblical Literature* III(3) (1992): 441–462.

Mark's skill as a storyteller—and interpreter of the events he narrates—is demonstrated in the artful way he organizes his account of Jesus' Passion. Peter's testing (14:37–38) and denial that he even knows Jesus (15:65–72) provide the frame for and ironic parallel to Jesus' trial before the Sanhedrin, the Jewish council headed by Caiaphas, the high priest. When Peter fulfills Jesus' prediction about denying him, the disciple's failure serves a double purpose: confirming Jesus' prophetic gifts and strengthening readers' confidence in Jesus' ability to fulfill other prophecies, including those of his resurrection (14:28) and reappearance as the glorified Son of Man (14:62).

Mark contrasts Peter's fearful denial with Jesus' courageous declaration to the Sanhedrin that he is indeed the Messiah and the appointed agent of God's future judgment (14:62). The only Gospel writer to show Jesus explicitly accepting a messianic identity at his trial, Mark may do so to highlight his theme that Jesus' messiahship is revealed primarily through humility and service, a denial of self that also effects humanity's salvation (10:45). Like the author of Hebrews, Mark sees Jesus' divine sonship earned and perfected through suffering and death (Heb. 2:9–11; 5:7–10).

At daybreak Friday, the "whole council held a consultation" (15:1)—perhaps implying that the night meeting had been illegal and therefore lacked authority to condemn Jesus—and sends the accused to Pontius Pilate, the Roman prefect or procurator who was in Jerusalem to maintain order during Passover week. Uninterested in the Sanhedrin's charge that Jesus is a blasphemer, Pilate focuses on Jesus' reputed political crime, seditiously claiming to be the Jewish king. After remarking that it is Pilate himself who has stated the claim, Jesus refuses to answer further questions. Because Mark re-creates almost the entire Passion story in the context of Old Testament prophecies, it is difficult to know if Jesus' silence represents his actual behavior or the author's reliance on Isaiah 53, where Israel's suffering servant does not respond to his accusers (Isa. 53:7).

As Mark describes the proceedings, Pilate is extremely reluctant to condemn Jesus and does so only after the priestly hierarchy pressures him to do so. Whereas the Markan Pilate maneuvers to spare Jesus' life, the historical Pilate (procurator of Judea from 26 to 36 C.E.), whom Josephus describes, rarely hesitated to slaughter troublesome Jews (cf. *Antiquities* 18.3.1–2; *The Jewish War* 2.9.4). When a mob demands that not Jesus but a convicted terrorist named **Barabbas** be freed, Pilate is pictured as having no choice but to release Barabbas (the first person to benefit from Jesus' sacrifice) and order the Galilean's crucifixion.

Stripped, flogged, mocked, and crowned with thorns, Jesus is apparently unable to carry the crossbeam of his cross, so Roman soldiers impress a bystander, **Simon of Cyrene,** to carry it for him (15:16–21). Taken to Golgotha ("Place of the Skull") outside Jerusalem, Jesus is crucified between two criminals (traditionally called "thieves" but probably brigands similar to those who formed the Zealot party in Mark's day). According to Pilate's order, his cross bears a statement of the political offense for which he is executed: aspiring to be the Jewish king—a cruelly ironic revelation of his true identity (15:22–32).

Although Mark's description of Jesus' undergoing a criminal's shameful death is almost unendurably harsh (see figure 7.5), his Passion story effectively conveys his dual purpose: creating a paradigm for Christians facing a similar fate and showing that out of human malice and blindness the divine goal is accomplished. The disparity between what witnesses to the Crucifixion think is happening and the saving work that God actually achieves through Jesus' death is expressed in Mark's report of Jesus' last words. Just before dying, Jesus cries out in Aramaic, *"Eli, Eli, lema sabachthani?":* "My God, My God, why hast thou foresaken me?" (15:33). In placing this question—a direct quotation of Psalm 22:1—on Jesus' lips, the author invites readers to remember the psalm in its totality. The psalmist opens his poem with a cry of despair, describing the savage attacks of enemies who try to destroy him. Midway through his song, however, the poet abruptly changes to a positive tone, ending in a joyous affirmation of God's reign over all nations of the earth (Ps. 22:19–31). In Mark's eschatological vision, the horror of Jesus' agony is similarly transformed by God's intervention to raise his Son in glory.

JESUS' BURIAL

Although some scholars believe that Mark's wealth of concrete detail indicates that he drew on a well-developed oral form of the Passion story for his Gospel, others think that the narrative of Jesus' last week is basically a Markan composition. In contrast to the geographical vagueness of much of his Galilean narrative, the author's Passion account is full of

Figure 7.5 *The Crucifixion* by Matthias Grunewald (c. 1470–1528). Painted on wood, this small version of Jesus' tortured death heightens the sense of the sufferer's physical pain and grief. Although his emphasis on Jesus' agony reflects Mark's account, Grunewald follows John's Gospel in showing Jesus' mother and the beloved disciple (as well as another Mary) present at the Cross. (Samuel H. Kress Collection. Photograph © 1988 Board of Trustees, National Gallery of Art, Washington)

the names of specific places and participants, from Gethsemane, to Pilate's courtyard, to Golgotha. As in all four Gospels, **Mary of Magdala** provides the key human link connecting Jesus' death and burial

and the subsequent discovery that his grave is empty (15:40–41, 47; 16:1). **Joseph of Arimathea,** a mysterious figure introduced suddenly into the narrative, serves a single function: to transfer Jesus' body from

Roman control to that of the dead man's disciples. Acquainted with Pilate, a member of the Sanhedrin and yet a covert supporter of Jesus' ministry, he bridges the two opposing worlds of Jesus' enemies and friends. Not only does Joseph obtain official permission to remove Jesus' body from the cross — otherwise it would routinely be consigned to an anonymous mass grave — but he also provides a secure place of entombment, a rock-hewn sepulcher that he seals by rolling a large flat stone across the entrance (15:42–47).

Postlude: The Empty Tomb

Because the Jewish Sabbath begins at sundown Friday, the day of Jesus' execution, the female disciples cannot prepare the corpse for interment until Sunday morning. Arriving at dawn, the women find the entrance stone already rolled back and the crypt empty except for the presence of a young man dressed in white. (Is he the same unidentified youth who fled naked from Gethsemane in 14:50–51?)

Mark's scene at the vacant tomb recalls themes recurring throughout his Gospel. Like the male disciples who could not understand Jesus' allusion to resurrection (9:9–10), the women are bewildered, unable to accept the youth's revelation that Jesus is "risen." Fleeing in terror, the women say "nothing to anybody" about what they have heard (16:8), leaving readers in suspense, wondering how the "good news" of Jesus' resurrection ever got started. The Gospel thus concludes with a frightened silence, eschewing any account of Jesus' postresurrection appearances (16:8).

MARK'S INCONCLUSIVENESS: RESURRECTION OR PAROUSIA?

Mark's belief in the nearness of Jesus' Parousia may explain why the risen Jesus does not manifest himself in the earliest Gospel. The mysterious youth in white tells the women how to find Jesus — the risen Lord has already started a posthumous journey "to Galilee," where Peter and the other disciples "will

see him" (16:6–7). Some scholars think that Mark, convinced that the political and social chaos of the Jewish revolt will soon climax in Jesus' return, refers not to a resurrection phenomenon but to the Parousia. Forty years after the Crucifixion, Mark's community may believe that their wandering through the wilderness is almost over: They are about to follow Jesus across Jordan into "Galilee," his promised kingdom.

Mark's inconclusiveness, his insistence on leaving his story open-ended, must have seemed as unsatisfactory to later Christian scribes as it does to many readers today. For perhaps that reason, Mark's Gospel has been heavily edited, with two different conclusions added at different times. All the oldest manuscripts of Mark end with the line stressing the women's terrified refusal to obey the young man's instruction to carry the resurrection message to Peter. In time, however, some editors appended postresurrection accounts to their copies of Mark, making his Gospel more consistent with Matthew and Luke (Mark 16:8b and 16:9–20).

Summary

Christianity's first attempt to create a sequential account of Jesus' public ministry, arrest, and execution, Mark's Gospel includes relatively little of Jesus' teaching. Focusing on Jesus' actions — exorcisms, healings, and other miracles — the author presents his mighty works as evidence that God's kingdom has begun to rule, breaking up Satan's control of suffering humanity. Writing under the shadow of Roman persecution and the impending Roman destruction of Jerusalem, Mark presents Jesus as an eschatological Son of Man, who will soon reappear to judge all people.

Mark's ironic vision depicts Jesus as an unexpected and unwanted kind of Messiah who is predestined to be misunderstood, rejected, and crucified — a Messiah revealed only in suffering and death. God, however, uses humanity's blindness and inadequacy to provide a ransom sacrifice in his Son, saving humankind despite its attempts to resist him.

QUESTIONS FOR REVIEW

1. According to tradition, who wrote the Gospel according to Mark? Why are modern scholars unable to verify that tradition? What themes in the Gospel suggest that it was composed after the Jewish revolt against Rome had already begun?

2. Outline and summarize the major events in Jesus' public career, from his baptism by John and Galilean ministry through his last week in Jerusalem. Specify the devices that Mark uses to connect the powerful miracle worker in Galilee with the seemingly powerless sacrificial victim in Jerusalem. Why does Mark devote so much space and detail to narrating the Passion story? Why does he have Jesus predict his own death three times?

3. Describe the three different categories Mark assigns the Son of Man concept. How is this concept related to earlier Jewish writings, such as the books of Ezekiel, Daniel, and 1 Enoch?

4. Define *parable,* and discuss Jesus' use of this literary form to illustrate his vision of God's kingdom. Why does Mark state that Jesus used parables to *prevent* people from understanding his message?

5. Explain a possible connection between the messianic secret concept and Mark's picture of the disciples as hopelessly inept and Jesus' opponents as mistakenly seeing him as the Devil's agent. What devices does the author employ to convey his view that Jesus *had to be misunderstood* for him to fulfill God's plan?

QUESTIONS FOR DISCUSSION AND REFLECTION

1. How does the historical situation when Mark wrote help account for the author's portrait of Jesus as a suffering Messiah whose disciples must also expect to suffer? Would the wars, insurrections, and persecutions afflicting Mark's community have stimulated the author's sense of eschatological urgency?

2. Why does Mark paint so unflattering a picture of Jesus' Galilean family, neighbors, and disciples, all of whom fail to understand or support him? Do you think that the author is trying to disassociate Christianity from its Palestinian origins in favor of his Gentile church's understanding of Jesus' significance?

3. Do you think that Mark's emphasis on Jesus' exorcisms—his battle with cosmic Evil—is an expression of the author's eschatology, his belief that in

Jesus' activities God's kingdom has begun and the End is near?

4. Discuss Mark's use of irony in his presentation of Jesus' story. List and discuss some incongruities between the spiritual reality that Jesus embodies and the way in which most people in the Markan narrative perceive him. In the literary world that Mark creates in his Gospel, how do appearance and reality conflict? How does Mark demonstrate that God achieves his purpose in Jesus even though political and religious authorities succeed in destroying him?

5. In your view, why does Mark end his Gospel so abruptly? Are there any clues in the Gospel that the author expects the Parousia to occur imminently? Are stories of Jesus' postresurrection appearances merely precursors of his return as eschatological judge?

TERMS AND CONCEPTS TO REMEMBER

Mark's eschatological urgency	Peter
	Judas Iscariot
Second Coming (Parousia)	demons and demonic possession
Galilee	Zoroastrianism
John the Baptist	messianic secret
exorcism	fall of Jerusalem
eschaton	Zealots
kingdom of God	Last Supper
Transfiguration	Eucharist
Sanhedrin (Great Council)	Passion
	Gethsemane
Son of God	Caiaphas
Son of Man	Pontius Pilate
parable	Golgotha
simile	Joseph of Arimathaea
allegory	

RECOMMENDED READING

Achtemeier, Paul J. "Gospel of Mark." In D. N. Freedman, ed., *The Anchor Bible Dictionary*, Vol. 4, pp. 541–557. New York: Doubleday, 1992. Applies the two-source hypothesis to Mark.

Bryan, Christopher. *A Preface to Mark: Notes on the Gospel in Its Literary and Cultural Settings.* New York: Oxford University Press, 1993. Links Mark with the oral tradition.

Funk, Robert W., and Hoover, Roy W. *The Five Gospels: The Search for the Authentic Words of Jesus.* A Polebridge Press Book. New York: Macmillan, 1993. A fresh, colloquial translation, with clear, scholarly annotations comparing Markan passages with parallels in Matthew, Luke, and Thomas.

Harrington, Daniel J. "The Gospel According to Mark." In R. E. Brown et al., eds., *The New Jerome Biblical Commentary*, pp. 596–629. Englewood Cliffs, N.J.: Prentice-Hall, 1990.

Kee, Howard C. *Community of the New Age: Studies in Mark's Gospel.* Philadelphia: Westminster Press, 1977. Reprint, Macon, Ga.: Mercer University Press, 1983. Examines the probable historical circumstances of Mark's community.

Kelber, W. H. *Mark's Story of Jesus.* Philadelphia: Fortress Press, 1979. A penetrating but succinct analysis of Mark's rendition of Jesus' life.

———. *The Oral and the Written Gospel: The Hermeneutics of Speaking and Writing in the Synoptic Tradition, Mark, Paul, and Q.* Philadelphia: Fortress Press, 1983. A major scholarly study of Mark's place in the Jesus tradition.

Ladd, George Eldon. *A Theology of the New Testament.* Grand Rapids, Mich.: Eerdmans, 1974.

Mann, C. S. *Mark: A New Translation, Interpretation, and Commentary.* Anchor Bible, Vol. 27. Garden City, N.Y.: Doubleday, 1986. Argues the Griesbach hypothesis that Mark is a conflation of Matthew and Luke.

Schmidt, Daryl D. *The Gospel of Mark: The Scholars Bible I.* Sonoma, Calif.: Polebridge Press, 1991. A vivid new translation with scholarly annotations.

Streeter, B. H. *The Four Gospels: A Study in Origins.* New York: Macmillan, 1924. A classic statement of the relationship of the Synoptic Gospels, arguing Mark's priority.

Tolbert, Mary Ann. *Sowing the Gospel: Mark's World in Literary-Historical Perspective.* Minneapolis: Fortress Press, 1989. Analyzes the literary character and structure of Mark's Gospel.

CHAPTER 8

Matthew's Portrait of Jesus
The Great Teacher

Do not suppose that I have come to abolish the Law and the prophets;
I did not come to abolish, but to complete. Matthew 5:17

Key Themes Most scholars believe that Matthew's Gospel is an expanded edition of Mark, which the author frames with accounts of Jesus' birth (chs. 1 and 2) and postresurrection appearances (ch. 28). Although retaining Mark's general sequence of events, Matthew adds five blocks of teaching material, emphasizing Jesus as the inaugurator of a New Covenant (26:26–29) who definitively interprets the Mosaic Torah and, through fulfilling specific prophecies in the Hebrew Bible, proves his identity as Israel's Messiah. Writing a decade or two after the Roman destruction of Jerusalem, Matthew somewhat softens Mark's portrait of an eschatological Jesus, adding parables that imply a delay in the Parousia (Second Coming) (chs. 24 and 25), an interval of indefinite length devoted to the missionary work of the Church *(ekklesia).* Matthew's principal discourses include the Sermon on the Mount (chs. 5–7), instructions to the Twelve (ch. 10), parables of the kingdom (ch. 13), instructions to the church (ch. 18), and warnings of Final Judgment (chs. 23–25).

If Mark was the first Gospel written, as most scholars believe, why does Matthew's Gospel stand first in the New Testament canon? The original compilers of the New Testament probably assigned Matthew the premier position for several reasons. It offers a more extensive coverage of Jesus' teaching than any other Gospel, making it the church's major resource in instructing its members. In addition, Matthew's Gospel was particularly important to early church leaders because it is the Gospel most explicitly concerned with the nature and function of the **Church** (Greek, *ekklesia*). The only Gospel even to use the term *ekklesia*, Matthew devotes two full chapters (chs. 10 and 18) to providing specific guidance to the Christian community.

Relation to the Hebrew Bible

The placement of Matthew's Gospel at the opening of the New Testament is also thematically appropriate because it forms a strong connecting link with the Hebrew Bible (Old Testament). Matthew starts his account with a genealogy to associate Jesus with the most prominent heroes of ancient

drives home the connection between prophecy and specific events in Jesus' life: "All this happened in order to fulfill what the Lord declared through the prophet . . . ," Matthew writes, then citing a biblical passage to support his contention (1:22–23; 2:15, 23; see box 8.1).

Matthew takes great pains to show that Jesus both taught and fulfilled the principles of the Mosaic Law (5:17–20). For these and other reasons, Matthew is usually regarded as the "most Jewish" of the Gospels. At the same time, the author violently attacks the leaders of institutional Judaism, condemning the Pharisees and scribes with extreme bitterness (ch. 23).

Authorship, Purpose, Sources, and Organization

Israel. Beginning with Abraham, progenitor of the Hebrew people, Matthew lists as Jesus' ancestors celebrated kings like David, Solomon, and Josiah. From the outset, the author intends to establish Jesus' credentials as the "seed" (descendant) of Abraham through whom God will bless all nations (Gen. 22:18) and as the heir of King David who fulfills the promise that David's line would rule "forever" (2 Sam. 7:16). Hence, he first identifies his subject as "son of David" and "son of Abraham" (Matt. 1:1)—in contrast to Mark's opening identification of Jesus as "Son of God" (Mark 1:1).

Matthew's wish to connect Jesus with the Hebrew Bible goes far beyond genealogical concerns. More than any other Gospel writer, he presents Jesus' life in the context of biblical Law and prophecy. Throughout the entire Gospel, Matthew stresses Jesus' fulfillment of ancient prophecies, repeatedly emphasizing the continuity between Jesus and the promises made to Israel, particularly to the royal dynasty of David. To demonstrate that Jesus' entire career, from conception to resurrection, was predicted centuries earlier by Bible writers from Moses to Malachi, Matthew quotes from, paraphrases, or alludes to the Hebrew Bible at least 60 times. (Some scholars have detected 140 or more allusions to the Hebrew Scriptures.) Nearly a dozen times, Matthew employs a literary formula that

Who was the man so deeply interested in Jesus' practice of the Jewish religion and simultaneously so fierce in his denunciation of Jewish leaders? As in Mark's case, the author does not identify himself, suggesting to most historians that the Gospel originated and circulated anonymously. The tradition that the author is the "publican" or tax collector mentioned in Matthew 9:9–13 (and called "Levi" in Mark 2:14) dates from the late second century C.E. and cannot be verified. The main problem with accepting the Apostle Matthew's authorship is that the writer relies heavily on Mark as a source. It is extremely unlikely that one of the original Twelve would depend on the work of Mark, who was not an eyewitness to the events he describes.

The oldest apparent reference to the Gospel's authorship is that of Papias (c. 140 C.E.), whom Eusebius quotes: "Matthew compiled the Sayings [Greek, *logia*] in the Aramaic language, and everyone translated them as well as he could" (*History* 3:39:16). As many commentators have noted, the Sayings, or *logia*, are not the same as the "words" [Greek, *logoi*] of Jesus, nor are they the same as the Gospel of Matthew we have today. Whereas scholars once believed that Matthew's Gospel was first written in Aramaic by the apostle who was formerly a tax collector, modern analysts point out that there is no evidence of an earlier Aramaic version of

Box 8.1

Representative Examples of Matthew's Use of the Septuagint (Greek) Version of the Hebrew Bible to Identify Jesus as the Promised Messiah

MATTHEW	HEBREW BIBLE SOURCE

"All this happened in order to fulfill what the Lord declared through the prophet. . . ." (Matt. 1:22)

1. "The Virgin will conceive and bear a son, and he shall be called Emmanuel." (Matt. 1:22)

2. "Bethlehem in the land of Judah, you are far from least in the eyes of the rulers of Judah; for out of you shall come a leader to be the shepherd of my people Israel." (Matt. 2:5–6)

3. So Joseph . . . went away . . . to Egypt, and there he stayed till Herod's death. This was to fulfill what the Lord had declared through the prophet: "I called my son out of Egypt." (Matt. 2:15)

4. Herod . . . gave orders for the massacre of all children in Bethlehem and its neighborhood, of the age of two years or less. . . . So the words spoken through Jeremiah the prophet were fulfilled: "A voice was heard in Rama, wailing and loud laments; it was Rachael weeping for her children, and refusing all consolation, because they were no more." (Matt. 2:16–18)

5. "He shall be called a Nazarene." (Matt. 2:23)

   [This statement does not appear in the Hebrew Bible; it may be a misreading of Isaiah 11:1.]

6. When he heard that John had been arrested, Jesus withdrew to Galilee; and leaving Nazareth he went and settled at Capernaum on the Sea of Galilee, in the district of Zebulun and Naphtali. This was to fulfill the passage in the prophet Isaiah which tells of "the land of Zebulun, the land of Naphtali, the Way of the Sea, the land beyond Jordan, heathen Galilee," and says:

   The people that lived in darkness saw a great light:
   light dawned on the dwellers in the land of death's dark shadow (Matt. 4:12–16)

7. And he drove the spirits out with a word and healed all who were sick, to fulfill the prophecy of Isaiah: "He took away our illnesses and lifted our diseases from us." (Matt. 8:16–17)

1. A young woman is with child, and she will bear a son and will call him Immanuel. (Isa. 7:14)

2. But you, Bethlehem in Ephrathah, small as you are to be among Judah's clans, out of you shall come forth a governor for Israel, one whose roots are far back in the past, in days gone by. (Mic. 5:2)

3. When Israel was a boy, I loved him;
   I called my son out of Egypt. (Hos. 11:1)

4. Hark, lamentation is heard in Ramah, and bitter weeping,
   Rachel weeping for her sons.
   She refuses to be comforted: they are no more.
   (Jer. 31:15)

5. Then a shoot shall grow from the stock of Jesse, and a branch [Hebrew, *nezer*] shall spring from his roots. (Isa. 11:1)

6. For, while the first invader has dealt lightly with the land of Zebulun and the land of Naphtali, the second has dealt heavily with Galilee of the Nations on the road beyond Jordan to the sea.

   The people who walked in darkness
   have seen a great light;
   light has dawned upon them,
   dwellers in a land as dark as death.
   (Isa. 9:1–2)

7. Yet on himself he bore our sufferings,
   our torments he endured,
   while we counted him smitten by God,
   struck down by disease and misery.

   (Isa. 53:4)

(continued)

Box 8.1 *(continued)*

MATTHEW	HEBREW BIBLE SOURCE

"All this happened in order to fulfill what the Lord declared through the prophet. . . ." (Matt. 1:22)

8. Jesus . . . gave strict injunctions that they were not to make him known. This was to fulfill Isaiah's prophecy:

> Here is my servant, whom I have chosen,
> my beloved on whom my favour rests;
> I will put my spirit upon him,
> and he will proclaim judgment among the
>   nations.
> He will not strive, he will not shout,
> nor will his voice be heard in the streets.
> He will not snap off the broken reed,
> nor snuff out the smouldering wick,
> until he leads justice on to victory.
> In him the nations shall place their hope.
>   (Matt. 12:16–21)

8. Here is my servant, whom I uphold,
> my chosen one in whom I delight,
> I have bestowed my spirit upon him,
> and he will make justice shine on the nations.
> He will not call out or lift his voice high,
> Or make himself heard in the open street.
> He will not break a bruised reed,
> or snuff out a smouldering wick;
> he will make justice shine on every race,
> never faltering, never breaking down,
> he will plant justice on earth,
> while coasts and islands wait for his teaching.
>   (Isa. 42:1–4)

9. In all his teaching to the crowds Jesus spoke in parables; in fact he never spoke to them without a parable. This was to fulfill the prophecy of Isaiah:

> I will open my mouth in parables;
> I will utter things kept secret since the world
>   was made. (Matt. 13:34–35)

9. Mark my teaching, O my people,
> listen to the words I am to speak.
> I will tell you a story with a meaning,
> I will expound the riddle of things past,
> things that we have heard and know,
> and our fathers have repeated to us.
>   (Ps. 78:2 — *not* in Isaiah)

10. Jesus instructs his disciples to bring him a donkey and her foal. "If any speaks to you, say 'Our Master needs them'; and he will let you take them at once." This was to fulfill the prophecy which says, "Tell the daughter of Zion, 'Here is your king, who comes to you riding on an ass, riding on the foal of a beast of burden.'" (Matt. 21:2–5)

[Matthew shows Jesus mounted on two beasts — the donkey and her foal. See Luke 19:29–36, where a single mount is mentioned.]

10. Rejoice, rejoice, daughter of Zion,
> shout aloud, daughter of Jerusalem;
> for see, your king is coming to you,
> his cause won, his victory gained,
> humble and mounted on an ass,
> on a foal, the young of a she-ass.
>   (Zech. 9:9)

11. *[Judas returns the bribe — "thirty silver pieces" — given him to betray Jesus.]*

. . . and in this way fulfillment was given to the saying of the prophet Jeremiah: "They took the thirty silver pieces, the price set on a man's head (for that was his price among the Israelites) and gave the money for the potter's field, so the Lord directed me."

11. *[Matthew is wrong in citing Jeremiah as the source of this passage, which, in the form he quotes it, does not appear in the Hebrew Bible. It is Zechariah who reports being paid "thirty shekels of silver," which he then donates to the Temple treasury]:*

So they weighed out as my wages thirty shekels of silver. Then the Lord said to me, "Throw it into the treasury" — this is the lordly price [the standard price of a slave] at which I was valued by them. So I took the thirty shekels of silver and threw them into the treasury in the house of the Lord.

[Jeremiah does record investing in a field near Jerusalem (Jer. 32:6–15) and refers to visiting a potter's house (Jer. 18:1–3), but neither he nor Zechariah provides support for Matthew's claim of prophetic fulfillment.]

the Gospel. Papias's use of *logia* may refer to an early collection of Jesus' sayings compiled by someone named Matthew, or it may allude to a list of messianic prophecies from the Hebrew Bible that a Christian scribe assembled to show that Jesus' life was foretold in scripture. Most scholars do not believe that Papias's description applies to the canonical Gospel of Matthew.

MATTHEW AND JUDAISM

The author remains unknown (we call him Matthew to avoid confusion), but scholarly analysis of his work enables us to gain some insight into his theological intentions and distinctive interests. Thoroughly versed in the Hebrew Bible, the writer is remarkably skilled at its exegesis (the explanation and critical interpretation of a literary text). Some scholars believe that he may have received scribal training, a professional discipline he utilizes to demonstrate to his fellow Jews that Jesus of Nazareth is the predicted Messiah. The author may refer to himself or to a "school" of early Christian interpreters of the Hebrew Scriptures when he states: "When, therefore, a teacher of the law [a scribe] has become a learner [disciple] in the kingdom of Heaven, he is like a householder who can produce from his store both the new and the old" (13:52–53). Matthew effectively combines "the new" (Christian teaching) with "the old" (Judaism). To him Jesus' teachings are the legitimate outgrowth of Torah study.

Recent scholarly investigations have demonstrated that several varieties of Jewish Christianity existed in the first-century church. The particular type to which Matthew belongs can only be inferred from examining relevant aspects of his Gospel. Some Jewish Christians demanded that all Gentile converts to the new faith keep the entire Mosaic Law or at least undergo circumcision (Acts 15:1–6; Gal. 6:11–16). Matthew does not mention circumcision, but he insists that the Mosaic Torah is binding on believers (5:17–20). In his view, Christians are to continue such Jewish practices as fasting (6:16–18), regular prayer (6:5–6), charitable giving (6:2), and making formal **sacrifices** (5:23). His account also implies that Mosaic purity laws, forbidding certain foods, apply to his commu-

nity. Matthew includes Mark's report of Jesus' controversy with the Pharisees over ritual hand washing but omits Mark's conclusion that Jesus declares all foods ceremonially clean (cf. 15:1–20 with Mark 7:1–23, especially 7:19).

Matthew depicts Jesus' personal religion as Torah Judaism, but he has no patience with Jewish leaders who disagree with his conclusions. He labels them "blind guides" and hypocrites (23:13–28). Despite his contempt for Jewish opponents, however, Matthew retains his respect for Pharisaic teachings and urges the church to "pay attention to their words" (23:3).

In his use of scriptural quotations and **pesher** (commentary), Matthew employs interpretative methods common to the Judaisms of his day. Like the writers at Qumran, the Essene community of monklike scholars who withdrew from the world to await the final battle between Good and Evil, Matthew interprets the prophecies of the Hebrew Bible as applying exclusively to his group of believers, whom he regards as the true Israel. He also commonly presents Jesus' teaching as a kind of midrash on the Torah. A detailed exposition of the underlying meaning of a biblical text, a **midrash** includes interpretations of Scripture's legal rules for daily life (called **Halakah**) and explanations of non-legal material (called **Haggadah**). At various points in his Gospel, Matthew shows Jesus providing halakic interpretations of the Torah (5:17–48), particularly on such legal matters as Sabbath observance and divorce (12:1–21; 19:3–12).

DATE AND PLACE OF COMPOSITION

The Gospel gives few clues to its precise time of origin, but Matthew apparently refers to Jerusalem's destruction as an accomplished fact (22:7). The author's hostility to the Jewish leadership and references to "their" synagogues (9:35; 10:17; 12:9; 13:54) may suggest that he wrote after the Christians already had been expelled from Jewish meeting places, an expulsion that occurred about 85 or 90 C.E.

The oldest citations from Matthew's Gospel appear in the letters of Ignatius, who was bishop of Antioch in Syria about 110–115 C.E. Ignatius's reference and the unusual prominence given Peter in

Box 8.2

Examples of Matthew's Editing of Markan Material*

Jesus' Baptism

Mark: It happened at this time that Jesus came from Nazareth in Galilee

and was baptized in the Jordan by John. At the moment when he came up out of the water, he saw the heavens torn open and the Spirit, like a dove, descending upon him. And a voice spoke from heaven: "Thou art my Son, my Beloved; on thee my favour rests." (Mark 1:9–11)

Matthew: Then Jesus arrived at the Jordan from Galilee, and came to John to be baptized by him. **John tried to dissuade him, "Do you come to me?" he said. "I need rather to be baptized by you." Jesus replied, "Let it be so for the present; we do well to conform in this way with all that God requires." John then allowed him to come.** After baptism Jesus came up out of the water at once, and at that moment heaven opened; he saw the Spirit of God descending like a dove to alight upon him; and a voice from heaven was heard saying, "**This is my Son,** my Beloved, on whom my favour rests." (Matt. 3:13–17)

In comparing the two accounts of Jesus' baptism, the reader will note that Matthew inserts a speech by John into the Markan narrative. Recognizing Jesus as "mightier" than himself, John is reluctant to baptize him. By giving John this speech, Matthew is able to stress Jesus' superiority to the Baptist. Matthew also changes the nature of Jesus' experience of the "Spirit" after his

baptism. In Mark, the heavenly voice is addressed directly to Jesus and apparently represents Jesus' own private mystical experience of divine sonship at the event. Matthew changes the "thou art," intended for Jesus' ears, to "this is," making the divine voice a public declaration heard by the crowds.

Jesus' Healings

Mark: That evening after sunset they brought to him all who were ill or possessed by devils; and the whole town was there, gathered at the door. He healed many who suffered from various diseases, and drove out many devils.

He would not let the devils speak, because they knew who he was. (Mark 1:32–34)

Matthew: When evening fell, they brought to him many who were possessed by devils;

and **he drove the spirits out with a word and healed all who were sick.**

to fulfill the prophecy of Isaiah: "He took away our illnesses and lifted our diseases from us." (Matt. 8:16–17)

In reproducing Mark's story, Matthew edits it in several ways that are characteristic of his particular concerns as an author: (1) He condenses Mark's narrative, omitting various details to focus on a single aspect of Jesus' miraculous power, in this case the exorcising of "devils." (2) He emphasizes the totality or comprehensiveness

of Jesus' power, changing Mark's "he healed many" to "healed all." (3) Most characteristically, he adds to the account a quotation from the Hebrew Bible, citing Isaiah's poem about the suffering servant (Isa. 53:4), to demonstrate that Jesus' activities fulfilled ancient prophecy.

*Matthew's chief editorial changes are printed in boldface type.

Jesus' Reception by His Neighbors in His Hometown of Nazareth

Mark: He left that place and went to his home town accompanied by his disciples. When the Sabbath came he began to teach in the synagogue; and the large congregation who heard him were amazed and said,
"Where does he get it from?", and, "What wisdom is this that has been given him?", and, "How does he work such miracles? Is not this the carpenter, the son of Mary, the brother of James and Joseph and Judas and Simon? And are not his sisters here with us?" So they [turned against] him. Jesus said to them, "A prophet will always he held in honour except in his home town, and among his kinsmen and family." He could work no miracle there, except that he put his hands on a few sick people and healed them; and he was taken aback by their want of faith. (Mark 6:1–6)

Matthew: Jesus left that place, and came to his home town, where he taught the people in their synagogue.

In amazement they asked,

"Where does he get this wisdom from, and these miraculous powers? **Is he not the carpenter's son? Is not his mother called Mary,** his brothers James, Joseph, Simon, and Judas? And are not all his sisters here with us? Where then has he got all this from?" So they [turned against] him, and this led him to say, "A prophet will always be held in honour, except in his home town, and in his own family." And **he did not work many miracles there: such was their want of faith.** (Matt. 13:54–58)

In editing Mark's account of Jesus' unsatisfactory reunion with his former neighbors in Nazareth, Matthew reproduces most of his source but makes some significant changes and deletions. He omits Mark's reference to the Sabbath, as well as Mark's brief list of Jesus' "few" deeds there and Jesus' apparent surprise at his fellow townsmen's refusal to respond to his healing efforts. Matthew also

substitutes the phrase "the carpenter's son" for Mark's "the son of Mary," with its implication of Jesus' illegitimacy. In both accounts, the Nazareans' familiarity with Jesus' background and family (naming four "brothers" and referring to two or more "sisters") is enough to make them skeptical of Jesus' claims to special wisdom or authority.

Jesus' Stilling of a Storm

Mark: [Immediately after miraculously feeding the multitudes who had gathered to hear him preach, Jesus sends the disciples by boat across the sea of Galilee to Bethsaida.] After taking leave of them [the crowds], he went up the hill to pray. It was now late and the boat was already well out on the water, while he was alone on the land. Somewhere between three and six in the morning, seeing them laboring at the oars against a head wind, he came toward them, walking on the lake. He was going to pass by them; but when they saw him walking on the lake, they thought it was a ghost and cried out; for they all saw him and were terrified.

Matthew: As soon as they had finished, he made the disciples embark and cross to the other side [of the Sea of Galilee] ahead of him, while he dismissed the crowd; then he went up the hill by himself to pray. It had grown late, and he was there alone. The boat was already some distance from the shore, battling a head wind and a rough sea. Between three and six in the morning he came towards them, walking across the lake. When the disciples saw him walking on the lake they were so shaken that they cried out in terror: "It is a ghost!" But at once Jesus spoke to them: "Take heart! It is I; do not be afraid."

(continued)

Box 8.2 (continued)

Jesus' Stilling of a Storm

Mark: But at once he spoke to them: "Take heart! It is I; do not be afraid." Then he climbed into the boat with them, and the wind dropped. At this they were utterly astonished, for they had not understood the incident of the loaves; their minds were closed. (Mark 6:45–52)

Matthew: Peter called to him: "Lord, if it is you, tell me to come to you over the water." "Come," said Jesus. Peter got down out of the boat and walked over the water towards Jesus. But when he saw the strength of the gale he was afraid; and beginning to sink, he cried, "Save me, Lord!" Jesus at once reached out and caught hold of him. "Why did you hesitate?" he said. "How little faith you have!" Then they climbed into the boat; and the wind dropped. **And the men in the boat fell at his feet, exclaiming "You must be the Son of God."** (Matt. 14:22–33)

Besides adding the episode involving Peter's impetuous attempt to imitate Jesus' power over nature, Matthew radically changes the disciples' reaction to their Master's miraculous control of the sea, symbol of primal chaos. Whereas the Markan disciples fail to perceive Jesus' divinity in his ability to subdue wind and storm — Mark says

that "their minds were closed" — the Matthean disciples immediately recognize Jesus as "Son of God." Matthew's editorial changes reflect not only his promotion of Peter's importance (see Matt. 16:13–19) but also his tendency to picture the disciples as better role models than Mark had portrayed them.

---

this Gospel (Matt. 16:16–19) suggest that it originated in Antioch, a city in which Peter had great influence (Gal. 2:11–14). Founded by Greek-speaking Jewish Christians in the late 30s C.E., during the first generation of Christianity the Antioch church was second only to that in Jerusalem (Acts 11:19–26; 15:2–35). The Antiochean congregation was also the stage on which two different wings of the early Christian community waged a vigorous battle over the status of Gentile converts. Whereas Paul advocated total equality for Gentiles, James (called "the Lord's brother") took a decidedly more conservative stance, insisting that Gentiles keep at least some Torah restrictions. Peter seems to have occupied a middle position between James and Paul, permitting Gentiles into the group but drawing the line at close association with them, particularly if they did not observe kosher food laws. Matthew's Gospel reflects his community's historical movement away from exclusively Jewish Christianity toward a ministry that focuses on Gentiles. In chapter 10, the Matthean Jesus orders his disciples not to

enter Gentile territories and to preach only to "the lost sheep of the house of Israel" (10:5–6). At the very end of his Gospel, however, Matthew pictures the risen Jesus issuing the "great commission" — to "make *all nations* my disciples" (28:19; italics added). Mediating between Torah-oriented traditions and a Hellenistic cosmopolitanism, Matthew produced a gospel appropriate for his transitional generation, between about 80 and 90 C.E.

THE AUTHOR'S PURPOSE

In composing his Gospel, Matthew has several major objectives. Three of the most important are demonstrating Jesus' credentials as Israel's true Messiah; presenting Jesus as the supreme teacher and interpreter of the Mosaic Torah, the principles of which provide ethical guidance for Matthew's particular Jewish-Christian community; and instructing that community — the church — in the kind of correct belief and behavior that will ensure Jesus' approval when he returns.

STRUCTURE AND USE OF SOURCES

Matthew accomplishes his multiple purposes by assembling material from several different sources to construct his Gospel. Using Mark as his primary source, he incorporates about 90 percent of the earlier Gospel into his account. Into the Markan outline, Matthew inserts five large blocks of teaching material. Many ancient Jewish authors, consciously paralleling the Torah (the "five books of Moses"), arranged their works into fivefold divisions, as did the editors of the Psalms. The first of Matthew's five collections is the most famous as well as the most commonly quoted, the Sermon on the Mount (chs. 5–7). The other four are instructions to the Twelve Apostles (ch. 10), parables on the kingdom (ch. 13), instructions to the Church (Matthew's Christian community) (ch. 18), and warnings of the Final Judgment (chs. 23–25).

The Q Source Some of the material in these five sections is peculiar to Matthew, such as the parables involving weeds in a grain field (13:24–30) and the unforgiving debtor (18:23–35). Other parts are similar or virtually identical to material found in Luke but not in Mark. Scholars believe that Matthew and Luke, independently of each other, drew much of their shared teaching from the now-lost Q (*Quelle* [Source]) document (see chapter 6). Containing a wide variety of sayings attributed to Jesus, including kingdom parables, instructions to the disciples, and (at least in its final edition) prophecies of impending judgment, the Q document is thought to have been compiled about 50–70 C.E. Scholars have reconstructed the supposed contents of Q in different ways, although no single reconstruction has won universal acceptance. Nonetheless, the Q hypothesis works well in accounting for the source of Jesus' sayings absent in Mark but present in both Matthew and Luke (see box 6.3).

The M Source In addition to Mark and Q (assuming its historicity), Matthew uses material found only in his Gospel. Scholars designate this material unique to Matthew as M (Matthean). M includes numerous sayings and parables, such as the stories

about the vineyard laborers (20:1–16) and many of the kingdom pronouncements in chapter 13 (13:24–30; 13:44–45; 13:47–52). Finally, Matthew frames his story of Jesus with a narrative of Jesus' birth and infancy (1:18–2:23) and a concluding account of two postresurrection appearances, the first to women near Jerusalem and the second to the "eleven disciples" in Galilee (28:8–20).

MATTHEW'S EDITING OF MARK

Before considering passages found only in Matthew, we can learn something of the author's intent by examining the way in which he edits and revises Markan material (see box 8.2). Although he generally follows Mark's chronology, Matthew characteristically condenses and shortens Mark's narrative. In fact, Matthew generally summarizes and abbreviates Mark's account, rather than the other way around. In the story of the epileptic boy, Matthew severely abridges Mark's version, recounting the episode in a mere five verses (17:14–18) compared with Mark's sixteen (Mark 9:14–29). Matthew is also significantly briefer in his telling of Jesus' healing of Peter's mother-in-law (8:14–15; Mark 1:29–31), the Gerasene demoniac (8:28–34; Mark 5:1–20), and the resuscitation of Jairus's daughter and the curing of the woman with a hemorrhage (9:18–26; Mark 5:21–43). In abbreviating Mark's version of events, Matthew typically omits much physical detail, as well as Jesus' emotional responses to the situation.

Emphasis on the Miraculous and Supernatural At the same time that he shortens Mark's description of Jesus' miracles, Matthew heightens the miraculous element, stressing that Jesus effected instant cures (9:22; 15:28; 17:18). In recounting Jesus' unfriendly reception in Nazareth, Matthew changes Mark's observation that Jesus "could work no miracle there" (Mark 6:5) to the declaration that "he did not work many miracles there," eliminating the implication that the human Jesus had any limit to his powers (13:58) (see box 8.2). He similarly omits Mark's definition of John's baptism as a rite "in token of repentance, for the forgiveness of sins" (3:2, 6, 11; Mark 1:4). Mark's exact phrase, "for the forgiveness

---

Box 8.3
Representative Examples of Material Found Only in Matthew

A "Table of Descent" [genealogy] listing Jesus' ancestors (1:1–17)

Matthew's distinctive version of Jesus' miraculous conception and birth at Bethlehem (1:18–2:23)

Some parables, sayings, and miracles unique to Matthew:

1. The dumb demoniac (9:32–34)
2. Wheat and darnel [weeds] (13:24–30)
3. Buried treasure (13:44)
4. The pearl of "special value" (13:45)
5. Catching fish in a net (13:47–50)
6. A learner with treasures old and new (13:51–52)
7. Earthly rulers collecting tax (17:25–26)
8. Finding a coin in a fish's mouth to pay Temple tax (17:27)

9. The unforgiving debtor (18:23–35)
10. Paying equal wages to all vineyard laborers (20:1–16)
11. The two sons and obedience (21:28–32)
12. The improperly dressed wedding guest (22:11–14)
13. The wise and foolish virgins (25:1–13)
14. The judgment separating sheep from goats (25:31–46)
15. Judas and the chief priests (27:3–10)
16. The dream of Pilate's wife (27:19)
17. The resurrection of saints (27:52–53)
18. The Easter morning earthquake (28:2)
19. The chief priests' conspiracy to deny Jesus' resurrection (28:11–15)

---

of sins," does appear in Matthew, but it is transferred to the Matthean Jesus' explanation of the ceremonial wine at the Last Supper (26: 26–28). The author may have effected this transposition to make sure that his readers understood that "forgiveness of sin" comes not from John's baptism but from Jesus' expiatory death.

Matthew's edition of the Passion narrative also intensifies the supernatural element. In Gethsemane, the Matthean Jesus reminds his persecutors that he has the power to call up thousands of angels to help him (26:53), a claim absent from Mark. Matthew's Christ allows himself to be arrested only to fulfill Scripture (26:54).

Matthew also revises Mark's crucifixion account, inserting several miracles to stress the event's cosmic significance. To Mark's plague of darkness and the rending of the Temple curtain, Matthew adds a violent earthquake, severe enough to open graves and permit suddenly resurrected "**saints**" (holy persons) to rise and walk the streets of Jerusalem (27:50–53). (This mysterious raising of saints is not mentioned elsewhere in the New Testament but probably appears here to express Matthew's

conviction that Jesus' death makes possible the resurrection of the faithful.) Matthew introduces yet another earthquake into his description of the first Easter morning, stating that the women disciples arrive at Jesus' tomb in time to see a divine being descend and roll away the stone blocking the tomb entrance. Mark's linen-clad youth becomes an angel before whom the Roman guards quake in terror (28:1–4). What Mark's account implies, Matthew's typically makes explicit, ensuring that the reader will not miss the hand of God in these happenings. Nor does Matthew leave the Galilean women wondering and frightened at the empty sepulcher. Instead of being too terrified to report what they have seen, in Matthew's version the women joyously rush away to inform the disciples (28:8; Mark 16:8). In this retelling, the women set the right example by immediately proclaiming the good news of Jesus' triumph over death (28:19).

ORGANIZATION OF MATTHEW'S GOSPEL

Because of the complex nature of the Matthean composition and the skill with which the author

Box 8.4
New Characters Introduced in Matthew

Joseph, husband of Mary (1:16, 18–25; 2:13–14, 19–23)

Herod the Great, Roman-appointed king of Judea (40–4 B.C.E.) (2:1–8, 16–19)

The Magi (astrologers or "wise men" from the east) (2:1–12)

Satan, the Devil (as a speaking character) (4:1–11)

Two blind men (9:27–31)

A dumb demoniac (9:32–34)

Revised list of the Twelve (10:1–4)

The mother of James and John, sons of Zebedee (20:20–21)

---

has interwoven Mark's narrative with Jesus' discourses (from Q and M), it is difficult to reduce Matthew to a clear-cut outline. Separating the book into convenient divisions and subdivisions in conventional outline form tends to distort and oversimplify its interlocking themes. One can, however, identify some of the major parts that make up the Gospel whole. The following gives a rough idea of Matthew's general structure:

1. Introduction to the Messiah: genealogy and infancy narratives (1:1–2:23)
2. The beginning of Jesus' proclamation: baptism by John; the temptation by Satan; inauguration of the Galilean ministry (3:1–4:25)
3. First major discourse: the Sermon on the Mount (5–7)
4. First narrative section: ten miracles (8:1–9:38)
5. Second major discourse: instructions to the Twelve Apostles (10)
6. Second narrative section: the Baptist's questions about Jesus; controversies with Jewish authorities (11:1–12:50)
7. Third major discourse: parables on the kingdom (13:1–52)
8. Third narrative section: from the rejection in Nazareth to the Transfiguration (13:53–17:27)
9. Fourth major discourse: instructions to the church (18)
10. Fourth narrative section: the Jerusalem ministry (19:1–22:46)
11. Fifth major discourse: warnings of Final Judgment (23–25)
12. Fifth and final narrative section: the Passion story and resurrection appearances (26:1–28:20)

Except for the birth narratives and final postresurrection apparitions, even a minimal outline makes clear that Matthew tells essentially the same story that we find in Mark and Luke (see box 6.1). Only by carefully scrutinizing Matthew's handling of his sources, the Hebrew Bible, Mark, M, and (presumably) Q can we appreciate the ways in which his Gospel is distinctive (see boxes 8.3 and 8.4).

Introduction to the Messiah: Infancy Narrative

Except for Matthew and Luke, no New Testament writers refer even briefly to the circumstances surrounding the birth of Jesus Christ. Nor do Matthew and Luke allude to Jesus' infancy in the main body of their Gospels. In both cases, the infancy narratives are self-contained units that act as detachable prefaces to the central narrative of Jesus' public ministry.

Matthew constructs his account (1:18–2:23) with phrases and incidents taken from the Hebrew

Bible. To him the infant Messiah's appearance gives new meaning to ancient biblical texts, fulfilling prophecy in many unexpected ways. The child is born to a virgin made pregnant by the Holy Spirit (1:18–19). To the author, this fulfills a passage from Isaiah 7:14, which in Hebrew states that "a young woman is with child, and she will bear a son. . . ." Matthew, however, quotes not the original Hebrew language version of the text, but an Old Greek translation in which "young woman" is rendered as *parthenos,* or "virgin." Historians believe that Isaiah's words originally referred to the birth of an heir to the then-reigning Davidic king, but Matthew sees them as forecasting the Messiah's unique manner of birth. Like other New Testament writers, Matthew reads the Hebrew Bible from an explicitly Christian viewpoint, consistently giving the Jewish Scriptures a christological interpretation. By making almost the entire Hebrew Bible foreshadow the Christ event, Matthew transforms it into a Christian document.

Matthew's concern to anchor Jesus' entrance into life firmly in the context of Scripture fulfillment is evident in his account of the mysterious "Magi" or "wise men" from the east who come to pay homage to the infant Jesus. Traditionally three in number (although Matthew does not say how many they were), the Magi were probably Babylonian or Persian astrologers who had studied the horoscope of Judah and concluded that it was then time for "the king of the Jews" to be born. Astrology was extremely popular with all classes of society in Greco-Roman times, and it was commonly believed that the appearance of unusual celestial bodies, such as comets or "falling stars," heralded the occurrence of major events on earth (Isa. 14:12–23; Job 38:23; Judg. 5:20).

Matthew's reference to the "star" that guides the Magi to Jesus' birthplace is puzzling. Modern scientists do not know what astronomical phenomenon Matthew has in mind, but a conjunction of the planets Jupiter and Saturn in the constellation Pisces (7 B.C.E.) may have been seen as a divine "sign" or portent. (No other New Testament writer or contemporary historian alludes to the "star of Bethlehem.") Noting that the star "stops" to hover over Jesus' birthplace (2:10)—behavior impossible for a genuine celestial body—some commentators

suggest that Matthew invites his readers to understand that an angel (traditionally likened to a star [Isa. 40:26; Rev. 12:4, 9]) actually directs the Magi.

In the Evangelist's account, the unnamed heavenly body leads the traveling astrologers to create a situation in which several biblical prophecies can be fulfilled. On reaching Jerusalem, the astrologers are brought before King Herod, who recognizes that their inquiry about a new Jewish king refers to the Messiah's birth in **Bethlehem,** King David's home city, foretold in Micah 5:2.

Herod's jealous attempt to kill the child (2:1–18) fulfills prophecy (Jer. 31:15), as does the holy family's flight into Egypt (Hos. 11:1). Matthew structures the entire episode to parallel the biblical story of Moses' infancy (Exod. 1:8–2:25). As the baby Moses survived the Egyptian pharaoh's murderous schemes, so the infant Jesus escapes another ruler's plot to kill God's chosen one. The analogy between the two figures is also intended to apply to Jesus' adult life. Like Moses, Jesus will be summoned from Egypt to deliver his people. Moses led Israel from Egyptian slavery to a covenant relationship with God; Jesus will free believers from sin and establish a New Covenant (2:13–15, 19–21; 19:27–29).

The Beginning of Jesus' Proclamation

Matthew gives no information about Jesus' life from the time of his family's settling in Nazareth (2:22–23) to the appearance of John the Baptist, a gap of approximately thirty years (Luke 3:1, 23). Although he starts his account of Jesus' adult career (3:1–4:25) at exactly the same point as Mark (1:1–13), Matthew edits Mark's baptism narrative to emphasize Jesus' superiority to John and to avoid any implication that Jesus needed forgiveness of previous sins (3:1–17). (See figures 8.1 and 8.2 for two distinctly different interpretations of the young Jesus.)

THE TEMPTATION

Mark (1:12–13) briefly alludes to Satan's tempting Jesus, but Matthew expands the scene to include a dramatic dialog between Jesus and the Evil One

Figure 8.1 *The Holy Family.* In depicting Jesus, Mary, and Joseph as indigenous Americans, the twentieth-century painter Fr. John B. Giuliani emphasizes both the archetypal sacredness of the family and the tradition of spirituality attained by pre-Columbian peoples of North America. (© Fr. John Guiliani. Used with permission of Bridge Building Images, P.O. Box 1048, Burlington, VT 05402)

(4:1–11). Whether he is viewed as an objective reality or a metaphor standing for human failure to obey God, Matthew's Satan attempts to deflect Jesus from the true course of his messiahship.

As Matthew and Luke (4:1–13) present it, the confrontation with Satan serves to clarify Jesus' concept of his messianic role. Representing false notions of the Messiah, Satan prefaces his first two challenges with the phrase "If you are the Son of God," a mean-spirited attempt to capitalize on any doubts that the human Jesus may have experienced about his origins or his future authority as God's agent. The first temptation deals with Jesus' personal hunger. Satan calls for Jesus to test the extent of his miraculous power by turning stones into bread, a ploy Jesus refutes by quoting the Torah principle that one lives spiritually on the word of God (Deut. 8:3). Some modern commentators have suggested that Jesus thereby rejects the temptation to undertake a messiahship exclusively focused on material good works, although he makes feeding the hungry and destitute an important part of his ministry.

The second temptation is a profound challenge to Jesus' consciousness of his own messianic identity. "If you are the Son of God," Satan demands, show that you can fulfill the terms of Psalm 91, a poem that unconditionally asserts that God will save from all harm the man he has chosen.

> For you the LORD [Yahweh] is a safe retreat;
> you have made the Most High your refuge.
> No disaster shall befall you,
> no calamity shall come upon your home.
> For he [Yahweh] has charged his angels
>   to guard you wherever you go,
>   to lift you on their hands
> for fear you should strike your foot
> against a stone. (Ps. 91:9–12)

The poem continues to reassure God's favorite that Yahweh will "lift him beyond danger" and "rescue him and bring him to honour" (Ps. 91:14–16). In Matthew's time, many Jews must have pointed out to Christians that Jesus' death on the cross was entirely contrary to the promises of divine protection given in this well-known psalm. In Matthew 4:6, the Devil quotes this scripture, and Jesus counters this "demonic" use of the Bible by citing the general Torah principle of not putting God to the test (Deut. 6:16).

the Messiah, who will not impose his rule by cruelty and violence. Satan is not to be "worshiped" by imitating his methods.

First Major Discourse: The Sermon on the Mount

In the temptation scene (4:1–11), Matthew shows Jesus repudiating some of the functions then popularly associated with the Messiah. In the Sermon on the Mount (chs. 5–7), Matthew demonstrates how radically different Jesus' concept of this messiahship is from the popular expectation of a conquering warrior-king. This long discourse, in which Jesus takes his seat on a Galilean hill, reminding the reader of Moses seated on Mount Sinai, is the New Testament's most extensive collection of Jesus' teachings and admonitions. Matthew's "sermon" is not the record of a single historical speech by Jesus, but a compilation of Jesus' sayings from several different sources. Some of the same teachings appear in Luke's Sermon on the Plain, the third Gospel's equivalent version of the discourse (Luke 6:17–7:1). Matthew collects the sayings in one place (5:1–8:1); Luke scatters them throughout his Gospel narrative (see box 9.3).

Matthew opens the discourse with a collection of **Beatitudes** ("blessings" or "happinesses"), assertions that certain classes of people—the sorrowful, the peacemakers, the hungry, the persecuted—uniquely enjoy divine favor. Jesus' statements significantly challenge assumptions typical of some Old Testament thought. Deuteronomy and Proverbs had argued that material prosperity and earthly success were signs of God's approval, whereas poverty and suffering were evidence of divine punishment. In the Beatitudes, Jesus reverses these traditional views, affirming that Israel's God takes the part of those suffering grief or loss.

Although Matthew presents Jesus as a staunch upholder of the Mosaic Torah, he is aware that other churches—primarily those established by Paul, who declared Christianity's independence of the Law covenant (see chapter 15)—do not share this conviction. Conceding that such nonobservant

Figure 8.2 This "Good Shepherd" is an early Christian painting of Christ on the ceiling of a crypt in the catacombs of St. Priscilla in Rome. Note that the artist pictures Jesus in a pose that would be familiar to a Greco-Roman audience. Like earlier renditions of Apollo, the Greek god of prophecy, intellect, music, and shepherds, the youthful Jesus carries a lamb on his shoulders to demonstrate his concern for his human flock. Compare John 10:1–18, Matthew 18:12–14, and Luke 15:4–7. (Courtesy of Benedettine Di Priscilla)

In a third and final attempt to subvert Jesus' understanding of his messianic role, Satan offers him worldly power on a vastly grander scale than King David, the Messiah's prototype, had enjoyed. All Jesus must do in return is "pay homage" to Satan, a demand that Jesus recognizes as undermining the essence of Judaism's commitment to one God (Deut. 6:13). A thousand years earlier, David had gained his kingdom through war and bloodshed, a procedure that Matthew recognizes as unsuitable to

believers are still part of "the kingdom of Heaven" (a term Matthew sometimes applies to the Church), the author nonetheless regards them as ranking below Torah loyalists:

> If any man therefore sets aside even the least of the Law's demands, and teaches others to do the same, he will have the lowest place in the kingdom of Heaven, whereas anyone who keeps the Law, and teaches others so, will stand high in the kingdom of Heaven. (Matt. 5:19)

THE ANTITHESES

To Matthew, Jesus gives the Torah renewed vitality by asking followers to go beyond mere obedience and to cultivate an inner grace that excels the old Mosaic requirements. The author shows Jesus illustrating the Torah's eternal validity in the six **antitheses,** a series of rhetorical statements in which Jesus formally contrasts opposing ideas in similar or parallel verbal structures. Matthew typically begins a statement with the declaration "you have learned that our forefathers were told" and balances it with Jesus' contrasting "but what I tell you is this: . . ." In this part of the sermon, Jesus contrasts Torah commandments with new interpretations based exclusively on his own personal authority: "You have learned that they [the biblical Israelites] were told 'Eye for eye, tooth for tooth.' But what I tell you is this: Do not set yourself against the man who wrongs you. If someone slaps you on the right cheek, turn and offer him your left" (5:38–39).

The *lex talionis,* or law of retaliation, that Jesus quotes is central to the Mosaic concept of justice and appears in three different Torah books (Exod. 21:23–25; Lev. 24:19–20; Deut. 19:21). Matthew's Jesus explicitly repudiates the concept, insisting that his people give up the power to avenge personal wrongs. Instead, the victim of wrongdoing is asked to surrender whatever an enemy wants to take. Although critics have accused Jesus of instituting a "slave morality" in which the strong exploit the weak, his intention may have been to end the cycle of retaliatory justice that can blight individual lives and entire nations alike.

In the final antithesis and its accompanying commentary (5:43–48), Jesus contrasts the command to love one's neighbor (Lev. 19:18) with the assumption that it is permissible to hate an enemy. Again, he demands a "higher righteousness" that surpasses mere legal compliance in order to encompass both friend and stranger in God-like love (5:43–45). Jesus urges his listeners to put no limit, legal or doctrinal, on their goodwill or affection because "there must be no limit to your goodness, as your heavenly Father's goodness knows no bounds" (5:48). Believers must imitate the heavenly Parent, who sends rain and sun to all, regardless of merit. Seeking first the kingdom (6:33) requires submission to these divine principles of beneficence.

JESUS' AUTHORITY

The sermon ends with Jesus' parable about the advantages of building one's life firmly on the rock of his teachings (7:24–27), after which, Matthew reports, the crowds "were astounded" because "unlike their own teachers he taught with a note of [his personal] authority" (7:28). Note that Matthew's phrase "when Jesus had finished this discourse," or a variation thereof, marks the conclusion of the four other blocks of teaching material in his Gospel (11:1; 13:53; 19:1; 26:1).

First Narrative Section: Ten Miracles

In the first long narrative section of his Gospel (8:1–9:38), based largely on Mark, Matthew concentrates on depicting Jesus' miraculous healings and exorcisms. To Mark's account of the cleansing of a leper (Mark 1:40–45), Matthew adds the story of a **centurion,** a Roman army officer in charge of 100 infantrymen (8:5–13; also Luke 7:1–10). Notice that Matthew connects this episode with references to the practice of converting Gentiles that existed in the author's own day. After expressing Jesus' astonishment that the Gentile soldier reveals a faith stronger than that of any Israelite, the author makes his point: non-Jews like the centurion will come to feast with Abraham and the other patriarchs, and Jews, once the favored people, will be left outside. Throughout his Gospel, Matthew pictures the Christian community as the "new Israel," replacing the old, which lost its privileges because it failed to recognize Jesus as the Messiah.

Second Major Discourse: Instructions to the Twelve Apostles

In his second major collection of ethical teaching, Matthew presents Jesus' instructions to the twelve chief disciples (listed by name in 10:2–4). Notice that the Twelve are sent exclusively to Jews and forbidden to preach to Gentiles or Samaritans (10:5–6), an injunction found only in Matthew. (By contrast, both Luke and John show Jesus leading his disciples on a brief Samaritan campaign [Luke 9:52–56; John 4:3–42].) The Twelve are to preach the kingdom's imminent appearance, the same apocalyptic message that the author attributes to both the Baptist (3:2) and Jesus at the outset of his career (4:17). While healing the sick, cleansing lepers, and raising the dead—thus replicating Jesus' spectacular miracles—the disciples are to expect hostility and persecution. This extended warning (10:16–26) seems to apply to conditions that existed in the author's generation, rather than in the time of Jesus' Galilean ministry. Matthew's apparent practice of combining Jesus' remembered words with commentary relating them to later experiences of the Christian community is typical of all the Gospel writers.

A strong eschatological tone pervades the entire discourse. Followers are to be loyal at the time of testing because destruction in Gehenna awaits the unfaithful. The New Testament name for a geographical location, the **"Valley of Hinnom,"** Gehenna is commonly rendered as "hell" in English translations, although it is uncertain that the later Christian notion of a metaphysical place of punishment accurately expresses the original meaning of Gehenna (see box 8.5). A site of human sacrifice in Old Testament times (Jer. 7:32; 1 Kings 11:7; etc.),

the Valley of Hinnom later housed a garbage dump that was kept permanently burning, a literal place of annihilation for "both soul and body" (Matt. 10:28; 18:8; 25:30, 46; etc.).

Equally arresting is the statement that before the Twelve have completed their circuit of Palestine "the Son of Man will have come" (10:23). Writing more than half a century after the events he describes, Matthew surprisingly retains a prophecy that was not fulfilled, at least not in historical fact. The author's inclusion of this apocalyptic prediction indicates that he may not have understood it literally. Matthew may have regarded the "Son of Man" as already spiritually present in the missionary activity of the Church. If so, this suggests that many of Matthew's other references to "the end of the age" and Jesus' Parousia (chs. 24 and 25) are also to be understood metaphorically.

Second Narrative Section: Questions and Controversies

JESUS AND JOHN THE BAPTIST

Matthew opens his second extended narrative (11:1–12:50) by discussing the relationship of Jesus to John the Baptist, whose fate foreshadows that of Jesus. Locked in Herod Antipas's prison and doomed to imminent martyrdom, John writes to inquire if Jesus is really God's chosen one (11:2–3). The Baptist's question contrasts strangely with his earlier proclamation of Jesus' high status (3:11–15) and may reflect a later competition between the disciples of Jesus and John in Matthew's day.

Matthew uses the incident to place the two prophets' roles in perspective, highlighting Jesus' superiority. Without answering John's question directly, Jesus summarizes his miracles of healing that suggest God's presence in his work (11:4–6). Matthew then contrasts the function and style of the two men, emphasizing Jesus' far greater role. Although John is the "destined Elijah" whose return to earth was to inaugurate the time of Final Judgment, he does not share in the "kingdom."

Box 8.5
Matthew's Use of Hell: Some Biblical Concepts of the Afterlife

The term that many English-language Bibles translate as "hell" is Gehenna (*gē hinnōm*) (Matt. 5:22, 29–30; 10:28; 23:15, 33), which originally referred not to a place of posthumous torment but to a specific geographical location, a ravine near Jerusalem. A valley bordering Israel's capital city on the southwest, Gehenna was named for the "sons of Hinnom (*gē ben(e) hinnōm*)," the biblical designation of an ancient Canaanite group that occupied the site before King David captured it about 1000 B.C.E. Gehenna had an evil reputation as the place where humans were sacrificed and burned as offerings to false gods, a practice that Israelite prophets vehemently condemned (Jer. 7:31; 19:11; 32:35; cf. 2 Kings 23:10; 2 Chron. 28:3; 33:5).

In time, perhaps influenced by Persian ideas about afterlife punishments in fire, some Jewish writers made Hinnom's valley (Gehenna) the symbol of God's eschatological judgment, where the wicked would suffer after death (1 Enoch 26:4; 27:2–3). A potent image of alienation from God, the earthly Gehenna was eventually associated with mythical concepts of an Underworld "lake of fire," the future abode of unrepentant sinners (2 Esd. 7:36; Rev. 20).

SHEOL AND HADES

The concept of eternal punishment does not occur in the Hebrew Bible, which uses the term **Sheol** to designate a bleak subterranean region where the dead, good and bad alike, subsist only as impotent shadows. When Hellenistic Jewish scribes rendered the Bible into Greek, they used the word Hades to translate Sheol, bringing a whole new mythological association to the idea of posthumous existence. In ancient Greek

myth, Hades, named after the gloomy deity who ruled over it, was originally similar to the Hebrew Sheol, a dark place underground in which all the dead, regardless of individual merit, were indiscriminately housed (see Homer's *Odyssey,* Book 11). By the Hellenistic period, however, Hades had become compartmentalized into separate regions: These included Elysium, a paradise for the virtuous, and Tartarus, a place of punishment for the wicked. Influenced by philosophers such as Pythagoras and Plato and the Orphic mystery religions (see chapter 3), Greek religious thought eventually posited a direct connection between people's behavior in this life and their destiny in the next: Good actions earned them bliss, whereas injustices brought fearful penalties.

HELL

Popular concepts of Hell derive from a variety of sources extending back in time to the earliest Mesopotamian and Egyptian speculations about the terrors of the next world. Although absent from the Hebrew Bible and most of the New Testament, a few scattered references to the concept (primarily involving Gehenna or a fiery lake) appear in the Synoptic Gospels and Revelation, as well as some noncanonical Jewish and Christian books, such as 1 and 2 Enoch and the Apocalypse of Peter. In general, pre-Christian mythologies and other extra-biblical sources supply most of the frightening imagery for such celebrated literary works as Dante's *Inferno* and Milton's *Paradise Lost,* as well as the "hellfire" sermons of many Puritan divines and their modern successors. The word itself, not found in the Bible, commemorates *Hel,* the fierce Norse goddess who reigned over the netherworld.

Perhaps because Matthew sees John operating independently of Jesus, he does not consider him a Christian. (Box 8.6 indicates the four Gospel authors' strikingly different views of John's role.)

John is a wild and solitary figure; Jesus is gregarious, friendly with Israel's outcasts, prostitutes, and "sinners." Enjoying food and wine with socially unrespectable people, Jesus provokes critics who accuse him of gluttony and overdrinking (11:7–19).

In Matthew's evaluation, neither John nor Jesus, representing two very different approaches to the religious life, can win the fickle public's approval.

HARSH SAYINGS

At the same time that he presents Jesus performing works of mercy and forgiveness (11:28–30), Matthew also includes harsh sayings very similar to

Box 8.6

John the Baptist as the Eschatological Elijah Figure

MATTHEW

"He is the man of whom Scripture says,

'Here is my herald, whom I send on ahead of you, and he will prepare your way before you.'

I tell you this: never has there appeared on earth a mother's son greater than John the Baptist, and yet the least in the kingdom of Heaven is greater than he.

"Ever since the coming of John the Baptist the kingdom of Heaven has been subject to violence and violent men are seizing it. For all the prophets and the Law foretold things to come until John appeared, and John is the destined Elijah, if you will but accept it. If you have ears, then hear." (Matt. 11:10–14)

MARK

[Popular speculations about John's return to life after his beheading by Herod Antipas:]
Now King Herod heard of it [Jesus' miracles], for the fame of Jesus had spread; and people were saying, "John the Baptist has been raised to life, and that is why these miraculous powers are at work in him." Others said, "It is Elijah." (Mark 6:14–15)

LUKE

"He is the man of whom Scripture says,

'Here is my herald, whom I send on ahead of you, and he will prepare your way before you.'

I tell you, there is not a mother's son greater than John, and yet the least in the kingdom of God is greater than he." (Luke 7:27–28)

"Until John, it was the Law and the prophets; since then, there is the good news of the kingdom of God, and everyone forces his way in." (Luke 16:16)

JOHN

This is the testimony which John gave when the Jews of Jerusalem sent a deputation of priests and Levites to ask him who he was. He confessed without reserve and avowed, "I am not the Messiah." "What then? are you Elijah?" "No," he replied. "Are you the prophet whom we await?" He answered "No."* "Then who are you?" they asked. "We must give an answer to those who sent us. What account do you give of yourself?" He answered in the words of the prophet Isaiah: "I am a voice crying aloud in the wilderness, 'Make the Lord's highway straight.'" (John 1:19–23)

*Note that John's Gospel denies the Baptist the roles of prophet and latter-day Elijah that the Synoptics accorded him.

---

the denunciations and threats of divine judgment uttered by the Baptist. When the towns of Chorazin and Bethsaida fail to repent after witnessing Jesus' miracles there, Jesus makes a sweeping statement that **Sodom,** which Yahweh destroyed by fire, would fare better on Judgment Day than they (11:20–24). Castigating his opponents as poisonous snakes, Jesus (12:33–37) seems to violate his own principles outlined in the Sermon on the Mount.

Third Major Discourse: Parables on the Kingdom

Matthew frames Jesus' third discourse with his version of Jesus' alienation from his family (12:46–50; Mark 3:31–35) and Jesus' rejection by the citizens of Nazareth (13:54–58; Mark 6:1–6). The author divides Jesus' parable teachings into two distinct episodes: the first public, the second private

(13:10–23). Notice that although only the Twelve are initiated into the secrets of God's rule, Matthew softens Mark's explanation of Jesus' reasons for speaking in parables. Instead of using figures of speech to prevent understanding (Mark 4:11–12), Matthew states that Jesus speaks metaphorically *because* most people have the wrong attitude and unconsciously shut their mental eyes and ears (13:11–15; Isa. 6:9–10). Note also that Matthew's version of the parable lesson explicitly states that the Twelve do understand and appreciate Jesus' teaching (13:16–17, 51–52), thus eliminating Mark's view of the disciples' chronic stupidity.

IMAGES OF THE KINGDOM

To Mark's original collection of kingdom parables, Matthew adds several comparisons in which the kingdom is likened to a buried treasure, a priceless pearl, a harvest of fish, and a field in which both grain and "darnel [weeds]" grow (13:24–30, 36–50). The last two introduce a distinctly Matthean concept: The kingdom (church) consists of a mixture of good and bad elements that will not be separated completely until the last day. The same theme reappears in Matthew's version of the parable about ungrateful guests (22:1–13; cf. Luke 14:16–23).

Third Narrative Section: From the Rejection in Nazareth to the Transfiguration

Matthew's third narrative section (13:53–17:27) slightly revises many incidents related in Mark's Gospel. Recounting Jesus' rejection by his fellow citizens of Nazareth, Matthew subtly modifies Mark's older account, calling Jesus "the carpenter's son" rather than the Markan "son of Mary" (Mark 6:3) and changing Mark's statement that Jesus "could work no miracle there" (Mark 6:5) to "did not work many miracles there" (13:54–58) (see box 8.2).

With minor changes, Matthew also follows Mark closely in his account of the Baptist's execu-

tion, the miraculous feeding of 5000 people, and the stilling of the Galilean storm (14:1–27; Mark 6:14–52). Note that Matthew's editing of this part of the Markan narrative entails a major change in Mark's order of events. The episode in which Jesus sends the Twelve on a missionary journey (Mark 6:7–13) does not appear in Matthew's third narrative section because he has already incorporated it into his version of Jesus' instructions to the Twelve (ch. 10). Matthew also revises other Markan passages dealing with the disciples. He embellishes Mark's account of Jesus' striding across the Sea of Galilee by adding that Peter also attempted to walk on water. More significantly, Matthew deletes Mark's reference to the disciples' "closed" minds, or "hard-heartedness," and replaces it with their positive recognition of Jesus as "Son of God" (14:28–33; Mark 6:52). He further modifies Mark's theme of the disciples' obtuseness by insisting that the Twelve fully comprehend the miracle of loaves and fishes (15:5–12; Mark 8:1–21). Most of these revisions to Mark's account—especially Matthew's deletion of Mark's criticisms of the Twelve—serve to enhance the disciples' role and reputation.

Describing Jesus' dispute with the Pharisees over ritual hand washing (taken from Mark 7:1–23), Matthew gives the debate a meaning significantly different from that in his Markan source. In Mark, the episode's climax is reached when the author interprets Jesus' words to mean that all foods are clean, including those the Torah forbids Jews to eat (7:19). Believing that Torah prohibitions remain in effect, Matthew drops Mark's climactic interpretation (15:1–11).

PETER AND THE CHURCH

One of Matthew's most celebrated additions to Mark's narrative appears in his version of Peter's recognition of Jesus' identity (16:13–29). Matthew's Peter not only confesses Jesus as the Messiah but identifies him as the Son of God (an element absent in Mark). Jesus' declaration that Peter is the rock upon which Jesus will build his Church appears only in Matthew, as does the promise to award Peter spiritual powers that are honored in heaven and on earth. Matthew's Jesus, however, makes no provision for the transmission of ecclesiastical authority to Peter's successors.

Despite his singling Peter out as foremost among the apostles ("ones sent out [by Jesus]"), Matthew retains Mark's tradition that Peter fundamentally misunderstands the nature of Jesus' messiahship. When Peter attempts to dissuade Jesus from a decision that will lead to his death in Jerusalem, Jesus again ironically addresses the apostle as "Satan" (16:21–23).

Fourth Major Discourse: Instructions to the Church

In chapter 18, Matthew assembles disparate sayings of Jesus and applies them to the Christian community of the writer's generation. Taken together, chapters 10 and 18 form a rudimentary instruction manual for the early Church. The author skillfully combines numerous small literary units to achieve his intended effect. A brief glimpse of the disciples' squabbling for power (18:1–2) introduces opposing images of a powerless child and a drowning man (18:2–7), which are quickly followed by pictures of self-blinding and the flames of Gehenna (18:8–9). The variety of literary forms gathered here makes the author's prescription for an ideal Christian community intensely vivid. The writer's devices include hyperbole (exaggeration for rhetorical effect) parable (the lost sheep and the unforgiving debtor [18:12–14, 23–35]), advice on supervising troublesome people (18:15–17); prophetic promises (18:10, 18–20), and direct commands (18:22). In Matthew's view of the Church, service, humility, and endless forgiveness are the measure of leadership. Practicing the spirit of Torah mercy, the Church is the earthly expression of divine rule (18:23–35), a visible manifestation of the kingdom.

Note that Matthew gives the individual "congregation" the right to exclude or ostracize disobedient members (18:15–17). During later centuries, this power of *excommunication* was to become a formi-

dable weapon in controlling both belief and behavior. Notice also that the same authority accorded Peter in Jesus' famous "keys of the kingdom" speech (16:16–20) is also given to individual congregation leaders (18:18).

Fourth Narrative Section: The Jerusalem Ministry

In this long narrative sequence (19:1–22:46), Matthew arranges several dialogs between Jesus and his opponents, interspersed with incidents on the journey south from Galilee to Jerusalem. The section opens with "some Pharisees" challenging Jesus on the matter of divorce. In Mark's version of the encounter, Jesus revokes the Torah provisions for divorce and forbids remarriage (Mark 10:1–12). Matthew modifies the prohibition, stating that "unchastity" or sexual unfaithfulness provides grounds for lawful divorce (19:3–9). He also adds a discussion with the disciples in which Jesus mentions several reasons for not marrying, including a commitment to remain single for "the kingdom" (19:10–12).

DISCIPLESHIP AND SUFFERING

After the third prediction of Jesus' impending death in Jerusalem (20:17–19), Matthew again stresses that suffering must precede the disciples' heavenly reward, as it does Jesus'. In Mark, the sons of Zebedee, James and John, directly ask Jesus for positions of honor in his kingdom, presumably to satisfy personal ambition (Mark 10:35–40). In Matthew's version of the episode, it is the apostles' mother who makes the request on their behalf (20:20–21). (Note that Jesus had already promised his followers that he would share his heavenly rule with them [19:27–29].) The prediction that the two sons of Zebedee will follow their leader to a martyr's death indicates that Matthew writes after both apostles had died (20:23). According to Acts (12:1–2), James was beheaded by **Herod Agrippa I,** who reigned as king of Judea 41–44 C.E. It may be that John was similarly executed at about that time.

ENTRANCE INTO JERUSALEM

Matthew prepares his readers for the significance of Jesus' Jerusalem experience by prefacing his account with a miracle found only in his Gospel. After Jesus restores sight to two blind men, they immediately become his followers—in contrast to the "blind" guides of Jerusalem (20:29–34). The author's determination to show that Jesus' actions match biblical prophecy in every detail causes him to create a somewhat grotesque picture of his hero's entrance into the holy city. Matthew quotes Zechariah's prophecy about the Messiah's arrival in full and inserts an additional phrase from Isaiah. However, he apparently misunderstands Zechariah's poetic use of parallelism. In Zechariah's poetic structure, "the foal of a beast of burden" on which the Messiah rides is parallel to and synonymous with the prophet's reference to "an ass" (Zech. 9:9; Isa. 62:11). To make Jesus' action precisely fit his concept of the prophecy, Matthew has Jesus mount not one but two animals simultaneously, "the donkey and her foal," for his triumphant ride into Jerusalem (21:1–11).

In his account of Jesus' Jerusalem ministry, Matthew generally adheres to Mark's narrative, although he adds some new material and edits Mark, usually to enhance his portrait of Jesus. After driving the moneychangers from the Temple, Jesus heals some blind men and cripples (21:14), miracles absent in Mark. During this brief period, Jesus is repeatedly hailed as "Son of David," one of Matthew's chief designations for his hero (1:1; 20:30; 21:9, 16). Matthew reproduces many of the Markan debates between Jesus and Jewish Torah experts on matters of paying taxes to Rome (22:16–22), the resurrection (22:23–33), and the law of love (22:34–40). However, he significantly edits Mark's report on Jesus' encounter with a friendly Torah instructor (Mark 12:28–34). Whereas Mark states that this congenial exchange prevented further attacks on Jesus, Matthew transfers Mark's comment to the conclusion of Jesus' re-

marks about the Messiah as David's "son" (22:46; Mark 12:35). Matthew has only harsh words for the Jerusalem authorities and declines to show Jesus on good terms with rival Jewish teachers.

THE CHURCH REPLACES ISRAEL

While studying Matthew's account of Jesus' last days, readers will discover that most of the author's changes and additions to Mark serve to express his extreme hostility toward Jewish leaders. In the author's bitter view, prostitutes and criminals stand a better chance of winning divine approval than do the Temple priests, Pharisees, or their associates (21:31).

Notice that the three parables that Matthew inserts into the Markan narrative serve to condemn the Jewish establishment. In the parable of the two sons, the disobedient youth represents Judaism (21:28–32). In a second parable, the "wicked tenants" who kill a landlord's son are the Jerusalem officials who reject Jesus (21:42–46). To Matthew, the vineyard owner's transfer of his estate to more deserving tenants means that God has abandoned Israel and adopted the Church as his new chosen people.

Matthew replays the same theme in the parable featuring guests who ungratefully ignore their invitations to a wedding party (the messianic banquet). Matthew's statement that the outraged host then burns down the ingrates' city (a rather excessive reaction) probably refers to the Romans' burning Jerusalem in 70 C.E. As in the wicked tenant parable, newcomers replace the formerly chosen group—the Church takes Israel's place (22:1–10).

Fifth Major Discourse: Warnings of Final Judgment

This fifth and final block of teaching material summarizes the Matthean Jesus' adverse judgment on Jerusalem, particularly its Temple and religious hierarchy (chs. 23–25). It opens with a blistering denunciation of the scribes and Pharisees—professional transmitters and interpreters of the law—upon whom Jesus is pictured as heaping **"seven woes,"** perhaps corresponding to the curses on a disobedient Israel listed in Deuteronomy 28. According to Matthew, Jesus blames the Pharisees and their associates for every guilty act—every drop of innocent blood poured out—in Israel's entire history. He condemns the religious leadership to suffer for their generation's collective wrongdoing, as well as that of their distant ancestors.

Matthew implies that the Roman devastation of Jerusalem in 70 C.E., an event that occurred during the author's lifetime, is tangible proof of God's wrath toward Israel (23:35–36). Matthew intensifies this theme in his version of Jesus' trial before Pilate (ch. 27); note that Matthew represents a Jerusalem crowd demanding the Messiah's crucifixion, hysterically inviting the Deity to avenge Jesus' blood upon them and their children (27:25). Matthew edits Mark's Passion narrative by adding that Pilate, symbol of imperial Rome, washed his hands of responsibility for Jesus' death—even while ordering Jesus' execution (27:24). All four Gospel writers shift the blame from the Roman government to the Jewish leadership, but only Matthew extends responsibility to the Jews' as-yet-unborn descendants.

Many commentators find an ethical paradox in Matthew's vindictive attitude toward his fellow Jews who did not accept Jesus as the national Messiah. Earlier in his Gospel, Matthew presents Jesus as repudiating the *lex talionis* (5:38–40), stressing instead the necessity of practicing infinite forgiveness (6:12, 14–16; 18: 21–35) and exercising mercy (5:7). In dealing with his church's opponents, however, Matthew judges without compassion, apparently regarding Jewish rejection of his Messiah as falling beyond the tolerable limits of charity. The author, in effect, reintroduces the old law of retaliation that Jesus himself rejected. Historically, the consequences of New Testament writers attributing collective guilt to the Jewish people helped fuel the waves of anti-Semitism that repeatedly swept through the Western world for centuries afterward. Throughout Europe, Jews were indiscriminately persecuted as "Christ-killers," often with the blessing of ecclesiastical authorities.

Since the Holocaust of World War II, when Nazi Germany led a campaign of genocide against European Jews, killing approximately 6 million men, women, and children, a number of church leaders—Catholic, Protestant, and Greek Orthodox—have publicly condemned the practice of anti-Semitism. In 1974, the Roman Catholic Church officially reminded Christendom that modern Jews are not responsible for Jesus' crucifixion.

To place Matthew's negative verdict on the first-century Jewish establishment in historical perspective, we must remember that he condemns only the Jerusalem leadership, not Judaism itself. Despite his dislike of Pharisaic customs, the author agrees with Pharisaic teaching. He reminds his readers to "pay attention to their words" and "do what they tell you," for they occupy "the seat of Moses" and their teachings are authoritative (23:1–3).

THE FALL OF JERUSALEM AND THE PAROUSIA

Signs of the Times The second part of Jesus' fifth discourse is based largely on Mark 13, the prediction of Jerusalem's impending destruction. Whereas Mark states that the disciples asked only about when the Temple would fall (Mark 13:1–4), Matthew expands the disciples' question to include an eschatological inquiry into Jesus' Second Coming (the Parousia) and the "end of the age," the End of human history as we know it (24:1–3). Jesus' reply is a good illustration of how first-century Jewish eschatology was incorporated into the Christian tradition.

Matthew's presentation of the "signal" or "signs" leading to Jesus' return is a complex mixture of first-century historical events, such as the Jewish War, and prophetic images from the Hebrew Bible, particularly Daniel, Joel, Zechariah, and the pseudepigraphical 1 Enoch. All three Synoptic writers link the Jewish revolt against Rome (66–73 C.E.) with supernatural portents of End time and Jesus' reappearance. Mark, the first to make this association of events, seems to have written at a period when the revolt had already begun (note the "battles" and "wars" in 13:7–8) and Jerusalem was about to fall. These cataclysmic events he called "the birth pangs of the new age." Both Matthew and Luke follow Mark's lead and connect these political upheavals with persecution of believers, perhaps allusions to Nero's cruel assault on Roman Christians (c. 64–65 C.E.) or Zealot violence against Jewish Christians who refused to support the revolt. The Synoptic authors concur that attacks on the Church, then a tiny minority of the Greco-Roman population, are of critical importance. The sufferings of the Christian community will bring God's vengeance on all humanity.

Matthew follows Mark in referring to the mysterious "abomination of desolation" as a warning to flee Judea (24:15), perhaps echoing a tradition that Jewish Christians had escaped destruction by leaving the holy city and seeking refuge in Pella, east of Jordan (see box 7.6). In his version of Mark's eschatological prediction, however, Luke omits the "abomination" sign and substitutes an allusion to Roman armies besieging Jerusalem (Luke 21:20–24).

Both Mark and Matthew are aware that in the white heat of eschatological expectation there were "many" false reports of the Messiah's return (Mark 13:21–23; Matt. 24:23–27). Some Christians must have experienced crushing disappointment when their prophets' "inspired" predictions of Jesus' reappearance failed to materialize. Thus, both Evangelists caution that even "the Son" does not know the exact date of the Parousia (Mark 13:32; Matt. 24:36). Matthew adds that when the Son does return, his coming will be unmistakable in its universality, "like lightning from the east, flashing as far as the west" (24:27).

Matthew preserves the "double-vision" nature of the Parousia found in Mark. Jesus' supernatural coming will be preceded by unmistakable "signs" that it is near (24:21–22, 29–35); at the same time, he will come without warning and when least expected (24:42–44). Although contradictory, both concepts apparently existed concurrently in the early church, which was deeply influenced by eschatological thinking.

Although the author of Revelation connects End time with cosmic catastrophe, other New Testament writers (perhaps aware of the repeated failure of attempts to calculate the date of the Parousia) stress that the Son's return is essentially unheralded (1 Thess. 5:1–5; 2 Peter 3:10).

Matthew probably wrote about two decades after Mark's Gospel was composed, but he retains the Markan tradition that persons who knew Jesus would live to see his predictions come true (24:34; Mark 13:30). To Matthew, the Roman annihilation of the Jewish state, which coincided with the emergence of the Christian church as an entity distinct from Judaism, may essentially have fulfilled Jesus' words, or at least an important part of his prophecy. From the writer's perspective, the "New Age" had already dawned with God's overthrow of Israel and the church's new and decisive role in future human history (28:19–20).

Parables of Jesus' Return   Chapters 24 and 25 contain three parables and a prophetic vision of Jesus' unannounced Parousia. Whatever their original meaning to Jesus, in Matthew they serve to illustrate believers' obligation to await faithfully and patiently their absent Lord's return. The first parable contrasts two servants, one of whom abuses his fellow employees until the master suddenly reappears to execute him (24:45–51)—a clear warning to church members to treat others honorably. The parable about a delayed bridegroom similarly contrasts two kinds of believers, those who are alert and prepared for the wedding event and those who are not. Note that the "bridegroom" is "late in coming," a hint that Christians must reconcile themselves to a delay in the Parousia (25:1–13).

The parable of the talents, in which a master's servants invest huge sums of money for him, emphasizes the necessary growth and productivity of the church during its Lord's prolonged absence (25:14–30). Once again, the servants—the master's Church—are unexpectedly called to account, in this case to demonstrate that they have significantly increased the value of the treasure entrusted to them.

The fourth and final judgment parable concerns not only the Church but also "the nations." The

Figure 8.3 *Christ Separating Sheep from Goats.* This early sixth-century mosaic illustrates Matthew's parable of eschatological judgment (Matt. 25:31–46). At his Parousia (Second Coming), an enthroned Jesus, flanked by two angels, divides all humanity into two mutually exclusive groups. The sheep are gathered in the favored position at Jesus' right hand, whereas the goats, at Jesus' left, are condemned to outer darkness for their failure to help others. (© Hirmer Fotoarchiv)

term *nations* refers primarily to Gentiles living without the Mosaic Law, but it may be intended to include all humanity—Jewish, Christian, and those belonging to other world religions as well. In the parable about separating worthy "sheep" and unworthy "goats," all are judged exclusively on their behavior toward Jesus' "little ones," Matthew's favored term for Christian disciples (25:31–46) (see figure 8.3).

Matthew's eschatological vision makes charitable acts, rather than "correct" religious doctrines, the standard of distinguishing good people from bad. In such passages, Matthew reflects the ancient Israelite prophets who regarded service to the poor

and unfortunate as acts of worship to God. The Book of James, which defines true religion as essentially humanitarian service to others (James 1:27), espouses a similar view.

Author's Purpose in the Judgment Parables By adding the four parables of judgment to his expansion of Mark 13 and by linking them to "the kingdom" (25:1, 14), Matthew shifts the apocalyptic emphasis from expectations about the Parousia to the function and duties of the Church. Note that Matthew places the parables of the alert householder, the trustworthy servant, and the talents among Jesus' predictions of the *eschaton.* By contrast,

Luke, who uses the same parables, places them among the general teachings of Jesus' pre-Jerusalem ministry (cf. Matt. 24:43–44 with Luke 12:39–40; Matt. 24:45–51 with Luke 12:42–46; and Matt. 25:14–30 with Luke 19:12–27).

Fifth and Final Narrative Section: The Passion Story and Resurrection

Matthew retells the story of Jesus' last two days on earth (Thursday and Friday of Holy Week) with the same grave and solemn tone we find in Mark. To the Gospel writers, Jesus of Nazareth's suffering, death, and resurrection are not only the most important events in world history but also the crucial turning point in humanity's relation to God. Although Matthew's Passion narrative (26:1–28:20) closely follows Mark's sequence of events, he adds a few new details, probably drawn from the oral tradition of his community. The treachery of Judas Iscariot is emphasized and linked to the fulfillment of a passage in Jeremiah, although the relevant text actually appears in Zechariah (Matt. 26:14–15; 20–25, 47–50; 27:3–10; Jer. 32:6–13; Zech. 11:12–13). The theme of a warning dream, used frequently in the birth story, is reintroduced when Pilate's wife, frightened by a dream about Jesus, urges her husband to "have nothing to do with that innocent man" (27:19).

MIRACULOUS SIGNS

To stress that the very foundations of the world are shaken by the supreme crime of crucifying God's son, Matthew reports that an earthquake accompanies Jesus' last moment and triggers a resurrection of the dead (27:50–53), an eschatological phenomenon usually associated with the Final Judgment. Although the author presumably includes the incident to show that Jesus' death opens the way for humanity's rebirth, neither he nor any other New Testament writer explains what eventually happens

to the reanimated corpses that leave their graves and parade through Jerusalem.

THE CENTURION'S REACTION

Whereas Mark reports that only one Roman soldier recognizes Jesus as God's son, Matthew states that both the centurion and his men confess Jesus' divinity (27:54). Perhaps Matthew's change of a single man's exclamation to that of a whole group indicates his belief that numerous Gentiles will acknowledge Jesus as Lord.

THE EMPTY TOMB

Despite some significant differences, all three Synoptic Gospels agree fairly closely in their account of Jesus' burial and the women's discovery of the empty tomb. Matthew, however, adds details about some Pharisees persuading Pilate to dispatch Roman soldiers to guard Jesus' tomb. According to Matthew, the Pharisees are aware of Jesus' promise to rise from the grave "on the third day" and arrange for a Roman guard to prevent the disciples from stealing the body and creating the false impression that Jesus still lives. In Matthew's account, the Romans guarding the tomb on Sunday morning actually see an angel descend from heaven, a sight that paralyzes them with terror.

THE PLOT TO DISCREDIT THE RESURRECTION

After the women discover the empty gravesite and then encounter Jesus himself, some guards report what has happened to the Jerusalem priests. According to Matthew, the Sadducean priests then plot to undermine Christian claims that Jesus has risen by bribing the soldiers to say that the disciples secretly removed and hid Jesus' corpse (27:62–66; 28:11–15).

Matthew implies that Jews of his day used the soldiers' false testimony to refute Christian preaching about the Resurrection. However, his counterargument that the Roman soldiers had admitted falling asleep while on duty is not convincing.

Severe punishment, including torture and death, awaited any Roman soldier found thus derelict. In 79 C.E., only a few years before Matthew wrote, soldiers guarding the gates of Pompeii preferred being buried alive during the cataclysmic eruption of Mount Vesuvius rather than face the consequences of leaving their posts without permission. A rumor about the possible theft of Jesus' body undoubtedly circulated, but probably not for the reasons that Matthew gives.

POSTRESURRECTION APPEARANCES AND THE GREAT COMMISSION

In Mark's Gospel, Jesus promises that after his death he will reappear to the disciples in Galilee (Mark 14:28; 16:7). After recording the women's dawn encounter with the risen Lord, Matthew then reports that Jesus also appeared to the Eleven at a prearranged mountain site in Galilee. Matthew observes that some disciples had doubts about their seeing Jesus, as if mistrusting the evidence of their own senses. The author seems to imply that absolute proof of an event so contrary to ordinary human experience is impossible.

Even though some disciples doubt, all presumably accept the final command of the One whose teachings are vindicated by his resurrection to life: They, and the community of faith they represent, are to make new disciples throughout the Gentile world (28:16–20). This commission to recruit followers from "all nations" further stresses Matthew's theme that the church has much work to do before Jesus returns. It implies that the author's tiny community had only begun what was to be a vast undertaking—a labor extending into the far-distant future.

Summary

In composing a new edition of Jesus' life, Matthew provides his community with a comprehensive survey of Jesus' teaching. The unknown author, who may have lived in Antioch or some other part of Syria in the 80s C.E., was a Jewish Christian who used scribal techniques to place Jesus' life and death in the context of ancient Jewish prophecy. Writing to demonstrate that Jesus of Nazareth is the expected Messiah foretold in the Hebrew Bible, Matthew repeatedly quotes or alludes to specific biblical passages that he interprets as being fulfilled in Jesus' career.

The author's concurrent emphasis on scriptural fulfillment and on Jesus' authoritative reinterpretation of the Mosaic Torah (Matt. 5–7) suggests that his work is directed primarily to an audience that sees itself, at least in part, still bound by Torah regulations. Jesus' comments on such matters as Sabbath observance (12:1–14) and divorce (19:3–12) can be seen as examples of Halakah characteristic of first-century Palestinian rabbinic teaching.

By incorporating a large body of teaching material into Mark's narrative framework, Matthew balances Mark's emphasis on Jesus' deeds—miracles of healing and exorcism—with a counterstress on the ethical content of Jesus' preaching. Instructions to the original disciples (chs. 10 and 18) are applied to conditions in the Christian community of Matthew's day.

Matthew retains the apocalyptic themes found in Mark, but he significantly modifies them. He links the eschatological "kingdom" to missionary activities of the early church, a visible manifestation of divine rule. Matthew's Gospel typically shifts the burden of meaning from speculations about the *eschaton* to necessary activities of the church during the interim between Jesus' resurrection and the Parousia. Thus, Matthew expands Mark's prediction of Jerusalem's destruction to include parables illustrating the duties and obligations of Jesus' "servant," the church (cf. Mark 13 and Matt. 24–25). The shift from eschatological speculation to concern for the indefinitely extended work of the church will be even more evident in Luke-Acts.

By framing Mark's account of Jesus' ministry and Passion with narratives of the Savior's birth and resurrection, Matthew emphasizes the divinely directed, supernatural character of Jesus' life. In Matthew, Jesus becomes the Son of God at conception and is the inheritor of all the ancient promises to Israel. He is the "son" of Abraham, heir to the Davidic throne, successor to the authoritative seat of Moses, and the embodiment of divine Wisdom. A guidebook providing instruction and discipline for the community of faith, Matthew's Gospel became the church's major source of *parenesis*—advice and instructive encouragement to the faithful.

QUESTIONS FOR REVIEW

1. Even if Mark's Gospel is an older work, what qualities of Matthew's Gospel can account for its standing first in the New Testament canon? How does Matthew connect his account with the Hebrew Bible?

2. Why do scholars believe it unlikely that one of the Twelve wrote Matthew's Gospel? From the content of the Gospel, what can we infer about its author and the time and place of its composition?

3. In his apparent use of Mark, Q, and other sources unique to his account, how does Matthew reveal some of his special interests and purposes? To stress his individual themes, what kinds of changes does he make in editing Mark's account?

4. In adding five blocks of teaching material to Mark's framework, how does Matthew emphasize Jesus' role as an interpreter of the Mosaic Torah? How does Matthew present Jesus' teachings as the standard and guide of the Christian community?

5. What elements from the Hebrew Bible does Matthew employ to create his accounts of Jesus' infancy and his Passion? How does the author's emphasis on the supernatural affect his portrait of Jesus?

6. Although he stresses that Jesus' personal religion is Torah Judaism, Matthew also presents his hero as founder of the church *(ekklesia)*. How "Jewish" and Torah-abiding did Matthew intend the church to be?

7. In editing and expanding Mark's prophecy of Jerusalem's fall and the *eschaton*, Matthew interpolates several parables of judgment. How do these parables function to stretch the time of the End into the far-distant future?

QUESTIONS FOR DISCUSSION AND REFLECTION

1. Stressing Jesus' kingdom message, Matthew devotes long sections to presenting a "kingdom ethic," which involves ending the cycle of retaliation and returning good for evil. If practiced fully today, would Jesus' teaching about giving up all possessions and peacefully submitting to unfair treatment successfully change modern society?

Can Jesus' policy of turning the other cheek be applied to relations among nations, or does it apply to individual relationships only? Did Jesus intend his ethic for a future ideal time, for dedicated members of the church, or for this imperfect world? Do you think that he expected everyone eventually to follow the principles in the Sermon on the Mount and thus bring about God's rule on earth?

2. With his frequent allusions to Gehenna's fires and a place of "outer darkness" where there is "wailing and grinding of teeth," Matthew makes more references to sinners' punishment in the afterlife than any other Gospel writer. As shown in chapters 10 and 18, he also seems more interested in maintaining church order and exercising control over church members than do the other Evangelists. Do you see any connection between these two concerns? Historically, does a religious institution attain greater power if it promotes a belief that it alone offers the means of escaping eternal torment? How large a role does fear of damnation play in eliciting obedience to ecclesiastical authority?

TERMS AND CONCEPTS TO REMEMBER

ekklesia	antitheses
Halakah	*lex talionis* (the law
Matthew's view of Peter's	of retaliation)
role in the church	Apostle
Q (*Quelle*) document	Gehenna
M (Matthew's special	Sheol
source)	Matthew's view of
Magi	scribes and Pharisees
Sermon on the Mount	Parousia
Beatitudes	great commission

RECOMMENDED READING

Beare, F. W. *The Gospel According to Matthew.* New York: Harper & Row, 1982. A standard introduction.

Brown R. E. *The Birth of the Messiah: A Commentary on the Infancy Narratives in Matthew and Luke.* New York: Doubleday, 1977. A thorough analysis of traditions surrounding Jesus' birth.

———. *The Death of the Messiah,* Vols. 1 and 2. New York: Anchor-Doubleday, 1994. An exhaustive analysis of the Gospel accounts of Jesus' arrest, trial, and execution by a leading Roman Catholic scholar.

Edwards, R. A. *Matthew's Story of Jesus.* Philadelphia: Fortress Press, 1985. An introductory study.

Ellis, P. F. *Matthew: His Mind and His Message.* Collegeville, Minn.: Liturgical Press, 1974.

Farmer, W. B. *Jesus and the Gospel: Tradition, Scripture, and Canon.* Philadelphia: Fortress Press, 1982. An argument for the primacy of Matthew's Gospel.

Gundry, R. H. *Matthew: A Commentary on His Literary and Theological Art.* Grand Rapids, Mich.: Eerdmans, 1982. A thorough scholarly analysis and exposition.

Johnson, S. E. "The Gospel According to St. Matthew, Introduction and Exegesis." In G. A. Buttrick, ed., *The Interpreter's Bible,* Vol. 7, pp. 231–625. New York and Nashville, Tenn.: Abingdon Press, 1951. Covers most major issues in the study of Matthew.

Kee, H. C. *Jesus in History: An Approach to the Study of the Gospels,* 2nd ed. New York: Harcourt Brace Jovanovich, 1977. A respected exploration of the Gospel texts.

Kingsbury, J. D. *Matthew: Structure, Christology, Kingdom.* Philadelphia: Fortress Press, 1975.

———. *Matthew as Story.* Philadelphia: Fortress Press, 1986. A more advanced analysis of the Gospel.

Meier, John P. *The Vision of Matthew: Christ, Church and Morality in the First Gospel.* Theological Inquiries. New York: Paulist Press, 1979.

———. "Matthew, Gospel of." In D. N. Freedman, ed., *The Anchor Bible Dictionary,* Vol. 4, pp. 622–641. New York: Doubleday, 1992. A lucid survey of current scholarship on the origin and purpose of Matthew's Gospel.

Senior, D. P. *What Are They Saying About Matthew?* New York: Paulist Press, 1983. A survey of critical approaches to interpreting Matthew.

Stendahl, Krister. *The School of St. Matthew and Its Use of the Old Testament.* Philadelphia: Fortress Press, 1968.

CHAPTER 9

Luke's Portrait of Jesus

A Savior for "All Nations"

But [Jesus] said, "In the world kings lord it over their subjects; and those in authority are called 'Benefactors.' Not so with you: on the contrary, the highest among you must bear himself like the youngest, the chief of you like a servant. . . . Here I am among you like a servant."

Luke 22:25–27

Key Themes The first part of a two-volume work (Luke-Acts), Luke's Gospel presents Jesus' career not only as history's most crucial event but also as the opening stage of an indefinitely extended historical process that continues in the life of the Church (Acts 1–28). Writing for a Greco-Roman audience, Luke emphasizes that Jesus and his disciples, working under the Holy Spirit, are innocent of any crime against Rome and that their religion is a universal faith intended for all people. The parables unique to Luke's Gospel depict the unexpected ways in which God's in-breaking kingdom overturns the normal social order and reverses conventional beliefs. After a formal preface and extended nativity account (chs. 1 and 2), Luke generally follows Mark's order in narrating the Galilean ministry (chs. 3–9); he then inserts a large body of teaching material, the "greater interpolation" (9:51–18:14), supposedly given on the journey to Jerusalem, returning to Mark for his narration of the Jerusalem ministry and Passion story (18:31–23:56). Luke's final chapter reports postresurrection appearances in or near Jerusalem (ch. 24).

The author of Luke-Acts is unique among New Testament writers, manifesting a breadth of historical vision comparable to that shown in the sweeping narrative of Israel's history from the conquest of Palestine to the first destruction of the Jewish state (the Hebrew Bible books of Joshua through 2 Kings). Like the final editors of Israel's historical books (sixth century B.C.E.), the writer of Luke-Acts lived at a time when Jerusalem and its Temple lay in ruins and Jews were enslaved to Gentiles. Babylon had demolished Solomon's Temple in 587 B.C.E., and Rome (labeled the new Babylon in Revelation) had obliterated its successor in 70 C.E. In both of these national disasters, the people of Israel lost their sanctuary, priesthood, and homeland. Both catastrophes raised similar questions about God's loyalty to his covenant people. In the bleak decades after 587 B.C.E., the authors of Psalm 89 and Lamentations questioned their God's faithfulness to his promises, while the author of Job demanded that

---

Yahweh, the Lord of history, justify his permitting the righteous and innocent to suffer as if they were guilty of unpardonable crimes.

About thirty years before Luke compiled his accounts of Jesus and the early church, Paul had insisted that his fellow Jews were still God's covenant people: "They are Israelites: they were made God's sons; theirs is the splendour of the divine presence, theirs the covenants, the law, the temple worship, and the promises" (Rom. 9:4). Paul was executed several years before the cataclysm of 70 C.E.; we do not know how he would have interpreted the event to other Jews. Luke, however, who was thoroughly acquainted with God's promises to Israel, attempted to place the Jews' seemingly inexplicable fate in historical and theological perspective. As L. T. Johnson notes in his essay on Luke-Acts (see "Recommended Reading"), Luke's two-volume narrative functions in part as a **theodicy,** a literary work that tries to reconcile beliefs about divine goodness with the irrefutable fact that evil and undeserved suffering characterize human experience.

As he indicates in his formal preface to the Gospel, Luke has pondered long over "the whole course of these events" and is determined to provide "a connected narrative" that will give readers "authentic knowledge" (1:3–4) about the interlocking stories of Judaism and nascent Christianity. Luke's wish to convey "authentic" information (a reliable meaning) through *kathexes* (proper sequential order) in writing his account suggests his moral purpose: Luke-Acts will demonstrate that God did indeed fulfill his promises to Israel before giving his new revelation to the Gentiles. Assured that God has been faithful to Israel, Gentiles can now rely on his promises made through the Church, a renewed Israel that includes both Jews and Greeks.

Luke thus begins his double volume — in length Luke-Acts makes up a full third of the New Testament — with a narrative about the conception of John the Baptist. As Luke presents John's nativity, the future baptizer of Jesus is the culminating prophetic figure in Israel's history. The author makes John's parents resemble Abraham and **Sarah** in Genesis: like their biblical prototypes, the Baptist's parents, **Zechariah** and **Elizabeth,** are aged and childless — until an angel appears to announce that the hitherto barren wife will conceive a son destined to be an agent of God's plan for humanity. As the son of Abraham and Sarah — **Isaac** — is the precious "seed" through whom the promised benefits to Israel will flow, so John is the connecting link between Israel's past and the future blessings bestowed by Jesus. John will fill the prophesied role of a returned **Elijah,** messenger of a New Covenant and precursor of Jesus (1:5–21). Because John's father Zechariah is a priest who devotedly officiates at the Temple — the location of Zechariah's angelic visitation — the Baptist's heritage is firmly planted at the exact center of Israel's religious tradition.

Midway through his Gospel, Luke makes John's transitional function explicit: "Until John, it was the Law and the prophets; since then there is the good news of the kingdom of God, and everyone forces his way in" (16:16). As the last of Israel's long line of prophets, John represents the Old Covenant (Torah and prophets). As the figure who introduces the new era of God's kingdom, John's successor — Jesus of Nazareth — stands at the precise center of time, the pivot on which world history turns.

Beginning his ministry with John's baptism, the Lukan Jesus completes it with extensive postresurrection appearances in which he interprets the Hebrew Bible as a christological prophecy, declaring that "everything written about me in the Law of Moses and in the prophets and psalms . . . [is now] fulfilled" (Luke 24:36–53). Jesus then commands his disciples to recruit followers from "all nations," creating a multicultural Gentile community (24:47; Acts 1:8).

In Luke's view, God *has* kept his biblical promises to Israel; the divine advantages that formerly were Israel's exclusive privilege can now be extended to others. Accordingly, Luke ends his history of the early church with Paul's declaration that "this salvation of God has been sent to the Gentiles; the Gentiles will *listen*" (Acts 28:28: italics added). It is significant that Paul is in Rome, the Gentile center of imperial power, when he asserts that henceforth he and his fellow missionaries will focus their efforts on Gentiles.

As Luke tells his story of Jesus' ministry and Christianity's birth, the characters' physical movement from one geographical location to another is thematically important. In the Gospel, Jesus' journey from Galilee to Jerusalem occupies almost ten chapters (9:51–19:44), a section into which Luke inserts many of his most distinctive teachings and parables. For Luke, Jerusalem is the sacred stage on which the drama of human salvation is acted out. It is the site of Zechariah's vision (1:8–22), the place where twelve-year-old Jesus first manifests his divine calling (2:41–51), the goal of Jesus' earthly journey (9:51; 13:33), and the predestined location of Jesus' exemplary death (18:31–32). Jerusalem is, moreover, the locale of *all* the Lukan Jesus' postresurrection appearances and his ascension to heaven.

In Acts, Jerusalem continues to be the focal point: It is the birthplace of Christianity, the nucleus of subsequent missionary activity, and the location of the infant church's first apostolic conference. Even when missionaries carry the word into Gentile territories, they almost invariably circle back to Jerusalem (cf. Acts 1:8; 12:25; 15:2; 18:22; 19:21; 20:16; 21:13). In Luke, virtually all journeys lead to or originate from the holy city—with the crucial exception of Paul's voyage to Rome. After showing Paul preaching "without [legal] restraint" in Rome, Luke abruptly ends his account. He does not continue the story with Paul's execution for sedition or Jerusalem's destruction, twin blows to the church that effectively eliminated both the chief missionary to the Gentiles and the original Jewish nerve center of Christianity. For Luke's purpose, it is enough to imply that Christianity metaphorically has outgrown its Jewish planting and has been transplanted abroad in order to thrive on Gentile soil.

Luke-Acts thus traces the course of a new world religion from its inception in a Bethlehem stable to its (hoped-for) status as a legitimate faith of the Roman Empire. By making Jesus' life the central act of a three-part drama that begins with Israel and continues with the Christian church, Luke offers a philosophy of history vital to Christianity's later understanding of its mission. Instead of bringing the world to an apocalyptic end, Jesus' career is a new beginning that establishes a heightened awareness of God's intentions for all humanity. The Lukan Jesus' triumph over death is closely tied to the disciples' job of evangelizing the world (24:44–53; Acts 1:1–8). In revising Mark's Gospel (Luke's principal source), the author creatively modifies Markan expectation of an immediate End to show that Jesus' essential work is continued by the believing community. Acts portrays the disciples entering a new historical epoch, the age of the Church, and thereby extends the new faith's operations indefinitely into the future. Acts concludes not by drawing attention to the Parousia, but with Paul's resolve to concentrate on ministering to Gentiles (28:27–28).

The Author and His Sources

DEDICATION TO THEOPHILUS

Luke addresses his Gospel to **Theophilus,** the otherwise unknown person to whom he also dedicates his sequel, the Book of Acts (1:1; Acts 1:1). Bearing a Greek name meaning "lover of God,"

Theophilus—whom Luke calls "your Excellency"—may have been a Greek or Roman official, perhaps an affluent patron who underwrote the expenses of publishing Luke's composition.

AUTHORSHIP AND DATE

The most important early reference to the author of Luke-Acts confirms that, like Mark, he was not an eyewitness to the events he narrates. In the Muratorian list of New Testament books (usually dated at about 200 C.E., although some recent scholarly studies place it in the fourth century), a note identifies the author of this Gospel as **Luke,** "the beloved" physician who accompanied Paul on some of the apostle's missionary journeys. The note also states that Luke did not know Jesus. In the late second century C.E., Irenaeus, a bishop of Lyon in Gaul (modern France), also referred to the author as a companion of Paul, presumably the same Luke named in several Pauline letters (Col. 4:14; Philem. 24; 2 Tim. 4:11). If the author of Luke-Acts is Paul's friend, it explains the "we" passages in Acts in which the narration changes from the third to the first person in describing certain episodes; presumably, he was a participant in these happenings (Acts 16:10–17; 20:5–15; 21:1–18; 27:1–28:16). Some commentators also argue for Lukan authorship on the basis of the writer's vocabulary, which includes a number of medical terms appropriate for a physician. Other scholars point out that the writer uses medical terms no more expertly than he employs legal or even maritime terminology.

The author nowhere identifies himself, either in the Gospel or Acts. His depiction of Paul's character and teaching, moreover, does not always coincide with what Paul reveals of himself in his letters. To many contemporary scholars, these facts indicate that the author could not be a person who knew the apostle well. Perhaps the most telling argument against Luke's authorship is that the writer shows no knowledge of Paul's letters. Not only does he never refer to Paul's writing, he alludes to none of Paul's distinctive teachings in any of the Pauline speeches contained in Acts. On the other hand, critics who uphold Lukan authorship point out that the physician associated with Paul for only brief periods and wrote long after Paul's death when the theological issues argued in Paul's letters were no longer as immediate or controversial as they had been. Luke's concern in Acts is not to reopen theological disputes but to smooth over differences that divided the early church and depict apostles and missionaries united in spreading the faith. Although many experts regard the writer of Luke-Acts as anonymous, others retain the traditional assumption that the historical Luke is the author.

Although the author's identity is not conclusively settled, for convenience we refer to him as Luke. Because of his interest in a Gentile audience and his ease in handling the Greek language (he has the largest vocabulary and most polished style of any Evangelist), the writer may have been a Gentile, perhaps the only non-Jewish Bible writer.

According to most scholars, Luke-Acts was written after 70 C.E., when Jerusalem was destroyed by the Roman armies under General (later, Emperor) Titus. In his version of Jesus' prediction of the holy city's fall (paralleling Mark 13 and Matthew 24), Luke reveals detailed knowledge of the Roman siege:

> But when you see Jerusalem encircled by armies, then you may be sure that her destruction is near. Then you who are in Judea must take to the hills; those that are in the city itself must leave it . . . because this is the time of retribution. . . . For there will be great distress in the land and a terrible judgment upon this people. They will fall at the sword's point; they will be carried captive into all countries; and Jerusalem will be trampled down by foreigners until their day has run its course.
>
> (21:20–24)

In this quoted passage, Luke substitutes a description of Jerusalem's siege for the cryptic "sign" (the "abomination of desolation") that Mark and Matthew allude to at this point in their accounts (see Mark 13:13–19; Matt. 24:15–22). Luke also refers specifically to the Roman method of encircling a besieged town, a military technique used in the 70 C.E. assault on Jerusalem:

> Your enemies will set up siege-works against you; they will encircle you and hem you in at every point; they will bring you to the ground, you and

Box 9.1
Luke's Editing and Restructuring of Mark

Because we have one of Luke's principal written sources, the Gospel of Mark, it is possible to learn something of Luke's authorial intentions by examining the way in which he characteristically revises the material he inherited. Although Luke is generally faithful to Mark, which constitutes about 35 percent of his narrative, he makes a number of significant changes in the Markan text. Besides omitting large sections of Mark's account (Mark 6:45–8:26 and 9:41–10:12), possibly to avoid repetitions, such as Mark's second version of the multiplication of loaves and fishes, Luke also typically deletes Markan passages that might reflect unfavorably on Jesus' family or disciples. Consistent with his exaltation of Mary in the birth stories (ch. 2), he omits Mark's story of Jesus' "mother and brothers" trying to interfere in his ministry (Mark 3:21, 33–34) and rewrites the Markan Jesus' statement about not being respected by his "family and kinsmen" (cf. Mark 6:4 and Luke 4:22, 24). Similarly, Luke excises Mark 8:22–26, an incident symbolic of the disciples' slowness to see or understand Jesus' identity, as well as Markan passages equating Peter with "Satan" (Mark 8:33) or dramatizing the disciples' ineptitude or cowardice (Mark 14:27, 40–41, 51–52).

In one of his most significant changes to the Markan sequence of events, Luke places Jesus' rejection in Nazareth at the outset of his ministry, rather than midway through it as do Mark (6:1–6) and Matthew (13:53–58). Luke also thoroughly rewrites the Nazareth episode, transforming it into a paradigm of his entire two-volume work. Previewing the church's mission to Gentile nations later described in Acts, Luke has Jesus antagonize his home town congregation by implying that God transfers his favor from the covenant people to non-Jews (Luke 4:25–29).

Another distinctive feature of Luke's Gospel anticipates the narrative thrust in Acts: the journey motif. Whereas Mark only briefly refers to Jesus' journey from Galilee to Jerusalem (Mark 10:17, 32–33), Luke repeatedly emphasizes the importance of Jesus' movements, devoting a full ten chapters to the trek (Luke 9:51–19:28). This restructuring of Mark's account prepares readers to see parallels to Paul's missionary travels in Acts, highlighting the continuity between Jesus' activities and those of his later followers. As

Jesus resolves to go to Jerusalem (Luke 9:51), so Paul similarly decides to travel to Rome (Acts 19:21), the city where a martyr's death, like that of Jesus, awaits him.

Luke's view of the centrality of Jerusalem also significantly shapes his narrative structure. It is the place where his Gospel account begins (Luke 1:8–22), the setting of Jesus' first public appearance (2:43, 46), the goal of Jesus' life journey (9:51), the only site appropriate for Jesus the prophet to die (13:33, a statement unique to Luke), and the location of *all* of Jesus' postresurrection appearances (24:1–53). Whereas Mark explicitly states that the risen Jesus will appear in Galilee (Mark 14:28; 16:7), Luke not only locates Jesus' resurrection and ascension to heaven in or near Jerusalem (Luke 24; Acts 1) but also makes it the center where Christianity first develops. As scholars have noted, in the Gospel, everything progresses toward Jerusalem, where the early church is born; beginning with the second half of Acts, however, everything moves *away* from Jerusalem — culminating in Paul's arrival in Rome, the imperial capital where the new faith finds its natural audience.

Because Luke presents Jesus' story as a prophetic model for the activities of the early church, the author introduces themes and incidents into the Gospel that later characterize Acts' picture of the church's relationship with Rome. The author emphasizes specific parallels between Jesus' dual trials — before the Sanhedrin and before a Roman governor — and similar trials in Acts, where Paul is hailed before both priestly and Roman courts (cf. Luke 22:66–23:25; Acts 22:25–23:19). Thus, Luke is the only Gospel writer to include in his Passion story an episode in which Jesus appears before Herod Antipas (Luke 23:6–12) — an incident that parallels and foreshadows Paul's similar hearing before another member of the Herodian dynasty, Herod Agrippa II (Acts 25:13–26:32). As the Roman magistrates before whom Paul appears declare him guiltless of any crime against the government (Acts 25:25; 26:30–32), so Pilate exonerates Jesus from the political charge of sedition (Luke 23:13–15, 22). Luke even changes Mark's report of the centurion's speech at the cross: Instead of perceiving Jesus' divine sonship, the Roman soldier now simply states that Jesus was legally "innocent" (cf. Mark 15:39; Matt. 27:54; Luke 23:47).

(continued)

Box 9.1 *(continued)*

Finally, Luke modifies Mark's narrative to express his theological view of Jesus. Besides deleting Mark's crucial statement about Jesus' dying sacrificially as a "ransom for many" (10:45) and emphasizing instead his example of service that will be a pattern for disciples later in Acts (Luke 22:27), Luke also eliminates Markan passages that show Jesus as too humanly vulnerable. In the Gethsemane scene, Luke severely edits the Markan description of Jesus' desperate anguish, totally eliminating his prayer to be spared the cup of

suffering (cf. Mark 14:32–42 and Luke 22:39–46). The famous verses that describe Jesus as "sweating blood" do not appear in some of the oldest and best Lukan manuscripts; later scribes may have inserted them to make Luke's account consistent with the other two Synoptics (see box 2.1). The Lukan Jesus thus utters no final cry of abandonment, but instead serenely commits his spirit to God (cf. Mark 15:33–37; Luke 23:46–47).

---

your children within your walls, and not leave you one stone standing on another. (19:43–44)

It would appear, then, that the Gospel was written at some point after the Jewish War of 66–73 C.E. and before 90 C.E., when publication made Paul's letters accessible to Christian readers. Many scholars place Luke-Acts in the mid to late 80s C.E. and favor Ephesus, a Greek-speaking city in Asia Minor with a relatively large Christian population, as the place of composition.

LUKE'S USE OF SOURCES

As a Christian living two or three generations after Jesus' time, Luke must rely on other persons' information, including orally transmitted recollections about Jesus and traditional Christian preaching. Besides using memories of "eyewitnesses" and later missionary accounts, the author depends on his own research skills—the labor he expends going "over the whole course of these events in detail" (1:1–4).

Luke is aware that "many" others before him produced Gospels (1:1). His resolve to create yet another suggests that he was not satisfied with his predecessors' efforts. As Matthew did, he chooses Mark as his primary source, but he omits several large units of Markan material (such as Mark 6:45–8:26 and 9:41–10:12), perhaps to make room for his own special additions. Adapting Mark to his creative purpose, Luke sometimes rearranges the sequence of individual incidents to emphasize his

particular themes. Whereas Mark placed Jesus' rejection at Nazareth midway through the Galilean campaign, Luke sets it at the beginning (4:16–30). Adding the Nazarenes' attempt to kill Jesus to Mark's account, he uses the incident to foreshadow his hero's later death in Jerusalem (see box 9.1).

In addition, Luke frames Mark's central account of Jesus' adult career with his own unique stories of Jesus' infancy (chs. 1 and 2) and resurrection (ch. 24). Luke further modifies the earlier Gospel by adding two extensive sequences of teaching material. The first section—called the "lesser interpolation" (6:20–8:3)—includes Luke's version of the Sermon on the Mount, which the author transfers to level ground. Known as the Sermon on the Plain (6:20–49), this collection of Jesus' sayings is apparently drawn from the same source that Matthew used, the hypothetical Q document. Instead of assembling Q material into long speeches as Matthew does, however, Luke scatters these sayings throughout his Gospel. Scholars believe that he observes Q's original order more closely than Matthew does.

Luke's second major insertion into the Markan narrative, called the "greater interpolation," is nearly ten chapters long (9:51–18:14). A miscellaneous compilation of Jesus' parables and pronouncements, this collection supposedly represents Jesus' teaching on the road from Galilee to Jerusalem. It is composed almost exclusively of Q material and Luke's special source, which scholars call L (Lukan). After this interpolation section, during which all narrative action stops, Luke returns to Mark's account at

Box 9.2
Representative Examples of Material Found Only in Luke

A formal preface and statement of purpose (1:1–4)

A narrative about the parents of John the Baptist (1:5–25, 57–80)

Luke's distinctive story of Jesus' conception and birth (1:26–56; 2:1–40)

Jesus' childhood visit to the Jerusalem Temple (2:41–52)

A distinctive Lukan genealogy (3:23–38)

The Scripture reading in the Nazareth synagogue and subsequent attempt to kill Jesus (4:16–30)

Details on the Roman siege of Jerusalem (19:43–44; 21:21–24)

Jesus' hearing before Herod Antipas (23:6–12)

The sympathetic criminal (23:39–43)

Jesus' postresurrection appearances on the road to Emmaus (24:13–35)

Some parables, sayings, and miracles unique to Luke:

1. A miraculous catch of fish (5:1–11)
2. Raising the son of a Nain widow (7:11–17)
3. Two forgiven debtors (7:41–43)
4. Satan falling like lightning from heaven (10:18)
5. The good Samaritan (10:29–37)
6. The friend asking help at night (11:5–10)
7. The rich and foolish materialist (12:13–21)
8. Remaining alert for the Master's return (12:36–38)
9. The unproductive fig tree (13:6–9)
10. Healing a crippled woman on the Sabbath (13:10–17)
11. Curing a man with dropsy (14:1–6)
12. A distinctive version of the kingdom banquet (14:12–24)
13. Counting the costs of going to war (14:31–33)
14. Parable of the lost coin (15:8–10)
15. The prodigal (spendthrift) son (15:11–32)
16. The dishonest manager (16:1–13)
17. Lazarus and the rich man (16:19–31)
18. Healing ten lepers (17:11–19)
19. The unjust judge (18:1–8)
20. The Pharisee and the tax collector (18:9–14)
21. Restoring the ear of a slave (22:47–53)

18:15 and then reproduces an edited version of the Passion story.

Like the other Synoptic writers, Luke presents Jesus' life in terms of images and themes from the Hebrew Bible, which thus constitutes another of the author's sources. In Luke's presentation, some of Jesus' miracles, such as his resuscitating a widow's dead son, are told in such a way that they closely resemble similar miracles in the Hebrew Scriptures. Jesus' deeds clearly echo those of the prophets Elijah and Elisha (1 Kings 17–19; 2 Kings 1–6). Luke introduces the Elijah–Elisha theme early in the Gospel (4:23–28), indicating that for him these ancient men of God were prototypes of the Messiah.

Although he shares material from Mark, Q, and the Hebrew Bible with Matthew, Luke gives his "connected narrative" a special quality by including many of Jesus' words that occur only in his Gospel (the L source). Only in Luke do we find such celebrated parables as those of the prodigal son (15:11–32), the lost coin (15:8–10), the persistent widow, the good Samaritan (10:29–32), and Lazarus and the rich man (16:19–31) (see box 9.2). These and other parables embody consistent themes, typically stressing life's unexpected reversals and/or God's gracious forgiveness of wrongdoers.

Despite the inclusion of some of Jesus' "hard sayings" about the rigors of discipleship, Luke's special material tends to picture a gentle and loving Jesus, a concerned shepherd who tenderly cares for his flock (the community of believers). Luke has been accused of "sentimentalizing" Jesus' message; however, the author's concern for oppressed people — the poor, the socially outcast, the women—is genuine and lends his Gospel a distinctively humane and gracious ambience.

SOME TYPICAL LUKAN THEMES

Luke makes his Gospel a distinctive creation by sounding many themes important to the self-identity and purpose of the Christian community for which he writes. Many readers find Luke's account especially appealing because it portrays Jesus taking a personal interest in women, in the poor, in social outcasts, and in other powerless persons. In general, Luke portrays Jesus as a model of compassion who willingly forgives sinners, comforts the downtrodden, and heals the afflicted. Luke's Jesus is particularly attentive to issues of social and economic justice. In numerous parables unique to his Gospel, Luke demonstrates that Jesus' kingdom ethic demands a radical change in society's present social and religious values. Some major themes that strongly color Luke's portrait of Jesus are described next.

The Holy Spirit   Luke is convinced that Jesus' career and the growth of Christianity are not historical accidents, but the direct result of God's will, which is expressed through the Holy Spirit. Luke uses this term more than Mark and Matthew together (fourteen times). It is by the Spirit that Jesus is conceived and by which he is anointed after baptism. The Holy Spirit leads him into the wilderness (4:1) and empowers his ministry in Galilee (4:14). The Spirit is conferred through prayer (11:13), and at death the Lukan Jesus commits his "spirit" to God (23:46).

The Holy Spirit reappears with overwhelming power in Acts 2 when, like a "strong driving wind," it rushes upon the 120 disciples gathered in Jerusalem to observe **Pentecost.** Possession by the Holy Spirit confirms God's acceptance of Gentiles into the Church (Acts 11:15–18). To Luke, it is the Spirit that is responsible for the rapid expansion of believers throughout the Roman Empire. Like Paul, Luke sees the Christian community as charismatic, Spirit-led, and Spirit-empowered.

Prayer   Another of Luke's principal interests is Jesus' and the disciples' use of prayer. Luke's infancy

Figure 9.1 *Virgin and Child.* This polychromed wooden sculpture from Africa shows the infant Jesus being nursed by Mary, a rendition illustrating the archetypal image of mother and child, nurturer and bearer of new life, as well as an image of black holiness. (© Boltin Picture Library)

narrative is full of prayers and hymns of praise by virtually all the adult participants. In his account of John's baptizing campaign, the Spirit descends upon Jesus not at his baptism as in Mark, but afterward while Jesus is at prayer (3:21). Similarly, Jesus chooses the disciples after prayer (6:12) and prays before he asks them who he is (9:18). The Transfiguration occurs "while he is praying" (9:29). Jesus' instructions on prayer are also more extensive than in other Gospels (11:1–13; 18:1–14). The Lukan stress on prayer carries over into Acts, in which the heroes of the early church are frequently shown praying (Acts 1:14, 24–26; 8:15; 10:1–16).

Jesus' Concern for Women   From the beginning of his account, Luke makes it clear that women play an

Figure 9.2 The Holy Family. The unknown years of Jesus' boyhood are given a Japanese setting in this twentieth-century painting on silk. Shouldering his share of the family's work, the young Jesus carries wood to help Joseph, his carpenter father, while Mary, his mother, is busy at her spinning wheel. The themes of productive labor, mutual assistance, and familial harmony dominate the domestic scene in Nazareth, providing a contrast to the adult Jesus' later rejection of family ties and obligations (Mark 3). (© Boltin Picture Library)

indispensable part in fulfilling the divine plan. Elizabeth, Zechariah's wife, is chosen to produce and raise Israel's final prophet, the one who prepares the way for Jesus. Her cousin Mary responds affirmatively to the Holy Spirit, conceiving and nurturing the world-savior (see figure 9.1). During his adult ministry, Jesus accepts many women disciples, praising those who, like **Mary,** the sister of **Martha,** abandon domestic chores to take their places among the male followers—a privilege Jesus declares "will not be taken from [them]" (10:38–42) (see figure 9.2). Galilean women not only follow Jesus on the path to Jerusalem but also financially support him and his male companions (8:2–3). As in Mark, it is these Galilean women who provide the human link between Jesus' death and resurrection, witnessing

the Crucifixion and receiving first the news that he is risen (23:49; 23:55–24:11).

Jesus' Affinity with the Unrespectable   Closely linked to Jesus' concern for women, who were legally powerless in Palestine, is his affinity with many similarly vulnerable people on the margins of society. "A friend of tax-gatherers and sinners" (7:34), the Lukan Jesus openly accepts social outcasts, including "immoral" women, such as an (apparently notorious) woman who crashes a Pharisee's dinner party and seats herself next to Jesus, bathing his feet with her tears, much to his host's indignation (7:37–50). Luke alone preserves one of Jesus' most provocative stories, in which the central character is an ungrateful son who consorts with prostitutes and sinks to groveling with swine — but who is unconditionally loved by his father (15:11–32). In Luke, Jesus not only conducts a brief ministry in **Samaria** (traditionally viewed as a center of religious impurity [9:52–56]) but also makes a **Samaritan** the embodiment of neighborly love (10:30–37).

Accused of being "a glutton and a drinker," Jesus personally welcomes "tax-gatherers and other bad characters" to dine with him, refusing to distinguish between deserving and undeserving guests (7:29–34; 15:1–2). In Luke's version of the great banquet, the host's doors are thrown open indiscriminately to "the poor, the crippled, the lame, and the blind," people incapable of reciprocating hospitality (14:12–24). To Luke, it is not the "poor in spirit" who gain divine blessing, but simply "the poor," the economically deprived for whom productive citizens typically show little sympathy (cf. 6:20–21 and 6:24–25).

Christianity as a Universal Faith

The author designs Luke-Acts to show that through Jesus and his successors, God directs human history to achieve humanity's redemption. Luke's theory of salvation history has a universalist aspect: From its inception, Christianity is a religion intended for "all nations," especially those peoples who have hitherto lived without Israel's Law and prophets. As **Simeon** prophesies over the infant Jesus, the child is destined to become "a revelation to the heathen [Gentiles]" (2:32). In Acts, the risen Christ's final words commission his followers to bear witness about him from Jerusalem "to the ends of the earth" (Acts 1:8).

Christianity as a Lawful Religion

Besides presenting Christianity as a universal faith, Luke works to show that it is a peaceful and lawful religion. In reporting Jesus' trial before the Roman magistrate and Paul's similar hearings before various other Roman officials, Luke is careful to mention that in each case the accused is innocent of any real crime. Although Pilate condemns Jesus for claiming to be "king of the Jews," an act of sedition against Rome, in Luke's Gospel, Pilate also affirms Jesus' innocence, explicitly stating that he finds the prisoner "guilty of no capital offence" (23:22). In Acts, Luke creates parallels to Jesus' trial in which the apostles and others are similarly declared innocent of subversion. Convinced that Christianity is destined to spread throughout the empire, Luke wishes to demonstrate that it is no threat to the peace or stability of the Roman government.

Jesus as Savior Finally, Luke presents Jesus in a guise that his Greek and Roman readers will understand. Matthew had labored to prove from the Hebrew Bible that Jesus was the Davidic Messiah. In the account of Jesus' infancy, Luke also sounds the theme of prophetic fulfillment. But he is aware as well that his Gentile audience is not primarily interested in a Jewish Messiah, a figure traditionally associated with Jewish nationalism. Although Mark and Matthew had declared their hero "Son of God," Luke further universalizes Jesus' appeal by declaring him "Savior" (1:69; 2:11; Acts 3:13–15). He is the only Synoptic writer to do so. Luke's term (the Greek *sōter*) was used widely in the Greco-Roman world and was applied to gods, demigods, and human rulers alike. Hellenistic peoples commonly worshiped savior deities in numerous mystery cults and hailed emperors by the title "god and savior" for the material benefits, such as health, peace, or prosperity, that they conferred upon the public. For Luke, Jesus is the **Savior** of repentant humanity, one who delivers believers from the consequences of sin, as the judges of ancient Israel "saved" or delivered their people from military oppressors. (The NEB translators therefore use the English noun *deliverer* for *sōter* in Luke [1:24, 69; 2:11].)

ORGANIZATION OF LUKE'S GOSPEL

A simple outline of Luke's structure follows:

1. Formal preface (1:1–4)
2. Infancy narratives of the Baptist and Jesus (1:5–2:52)
3. Prelude to Jesus' ministry: baptism, genealogy, and temptation (3:1–4:13)
4. Jesus' Galilean ministry and the "lesser interpolation" (4:14–9:50)

> ### Box 9.3
> ### New Characters Introduced in Luke
>
> Elizabeth and the priest Zechariah, parents of the Baptist (1:5–25, 39–79)
>
> Gabriel, the angel who announces Jesus' virginal conception (1:26–38)
>
> Augustus, emperor of Rome (2:1–2)
>
> Simeon, who foretells Jesus' messiahship (2:25–35)
>
> Anna, an aged prophetess (2:36–38)
>
> The widow of Nain (7:11–16)
>
> The unidentified sinful woman whom Jesus forgives (7:36–50)
>
> The sisters Mary and Martha (10:38–39)
>
> Zacchaeus, the wealthy tax collector (19:1–10)
>
> Herod Antipas, as one of Jesus' judges (22:7–12; also 9:7–9)
>
> Cleopas and another unidentified disciple (24:13–35)
>
> Additional minor characters, including a crippled woman (13:10–17), a man with dropsy (14:1–4), and ten lepers (17:11–19)

5. Luke's travel narrative: Jesus' teachings on the journey to Jerusalem (the "greater interpolation" [9:51–18:14])
6. The Jerusalem ministry: Jesus' challenge to the holy city (18:31–21:38)
7. The final conflict and Passion story (22:1–23:56)
8. Epilog: resurrection appearances in the vicinity of Jerusalem (24:1–53)

In examining Luke's work, we focus primarily on material found only in his Gospel, especially the narrative sections and parables that illustrate distinctively Lukan themes (see box 9.3 for new characters introduced in Luke). Because we have already discussed the preface, we begin with one of the most familiar and best-loved stories in the entire Bible — the account of Jesus' conception and birth.

Infancy Narratives of the Baptist and Jesus

We do not know Luke's source for his infancy narratives (1:5–2:52), but he apparently drew on a tradition that differed in many details from Matthew's

account. The two writers agree that Jesus was born in Bethlehem to **Mary,** a virgin, and **Joseph,** a descendant of David (see figure 9.3). Apart from that, however, the two Evangelists relate events in a strikingly different manner.

In composing his infancy narratives, Luke adopts a consciously biblical style, writing in the old-fashioned Greek of the Septuagint Bible. The effect is like reading the birth stories in the archaic language of the King James Version and most of the rest of the Gospel in more contemporary English. Luke's purpose here, however, is more than merely stylistic: He is echoing the ancient Scriptures, both by his style and by quoting extensively from the Hebrew prophets, because what he relates in these passages is the climactic turn of history: "Until John, it was the Law and the prophets, since then there is the good news of the kingdom" (16:16). Whereas the Baptist will serve as the capstone of Israel's ancient prophetic tradition, in Jesus, God will both fulfill his promises to Israel and begin the climactic process of human salvation.

THE BIRTH OF JOHN THE BAPTIST

In depicting John's aged parents, Elizabeth and Zechariah, Luke highlights their exemplary piety and devotion to the letter of Israel's religion.

Figure 9.3 *Virgin and Child.* In this conception of Mary and the infant Jesus, the artist pictures the Madonna as an archetypal image of abundance and fertility, giving her a crown to depict her queenly status and surrounding her with flowers to suggest her association with natural fecundity. This twentieth-century rendition of the Virgin by F. Botero of Columbia effectively demonstrates her thematic connection with nurturing goddesses of pre-Christian antiquity. (© Fernando Botero, courtesy, Marlborough Gallery)

Described as "upright and devout, blamelessly observing all the commandments and ordinances of the [Torah]" (1:6), Zechariah and Elizabeth represent the best in Judaism.

In narrating his parallel accounts of John's and Jesus' nativities, Luke is the only New Testament writer to state that their respective mothers are blood relatives (1:36). The later adult association between John and Jesus is thus foreshadowed by their physical kinship, their mothers' friendship, and the similar circumstances of their births.

THE ROLE OF MARY

Luke interweaves the two nativity accounts, juxtaposing **Gabriel**'s visit to Mary (1:26–38) (the **Annunciation**) with Mary's visit to her cousin Elizabeth, a meeting that causes the unborn John to stir in his mother's womb at the approach of the newly conceived Jesus. As Mary had been made pregnant by the Holy Spirit, so Elizabeth at their encounter is empowered by the Spirit to prophesy concerning the superiority of Mary's child. This emphasis on women's role in the divine purpose (note also the prophetess Anna in 2:36–38) is a typical Lukan concern. Also significant is Luke's hint about Mary's family background. Because Elizabeth is "of priestly descent," which means that she belongs to the tribe of Levi, it seems probable that Mary also belongs to the Levitical clan rather than the Davidic tribe of Judah. Like that of Matthew, Luke's genealogy traces Jesus' Davidic ancestry through Joseph (1:5; 3:23–24).

In relating the two infancy stories, Luke subtly indicates the relative importance of the two children. He dates John's birth in King Herod's reign (1:5). By contrast, when introducing Jesus' nativity, the author relates the event not to a Judean king, but to a Roman emperor, Augustus Caesar (2:1). Luke thus places Jesus in a worldwide (as opposed to a local Jewish) context, suggesting both the universal scope of Jesus' significance and the babe's ultimate destiny to rule all humanity.

In telling of Jesus' circumcision and Mary's ritual purification (2:21–24), Luke stresses another theme important to his picture of Jesus' Jewish background: Not only relatives like Elizabeth and Zechariah but also Jesus' immediate family observe the Mosaic Law scrupulously. His parents obey every Torah command (2:39), including making a yearly pilgrimage to the Jerusalem Temple for Passover (2:41–43). The author's own view is that most of the Torah's provisions no longer bind Christians (Acts 15), but he wishes to emphasize that from birth Jesus fulfilled all Torah requirements.

LUKE'S USE OF HYMNS

Throughout the infancy stories of Jesus and the Baptist, Luke follows the Greco-Roman biographer's practice of inserting speeches that illustrate themes vital to the writer's view of his subject. The long poem uttered by Zechariah—known by its Latin name, the Benedictus (1:67–79)—combines scriptural quotations with typically Lukan views

about Jesus' significance. The same is true of the priest Simeon's prayer, the Nunc Dimittis (2:29–32) and prophecy (2:23–25). Some of the speeches ascribed to characters in the nativity accounts may be rewritten songs and prayers first used in Christian worship services. These liturgical pieces include the angel Gabriel's announcement to Mary that she will bear a son, the Ave Maria (1:28–33), and Mary's exulting prayer, the **Magnificat** (1:46–55). Mary's hymn closely resembles a passage from the Hebrew Bible, the prayer Hannah recites when an angel foretells the birth of her son, Samuel (1 Sam. 2:1–10). In its present form, this hymn may be as much a composition of the early church, conceived as an appropriate biblical response to the angel's visit, as a memory of Mary's literal words. Nonetheless, Luke implies that Jesus' mother may have been a source of this tradition, noting that she reflected deeply on the unusual circumstances surrounding her son's birth (2:19; see also 2:51).

Luke includes the only tradition about Jesus' boyhood contained in the New Testament, an anecdote about the twelve-year-old boy's visit to the Temple in which he impresses some learned scribes with the acuteness of his questions and understanding (2:41–52). The statement that Jesus "advanced in wisdom and in favor with God and men" (2:52) almost exactly reproduces the Old Testament description of young Samuel (1 Sam. 2:26) and is probably a conventional observation rather than a historically precise evaluation of Jesus' youthful character. For Luke, this Temple episode serves primarily to anticipate Jesus' later ministry at the Jerusalem sanctuary.

Jesus' Galilean Ministry and the "Lesser Interpolation"

JESUS' REJECTION IN NAZARETH

After describing John's baptism campaign and Jesus' temptation by Satan (3–4:13), Luke introduces Jesus' public career in a way that significantly revises Mark's order of events. Whereas Matthew closely follows Mark in placing Jesus' rejection in Nazareth after the Galilean campaign is already well under way (cf. Mark 6:1–6; Matt. 13:53–58), Luke transfers this episode almost to the beginning of Jesus' ministry (4:16–30). The Evangelist makes this change in his source not to provide a more factually accurate biography, but probably for the same reason that the author of John's Gospel switches his account of Jesus' assault on the Temple from the time of Jesus' final entry into Jerusalem (as all three Synoptics have it) to the beginning of his career: He wants his readers to understand the event's thematic or theological meaning. (See chapter 10 for a discussion of John's probable motives in repositioning the Temple incident.)

In this highly dramatic scene of conflict between Jesus and the residents of his home town, Luke extensively rewrites Mark's account. Besides eliminating Mark's implication that Jesus' family failed to recognize his worth and inserting a quotation from Isaiah that expresses Luke's view of Jesus' prophetic role, the author creates a speech for Jesus that outrages the people of Nazareth. Taking full authorial advantage of his first opportunity to show the adult Jesus interacting with his contemporaries, Luke uses the occasion of Jesus' visit to the Nazareth synagogue to give readers a thematic preview of his entire two-volume work. By adding that Jesus' former neighbors try to kill him (an element absent in Mark and Matthew, who merely report that Nazareth's residents showed him little respect), Luke foreshadows Jesus' later rejection and death in Jerusalem. By having Jesus deliver a sermon in which two of Israel's greatest prophets, Elijah and Elisha, perform their most spectacular miracles to benefit Gentiles, not native Israelites, Luke anticipates the church's future mission to Gentile nations, developments he will narrate in the Book of Acts.

Even more important to Luke is his vision of Jesus' essential calling, which he evokes in the quotation from Isaiah: Jesus is empowered by the same divine Spirit that motivated Israel's prophets, and he will pursue the same kind of work they did, offering aid and comfort to people suffering the harsh realities of economic and political oppression, explicitly "the poor" and downtrodden. Restoring vision to persons metaphorically imprisoned or blind

and helping "broken victims go free," Jesus proclaims God's favor to those whom society typically ignores or exploits. Characteristically, Luke omits Isaiah's reference to divine "vengeance" (Isa. 61:1–2; 58:6).

THE "LESSER INTERPOLATION"

For the next two chapters (4:31–6:11), Luke reproduces much of the Markan narrative dealing with Jesus' miracles of healing and exorcism. Despite violent opposition in Nazareth, Jesus draws large crowds, healing many and preaching in numerous Galilean synagogues. Luke transposes the Markan order, however, placing Jesus' calling of the Twelve after the Nazareth episode (6:12–19). This transposition serves as an introduction to Jesus' first public discourse, the Sermon on the Plain (6:20–49). The Sermon begins a long section (called the "lesser interpolation") in which the author interweaves material shared with Matthew (presumably from Q) with material that appears only in his own Gospel (6:20–8:3).

Luke's Sermon on the Plain   Resembling an abbreviated version of Matthew's Sermon on the Mount (see box 9.4), the Lukan discourse begins with briefer forms of four Beatitudes, all of which are in the second person and hence directed at "you" (the audience/reader). Matthew had phrased the Beatitudes in the third person ("they") and presented them as blessings on people who possessed the right spiritual nature, such as "those who hunger and thirst to see right prevail" (Matt. 5:6). By contrast, Luke "materializes" the Beatitudes, bluntly referring to physical hunger: "How blest are you who now go hungry; your hunger shall be satisfied" (6:21). His "poor" are the financially destitute, the powerless who are to receive the "kingdom of God."

Luke follows the Beatitudes with a list of "woes" ("alas for you") in which the "rich" and "well-fed" are cursed with future loss and hunger. Persons happy with the present social order are destined to regret their former complacency (6:24–26). This harsh judgment on people whom society generally considers fortunate occurs only in Luke and represents one of Luke's special convic-

Box 9.4
Comparison of the Beatitudes in Matthew and Luke

MATTHEW	LUKE
How blest are these who know their need of God [the "poor in spirit"]; the kingdom of Heaven is theirs.	How blest are you who are in need ["the poor"]; the kingdom of God is yours.
How blest are those of a gentle spirit; they shall have the earth for their possession.	
How blest are those who hunger and thirst to see right prevail; they shall be satisfied.	How blest are you who now go hungry; your hunger shall be satisfied.
How blest are those who show mercy; mercy shall be shown to them.	
How blest are those whose hearts are pure; they shall see God.	
How blest are the peacemakers; God shall call them his [children].	
How blest are those who have suffered persecution for the cause of right; the kingdom of Heaven is theirs.	How blest you are when men hate you, when they outlaw you and insult you, and ban your very name as infamous, because of the Son of Man. On that day be glad and dance for joy; for assuredly you have a rich reward in heaven; in just the same way did their fathers treat the prophets.
How blest you are, when you suffer insults and persecution and every kind of calumny for my sake. Accept it with gladness and exultation, for you have a rich reward in heaven; in the same way they persecuted the prophets before you. (Matt. 5:3–12)	
	[The "Woes"]
	But alas for you who are rich; you have had your time of happiness.
	Alas for you who are well-fed now; you shall go hungry.
	Alas for you who laugh now; you shall mourn and weep.
	Alas for you when all speak well of you; just so did their fathers treat the false prophets. (Luke 6:20–26)

tions: The kingdom will bring a radical reversal of presently accepted values and expectations. The author does not specify his objections to the wealthy as a class, but in material exclusive to his Gospel he repeatedly attacks the rich, predicting that their present affluence and luxury will be exchanged for misery.

Reversals of Status for Rich and Poor In pleading the cause of the poor against the rich, Luke also includes his special rendering of Jesus' command to love one's enemies (6:32–36; cf. Matt. 5:43–48). One must practice giving unselfishly because such behavior reflects the nature and purpose of God, who treats even the wicked with kindness (6:32–36).

As the Lukan parables typically illustrate unexpected reversals of status between the rich and poor, so do they teach generosity and compassion — qualities that to Luke are literally divine (6:35–36).

To Luke, Jesus provides the model of compassionate behavior. When Christ raises a widow's son from the dead (7:11–17), the miracle expresses the twin Lukan themes of God's special love for the poor and unfortunate (especially women) and Jesus' role as Lord of the resurrection. (Be sure to note the awe-inspiring quality that Luke imparts to this scene, as well as Jesus' empathy for the grieving mother.) By including this episode (unique to his Gospel), the author reminds his readers of the joy they will experience when Jesus appears again to restore life to all.

The Importance of Women Luke commonly uses Jesus' interaction with women to reveal his concept of Jesus' character, stressing his hero's combination of authority and tenderness. After providing ultimate comfort to the sorrowing widow at Nain, Jesus reveals similar compassion for a prostitute, to whom he imparts another form of new life. All four Gospels contain an incident in which a woman anoints Jesus with oil or some other costly ointment (Mark 14:3–9; Matt. 26:6–13; John 12:1–8). In Luke (7:36–50), however, the anointing does not anticipate preparation for Jesus' burial, as it does in the other Gospels, but is an act of intense love on the unnamed woman's part. Set in the house of a Pharisee where Jesus is dining, the Lukan version focuses on the woman's overwhelming emotion and on the typically Lukan theme of compassion and forgiveness. To Luke, the "immoral" woman's love proves that "her many sins have been forgiven."

In John, the woman is identified as Mary, sister of Martha and **Lazarus,** but there is no hint of her possessing a lurid past. It would appear that Jesus' emotional encounter with a woman who lavished expensive unguents upon him impressed onlookers enough to remember and transmit it orally to the early Christian community, but — as in the case of many other of Jesus' actions and sayings — the precise context of the event was forgotten. Each Gospel writer provides his own explanatory frame for the incident (cf. Luke 7:36–50; Mark 14:3–9; Matt. 26:6–13; John 12:1–8).

Fittingly, the first extensive interpolation of Lukan material concludes with a summary of the part women play in Jesus' ministry. Accompanying him are numerous female disciples, Galilean women whom he had healed and who now support him and the male disciples "out of their own resources" (8:1–3).

Luke's Travel Narrative: Jesus' Teachings on the Journey to Jerusalem

Luke begins this long section (9:51–18:14) with Jesus' firm resolution to head toward Jerusalem and the final conflict that will culminate in his death and resurrection. Although ostensibly the record of a journey from Galilee to Judea, this part of the Gospel (traditionally known as the "greater interpolation") contains little action or sense of forward movement. Emphasizing Jesus' teaching, it is largely a miscellaneous collection of brief anecdotes, sayings, and parables. Here the author intermixes Q material with his individual source (L), including most of the parables unique to his Gospel.

At the beginning of this section, Luke records two incidents that preview later developments in Acts. On his way south to Jerusalem, Jesus passes through Samaria, carrying his message to several villages. In Matthew (10:5–6), Jesus expressly forbids a mission to the Samaritans, bitterly hated by Jews for their rival interpretations of the Mosaic Law. Luke, however, shows Jesus forbidding the disciples to punish an inhospitable Samaritan town and instead shows him conducting a short campaign there (9:52–56).

Along with the celebrated story of the "good Samaritan," this episode anticipates the later Christian mission to Samaria described in Acts 8. Jesus' sending forth seventy-two disciples to evangelize the countryside (10:1–16) similarly prefigures the future recruiting of Gentiles. In Jewish terminology, the number seventy or seventy-two represented the sum total of non-Jewish nations. As the Twelve sent to proselytize Israel probably symbolize the traditional twelve Israelite tribes (9:1–6), so the activity of the seventy-two foreshadows Christian expansion among Gentiles of the Roman Empire.

Luke's Jesus experiences a moment of ecstatic triumph when the seventy-two return from conducting a series of successful exorcisms. Possessed by the Spirit, he perceives the reality behind his disciples' victory over evil. In a mystical vision, Jesus sees Satan, like a bolt of lightning, hurled from heaven. Through the disciples' actions, Satan's influence is in decline (although he returns to corrupt Judas in 22:23).

In this context of defeating evil through good works, Jesus thanks God that his uneducated followers understand God's purpose better than the intellectually elite. In this passage, Luke expresses ideas that are more common in John's Gospel: Only Christ knows the divine nature, and only he can reveal it to those whom he chooses (10:17–24; cf. Matthew's version of this prayer in Matt. 11:25–27).

PARABLE OF THE GOOD SAMARITAN

Luke is aware, however, that "the learned and wise" are not always incapable of religious insight. In 10:25–28, a Torah expert defines the essence of the Mosaic Law in the twin commands of love God (Deut. 6:5) and neighbor (Lev. 19:18). Confirming the expert's perception, Jesus replies that, in loving thus, the man "will live." In this episode, Luke provides a good example of the way in which he adapts Markan material to his theological purpose. Mark places this dialog with the Torah instructor in the Jerusalem Temple and stresses Jesus' approval of the speaker's view that the "law of love" is the epitome of Judaism (Mark 12:28–31). Luke changes the site of this encounter from the Temple to an unidentified place on the road to Jerusalem and uses it to introduce his parable of the good Samaritan. The author creates a transition to the parable by having the instructor ask Jesus to explain what the Torah means by "neighbor."

Instead of answering directly, Jesus responds in typical rabbinic fashion: He tells a story. The questioner must discover his neighbor's identity in Jesus' depiction of a specific human situation. Analyzing the tale of the good Samaritan (10:29–35), most students will find that it not only follows Luke's customary theme of the unexpected but also introduces several rather thorny problems.

Ethical Complexities   Jesus' original audience would have seen enormous ethical complexities in this parable. The priest and **Levite** face a real dilemma: When they find the robbers' victim, they do not know whether the man is alive or dead. If they so much as touch a corpse, the Torah declares them ritually unclean, and they will be unable to fulfill their Temple duties. In this case, keeping the Law means ignoring the claim of a person in need. The priest's decision to remain faithful to Torah requirements necessitates his failure to help.

By making a Samaritan the moral hero of his story, Jesus further complicates the issue. In Jewish eyes, the Samaritans, who claimed guardianship of the Mosaic Law, were corruptors of the Torah from whom nothing good could be expected. (Note that a Samaritan village had refused Jesus hospitality because he was making a pilgrimage to Jerusalem, site of the Temple cult that the Samaritans despised [10:52–56].) Finally, Jesus' tale stresses a typical Lukan reversal: The religious outsider, whom the righteous hold in contempt, is the person who obeys the Torah's essential meaning—to act as God's agent by giving help to persons in need.

When Jesus asks the Torah expert which person in the tale behaves as a neighbor, the expert apparently cannot bring himself to utter the hated term *Samaritan*. Instead, he vaguely identifies the hero as "the one who showed [the victim] kindness." Jesus' directive to behave as the Samaritan does—in contrast to the priest and the Levite—contains a distinctly subversive element. When the Samaritan helps a Jew (the victim had been traveling from Jerusalem), he boldly overlooks ethnic and sectarian differences in order to aid a religious "enemy."

By constructing this particular situation, Jesus forces the Torah instructor (and Luke his reader) to

Box 9.5

The Lord's Prayer and the Golden Rule in the Gospels of Matthew and Luke

The Lord's Prayer

Matthew: Our Father in heaven
thy name be hallowed;
thy kingdom come,
thy will be done,
on earth as in heaven.
Give us today our daily bread.
Forgive us the wrong we have done,
as we have forgiven those who have
    wronged us.
And do not bring us to the test,
but save us from the evil one.
        (Matt. 6:9–13)

Luke: Father, thy name be hallowed;
thy kingdom come.
Give us each day our daily bread.
And forgive us our sins,
for we too forgive all who have done
    us wrong.
And do not bring us to the test.
        (Luke 11:2–4)

The Golden Rule

Matthew: Always treat others as you would like
them to treat you: that is the Law and the
prophets. (Matt. 7:12)

Luke: Treat others as you would like them to treat
you. (Luke 6:31)

Note that Matthew's versions appear to include interpretative comments, a midrash on Luke's simpler tradition of Jesus' words.

recognize that a "neighbor" does not necessarily belong to one's own racial or religious group but can be any person who demonstrates generosity and human kindness. (From the orthodox view, the Samaritan belongs to a "false" religion; he is not only a foreigner but a "heretic" as well.) An even more subversive note is sounded when the parable implies that the priest's and Levite's faithful adherence to biblical rules is the barrier that prevents them from observing religion's essential component, which the Torah expert had correctly defined as the love of God and neighbor.

MARY AND MARTHA

Note that Luke follows the Samaritan parable with a brief anecdote about Jesus' visit at the house of two sisters, Mary and Martha (10:38–42). In its own way, this episode draws a similar distinction between

strict adherence to duty and a sensitivity to "higher" opportunities. The Lukan Jesus commends Mary for abandoning her traditional woman's role and joining the men to hear his teaching. The learning experience will be hers to possess forever.

INSTRUCTIONS ON PRAYER

Luke places a greater emphasis on prayer than any other Synoptic author. Although his version of the Lord's Prayer is much shorter than Matthew's (see box 9.5), he heightens its significance by adding several parables that extol the value of persistence. Petitioning God is implicitly compared to pestering a friend until he gives what is asked (11:5–10). The same theme reappears in the parable of the importunate or "pushy" widow (18:1–8) who seeks justice from a cynical and corrupt judge. An unworthy representative of his profession, the judge cares nothing about God or public opinion—but he finally grants the widow's petition because she refuses to give him any peace until he acts. If even an unresponsive friend and unscrupulous judge can be hounded into helping one, how much more is God likely to reward people who do not give up talking to him (18:7–8)?

Luke contrasts two different kinds of prayer in his parable of the Pharisee and a "**publican**" (tax-gatherer) (18:9–14). In Jesus' day, the term *tax-gatherer* was then a synonym for sinner, one who betrayed his Jewish countrymen by hiring himself out to the Romans and making a living by extorting money and goods from an already-oppressed people. Notice that the parable contrasts the Pharisee's consciousness of religious worth with the tax collector's confession of his failings. In Luke's reversal of ordinary expectations, it is the honest outcast who wins God's approval and not necessarily the conventionally good person.

LUKE'S VIEWS ON RICHES AND POVERTY

More than any other Gospel writer, Luke stresses forsaking worldly ambition for the spiritual riches of the kingdom. The Lukan Jesus assures his followers that if God provides for nature's birds and flowers, he will care for Christians. He urges his disciples to sell their possessions, give to the poor, and thus earn "heavenly treasures" (12:22–34).

Luke's strong antimaterialism and apparent bias against the rich is partly the result of his conviction that God's judgment may occur at any time. The rich fool dies before he can enjoy his life's work (12:13–21), but Christians may undergo judgment even before death. The Master may return without warning at any time (12:35–40). Rather than accumulating wealth, believers must share with the poor and the socially unwanted (14:12–14). Luke also emphasizes that the deformed and unattractive, rejects and have-nots of society, must be the Christian's primary concern in attaining Jesus' favorable verdict (14:15–24).

LAZARUS AND THE RICH MAN

Reversals in the Afterlife The Lukan Jesus makes absolute demands upon his disciples: None can

belong to him without giving away everything he owns (14:33). In his parable of **Lazarus** and the rich man, Luke dramatizes the danger of hanging on to great wealth until death parts the owner from his possessions (16:19–31). Appearing only in Luke's Gospel, this metaphor of the afterlife embodies typically Lukan concepts. It shows a rich man experiencing all the posthumous misery that Jesus had predicted for the world's comfortable and satisfied people (6:24–26) and a poor beggar enjoying all the rewards that Jesus had promised to the hungry and outcast (6:20–21). Demonstrating Luke's usual theme of reversal, the parable shows the two men exchanging their relative positions in the next world.

In reporting Jesus' only parable that deals with the contrasting fates of individuals after death, Luke employs ideas typical of first-century Hellenistic Judaism. The author's picture of Lazarus in paradise and the rich man in fiery torment is duplicated in Josephus's contemporary description of Hades (the Underworld).

Notice that Luke charges the rich man with no crime and assigns the beggar no virtue. To the author, it appears that present social conditions—the existence of hopeless poverty and sickness alongside the "magnificence" and luxury of the affluent—demand a radical change when God rules the world completely. The only fault of which the rich man is implicitly guilty is his toleration of the extreme contrast between his own abundance and the miserable state of the poor. For Luke, it appears to be enough. The author's ideal social order is the commune that the disciples establish following **Pentecost,** an economic arrangement in which the well-to-do sell their possessions, share them with the poor, and hold "everything in common" (Acts 2:42–47).

Luke modifies his severe criticism of great wealth, however, by including Mark's story of Jesus' advice to a rich man. (He returns to the Markan narrative again in 18:15.) If wealth disqualifies one for the kingdom, who can hope to please God? Note that Jesus' enigmatic reply—all things are possible (18:18–27)—leads to the concept of divine compensation. Persons who sacrifice family or home to seek the kingdom will be repaid both now (presumably referring to the spiritual riches they enjoy in church fellowship) and in the future with eternal life (18:28–30).

JESUS' LOVE OF THE UNHAPPY AND THE OUTCAST

All the Gospel authors agree that Jesus sought the company of "tax-gatherers and sinners," a catchall term referring to the great mass of people in ancient Palestine who were socially and religiously unacceptable because they did not or could not keep the Torah's requirements. This "unrespectable" group stood in contrast to the Sadducees, the Pharisees, the scribes, and others who conscientiously observed all Torah regulations in their daily lives. In the Synoptic Gospels, Jesus ignores the principle of contamination by association. He eats, drinks, and otherwise intimately mixes with a wide variety of persons commonly viewed as both morally and ritually "unclean." At one moment we find him dining at the homes of socially honored Pharisees (7:36–50) and the next enjoying the hospitality of social pariahs like **Simon** the leper (Matt. 26:6–13) and Zacchaeus the tax collector (19:1–10). Jesus's habitual associations lead some of his contemporaries to regard him as a pleasure-loving drunkard (7:34). According to Luke, Jesus answers such criticism by creating parables that illustrate God's unfailing concern for persons the "righteous" dismiss as worthless (see box 9.6).

PARABLES OF JOY AT FINDING WHAT WAS LOST

One of the ethical highlights of the entire New Testament, Luke 15 contains three parables dramatizing the joy human beings experience when they recover something precious they had thought forever lost.

The Lost Sheep   The parable of the lost sheep (also in Matt. 18:10–14) recounts a shepherd's delight in finding a strayed animal. In Luke's version, emphasis falls on the celebration that follows the shepherd's find: "friends and neighbors" are called together to rejoice with him (15:1–7).

A Lost Coin   A second parable (15:8–10) invites us to observe the behavior of a woman who loses one of her ten silver coins. She lights her lamp (an extravagant gesture for the poor) and sweeps out her entire house, looking in every corner, until she finds the coin. Then, like the shepherd, she summons "friends and neighbors" to celebrate her find. Although Luke sees these two parables as allegories symbolizing heavenly joy over a "lost" sinner's repentance (15:7, 10), they also reveal Jesus' characteristic tendency to observe and describe unusual human behavior. Both the shepherd and woman exhibit the intense concentration on a single action — searching for lost property — that exemplifies Jesus' demand to seek God's rule first, to the exclusion of all else (6:22; Matt. 6:33).

The Prodigal Son   One of the most emotionally moving passages in the Bible, the parable of the prodigal son might better be called the story of the forgiving father, for the climax of the narrative focuses on the latter's attitude to his two very different sons. Besides squandering his inheritance "with his women" (15:30), the younger son violates the most basic standards of Judaism, reducing himself to the level of an animal groveling in a Gentile's pigpen. Listing the young man's progressively degrading actions, Jesus describes a person who is utterly insensitive to his religious heritage and as "undeserving" as a human being can be. Even his decision to return to his father's estate is based on an unworthy desire to eat better food.

Yet the parable's main focus is not on the youth's unworthiness, but on the father's love. Notice that when the prodigal (spendthrift) is still "a long way off," his father sees him and, forgetting his dignity, rushes to meet the returning son. Note, too, that the father expresses no anger at his son's shameful behavior, demands no admission of wrongdoing, and inflicts no punishment. Ignoring the youth's contrite request to be hired as a servant, the parent instead orders a lavish celebration in his honor.

The conversation between the father and his older son, who understandably complains about the partiality shown to his sibling, makes the parable's theme even clearer. Acknowledging the older child's superior claim to his favor, the father attempts to explain the unlimited quality of his affection (15:11–32). The

Box 9.6
The Parable of the Great Banquet: Three Authorial Interpretations

Three Gospels—the canonical Matthew and Luke and the apocryphal Thomas—preserve three strikingly different versions of a parable in which guests who are first invited to a great dinner party fail to respond and are unexpectedly replaced by strangers recruited from the streets. Each of the three versions is distinguished by the distinctive concerns of the individual Gospel writer.

MATTHEW	LUKE	THOMAS
Then Jesus spoke to them again in parables: "The kingdom of Heaven is like this. There was a king who prepared a feast for his son's wedding; but when he sent his servants to summon the guests he had invited, they would not come. He sent others again, telling them to say to the guests, 'See now! I have prepared this feast for you. I have had my bullocks and fatted beasts slaughtered; everything is ready; come to the wedding at once.' But they took no notice; one went off to his farm, another to his business, and the others seized the servants, attacked them brutally, and killed them. The king was furious; he sent troops to kill those murderers and set their town on fire. Then he said to his servants, 'The wedding-feast is ready; but the guests I invited did not deserve the honour. Go out to the main thoroughfares, and invite everyone you can find to the wedding.' The servants went out into the streets, and collected all they could find, good and bad alike. So the hall was packed with guests. "When the king came in to see the company at the table, he observed one man who was not dressed for a wedding. 'My friend,' said the king, 'how do you come to be here without your wedding clothes?' He had nothing to say. The king then said to his attendants, 'Bind him hand and foot; turn him out into the dark, the place of wailing and grinding of teeth.' For though many are invited, few are chosen." (Matt. 22:1–14)	One of the company, after hearing all this, said to him, "Happy the man who shall sit at the feast in the kingdom of God!" Jesus answered, "A man was giving a big dinner party and had sent out many invitations. At dinner-time he sent his servant with a message for his guests, 'Please come, everything is now ready.' They began one and all to excuse themselves. The first said, 'I have bought a piece of land and I must go and look over it; please accept my apologies.' The second said, 'I have bought five yoke of oxen, and I am on my way to try them out; please accept my apologies.' The next said, 'I have just got married and for that reason I cannot come.' When the servant came back he reported this to his master. The master of the house was angry and said to him, 'Go out quickly into the streets and alleys of the town, and bring me in the poor, the crippled, the blind, and the lame.' The servant said, 'Sir, your orders have been carried out and there is still room.' The master replied, 'Go out on to the highways and along the hedgerows and make them come in; I want my house to be full. I tell you that not one of those who were invited shall taste my banquet." (Luke 14:15–24)	Jesus said, "A person was receiving guests. When he had prepared the dinner, he sent his slave to invite the guests. The slave went to the first and said to that one, 'My master invites you.' That one said, 'Some merchants owe me money; they are coming to me tonight. I have to go and give them instructions. Please excuse me from dinner.' The slave went to another and said to that one, 'My master has invited you.' That one said to the slave, 'I have bought a house, and I have been called away for a day. I shall have no time.' The slave went to another and said to that one, 'My master invites you.' That one said to the slave, 'My friend is to be married, and I am to arrange the banquet. I shall not be able to come. Please excuse me from dinner.' The slave went to another and said to that one, 'My master invites you.' That one said to the slave, 'I have bought an estate, and I am going to collect the rent. I shall not be able to come. Please excuse me.' The slave returned and said to his master, 'Those whom you invited to dinner have asked to be excused.' The master said to his slave, 'Go out on the streets and bring back whomever you find to have dinner.' "Buyers and merchants [will] not enter the places of my Father." (Thom. 64)

(continued)

Box 9.6 *(continued)*

In Matthew's version of the parable, a king issues invitations to a sumptuous wedding feast for his son. Not only are the ruler's supposed friends indifferent to his hospitality, some kill the servants who invited them. Furious, the ruler then dispatches armies to destroy those who murdered his emissaries and "burn their city." The king's overreaction to his spurned generosity is even more extreme when one of the rabble brought in to replace the ungrateful guests shows up without the proper festal garments, a social faux pas for which he is tied up and thrown into a "frighteningly dark" prison.

Setting the parable in the narrative context of Jesus' rejection by the Jerusalem authorities, Matthew transforms it into a historical allegory of God's relationship with Israel. When the covenant people reject the invitation to his son's (Jesus') messianic banquet, God's anger results in the Roman destruction of Jerusalem and the replacement of his former people by a new crowd that includes "good and bad alike," the Matthean religious community. The divine host's arbitrary casting of the improperly dressed guest—who could not reasonably have been expected to be carrying a set of formal attire when he was suddenly dragged to a stranger's wedding—may derive from another (otherwise lost) parable. The supernatural darkness to which the fashion felon is consigned is one of Matthew's characteristic images.

Luke introduces the parable as simply a "big dinner party" given by an ordinary (but presumably rich) host whose prospective guests all turn down his last-minute invitation. The three guests' stated excuses for not attending are entirely reasonable: All are busily engaged in life's ordinary pursuits, tending to their farms, their animals, and their marriages. The spurned host then invites a typically Lukan category of guests—the poor, crippled, lame, and blind, precisely the kind of commonly devalued people that Jesus had already instructed his followers to include in their feasts (cf. Luke 14:12–14). As Matthew had turned a parable involving ungrateful guests into a polemic against the Jerusalem establishment and a justification for Jerusalem's destruction, so Luke makes it into a plea for the social outcasts—those who can't repay one's hospitality—whose cause he espouses throughout his Gospel.

Whereas most traditional folk narratives feature a set of three actions, as does Luke's story of three rejected invitations in his version of the parable, that contained in Thomas breaks the usual pattern by including four guests and their reasons for not attending. All four invited guests are people of property, homeowners, landlords, and financiers, members of the economically successful class of whom most early Christian writers are profoundly suspicious. Thomas's bias is clearly apparent in the parable's final line: The commercial class—"buyers and merchants"—are not God's kind of people.

In its three variations, the banquet parable has one consistent theme: The host has everything ready and, without warning his chosen guests in advance, suddenly demands that they drop everything and come to enjoy his good things. When, busily employed elsewhere, they fail to appreciate his offer, the disappointed host unexpectedly opens his house to people who could not previously consider themselves eligible—loiterers in the marketplace, social pariahs, and anybody who had no place else to go. Despite the Gospel writers' editorial revisions, themes characteristic of Jesus' authentic parables, including God's incalculable ways of intervening in human lives and the reversals of normal expectations his appeals create, are embedded in the "sweet unreasonableness" of this tale.

---

father's nature is to love unconditionally, making no distinction between the deserving and the undeserving recipients of his care. The parable expresses the same view of the divine Parent, who "is kind to the ungrateful and wicked," that Luke pictured in his Sermon on the Plain (6:35–36).

Like many of Jesus' authentic parables, this tale ends with an essential question unanswered: How will the older brother, smarting with natural resentment at the prodigal's unmerited reward, respond to his father's implied invitation to join the family revel? As Luke views the issue, Jesus' call to sinners was remarkably successful; it is the conventionally religious who too often fail to value an invitation to the messianic banquet.

PARABLE OF THE DISHONEST STEWARD

Luke's parables not only surprise us by turning accepted values upside down, consigning the fortunate rich to torment and celebrating the good fortune of the undeserving, but they can also puzzle us. Luke follows the parable of the prodigal son with a mind-boggling story of a dishonest and conniving businessman who cheats his employer and is commended for it (16:1–9).

Teaching none of the conventional principles of honesty or decent behavior, this parable makes most readers distinctly uncomfortable. Like the prodigal son, the steward violates the trust placed in him and defrauds his benefactor. Yet, like the prodigal, he is rewarded by the very person whom he has wronged. The unexpected is what happens. This upsets our basic notions of justice and fair play, as the prodigal's elder brother was upset by having no distinction drawn between his moral propriety and the younger brother's outrageous misbehavior. The meaning Luke attaches to this strange parable—worldly people like the steward are more clever than the unworldly—does not explain the moral paradox. We must ask in what context, in response to what situation, did Jesus first tell this story? Is it simply another example of the unexpected or a paradigm of the bewilderingly unacceptable that must happen when the kingdom breaks into our familiar and convention-ridden lives? Clearly, Luke's readers are asked to rethink ideas and assumptions previously taken for granted.

Figure 9.4 Bust of the Emperor Tiberius (14–37 C.E.). According to Luke, Jesus was "about thirty years old" when he began his Galilean campaign during the fifteenth year of Tiberius's reign (c. 27–29 C.E.) (Luke 3:1, 23). (© British Museum)

The Jerusalem Ministry: Jesus' Challenge to the Holy City

This segment of Luke's narrative (18:31–21:38) focuses on Jesus' teaching in or near Jerusalem (see figure 9.4). The disciples excitedly anticipate great events once Jesus arrives in the holy city (19:11). Luke, however, presents the Jerusalem ministry in a way that redefines apocalyptic hopes and interprets Jesus' kingdom teaching in the light of present realities. In Luke's version of the prophecy, foretelling the Jewish revolt and Jerusalem's destruction, the author carefully distinguishes between historical events that have already occurred and cosmic portents that belong to the future.

CONFLICTING BELIEFS ABOUT THE PAROUSIA

Luke's account of Jesus' teachings about the kingdom and Jerusalem's fall seems to modify two popular ideas about the nature of End time and the Parousia. One is a belief that the Parousia has already happened, a concept also discussed in Paul's second letter to the church at **Thessalonica,** a town in northern Greece (2 Thess. 2:1–12). Apparently, some believed that the Second Coming was accomplished by Jesus' death, resurrection, and **ascension** into heaven, followed by his outpouring of the Holy Spirit upon the church. (We find a similar concept in John's Gospel.) A more common view held that the Parousia was extremely near and would occur within the lifetimes of people then living. Luke does not reject the traditional view that Jesus' return will involve a supernatural event bringing history as we know it to a close. His Gospel retains elements of primitive Christian **apocalypticism,** including instructions to be constantly alert and prepared for the *eschaton,* but he also distances the End, placing it at some unknown time in the remote future.

LUKAN SAYINGS ABOUT THE KINGDOM

In Luke's Gospel, we find Jesus' sayings about the imminence of the kingdom intermixed with exclusively Lukan material about the kingdom being already a reality present in Jesus' miraculous deeds and teaching. When the Pharisees accuse Jesus of exorcising demons by the power of "Beelzebub [Satan]," he answers, "If it is by the finger of God that I drive out the devils, then be sure the kingdom of God has already come upon you" (11:20). Jesus thus challenges onlookers to see in his successful fight against Evil the inbreaking reign of God. A similar concept of the kingdom appears in Jesus' answer to those Pharisees who ask when God's dominion will begin: "You cannot tell by observation when the Kingdom of God comes. There will be no saying, 'Look, here it is!' or 'there it is!'; for in fact the kingdom of God is among you [or in your midst]" (17:20–21). Because God rules through Jesus, the Son's work of healing and expelling devils means that the kingdom now reigns. Luke follows this saying with statements that emphasize the unexpectedness and unpredictability of the "Son of Man's" reappearance. Readers are told not to believe premature reports of Jesus' arrival, for the world will continue its normal way until the Parousia suddenly occurs. Though (in this tradition) coming without signs, it is as unmistakable as "the lightning flash that lights up the earth from end to end" (17:22–30).

In his editing of Mark's apocalyptic passages, Luke reveals his intent to modify earlier expectations. At the outset of his Gospel, he omits Mark's reference to Jesus' warning about the kingdom's nearness, replacing it with Jesus' announcement of his peaceful messiahship in the Nazareth synagogue (Mark 1:14–15; Luke 4:16–22). Luke presents an edited form of the proclamation in 10:9, 11, but in the context of the disciples' healing ministry, harmonizing with the concept of the kingdom's being present in Jesus' activity. The apocalyptic declaration that some standing beside Jesus would not die before experiencing the kingdom (Mark 9:1) is preserved, but in the context of the Transfiguration, which reveals Jesus' divine kingship (9:27).

THE FALL OF JERUSALEM AND THE PAROUSIA

Luke also retains Mark's apocalyptic prediction of Jerusalem's destruction (Mark 13) but edits it extensively to show that a period of indefinite length intervenes between the city's fall and the actual Parousia (ch. 21). Luke is aware that many of Jesus' followers expected his ministry to culminate in God's government being established visibly on earth. The author reports that "because he [Jesus] was now close to Jerusalem . . . they thought the reign [or kingdom] of God might dawn at any moment" (19:11), an expectation that persisted in the early church (Acts 1:6–7). Luke counters this belief with a parable explaining that their Master must go away "on a long journey" before he returns as "king" (19:12–27). (This parable of "talents," or servants investing money for their absent master, is used by Matthew [25:14–30] for the same purpose of explaining the delayed Parousia.)

Jerusalem's Fall Is Not the End   Luke makes the point even clearer in his description of the Jerusalem siege. Christians are to flee the doomed city, knowing that "the end does not follow immediately" (21:9, 20–23). The author separates historical events preceding Jerusalem's destruction from cosmic events that signal Jesus' return. After the Romans decimate the city and burn the Temple, an indefinitely extended period of secular history will intervene. Luke's Jesus states that "Jerusalem will be trampled down by foreigners until their day has run its course" (21:24). This reference to an epoch of Gentile domination occurs only in Luke and replaces the apocalyptic "sign" of the "abomination of desolation" that appears at this point in Mark's prophecy of the End (Mark 13:14; Matt. 24:15). In Luke's modified apocalypse, an age of "foreign" (Roman) control will intervene between Jerusalem's fall in 70 c.e. and the Parousia. In Acts, Luke shows the church's representatives exploiting the Gentiles' "day" or "time" by evangelizing the Roman Empire.

Two Stages of the End   Luke's revision of Mark 13 suggests that the author divides apocalyptic time into two distinct stages. The first stage involves the Jewish revolt and Jerusalem's fall; the second involves the Parousia. Note that Luke uses mythic and astronomical language to characterize events during the second stage. In this passage (21:25–28), he borrows terms from Jewish apocalyptic writers and follows Mark in citing cosmic phenomena — "portents in sun, moon and stars" — that herald the last day. Foreign powers (Gentile nations) no longer will dominate but will become powerless with fear. The climactic event is the reappearance of the Son of Man, who then will possess a might and splendor eclipsing that of Gentile rulers. Only after the terrifying celestial display begins can the faithful regard their freedom as near.

Although he had previously included the celebrated assertion that there would be no convincing "sign" of the End (17:21), Luke now cites Mark's simile of the fig tree. When the tree buds, one knows summer is near — thus, when the believer sees the prophesied events occurring, he knows that the "kingdom" (here synonymous with the Parousia) is close. Luke also reproduces Mark's confident declaration that "the present generation will live to see it all" (21:32). In its reedited context, however, the assertion that a single generation would witness the death throes of history probably applies only to the cosmic "portents" that immediately precede the Son's arrival. Luke's modified eschatology does not require that the "generation" that witnessed Jesus' ministry and/or Jerusalem's destruction be the same group living when the Parousia takes place. Even so, the believer must remain awake at all times because the final day will dawn on all humanity with universal impact (21:34–36).

The Final Conflict and Passion Story

LUKE'S INTERPRETATION OF THE PASSION

Although Luke's account of Jesus' last days in Jerusalem roughly parallels that of Mark (14:1–16:8), it differs in enough details to suggest that Luke may have used another source as well. In this section (22:1–23:56), Luke stresses a theme that will also dominate Acts: Jesus, like his followers after him, is innocent of any sedition against Rome. Luke interprets Jesus' death as an act of legal murder brought about by the Jewish leadership. More than in any other Gospel, Pilate is represented as reluctant to condemn Jesus, repeatedly declaring that the accused is not guilty of a "capital offence." Only when pressured by a Jerusalem mob does Pilate consent to Jesus' crucifixion.

Besides insisting on Jesus' innocence, Luke edits the Markan narrative (or another tradition parallel to that contained in Mark) to present his own theology of the cross. Mark had stated that Jesus' death was sacrificial: His life is given "as a ransom for many" (Mark 10:45). In the Lukan equivalent of this passage (placed in the setting of the Last Supper), Jesus merely says that he comes to serve (cf. Mark 10:42–45 and Luke 22:24–27). Unlike some other New Testament writers, Luke does not see Jesus' Passion as a mystical atonement for human sin. Instead, Jesus appears "like a servant," providing an example for others to imitate, the first in a line of Christian models that includes Peter, Stephen, Paul, and their companions in the Book of Acts.

THE LAST SUPPER

Mark's report of the Last Supper (Mark 14:17–25) closely parallels that described in Paul's first letter to the Corinthians (1 Cor. 11:23–26). Luke's version introduces several variations: In the Lukan ceremony, the wine cup is passed first and then the unleavened bread. The author may present this different order in the ritual because he wants to avoid giving Jesus' statement about drinking wine again in the kingdom the apocalyptic meaning that Mark gives it. Luke also omits the words interpreting the wine as Jesus' blood, avoiding any suggestion that Jesus sheds his blood to ransom humanity from sin or that he gives his blood to establish a New Covenant. In Luke, Jesus' only interpretative comment relates the bread (Eucharist) to his "body" (22:17–20). The author also inverts Mark's order by having Jesus announce Judas's betrayal after the ritual meal, implying that the traitor was present and participated in the communion ceremony.

JESUS' FINAL ORDEAL

In his report of Jesus' arrest, trials, and crucifixion, Luke makes several more inversions of the Markan order and adds new material to emphasize his characteristic themes. Softening Mark's harsh view of the disciples' collective failure, Luke states that they fell asleep in Gethsemane because they were "worn out by grief" (22:45–46). In this scene, the author contrasts Jesus' physical anguish—he literally sweats blood—with the spiritual help Jesus receives from prayer. After asking the Father to spare him, Jesus perceives "an angel from heaven bringing him strength," after which he prays even more fervently. In extremity, Jesus demonstrates the function of prayer for those among the Lukan community who suffer similar testing and persecution (22:39–44).

In describing Jesus' hearing before the Sanhedrin, Luke makes several changes in the Markan sequence of events. In Mark, the High Priest questions Jesus, Jesus is then physically abused, and Peter denies knowing him (Mark 14:55–72). Luke places Peter's denial first, the beating second, and the priest's interrogation third (22:63–71). Instead of announcing his identity as Messiah as in Mark, the Lukan Jesus makes only an ambiguous statement that may or may not be an admission. Luke also rephrases Jesus' allusion to the "Son of Man" to show that with Jesus' ministry, the Son's reign has already begun (22:67–71).

Herod Antipas   In Luke, the Sanhedrin can produce no witnesses and no conviction on charges of blasphemy. Its members bring Jesus to Pilate strictly on political terms: The accused "subverts" the Jewish nation, opposes paying taxes to the Roman government, and claims to be the Messiah, a political role. When Pilate, eager to rid himself of this troublesome case, learns that Jesus is a Galilean and therefore under the jurisdiction of Herod Antipas, he sends the prisoner to be tried by Herod, who is in Jerusalem for the Passover (23:6–12). Found only in Luke, the Herod episode serves to reinforce Luke's picture of an innocent Jesus. Pilate remarks that neither he nor Herod can find anything in Jesus' case to support the Jews' charge of "subversion" (23:13–15).

In Luke's eyes, only the Jewish leaders are responsible for Jesus' condemnation. Twice Pilate declares that the prisoner "has done nothing to deserve death" (23:15) and is legally "guilty of [no] capital offence" (23:22). The Roman procurator, whom other contemporary historians depict as a ruthless tyrant contemptuous of Jewish public opinion, is here only a weak pawn manipulated by a fanatical group of his Jewish subjects.

Last Words on the Cross   In recounting Jesus' crucifixion, Luke provides several "last words" that illustrate important Lukan themes. Only in this Gospel do we find Jesus' prayer to forgive his executioners because they do not understand the significance of their actions (23:34). Because Luke regards both Jews and Romans as acting in "ignorance" (see Acts 2:17), this request to pardon his tormentors encompasses all parties involved in Jesus' death. Besides illustrating Jesus' heroic capacity to forgive, this prayer shows Luke's hero vindicating his teaching that a victim must love his enemy (6:27–38) and end the cycle of hatred and retaliation that perpetuates evil in the world. To Luke, Jesus' death enacts the supreme parable of reversal, forgiveness, and completion.

Even in personal suffering, the Lukan Jesus thinks not of himself, but of others. Carrying his cross on the road to **Calvary,** he comforts the women who weep for him (23:26–31). He similarly consoles the man crucified next to him, promising him an immediate reward in **paradise** (23:43).

(Note that this fellow sufferer has recognized Jesus' political innocence [23:41].) The Messiah's last words are to the Father whose Spirit he had received following baptism (3:21; 4:1, 14) and to whom in death he commits his own spirit (23:46–47).

Except for the symbolic darkness accompanying the Crucifixion (23:44–45), Luke mentions no natural phenomena comparable to the great earthquake that Matthew records. Consequently, the Roman centurion does not recognize in Jesus a supernatural being, "a son of God," as in Mark and Matthew (Mark 15:39; Matt. 27:54). The centurion's remark refers not to Jesus' divinity but to the political injustice of his execution. "Beyond all doubt," he says, "this man was innocent" (23:47). This account of Jesus' death dramatizes two major Lukan themes: Jesus, rather than being a sacrifice for sin, is an example of compassion and forgiveness for all to emulate. He is also, like his followers, completely innocent of any crime against Rome.

Like Matthew, Luke generally follows Mark's order through Jesus' burial and the women's discovery of the empty tomb. Omitting any Matthean reference to supernatural phenomena such as an Easter morning earthquake or the appearance of an angel that blinds the Roman guards, Luke diverges from Mark only in that the women report what they have seen to the Eleven, who do not believe them (23:49–24:11). (No Gospel writer except Mark has the women keep silent about their observation.)

Epilog: Postresurrection Appearances in the Vicinity of Jerusalem

Because early editions of Mark contain no resurrection narrative, it is not surprising that Matthew and Luke, who generally adhere to Mark's order through the discovery of the empty sepulcher, differ widely in their reports of Jesus' postresurrection appearances. Consistent with his emphasis on Jerusalem, Luke omits the Markan tradition that Jesus would reappear in Galilee (Mark 16:7; Matt. 28:7, 16–20) and places all the disciples' experiences of the risen Jesus in or near Jerusalem.

In concluding his Gospel, the author creates two detailed accounts of Jesus' posthumous teaching that serve to connect Jesus' story with that of the believing community for whom Luke writes. The risen Jesus' words are not a final farewell but a preparation for what follows in Luke's second volume, the Book of Acts. Because Luke wishes to show that Jesus' presence and power continue unabated in the work of the early church, he describes Jesus' last instructions in terms that directly relate to the ongoing experience of the church. For Luke, the disciples' original experience of their risen Lord is qualitatively the same spiritually renewing experience that believers continue to enjoy in their charismatic community. Even after ascending to heaven, Jesus remains present in the church's characteristic activities: sharing sacramental meals, studying Scripture, and feeding the poor.

In narrating Jesus' first appearance on the road to **Emmaus** (a few miles from Jerusalem), Luke emphasizes the glorified Lord's relationship to followers left behind on earth. The two disciples, Cleopas and an unnamed companion (perhaps a woman), who encounter Jesus do not recognize him until they dine together. Only in breaking bread—symbolic of the Christian Communion ritual—is Jesus' living presence discerned.

In Luke's second postresurrection account, the disciples are discussing Jesus when he suddenly appears in their midst, asking to be fed—it has been more than three days since the Last Supper, and he is hungry. The Lukan disciples' offering Jesus a piece of cooked fish makes several points: Their job is to care for the poor and hungry whom Jesus had also served; they have fellowship with Jesus in communal dining; and they are assured that the figure standing before them is real—he eats material food—and not a hallucination. By insisting on Jesus' physicality, Luke also firmly links the heavenly Christ and the human Jesus—they are one and the same.

Perhaps most important for Luke's understanding of the way in which Jesus remains alive and present is the author's emphasis on studying the Hebrew Bible in order to discover the true significance of Jesus' career. At Emmaus, Jesus explains "the passages which referred to himself in every part of the scriptures" (24:27), thus setting his listeners' "hearts on fire" (24:32). In Jerusalem he repeats these lessons in biblical exegesis, interpreting the Torah, Prophets, and Writings as christological prophecies (24:44), an innovative practice that enabled Christians to recognize Jesus in the Mosaic revelation. Luke also connects these postresurrection teachings with the church's task: Jesus' death and resurrection, foretold in Scripture, are not history's final act but the beginning of a worldwide movement. The disciples are to remain together in Jerusalem until Jesus sends the Holy Spirit, which will empower them to proclaim God's new dispensation to "all nations" (24:46–49; fulfilled in Acts 1–2).

Summary

The author of the Gospel traditionally ascribed to Luke, traveling companion of the apostle Paul, wrote primarily for a Gentile audience. His portrait of Jesus reveals a world *sōter* ("savior" or "deliverer"), conceived by the Holy Spirit, who opens a new era in God's plan for human salvation. As John the Baptist represents the culmination of Israel's role in the divine plan, so Jesus—healing, teaching, and banishing evil—inaugurates the reign of God, the "kingdom," among humanity.

Emphasizing God's compassion and willingness to forgive all, the Lukan Jesus provides a powerful example for his followers to imitate in service, charity, and good works. An ethical model for Jews and Gentiles alike, Jesus establishes a Spirit-led movement that provides a religion of salvation for all people. The primitive belief that the Son of Man would return "soon" after his resurrection from the dead is replaced with Luke's concept of the disciples' role in carrying on Jesus' work "to the ends of the earth," a commission that extends the time of the End indefinitely into the future. In the meantime, a law-abiding and peaceful church will convey its message of a Savior for all nations throughout the Roman Empire—and beyond.

QUESTIONS FOR REVIEW

1. Describe some of Luke's major themes and concerns. How do parables that appear only in Luke's Gospel, such as Lazarus and the rich man and the prodigal son, illustrate typically Lukan ideas?

2. Describe the roles that women play in Luke's account. Which women, absent in Mark and Matthew, appear in Luke's version of Jesus' ministry? What qualities of Jesus does their presence elicit?

3. Evaluate the evidence for and against the tradition that Luke, Paul's traveling companion, wrote the Gospel bearing his name. Because the author was aware that "many" other accounts of Jesus' life and work had already been composed, why did he—who was not an eyewitness to the events he describes—decide to write a new Gospel? Does the fact that the writer added the Book of Acts as a sequel to his Gospel narrative suggest something about his purpose?

4. In the Greco-Roman world, historians and biographers often composed long speeches to illustrate their characters' ideas, ethical qualities, and responses to critical events. Do you find any evidence that Luke uses this method in the Gospel and/or Acts?

5. Show some of the specific ways that Luke's version of Jesus' arrest, trial, and execution reflects an awareness of the political realities with which the Christian community had to deal. How does Luke take pains to show that Jesus is innocent of sedition against Rome?

QUESTIONS FOR DISCUSSION AND REFLECTION

1. Much of the material that appears only in Luke's Gospel highlights Jesus' concern for women, the poor, and the socially outcast. The parables unique to his account—such as the prodigal son, the good Samaritan, and Lazarus and the rich man—stress unexpected reversals of society's accepted norms. What view of Jesus' character and teaching do you think Luke wishes to promote?

2. Compare Matthew's Sermon on the Mount (Matt. 5–7) with Luke's similar Sermon on the Plain (ch. 6). When Luke's version of a saying differs from Matthew's, which of the two do you think is probably closer to Jesus' own words? Do the different versions of the same saying—such as Jesus' blessing of the poor—also illustrate the individual Gospel writer's distinctive viewpoint?

3. Luke's Gospel emphasizes such themes as prayer, the activity of the Holy Spirit, the kingdom's reversal of normal expectations, the rejection of wealth and other material ambitions, Jesus' compassion, and the divine joy in human redemption. How do these themes relate to the author's belief that Jesus' ministry completes the purpose of Israel's revelation and begins a "new age" leading to the kingdom?

4. Luke consistently shows Jesus gravitating toward economically and politically powerless persons, including women, social outcasts, and the poor. Do you think that the Lukan Jesus' example of concern for socially marginal and "unrespectable" people—such as prostitutes, notorious sinners, and tax collectors who collaborated with the "evil empire" of Rome—is sufficiently recognized or honored by today's political and religious leaders? Can someone be a Christian and *not* follow Jesus' example of siding with the poor and oppressed? Explain your answer.

5. In editing Mark's prophecy of Jerusalem's fall and Jesus' Second Coming, how does Luke modify his predecessor's emphasis on the nearness of End time? Are Luke's changes in Mark's apocalyptic viewpoint consistent with his writing a second book about the purpose and goals of the early Christian church (the Book of Acts)?

TERMS AND CONCEPTS TO REMEMBER

Luke-Acts as a two-volume work
Theophilus
Luke (Paul's traveling companion)
Luke's research methods
L (Lukan) source
Luke's distinctive themes
role of the Holy Spirit
Luke's interest in women
Savior *(sōter)*
Elizabeth and Zechariah
Simeon and Anna
Benedictus
Nunc Dimittis
Magnificat
"lesser interpolation"
Sermon on the Plain
"greater interpolation"
parables of forgiveness, reversal, and the unexpected
Luke's interpretation of Jesus' ministry and death
Luke's modification of Mark's apocalyptic urgency

RECOMMENDED READING

Conzelmann, Hans. *Theology of St. Luke.* Translated by G. Buswell. New York: Harper & Row, 1960. An influential and incisive analysis of Luke's theological purposes.

Danker, F. W. *Luke.* Philadelphia: Fortress Press, 1976. A good general introduction.

Edwards, O. C., Jr. *Luke's Story of Jesus.* Philadelphia: Fortress Press, 1981.

Fitzmyer, J. A., ed. *The Gospel According to Luke,* Vols. 1 and 2 of the Anchor Bible. Garden City, N.Y.: Doubleday, 1981, 1985.

Johnson, Luke Timothy. "Luke-Acts, Book of." In D. N. Freedman, ed., *The Anchor Bible Dictionary,* Vol. 4, pp. 403–420. New York: Doubleday, 1992. A lucid summary of current scholarly studies of Luke's two-volume work.

Karris, Robert J. "The Gospel According to Luke." In R. E. Brown et al., eds., *The New Jerome Biblical Commentary,* pp. 675–721. Englewood Cliffs, N.J.: Prentice-Hall, 1990. Provides detailed commentary on Lukan accounts.

Leaney, A. R. C. *A Commentary on the Gospel According to St. Luke,* 2nd ed. Harper's New Testament Commentary. London: Black, 1966.

Talbert, C. H. *Reading Luke: A Literary and Theological Commentary on the Third Gospel.* Los Angeles: Crossroads, 1982.

———. *Luke-Acts: New Perspectives from the Society of Biblical Literature Seminar.* New York: Crossroads, 1984.

Tiede, David. *Prophecy and History in Luke-Acts.* Philadelphia: Fortress Press, 1980.

CHAPTER 10

John's Portrait of Jesus

Divine Wisdom Made Flesh

He who has faith in me will do what I am doing; and he will do greater things still. . . . Your Advocate [Paraclete], the Holy Spirit . . . will teach you everything, and will call to mind all that I have told you.

John 14:12, 26

Key Themes In John's Gospel, the order of events and the portrayal of Jesus and his teaching are strikingly different from those in the Synoptic accounts. Whereas the Synoptics depict Jesus as an eschatological healer-exorcist whose teachings deal primarily with Torah reinterpretation, John describes Jesus as an embodiment of heavenly Wisdom who performs no exorcisms and whose message centers on his own divine nature. In John, Jesus is the human form of God's celestial Word, the cosmic expression of divine Wisdom by which God created the universe. As the Word incarnate (made flesh), Jesus reveals otherwise unknowable truths about God's being and purpose. To John, Jesus' crucifixion is not a humiliating ordeal (as Mark characterizes it), but a glorification that frees Jesus to return to heaven. John's Gospel preserves no tradition of a Second Coming (the Parousia). Instead, it argues that the risen Christ is eternally present in the invisible form of a surrogate — the Paraclete, or Holy Spirit, who continues to inspire and direct the believing community.

From the moment we read the opening lines of John's Gospel — "When all things began, the Word already was. The Word dwelt with God, and what God was, the Word was" (1:1) — we realize that we have entered a world of thought strikingly different from that of the Synoptic Gospels. "Word," which John uses to denote the state of Jesus' preexistence in heaven before he came to earth, translates the Greek term *Logos*. A philosophical concept with a long pre-Christian history, **Logos** can mean anything from a divine utterance to the principle of cosmic reason that orders and governs the universe. To John, it is the infinite wisdom of God personified.

Identifying his hero with the Greek Logos concept is only the first of John's many astonishing innovations in retelling Jesus' story. While the three Synoptics give remarkably similar accounts of their subject's life, John creates a portrait of Jesus that differs in both outline and content from the other Gospels. Ninety percent of John's material appears exclusively in his account and has no

The author clearly states his purpose: to inspire faith in Jesus' divinity. He describes Jesus' miracles—which he calls "signs"—"in order that you may hold faith that Jesus is the Christ, the Son of God, and that through this faith you may possess life by his name" (20:31). This declaration follows the Gospel's climactic scene—a postresurrection appearance in which the reality of Jesus' living presence conquers the doubts of his most skeptical disciple, Thomas. Confronted with a sudden materialization of the risen Jesus, Thomas recognizes him as "My Lord and my God!"—a confession of faith that the reader is intended to echo.

Authorship

Since the late second century C.E., the Gospel of John (commonly labeled the Fourth Gospel to distinguish it from the Synoptics) has been attributed to the apostle John, son of Zebedee and brother of James. In the Synoptics, John and James are Galilean fishermen and, along with Peter, form an inner circle of Jesus' most intimate followers. The most prominent of the Twelve, the three are present when Jesus raises Jairus's daughter (Mark 5:37), at the Transfiguration (Mark 9:2), and with Jesus in the garden of Gethsemane when he is arrested (Mark 14:33). Jesus nicknames John and his brother "Boanerges," meaning "sons of thunder," perhaps for their aggressive temperaments, as when they ask Jesus to send fire to consume a Samaritan village (Luke 9:54) or demand first place in his kingdom (Mark 10:35–40). Writing in the mi-50s C.E., Paul describes John as one of the three "pillars" in the Jerusalem church (Gal. 2:6–10) during its formative period.

According to one church tradition, John eventual settled in Ephesus, where he lived to an exceptional old age, writing his Gospel, three letters, and the Book of Revelation. These five works are known collectively as the "Johannine literature."

The tradition ascribing authorship to the son of Zebedee is relatively late. Before about 180 C.E., church writers do not mention the Gospel's existence. After that date, some leading churchmen

parallel in the Synoptics. The Fourth Gospel offers a different chronology of Jesus' ministry, a different order of events, a different teaching, and a distinctly different teacher. Instead of Mark's humble carpenter-prophet, John presents a divine hero whose supernatural glory radiates through every speech he utters and every miracle he performs. John's Jesus is a being of light even while walking the earth.

The Gospel of John is so different from the Synoptics that most scholars view it as fundamentally not a portrait of the historical Jesus, but as a profound meditation on his theological significance. The community that produced this Gospel held a uniquely high view of Jesus' divinity, in some respects virtually equating him with God. John's high Christology derives largely from a conviction that after Jesus' death, the Paraclete (Holy Spirit) revealed Jesus' true nature to the author's particular group. The **Paraclete,** which can be translated as "Advocate" or "Comforter," is the guiding force that shapes this Gospel's vision of Jesus, enabling the writer to reinterpret traditions about Jesus in order to convey his real identity as the cosmic Christ (14:26; 15:26).

accept it as John's composition, although others doubt its authenticity. Some even suggest that it was the work of Cerinthus, a Gnostic teacher.

One church leader, Clement of Alexandria, states what became the official view of John's origin. Clement (about 200 C.E.) recognized the salient differences between the Synoptics and John and noted that after the other Evangelists had preserved the "facts of history," John then wrote "a spiritual Gospel." Both traditionalists and modern critics agree with Clement on two counts: that John's Gospel was the last one written and that it profoundly "spiritualizes" its portrayal of Jesus.

PROBLEMS WITH THE TRADITIONAL THEORY

Most contemporary scholars doubt that the apostle John wrote the document bearing his name. The Gospel itself does not mention the author's identity, stating instead that it is based on the testimony of an anonymous disciple "whom Jesus loved" (21:20–24). Tradition identifies this "Beloved Disciple" with John (whose name does not appear in the Gospel), but scholars can find no evidence to substantiate this claim. Jesus predicted that John would suffer a death similar to his (Mark 10:39), whereas the Gospel implies that its author, unlike Peter, James, and John, did not die a martyr's death (21:20–22). Many historians suggest that Herod Agrippa may have executed the apostle John along with his brother James about 41–43 C.E. (Acts 12:1–3).

Some critics propose that another John, prominent in the church at Ephesus about 100 C.E., is the author. Except that he was called "John the Elder" (presbyter), we know nothing that would connect him with the Johannine writings. Lacking definite confirmation of traditional authorship, scholars regard the work as anonymous. For convenience, we refer to the author as John.

THE BELOVED DISCIPLE

Although the Gospel text does not identify its author, editorial notes added to the final chapter associate him with the unnamed Beloved Disciple, suggesting that at the very least this disciple's teachings are the Gospel's primary source (21:23–24). Whether or not this anonymous personage was a historical character, he is certainly an idealized figure, achieving an intimacy and emotional rapport with Jesus unmatched by Peter or the other disciples. In the Gospel, he does not appear (at least as the one "Jesus loved") until the final night of Jesus' life, when we find him at the Last Supper, lying against his friend's chest (13:23). (The Twelve dined in the Greco-Roman fashion, reclining two-by-two on benches set around the table.)

Designed to represent the Johannine community's special knowledge of Christ, the Beloved Disciple is invariably presented in competition with Peter, who may represent the larger apostolic church from which the disciple's exclusive group is somewhat distanced. At the Last Supper, the Beloved Disciple is Peter's intermediary, transmitting to Jesus Peter's question about Judas's betrayal (13:21–29). Acquainted with the high priest, he has access to Pilate's court, thus gaining Peter's admittance to the hearing, where Peter denies knowing Jesus (18:15–18). The only male disciple at the cross, he receives Jesus' charge to care for Mary, becoming her "son" and hence Jesus' "brother" as well (19:26–27).

Outrunning Peter to the empty tomb on Easter morning, he arrives there first and is the first to believe that Jesus is risen (20:2–10). In a boat fishing with Peter on the Sea of Galilee, the disciple is the first to recognize the resurrected Jesus standing on the shore, identifying him to Peter (21:4–7). Peter, future "pillar" of the Jerusalem church, is commissioned to "feed" (or spiritually nourish) Jesus' "sheep" (his future followers), but Jesus has a special prophecy for the Beloved Disciple's future: He may live until the Master returns (21:20–22). (This reference to the Second Coming is virtually unique in John's Gospel.)

Editorial comments appended to the Gospel, apparently after the favored disciple's death, indicate how the Johannine church interpreted Jesus' prophecy. The editor notes that, although Jesus' remark had circulated among "the brotherhood" (the community in which the Gospel originated), the saying did not mean that the "disciple would not die." It meant only that Jesus' intentions for his favorite did not involve Peter (21:21–23). The editor's comments hint at the differences between the Johannine and most apostolic Christian communities, which, during the first century C.E., were generally independent of one another. The disciple's "brotherhood" would produce a Gospel promoting Jesus' theological meaning in ways that paralleled the Petrine churches' teachings but revealing, they believed, Jesus' "glory" (1:14) more fully than other Gospel accounts.

PLACE AND DATE OF COMPOSITION

Despite its use of Hellenistic terms and ideas, recent studies indicate that John's Gospel is deeply rooted in Palestinian tradition. It shows a greater familiarity with Palestinian geography than the Synoptics and reveals close connections with first-century Palestinian Judaisms, particularly concepts prevailing in the Essene community at Qumran. Study of the Dead Sea Scrolls from Qumran reveals many parallels between Essene ideas and those prevailing in the Johannine community (see box 10.1). Essene writers and the author of John use a remarkably similar vocabulary to express the same kind of ethical dualism, dividing the world up into two opposing groups of people: those who walk in the *light* (symbolizing truth and goodness) and those who walk in *darkness* (symbolizing deceit and evil). In comparing John with the Dead Sea Scroll known as the *Rule of the Community,* scholars find not only an almost identical use of distinctive terms but also a comparable worldview that sees the universe as a battleground of polar opposites. In this dualistic Cosmos, the devil (synonymous with "liar") and his "spirit of error" oppose Jesus' "spirit of truth" (cf. John 8:44; 12:35; 14:17; 15:26 with *Rule of the Community* 1QS 3.13, 17–21).

The Qumran and Johannine communities are also alike in that each owes a saving enlightenment to its respective founder. As the mysterious Teacher of Righteousness had earlier brought the light of

true understanding to the Essenes, so the Johannine Jesus —"the light of the world"— came to illuminate humanity's mental and spiritual darkness. The unidentified Essene teacher, of course, received nothing comparable to the exaltation the Johannine writer accords Jesus. Given the two groups' claims to exclusive knowledge, it is inevitable that their literature expresses a rigorously sectarian attitude. Both the Dead Sea Scrolls and the Johannine writings view their respective groups, tiny as they were, as the *only* guardians of light and truth in a fatally benighted world.

Before the Dead Sea Scrolls were discovered, many scholars believed that John's Gospel —with its seemingly Platonic dualism and use of Greek philosophical terms such as Logos —originated in a Hellenistic environment, perhaps in Ephesus, the traditional home of the apostle John during his old age. A wealthy seaport and capital of the Roman province of Asia (western Turkey), **Ephesus** was a crossroad of Greek and Near Eastern ideas. With a large colony of Jews, it was a center for Paul's missionary work, as well as the base of a John the Baptist sect (Acts 19:1–7). If the Gospel was composed in an area where the Baptist was regarded as Jesus' superior, it would account for the writer's severe limitation of the Baptist's role in the messianic drama, reducing his function to that of a mere "voice" bearing witness to Jesus (1:6–9, 19–28). The many similarities between Essene and Johannine thought, however, now incline many scholars to fix the Gospel's place of composition (at least its first edition) in Palestine or Syria.

Some critics once thought that John's Gospel was composed late in the second century (when Christian authors first mention it). However, tiny manuscript fragments of John discovered in the Egyptian desert have been dated at about 125 and 150 C.E., making them the oldest surviving part of a New Testament book. Allowing time for the Gospel to have circulated abroad as far as Egypt, the work could not have originated much later than about 100 C.E. The Gospel's references to believers' being expelled from Jewish synagogues (9:22, 34–35)—a process that began about 85 or 90 C.E. —suggest that the decisive break between

Box 10.1
The Johannine Community:
A Distinctive Group Within Early Christianity

Most scholars believe that the Gospel of John, as well as the Epistles of 1, 2, and 3 John (see chapter 18), originated in a somewhat marginal Christian community distinguished by a uniquely high Christology. The Gospel's final chapter, apparently an epilog added by a later editor, ascribes the Gospel to a disciple whom Jesus loved (21:24), one who had been present at the Last Supper and the Crucifixion (13; 19:25–27). Close study of the Gospel and Epistles suggests that a variety of Jewish or other Palestinian groups, including former disciples of John the Baptist, Samaritans, Essenes, and proto-Gnostics, influenced different stages of the community's development and hence of the Gospel's composition. Several eminent New Testament scholars, notably Raymond E. Brown in *The Community of the Beloved Disciple* and J. L. Martyn in *History and Theology in the Fourth Gospel,* have employed sociohistorical methods to reconstruct the evolution of the eclectic group that produced the Johannine literature (see "Recommended Reading").

Although scholars do not agree on the Johannine group's precise stages of development—no one knows when or where it originated or why it produced an interpretation of Jesus so different from the Synoptic model—most accept some general inferences about the community. Like most early Christian believers, members of what would become the Johannine community were Jews with connections to local synagogues. They probably differed from their compatriots only in their belief that Jesus of Nazareth was the promised Davidic Messiah, a God-sent prophet in the tradition of Elijah and Elisha (a relatively low Christology). The galvanizing force behind this group may have been one of Jesus' followers who later became known as the Beloved Disciple.

At some point relatively early in its growth, some members introduced ideas typical of the Qumran teachings, with their dualistic concepts of cosmic opposites: Light-Dark, Good-Evil, Truth-Lie, Spirit-Flesh, and children of God (the believers' sect) versus spawn of the devil (the believers' religious critics). As the community promoted an increasingly exalted view of Jesus, identifying him with the heavenly Wisdom by which the universe was created, its burgeoning claims for Jesus' divinity brought it into open conflict with some synagogue leaders, who probably saw Johannine Christology as a threat to Jewish monotheism. Conflict with orthodox Judaism may have been exacerbated as Samaritans—whom Jews regarded as heretics—also influenced the community, their presence reflected in the Gospel's stories of Samaritan

church and synagogue was already in effect when it was written. Hence, the Gospel is usually dated between about 90 and 100 C.E.

RELATION TO THE SYNOPTIC GOSPELS

Despite some verbal parallels to Mark (cf. John 6:7 and Mark 6:37; John 12:3 and Mark 14:3, 5), most scholars do not think that the author of John's Gospel drew on the earlier Gospels. A few scholars, however, such as Thomas Brodie (see "Recommended Reading"), argue that the author created his account by appropriating material from the Synoptics and thoroughly transforming it. By carefully analyzing John's presumed reworking of his sources (primarily Mark, Matthew, Ephesians, and the Mosaic Torah), Brodie concludes that John's Gospel is basically a theolog-

ical reinterpretation of previously existing traditions about Jesus' life and meaning. Instead of deriving from a marginal Christian group, the supposedly independent Johannine community, John's narrative actually represents mainstream Christianity.

The enormous differences between the Synoptics and the Fourth Gospel, however, persuade most scholars that John's vision of Jesus does not derive from the older canonical Gospels (see boxes 10.2 and 10.3). Concentrating on Jesus as a heavenly revealer of ultimate truth, John does not present his hero in Synoptic terms. The writer avoids most of the major themes and events that the Synoptic accounts employ to delineate Jesus' character and teaching.

Even a cursory review of major Synoptic incidents and motifs that do not appear in John's

conversions (John 4) and Jewish accusations that Jesus was a Samaritan (8:48).

Incorporating the Signs Gospel, a narrative of Jesus' public miracles, the first edition of John's Gospel probably appeared in the 90s C.E., shortly after Johannine Christians were expelled from the synagogue (John 9). By that time, Johannine Christology had acquired elements that anticipated later Gnostic doctrines, including a belief that Jesus was God's Eternal Word who descended from heaven to reveal divine knowledge (1:1–4, 14; 17:3), reascended to his celestial place of origin, and caused followers to be "born from above." Under the guidance of the Beloved Disciple, the community also emphasized the continuing reality of Jesus' postascension presence, the Paraclete, which illuminated their understanding of Jesus' divine nature.

After their insistence on Jesus' near-equality to God had alienated them from the synagogue, further speculation on Jesus as pure spiritual Being apparently produced a decisive split within the community membership, a division reflected in the Epistles of 1 and 2 John. Perhaps about 100–110 C.E., the anonymous writer of 1 John berated a segment of his group that had withdrawn from the Johannine community, accusing them of capitulating to the world and being anti-Christs. He states that the secessionists deny that Jesus has come "in the flesh" (in genuinely human form), suggesting that the author's opponents were proto-Gnostic Christians who viewed Christ as entirely spirit. A Johannine editor, not the Gospel's original author, may have appended chapter 21 to the Gospel during this period; the appendix insists that the Being who descended from heaven was also physically human (the risen Jesus eats breakfast with his followers) and that the Beloved Disciple lends his authority to the editor's group because that disciple is the Gospel's principal source.

After their bitter parting, the two Johannine groups moved in different directions. The secessionists, who took John's Gospel with them, seem to have evolved into full Gnosticism, accounting for the historical fact that the Fourth Gospel was widely used in Gnostic circles. The first commentary written on John's Gospel was by a Gnostic scholar, Heracleon, who lived near the close of the second century C.E.

The other Johannine group, which had produced the Epistles denouncing an extreme Gnostic interpretation of Jesus, eventually merged with the proto-orthodox church, bringing their Gospel and its revolutionary view of Jesus' relationship to the Father with them. Accepted only slowly by the international church, John's Gospel became the work that ultimately defined Christian belief in Jesus' dual nature, paving the way for the post–New Testament dogma of the Trinity.

Gospel would produce a long list of differences. A dozen representative examples follow, along with brief suggestions about the author's possible reasons for not including characteristic Synoptic material.

1. John has no birth story or reference to Jesus' virginal conception, perhaps because he sees Christ as the eternal Word (Logos) who "became flesh" (1:14) as the man Jesus of Nazareth. John's doctrine of the **Incarnation** (the spiritual Logos becoming physically human) makes the manner of Jesus' human conception irrelevant.

2. John contains no record of Jesus' baptism by John, emphasizing Jesus' independence of and superiority to the Baptist.

3. John includes no period of contemplation in the Judean wilderness or temptation by Satan. His Jesus possesses a vital unity with the Father that makes worldly temptation impossible.

4. John never mentions Jesus' exorcisms, preferring to show Jesus' overcoming Evil through his personal revelation of divine truth rather than through the casting out of demons (which plays so large a role in Mark's and Matthew's reports of his ministry).

5. Although he reports some friction between Jesus and his brothers (7:1–6), John does not reproduce the Markan tradition that Jesus' family thought he was mentally unbalanced or that his neighbors at Nazareth viewed him as nothing extraordinary (Mark 3:20–21, 31–35; 6:1–6). In John, Jesus meets considerable opposition, but he is always too commanding and powerful a figure to be ignored or devalued.

Box 10.2
Representative Examples of Material Found Only in John

1. Doctrine of the Logos: Before coming to earth Jesus preexisted in heaven, where he was God's mediator in creating the universe (1:1–18).

2. Miracle at Cana: Jesus changes water into wine (the first "sign") (2:1–12).

3. Doctrine of spiritual rebirth: conversation with Nicodemus (3:1–21; see also 7:50–52; 19:39).

4. Jesus is the water of eternal life: conversation with the Samaritan woman (4:1–42).

5. Jesus heals the invalid at Jerusalem's Sheep Pool (5:1–47).

6. The "I am" sayings: Jesus speaks as divine Wisdom revealed from above, equating himself with objects or concepts of great symbolic value, such as "the bread of life" (6:22–66), "the good shepherd" (10:1–21), "the resurrection and the life" (11:25), "the way," "the truth" (14:6), and "the true vine" (15:1–17).

7. Jesus, light of the world, existed before Abraham (8:12–59).

8. Cure of the man born blind: debate between church and synagogue (9:1–41).

9. The raising of Lazarus (the seventh "sign") (11:1–12:11).

10. A different tradition of the Last Supper: washing the disciples' feet (13:1–20) and delivering the farewell discourses; promise of the Paraclete, the Spirit that will empower the disciples and interpret the meaning of Jesus' life (13:31–17:26).

11. Resurrection appearances in or near Jerusalem to Mary Magdalene and the disciples, including Thomas (20:1–29).

12. Resurrection appearances in Galilee to Peter and to the Beloved Disciple (21:1–23).

6. John presents Jesus' teaching in a form radically different from that of the Synoptics. Both Mark and Matthew state that Jesus "never" taught without using parables (Mark 4:34; Matt. 13:34), but John does not record a single parable of the Synoptic type (involving homely images of agricultural or domestic life). Instead of brief anecdotes and vivid comparisons, the Johannine Jesus delivers long philosophical speeches in which Jesus' own nature is typically the subject of discussion. In John, he speaks both publicly and privately in this manner, in Galilee as well as in Jerusalem.

7. John includes none of Jesus' reinterpretations of the Mosaic Law, the main topic of Jesus' Synoptic discourses. Instead of the many ethical directives about not divorcing, keeping the Sabbath, ending the law of retaliation, and forgiving enemies that we find in Mark, Matthew, and Luke, John records only one "new commandment"—to love. In both the Gospel and the letters, this is Jesus'

single explicit directive; in the Johannine community, mutual love among "friends" is the sole distinguishing mark of true discipleship (13:34–35; 15:9–17).

8. Conspicuously absent from John's Gospel is any prediction of Jerusalem's fall, a concern that dominated the Synopticists' imagination (Mark 13; Matt. 24–25; Luke 21).

9. Nor does John contain a prophecy of Jesus' Second Coming, substituting a view that Jesus is already present among believers in the form of the Paraclete, the Holy Spirit that serves as Christians' Helper, Comforter, or Advocate (14:25–26; 16:7–15). To John, Jesus' first coming means that believers have life now (5:21–26; 11:25–27). Presenting a realized eschatology, a belief that events usually associated with the *eschaton* (world's End) are even now realized or fulfilled by Jesus' spiritual presence among believers, John does not stress a future eschatological return.

Box 10.3
Characters Introduced or Given New Emphasis in John

Andrew, Peter's brother, as a speaking character (1:40–42, 44; 6:8–9; 12:20–22)

Philip, one of the Twelve (1:43–49; 6:5–7; 12:20–22; 14:8–11)

Nathanael, one of the Twelve (1:45–51)

Mary as a participant in Jesus' ministry (2:1–5) and at the cross (19:25–27)

Nicodemus, a leading Pharisee (3:1–12; 7:50–52; 19:39)

A Samaritan woman (4:7–42)

A paralyzed man cured in Jerusalem (5:1–15)

Jesus' unbelieving "brothers" (7:2–10)

The woman taken in adultery (8:3–11; an appendix to John in NEB)

A man born blind (9:1–38)

Lazarus, brother of Mary and Martha (11:1–44; 12:1–11)

An unidentified disciple whom "Jesus loved" (13:23–26; 18:15–16; 19:26–27; 20:2–10; 21:7, 20–24)

Annas, father-in-law of Caiaphas, the High Priest (18:12–14, 19–24)

---

10. Although he represents the sacramental bread and wine as life-giving symbols, John does not preserve a communion ritual or the institution of a New Covenant between Jesus and his followers at the Last Supper. Stating that the meal took place a day before Passover, John substitutes Jesus' act of humble service—washing the disciples' feet—for the Eucharist (13:1–16).

11. As his Jesus cannot be tempted, so John's Christ undergoes no agony before his arrest in the garden of Gethsemane. Unfailingly poised and confident, Jesus experiences his painful death as a glorification, his raising on the cross symbolizing his imminent ascension to heaven. Instead of Mark's cry of despair, in John, Jesus dies with a declaration that he has "accomplished" his life's purpose (19:30).

12. Finally, it must be emphasized that John's many differences from the Synoptics are not simply the result of the author's trying to "fill in" the gaps in his predecessors' Gospels. By carefully examining John's account, we see that he does not write to supplement earlier narratives about Jesus, but that both his omissions and inclusions are determined almost exclusively by the writer's special theological convictions (20:30–31; 21:25). From his opening

hymn praising the eternal Word to Jesus' promised reascension to heaven, every part of the Gospel is calculated to illustrate Jesus' glory as God's fullest revelation of his own ineffable Being.

DIFFERENCES IN THE CHRONOLOGY AND ORDER OF EVENTS

Although John's essential story resembles the Synoptic version of Jesus' life—a public ministry featuring healings and other miracles followed by official rejection, arrest, crucifixion, and resurrection—the Fourth Gospel presents important differences in the chronology and order of events. Significant ways in which John's narrative sequence differs from the Synoptic order include the following:

1. The Synoptics show Jesus working mainly in Galilee and coming south to Judea only during his last days. By contrast, John has Jesus traveling back and forth between Galilee and Jerusalem throughout the duration of his ministry.

2. The Synoptics place Jesus' assault on the Temple at the end of his career, making it the incident that consolidates official hostility toward him; John sets it at the beginning (2:13–21).

3. The Synoptics agree that Jesus began his mission after John the Baptist's imprisonment, but John states that their missions overlapped (3:23–4:3).

4. The earlier Gospels mention only one Passover and imply that Jesus' career lasted only about a year; John refers to three Passovers (2:13; 6:4; 11:55), thus giving the ministry a duration of three to nearly four years.

5. Unlike the Synoptics, which present the Last Supper as a Passover celebration, John states that Jesus' final meal with the disciples occurred the evening before Passover and that the Crucifixion took place on Nisan 14, the day of preparation when paschal lambs were being sacrificed (13:1, 29; 18:28; 19:14). Many historians believe that John's chronology is the more accurate, for it is improbable that Jesus' arrest, trial, and execution took place on Nisan 15, the most sacred time of the Passover observance.

Although most scholars consider the Synoptics more reliable sources of Jesus' actual teaching, many believe John is right about the length of Jesus' career and about the day on which he was crucified.

JOHN'S PURPOSE AND METHOD

As an author, John states that his goal is to elicit belief in his community's distinctively high Christology (17:3–5; 20:30–31), but other purposes also can be inferred from studying the text. The author commonly refers to his fellow countrymen as "the Jews [Judeans]," as if they are a group from which he is entirely disassociated. His picture of an "innocent" Pontius Pilate and his placing the full responsibility for Jesus' execution on the Jerusalem leadership probably echoes the hostility existing between the author's community and Jewish leaders in the decades following 70 C.E., when the church and synagogue became bitterly divided. John's claim of divinity for Jesus could only have increased the antagonism, as his subject's Jerusalem speeches suggest (chs. 7–9, 12, 16, 18). The Johannine community's expulsion from local synagogues seems to have had an almost traumatic impact on the writer, who reacts by dramatizing his group's spiritual superiority to their synagogue critics (compare John 3:9–11 and 9:18–35).

Relation to Gnostic Ideas   Although he maintains Jesus' supernatural character, John also refutes Gnostic Christians who view Christ as pure spirit. As noted in chapter 1, Gnosticism was a movement in the early church that developed into Christianity's first major heresy. Gnostic thinkers see the universe as consisting of two mutually exclusive realms. The invisible world of spirit is pure and good, and the physical world is inherently evil, the inferior creation of a lesser god (whom some Gnostics identify with Yahweh). According to Gnostic belief, human beings gain salvation only through special knowledge (*gnosis*), imparted to a chosen elite through communion with spiritual beings. A divine redeemer (presumably Christ) descends from the spirit realm to transmit saving knowledge to persons whose souls are sufficiently disciplined to escape the body's earthly desires. Transcending the material world's false reality, the soul can then perceive the eternal truths of the spirit.

A mixture of elements from marginal Judaism, Greek mystery cults, and Christianity, Gnosticism held a number of diverse views about Christ. One branch of Gnosticism, called **Docetism** (a name taken from the Greek verb "to seem") argued that Christ, being good, could not also be human; he only *seemed* to have a physical body. The Docetists contended that as God's true son, Christ was wholly spiritual, ascending to heaven while leaving another's body on the cross.

Although he uses typically Gnostic terms, John avoids Gnosticism's extremism by insisting on Jesus' physical humanity (1:14). Even after the Resurrection, Jesus displays fleshly wounds and consumes material food (chs. 20–21). To show that Jesus was a mortal person who truly died, John eliminates from his Passion story the tradition that Simon of Cyrene carried Jesus' cross (lest the reader think that Simon might have been substituted for Jesus at the Crucifixion). John also adds a new incident in which a Roman soldier pierces Jesus' side, confirming physical death (ch. 20).

Despite the inclusion of details to confound Gnostic misinterpretations, John's Gospel was popular in many Gnostic circles (which may account for its relatively slow acceptance by the church at large). Besides the metaphysical doctrine of Christ's preexistence, John contains many statements expressing classic Gnostic ideas. Knowing the divine beings—Father and Son—is equated with "eternal life" (17:3). The assertion that "the spirit alone gives life; the flesh is of no avail" (6:63) and the emphasis on spiritual rebirth (ch. 3) strikingly parallel Gnostic notions.

John's Portrayal of Jesus' Teaching

The author's presentation of Jesus' teaching, both public and private, differs so completely from the Synoptic accounts that many readers may wonder how closely John reflects Jesus' actual words. If the Galilean prophet consistently spoke in parables and short, proverbial statements—as Mark, Matthew, and Luke insist that he did—why does John show him delivering only long metaphysical discourses about himself? Is John trying to reproduce Jesus' speeches as they were originally uttered, or does he have another purpose?

The Role of the Paraclete

The author gives a clue to his method in the series of farewell speeches that Jesus delivers at the Last Supper (chs. 14–17). A mixture of comforting promises, prayers, and metaphors of union between God and believing humanity, these discourses present Jesus as explaining precisely why he must leave his disciples on earth while he dies and ascends to heaven. His death is not a permanent loss, for he returns to the Father only in order to empower his earthly disciples with the Paraclete, the Holy Spirit, which acts as his surrogate among them.

John believes that his community possesses that promised Spirit and that it operates on his group exactly as Jesus had foretold. In John's view, the Spirit allows his community to perform several functions that serve the dual purpose of linking members to the human Jesus (now dead) and to the glorified Jesus, whose Spirit still lives among them. The Spirit inspires believers to continue Jesus' miraculous work of healing; it answers their prayers for power and knowledge; it provides defenses against their opponents' hostile criticism; and—most important for the presentation of Jesus' teachings—it enables the "brotherhood" to interpret Jesus' life in its full theological significance (14:12–26).

Speaking as if the Paraclete were a second self, John's Jesus refers to "the Spirit of truth" as a divine person who will bear witness to Christ's identity, revealing him far more fully than is possible during Jesus' human incarnation. One of the Paraclete's main purposes is to unveil Jesus' true likeness, to paint his portrait in supernal colors. Thus, John represents Jesus as saying that "he [the Paraclete] will glorify me," making Jesus' cosmic meaning known to the author's privileged group (16:12–15).

Directed by the Paraclete, the author's community not only preserves traditions about Jesus of Nazareth but experiences Spirit-directed insights into Jesus' character and nature. The author's task in this Gospel is not to record external facts about his subject's earthly biography, but to create a portrait of Jesus that duplicates what the Paraclete reveals. Because the Paraclete's function is to define Jesus' glory—both its heavenly origin and its continuing presence on earth—John's account must meet the formidable challenge of portraying the real Jesus, delineating both the man and his celestial splendor. (Compare John's method with Luke's similar implication that Jesus' real story can be told only in terms of his postresurrection divinity [Luke 24:25–27, 44–53].)

The speeches in John are thus a creative assimilation of Jesus' remembered words into highly developed confessions of faith in his divine nature and cosmic status. As they stand in the Gospel, they are probably largely the author's creation—sublime tributes to Jesus' unique role in human redemption.

Many scholars have noted that John's Gospel presents Jesus not as a figure of the recent historical past, but as an immortal being who still lives within the community of faith. Promised that Jesus' followers will accomplish "greater things" than the human Jesus (14:12), the author and his church perceive Jesus' continuing presence in their own ministries. Thus, in John's Gospel, Jesus' speeches and the dialogs with his opponents manifest a double vision, a two-level drama. In John's vision of events, the human Jesus of the past and the believers of the present perform the same Spirit-directed work.

Chapter 9 offers a good example of John's method. In recounting Jesus' restoration of sight to a man born blind, John skillfully combines memories of

Jesus' healing ministry with the similar miraculous works his own community performs. The two elements—Jesus and his later disciples—can be equated in John's narrative because the same Paraclete operates through both parties. An awareness that John uses a double vision, combining historical past and present in telling his story, will help the reader understand the diverse elements present in this difficult chapter. Notice that the curative miracle is followed by a series of debates and confrontations between the cured man, his parents, and officials of his synagogue. The Jewish officials' interrogation of the man reproduces circumstances prevailing not in Jesus' day, but in the writer's own time, when Torah authorities cross-examined Jews suspected of regarding Jesus as the Jewish Messiah. (Do not overlook the references to the expulsion of Jesus' followers from the synagogue [9:23, 34], a situation that did not develop until well after Jerusalem's destruction in 70 C.E.)

The conversation with the Pharisee Nicodemus in chapter 3 reveals a similar conflation (blending) of Jesus' past actions with the Johannine community's ongoing ministry. Jesus' pretended astonishment that one of Israel's most famous teachers does not understand the Spirit that motivates Jesus' followers echoes the late-first-century debate between the Jewish authorities and the author's group. Using the first-person plural "we" to signify the whole believing community, John affirms that his community experiences the Spirit's power, while "you" (the disbelieving opponents) refuse to credit the Johannine testimony (3:9–11). The reader will also observe that in this dialog Jesus speaks as if he has already returned to heaven (3:13), again reflecting a conviction of the author's community.

ORGANIZATION OF JOHN'S GOSPEL

John's Gospel is framed by a prolog (1:1–51) and an epilog (21:1–25). The main narrative (chs. 2–20) divides naturally into two long sections: an account of Jesus' miracles and public speeches (chs. 2–11) and an extended Passion story emphasizing Jesus' final prayers and speeches to the disciples (chs. 12–20). Because John regards Jesus' miracles as "signs" or public evidence of his hero's supernatural character, the first section is called the Book of

Signs. Many scholars believe that the author uses a previously compiled collection of Jesus' miraculous works as a primary source (see below). Because it presents Christ's death as a "glorious" fulfillment of the divine will, some commentators call the second part the Book of Glory.

The Gospel is outlined as follows:

1. Prolog: Hymn to the Logos; testimony of the Baptist; call of the disciples (1:1–51)
2. The Book of Signs (2:1–11:57)
   a. The miracle at Cana
   b. Cleansing the Temple
   c. Dialog with Nicodemus on spiritual rebirth
   d. Conversation with the Samaritan woman
   e. Five more miraculous signs in Jerusalem and Galilee; Jesus' discourses witnessing to his divine nature
   f. The resurrection of Lazarus (the seventh sign)
3. The Book of Glory (12:1–20:31)
   a. The plot against Jesus
   b. The Last Supper and farewell discourses
   c. The Passion story
   d. The empty tomb and resurrection appearances to Peter and the beloved disciple
4. Epilog: postresurrection appearances in Galilee; parting words to Peter and the Beloved Disciple (21:1–25)

Hymn to the Word (Logos)

John's opening hymn to the Word introduces several concepts vital to his portrait of Christ. The phrase "when all things began" recalls the Genesis creation account when God's word of command—"Let there be light"—illuminated a previously dark universe. In John's view, the prehuman Christ is the creative Word (divine wisdom, cosmic reason) whom God uses to bring heaven and earth into existence. "With God at the beginning," the Word is an integral part of the Supreme Being—"what God was, the Word was" (1:1–5).

John's supreme irony is that the very world that the Word created rejects him, preferring spiritual "darkness" to the "light" he imparts. Nonetheless, the Word "became flesh"—the man Jesus—and temporarily lived among humans, allowing them to witness his "glory, such glory as befits the Father's only Son" (1:10–14).

GREEK AND JEWISH BACKGROUND

As noted previously, Logos (Word) is a Greek philosophical term, but John blends it with a parallel Hebrew tradition about divine Wisdom that existed before the world began. According to the Book of Proverbs (8:22–31), Wisdom (depicted as a gracious young woman) was Yahweh's companion when he created the universe, transforming the original dark **Chaos** into a design of order and light. As Yahweh's darling, she not only was his intimate helper in the creative process but also became God's channel of communication with humanity. As Israel's wisdom tradition developed in Hellenistic times, Wisdom was seen as both Yahweh's agent of creation and the being who reveals the divine mind to the faithful (Ecclus. 24; Wisd. of Sol. 6:12–9:18).

In the Greek philosophical tradition, Logos is also a divine concept, the principle of cosmic reason that gives order and coherence to the otherwise chaotic world, making it accessible to human intellect. The Logos concept had circulated among Greek thinkers since the time of the philosopher Heraclitus (born before 500 B.C.E.). In John's day, Logos was a popular Stoic term, commonly viewed as synonymous with the divine intelligence that created and sustained the universe.

These analogous Greek and Hebrew ideas converge in the writings of Philo Judaeus, a Hellenistic Jewish scholar living in Alexandria during the first century C.E. A pious Jew profoundly influenced by Greek rationality, Philo attempted to reconcile Hellenic logic with the revelation contained in the Hebrew Bible. Philo used the Hebrew concept of Wisdom as the creative intermediary between the transcendent Creator and the material creation. However, he employed the Greek term *Logos* to designate Wisdom's role and function. (Philo may have preferred *Logos* because it is masculine in Greek, whereas Wisdom [*Sophia*] is feminine.) Philo's interpretation can be illustrated by an allegorical reading of Genesis 1, in which God's first act is to speak—to create the Word (Logos)—by which power the **Cosmos** is born.

In identifying the prehuman Christ with Philo's Logos, John equates Jesus with the loftiest philosophical ideal of his age. His Christ is thus superior to every other heavenly or earthly being, all of whom owe their creation to him. John's Jesus not only speaks the word of God, he is the Word incarnate. From the author's perspective, Jesus' human career is merely a brief interlude, a temporary descent to earth preceded and followed by eternal life above (3:13). (Compare John's Logos doctrine with similar ideas discussed in Phil. 2 and Col. 1–2; see also figure 10.1.)

JESUS AND DIVINE WISDOM

After the prolog, John does not again refer explicitly to Jesus as the Word. He does, however, repeatedly link his hero to the concept of divine Wisdom, a personification of God's creative intelligence (see box 10.4). In the Hebrew Bible, Wisdom is both the means by which God creates and the channel through whom he communicates to humankind. Hebrew Bible writers characteristically picture Wisdom speaking in the first person, using the phrase "I am" and then defining her activities as God's agent. John casts many of Jesus' speeches in exactly the same form, beginning with a declaration "I am" and then typically equating himself with a term of great religious significance. Compare some of Wisdom's speeches with those of the Johannine Jesus:

> The Lord created me the beginning of his works,
> before all else that he made, long ago.
> Alone, I was fashioned in times long past,
> at the beginning, long before earth itself.
> (Prov. 8:22–23)

Identifying Wisdom with God's verbal command to create light (Gen. 1:3), the author of Ecclesiasticus represents her as saying:

> I am the word which was spoken by the Most
> High; . . .
> Before time began he created me,
> and I shall remain for ever. . . .
> (Ecclus. 24:3, 9)

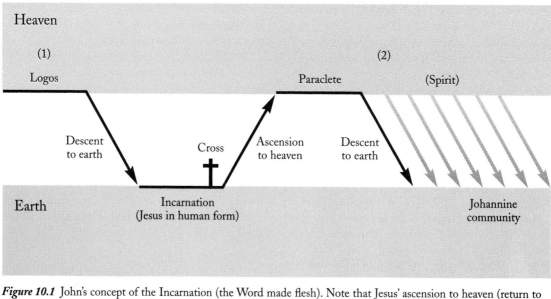

Figure 10.1 John's concept of the Incarnation (the Word made flesh). Note that Jesus' ascension to heaven (return to his place of spiritual origin) is followed by a descent of the Paraclete, Jesus' Spirit—an invisible surrogate that inspires the Johannine brotherhood. Whereas Jesus' human presence on earth was brief, John implies that the Paraclete abides permanently with the believing community.

Sent by God to live among his people, Israel, Wisdom invites all to seek her favor:

> Come to me, you who desire me,
> and eat your fill of my fruit; . . .
> Whoever feeds on me will be hungry for more,
> and whoever drinks from me will thirst for more.
> (Ecclus. 24:19, 21–22; cf. John 4:13–15)

JESUS AND YAHWEH

Jesus' "I Am" Pronouncements Besides associating Jesus with the Hebrew principle of eternal Wisdom, John's "I am" speeches also express an important aspect of his Christology. They echo Yahweh's declaration of being to Moses at the burning bush (Exod. 3:14), in which God reveals his sacred personal name. In the Hebrew Bible, only Yahweh speaks of himself (the "I am") in this manner. Hence, Jesus' reiterated "I am . . . the bread of life" (6:35), "the good shepherd" (10:11), "the resurrection and the life" (11:25), or "the way," "the truth," and "the life" (14:6) stress his unity with God, the eternal "I am" (see box 10.5).

John attributes much of "the Jews'" hostility toward Jesus to their reaction against his apparent claims to divinity. When Jesus refers publicly to his prehuman existence, declaring that "before Abraham was born, I am," his outraged audience in the Temple attempts to stone him for blasphemy (8:56–59). Most scholars doubt that Jesus really made such assertions. According to this view, the attempted stoning represents Jewish leaders' response to the preaching of John's group, which made extraordinarily high claims about Jesus' divine nature.

ROLE OF THE BAPTIST

Readers will notice that John repeatedly interrupts his Logos hymn to compare the Baptist unfavorably to Jesus. Insisting on the Baptist's inferiority, the author has him bear witness against himself: He is neither a prophet nor the Elijah figure, but only "a voice" whose sole function is to announce Jesus. Thus, the Baptist bears witness to seeing the Holy Spirit descend upon Jesus, a phenomenon that

Box 10.4

Wisdom Speeches in the Hebrew Bible as Models for the Johannine Jesus

Wisdom searches the streets for those willing to
    receive her:
Hear how Wisdom lifts her voice
and Understanding cries out.
She stands at the cross-roads, . . .
beside the gate, at the entrance to the city . . .
"Men, it is to you I call,
I appeal to every man: . . .
Listen! For I will speak clearly,
you will have plain speech from me;
for I speak nothing but the truth . . .
I am Wisdom, I bestow shrewdness
and show the way to knowledge and prudence . . .
I have force, I also have ability;
understanding and power are mine.
Through me kings are sovereign
and governors make just laws . . .
from me all rulers on earth derive their nobility.
Those who love me I love,
and those who search for me find me.

    . . .

The Lord created me the beginning of his works,
before all else that he made, long ago.
Alone, I was fashioned in times long past,
at the beginning, long before earth itself.
When there was yet no ocean I was born . . .
When he set the heavens in their place I was there,
when he girdled the ocean with the horizon,
when he fixed the canopy of clouds overhead
and set the springs of ocean firm in their place . . .
Then I was at his side each day, his darling and
    delight,
playing in his presence continually,
playing on the earth, when he had finished it,
while my delight was in mankind . . .
Happy is the man who keeps to my ways,
happy the man who listens to me, . . .
for he who finds me finds life
and wins favor from [Yahweh],
while he who finds me not, hurts himself
and all who hate me are in love with death."
                (Prov. 8:1–7, 12–17, 22–36)

Hear the praise of Wisdom from her own
    mouth, . . .
in the presence of the heavenly host:
"I am the word (Logos) which was spoken by the
    Most High:

it was I who covered the earth like a mist.
My dwelling-place was in high heaven;
my throne was in a pillar of cloud. . . ."
Then the Creator decreed where I should dwell.
He said, "Make your home in Jacob;
find your heritage in Israel." . . .
"Before time began he created me,
and I shall remain for ever. . . .
I took root among the people whom the Lord had
    honoured
by choosing to be his special possession. . . .
Come to me, you who desire me,
and eat your fill of my fruit. . . .
Whoever feeds on me will be hungry for more,
and whoever drinks from me will thirst for more."
                (Ecclus. 24:1–12, 18–21)

For in wisdom there is a spirit intelligent and holy,
unique in its kind, yet made up of many parts, subtle,
free-moving, lucid, spotless, clear, invulnerable, loving
what is good, . . . kindly towards men, . . . all-
powerful, all-surveying, and permeating all intelligent,
pure, and delicate spirits. . . . She is the brightness
that streams from everlasting light, the flawless mirror
of the active power of God and the image of his
goodness. She is one, yet can do everything, herself
unchanging, she makes all things new, age after age
she enters into holy souls, and makes them God's
friends and prophets, for nothing is more acceptable
to God but the man who makes his home with
wisdom.

She is initiated into the knowledge that belongs to
God and she decides for him what he shall do. . . .
Through her I shall have immortality, and shall leave
an undying memory to those who come after me. I
shall rule over my peoples, and nations will become
my subjects.

Send her forth from the holy heavens, and from
thy glorious throne bid her come down, so that she
may labour at my side and I may learn what pleases
thee. For she knows and understands all things, and
will guide me presently in all I do, and guard me in
her glory. So shall my life's work be acceptable, and I
shall judge thy people justly, and be worthy of my father's throne.
            (Wisd. of Sol. 7:22–28; 8:4, 13; 9:10–12)

Box 10.5
Isis and the "I Am" Statements in John

Yahweh's declaration of being as the immortal "I am" in Exodus 3 and Lady Wisdom's assertion of her cosmic role in Proverbs 8 and the deuterocanonical books of Wisdom and Ecclesiasticus provide a biblical model for John's "I am" speeches. In Hellenistic culture, the closest parallel to these Johannine statements occurs in hymns honoring Isis, an Egyptian mother goddess who, in John's time, was recognized as a universal deity throughout the Greco-Roman world. One text from the first or second century c.e. pictures Isis asserting her divine preeminence:

I am Isis, the mistress of every land . . .
I gave and ordained laws for men, which no one is
      able to change . . .
I am she who findeth fruit for men . . .

I divided the earth from the heaven.
I shows the paths of the stars,
I ordered the course of the sun and the moon . . .
I made strong the right . . .
I broke down the governments of tyrants.
I made an end to murders . . .
I ordained that the true should be thought good . . .
With me the right prevails . . .

Although the exact form of the Johannine declarations, "I am the . . ." does not occur in this hymn, it does appear in another fragmentary Isis text, where she affirms her eternity: "I am the deity that had no beginning . . . I am the truth, I am the creator and the destroyer." (Compare John 14:6, where Jesus says, "I am the way, the truth, and the life.")

Mark reports as Jesus' inward or private experience of his calling (Mark 1:10–11) (see box 8.5).

Contrary to the Markan tradition of a hidden Messiah whose identity is only gradually revealed, John has the Baptist immediately hail Jesus as the "Lamb of God . . . who takes away the sin of the world." In John, Jesus is recognized as "God's Chosen One" right from the start (1:6–9, 19–36).

The Book of Signs

John structures his account of Jesus' public ministry around seven signs—miracles that illustrate Jesus' supernatural power—to demonstrate his hero's divinity. The Johannine emphasis on signs contrasts emphatically with the Markan Jesus' curt refusal to give *any* miraculous demonstration of his identity (Mark 8:11–12; cf. Matt. 12:38–40, where the "sign of Jonah"—the prophet's escape from death—is the one sign allowed Jesus' generation).

Many scholars believe that in composing his narrative the Johannine author used an older document, known as the **Signs Gospel.** According to this theory, the Signs Gospel was a straightforward

narrative that depicted Jesus' performing (probably seven) wondrous deeds calculated to show that he was the Messiah (see box 10.6). Some scholars think that the Signs Gospel was the first written account of Jesus' public ministry, composed about the same time as Q, the similarly hypothetical collection of Jesus' sayings. Presumably compiled by a group of Jewish Christians about 50–60 c.e., it served as the narrative framework for the present Gospel of John. Advocates of this theory believe that the Johannine author merely inserted his elaborate dialogs and lengthy speeches into the Signs Gospel, usually without deleting or changing much of the original wording. Scholars therefore were able to attempt reconstructing the text of the earlier Gospel that was John's principal source. Although the Signs Gospel has not survived as an independent account, it seems to be preserved embedded in the canonical Gospel of John (see R. J. Miller and R. T. Fortna in "Recommended Reading").

THE MIRACLE AT CANA

The first Johannine sign occurs at the Galilean town of Cana (not mentioned in the Synoptics), where

---

Box 10.6
The Signs Gospel

Many scholars believe that the author of John's Gospel used an earlier narrative of Jesus' miraculous deeds known as the Signs Gospel. The author's hypothetical source contained accounts of the following miracles (listed here in the Johannine order):

1. Turning water into wine at Cana (in Galilee, 2:1–11)

2. Healing an official's son (in Galilee, 2:12a; 4:46b–54)

3. Healing a crippled man (in Jerusalem, 5:2–9)

4. Feeding 5000 people (in Galilee, 6:1–15)

5. Walking on water (in Galilee, 6:16–25)

6. Restoring sight to a blind man (in Jerusalem, 9:1–8)

7. Raising Lazarus from the dead (near Jerusalem, 11:1–45)

Some scholars also think that the disciples' huge catch of fish (21:1–14) was originally a Galilean miracle that the Gospel's final editor incorporated into his appended account of Jesus' postresurrection appearances.

Jesus, attending a wedding with his mother, changes water into wine. At first glance, this "miracle" resembles the magic tricks that priests of Dionysus (Bacchus), the Greco-Roman god of wine and inspiration, performed to impress gullible onlookers. To John, however, the act is deeply symbolic.

First, Jesus' producing a vintage wine of high quality suggests the superiority of his celebration of life (10:10–11) to the cheerless doctrine of his Jewish predecessors. The fact that it occurs at a marriage festival, the joyful union of man and woman, reminds us that Jesus is the "bridegroom," whose presence brings happiness (3:29; Mark 2:19–20). Most important, the wine represents the sacramental beverage of the Christian communion, the drink symbolizing the blood Jesus sheds on the cross (2:1–11)—a beverage producing both spiritual intoxication and a solemn transcendence of mortality.

ASSAULT ON THE TEMPLE

Reversing the Synoptic order, John shows Jesus driving moneychangers from the Temple during a Passover at the outset of his ministry. For John, the episode's significance is Jesus' superiority to the Jerusalem sanctuary. The Temple is no longer sacred because the Holy Spirit now dwells in Jesus' person rather than the shrine King Herod constructed. Jesus' physical body may be destroyed, but unlike the Herodian edifice he will rise again as proof that God's Spirit imbues him (2:13–25).

DIALOG WITH NICODEMUS

Jesus' conversation with **Nicodemus,** a Pharisee and member of the Jewish Council (Sanhedrin), typifies John's method of presenting Jesus' teaching (3:1–21). In most of the Johannine dialogs, Jesus uses a figure of speech or metaphor that the person with whom he speaks almost comically misinterprets, usually taking Jesus' words literally. John then has Jesus explain his metaphoric meaning, commonly launching a long monolog in which Christ discourses on his metaphysical nature and unique relationship with the Father.

Thus, when Jesus remarks that unless one is "born over again"—or, in an alternative translation, "born from above"—he cannot "see the kingdom of God," Nicodemus mistakenly thinks he refers to reemerging from the womb. Jesus then explains that he means rebirth "from water and spirit," referring to the spiritual renewal that accompanies Christian baptism. Found only in John, this doctrine of becoming "born again" resembles beliefs characteristic of Gnosticism and Greek mystery religions. In both cults, converts undergo initiation rights, commonly involving purification by water, to achieve the soul's new birth on a higher plane of existence, leading eventually to immortality. In the case of being "born from above," initiates experience the Gnostic truth that their souls (or true selves) are of heavenly origin and hence intrinsically divine and eternal.

Perhaps aware of non-Christian parallels to this teaching, the author stresses that Jesus is uniquely qualified to reveal spiritual truths. He is intimately acquainted with the unseen world because heaven is his natural environment, the home to which he will return when "lifted up [on the cross]" (3:12–15).

In perhaps the most famous passage of the New Testament, Jesus states his purpose in coming to earth. God so intensely loves the world that he sends his Son not to condemn it, but to save it, awakening in humanity a faith that gives "eternal life." Believers pass the test for eternal life through their attraction to Jesus' "light," while others judge themselves by preferring the world's "darkness" (3:16–21). Here, John's attitude toward the world is positive, although elsewhere he expresses an ambiguous attitude toward its mixed potential for good and evil. Representing Jesus' ministry and crucifixion as the world's time of judgment (12:31), he declares that Christians are "strangers in the world" (17:16).

Despite acknowledging the world's capacity to believe (17:21, 23), the author shows Jesus telling Pontius Pilate that his "kingdom does not belong to this world"—at least not the kind of system that Pilate and the Roman Empire represent (18:36).

CONVERSATION WITH THE SAMARITAN WOMAN

Luke emphasizes Jesus' warm relationships with women, who are numbered among his most faithful disciples. John further explores Jesus' characteristic openness to women, with whom he converses freely, teaching them on the same level he instructs his male followers. As in Luke, John shows Jesus ignoring the rigid social conventions that segregate the sexes, even to the point of speaking intimately with prostitutes and others of questionable reputation.

Astonishing the disciples by his violation of the social code (4:27), Jesus publicly discusses fine points of theology with a Samaritan woman who gives him water to drink at Jacob's well. Recalling the deep hostility then existing between Jews and

Samaritans (see chapter 9), we understand the woman's surprise at Jesus' willingness to associate with her. She assumes that he is a prophet and seizes the opportunity to learn from him (see figure 10.2). As Jesus later instructs Martha in the mysteries of the Resurrection (11:17–27), so he reveals to the Samaritan woman that he is the "living water" that satisfies humanity's spiritual thirst. Disclosing that neither the Jerusalem Temple nor the Samaritans' rival shrine at Mount Gerizim is the only right place to worship, Jesus teaches her that "spirit and truth" transcend the claims of any earthly sanctuary.

John uses this episode to illustrate several provocative ideas. Although the woman is "immoral" (she has had five husbands and now lives with a man to whom she is not married), Jesus selects her to fill an important role. She is not only the first non-Jew to whom he reveals that he is the Christ (4:25–26) but also the means by which "many Samaritans" become believers (4:39). The woman's rush to inform her fellow villagers about Jesus anticipates Mary Magdalene's later role as prophet to the male disciples when she brings the news that their crucified Lord still lives (20:1–2, 10–18).

THE WOMAN TAKEN IN ADULTERY

Because it does not appear in the oldest New Testament manuscripts, editors of the New English Bible relegate the story of the adulterous woman (8:1–11) to an appendix following chapter 21. In some manuscripts, the incident shows up in Luke, where it well suits the Lukan theme of forgiveness. The anecdote in which Pharisees demand that Jesus judge a woman "caught in the very act" of illicit sex was apparently a well-known tradition that had difficulty finding a home in the canonical Gospels, perhaps because many early Christians found it shocking.

Asked to endorse the Torah rule that prescribed death by stoning for adulterers (Lev. 20:10; Deut. 22:20–21), Jesus turns the responsibility for deciding the woman's fate back on her accusers. Only the person who is "faultless" (without sin) is qualified to enforce the legal penalty. Forcing those who

Figure 10.2 This Ravenna mosaic shows Jesus conversing with a Samaritan woman drawing water from Jacob's well (John 2). Both Luke and John emphasize Jesus' characteristic concern for women. (© Scala/Art Resource, NY)

would judge her to examine their own consciences, Jesus finds that the assembled crowd melts away, leaving him alone with the accused. He neither condemns nor imposes penance on the woman, merely instructing her not to "sin again." Neither blamed nor lectured, she is left to ponder the meaning of her rescue. Whether this episode belongs in John or not, it is consistent with Jesus' nonjudgmental attitude toward individual "sinners" in all four Gospels.

FURTHER SIGNS AND MIRACLES

Jesus' second sign is his curing a nobleman's dying son in Cana (4:46–54). His third is his healing a crippled man at the Sheep Pool in Jerusalem, a controversial act because it occurs on the Sabbath (5:1–15). Criticism directed at Jesus' alleged Sabbath breaking provides the opportunity for an extended discourse on his special relation to the Father. In John's view, God's work (sustaining the universe) continues unceasingly and provides a

model that the Son imitates in ministering to God's human creation (5:16–17).

When accused of claiming "equality with God," Jesus clarifies the nature of his authority. The Son initiates "nothing" on his own; he can only imitate the Father. As God creates life, so the Son grants "eternal life" to those trusting him. In Jesus' ministry, the long-hoped-for resurrection to immortality is already a present reality (5:18–26). Emphasizing his dependence on the Father who sent him, Jesus states that he acts as he is told, dutifully obeying a superior intelligence (5:30). Those who reject him also misread the Hebrew Bible that anticipated God's ministry through him. If his critics really understood the Torah (including the Sabbath's true meaning), they would believe him (5:31–47).

John's presentation of the next two signs parallels the Synoptic tradition, but they are followed by a typically Johannine speech in which the author significantly reinterprets their meaning. The miraculous feeding of 5000 people (the fourth sign) is the only miracle that appears in all four Gospels

(6:1–12; Mark 6:30–44; Matt. 14:13–21; Luke 9:10–17). As in Mark, the miracle is immediately followed by Jesus' walking on water (John's fifth sign) (6:16–21; Mark 6:47–51).

The scene in which Jesus identifies himself with life-giving bread probably reflects the situation in John's day, when his community argued bitterly with other Jews about the Christian communion ritual. Jesus asserts that the only way to gain eternal life is to eat his flesh and drink his blood. Many persons, including Christians, take offense at what seems to them an absurd recommendation of cannibalism. John's church apparently taught that the sacramental bread and communion wine literally became Jesus' body and blood (6:25–65), in a process called *transubstantiation.* Even centuries after John's time, numerous outsiders charged that Christians practiced bloodthirsty rites, including cannibalism, during their secret meetings.

Jesus' sixth sign—restoring sight to a blind man (9:1–41)—illustrates John's theme that Christ is "the light of the world" (8:12). His gift of sight dispels the darkness that afflicted the man and reflects Jesus' identity as the Word that originally brought light out of dark Chaos at the world's creation (Gen. 1:1–5). As mentioned previously, this lengthy episode probably mingles traditions about Jesus' healings with similar miraculous cures performed by Christian prophets in John's church. The dialog in the synagogue that follows the miracle illustrates the tension that prevailed between church and synagogue in John's day.

THE RAISING OF LAZARUS

The seventh and most spectacular miracle—raising Lazarus from the dead (11:1–44)—demonstrates another Johannine conviction, that Jesus possesses irresistible power over life and death. Concluding the Book of Signs, the narrative of Lazarus' miraculous resuscitation also functions to connect Jesus' good works with his arrest and crucifixion. As John relates it, Jesus' ability to raise a man who has been dead for four days is the act that consolidates Jewish opposition to him and leads directly to his death (11:45–53).

Although no other canonical Gospel mentions the Lazarus episode, John may draw upon a primitive resuscitation story that was once part of Mark's narrative (see "The Secret Gospel of Mark" [box 10.7] for an early parallel to the Lazarus miracle). Certain elements of John's account appear in Luke, who includes Mary and Martha (Lazarus's sisters) among Jesus' followers (Luke 10:38–42) but apparently is unaware that they have a brother named Lazarus. (Luke, however, uses the name Lazarus in his parable about death and the afterlife [Luke 16:19–31].) Whatever the historical foundation of the Lazarus incident, John uses it to prove that Jesus is Lord of the resurrection. In a climactic "I am" speech, Jesus declares, "I am the resurrection and I am life. If a man has faith in me, even though he die, he shall come to life; and no one who is alive and has faith shall ever die" (11:25). In dramatic fulfillment of his claims, Jesus orders Lazarus to rise from his tomb, showing all witnesses present that the eschatological hope of life comes through Jesus now (11:1–44).

In John's account, the raising of Lazarus serves multiple literary and theological purposes. As a turning point in the Gospel narrative, it has the same function as the assault on the Temple in the Synoptics: The incident provokes hostility toward Jesus and ignites a fatal conspiracy leading to his execution. As the episode linking the Book of Signs with the Book of Glory (the story of Jesus' Passion), the Lazarus account operates as a preview of Jesus' death and resurrection. Like Lazarus, Jesus will be entombed in a cave from which a great stone—signifying death's finality—will be rolled away as he rises to immortal life. In the Johannine narrative, Martha's confession of faith in Jesus' divine sonship—made just before Lazarus's resuscitation—anticipates Thomas's more complete recognition of the risen Jesus' true divinity (11:27; 20:28).

The raising of Lazarus is also a perfect demonstration of John's realized eschatology. Events traditionally assigned to the *eschaton,* such as the dead obeying a divine summons to exit from their graves, now occur during Jesus' ministry. "As the Father raises the dead and gives them life, so the Son gives life to men," Jesus had earlier declared (5:21), adding that those who trust him *already* possess "eternal life, and [do] not come up for judgment, but [have] already passed from death to life" (5:24). For the Johannine writer, "the time is already here,

Box 10.7
Secret Mark: A Source for John's Account of the Raising of Lazarus?

The Secret Gospel of Mark consists of a fragment that Clement of Alexandria (c. 180–200 C.E.) copied into a letter concerning a "secret" edition of canonical Mark used by some Christians in Egypt. Clement's excerpt was preserved in a manuscript transcribed during the eighteenth century and discovered by the New Testament scholar Morton Smith in 1958. Because Jesus' raising of Lazarus—a man who had been dead for four days and hence in a state of rapid decomposition—is the most spectacular miracle attributed to him, it seems inexplicable that the Synoptic writers never mention it. The existence of Secret Mark, however, shows that this story of Jesus' resurrecting a man whom "he loved" was once part of the Synoptic tradition, at least in Egypt. The fact that the earliest fragments of John's Gospel were found in Egypt (and the tradition, recorded by Eusebius, that Mark was the first to bring Christianity to that country) may suggest some otherwise unknown connection between the Secret Mark account and the composition of John 11.

Whether the author of John was familiar with Secret Mark or knew of the oral tradition behind it, it seems likely that he borrowed the names of Lazarus's sisters, Mary and Martha, from the same oral or written tradition found in Luke (10:38–41), whose Gospel does not mention that they had a brother. The name Lazarus (the beggar who died and went to the paradise of **Abraham's bosom**)—the only character given a name in one of Jesus' parables—also occurs in Luke (16:19–26).

THE SECRET GOSPEL OF MARK

Fragment 1: To be located between Mark 10:34 and 10:35.

[1]And they come into Bethany, and this woman was there whose brother had died. [2]She knelt down in front of Jesus and says to him, "Son of David, have mercy on me." [3]But the disciples rebuked her. [4]And Jesus got angry and went with her into the garden where the tomb was. [5]Just then a loud voice was heard from inside the tomb. [6]Then Jesus went up and rolled the stone away from the entrance to the tomb. [7]He went right in where the young man was, stuck out his hand, grabbed him by the hand, and raised him up. [8]The young man looked at Jesus, loved him, and began to beg him to be with him. [9]Then they left the tomb and went into the young man's house. (Incidentally, he was rich.) [10]Six days later Jesus gave him an order; [11]and when evening had come, the young man went to him, dressed only in a linen cloth. [12]He spent that night with him, because Jesus taught him the mystery of God's domain. [13]From there [Jesus] got up and returned to the other side of the Jordan.

Fragment 2: To be located between 10:46a ("Then they came to Jericho") and 10:46b ("As he was leaving Jericho . . .")

[1]The sister of the young man whom Jesus loved was there, along with his mother and Salome, [2]but Jesus refused to see them.

1:7a This *young man* seems to play a rather important role in Mark. Most notably, his reappearance in the empty tomb announcing to the women Jesus' resurrection suggests that this story of his own resurrection serves to foreshadow Jesus'.

1:7b The action is comparable to that found in Mark 5:41; 9:27.

1:7c *Grabbed him by the hand* could be linked with what follows in v. 8, rather than with what precedes: "Grabbing him by the hand, the young man . . ."

1:10 *gave him an order:* The meaning of the Greek is obscure; it may imply that Jesus gave the young man instructions.

1:11 *dressed only in a linen cloth:* The text reads literally: "a linen cloth having been draped over the naked body." The Markan "young man" appears so dressed also in Mark 14:51. The significance of the linen cloth worn over a naked body is a longstanding riddle in Markan scholarship. It may be some sort of early Christian baptismal garb. Hippolytus, *Apostolic Tradition* 21.11, specifies that in the ceremony of baptism both the catechuman and the presbyter are to stand in the water naked.

2:1a The *young man* is the same one as in the first fragment.

From Robert J. Miller, ed., *The Complete Gospels,* 2nd ed. (San Francisco: HarperSanFrancisco, 1994) p. 411.

---

when the dead shall hear the voice of the Son of God, and all who hear shall come to life" (5:25). In John's view, the life-imparting final resurrection is currently taking place among believers: "No one,"

Jesus assures Martha, "who is alive and has faith shall ever die" (11:26). In thus reinterpreting the timing and nature of resurrection, the author transfers fulfillment of eschatological prophecies about eternal life from the indefinite future—the End of the world—to the concrete here and now.

In grim contrast to the joyous belief that greets Jesus' miracle, John shows some Jerusalem leaders plotting Jesus' death. Jesus' opponents fear that if the Jewish people accept his messiahship (making him "king of the Jews") their response will incite the Romans to destroy their state and place of worship. (This passage refers to the Roman destruction of Jerusalem in 70 c.e.) Caiaphas, the High Priest, proposes that eliminating Jesus will spare the nation that ordeal. Caiaphas's remark—that "it is more to your interest that one man should die for the people, than that the whole nation should be destroyed"—is deeply ironic. While justifying the plot to kill Jesus, the High Priest unwittingly expresses the Christian belief that Jesus' death redeems the world (11:47–53).

The Book of Glory

The second section of John's Gospel—the Book of Glory (chs. 12–20)—may be based on a Passion narrative that had already been added to the primitive Signs Gospel when John incorporated the older work into his expanded account. If scholars are correct in assuming John's use of an earlier document, the Johannine author thoroughly transforms his source, radically reinterpreting the meaning of Jesus' last days. Connecting the Book of Glory with the miraculous signs previously reported, John opens this section by showing Jesus at dinner with friends, celebrating Lazarus's return to life. The festive meal unites several important themes, looking back to Jesus' feeding the multitudes and the resurrection of Lazarus and looking forward to the Last Supper and Jesus' own death. Even while rejoicing in one man's escape from the tomb, the dinner guests are forewarned of their leader's imminent death when Lazarus's sister Mary anoints Jesus' feet with expensive perfume. Christ approves her prophetic action as preparing his body for burial, for his hour of "glory" is near at hand.

Whether following different sources or reworking the older Synoptic tradition, John pictures Jesus' final days in a way that transforms the Mes-

siah's betrayal and suffering into a glorious triumph. After his messianic entry into Jerusalem (John adds the detail of the crowds' waving palm branches that gives Palm Sunday its name) (12:12–19), Jesus foretells his death in terms resembling Mark's description of the agony in Gethsemane (14:32–36) but reinterpreted to stress the Crucifixion's saving purpose: "Now my soul is in turmoil, and what am I to say? Father, save me from this hour. No, it was for this that I came to this hour. Father, glorify thy name" (12:27–28). When a celestial voice affirms that God is glorified in Christ's actions, Jesus interprets his "lifting up" (crucifixion) as God's predestined means of drawing all people to him, a process of human salvation that cannot occur without his death (12:28–33).

THE LAST SUPPER AND FAREWELL DISCOURSES

Perhaps because he has already presented his view of Jesus as the "heavenly bread" that gives life to those who partake of it (6:26–58), John's account of the Last Supper contains no reference to Jesus' distributing the ceremonial bread and wine (the Eucharist). Instead, John's narrative dramatizes a concept found also in Luke's Gospel—that Jesus comes "like a servant" (Luke 22:27). Given the author's view that Christ shares the nature of the Supreme Being (1:1), Jesus' taking the role of a domestic slave, washing his disciples' travel-stained feet, is extremely significant. The Master's humility both demonstrates God's loving care for the faithful and sets an example of humble service for the Johannine community (13:3–17).

After Judas Iscariot leaves the group to betray his Master (a treachery that John believes is predestined), Jesus delivers a series of farewell speeches intended to make clear the way in which his ministry reveals the Father and to place Jesus' inevitable death in proper perspective. Summarizing the divine purpose fulfilled in his life, Jesus gives the "new commandment" of love that distinguishes his people from the rest of the world (13:34–35). Christ's ultimate "act of love" is surrendering his life for his friends' benefit (15:11–14).

With his example of love opening the true "way" to the Father, the Johannine Jesus faces death as a transfiguring experience. In John's view, Jesus' death and return to heaven will permit believers to experience life with God (14:1–6) and simultaneously will allow God to live with them (14:23). Because the divine Parent dwells in him, Christ can reveal God fully—to see Jesus in his true meaning is to see the Father (14:7–11). John insists on Jesus' unique relationship to God—he and the Father "are one," but it is a unity of spirit and purpose that also characterizes the disciples (17:12, 20–21). Despite his close identification with the Deity, John's Jesus does not claim unequivocal equality with God. He simply states that "the Father is greater than I" (15:28).

SENDING THE PARACLETE (HOLY SPIRIT)

With John's emphasis on the disciples' mystic union with Christ (15:5–10; 17:12, 20–22) and the superiority of the unseen spirit to mere physical existence (6:63), it is not surprising that he presents a view of Jesus' return that differs strikingly from that in the Synoptics. Instead of an eager anticipation of the Second Coming (as in Mark 13, Matt. 24–25, or Luke 21), John teaches that Jesus is already present, inspiring the faithful. Brief allusions to Christ's reappearance after death (14:3) are fulfilled when he sends the disciples the Paraclete. The Paraclete, variously translated as "Advocate," "Helper," "Counselor," or "Comforter," is synonymous with "the Spirit of Truth" (14:17) and "the Holy Spirit" (14:26). Although unbelieving humanity will see him no more, he remains eternally present with the faithful (14:16–26). An invisible counterpart to Jesus, the Paraclete enables the disciples to understand the true significance of Jesus' teaching (16:1–15). By implication, the Paraclete also empowers the author to create a Gospel that fully portrays Jesus' glory.

By its presence in the Johannine community's preaching, the Paraclete operates to judge the world's unbelief. Affirming that Jesus is present simultaneously with the Father and with believers, the Paraclete also witnesses to the invincibility of good, resisting the spiritual darkness that claimed Jesus' physical life and now threatens his followers.

In John's view, Jesus imparts the promised Advocate (Paraclete) at his resurrection, merely by breathing on the disciples and saying, "Receive the Holy Spirit" (20:21–23). The risen Lord's action recalls the creation scene in Genesis 2 when Yahweh breathes into Adam's nostrils "the breath of life," making him an animate being or "living creature." As John's Gospel begins with the Word creating the universe (1:1–5), so it closes with the Word breathing the pure spirit of life into his renewed human creation.

John's Interpretation of the Passion

John's narration of Jesus' arrest, trial, and crucifixion is so different from the Synoptic accounts that some scholars believe that he based his Passion story on an independent tradition. A majority, however, think that the differences result primarily from John's mystical interpretation of Jesus' last hours. Although the author is probably historically correct when he places the date of Jesus' execution the day *before* Passover, his narration is governed principally by theological considerations, such as viewing Jesus' being "lifted up" on the cross as the predestined first stage of his hero's reascent into heaven. John ironically places his general understanding of Jesus' death—that he dies to redeem both the Jewish nation and all God's "scattered children" (11:49–53)—on the lips of Caiaphas, whose words the author regards as inspired prophecy.

John's Passion narrative is pervasively shaped by the author's high Christology and his wish to shift responsibility for Jesus' death—here a legalized murder—to his Jewish opponents. Mark's Gospel had already wrestled with the problem of reconciling his portrait of Jesus as a powerful miracle worker in Galilee with the fact of Jesus' apparent helplessness before his enemies in Jerusalem (see chapter 7). After depicting Jesus as a figure of virtually irresistible force throughout his Gospel, John faces an even greater problem in explaining how this incarnation of divine Wisdom became his adversaries' mortal victim. John resolves the potential dilemma by affirming the paradox inherent in Jesus' circumstance: Even in Jerusalem, Jesus retains his superhuman power but voluntarily refuses to use it in order to fulfill scriptural predictions that God's Son must die to save others.

The author emphasizes the disparity between Jesus' divine nature and willing victimhood, portraying Jesus as being in full control of the situation. Foreknowing exactly what will happen to him, the Johannine Christ boldly seeks out the soldiers and Temple police who, in the darkness of Gethsemane, are searching for him (18:4). When told they are looking for Jesus of Nazareth, Jesus replies, "I am he," a revelation of divine identity that causes the soldiers to recoil and fall to the ground (18:4–8). The last of Jesus' "I am" statements, this declaration echoes John's earlier association of Jesus with Israel's God of the Covenant (8:58; cf. Exod. 3:8–16), a claim to divinity that triggers an attempt to stone the apparent blasphemer. Those plotting Jesus' downfall only *seem* to be in charge. Pilate, the representative of Roman imperial power, is specifically informed that his role as dispenser of life or death is only illusory (19:10–11).

Instead of fleeing in terror as they do in the Synoptics, the Johannine disciples are simply dismissed by their Master, who prevents their arrest to fulfill Scripture — the Messiah will lose no one entrusted to him. The author then interweaves the story of Peter's denial with his unique account of Jesus' interrogation before **Annas,** father-in-law of the High Priest Caiaphas (18:8–17). (Unlike the Synoptics, John does not show Jesus formally tried before the full Sanhedrin, but only given an informal hearing at the High Priest's private residence.)

It is in his version of Jesus' appearance before Pontius Pilate that John most explicitly mirrors his community's estrangement from the Jewish community. Only John states that Pharisees, as well as Temple priests, are involved in Jesus' indictment before the Roman procurator. Presenting events in a strangely implausible way, John shows a frightened and harried Pilate dashing back and forth between a Jewish crowd outside his palace and the accused prisoner inside. (John states that Jewish priests could not enter a Gentile's quarters because such contact would make them ritually unclean for the upcoming Passover.) In his desire to foster good relations with Rome, Luke had depicted a Pilate technically innocent of arranging Jesus' death

(Luke 23:1–25), but John goes much further. His Pilate is literally run ragged shuttling between accommodation of the priests who demand Jesus' execution and his sympathetic support of the "king" whom they wish to kill (18:28–19:16). In John's account, Pilate makes no fewer than *eight* attempts to persuade Jesus' priestly accusers (John inaccurately labels them collectively as "Jews") that Jesus is guilty of no crime (cf. 18:31, 38–39; 19:4–6, 12, 14–16). Only after the crowd threatens to accuse Pilate himself of sedition against Rome for championing Jesus' cause (19:12) and insists that their nation has no ruler but the Roman emperor (19:15–16) does Pilate reluctantly submit and turn Jesus over for execution. John also has Pilate symbolically vindicate Jesus' claim to be the rightful Jewish king by refusing to revise a public notice of the crime for which Jesus was crucified (19:19–22).

John's picture of the Crucifixion includes a number of his distinctive concerns. The Johannine Jesus carries his crossbeam all the way to Golgotha, thus precluding any Gnostic or other claim that someone else, such as Simon of Cyrene or even Judas, died in his stead (19:17). In an incident recounted nowhere else, John has a Roman soldier thrust his lance into Jesus' side, initiating a torrent of blood and water. This wounding not only confirms Jesus' physical death (lest one think that Christ only seemed to perish) but also provides typical Johannine symbols of sacramental wine (blood) and truth (water and spirit), emblems that nourish the community of faith (cf. 4:10–14; 6:53–58; 7:37–39).

Besides the small group of Galilean women who witness the Crucifixion in the Synoptic tradition, John adds the figures of Jesus' mother and the Beloved Disciple. Mary (who is never named in this Gospel) apparently fills a symbolic function: Appearing only twice — at the joyous wedding in Cana where water is turned into wine and at the cross where water and blood flow from Jesus — Mary may signify the believing community that benefits from the sacramental emblems of shed blood and crucified body. Only in John's account does Jesus place her (the Church) under the care of the Beloved Disciple, the one who personally testifies to the significance of Jesus' sacrificial death (19:25–27). (See box 10.8 for a comparison of

Box 10.8
Jesus' Last Words: A Summary of the Evangelists' Beliefs About Him

Jesus' final utterances, compiled from the four different Gospel accounts of his crucifixion, are traditionally known as the "seven last words on the cross." Whereas Mark and Matthew agree that Jesus is almost entirely silent during his agony, crying out only once—in Aramaic—to ask why God has deserted him, Luke and John ascribe several short speeches to their dying hero, showing him in full control of his final hours. The particular statements that each Evangelist has Jesus voice represent that author's individual understanding of Jesus' nature and the meaning of his death.

MARK (15:34)

Eloi, Eloi, lema sabachthani?
(My God, my God, why have you forsaken me?)

MATTHEW (27:46)

Eli, Eli, lema sabachthani?
(My God, my God, why have you forsaken me?)

LUKE (23:34, 43, 46)

Father, forgive them [Roman executioners]; they do not know what they are doing.

Truly I tell you: today you [the sympathetic felon next to him] will be with me in Paradise.
Father, into your hands I commit my spirit.

JOHN (19:26–27, 28, 30)

Mother, there is your son . . . There is your mother. [placing Mary (the church) in the future care of the Beloved Disciple (the Johannine community)]
I am thirsty [to fulfill scripture].

It is accomplished!

Writing to a vulnerable group then undergoing hardship and suffering, Mark devotes much of his Gospel to a bleak description of Jesus' Passion, emphasizing that if God permitted his son to endure pain and humiliation, the disciples may expect no better fate. Jesus' cry of despair anticipates his persecuted followers' sense of similarly being abandoned by God. Although Matthew modifies the Passion story to underscore its fulfillment of biblical prophecy, he retains Mark's stress on Jesus' solitary and extreme anguish.

Luke, who presents Jesus as a model of self-sacrificing service to others, thoroughly edits the Passion narrative to highlight Jesus' innocence of any crime against Rome and to illustrate the themes of forgiveness and spirituality that color his portrait of Jesus. Unlike Mark's account, in which Jesus appears almost numb with shock at his brutal treatment, Luke's Jesus is neither silent nor despairing: he speaks repeatedly and confidently, as if he were already enthroned as eschatological judge. He pardons his Roman tormenters, absolving them of responsibility for his execution, and comforts the felon crucified next to him, granting him a posthumous reward in Paradise. Because Luke presents Jesus as led by the Holy Spirit throughout his earthly ministry, it is thematically appropriate for him to show, at the end, Jesus calmly relinquishing his own spirit to God.

Consistent with his picture of Jesus as fully aware of his divine nature, including his prehuman existence in heaven, John paints a Jesus absolutely untroubled by doubt or dejection. Acting out the purpose for which he descended to earth, John's Jesus remains in complete charge of his destiny, allowing soldiers to capture him only to fulfill the divine will (John 18:4–9). The Johannine Jesus thus undergoes no agony in Gethsemane or despair on the cross. In contrast to Mark's picture of lonely abandonment, John shows Jesus accompanied by his mother and his favorite disciple, whose future lives together he arranges. When he says he thirsts, it is not because he experiences ordinary human suffering, but only to fulfill prophecy. His moment of death is simultaneously his "hour of glory," when he can announce that he has accomplished all the Father sent him to do. In his serene omniscience, the Johannine Jesus seems altogether a different being from Mark's disconsolate Son of Man.

Figure 10.3 *Crucifixion.* A modern Japanese artist offers a highly stylized interpretation of Jesus' crucifixion. Two figures, possibly representing Jesus' mother and the Beloved Disciple, kneel in adoration of the incarnate Word of God. (© Boltin Picture Library)

Gospel accounts of Jesus' last words.) By designating the Beloved Disciple as Mary's honorary son, John also makes him Jesus' brother, in effect Jesus' successor as leader of the Johannine community (see figure 10.3).

POSTRESURRECTION APPEARANCES IN JERUSALEM

Although John apparently follows the same tradition that Luke used, placing Jesus' resurrection appearances in and around Jerusalem (instead of Galilee as in Mark and Matthew), he modifies the story to illustrate his characteristic themes. On the first Easter Sunday, Mary Magdalene is alone when she discovers that Jesus' corpse has vanished from Joseph of Arimathaea's garden tomb where it had

been placed late the previous Friday. Prophet of her Lord's resurrection, she is the first to report the empty tomb and the first to see the risen Jesus, announcing these glad tidings to the male disciples (20:1–2, 10–18).

Following Jesus' Sunday evening appearance to the disciples, infusing them with the Holy Spirit, he appears again to "doubting Thomas," vanquishing his skepticism. (Note that the Beloved Disciple believes that Jesus lives even before physical proof is offered, illustrating the Johannine community's cultivation of faith [20:8–9, 26–29].) His "light" having "overcome" the world's spiritual darkness, Jesus also conquers death. His resurrection is the final victorious "sign" toward which all his earlier miracles pointed.

Epilog: Postresurrection Appearances in Galilee

Most scholars believe that the Fourth Gospel originally ended at 20:31 with the author's stated purpose of inspiring faith. Chapter 21, which records traditions about Jesus' posthumous appearances in Galilee, seems to be the work of an editor, who may have prepared the Gospel manuscript for publication. This redactor also emphasizes the complementary roles of Peter, leader of the Twelve, and the unidentified "disciple whom Jesus loved."

When Jesus appears to share an early morning breakfast of bread and fish (again demonstrating that the risen Christ is not a ghost or other disembodied spirit), he questions Peter about the depth of his love. Using three different Greek verbs for "love," Jesus emphasizes that love for him means feeding his "lambs." Thus, Peter and the Church are to provide spiritual and other care for future believers, the "other sheep" (10:16), including Gentiles, who will soon join the apostolic fold (21:4–17). (Note the contrasting fates predicted for Peter [20:18–19] and the Beloved Disciple [20:20–23].)

The Gospel concludes with the editor's musing on the vast oral tradition surrounding Jesus. If his entire career were to be recorded in detail, the "whole world" could not contain "the vast number of books that would be produced" (21:25).

In the New Testament book called 1 John, the writer successfully defends the Johannine community's Christology and behavioral ethics against (apparently) Gnostic opponents. 1 John's defense of the Fourth Gospel's portrayal of Jesus helped clear the way for the Gospel's eventual acceptance into the Christian canon. The Johannine view of a celestial preexistent Christ, who on earth was also fully human (the Word of God "made flesh"), adds a whole new dimension to Jesus' theological significance, one absent from the Synoptic tradition. By presenting Christ as God's agent of creation who, in the Incarnation, bridges the realms of spirit and matter to reveal ultimate knowledge, John imparts to Jesus a universality unmatched in earlier Gospels.

Summary

Although John's Gospel may have originated on the fringes of the Christian community in a group influenced by Essene sectarianism and proto-Gnostic ideas, it eventually provided mainstream Christianity with concepts crucial to its later theological development. The Synoptics had in effect divided Jesus' messiahship into two essentially different parts: a career in the recent past as a sacrificial servant and a future Second Coming as the virtually omnipotent Son of Man. The failure of the Parousia to occur during the lifetimes of Jesus' original followers may have created a crisis of belief that John's transformation of Jesus' story effectively addresses. In John's Gospel, Jesus accomplishes everything necessary for the Messiah in a single earthly coming. Events normally associated with the *eschaton*—divine judgment, spiritual regeneration, resurrection, and the giving of full knowledge—all take place during Jesus' historic ministry. John's vision does not emphasize Jesus' future return because the Johannine Christ had already achieved his disciples' redemption and, in the form of the Paraclete, is eternally present with believers. Only once in the main body of his Gospel does the author briefly refer to Christ's reappearance: In John 14:3, Jesus states that he will "come again" to receive his disciples, taking them to dwell with him in his Father's heavenly abode. This promised return, however, is only to collect the faithful—perhaps at the hour of death—and makes no allusion to eschatological events of the Synoptic type (cf. 21:23).

At the very end of Matthew's Gospel, the risen Jesus promises his disciples to be always with them "to the end of time" (Matt. 28:20). Luke also frames his resurrection accounts to suggest that Jesus remains present in such Christian practices as Bible study and communal meals (Luke 24). But only John portrays the advent of the Paraclete as if "he" were Jesus' double (15:26–27), fulfilling believers' desire for a continuing presence (14:10–26).

Besides helping resolve the problem of a delayed Second Coming, John's Gospel also succeeds in portraying Jesus as so unique and exalted that he can have no rivals: No prophet, lawgiver, angel, or other heavenly being possesses his relationship to God. More than any single book in the New Testament, this Gospel lays the foundations for later theological interpretations of Christ's nature and function. In post-New Testament times, theologians came to see Christ as the Second Person in the **Trinity** (a term that does not appear in canonical Scripture), coequal, consubstantial, and coeternal with the Father. Although the Johannine writings do not articulate so formal a dogma, historically John's high Christology profoundly influenced Christianity's eventual understanding of its Master.

QUESTIONS FOR REVIEW

1. Evaluate the arguments for and against the Apostle John's responsibility for the Gospel traditionally attributed to him. Describe the role of the Beloved Disciple and his relationship to the Fourth Gospel.

2. List and define some of the major differences between the Gospel of John and the Synoptic Gospels. Compare Jesus' manner of speaking and use of parables in Mark with his long philosophical discourses in John. In composing Jesus' Johannine speeches, do you think that the author was influenced by the form of Wisdom's speeches in Proverbs, Ecclesiasticus, and the Wisdom of Solomon?

3. In presenting Jesus as a spiritual redeemer descended from heaven, John reflects or parallels some Gnostic ideas. In what specific ways does John's Gospel resemble — or differ from — Gnostic teachings?

4. John's Gospel contains almost no apocalyptic teaching and has no prediction of Jesus' Second Coming. Does John's teaching about the Advocate, or Paraclete, render a belief in Jesus' eschatological return unnecessary?

5. Name several of the seven "signs" or miracles that Jesus performs to demonstrate his divinity. How does the raising of Lazarus lead to Jesus' death?

6. What is the purpose of Jesus' "I am" speeches? What do they reveal about him?

QUESTIONS FOR DISCUSSION AND REFLECTION

1. The "brotherhood," or Christian community, that produced John's Gospel preserved traditions about Jesus that roughly paralleled but significantly differed from those on which the Synoptic Gospels are based. Why do you suppose the Johannine community so strongly identified Jesus with the divine Wisdom that God used to create the universe (Prov. 8)? How does John's introductory Hymn to the Logos (Word) express the author's view of Jesus' prehuman existence and divine nature?

2. More than any other single New Testament book, the Gospel of John has influenced subsequent Christian thought about Jesus' divinity. What specific Johannine teachings do you think most contributed to the conception of the Trinity — the doctrine that defines the Christian God as embodying the triune Being: Father, Son, and Holy Spirit?

In discussing the idea that the heavenly being (Logos) who became the human Jesus had no beginning but dwelt from eternity with the Father, interpret such diverse Johannine statements as "he who has seen me has seen the Father" and "the Father is greater than I am."

3. The idea that Jesus is divine — to be identified with the God of the Hebrew Bible — is perhaps the chief source of division between monotheistic Jews and orthodox Christians. Is Jesus' "full divinity" a major preoccupation of the Synoptic writers? How does John's claim of Jesus' virtual godhood work to separate today's Jews and Christians?

TERMS AND CONCEPTS TO REMEMBER

Incarnation	Isis
Holy Spirit	Book of Signs
high Christology	transubstantiation
Gnosticism	Book of Glory
Paraclete (the Advocate)	Jesus' hour of "glory"
Logos (Word)	washing the disciples'
heavenly Wisdom	feet
(Prov. 8)	Annas
Philo Judaeus	Crucifixion

RECOMMENDED READING

Baltz, Frederick W. *Lazarus and the Fourth Gospel Community.* Lewiston, N.Y.: Mellen Biblical Press, 1995. Presents evidence that Lazarus was the Beloved Disciple, whom the author identifies with the historical figure Eleazar, son of Boethus, whose sisters, Miriam and Martha, appear briefly in rabbinical literature.

Brodie, Thomas L. *The Quest for the Origin of John's Gospel: A Source-Oriented Approach.* New York: Oxford University Press, 1993. Argues that John composed his Gospel by theologically transforming the Synoptic accounts.

Brown, R. E. *The Gospel According to John,* Vols. 29 and 29a of the Anchor Bible. Garden City, N.Y.: Doubleday, 1966, 1970. Provides the most complete historical and theological background and the most thorough commentary on John's Gospel.

——. *The Community of the Beloved Disciple.* New York: Paulist Press, 1979. A readable and insightful study of the Christian group that produced the Gospel and the Letters of John.

——. *The Epistles of John,* Vol. 30 of the Anchor Bible. Garden City, N.Y.: Doubleday, 1982. A thoroughly annotated edition.

Bultmann, Rudolf. *The Gospel of John.* Translated by G. R. Beasley-Murray. Philadelphia: Westminster Press, 1971. A somewhat dated but seminal interpretation.

Caird, G. B. "Letters of John." In *The Interpreter's Dictionary of the Bible,* Vol. 2, pp. 946–952. Nashville, Tenn.: Abingdon Press, 1962.

Cullman, Oscar. *The Johannine Circle.* Translated by John Bowden. Philadelphia: Westminster Press, 1976. Explores the Gospel's possible source.

Dodd, C. H. *Historical Tradition in the Fourth Gospel.* Cambridge: Cambridge University Press, 1963.

——. *The Interpretation of the Fourth Gospel.* Cambridge: Cambridge University Press, 1965.

Fortna, R. T. *The Fourth Gospel and Its Predecessor: From Narrative Source to Present Gospel.* Philadelphia: Fortress Press, 1988. The definitive analysis of the hypothetical Signs source underlying John's Gospel.

Haenchen, Ernst. *A Commentary on the Gospel of John,* Vols. 1 and 2. Hermeneia Commentary. Translated by R. W. Funk. Philadelphia: Fortress Press, 1984.

Kysar, Robert. *John, the Maverick Gospel.* Atlanta: John Knox Press, 1976. An influential study of the Fourth Gospel.

——. "John, Epistles of." In D. N. Freedman, ed., *The Anchor Bible Dictionary,* Vol. 3, pp. 900–912. New York: Doubleday, 1992. Relates circumstances of the Gospel's composition to later epistles.

——. "John, the Gospel of." In D. N. Freedman, ed., *The Anchor Bible Dictionary,* Vol. 3, pp. 912–931. New York: Doubleday, 1992. A thoughtful review of Johannine literature and scholarship.

Martyn, J. L. *History and Theology in the Fourth Gospel,* 2nd ed. Nashville, Tenn.: Abingdon Press, 1979. A brilliant interpretation of John's method of composition that focuses on John 9.

Miller, Robert J., ed. *The Complete Gospels,* 2nd ed. San Francisco: HarperSanFrancisco, 1994.

Olson, A. M., ed. *Myth, Symbol and Reality.* Notre Dame, Ind.: University of Notre Dame Press, 1981. Includes essays on the Logos.

Perkins, Pheme. "The Gospel According to John." In R. E. Brown et al., eds., *The New Jerome Biblical Commentary,* pp. 942–985. Englewood Cliffs, N.J.: Prentice-Hall, 1990. An insightful commentary on the Gospel.

——. "The Johannine Epistles." In R. E. Brown et al., eds., *The New Jerome Biblical Commentary,* pp. 986–995. Englewood Cliffs, N.J.: Prentice-Hall, 1990.

Schnackenburg, Rudolf. *The Gospel According to John,* Vols. 1–3. Various translators. New York: Seabury Press, 1980, and Crossroads, 1982. Challenging but insightful analysis.

Smith, D. M., Jr. *Johannine Christianity: Essays on Its Setting, Sources, and Theology.* Columbia: University of South Carolina Press, 1984.

CHAPTER 11

The Continuing Quest for the Historical Jesus

"Who do [people] say I am?"
Jesus questions his disciples

Mark 8:28

Key Themes Because the Evangelists present Jesus' life almost exclusively in theological terms and non-Christian first-century writers refer only briefly to his existence, scholars face a formidable challenge in trying to distinguish the Jesus of history from the Christ of faith. In their ongoing quest to recover the historical Jesus, scholars have developed criteria by which they hope to evaluate the authenticity of words and actions the early church ascribed to Jesus. Although most scholars generally agree on a methodology for screening traditions to find Jesus' authentic voice, they have reached strikingly different conclusions about his essential teachings and self-identity, particularly on the issue of his eschatology.

After reading four different accounts of Jesus' ministry—all of which are believers' tributes to his supernatural identity—students may wonder who the "real" Jesus of Nazareth may have been. Comparing Mark's Gospel with that of John, attentive readers see a great disparity in the way the two Evangelists present their subject. In Mark, Jesus is primarily an exorcist and healer who teaches, in brief parables and vivid figures of speech, about God's dawning rule. Framing Jesus' message in terms of an imminent eschatological judgment, Mark emphasizes a gradually revealed messiahship of human weakness and suffering.

In John, neither Jesus' innate divinity nor his ultimate triumph are ever in doubt: He is proclaimed God's sacrificial "lamb" from the outset of his public career. The Johannine Jesus performs no exorcisms and creates no parables. Instead of earthy similes based on peasant life, he speaks in extended monologs about the mystery of his divine nature

and his journeys from and back to heaven. To many, John's picture of an omniscient incarnation of celestial Wisdom is irresistible. His vision of Christ, a paradigm of cosmic power and absolute certainty, is probably the one that most attracts believers.

For all its spiritual appeal, however, John's depiction of Jesus' character and teaching seems too focused on the glory of the risen Christ to offer a realistic assessment of the historical person. Even Mark, with its emphasis on demonic possession, the impending *eschaton,* and Jesus' foreknowledge of the precise circumstances of his death, appears far removed from the normal standards of historicity.

New Testament scholars recognize that the Gospel authors do not attempt to record an objective, purely factual biography of Jesus but in their individual ways *interpret him theologically.* Aware of this fact, students often ask if it is possible to find the authentic man amid the sometimes conflicting sayings and deeds that the Evangelists attribute to their hero. Are there any "unbiased" historical sources that give us reliable information about the human Jesus?

Early Historical References to Jesus

Unfortunately, non-Christian writers tell us almost nothing about the Nazarene except that he existed, was crucified under Pilate, and inspired a new religious movement in the Roman Empire. The earliest writer to mention Jesus is Tacitus, a Roman senator and historian of the first century C.E., who seems to have based his report largely on secondhand evidence. His single allusion to Jesus is tantalizingly brief, stating merely that Jesus "had been executed in Tiberius's reign by the governor of Judaea, Pontius Pilate" (*Annals* 15.44). Tacitus's statements about Jesus and his followers are incidental to the historian's main purpose—illustrating the cruelty and corruption of Nero, who tried to blame the Christians for a great fire that consumed much of Rome about 64 C.E.:

> Nero had self-acknowledged Christians arrested. Then, on their information, large numbers of others were condemned—not so much for incendiarism as for their anti-social tendencies. Their deaths were made farcical. Dressed in wild animals' skins, they were torn to pieces by dogs, or crucified, or made into torches to be ignited after dark as substitutes for daylight. . . . Despite their guilt as Christians, and the ruthless punishment it deserved, the victims were pitied. For it was felt that they were being sacrificed to one man's brutality rather than to the national interest.
>
> (*Annals* 15.44)

Nero's persecution, which was apparently confined to the imperial capital, represents the Roman government's first official recognition of the new faith. That even an enlightened author such as Tacitus could regard Christians as so "notoriously depraved" that they deserved the death penalty indicates the extent to which Rome's ruling classes misunderstood the Jesus movement. Given first-century officialdom's ignorance of early Christian

beliefs, it is likely that few educated non-Christians were in a position to know the facts of Jesus' life and teachings.

Suetonius, another Roman historian, records that even before Nero, the emperor **Claudius** (reigned 41–54 C.E.) had expelled the Jews from Rome because of trouble arising from "Chrestus" (probably a variant spelling of Tacitus's "Christus" [the Greek *Christos*, or Christ]) (*Twelve Caesars* 25). The alleged "constant rioting" that Claudius punished about 49 C.E. may have resulted from conflicts between Roman Jews and Jewish-Christian missionaries who brought their innovative religion from Palestine. (The author of Acts refers to Claudius's expulsion of Jews, including Priscilla and Aquila, who met Paul in Corinth about 50 C.E. [Acts 18:2].)

Flavius Josephus, the first-century Jewish historian who interpreted his people's customs to a Greco-Roman audience, twice mentions Jesus. With its later Christian interpolations deleted, Josephus's comments originally may have run as follows:

> Now there was about this time [the administration of Pontius Pilate (26–36 C.E.)], Jesus, a wise man, . . . a doer of wonderful works, a teacher of such men as receive the truth with pleasure. He drew over to him . . . many of the Jews, . . . and when Pilate, . . . had condemned him to the cross, those that loved him at the first . . . [believed] that he appeared to them alive again the third day. . . . [A]nd the tribe of Christians, so named from him, are not extinct at this day.
>
> (*Antiquities* 18.3.3)

Josephus's second reference deplores the illegal execution of James, "the brother of Jesus, who was called Christ" (*Antiquities* 20.9.1). Although from a later date, allusions to Jesus in the Talmud, which condemns him for sorcery and "for leading Israel astray," similarly attest to Jesus' historicity.

Pliny the Younger, who governed the Roman province of **Bithynia** (north-central Turkey) from about 111 to 115 C.E., wrote to the emperor **Trajan** for advice about dealing with Christians who refused to participate in "emperor worship," a public ritual then popularly regarded as much an expression of patriotism as of religious commitment. Pliny's letter notes that Christians gathered to "partake of a meal [the Eucharist or Holy Communion]" and to sing "a hymn to Christ, as if to a god" (*Letters* 97), adding that cities, villages, and even the rural districts had been "thoroughly infected" by the "seditious" cult.

Whereas the Greco-Roman authors' cursory allusions to Jesus tend to confirm his martyrdom under Pilate and posthumous influence, they offer almost no information with which to construct a biography. Virtually everything we can learn about Jesus derives from the New Testament and a few other Christian documents, such as the **apocryphal Gospel** of Thomas. The writers of these works are not objective historians, but believers who regarded Jesus as qualitatively different from every other human being. To them, Jesus is "the image of the invisible God" in whom "the complete being of the Godhead dwells embodied" (Col. 1:15–20; 2:9–10). He is the Incarnation of the Logos, the preexistent Word, who so fully reveals the Creator that he is represented as saying that "anyone who has seen me has seen the Father" (John 14:9).

These devotional affirmations of Jesus' metaphysical nature cannot be affirmed scientifically, but must remain an expression of faith. Supernatural events that by definition occur outside life's normal historical process, such as Jesus' miraculous ability to control a storm, walk on water, or rise from the dead, cannot be studied in themselves, but only in their conceptual development within the primitive Christian community. Scientific analysis cannot deal with Jesus conceived as divinity but must approach the living man only as the legitimate object of historical inquiry, leaving to theologians the task of interpreting the paradox of Jesus as both completely human and fully divine.

A Survey of the Historical Search for the "Real" Jesus

Although some European rationalists, particularly eighteenth-century English Deists, had questioned the historical reliability of the Gospels, the first major critic to subject traditional ideas about Christian origins to systematic analysis was Hermann Samuel Reimarus (1694–1768). Reimarus, whose work was not published until after his death, argued that the "real" Jesus was a Jewish revolutionary who failed to overthrow the Romans and was instead executed by them. After stealing and hiding his body, Jesus' disciples proclaimed that he was divine and would soon reappear amid clouds of glory. According to Reimarus, Christianity is based on a double misrepresentation: the failure of Jesus' actual political aspirations and the failure of his disciples' eschatological predictions. A few modern scholars, such as S. G. Brandon, have also argued that Jesus was an anti-Roman Zealot, but this view is not widely accepted.

Although Reimarus's study was largely an anti-Christian polemic, it served the purpose of raising questions about the historical Jesus' actual teachings and intentions. David Friedrich Strauss (1808–1874) continued Reimarus's attempt to distinguish between the human Jesus and the church's theological claims about him. Advocating a scientific skepticism that rejected belief in miracles or other forms of the supernatural, Strauss focused on the composite nature and Christological purpose of the Gospels, concluding that they presented Jesus in mythological rather than historical terms. The publication of Strauss's *Life of Jesus Critically Examined* (1835) cost the author his university position and triggered an attack by conservative theologians that continued until Strauss's death.

H. J. Holtzmann (1832–1910) was another nineteenth-century German scholar who approached the historical Jesus by studying different layers of tradition in the Synoptic Gospels. Holtzmann's detailed use of source criticism and his conclusion that Mark is the earliest Gospel offered a methodology and hypothesis that have influenced New Testament scholarship ever since. Johannes Weiss (1863–1914) pursued the historical Jesus by concentrating on his preaching of the "kingdom of God," an eschatological message announcing the world's imminent End. By placing Jesus in the context of first-century Jewish eschatological expectations, Weiss made scholars aware that a viable historical reconstruction of Jesus requires studying him in a first-century Palestinian environment.

Even a figure as distinctive as Jesus cannot be properly viewed out of his particular time and place.

Weiss's thesis of an eschatological Jesus was adopted and extensively developed by Albert Schweitzer (1875–1965), whose monumental *Quest of the Historical Jesus* (1906/1961) both defined the movement and, for nearly a half-century, immobilized it. Schweitzer's book had a revolutionary impact, shattering many people's traditional image of Jesus. To unveil the man of history, Schweitzer used the relatively new techniques of form criticism, the research method that attempts to discover the older oral form of a tradition as it existed before becoming embedded in a written Gospel.

Schweitzer's Jesus is dominated by a conviction that he is God's chosen instrument to announce the impending consummation of history. Burning with eschatological zeal, he demands that followers abandon all earthly ties and work with him to hasten the arrival of God's kingdom, which will overturn the present satanic world order and usher in the New Age. Jesus' driving goal is to fulfill the prophetic conditions that will bring about a supernaturally inspired chain of events culminating in his cosmic reign as the Son of Man. When Jesus' early expectations do not materialize (Matt. 10:22–23), he marches to Jerusalem, confident that he can compel the kingdom's appearance through his voluntary death, the final "tribulation" leading to God's direct imposition of his sovereignty. The anticipated divine intervention does not occur, however, and Jesus is crushed by the system he defies.

Schweitzer's reading of Jesus as a devoted but misguided apocalyptist made Christianity's core figure seem irrelevant to the modern worldview. No matter how sincere, a prophet whose eschatological predictions had been disproved by the world's stubborn failure to end had little to say to twentieth-century thinkers accustomed to scientific rationalism. As a result of this uncongenial historical Jesus, scholars for the next several decades concentrated almost exclusively on the Gospels, employing form criticism and similar techniques to disentangle Palestinian traditions of the Jesus movement from later Hellenistic strands. The Jesus of history, apparently tied to an outmoded and unacceptable eschatology, was ignored while theologians focused on the postresurrection Christ of faith.

Rudolf Bultmann (1884–1976) is perhaps the single most influential New Testament scholar since Schweitzer. In his *Jesus and the Word* (1934) and *Jesus Christ and Mythology* (1958), Bultmann provided an exhaustive analysis of the different literary forms contained in the Synoptic Gospels, arguing that in most cases the material indicates an origin not in the life of Jesus but in the life of the early church. Bultmann also argued that the Gospels largely present Jesus in terms of Hellenistic **mythology**, portraying him as a supernatural figure who descends from heaven to reveal divine Wisdom. According to Bultmann, one can make Jesus' essentially timeless message relevant to modern believers only by translating the Gospels' mythic language into the principles of twentieth-century existentialism. Although it is both impossible and undesirable to recover the finite historical personality of Jesus himself, the universal concept for which Jesus stands can still summon people to make an existentialist decision of ethical commitment. For Bultmann, the human Jesus espoused a form of Judaism, while Christianity is essentially a Hellenistic creation, thus rendering the historical Jesus of only marginal significance to faith in the risen Christ.

Renewing the Quest

It was not until 1953 that scholars began to undertake a new search for the Jesus of history. In a speech that year, Ernst Käsemann declared that Christian faith must not be divorced from its historical roots in the human Jesus. The renewed quest has inspired a host of scholars seeking to reconstruct the teachings and actions of Jesus, including J. Jeremias. Jeremias examined Jesus' sayings by means of linguistic and form-critical analysis, hoping to find a middle ground between the imminent eschatology of Schweitzer (the End is near, but not yet) and the realized eschatology of C. H. Dodd (the kingdom is actually present in the ministry of Jesus). Although he did not resolve the problem of recovering Jesus' historical message, Jeremias proposed a middle way that has influenced other scholars. Jesus' kingdom is actually in the process of fulfillment: In one respect, it is yet to come; in another, it is already present in Jesus' healing and teaching.

The Continuing Scholarly Debate

The international scholarly community remains deeply divided on the issue of the historical Jesus' actions and teachings. A large number of distinguished scholars, including E. P. Sanders and Paula Fredriksen (see "Recommended Reading"), are convinced that Jesus' message emphasized an imminent eschatological judgment. According to this view, Jesus assaulted the Temple moneychangers because he believed (as the Hebrew prophets Micah and Jeremiah had earlier proclaimed) that God planned to destroy the Jerusalem sanctuary and raise a new one in the dawning New Age—an eschatological event that would occur in the immediate future! Similarly, Jesus' intensification of Torah ethics—insisting on purity of motive as well as deed (Matt. 5–7)—served to prepare a faithful remnant of Israel for the coming kingdom. Like the Essenes, Jesus and his followers—symbolizing the renewed twelve tribes of Israel—saw themselves as a divinely supported group ethically purifying itself for the final consummation of history. If the historical Jesus in fact preached that God was about to bring an adverse judgment against both Jewish and Roman authorities—and replace them with direct divine rule—this pronouncement can plausibly account for his arrest and execution. Although Jesus apparently did not advocate armed rebellion against the Roman-Sadducean alliance, his message of the established order's impending doom and the crowds that enthusiastically responded to the promise of their exploiters' overthrow would be enough to make Pilate eliminate this potential threat to the present system.

This picture of an eschatological Jesus not only explains Pilate's decision to crucify one who may have aspired to be king in God's new order but also places Jesus firmly within the context of first-century Palestinian Judaism. Like the Essenes and John the Baptist, Jesus was motivated by a vision of God's imminent intervention in history to restore a repentant and purified Israel. By continuing John's warning of a rapidly approaching eschatological judgment, Jesus similarly antagonized the ruling powers and met a similar fate.

The Work of the Jesus Seminar

Whereas many scholars view the historical Jesus as having anticipated an imminent *eschaton*, others insist that his teaching had little to do with popular eschatology. Prominent among the exponents of a noneschatological Jesus is the Jesus Seminar, a group of about one hundred leading North American New Testament scholars. Many researchers think that the work of the Jesus Seminar is particularly important because it is the only scholarly group that has collectively analyzed each and every word and action ascribed to Jesus, in both canonical and noncanonical sources, during the first three centuries C.E. (see figure 11.1). It has also taken the lead in making the results of its investigations known to a large audience outside the academic community.

Like other participants in the scholarly quest for the historical Jesus, members of the Jesus Seminar employed a set of criteria by which to evaluate the probable authenticity of sayings and deeds attributed to Jesus. The methodology for distinguishing Jesus' words from those of later followers who preached about him and whose declarations of faith were ultimately incorporated into Jesus' Gospel speeches includes several important standards of evidence (see box 11.1).

Because Jesus directed his teaching—in Aramaic—to a rural and largely illiterate peasant audience in first-century Galilee, the first criterion is that of *orality*. Jesus' authentic words, which were not written down until two or three decades after he spoke them, would have had to be vivid and striking enough to be remembered and repeated by unlettered hearers. Genuinely historical sayings, then, will be attention-getting and memorable, such

Figure 11.1 Head of Christ, artist unknown. This mosaic portrait of Jesus is composed of hundreds of tiny fragments of stone or tile arranged to create the lineaments of a human face. The result is not a realistic picture of an individual, but a highly stylized representation of a type of humanity. The stern and grimly determined face shown here well embodies Mark's image of a Messiah predestined to endure rejection and suffering. As the artist assembled many different pieces of material to achieve this stereotype, so today's scholars work to assemble a coherent picture of the historical Jesus from thousands of literary fragments embedded in both canonical and noncanonical sources. (Michos Tzovaras/Art Resource, NY)

as Jesus' advising people to get a beam out of their own eye before looking for a speck in someone else's. Jesus appears to have favored **aphorisms**— brief, pithy sayings that challenged or overturned conventional wisdom, forcing people to think about the world in new ways. "It is not what goes into a person that defiles," he said, "but what comes out" (Mark 7:15, Scholars Version)—an almost scatological criticism of biblical dietary laws. Although they resemble **proverbs** in form, Jesus' aphorisms are typically nonproverbial in rejecting common-

sensical assumptions or customs, such as his declaration: "It's easier for a camel to squeeze through a needle's eye than for a wealthy person to get into God's domain" (Mark 10:25, SV). Such statements not only provoke a double-take among typical listeners but also reverse traditional assurances that wealth is a divine blessing (Prov. 6:6–11; 10:15; 24:30–34; Job 42:12; Deut. 28:1–14).

Besides speaking in aphorisms that typically shock with their audacity or provoke with their rejection of familiar, everyday expectations, Jesus also

Box 11.1
Criteria for Testing the Authenticity of Jesus' Sayings

Scholars have developed a series of criteria by which to distinguish Jesus' authentic sayings from those ascribed to him in the Gospels. The Gospels appear to include at least four levels of the Jesus tradition: (1) Jesus' historical words; (2) sayings attributed to him during the period of oral transmission by Christian preachers and missionaries; (3) sayings modified and assembled in pre-Gospel written collections, such as Q (the hypothetical sayings document) or the first edition of the Gospel of Thomas (also a sayings source); and (4) speeches created for Jesus by the Gospel authors as they told his story. In the fourth category, many of Jesus' conversations or public debates with adversaries seem to be a function of the Gospel narrative and were created by the Evangelists to provide an approximation of what Jesus might have said on particular occasions. Although such Gospel dialogs may represent ideas not entirely dissimilar to Jesus' original teachings, scholars do not think that such narrative devices accurately recorded Jesus' actual words. Among the methods for testing authenticity proposed by the late Norman A. Perrin, members of the Jesus Seminar, and other scholars are the following criteria:

1. *Orality.* Because Jesus taught orally, to be remembered his ideas must have been vividly worded to achieve maximum impact on his largely illiterate Galilean audiences. To be remembered and quoted repeatedly during a long period of oral transmission, Jesus' sayings must have been strikingly memorable.

Examples of brief, highly quotable sayings include Jesus' declarations that it is easier for a camel to squeeze through the eye of a needle than for a rich man to enter God's kingdom (Mark 10:25; Matt. 19:24; Luke 18:25), that one should pay Caesar [the government] his due but give God what belongs to God (only in Mark 12:17), and that prophets are honored everywhere except on their home turf and among their relations (Mark 6:4; Matt. 13:15; John 4:44; G. Thom. 33) (this last also meets the criterion of multiple attestation).

2. *Form.* Jesus' best remembered sayings were cast in the form of concise aphorisms and parables that drew on familiar practices of rural peasant life. He used concrete images and made unexpected compar-

isons, freely employing such rhetorical devices as hyperbole, metaphor, humor, and paradox. Contrary to the Johannine picture, he apparently did not deliver long philosophical discourses.

Aphorisms that employ humor, hyperbole, or paradox include advice on taking a "plank" out of one's eye (Matt. 7:3–5; Luke 6:41–42; G. Thom. 26), being sly as a snake and simple as a dove (Matt. 10:16; G. Thom. 39), and robbing a strong man (Mark 3:27; Matt. 12:29; Luke 11:21–22; G. Thom. 35).

Many authentic sayings take the form of parables using images from agricultural or domestic life, such as the brief narratives that involve the sowing of seeds (Mark 4:3–8; Matt. 13:3–8; Luke 8:5–8a; G. Thom. 9), the mustard plant (Mark 4:30–32; Matt. 13:31–32; Luke 13:18–19; G. Thom. 20), the unproductive fig tree (Luke 13:6–9), and a woman's lost coin (Luke 15:8–10).

3. *Distinctiveness.* Jesus' aphorisms differed from both common Palestinian-Jewish beliefs or practices and later formulations of the Hellenistic church. His genuine teachings probably sounded peculiar, even outrageous, to his original hearers. Jesus' sayings tended to defy conventional wisdom and overturn normal ways of looking at the world. Authentic statements tend to challenge accepted social values and reverse ordinary expectations. (Of course, Jesus probably also spoke unmemorably about routine matters, but such discourse would not reveal his unique voice or typical idiom.)

Luke preserves some of Jesus' most distinctive teachings, including the parables of the prodigal son (Luke 15:11–32), the good Samaritan (Luke 10:30–35), the clever but dishonest steward (Luke 16:1–8a), the unjust judge (Luke 18:1–8), and the Pharisee and the tax collector (Luke 18:9–14a).

4. *Dissimilarity.* A somewhat different aspect of the distinctiveness test, the criterion of dissimilarity holds that a saying may be authentic if it differs significantly from both first-century Judaisms and early Christianity. Jesus' use of the Aramaic term *Abba* (an informal term for "father") (Mark 14:36; Luke 11:2) differs from the church's more formal way of addressing the Deity (Matt. 6:9) and probably represents Jesus' distinctive practice.

The obvious weakness in the dissimilarity criterion is that many of Jesus' characteristic teachings, including his emphasis on love, were also shared by other Palestinian teachers of his day (Mark 12:28–34). In fact, historians find Judean parallels to virtually all of Jesus' ethical pronouncements. Many scholars now believe that Jesus is best understood when seen operating in his first-century Palestinian-Jewish environment. Recent studies have shown that Jesus has much in common with the Essenes and Pharisees, in both the content and the parabolic style of his teachings.

5. *Multiple attestation.* This standard for determining reliable material considers the variety of different sources in which a particular statement or teaching occurs. If a saying appears in Mark, the Q document, and the Gospel of Thomas—all of which are presumed to be independent of one another—it is likely to be genuine. Jesus' emphasis on the kingdom of God appears to be confirmed by its frequent appearance in all three of these sources. (The specific form or interpretation of an individual kingdom pericope, however, is open to question. Each Christian writer or editor tends to modify individual sayings when incorporating them into a written text.) The criterion of multiple attestation also affirms several other traditions, such as Jesus' interest in women, the poor, and social outcasts such as lepers, tax collectors, prostitutes, and other "sinners." The tradition that Jesus performed healings, emphasized Wisdom precepts, and challenged both religious and political authority structures is also multiply attested.

Examples of material found in different sources, such as Mark, Q, and/or Thomas, include the parable of the dinner party (Matt. 22:1–14; Luke 14:16–24; G. Thom. 64); the perplexing command to hate one's relatives (Matt. 10:37; Luke 14:26; G. Thom. 55 and 101); asking, seeking, and finding (Matt. 7:7–8; Luke 11:9–10; G. Thom. 2 and 94); new wine and old wineskins (Mark 2:22; Luke 5:37–38; G. Thom. 47); and blessing the hungry (Matt. 5:6; Luke 6:21a; G. Thom. 69).

6. *Coherence.* This standard allows the scholar to regard material as potentially authentic if it resembles material already established by the criteria of orality, distinctiveness, and multiple attestation. If a saying or action is consistent with themes and concepts generally recognized as genuine, it, too, may be accepted. Many of the sayings designated as gray (probably not from Jesus) by the Jesus Seminar, for example, include some statements that approximate ideas in genuine sayings. (In many cases, the gray verdict simply represented a lack of scholarly consensus: The Seminar members' negative votes canceled out positive ones.)

7. *Awkwardness.* Some scholars believe that a tradition about Jesus, which the early church apparently found awkward or problematic—such as the reputed irregularity of Jesus' birth, his baptism by John for "remission of sins," his proclivity for associating with notorious sinners, and (above all) his shameful execution by a Roman governor—is likely to be authentic. Traditions that church apologists found embarrassing or difficult to explain caused too much general discomfort for believers to have added them as accretions to Jesus' story. This criterion of discomfort is particularly helpful in evaluating the plausibility of Jesus' actions, including his inability to win over most of his contemporaries and his controversial behavior in the Temple.

Potentially embarrassing traditions about Jesus include his baptism by John (Mark 1), his family's belief that he behaved irrationally (Mark 3:21, 31–35), his inability to heal those who do not trust him (Mark 6:5), his alleged reputation as a drunkard and a glutton who cultivated bad company (Matt. 11:16–19; Luke 7:31–35), his refusal to be called good (Mark 10:18, changed in Matt. 19:16–17), and the brutal fact of his crucifixion as a threat to the Roman government.

8. *Linguistic and environmental evidence.* This criterion uses linguistic and cultural evidence to eliminate sayings incorrectly ascribed to Jesus by later followers. If a Greek-language form underlies the pre-Gospel oral version of a particular saying, it cannot be authentic. Scholars agree that Jesus spoke a Galilean dialect of Aramaic and expressed his ideas in the context of a Jewish-Palestinian setting. Thus, sayings that reveal a Greco-Roman background are probably the creation of later Hellenistic disciples. The presence of a Hebrew or Aramaic form in a given saying may increase the probability of its genuineness but not prove it. The earliest Christians were Palestinian Jews who shared Jesus' linguistic and cultural environment.

(For a partial list of sayings that many scholars believe form an authentic core of Jesus' teachings, see box 11.3.)

used parables to convey his message. Scholars of the Jesus Seminar found that Jesus characteristically used exaggeration—huge sums of money in the parable of the unforgiving steward (Matt.18:23–35)—or surprise reversals of accepted values—a despised Samaritan turns out to be the moral hero of another famous parable (Luke 10:30–35). To distinguish Jesus' true voice from that of Christian preachers who modified his words in oral transmission or Gospel authors who fitted them into their theological preconceptions, Seminar members concluded that it was necessary to look for sayings that were peculiar to Jesus' distinctive style. This criterion resembles that of *dissimilarity*—sayings that differ from both typically Jewish *and* Christian teachings of the first century C.E. are more likely to prove authentic. In addition, sayings that are found in two or more different sources that are independent of each other, such as Mark, the Q document, *and* the Gospel of Thomas (or some other early noncanonical writing not derived from the Synoptics), have some chance of being genuine. This standard of *multiple attestation* suggests that if different groups (presumably with different Christologies) have preserved the same saying, it may go back to Jesus. As a result of this methodological screening, only about 20 percent of the words attributed to Jesus by Gospel writers were judged to have originated with him.

When meeting in conference to present detailed arguments for or against a statement ascribed to Jesus, members of the Jesus Seminar voted on the authenticity of individual sayings by dropping beads of different colors into a ballot box. A red bead meant that a member regarded the saying as unequivocally the historical words of Jesus. A pink bead indicated that the member believed that Jesus had said something very close to the recorded saying. A gray bead reflected serious doubt about the saying's genuineness. A black bead was a declaration that a saying definitely did not come from Jesus. By this means, the scholars were able to achieve a consensus: Virtually none of the sayings that picture Jesus as a prophet of eschatological doom represent his historical teaching. The long meditative Johannine speeches in which Jesus speaks of his divine nature were similarly judged to reflect the Evangelist's

Christological vision; the scholars voted them all black.

Results of the Seminar's work were published in *The Five Gospels* (1993), which features colloquial translations of the Greek texts and adds Thomas to the canonical four as a source of some reliable material. Subtitled *The Search for the Authentic Words of Jesus,* the book prints Jesus' words in red, pink, gray, or black, depending on the scholars' verdicts about their respective genuineness. Using only the sayings printed in red or pink to create a portrait of the historical Jesus, one will find him presented as a compassionate sage, a wisdom teacher deeply concerned with social justice—particularly for the poor and powerless—and with each person's intimate relationship with God.

Members of the Jesus Seminar believe that they have stripped away the Synoptic Gospels' eschatological overlay and the Johannine Gospel's high Christology to reveal a more unified and focused character portrait than is possible if one uncritically accepts *all* the claims the Evangelists make about their subject. In the view of some readers, the Seminar's red-letter Jesus seems more human and historically credible than John's omniscient figure who descends from heaven and serenely embraces his cross as the necessary means of reclaiming his preexistent divinity. For some critics, discovering Jesus as a wisdom teacher, even a kind of Hellenistic-Jewish-Cynic philosopher, removes the embarrassment of regarding him as an apocalyptist whose promise to return (within his disciples' lifetimes) as the eschatological Son of Man was not kept.

Other scholars doubt that rescuing a historical figure from his eschatological misconceptions is a reputable criterion for scholarship. Many scholars point out that if Jesus did not advocate an eschatological viewpoint, it is extremely difficult, if not impossible, to fit him into his historical environment. There is general scholarly agreement that Jesus' immediate predecessor, John the Baptist, warned Judah of an impending divine visitation and that Jesus' most influential interpreter, the apostle Paul, eagerly anticipated Jesus' imminent return as eschatological judge (see chapters 13 and 14). With Jesus' career closely bracketed by two such proponents of the approaching *eschaton,* advocates of a

Figure 11.2 *The Baptism of Christ.* In this late fifteenth-century wood carving, an anonymous sculptor imaginatively re-creates Jesus' ecstatic expression as he receives baptism from John. Showing Jesus as a bearded youth with thick, flowing hair, the artist suggests the overwhelming effect of the Holy Spirit that descends upon the young Nazarene, perhaps awakening him to a new awareness of his divine sonship. (© Boltin Picture Library)

noneschatological Jesus face a formidable challenge in explaining the continuity (or lack of it) in the sequence from John to Jesus to Paul.

The work of the Jesus Seminar has helped rekindle public interest in recovering the "real" Jesus, but the scholarly community is still far from achieving consensus on who Jesus believed he was or exactly what he taught. Some scholars have recently attacked the Seminar's conclusions, but thus far without providing a more persuasive critical method for separating the Jesus of history from the Christ of faith. Students wishing to explore the issue further may find it helpful to start with E. P. Sanders's *The Historical Figure of Jesus,* Paula Fredriksen's *From Jesus to Christ,* and Marcus Borg's *Jesus: A New Vision.* Borg's *Jesus at 2000* offers a bal-

anced survey of up-to-date scholarship on the renewed quest, while recent works by Robert Stein, Ben Witherington III, and Luke Timothy Johnson provide a strongly conservative approach to Jesus research. John P. Meier's comprehensive three-volume study (in progress) on the historical Jesus and J. Dominic Crossan's two books on the subject present strikingly different portraits of Jesus' self-identity and motivation (see "Recommended Reading").

As many commentators have noted, the picture of Jesus one attempts to paint typically says more about the painter than it does about the subject. Almost all attempts to reconstruct Jesus' personal character and motivation tend to be projections of qualities that the individual researcher consciously or unconsciously accepts as valuable. Students and scholars alike generally assume that Jesus, when found, will be relevant to contemporary needs and expectations. Most persons still reject the possibility that Jesus was too limited by his exclusively religious preoccupations to have anything truly meaningful to say to our largely secular and technological society.

The theory that presents Jesus as a fanatic, deluded and doomed by eschatological obsessions, however, does not satisfy most New Testament readers. Among many other considerations, the man embodied in the Gospels seems far too profound and insightful to attempt forcing an egocentric and literalist eschatology into historical fulfillment. The Jesus-as-apocalyptist view sees him as entirely the product of his own time. But the opposing theory of a noneschatological Jesus, a benign Wisdom teacher who championed the rights of the oppressed, creates a Jesus who is highly congenial to the modern temperament.

To scholars who see Jesus as having promoted a realized eschatology, Jesus' challenge to discern that God's kingdom reigns now — if people can get over their spiritual blindness and recognize its transcendent power — is intellectually attractive. Perpetuating the Johannine doctrine of cultivating eternal life in the present, this view has the advantage of presenting a Jesus who transcends his ancient Palestinian milieu to speak directly to contemporary experience. Most scholars, however, advise us to beware of discovering a Jesus who appears too acceptable by today's standards. No matter how much Jesus may have differed from his peers, the historical person was a first-century rural Jew and, in many ways, would undoubtedly seem disturbingly alien to late twentieth-century sensibilities.

Some General Agreements About the Historical Jesus

Although scholars have not achieved a consensus about Jesus' primary teachings, many do agree on the general outline of his life. The Gospel traditions contain numerous data about Jesus that are relatively "theology-free," particularly biographical information that is not cited as a fulfillment of biblical prophecy or a promulgation of christological doctrine. We may accept the tradition, then, that Jesus was born late in the reign of Herod the Great (between 6 and 4 B.C.E.); that he was raised in Nazareth (which is not mentioned in the Hebrew Bible); that he was the presumed son of Joseph, a carpenter, and his wife, Mary; and that he had brothers (or close relatives) named James (a future leader of the Jerusalem church), Joseph, Simon, and Judas (Jude), and an unknown number of sisters (or stepsisters) (Mark 6; Matt. 13:55). If Jesus and his putative father were carpenters, it probably means that the family had lost its hereditary land, which reduced them to a social status below that of Galilee's land-owning peasants.

When "about thirty years old" (Luke 3:1), Jesus came to John the Baptist for baptism in the River Jordan (about 27 or 29 C.E., depending on how one calculates Luke's "fifteenth year of the emperor Tiberius") (see figure 11.2). Mark's report that John baptized Jesus "in token of repentance for the forgiveness of sins" (Mark 1:4) is not an event that the early church would have invented. Because official doctrine held that Jesus was "sinless" and superior to the Baptist, Mark's baptismal story could not have emerged unless there was a firm tradition that Jesus had indeed submitted to John's ministrations. Some scholars think it likely that Jesus was, for an indefinite period, a disciple of the Baptist and did not begin his own ministry until after Herod Antipas had arrested and beheaded the prophet. Although it is impossible to confirm this theory, it appears that Jesus held the Baptist in the highest regard, perhaps regarding him as a mentor.

Following his baptism and perhaps an interlude of solitary meditation, Jesus began proclaiming a distinctive variation of the Baptist's message — the kingdom of God is near (or perhaps already present). In Jesus' proclamation, God's burgeoning rule reversed ordinary social values and encompassed people who were typically devalued by respectable society. The Synoptic tradition consistently shows Jesus as an active friend of the poor and outcast, going out of his way to share meals with known "sinners" and other disreputable people. Jesus' penchant for unsavory associations — along with his reputation as "a glutton and a drinker" — passes the credi-

Box 11.2
Developing Views of Jesus as the "Son of God"

Individual New Testament writers preserve different stages of a Christian concept that apparently developed over time—the conviction that Jesus was the "Son of God." As the passages listed below indicate, Jesus' divine sonship was interpreted in various ways. To understand the Christian authors' evolving views, we must start where they did, with the Hebrew Bible.

1. *The Davidic kings as God's adopted sons.* According to the covenant made with David's royal dynasty, the kings of Israel—Yahweh's anointed ones or "messiahs"—enjoyed a special relationship with their God, comparable to that of a son with his father. Speaking of David's heirs, Yahweh promises, "I will be his father, and he shall be my son . . . My love will never be withdrawn" (2 Sam. 7:14–15). Psalm 2, sung at the enthroning of one of David's descendants, expresses a similar view of the filial bond between king and God. Yahweh tells his "anointed" ruler (messiah): "You are my son . . . this day [the date of his crowning] I become your father" (Ps. 2:7). Thus, the Davidic king's coronation was simultaneously the time of his becoming God's "son" by adoption.

2. *Son by resurrection.* The oldest recorded Christian interpretation of Jesus' sonship—Paul's letter to the Romans (mid-50s C.E.)—states that Jesus "was declared Son of God by a mighty act in that he rose from the dead" (Rom. 1:3). In this passage, Paul follows Israel's ancient tradition that David's ultimate heir—the Messiah—would also in some sense become God's Son. As Paul expresses the concept, Jesus receives sonship at his resurrection, the Deity's miraculous confirmation of his messianic worthiness. The author of Acts preserves a similar view, representing Peter shortly after the Resurrection as saying that by exalting Jesus to his "right hand," "God has made this Jesus . . . both Lord and Messiah" (Acts 2:36). The oldest layer of preserved tradition suggests that the first Christians saw Jesus, like Israel's anointed kings, becoming God's Son by adoption, a reward conferred at his resurrection and ascension to heaven.

3. *Jesus' own witness.* The early church's identification of Jesus as a divine Son was undoubtedly stimulated by Jesus' practice of addressing God as *Abba,* an Aramaic term children used to express intimacy with their male parent (Mark 14:36; Luke 11:2). Closer to "daddy" than the more formal "father," *Abba* suggests Jesus' sense of personal closeness to the Deity. Paul attests to his church's continued use of the word (Rom. 8:15; Gal. 4:6).

4. *Jesus' adoption at baptism.* If Mark's Gospel (mid-60s C.E.) were our only Gospel, we might conclude that Jesus was designated God's Son at his baptism (Mark 1:11), apparently through adoption and anointing by the Holy Spirit. In Mark, the demons recognize Jesus' relationship to God (3:11–12), but no human being acknowledges it until he has proven his faithfulness unto death (15:39). Jesus' final act of filial devotion affirms his divine sonship (an idea also expressed in Hebrews [2:20; 5:7–9]).

5. *Sonship at conception.* Adding infancy narratives to their accounts of Jesus' life, Matthew and Luke (mid-80s C.E.) push the beginning of Jesus' sonship back in time, to the moment of his conception (Matt. 1:10; Luke 2:26–35). Matthew and Luke interpret Yahweh's promise to become as a father to the Davidic "son" (2 Sam. 7; Ps. 2) as meaning more than mere adoption; they see the Heavenly Voice at Jesus' baptism as simply confirming the biological fact of divine parentage.

6. *The son as creative Word.* Eschewing traditions of Jesus' virginal conception, John's Gospel, the last one written (mid-90s C.E.), declares that Jesus existed as God's Son long before he came to earth, even before the universe came into being (John 1:1–18). A variation of the concept appearing in Colossians (1:15–20; 2:9–10), John's doctrine of Jesus' eternal deity and sonship ultimately became the Christian standard of belief.

bility test because no believer would invent such tales (Matt. 10:18–19; Luke 15:1–3; 7:33–8:3). Some commentators have even suggested that Jesus' parable of the prodigal son—which features a young man who squanders his inheritance in riotous living, much to the dismay of his disapproving brother— may hint at a situation in Jesus' own life before he underwent John's cleansing baptism. Although anything said about Jesus before his association with the Baptist is necessarily conjectural, the twin traditions of his public repentance and his unfailing sympathy for social pariahs suggest that he knew this class of people well (and may once have been counted among them). His family's objections to Jesus' suddenly embarking on a controversial ministry and his neighbors' doubts about his new-found prophetic claims (Mark 3:20–21, 31–35; 6:1–6) also suggest that Jesus' early life was qualitatively different from his later career. The antifamily sentiments Jesus repeatedly expressed—including the "hard sayings" about hating father and mother and leaving "the dead to bury their dead"—emphasizes a sharp break with his former connections and way of life.

Whereas Jesus' Nazarene acquaintances had defined (and thereby limited) him in terms of his occupation and blood ties—he was merely "Mary's son," "the carpenter"—Jesus seems to have attained a radically new identity: He called God *Abba* (father). This divine-Parent/human-child relationship appears to underlie some of his most distinctive pronouncements, such as his injunction to be as giving and gracious to other mortals as God is to all his children, regardless of their merits (Matt. 5:44–48). The paradoxical command to "Love your enemies!" is practicable because God perceives human "enemies" as potential allies and friends.

Jesus' invitation to share in the divine relationship seems to have been remarkably inclusive: He breaks bread with Pharisees, lepers, tax collectors, slaves, women, and children (who, in the Greco-Roman world, were at the bottom of the social hierarchy). While raising their spirits, he also shows concern for their bodies: *All* the traditions agree that Jesus was a healer. How Jesus accomplished his healings and exorcisms is not known, but people he helped were convinced that he had changed them for the better, not least by validating their intrinsic worth and accepting some of them among his disciples. Issuing witty, provocative statements that challenged widely accepted values and attitudes, baiting religious authorities, and imparting a sense of physical and spiritual health to persons desperately in need of curative attention, Jesus, whether he wished to or not, could not help attracting followers.

Pursuing an itinerant life of deliberately chosen poverty and wandering randomly through Galilee from village to village, Jesus inevitably drew around him a mixed group of Galilean fishermen, farmers, women, and other ordinary working people. In parables and other figures of speech, he illustrated the desirability of living under God's kingdom—or perceiving the reality of divine rule, despite the oppression of secular authority, in the worlds of nature and human society. Although the Synoptic writers imply that the Galilean campaign lasted about a year, John's Gospel may be right in stating that it extended over at least three years and included several visits to Jerusalem.

While attracting throngs of mostly powerless admirers, Jesus also aroused powerful opposition. Jesus' apparent habit of relying on his own authority to pronounce on religious observances, such as Sabbath keeping—so different from the rabbinic tradition of citing the honored view of one's predecessors—irritated some and outraged others. Whereas many disciples were probably delighted with Jesus' authoritative dismissal of some purity laws and criticism of the Temple's priestly administration, some influential Sadducean officials in Jerusalem were undoubtedly suspicious of his motives. The priestly leadership may have regarded him as blasphemous and a potential threat to the delicate balance between Roman rule and Jewish welfare.

Jesus' healings, his preaching about God's kingdom, and his drawing of large, unruly crowds may have inspired some persons who particularly hated Roman occupation of the Holy Land to speculate that he was Israel's Messiah—the promised deliverer who would rid them of Gentile domination. John's report that a crowd wanted to proclaim him "[a Davidic] king" (John 6:15) and Luke's observation that as Jesus approached Jerusalem to celebrate Passover there, his disciples "thought the reign of God might dawn at any moment" (Luke 19:11) may echo actual historical conditions. Although most scholars do not think that Jesus presented himself as Israel's Messiah, some of his followers may have viewed him as the one prophesied to restore David's monarchy (see box 11.2). If such claims were being circulated on Jesus' behalf, it would explain Pilate's action in executing Jesus on the charge of treason, pretending to be "king of the

Jews." To the Roman procurator, Jesus was merely another messianic (royal) claimant, such as those who led popular uprisings after Herod the Great's death (see chapter 5).

Jesus' crucifixion under Pilate, which Tacitus and other non-Christian historians confirm, was not the kind of death—public, shameful, and associated with slaves and criminals—believers would fabricate for their leader. In the considered opinion of many Jews, the fact that Jesus was crucified meant that he *could not* have been the Messiah: No passage in the Hebrew Bible even hinted that the Messiah would die, let alone be executed as a felon by Gentile agents. (Proof texts that Christians later cited, such as the suffering servant poem in Isaiah 53 or Psalm 22, to explain Jesus' death are not specifically messianic prophecies.) Paul candidly describes the awkward fact of Jesus "nailed to the cross" as a "scandal"—a "stumbling block to Jews" and "sheer folly" to the Greeks (1 Cor. 1:23, 18). The humiliating fact of Jesus' crucifixion—so contrary to scriptural expectations—was probably the chief obstacle that kept most Jews from taking Christian preaching about him seriously. Some scholars believe that the first narrative about Jesus' miracles (and perhaps including his Passion)—the hypothetical Signs Gospel presumably later incorporated into John's Gospel—was composed to demonstrate that Jesus *was* Israel's Anointed One and that he was killed only because people refused to believe in his wondrous deeds (see chapter 10).

Jesus' Teaching About the Kingdom

Jesus' attempts to convey his vision of God's kingdom inspired some of his most celebrated parables and figures of speech. The English phrase "kingdom of God" translates the Greek expression *basileia tou theou*. *Basileia* refers primarily to the act or process of ruling, a quality or privilege that distinguishes a king or other ruler. To have *basileia* is to possess control, power, freedom, and independence. The biblical God, whose infinite kingship Israel's thinkers take for granted, has these attributes in abundance. Psalm 145 proclaims Yahweh's universal sovereignty:

> All thy creatures praise thee, Lord [Yahweh],
>   and thy servants bless thee.
> They talk of the glory of thy kingdom
>   and tell of thy might,
> they proclaim to their fellows how mighty are thy
>   deeds,
>   how glorious the majesty of thy kingdom.
> Thy kingdom is an everlasting kingdom, and thy
>   dominion stands for all generations.
>   (Ps. 145:11–12)

Israel's God is thus the supreme possessor of *basileia*, a concept that must be kept in mind when considering Jesus' possible intentions as he combines his kingdom teaching with assertions of his own autonomy and dominion.

Although he is never shown defining what he means by the term, in the Gospels Jesus is pictured using *basileia tou theou* in four major ways: (1) to express the kingdom's preeminence; (2) to defend his personal authority to represent the kingdom and interpret the divine will; (3) to imply the nature of his self-awareness—the views he holds about his relationship with God and the meaning of kingship; and (4) to proclaim the kingdom's radical demand for total commitment. Because it dominates his message throughout the Synoptic Gospels, we will concentrate on the first category, emphasizing those sayings that scholars believe are most likely to stem from the historical Jesus.

In the Sermon on the Mount, Matthew presents Jesus as giving top priority to seeking the kingdom. The disciple who puts God's kingdom and his "justice [righteousness]" "before everything else" will also receive all that ordinary life requires (Matt. 6:33). Matthew and the other Synoptic writers then present such a variety of conflicting, even contradictory, references to the kingdom that it is difficult to harmonize these disparate statements into a coherent view of what is meant. In different pericopes, the Synoptic Jesus speaks as if the kingdom were (1) a prophesied future event, (2) an unexpected occurrence, (3) a hidden power that grows slowly, (4) a present reality, and (5) physically present but unnoticed.

THE KINGDOM AS A FUTURE EVENT

The Synoptic writers typically emphasize the eschatological nature of the kingdom, presenting Jesus' message as a continuation of John the Baptist's warning of imminent divine judgment (cf. Matt. 3:3 and 4:17). In the Synoptic view, the kingdom is so close that people who first heard it proclaimed will live to see "the kingdom of God already come in power" (Mark 9:1; Matt. 16:28; Luke 9:27). All three Synoptic authors link Jesus' death with the kingdom's nearness. At the Last Supper, Jesus tells the disciples that he will never again drink "from the fruit of the vine until the day when I drink it new in the kingdom of God" (Mark 14:25; Matt. 26:19; Luke 22:16, 18).

THE KINGDOM AS AN UNEXPECTED EVENT

In their apocalyptic predictions that link Jerusalem's fall and Jesus' return in glory, the Synoptic Gospels also implicitly associate the Parousia with the kingdom's arrival (cf. Mark 13, Matt. 24, and Luke 21). These passages anticipating the *eschaton* are inherently paradoxical: While asserting that spectacular portents will herald the End, they also emphasize the suddenness and unexpectedness of divine intervention. Thus, the kingdom appears stealthily, "like a thief in the night," its abrupt materialization a striking contrast to the parables stressing its quiet growth (Mark 13:33; Matt. 24:42; 25:13; Luke 12:40; 21:36). These and other texts that relate the kingdom to the Second Coming incorporate traditional themes of Hellenistic-Jewish eschatology, including world judgment and resurrection. In this context, the kingdom's appearance signifies the End of history as we know it and the inception of a radically "New Age." As noted previously, scholars continue to debate the extent to which the Synoptic writers' eschatological expectations accurately mirror Jesus' historical views of the kingdom.

THE KINGDOM AS A HIDDEN POWER THAT GROWS SLOWLY

Many of the best-known parables depict the kingdom as a hidden power that grows slowly until it achieves greatness. In contrast to the apocalyptic tradition—in which God's kingdom bursts suddenly and catastrophically into human affairs (Dan. 2:44)—Jesus' kingdom parables typically reject destruction imagery in favor of similes depicting serene germination. Jesus compares the kingdom to a tiny mustard seed that develops "underground," gradually maturing into a "tree" that shelters wildlife (Mark 4:30–32; Matt. 13:31–32; Luke 13:18–19; G. Thom. 20). That the mustard plant is a weed farmers do not want taking over their fields perhaps adds an ironic dimension to Jesus' simple analogy.

The parable of "leaven" that causes bread dough to rise and expand also suggests the kingdom's slow and quiet maturation (Matt. 13:33; Luke 13:20–21; G. Thom. 96). The parables comparing the kingdom to seeking what is lost or unexpectedly finding an invaluable object—a pearl, a buried treasure, a lost coin—highlight a gradual and *private* process on the part of individuals. In parables of this kind, a solitary figure—a widow, a lone merchant, a shepherd—takes time to focus on the process of discovery, a quiet personal search that ends in rejoicing (Matt. 13:44; 18:12–13; Luke 15:4–6; G. Thom. 107). Employing images of life as it is daily lived, Jesus' parables of planting, growing, and recognizing unforeseen treasures have little affinity with apocalyptic violence (see box 11.3).

THE KINGDOM AS A PRESENT REALITY

Jesus' metaphors of seeking and finding harmonize with pronouncements in which he declares the kingdom a present reality. In Luke 11:20, he tells opponents, "But if it is by the finger of God that I drive out the devils, then be sure that the kingdom has already come upon you" (see also Matt. 12:28). Expelling demons, traditionally an eschatological act, is here equated with psychological healing and spiritual power, an expression of God's invisible dominion. Jesus' response to the Baptist's disciples,

Box 11.3
The Authentic Voice of Jesus

These are a few of approximately one hundred sayings that meet the Jesus Seminar's criteria for genuineness (all quotations are from the Scholars Version):

Love your enemies. . . . God causes the sun to rise on both the bad and the good, and sends rain on both the just and the unjust. Tell me, if you love those who love you, why should you be commended for that? Even the [tax] collectors do that. (Matt. 5:44–46)

Congratulations, you poor! God's domain belongs to you.

Congratulations, you hungry! You will have a feast.

Congratulations, you who weep now! You will laugh. (Luke 6:20–21)

When someone strikes you on the cheek, offer the other as well. When someone takes away your coat, don't prevent that person from taking your shirt along with it. . . . Give to everyone who begs from you. (Luke 6:29–30)

Forgive, and you'll be forgiven. (Luke 6:37b)

Foxes have dens, and birds of the sky have nests; but the son of Adam has nowhere to rest his head. (Luke 9:58)

You won't be able to observe the coming of God's imperial rule. People are not going to be able to say, "Look, here it is!" or "Over there!" On the contrary, God's imperial rule is right here in your presence. (Luke 17:20–21)

Every government divided against itself is devastated, and a house divided against a house falls. If Satan is divided against himself—since you claim that I drive out demons in Beelzebub's name—how will his domain endure? If I drive out demons in Beelzebub's name, in whose name do your own people drive (them) out? In that case, they will be your judges. But if by God's finger I drive out demons, then for you God's imperial rule has arrived. (Luke 11:17–20)

What does Heaven's imperial rule remind me of? It is like leaven which a woman took and concealed in fifty pounds of flour until it was all leavened. (Luke 13:20–21)

To what should we compare God's imperial rule, or what parable should we use for it? Consider the mustard seed: When it is sown on the ground, though it is the smallest of all the seeds on the earth, yet when it is sown, it comes up, and becomes the biggest of all garden plants, and produces branches, so that the birds of the sky can nest in its shade. (Mark 4:30–32)

Heaven's imperial rule is like treasure hidden in a field: when someone finds it, that person covers it up again, and out of sheer joy goes and sells every last possession and buys that field. Again, Heaven's imperial rule is like some trader looking for beautiful pearls. When that merchant finds one priceless pearl, he sells everything he owns and buys it. (Matt. 13:44–45)

That's why I tell you: don't fret about life—what you're going to eat—or about your body—what you're going to wear. Remember, there is more to living than food and clothing. Think about the crows: they don't plant or harvest, they don't have storerooms or barns. Yet God feeds them. You're worth a lot more than the birds! . . . Think about how the lilies grow: they don't slave and they never spin. Yet let me tell you, even Solomon at the height of his glory was never decked out like one of these. If God dresses up the grass in the field, which is here today and tomorrow is tossed into an oven, it is surely more likely (God cares for) you, you who don't take anything for granted. (Luke 12:22–28)

So I tell you, ask—it'll be given to you; seek—you'll find; knock—it'll be opened for you. Rest assured: everyone who asks receives; everyone who seeks finds; and for the one who knocks it is opened. (Luke 11:9–10)

No man can be a slave to two masters. No doubt that slave will either hate one and love the other, or be devoted to one and disdain the other. You can't be enslaved to both God and a bank account. (Matt. 6:24; Luke 16:13)

There was a rich man whose fields produced a bumper crop. "What do I do now?" he asked himself, "since I don't have any place to store my crops. I know," he said, "I'll tear down my barns and build larger ones so I can store all my grain and my goods. Then I'll say to myself, "You have plenty put away for years to come. Take it easy, eat, drink, enjoy yourself." But God said to him, "You fool! This very night your life will be demanded back from you. All this stuff you've collected—whose will it be now?" (Luke 12:16–20)

Figure 11.3 *The Apache Christ.* Pictured as a Native American holy man, this figure shows Christ on a mountaintop sacred to the Mescalero Apaches. A solar symbol is painted on his left palm, while he holds a deer hoof rattle in his right hand. Like John of Patmos, who images Christ adorned with pre-Christian astrological symbols, this contemporary artist combines biblical and other sacred motifs to depict a divine "Giver of Life." (© Robert Lentz. Used with permission of Bridge Building Images, P.O. Box 1048, Burlington, VT 05402)

who inquire if he is really the Messiah, similarly implies that Jesus' present activity is a realization of the kingdom. When John's disciples behold the blind restored to sight, the deaf restored to hearing, and the dead raised to life, we know that God now reigns (Matt. 11:2–6; Luke 7:22–23). When the seventy-two disciples return from a successful campaign of exorcisms, Luke has Jesus declare that he now sees Satan falling "like lightning" from heaven (Luke 10:18). The spiritual healings performed by Jesus and his followers are a defeat of Evil and a manifestation of divine sovereignty.

THE KINGDOM AS PHYSICALLY PRESENT YET UNNOTICED

Luke preserves Jesus' most explicit statement about the kingdom's already being present: "You can not tell by observation when the kingdom of God comes. There will be no saying, 'Look, here it is!' or 'there it is!'; for in fact the kingdom of God is among you" (or "right there in your presence") (Luke 17:20). With this startling declaration, Jesus informs the Pharisees that in his person and healing activity, they can witness the kingdom in operation. Divine rule, Jesus adds, is as immediately obvious and universal as sheet lightning that flashes over the entire sky (Luke 17:22–24). The same perception of the kingdom's paradoxically elusive yet pervasive presence is also found in the Gospel of Thomas: "It will not come by watching for it. It will not be said, 'Look, here!' or 'Look, there!' Rather, (the Father's) imperial rule is spread out upon the earth, and people don't see it" (G. Thom. 113). As Jesus implies in his calling the disciples' attention to the beauty of the flowers growing in a field or the fall of a sparrow, God rules the world unnoticed by unperceptive or unappreciative humans (see figure 11.3).

Luke's assertion that the kingdom rules everywhere, even among Jesus' opponents, has another parallel in the Thomas Gospel. Here Jesus is represented as saying that

the Kingdom is inside you, and it is outside of you. When you come to know yourselves, then you will become known, and you will realize that it is you who are the sons of the living Father. But if you do not know yourselves, you dwell in poverty and it is you who are that poverty.

(G. Thom. 3)

Whereas the Lukan saying depicts the kingdom appearing through Jesus' presence, that in Thomas seems to equate it with a state of heightened spiritual awareness. Knowing the true "self" (the divine "image" within each person) means awakening to one's kinship with God. Remaining ignorant of "the god within" is "poverty." Despite alleged Gnostic elements in the Thomas saying, this concept of an indwelling divine spirit—perhaps similar to what Paul called the "mystery" of "Christ in [the believer]" (Col. 1:27)—may represent an integral part of Jesus' kingdom concept.

Scholars who champion a noneschatological Jesus believe that the historical Galilean did not preach about a future eschatological kingdom of God, violently imposed by divine intervention. Instead, he taught that God's rule is presently active in creation but difficult for most people to perceive. According to this view, Jesus had a highly subtle sense of time, a vision of divine immanence in which God's eternal presence operates unseen, drawing and guiding into his dominion those who respond to his will. Entering God's domain means discerning and embracing the simultaneity of present and future, which conflate into a profound sense of the unbroken continuity of divine rule.

Many other scholars object that if Jesus' concept of seeking the kingdom meant a persistent quest for recognizing God's "finger" at work in the overfamiliar world, how can one account for an apocalyptically oriented John the Baptist, an eschatologically driven Paul, and an early Church that expected Christ's Second Coming to occur at any moment (see 1 Thess. 4:15–17; Mark 13)? Would it not be more reasonable to assume that Jesus was an eschatological prophet similar to his predecessors, many Jewish contemporaries, and his successors? One possible defense of a noneschatological view of Jesus is that the Gospel traditions make it clear that even his closest followers did not understand him. Misconstruing his complex and subtle vision of divine sovereignty, more pedestrian followers simply applied their inherited eschatological ideas to the one they accepted as Lord. Indeed, if Jesus had *not* taught that the kingdom reigns now in those doing the divine will, how did his apocalyptist followers conceive of such sayings as those expressed in Luke 11:20 and 17:20–21 and the Gospel of Thomas 3 and 113? Because these sayings run against the trend of later eschatologically oriented Christianity, they pass the test of distinctiveness and may well represent Jesus' actual views. Still other scholars observe that like many first-century Jews, Jesus may have promoted a double vision of the kingdom: God rules now through the work of his servants, but full implementation of *divine* sovereignty lies ahead in the future.

Wisdom and the Kingdom of God

In contrast to Mark and Matthew, who were apparently inspired by the apocalyptic disaster that befell Judea in 70 c.e., the authors of John and Thomas show that it was possible to follow a Jesus who was fundamentally an exponent of divine Wisdom rather than a purveyor of eschatological judgment. The Johannine writer rarely mentions the kingdom as an integral part of Jesus' teaching, but he may convey a significant historical truth when he makes the nature of Jesus' personal kingship the crucial issue on which Pilate's execution of Jesus hinges (John 18:33–19:22). During the confrontation with Pilate, the Johannine Jesus states that his kingdom is not of this world—that it is not political—but he fails to define either his government or his own kingly role (John 18:36).

John nonetheless gives his readers a relatively clear idea of what Jesus' kingdom involves. From the outset of his Gospel, the author identifies Jesus with the eternal Word, the expression of immortal Wisdom by and through which God created the universe (John 1:1–18; Prov. 8:22–36). In his person, Jesus reveals and shares with others the vital Wisdom by which God rules and communicates his will. As noted in chapter 10, John firmly links Jesus with Israel's **wisdom literature,** the teachings of which associate the wise person with God's *basileia*—heavenly kingship.

Box 11.4
Resurrection Traditions in Paul and the Gospels

The oldest surviving account of Jesus' postresurrection appearances occurs in Paul's first letter to the Corinthians, which contains a tradition "handed on" to Paul from earlier Christians. None of the Gospels' resurrection narratives, written fifteen to forty years after the date of Paul's letter, refers to Jesus' manifestations to his kinsman James or to the "over 500 brothers" who simultaneously beheld him (cf. 1 Cor. 15:3–8.)

PAUL (c. 54 c.e.)	MARK (c. 66–70 c.e.)	MATTHEW (c. 85 c.e.)	LUKE (c. 85–90 c.e.)	JOHN (c. 90–100 c.e.)
Jesus appears to Cephas (Peter) to "the Twelve" to "over 500" to James (Jesus' "brother") to "all the Apostles" to Paul (as an *apokalypsis,* or "revelation," Gal. 1:15–16)	No postresurrection account in original text [Two accounts were added later: Mark 16:8b and 16:9–19, in which Jesus appears first to Mary Magdalene, and then to the Eleven.]	No parallels Jesus appears to "the eleven disciples" [minus Judas Iscariot] "in Galilee"	Reference to "Simon [Peter]" to "the Eleven" (in Jerusalem) Jesus appears to "Cleopas" and an unnamed disciple on the road to Emmaus (near Jerusalem)	No parallels Jesus appears to Mary Magdalene (in Jerusalem) to "the disciples," particularly Thomas (in Jerusalem) to "the sons of Zebedee," Simon Peter, and the "Beloved Disciple" (in Galilee)

The apocryphal Wisdom of Solomon expresses the affinity between Wisdom and divine kingship that may have influenced John's view of Jesus:

> For she [Wisdom] ranges [the earth] in search of those who are worthy of her; . . . The true beginning of wisdom is the desire to learn, and a concern for learning means the keeping of her laws; to keep her laws is a warrant of immortality; and immortality brings a man near to God. Thus the desire of wisdom leads to kingly stature [a *basileia*]. (Wisd. of Sol. 6:16–20)

Notice that learning and keeping God's wise laws, the principles by which he orders the cosmos, lead to eternal life and make the obedient possessor of Wisdom a king.

Wisdom also reveals the kingdom of God:

> She [Wisdom] guided him [Jacob, the embodiment of Israel] on straight paths; she showed him

the *basileia tou theou* [literally, the kingdom or sovereignty of God]. (Wisd. of Sol. 10:10)

In Israel's wisdom writings, Wisdom (Sophia, a personification of God's primary attribute) imparts knowledge, divine favor, and immortal life (Prov. 2:1–10; Job 28:12–23; Ecclus. 24; Wisd. of Sol. 8:4, 13). She discloses secrets of the unseen world to those who seek her, satisfying their intellectual and spiritual thirst (Wisd. of Sol. 7:17–29). The references to Jesus' unveiling the "secret" or "mystery of the kingdom of God" in Mark (4:11) and Secret Mark (2:10) may preserve a parallel to the Johannine tradition that Jesus' teaching focuses not on the eschatological but on Wisdom's revelation of previously hidden cosmic truths.

According to this view of Jesus' kingdom message, Jesus teaches that followers must come under God's rule by imitating and participating in the divine *basileia*. As noted previously, *basileia* implies kingly autonomy, freedom, and self-deter-mination—living one's life as the master of one's situation. The Johannine Jesus tells his followers that he had already "conquered the world" (John 16:33). The self-confidence or "authority" with which Jesus habitually teaches may derive from his profound sense of possessing the celestial Wisdom that sets people free (Matt. 7:28–29; Mark 1:22; John 8:22). At liberty to proclaim his personal views on the Torah, he inevitably antagonizes many rival teachers of the Law. As a sage through whom Wisdom speaks, he is also free to recognize his own kingship—the *basileia* that Wisdom imparts (Wisd. of Sol. 6:17–20; 10:10). If Jesus publicly equated his wisdom teaching with kingship, the connection may have inspired Pilate's suspicion. As governor for Rome, Pilate could tolerate no Jew claiming to be a king of any kind.

The Johannine Jesus informs his disciples that he fully reveals the Father, the supreme reality with whom he—and they—enjoy a life-giving unity (John 17:1–8, 20–23). Spiritual union with the Deity confers a power upon Jesus' disciples that will enable them to accomplish greater deeds than he (John 14:10–14). The arrival of the Paraclete, or Spirit of Truth, endows believers with additional heaven-sent Wisdom and allows them to continue imitating Jesus' example of kingly rulership. Indeed, the Paraclete manifests the same power of *basileia* that characterizes Jesus (John 16:7–15). Initiated into the mystery of divinity and empowered by the Spirit, the Johannine disciple possesses a kingdom authority resembling that of Jesus himself (John 14:12–21).

Summary

Given the diverse theological backgrounds and varying degrees of personal skepticism in today's scholarly community, it seems unlikely that wide-spread agreement concerning Jesus' exact ideas about the kingdom will soon be reached. Some scholars point out that intense eschatological ex-pectations, particularly in first-century Palestine,

were not incompatible with wisdom teaching. From this perspective, Jesus may have been both a sage and a relatively traditional eschatological prophet in the manner of John the Baptist. If this view is cor-rect, there would be a direct line from the Baptist to Jesus' Synoptic proclamation and to Paul's fervent expectations of Christ's swift return. A growing number of scholars, however, question whether the historical Jesus resembled either the Baptist or Paul in worldview or kingdom teachings. Some com-mentators believe that Paul's eschatological bent may be partly a carry-over from his Pharisaic her-itage and partly a result of his assumption that Jesus' resurrection signaled the beginning of End time, an idea that may derive from Daniel's apoca-lypse (Dan. 12:1–3) (see box 11.4).

Scholars in large part agree that the historical Jesus taught about God's kingdom (whatever his precise meaning by the phrase), but most question the belief that he taught about himself. Although he seems to have perceived the world and his mis-sion from the vantage point of one who holds a pe-culiarly close relationship to God, he is not believed to have called himself Christ, Son of God, or the Holy One of Israel. All these honorific titles, schol-ars believe, were bestowed on him posthumously by a community that—in retrospect—recognized him as Israel's Messiah and God's chief agent, the means by which the Deity reconciles humanity to himself. In telling Jesus' story so that readers could understand his true significance, it was natural for the Gospel writers to apply titles such as Christ and Son of God to the historical figure. In the Evange-lists' view, they could not write the truth about who Jesus was unless they presented him in the light of his resurrection and glorification. The Galilean prophet and teacher who had challenged the world's norms in the name of a radical egalitarian-ism for all God's children was—by his continuing life in the believing community—vindicated as di-vine, the Wisdom and love of God made flesh.

QUESTIONS FOR REVIEW

1. Define the problem confronting scholars in their quest to find the historical Jesus. In what ways do the four Gospel writers' theological portraits of

Jesus make it difficult to determine exactly what the man Jesus said and did? Besides the Gospels, which were written by believers in Jesus' unique divinity, what other first-century sources do we have that might help illuminate his life?

2. When did the modern quest to discover the "real" Jesus begin, and what are its goals? Describe the picture of an "apocalyptic" Jesus that Albert Schweitzer drew in his famous *Quest of the Historical Jesus.* What different conclusions about Jesus' teachings have some later scholars drawn? Describe the work of the Jesus Seminar.

3. Summarize some of the criteria scholars use to screen for authenticity the Gospel sayings ascribed to Jesus, including the tests of orality, distinctiveness, dissimilarity, and awkwardness (the "embarrassment" factor). What standards can we use to distinguish between what Jesus himself taught and what the believing community may have attributed to him later?

4. Describe some areas in which scholars generally agree about the historical Jesus. Review Jesus' teaching about the "kingdom of God" as it appears in the Synoptic Gospels.

5. Moving from the earliest to the latest canonical statements about Jesus as the "Son of God," summarize evolving New Testament views about Jesus' relation to the Father. How did Jesus' use of the term *Abba,* the concept that Davidic kings became God's sons by adoption at the time of their coronation and anointing, and Paul's implication that Jesus became "Son of God" at his resurrection and ascension to heaven contribute to the idea of Jesus' divinity? Describe the important differences between the way Mark introduces Jesus' sonship and John's doctrine of preexistence and incarnation.

QUESTIONS FOR DISCUSSION AND REFLECTION

1. Is it possible to reconstruct a coherent picture of Jesus and his teaching using the source materials currently available? What sources do you regard as most trustworthy, as most likely to represent Jesus as he might have been rather than as he appeared to the believing community that worshiped him?

2. Teachings about the kingdom or rule of God are central to Jesus' message. After analyzing the different kinds of kingdom sayings found in the Gospels, do you find a consistent pattern of meaning in some or all of the sayings? Are readers likely to project their own values onto the recorded sayings and accept or stress only those that accord with their own preconceptions?

3. Do we possess any sure means of finding out what Jesus actually thought about himself and his purpose? In reading the four Gospels, do you find any clues that reliably indicate the nature of Jesus' own self-awareness?

4. Contrast the Synoptic portrait of Jesus as an apocalyptic exorcist and preacher with John's portrayal of Jesus as a revealer of heavenly wisdom. How would you distinguish Mark's idea of Jesus' kingdom from John's concept of Jesus' kingship?

5. The communities that produced the Synoptic Gospels clearly had very different traditions about Jesus from those treasured in the group that created John's Gospel. How do you account for such divergent views about Jesus' nature and teaching in two roughly contemporaneous Christian communities? In what ways do these divergent traditions about Jesus' teaching make it difficult to define the term *kingdom* as Jesus uses it?

TERMS AND CONCEPTS TO REMEMBER

Albert Schweitzer
realized eschatology
criteria for testing Jesus'
  authentic sayings
basileia tou theou
  (kingdom of God)

Jesus as apocalyptist
the relationship of divine
  Wisdom and *basileia*

RECOMMENDED READING

Borg, Marcus J. *Jesus: A New Vision.* San Francisco: Harper & Row, 1988. A scholarly and perceptive study showing that the historical Jesus' message was not primarily eschatological.

———. *Jesus at 2000.* San Francisco: HarperSanFrancisco, 1996. A collection of scholarly papers debating Jesus' historical, religious, and cultural significance on the two thousandth anniversary of his birth.

———. "Jesus, Teaching of." In D. N. Freedman, ed., *The Anchor Bible Dictionary,* Vol. 3, pp. 804–812. New York: Doubleday, 1992. A concise survey of Jesus' major teachings.

Bultmann, Rudolf. *History of the Synoptic Tradition,* rev. ed. Translated by John Marsh. San Francisco: Harper & Row, 1961. A major achievement in New Testament scholarship; shows how the Evangelists reinterpreted Jesus mythically.

Carlston, Charles E. "Jesus Christ." In P. J. Actemeier, ed., *Harper's Bible Dictionary*, pp. 475–487. San Francisco: Harper & Row, 1985. A good introduction to the subject; offers a clear survey of Jesus' principal teachings.

Chilton, Bruce, and Evans, Craig A., eds. *Studying the Historical Jesus: Evaluations of the State of Current Research*. Kinderhook, N.Y.: Brill, 1994. A collection of valuable essays by major New Testament scholars.

Crossan, John Dominic. *The Historical Jesus: The Life of a Mediterranean Peasant*. San Francisco: HarperSanFrancisco, 1991. A distinctive scholarly interpretation of Jesus as a sage advocating radical social egalitarianism.

——. *Jesus: A Revolutionary Biography*. San Francisco: HarperSanFrancisco, 1994. A distillation of Crossan's earlier book for the general reader.

Falk, Harvey. *Jesus the Pharisee: A New Look at the Jewishness of Jesus*. New York: Paulist Press, 1985. Shows the many similarities between the teachings of Jesus and those of the Pharisees, including parallels in both form and content.

Fredriksen, Paula. *From Jesus to Christ: The Origins of the New Testament Images of Jesus*. New Haven, Conn.: Yale University Press, 1988. Traces the historical process by which the human Jesus became the divine Christ.

Funk, Robert W., and the Jesus Seminar. *The Acts of Jesus: What Did Jesus Really Do?* San Francisco: HarperSanFrancisco, 1998. A radical evaluation of Jesus' historical actions that portrays Jesus as a healer, exorcist, and Wisdom teacher who associated with social outcasts.

Funk, Robert W.; Hoover, Roy W.; and the Jesus Seminar. *The Five Gospels: The Search for the Authentic Words of Jesus*. A Polebridge Press Book. New York: Macmillan, 1993. Features a highly colloquial translation of the canonical Gospels and Thomas, with Jesus' authentic words printed in red or pink, doubtful sayings in gray, and speeches ascribed to him by tradition or Gospel authors in black.

Jacobson, Arland D. *The First Gospel: An Introduction to Q*. Sonoma, Calif.: Polebridge Press, 1992. A study and tentative reconstruction of material in the hypothetical sayings source.

Johnson, Luke T. *The Real Jesus: The Misguided Quest for the Historical Jesus and the Truth of the Traditional Gospels*. San Francisco: HarperSanFrancisco, 1995. Challenges the Jesus Seminar's methodology without providing a persuasive alternative.

Josephus, Flavius. *Josephus: Complete Works*. Translated by W. Whiston. Grand Rapids, Mich.: Kregel, 1960. A dated translation but containing the complete texts of *The Antiquities of the Jews* and *The Jewish War;* brief references to Jesus, John the Baptist, and Jesus' brother James.

——. *The Jewish War,* rev. ed. Translated by G. A. Williamson. Edited by E. M. Smallwood. New York: Penguin Books, 1981. A modern translation of Josephus's eyewitness account of the Jewish revolt and its consequences.

Kee, Howard C. *Jesus in History,* 2nd ed. New York: Harcourt Brace Jovanovich, 1977.

Kloppenborg, John S. *The Formation of Q*. Philadelphia: Fortress Press, 1987. Analyzes the stages or levels of oral tradition contained in the hypothetical sayings source.

Kloppenborg, John S.; Meyer, Marvin W.; Patterson, Stephen J.; and Steinhauser, Michael G., *Q Thomas Reader*. Sonoma, Calif.: Polebridge Press, 1990.

Koester, Helmut. *Ancient Christian Gospels: Their History and Development*. Philadelphia: Trinity Press International, 1990. A thorough and detailed study of the Gospels' literary evolution; for more advanced students.

Mack, Burton I. "The Kingdom Sayings in Mark." *Forum* 3, no. 1 (1987): 3–47. Argues that Jesus' kingdom teachings were not eschatological.

Meier, John P. "Jesus." In R. E. Brown et al., eds., *The New Jerome Biblical Commentary*, pp. 1316–1328. Englewood Cliffs, N.J.: Prentice-Hall, 1990. A concise introductory essay.

——. *A Marginal Jew: Rethinking the Historical Jesus*, vols. 1 and 2. The first two volumes of a projected three-part biography by an eminent New Testament scholar, the most comprehensive study to date.

Meyer, Ben. "Jesus Christ." In D. N. Freedman, ed., *The Anchor Bible Dictionary*, pp. 773–796. New York: Doubleday, 1992. Provides a good introductory review of contemporary scholarship on Jesus' life and teachings.

Miller, Robert J. *The Complete Gospels: Annotated Scholars Version*, 2nd ed. San Francisco: HarperSanFrancisco, 1994. Includes all known Gospels, including fragments, produced during the first three Christian centuries.

Patterson, Stephen J. *The Gospel of Thomas and Jesus*. Sonoma, Calif.: Polebridge Press, 1993. Argues that the first edition of Thomas dates to the middle of the first century C.E. and contains authentic sayings of Jesus.

Rivkin, Ellis. *What Crucified Jesus? The Political Execution of a Charismatic*. Nashville, Tenn.: Abingdon Press, 1984. A Jewish scholar's investigation into the social and political forces that led to Jesus' execution by Rome.

Robinson, James M., ed. *The Nag Hammadi Library*, 3rd ed. San Francisco: Harper & Row, 1988. Contains English translations of Christian documents found at Nag Hammadi.

Robinson, John A. T. *Jesus and His Coming*. Philadelphia: Westminster Press, 1979. Argues that Jesus was not an apocalyptist and that beliefs about his Second Coming developed from a misunderstanding of his teachings.

Sanders, E. P. *Jesus and Judaism*. Philadelphia: Fortress Press, 1985. A scholarly and highly readable evaluation of the Gospel traditions about Jesus and his message, particularly about the kingdom and its original meaning in the context of Palestinian Judaisms.

——. *The Historical Figure of Jesus*. New York: Viking Press, 1994. A readable work of solid scholarship.

——. "The Life of Jesus." In Hershel Shanks, ed., *Christianity and Rabbinic Judaism*, pp. 41–83. Washington, D.C.: Biblical Archaeology, 1992. A lucid and commonsensical study of what we may know about the historical Jesus by a major New Testament scholar.

Sanders, E. P., and Davies, Margaret. *Studying the Synoptic Gospels*. Philadelphia: Trinity Press International, 1989.

Schweitzer, Albert. *The Quest of the Historical Jesus: A Critical Study of Its Progress from Reimarus to Wrede*. New York: Macmillan, 1961. The German original was published in 1906, but the issues Schweitzer raises in this monumental project still influence scholars' search for the real figure of history.

Sheehan, Thomas. *The First Coming: How the Kingdom of God Became Christianity*. New York: Random House, 1986. A scholar's careful and innovative account of historical and theological developments that transformed the Jesus of history into the Christ of faith.

Stein, Robert H. *Jesus the Messiah*. InterVarsity Press, 1996.

Tatum, W. Barnes. *In Quest of Jesus: A Guidebook*. Atlanta: John Knox Press, 1982. A helpful guide for beginners.

Witherington, Ben, III. *The Jesus Quest: The Third Search for the Jew of Nazareth*. Downers Grove, Ill.: InterVarsity, 1995. A conventional defense of traditional religious views of Jesus.

Wright, N. T. "Jesus, Quest for the Historical." In D. N. Freedman, ed., *The Anchor Bible Dictionary*, pp. 796–802. New York: Doubleday, 1992. A survey of scholars' efforts to discover the Jesus of history, including the work of the Jesus Seminar.

——. *The Original Jesus*. Grand Rapids, Mich.: Eerdmans, 1996. A conservative evaluation of the historical Jesus.

Aids for Comparing Gospel Texts

Aland, Kurt, ed. *Synopsis of the Four Gospels,* English ed. New York: United Bible Societies, 1985. A helpful presentation of parallels among the four canonical Gospels.

Crossan, John D., ed. *Sayings Parallels: A Workbook for the Jesus Tradition*. Philadelphia: Fortress Press, 1986. A comprehensive collection of Jesus' sayings arranged to include texts for all four canonical Gospels plus those from apocryphal sources, including the Gospel of Thomas and the Apocryphon of James.

Funk, R. W. *New Gospel Parallels*. Vols. 1 and 2, *Foundations & Facets*. Philadelphia: Fortress Press, 1985. A major achievement in New Testament scholarship. Volume 1 provides parallels to the three Synoptic Gospels. Volume 2 assembles parallels to the Gospels of John, Thomas, and Peter, the Infancy Gospel of Thomas, the Protoevangelium of James, the Acts of Pilate, and various manuscript fragments.

CHAPTER 12

Acts of the Apostles

You will bear witness for me in Jerusalem, and all over Judaea and Samaria, and away to the ends of the earth.

Jesus to the Jerusalem disciples Acts 1:8

Key Themes In the Book of Acts, Luke continues his two-part narrative of Christian origins, depicting characters who, like Jesus, are models of Christian behavior and service. This theologically shaped history of the early church emphasizes many of the same themes that dominated Luke's Gospel: (1) God's ancient promises to Israel through Abraham and Moses are fulfilled in the life and work of Jesus and his successors, who constitute a Spirit-blessed community, the new Israel. (2) Emphasizing that "the new Way (Christianity)" is a universal means of salvation encompassing all nations, Jewish and Gentile alike, Luke first shows biblical promises being fulfilled when the Jewish disciples are empowered by the Holy Spirit at Pentecost (2:1–47). (3) The author then illustrates the step-by-step process by which divine promises

were extended to non-Jewish peoples, beginning with campaigns in Samaria and Syria (8:1–12:25). The climactic events of this first section are the conversions of Paul, a Pharisee (ch. 9), and Cornelius, a Roman soldier, the first Gentile anointed by the Holy Spirit (chs. 10–11).

In the second part of Acts (chs. 13–28), Luke focuses almost exclusively on the travels of Paul, who leads a successful mission to Gentiles in Asia Minor and then carries the new religion into Europe, arriving in Rome about 60 C.E. Arguing that Christianity is a natural extension of Judaism that offers no threat to the Roman state, Luke designs his narrative to demonstrate that the church's task is to create an international and ethnically diverse community, a work that extends indefinitely into the future (28:28).

In the Book of Acts, the author of Luke's Gospel continues his story of Christian origins. Writing to the same Theophilus, he creates an exciting history that is also a defense of early Christianity. As a history, Acts does not attempt to provide a comprehensive record of its subject. The author lists the names of the original Eleven apostles (1:13) but tells us almost nothing about most of them. Instead, he organizes his book to focus on only two representa-

tive figures from the earliest Christian period. The apostle Peter, representing Jewish Christianity and the Jerusalem church, dominates the first half of Acts (chs. 1–12). Paul, representing the church's mission to Hellenistic Jews and Gentiles, is the major character of the second half (chs. 13–28). Whatever the author (whom we call Luke) may have known about the activities of other apostles and their companions, he does not include their stories in his narrative. His

---

THE BOOK OF ACTS

Author: Traditionally Luke, companion of Paul (see chapter 9). The same person who wrote the Gospel ascribed to Luke, name unknown.

Date: About 90 c.e.

Place of Composition: Unknown, perhaps Antioch or Ephesus.

---

history is thus highly selective, giving us primarily the "acts," or deeds, of only two great leaders and their immediate associates.

As a defense of Christianity, Acts further develops the same themes we found in Luke's Gospel. Directed at a Greek-speaking audience, Acts presents the new religion as both the natural fulfillment of Judaism and a universal faith intended for all nations. Peaceful and law-abiding, Christians are commissioned by the Holy Spirit to bring "the new Way" (9:2) to both Jews and Gentiles throughout the Roman Empire. The author emphasizes that the apostles and missionaries continue essentially the same ministry that Jesus had begun. Led by the same Spirit, members of the Christian community perform similar miraculous works — exorcisms, healings, and resuscitations of the dead — thereby demonstrating divine gifts almost identical to those of Jesus. To Luke, the church preserves and maintains the same ethical and spiritual quality that distinguished Jesus' career.

The Divine Plan of Humanity's Salvation

The incidents from early Christianity that Luke chooses to include in Acts are structured to express the author's major theme: the Spirit-directed growth of the church and its expansion westward from Palestine to Italy. In general, the book is arranged chronologically, showing the religion's incremental expansion into new geographical areas. Luke's organizing purpose is stated in Acts 1:8, in which the risen Jesus gives the disciples his final command: They are to "bear witness" to him "in Jerusalem, and all over Judaea and Samaria, and away to the ends of the earth."

LUKE'S MAJOR THEME: GOD'S SPIRIT OPERATING IN HUMAN HISTORY

Acts begins in Jerusalem (chs. 1–7), records a mission to Samaria (ch. 8), gives a detailed account of Paul's three missionary journeys throughout Asia Minor and Greece, and concludes with Paul's arrival in Rome, heart of the Roman Empire, and perhaps representing "the ends of the earth" (chs. 13–28). The narrative shift from Jerusalem to Rome reflects the historical development in which the new faith was transmitted from its Jewish founders to Gentile communities.

By tracing Christianity's course from its Palestinian roots to Gentile soil, Luke is able to illustrate the manner in which God has kept his biblical promises to Israel. Jesus and his Jewish followers are the fulfillment of Israel's prophetic goals, a demonstration of God's faithfulness that will reassure Theophilus and other Gentiles who join their ranks. At the end of his Gospel and the beginning of Acts, Luke takes pains to remind readers of Israel's hopes for a Davidic king. The disciples approaching Jerusalem wonder if the kingdom is at last about to materialize (Luke 19:11), a question they reformulate to Jesus immediately before his ascension to heaven: "Lord, is this the time when you are to establish once again the sovereignty of Israel?" (Acts 1:6). Jesus' answer — that they must remain in Jerusalem to "receive power" from above and then evangelize the earth — implies a positive response to their question. In Luke's view, God indeed does reestablish his rule over true citizens of Israel, the Jewish disciples of Jesus who represent the covenant people.

Luke further highlights the theme of Israel's restoration when the Eleven elect a replacement for Judas Iscariot (who has committed suicide), thus re-creating a leadership of Twelve, symbolic of Israel's twelve tribes (1:23–26). Once this continuity between Israel and the Christian community has been affirmed, however, Luke never again refers to the replacement (Matthias) or to any of the Twelve except for Peter and (briefly) John. (James, John's brother, is mentioned only to record his beheading by Herod Agrippa I [12:2].)

At Pentecost, when the Lukan Peter states that God's eschatological promise of Israel's Spirit-anointing is fulfilled (2:14–36), 3000 Jews join the Galilean disciples (2:37–41). Throughout both his Gospel and Acts, Luke is careful to distinguish the Jewish people, many of whom accept Jesus as the national Messiah, from a minority of their priestly leaders who had advocated Jesus' execution. Not only had the Jews as a whole—including their "rulers"—acted in ignorance of Jesus' identity, but it was also God's foreordained will that the Messiah *had* to suffer—no human action could have prevented it (3:17–24).

Peter's second Jerusalem speech emphasizes the Lukan theme that Jews remain "the heirs of the prophets" and "within the covenant" that God made with Abraham. Hence, God sent his "servant" and offered his "blessing" to them first, keeping the vow he had sworn to Israel's patriarchs and prophets (3:25–26). As Luke presents his history of salvation, Jerusalem and its Temple—where Pharisees and Jewish Christians worship side-by-side—are the nucleus of God's redemptive acts for all humanity.

Even when traveling in Gentile territories, the Lukan Paul consistently offers his message first to members of the local synagogue before proselytizing Syrians or Greeks. Although Paul repeatedly threatens to devote himself entirely to recruiting Gentile believers, he continues to minister to fellow Jews. At the end of Acts, however, Paul cites a portentous verse from Isaiah 6 about God's people being deaf and blind to his prophetic word. (This is the same passage that Mark had used to explain why Jesus spoke in parables—to *prevent* his hearers from understanding him [cf. Mark 4:10–12 and Acts 28:23–27].) When an exasperated Paul declares that henceforth he will concentrate all his efforts on "the Gentiles" because "the Gentiles will listen" (28:28), he expresses an unforeseen twist of history. By the time Luke wrote the sequel to his Gospel, Christianity, originally a Jewish phenomenon, had become a faith dominated by Gentiles. In this paradoxical event, Luke saw God's will accomplished: the gathering of every ethnic and national group into a universal worshiping community.

LUKE'S USE OF SPEECHES

Like other historians of his day, Luke ascribes long, elaborate speeches to his leading characters, such as Peter, Stephen, James, and Paul. But whoever the speaker, most of the speeches sound much alike in both style and thought. This similarity among Acts' many discourses, as well as the fact that they seem to reflect attitudes prevalent in the author's time rather than those of the historical figures he describes, suggests to most scholars that they are largely Luke's own compositions. In the absence of exact transcriptions of apostolic speeches, many of which were delivered amid noisy and unruly crowds, Luke apparently follows the standard practice of Greco-Roman authors by supplementing what was remembered with material of his own creation. Ancient historians and biographers like Thucydides, Livy, Tacitus, and Plutarch commonly advanced their narratives through speeches put in the mouths of historical characters. The classical writer composed such discourses based on his conception of the speaker's character and major concerns at the time the speech was given. He was not expected to reproduce a particular speech exactly as it was delivered. Thucydides explains the historian's method clearly and briefly:

> I have found it difficult to remember the precise words used in the speeches which I listened to myself and my various informants have experienced the same difficulty; so my method has been, while keeping as closely as possible to the general sense of the words that were actually used, to make the speaker say what, in my opinion, was called for by each occasion.
>
> (*The Peloponnesian War* I.22)

In short, while attempting to reproduce the "general sense" of what people said, Thucydides created their speeches according to his understanding of what "was called for by the occasion," the author's opinion of what was appropriate to a given situation. Although we cannot know the extent to which Luke's speeches reflect ideas expressed in generations before his time, they serve the important purpose of illustrating character and preserving aspects of early apostolic teaching.

ORGANIZATION OF THE BOOK OF ACTS

Luke arranges his narrative in ten major sections:

1. Prolog and account of the ascension (1:1–11)
2. Founding of the Jerusalem church (1:12–2:47)
3. Work of Peter and the apostles (3:1–5:42)
4. Persecutions of the "Hellenist" Jewish Christians and the first missions (6:1–8:40)
5. Preparation for the Gentile mission: the conversions of Paul and Cornelius (9:1–12:25)
6. First missionary journey of Barnabas and Paul: the Jerusalem conference (13:1–15:35)
7. Paul's second missionary journey: evangelizing Greece (16:1–18:21)
8. Paul's third missionary journey: revisiting Asia Minor and Greece (18:22–20:38)
9. Paul's arrest in Jerusalem and imprisonment in Caesarea (21:1–26:32)
10. Paul's journey to Rome and his preaching to Roman Jews (27:1–28:31)

Prolog and Account of the Ascension

In his introduction to Acts (1:1–11), Luke refers to the "first part" of his work (the Gospel) and then picks up where his earlier story of Jesus leaves off. Before ascending to heaven, the resurrected Jesus remains on earth for "forty days," a number that symbolizes the period of time required to accomplish a major religious undertaking. (Moses remained on Mount Sinai for forty days while receiving the Torah, and Jesus' wilderness temptation was of similar duration.)

Although his report of Jesus' postresurrection instruction is tantalizingly brief, Luke includes some major themes. The risen Jesus offers fresh insights into the nature of his kingdom, which is not the restoration of the Jewish state that the disciples had anticipated (Luke 19:11; Acts 1:3, 6–7). Contrary to apocalyptic expectations, God's rule expands gradually as the Christian message slowly permeates Greco-Roman society. The historical process must begin in Jerusalem, but the Spirit will empower believers to carry their faith throughout the earth (1:1–8).

Luke is the only New Testament writer to describe Jesus' ascent to the spirit world. He presents it as a quasi-physical movement skyward, culminating in Jesus' disappearance into the clouds (symbolic of the divine presence [Exod. 40:34–35; 1 Kings 8:10; Dan. 7:13]). Note that Luke makes the peaceful ascension a prophetic model of Jesus' quiet return (the Parousia) (1:9–11).

Founding the Jerusalem Church

THE APOSTLES

Luke is also the only New Testament author to record that the Eleven chose a replacement for Jesus' betrayer, Judas Iscariot (1:12–26). (Contrast Luke's version of Judas's suicide with Matthew's strikingly different account [Matt. 27:5].) In this episode, the author refers to two concepts important to the early church. By replacing Judas with **Matthias,** the disciples respect Jesus' example of appointing twelve followers to represent Israel's original twelve tribes. This passage also defines Luke's understanding of an apostle, a person who had physically accompanied Jesus during his entire ministry and also witnessed his resurrection (1:21–22). Because Paul had not personally known Jesus, Luke almost never calls him an apostle, although Paul himself passionately fought to make others acknowledge his right to that title (Gal. 1).

Notice that after Matthias's selection, the author says nothing more about him. He is equally silent about most of the other apostles, briefly mentioning the sons of Zebedee, James and John, but offering no hint of their characters or roles in the church. As a historian, Luke describes only those persons whose activities illustrate his thesis of the church's direct expansion from its Jewish starting point to its

Box 12.1
Some Representative Events That Shaped the World of the Early Church

THE EVOLUTION OF THE CHRISTIAN COMMUNITY AND ITS SCRIPTURES

c. 30 or 33 c.e. A number of Jesus' followers are convinced that they have seen him risen from the dead. Gathered in Jerusalem, a commune of believers is inspired to begin carrying the oral gospel of Jesus' resurrection to Jews and (somewhat later) Gentiles. The Christian church is born.

c. 3–35 c.e. Saul of Tarsus, a zealous Pharisee then persecuting Christian "heretics," experiences a vision of the risen Jesus on the road to Damascus.

50–62 c.e. Paul, now the preeminent Christian missionary to the Gentiles, composes a series of letters to various Christian communities in the eastern Mediterranean region. These letters are the earliest parts of the New Testament to be written.

c. 62 c.e. James, Jesus' kinsman, is killed in Jerusalem.

c. 64–65 c.e. Following a major fire in Rome, the emperor Nero persecutes Christians there. According to tradition, Peter and Paul are martyred then.

c. 66–70 c.e. The first account of Jesus' public ministry is written (the Gospel According to Mark).

66–73 c.e. Led by the Zealot party of dedicated revolutionaries, the Palestinian Jews revolt against Roman tyranny. Titus, son of the new emperor Vespasian, captures and destroys Jerusalem and its Temple (70 c.e.). The Jewish loyalists holding the besieged fortress of Masada commit mass suicide (73 c.e.).

THE POST-APOSTOLIC AGE

c. 80–85 c.e. The Gospel of Matthew is written (in Antioch?).

c. 85–90 c.e. Luke-Acts is published.

c. 80–100 c.e. The books of James, Hebrews, and (possibly) 1 Peter are written.

c. 90 c.e. Leading rabbis and Jewish scholars hold a council at Jamnia; the third part of the Hebrew Bible, the Writings, is defined. Christians are expelled from Jewish synagogues.

c. 90 c.e. The Letter to the Ephesians is included among Paul's correspondence.

c. 90–100 c.e. The Gospel of John is produced by the Johannine community. Letter of 1 Clement is written in Rome.

c. 95 c.e. Persecutions of the emperor Domitian (81–96 c.e.) cause John of Patmos to write the Book of Revelation.

c. 100–110 c.e. Letters of John are written.

c. 100–130 c.e. The Didache, Shepherd of Hermas, and Epistles of Ignatius are written. Canonical New Testament books of 1 and 2 Timothy, Titus, and Jude appear.

132–135 c.e. The bar Kochba rebellion against Rome is crushed by the emperor Hadrian (117–138 c.e.).

c. 130–150 c.e. 2 Peter is written.

367 c.e. Bishop Athanasius of Alexandria publishes a list of twenty-seven New Testament books corresponding to the present New Testament canon.

Gentile destination. (See box 12.1 for a list of events that shaped the world of the early church.)

THE HOLY SPIRIT AT PENTECOST

Luke presents the disciples' experience at Pentecost (a Jewish harvest festival held fifty days after Passover) in terms of prophetic fulfillment (2:1–47). The Holy Spirit's descent upon a tiny group of 120 disciples vindicates Jesus' promise to equip them with supernatural power (1:8; Luke 24:29), and it fulfills Joel's ancient prediction that God would

someday infuse all kinds of people with his Spirit (Joel 2:28–32) (see figure 12.1). Its presence symbolically rendered as wind and flame, the Spirit empowers the disciples to **speak in tongues.** This phenomenon of religious ecstasy, the believer's outpouring of strange sounds (called *glossolalia*), came to characterize the early church and was generally regarded as a sign of God's presence (11:14–18; cf. Paul's discussion of "ecstatic speech" in 1 Cor. 14). According to Luke, the pentecostal miracle enabled recipients of the Spirit to converse in foreign languages they had previously been unable to speak,

Figure 12.1 *The Descent of the Holy Spirit at Pentecost* by El Greco. Like a rushing wind and hovering tongues of flame, the Holy Spirit anoints disciples gathered in an "upper room" in Jerusalem. For the author of Acts, this event parallels the Spirit's descent at Jesus' baptism, empowering the early church to carry on Jesus' work. (© Museo del Prado, Madrid. All rights reserved.)

although some onlookers accuse the inspired disciples of being "drunk" and uttering unintelligible nonsense (2:1–13).

Observe that Luke has Peter, chief of the apostles, deliver Acts' first major speech to interpret the pentecostal experience (2:14–20). Peter's discourse illustrates several Lukan themes. The pentecostal Spirit is the phenomenon that Joel had foreseen as a sign of the last days. It is bestowed upon all believers, regardless of age or gender—women prophesy equally with men.

The Lukan Peter says that the Spirit-giving event is linked to "portents in the sky" and other astronomical displays foretold in Joel's prophecy. Interestingly, Luke represents Peter as equating the disciples' religious ecstasy with Joel's vision of cosmic upheaval, such as the sun's being darkened and the moon's turning to blood. (This interpretation of the astronomical "portents" as purely metaphorical suggests that the author's references to identical phenomena in Luke 21:25–28 may also be seen as figurative rather than as forecasts of literal events in future history.) Luke's main point, however, is that God has anointed his church, giving it the power to preach in every known tongue, the many languages of Pentecost representing the universality of the Christian mission.

Peter's long speech expresses another important Lukan theme. Jesus' death occurred "by the deliberate will and plan of God"—and was thus a theological necessity (2:23). God has vindicated his "servant" by raising him from the dead and placing him at God's "right hand" (the position of favor and power) in heaven. Linking this exaltation of Jesus with Davidic themes from the Psalms, Peter declares that by resurrecting Jesus, God has made him "both Lord and Messiah." Because Luke believes that Jesus was Messiah during his lifetime, the author may here preserve a very early Christian belief that Jesus—the "man singled out by God"—became confirmed as Messiah only on his ascension to heavenly glory (2:22, 36; see box 11.2).

THE JERUSALEM COMMUNE

Stressing a theme prominent in his Gospel, the author connects the Spirit's presence with its recipients' subsequent way of life, particularly their social and economic arrangements. The overwhelming "sense of awe" that believers feel is translated into the work of creating an ideal community without rich or poor.

Luke reports that the faithful sold their possessions so that money and goods could be distributed according to individual members' needs. Holding "everything" "in common" (2:43–45; 4:32–35), the Jerusalem community meets Jesus' challenge to sacrifice material possessions to attain true discipleship (Luke 18:18–30). As a result of establishing the kingdom's economic ethic as its standard, the Jerusalem church commonly depended on financial help from Gentile churches to sustain its ideal (Gal. 2:10; Rom. 15:25–28).

The Work of Peter and the Apostles

In the next section (3:1–5:42), Luke reports the activities of Peter and some of his Jerusalem associates. Peter's healing a crippled man by invoking Jesus' authority (3:1–10) demonstrates that the disciples continue their leader's work. Reporting a second Petrine speech (3:11–26), delivered in the Temple precincts, Luke interprets the miracle's significance. God wishes to reconcile Judaism with its infant daughter, the church. Jesus' resurrection, to which Peter and his associates are living witnesses (2:32; 3:15), proves the validity of the disciples' faith and opens the way to a unity of Jew and Jewish Christian. Luke insists that the persons who condemned Jesus did so "in ignorance." The Jerusalem leaders acted blindly because God, for his own mysterious reasons, had already determined that his "servant" must die (3:13–18). Perhaps because the Deity is the ultimate cause of Jesus' death, he now offers forgiveness to those who unwittingly carried out his will (3:17–19; Luke 23:24). As Luke portrays the situation, at this critical moment in Jewish-Christian relations, union of the two parties is possible.

Part of Israel does join the Christian fold. Luke rekindles the excitement of these early days as he records large numbers of Jews flocking to the church (4:4). In contrast to the people's enthusiastic response, Luke also shows the Jerusalem leadership hardening its position and attempting to halt the new movement.

In reading this section of Acts (chs. 3–5), notice that Luke heightens the sense of dramatic tension and conflict by presenting several direct confrontations between the apostles and the Jewish authorities. Note, too, that the author attributes much of the church's trouble to the Sadducee party, whose priests control the Temple (4:1–6; 5:17–18). By contrast, many Pharisees tend to tolerate or even champion some Christian activities (5:34–40; 23:6–9). During Peter's second hearing before the Sanhedrin, the Pharisee Gamaliel, a famous first-century rabbinical scholar, is represented as the protector of the infant church.

Seeing "the new Way" as divinely supported, Luke shows that its growth cannot be stopped. After the High Priest (identified as Annas in 4:6) imprisons the apostles, celestial forces intervene to release them (5:17–26). Whether employing human agents like Gamaliel or angels from heaven, the Deity acts decisively to ensure the church's survival and expansion.

Persecution of the Hellenist-Jewish Christians: The First Missions

While the Sadducees attack it from without, the Jerusalem community simultaneously experiences internal trouble (6:1–8:40). Strife breaks out between two different ethnic groups within the church. Although Luke only hints at the cause of this disagreement, he makes it clear that two distinct parties emerge: the **Hellenists,** who are Greek-speaking Jews of the Diaspora, and the "Hebrews," who are Aramaic-speaking Jews apparently native to Palestine. Some historians believe that this division reflects first-century Judaism's prevailing social and religious distinction between Palestinian Jews and Jews from foreign countries who have more thoroughly adopted Greek ideas and customs.

Because he wishes to picture the Jerusalem church as a model for later Christianity, Luke portrays the incipient conflict as being resolved by an orderly administrative process. Notice that the Twelve act unanimously to elect seven Greek-speaking disciples to represent the Hellenists (6:1–6).

STEPHEN: THE FIRST CHRISTIAN MARTYR

Although he implies that the seven leaders were elected to supervise the church's communal meals, Luke soon reveals that the seven were mainly proclaimers of the Gospel. Because of his public preaching, the chief Hellenist, **Stephen,** becomes the focus of Sadducean hostility. The priestly opposition accuses Stephen of attacking the Temple cult and subverting the Mosaic Torah, charges that also had been leveled against Jesus (6:8–15).

The account of Stephen's trial and public stoning effectively links the first part of Luke's history, centered in Jerusalem, with the second part, which records Christianity's outward expansion into Gentile territory. The author fashions Stephen's speech (7:2–53) as a Hellenist's severely critical indictment of Jerusalem's religious institutions. Stephen accuses the Temple leadership of "fighting against the Holy Spirit" (to Luke, the supreme offense), murdering the Messiah, and failing to keep the Torah (7:2–53). The episode concludes with typically Lukan themes: In prayer, the dying Stephen—the first Christian **martyr**—experiences a vision of heaven and, echoing Jesus' words on the cross, asks God to forgive his executioners (7:54–60).

The author contrasts Stephen's ecstatic vision with the angry presence of "a young man named Saul," who guards the cloaks of those stoning the victim. Luke's contrast of the two men, each zealous in his faith, is deeply ironic. The young Saul will become Paul the Apostle, Christianity's most famous missionary, and eventually suffer martyrdom himself. His presence at this point in the Lukan history connects the narrative about Stephen, a Greek-educated Christian Jew, with Paul's mission to Greek-speaking Gentile nations, a development recorded in the second half of Acts.

Demonstrating that the church's enemies cannot seriously interfere with its progress, Luke states that the Sadducean priests' efforts to block "the new Way" have the opposite effect. The persecution that follows Stephen's execution drives the Greek-speaking Jewish Christians from Jerusalem, but this event only serves to spread the faith into receptive new areas. (Note that although the Hellenists are expelled from the holy city, the Aramaic-speaking disciples are permitted to remain.) Contrary to their expectations, the priests' hostile action becomes the means by which Jesus' order to plant the faith in Judea and Samaria (1:8) is obeyed.

THE SAMARITAN MISSION

In his parable of the generous Samaritan, Luke (10:29–37) indicates Jesus' goodwill toward that despised group and anticipates Christianity's later growth in Samaria. In Acts, Luke portrays the Samaritan mission mainly through the work of a single figure, **Philip,** one of Stephen's Hellenist associates. Focusing on two of Philip's new converts, the author illustrates the increasing ethnic (and ethical) diversity of the church as it takes in the mixed population living outside Judea. The first convert is **Simon Magus,** a notorious magician who later tries to buy Peter's gift of imparting the Holy Spirit, an attempt the apostle severely rebukes (8:4–24). In legends that developed after New Testament times, Simon became a sinister figure involved in black magic and the occult. According to some historians, he is the prototype of Faust, the medieval scholar who—to gain forbidden knowledge—sells his soul to the devil.

The Simon Magus episode suggests the moral risks taken as the church absorbed potential troublemakers from the Hellenistic world; Philip's second major convert represents a significant breakthrough for the new religion. Occurring south of Jerusalem rather than in Samaria, Philip's conversion of an Ethiopian eunuch forms the climax of his career. According to the Mosaic Torah, a eunuch (a sexually mutilated male) was excluded from full Israelite citizenship. Despite the prejudice against him, however, this eunuch is a "God-fearer," a term Luke uses to denote a class of Gentiles who have adopted the Jewish religion without undergoing circumcision or keeping all the dietary requirements.

Notice that Luke sets up the scene to illustrate several characteristic themes. The author shows

Philip encountering the Ethiopian while he is reading a singularly appropriate passage from the Hebrew Bible—Isaiah 53. This poem describes an anonymous servant of God who suffers unjustly and offers Philip the perfect opportunity to identify Isaiah's mysterious servant with Jesus, who, though innocent, endured comparable suffering. Throughout this section of Acts, Luke repeatedly refers to Jesus as a "servant" (3:13, 26; 4:27, 30), the only New Testament writer to do so (cf. Luke 22:26–27). Notice that Luke omits Isaiah's allusions to the "servant" bearing punishment for others' sins, probably because the author does not interpret Jesus' death as a ransom or atonement for sinful humanity.

In depicting the primitive church's missionary efforts, Luke emphasizes the Spirit's directing role. Evangelists like Philip (and later Paul) go exactly where and to whom the Holy Spirit guides them, moving almost erratically from place to place. After Philip baptizes the eunuch, we are told that "the Spirit snatched Philip away, and the eunuch saw no more of him . . ." (8:39).

Preparation for the Gentile Mission: The Recruitment of Paul and Cornelius

PAUL'S VISION OF JESUS

As a literary artist, Luke skillfully prepares the reader for the historic transformation of Christianity from a movement within Judaism to an independent world religion. He does this by recording the recruitment of two different men whose acceptance of the new faith foreshadows the Gentile mission (9:1–12:25). The most dramatic event is the encounter of Saul (Paul) with the risen Lord on the road to **Damascus.** The author regards Paul's experience as crucially important and gives no fewer than three separate accounts of the incident (9:3–8; 22:6–11; 26:12–19). Luke clothes the event in supernatural images—a blinding light and heavenly voice—although Paul's only surviving reports of what happened are much more subdued (cf. Gal. 1:12, 15–16; 1 Cor. 15:8–9).

In Luke's historical scheme, Paul becomes God's agent (9:15), explicitly chosen to bring "the Way" (as Greek-speaking Christians first called their faith) to non-Jewish nations. As a result of the mystical experience that transformed his view of Jesus, Paul now suffers the same kind of persecution he had inflicted on others. Note Luke's reference to two separate plots on Paul's life, which he foils by escaping first from Damascus and then from Caesarea (9:24–30).

PETER'S CALL TO BAPTIZE A GENTILE

Luke devotes two full chapters (10–11) to narrating the conversion of **Cornelius,** a Roman military officer and the first Gentile Christian. To Luke, admitting the uncircumcised Gentile into the Christian fold represents one of the most important developments in religious history. The author's manner of telling the story reveals how crucial he believes the event to be. By this point in Luke-Acts, the reader has probably realized that whenever Luke wishes to emphasize the significance of an event, he describes it in terms of supernatural phenomena. At both Jesus' birth (Luke 1–2) and that of the church at Pentecost (Acts 2), the invisible spirit realm directly impinges on the human world. (The Resurrection and the apostles' escape from death in prison are two other examples.) Thus, Cornelius and Peter, whom God calls to baptize him, experience inspired dreams and visions that symbolically convey God's intent to make Gentiles as well as Jews his own people.

Stressing his view that the Spirit's presence validates a religious decision, Luke shows Cornelius and his entire household speaking in tongues exactly as the Jewish Christians had at Pentecost. As he had at the church's spiritual baptism, Peter again interprets the incident's religious meaning—the equal worth of Jews and Gentiles in God's sight (10:35–48). Peter's statement also clarifies the meaning of his dream: God declares all animal foods "clean" and acceptable, as well as the Gentile people who eat them. Dietary restrictions are no longer a barrier between Jew and non-Jew.

Typically Lukan themes dominate the Cornelius-Peter episode. Both men receive their respective visions while at prayer. The Spirit arranges and guides the human participants in this momentous conversion, empowering Jew and Gentile alike. The reader will also note that Luke preserves words of the resurrected Jesus directing believers how to behave at moments crucial to the evolving church. Speaking through trances or visions to Paul (9:4–6), Ananias (9:10–16), Cornelius (10:3–6), and Peter (10:10–16), the risen Lord continues to instruct his disciples (cf. Luke 24:25–27, 44–50). Luke thus shows the intimate communication prevailing between the Lord and his people.

HEROD AGRIPPA

Luke concludes this section by describing the attack on the Jerusalem church's leadership by Herod Agrippa I. A grandson of Herod the Great, Herod Agrippa reigned briefly (41–44 C.E.) over a reunited Jewish state. Although the emperor Claudius, who had appointed him king, supported Herod's rule, the puppet ruler was unpopular among his Jewish subjects. Herod apparently cultivated support from the Sadducees by persecuting their opponents, including Christians. Luke states that he beheaded James, brother of John, and also imprisoned Peter. After recording Peter's miraculous escape from prison, the author dramatizes Herod's punishment. Hailed publicly as "a god" by a fawning crowd, the king is instantly afflicted with a loathsome and fatal disease "because he had usurped the honour due to God" (12:1–24). Herod's miserable death, like that of Judas, illustrates the fate of persons who oppose the Spirit.

The First Missionary Journey of Barnabas and Paul: The Jerusalem Conference

According to Acts 11, the initial persecution and scattering of Hellenistic Jewish Christians eventually led to the formation of a mixed Jewish-Gentile church in Antioch, Syria. A prosperous city situated on the main trade and travel routes of the east-

ern Mediterranean, Antioch rapidly became the center for a hugely successful mission to the Gentiles (13:1–15:35). Paul and **Barnabas,** a Greek-speaking Jewish Christian from Cyprus, made the city their headquarters. It was here that followers of "the Way" first received the name of Christians (11:22–26).

In Acts 13, Luke shows Barnabas and Paul leaving Antioch to begin their first missionary tour of Asia Minor (see figure 12.2). According to this account, the two made it their practice to preach first in Jewish synagogues and, when rejected there, to turn then to a Gentile audience (13:46–48; 18:6; 28:28). Luke's version of Paul's speech in Pisidian **Antioch** (in Asia Minor) shows little sensitivity to Paul's characteristic teaching on the saving power of Christ or his anticipation of an early Parousia. (Compare Acts' account with Paul's letters to the Thessalonians and Corinthians.) Many scholars believe that the speeches in Acts reflect the Hellenistic preaching typical of the author's own time, late in the first century C.E.

Luke announces that Barnabas and Paul opened "the gates of faith to the Gentiles" (14:27), but he is not above remarking on the religious gullibility of some pagans. When Paul and Barnabas are evangelizing in **Lystra,** a Roman colony in Asia Minor, they are mistaken for gods in human form. After Paul miraculously heals a crippled man, the populace decides that he must be **Mercury** (Hermes), messenger of the Olympian gods, and that Barnabas is Jupiter (Zeus), king of the immortals. The pagan crowd's fickleness, however, matches its credulity. At one moment, the Lystrans are ready to offer sacrifices to Barnabas and Paul, but at the next — persuaded by some visiting Jews — they stone Paul and leave him for dead (14:8–30). Apparently indestructible, Paul recovers quickly and completes his missionary tour, returning to Antioch.

THE FIRST CHURCH CONFERENCE

The great success that Barnabas and Paul have in converting large numbers of Gentiles brings the church its first major crisis (15:1–25). In Antioch, many Jewish Christians insist that unless the new converts become circumcised they "[can] not be saved" (15:1). In Jerusalem, Christian Pharisees

CAPPADOCIA

Antioch LYCAONIA

Iconium

PHRYGIA PISIDIA Lystra

Perga PAMPHYLIA Derbe CILICIA

Attalia Tarsus

Seleucia Antioch

Salamis

Paphos *CYPRUS*

SYRIA

Sidon

MEDITERRANEAN Tyre Damascus

Ptolemais Sea of
Galilee

SEA Caesarea

Joppa
Jamnia

Jerusalem Dead
Sea

0   25   50 Miles

0   25   50 Kilometers

Figure 12.2 Paul's first missionary journey. According to
Acts, Paul made three major tours through the northeastern Mediterranean region. Although the account in
Acts may oversimplify Paul's complex travel itineraries, it
correctly shows him focusing his efforts on major urban
centers in Asia Minor (modern Turkey).

argue that Gentile converts "must be circumcised
and told to keep the Law of Moses" (15:5). 'According to Genesis, circumcision is required of all Israelite males if they are to be part of the covenant
community (Gen. 17:9–14). Because this ritual
mark on the organ of procreation distinguishes
Jews as heirs of Yahweh's promises to Abraham,
Jewish Christians naturally see it as a prerequisite
to entering the kingdom. In their opinion, foreigners must become Jews before they can be Christians. Paul and Barnabas oppose this notion with
"fierce dissension and controversy" (15:2).

The battle between advocates of the Mosaic
Torah and Hellenistic Christian Jews like Barnabas
and Paul gives Luke an opportunity to create a
model, or paradigm, for dealing with such contro-

versies in the church. By the time he wrote Acts,
the issue had long been decided in favor of the
Gentiles. Paul's advocacy of "freedom" from the
"bondage" of the Mosaic Torah had triumphed over
the "circumcision party." Thus, Luke presents the
controversy as considerably less intense than it actually was and simplifies the historical situation by
picturing a peaceful and unanimous resolution of
the problem.

The first church conference, held in Jerusalem
about 49 C.E. to decide the circumcision issue, provides Luke's model of orderly procedure. Initiating
the conference, Antioch sends delegates, including
Barnabas and Paul, to Jerusalem, and the Jerusalem
"apostles and elders" investigate the problem, permitting an extended debate between the two sides.
Peter, representing Palestinian apostolic authority,
delivers a speech reminding his fellow Jews that the
Spirit had been given to the Gentile Cornelius the
same as it had to Jewish Christians. Peter advises
against laying the Torah "yoke" upon converts. The
entire congregation then listens to Barnabas and
Paul plead their case for the Gentiles.

According to Luke, James (Jesus' "brother" or
kinsman), the person who later succeeds Peter as
head of the Jerusalem church, essentially decides
the issue. (See box 12.2 for a history of the leadership in the early Jerusalem church.) Although Acts
pictures James as a "moderate," accepting of Gentiles who do not observe Torah rules, Paul's letters
paint him as a strongly conservative Jew, advocating
circumcision for all (Gal. 2). Notice that Luke presents James as using his prestige to influence the
Jerusalem church to accept Gentiles without imposing Torah restrictions.

The Lukan James, however, does insist upon the
observation of some Jewish dietary laws by Gentiles. The Jacobean regulations seem based largely
on Torah rules from Leviticus, in which both Jews
and foreigners living in Israel are forbidden to eat
blood or meat that has not been drained of blood
(Lev. 17–18). Recognizing that Gentiles are accustomed to a more sexually permissive culture than
are Jews, James also forbids "fornication" or sexual
misconduct (15:13–21). In James' speech, Luke
shows a basic victory for one party (the Gentile
side), accompanied by a compromise that is sensitive to the consciences of the losing sides.

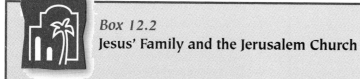

Box 12.2
Jesus' Family and the Jerusalem Church

In describing Jesus' return to Nazareth, Mark lists four of Jesus' "brothers" (or close kinsmen) by name: James, Joseph, Judas, and Simon, as well as at least two unidentified "sisters" (6:3). Mark's report that Jesus' "mother and his brothers" attempted to interfere with his ministry (3:21, 31–35) is consistent with the New Testament tradition that none of Jesus' family followed him until after his resurrection. Paul cites James as one of the prominent individuals to whom Jesus made a postresurrection appearance (1 Cor. 15:7), which was undoubtedly the experience that made James a disciple. (Acts 1:14 states that Mary, Jesus' mother, and "his brothers" assembled with the Twelve in Jerusalem shortly after the Ascension; they were presumably also present at the community's Spirit-anointing at Pentecost.)

When Paul made his postconversion visit to Jerusalem (probably about 35 C.E.), he found that "James the Lord's brother" was already an acknowledged leader of the Jerusalem church (Gal. 1:18–19). At the time of Paul's second Jerusalem visit (about 49 C.E.), James was recognized as one of three "reputed pillars of our society" (along with the apostles Cephas [Peter] and John) (Gal. 2:6–10). After Peter and John had left Jerusalem, James assumed undisputed leadership of the mother church (Acts 15:13–21; 21:18–26).

The author of Acts does not record the executions of any of his leading missionary characters, including Peter and Paul (who were probably martyred in Rome under Nero). But the Jewish historian Josephus reports that James, "the brother of Jesus, who was called Christ," was illegally brought to trial by some Sadducees and stoned to death (c. 62 C.E.; Josephus, *Antiquities* 20.9.1).

In *The History of the Church*, Eusebius reports that James, who "was called Christ's brother," was the first **bishop** (overseer) of Jerusalem and known to his fellow Jewish Christians as James the Righteous. He also records a version of James's death different from that given in Josephus. Quoting Clement, a late first-century writer, Eusebius states that James was hurled down from "the parapet [Temple walls?] and beaten to death with a fuller's club" (*History* 2.1, 23; 3.5, 11; 4.5, 22; 7.19).

According to another (unverifiable) tradition preserved in Eusebius, even after James's death, Jesus' relatives continued to play influential roles in the Jerusalem church. Shortly after the Romans destroyed Jerusalem (c. 70 C.E.), Eusebius says, "apostles and disciples of the Lord who were still alive" gathered together from different parts of the country, along with "kinsmen of the Lord, for most of them were still living." Their purpose was to appoint a successor to James who would preside over Christians in postwar Jerusalem. As Luke represents Christians voting unanimously twenty years earlier at the first Jerusalem council (Acts 15), so Eusebius states that Jesus' disciples and family members, forty years after his death, voted "unanimously" for Jesus' cousin, Symeon, to "occupy the throne" of the Jerusalem church. (Because Eusebius does not ordinarily refer to a bishop's "throne," the Jerusalem congregation may have accorded royal or Davidic status to Jesus' heirs.) Eusebius adds that Symeon was a son of Clopas (John 19:25), who was supposedly a brother of Joseph, Jesus' putative father (*History* 3.11).

According to Eusebius's source, an early church historian named Hegesippus, Symeon remained head of the Jerusalem church until persecutions under the emperor Trajan (98–117 C.E.), when, at age 120, he was tortured and crucified for being both a Davidic descendant and a Christian. Symeon was then succeeded by another Jewish Christian, Justus; Eusebius does not mention whether he, Jerusalem's third bishop, was also a member of Jesus' family (*History* 3.32, 35).

To his testimony about members of Jesus' family taking leadership roles in the early church, Eusebius adds an anecdote about the grandsons of Jude (Judas)—"the brother, humanly speaking, of the Savior." Again citing Hegesippus as his source, Eusebius states that the emperor Domitian (81–96 C.E.) ordered a search made for royal descendants of David who might push messianic claims to restore the Jewish throne. According to Hegesippus's account, when Jude's grandsons were brought before Domitian, the emperor dismissed them contemptuously when he found that they were poor peasants with work-worn, callused hands. After this close call with Roman authority (they were more fortunate than Symeon in Trajan's reign), the two apparently took a more active part in the Christian community, becoming church leaders (*History* 3.19–20). The lingering influence of James and Jude in the Christian tradition is evident in the two New Testament books ascribed to them (see chapter 18).

The author completes his example of model church procedures by illustrating the manner in which James's recommendation is carried out. Themes of unity and cooperation dominate Luke's account: The "whole church" agrees to send "unanimously" elected delegates back to Antioch with a letter containing the Jerusalem church's directive. Characteristically, Luke notes that the decision of this precedent-setting conference is also "the decision of the Holy Spirit" (15:22–29). To the author, the church's deliberations reflect the divine will.

PAUL'S INDEPENDENCE OF THE APOSTOLIC CHURCH

Luke's picture of Paul's cooperative relationship with the apostolic leadership in Jerusalem differs significantly from the account in Paul's letters. According to Luke, shortly after his conversion Paul went to Jerusalem, where he "tried to join the body of disciples there" but was rebuffed. After Barnabas took this zealous convert under his wing, however, Luke implies that Paul became an accepted member of Jerusalem's Christian community (9:26–30). In his own version of events, Paul categorically denies that he had early contact with the Jerusalem church or that his teaching about Jesus owed anything to his apostolic predecessors. After describing his private "revelation" of the risen Jesus, Paul states, "without consulting any human being, without going up to Jerusalem to see those who were apostles before me, I went off at once to Arabia, and afterwards returned to Damascus" (Gal. 1:17). Three years later, Paul notes, he did make a trip to Jerusalem "to get to know Cephas [Peter]," but he did not confer "with any other of the apostles, except James, the Lord's brother" (Gal. 1:18–19). When Paul immediately adds, "What I write is plain truth; before God I am not lying" (Gal. 1:20), it is clear that he rejects any suggestion that he was ever under the influence or jurisdiction of the Jerusalem leadership.

Given Luke's policy of depicting Paul as an obedient churchman, willingly subject to apostolic decrees, it is not surprising that Acts' picture of the Jerusalem conference contrasts markedly with Paul's eyewitness report (Gal. 2:1–10). Whereas Acts shows the Gentile-Torah issue peacefully and unanimously settled, Paul declared that "not for one moment" did he compromise his position that Gentile Christians should live absolutely free of Torah "bondage." According to Galatians, Paul accepted no restrictions, whereas Acts states that he unhesitatingly agreed to James's four Torah prohibitions. In addition, Paul reveals an attitude toward eating meat sacrificed to Greco-Roman gods that differs from that ascribed to him in Acts (1 Cor. 8:8; 10:27).

Some historians believe that the apostolic decree involving dietary matters may have been issued at a later Jerusalem conference, one that Paul did not attend. In this view, Luke has combined the results of two separate meetings and reported them as a single event. Later in Acts, the author seems aware that Paul did not know about the Jerusalem church's decision regarding Torah-prohibited meats. During Paul's final Jerusalem visit, James is shown speaking about the dietary restrictions as if they were news to Paul (21:25).

Paul's Second Missionary Journey: Evangelizing Greece

Luke devotes the remainder of Acts to recording Paul's missionary journeys and confrontations with Jewish and Roman authorities. Stressing Christianity's acceptability to the Greco-Roman world, the author structures the book's second half to illustrate three basic themes: (1) The Spirit controls the church's growth, precisely instructing missionaries on where they may or may not travel (16:6–10); (2) when Christian preachers are not interfered with, Gentiles respond favorably to the new religion, which enjoys a huge success throughout Asia Minor and Greece; and (3) from its beginnings, Christianity is familiar to Roman officials, who invariably see it as no threat to the imperial government. As Luke tells the story, only ignorant mobs or envious Jewish leaders oppose the faith and incite Roman authorities to suppress it.

These themes dominate Luke's account of Christianity's spread from Asia into Greece (16:1–18:2). After quarreling with Barnabas (15:36–40; cf. Gal. 2:13) and recruiting new companions, **Silas** and

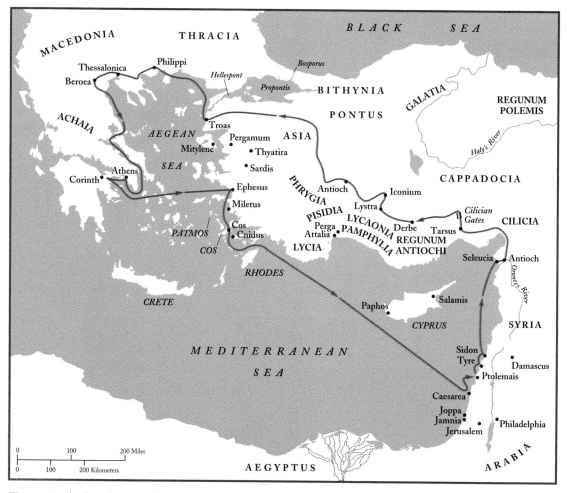

Figure 12.3 As Acts depicts it, Paul's second missionary journey brought Christianity to Europe, with new cells of Christians established in Philippi, Thessalonica, and Corinth. Note that Antioch in Syria is Paul's missionary headquarters.

Timothy, Paul has a vision in which Macedonian Greeks appeal for his help (16:9–10). Accepting the vision as a divine command, Paul and his new partners cross into Macedonia, a Roman province in northern Greece (see figure 12.3). (At this point, the author begins to speak in the first-person plural; his use of "we" and "us" suggests either that he was an eyewitness to this part of Paul's journey or that he incorporates another party's travel journal into his narrative.) In **Philippi,** where Paul establishes the first Christian church in Europe, an irate slaveholder accuses the missionaries of illegally

trying to convert Romans to Judaism. Wrongfully flogged and imprisoned, Paul and Silas assert their legal rights as Roman citizens, who are protected from punishment without a trial. Luke uses this incident to show that (1) only personal malice causes Paul's arrest; (2) God protects his agents, in this case sending an earthquake to open their prison doors; and (3) Philippi's legal authorities have no case against Paul or his associates.

After establishing another church at Thessalonica, Paul moves southward to **Athens,** famous for its magnificent artwork and schools of philoso-

Figure 12.4 A reconstruction of the Athenian Acropolis. According to Acts 17, Athenian philosophers invited Paul to explain his new religion at the Areopagus (Hill of Ares), a public forum located on a spur of the Acropolis. Named for Athene, goddess of wisdom, Athens was celebrated for encouraging freedom of thought and speech. (© AKG Photo)

phy (see figure 12.4). A university city emphasizing free speech and tolerance of diverse ideas, Athens is the only place on Paul's itinerary where he is neither mobbed nor arrested. Instead, he is politely invited to speak at the **Areopagus,** an open-air court where speakers can express their views. In a celebrated speech, Paul identifies the Athenians' "unknown god" as the Judeo-Christian Creator. Representing Paul as quoting two ancient Greek poets on the unity of humankind, Luke incorporates their insights into the Christian message. At Paul's allusion to Jesus' physical resurrection, however, the Athenians lose interest, perhaps because their philosophers commonly taught that the body has no part in a future immortal state. Only a few among Paul's audience are converted or baptized (17:16–34).

Paul enjoys much greater success in **Corinth,** a prosperous Greek seaport notorious for its materialism and houses of prostitution. Luke enables his readers to fix the approximate time of Paul's arrival—the early 50s C.E.—by his reference to two secular events that coincided with the apostle's visit. Luke notes that two Jewish Christians, **Aquila** and **Priscilla,** were in Corinth following the emperor Claudius's decree expelling all Jews from the capital. Claudius issued this edict about 49 C.E. The author also mentions that **Gallio** was then **proconsul** (governor) of Achaia, the Greek province in which Corinth is located. Archaeologists (scientists who study the remains of ancient cultures) recently found an inscription that enables them to place Gallio's term between about 51 and 53 C.E. This

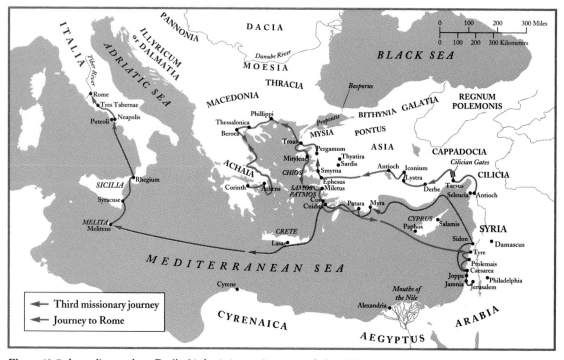

Figure 12.5 According to Acts, Paul's third missionary journey ended with his arrest in Jerusalem and two-year imprisonment in Caesarea. The bottom line shows the route of Paul's sea voyage to Rome, where he was taken to be tried in the imperial courts.

find is extremely important because it gives us one of the few relatively precise dates in Paul's career.

As in the episode at Philippi, Luke presents Paul's Corinthian visit as another illustration of his major themes—the new religion is both Spirit-directed and lawful. In a night vision, the Lord directs Paul to remain in Corinth despite persecution. When Paul is arrested and brought before Gallio, the governor dismisses Jewish charges against the missionary as irrelevant to Roman law. Legally exonerated, Paul and his companions continue their work unhindered (18:1–17).

Paul's Third Missionary Journey: Revisiting Asia Minor and Greece

In depicting Paul's third missionary journey (18:21–20:38) in which the apostle revisits churches he had founded in Asia Minor and Greece (see figure

12.5), Luke concentrates on Paul's activities in Ephesus (see figure 12.6). A thriving port city on the west coast of Asia (modern Turkey), Ephesus had an ethnically mixed population and a great variety of religious cults. Luke demonstrates the social and religious complexity of this cosmopolitan center by having his hero encounter a wide diversity of religionists there, both Jewish and Gentile.

The author hints that even Christianity in Ephesus differs from that found elsewhere, being influenced by Jewish followers of John the Baptist. Luke records two separate incidents in which members of a Baptist-Christian group are apparently brought into line with Pauline doctrine. The first involves the eloquent **Apollos,** an educated Jew from Alexandria, who delivers persuasive sermons about Jesus—but knows "only John's baptism." Hearing him in the Ephesus synagogue, Priscilla and Aquila "take him in hand," presumably bringing his ideas into harmony with Paul's teaching. After Apollos departs for Corinth (see 1

Figure 12.6 The Amphitheater at Ephesus. A wealthy Greco-Roman seaport in Asia Minor (western Turkey), Ephesus was the site of one of the seven wonders of the ancient world, the lavish marble Temple of Artemis (the Roman Diana). According to Acts 19, Ephesian silversmiths staged a riot in the amphitheater when Paul's Christian message threatened to subvert the worship of Artemis— and the prosperity of the silversmiths, who profited from selling miniature silver replicas of the goddess's statue and shrine to tourists. (Courtesy of Sonia Halliday Photographs, photo by F. H. C. Birch)

Cor. 1), Paul finds another group of Ephesian Christians observing "John's baptism." On their being rebaptized in Jesus' name, the converts receive the Holy Spirit, confirming the superiority of Jesus to his forerunner.

Luke further illustrates Christianity's superiority by contrasting Paul's astonishing ability to heal with the inability of some Jewish competitors. The apostle's spiritual power is so great that articles of clothing that had touched his skin are used to heal the sick and cast out "evil spirits." By contrast, seven Jewish exorcists trying to expel demons by invoking Jesus' authority fail ignominiously. Defying the exorcists, the possessed man strips all seven and hurls them naked from his house (19:11–17).

In religion, Ephesus's greatest pride was its enormous temple dedicated to **Artemis** (the Roman Diana), one of seven wonders of the ancient world (see figure 12.7). Although bearing a Greek name, the Ephesian Artemis was a mother goddess closely related to other Near Eastern fertility deities such as

Cybele and Ashtoreth. Paul's success in converting Ephesians brings him into conflict with the goddess's worshipers. Jewish-Christian monotheism, proclaiming the existence of only one God, threatens to hurt the business of Ephesian silversmiths who make their living selling replicas of Artemis and her shrine.

Duplicating the trial scene at Corinth, Luke states that Ephesian officials find the missionary innocent of disturbing the city's peace. Once again, attempts to harm the disciples backfire against the persecutors (19:23–41).

Luke frames Paul's adventures in Ephesus with intimations of the apostle's final journey—to Rome. As Luke had pictured Jesus turning his face resolutely toward Jerusalem and the servant's death that awaited him there (Luke 9:51), so the author shows Paul determined to complete his last tour and head for the imperial capital (19:21–22). After revisiting Greece (20:1–16), Paul calls the Ephesian church leaders to meet him in Miletus, an ancient

Figure 12.7 The cult statue of Artemis (Diana) at Ephesus. Although the Greeks honored Artemis as the virgin patron of wildlife and the hunt, Ephesian sculptors depicted her as a Near Eastern fertility goddess, decorating the torso of her statue with images of breasts, eggs, or perhaps the testicles of bulls that were sacrificed on her altar. The Roman Diana was also identified with the feminine symbol of the moon. (© Alinari/Art Resource, NY)

Greek city on the west coast of Asia Minor. There, Paul delivers a farewell speech, predicting his imminent imprisonment and implying a coming martyrdom. In this speech, Luke stresses holding to the apostolic teaching that Paul represents and resisting heresy (20:17–38).

Paul's Arrest in Jerusalem and Imprisonment in Caesarea

In this section, Luke foreshadows Paul's death, although he never explicitly refers to it (21:1–26:32). On his way to Jerusalem, presumably to deliver the money collected from the Pauline churches for the "poor" of Jerusalem's Christian commune, Paul encounters a prophet who foretells the apostle's fatal "binding" (arrest) there. Stressing the resemblance between Jesus and his later followers, Luke shows Paul expressing his willingness to die in Jerusalem. (Compare Paul's misgivings about the fatal return to Jerusalem in Romans 15.)

Ironically, the apostle to the Gentiles seals his fate by cooperating with the Palestinian-Jewish Christians of Jerusalem. When Paul bows to James's influence and agrees to undergo purification rites in the Temple to prove his faithfulness to Torah regulations, his presence in the sanctuary incites a riot. The Roman soldiers who intervene in the fray save Paul's life but also place him in protective custody (21:18–36). From this incident through the end of his story, Luke's hero is a prisoner of the Roman government.

CHRISTIANITY AND THE STATE

Paul's arrest and his hearings before various magistrates illustrate Luke's focus on Christianity's legal relation to the empire. The author consistently represents Roman officials as generally favoring the new religion. A Roman army officer permits Paul to explain his mission to a Jewish crowd (21:37–22:21), occasioning a speech in which Paul gives a second version of his mystical experience on the road to Damascus. When he discovers that Paul is a Roman citizen, a legal status that entitles him to protection from punishment without a proper trial,

the same army commander (later identified as Lysias) personally escorts his prisoner to the Sanhedrin to answer charges the Jews had brought against him.

In reporting Paul's Sanhedrin appearance, Luke shows that the Jerusalem leaders divide along party lines as they had during Peter's two hearings. The similarity of Paul's religious doctrines and those of the Pharisees is indicated by the fact that Paul has no qualms about identifying himself with them, and they take his part. As before, it is the Sadducean priests who must vehemently oppose the Christian "heresy."

In reading Luke's description of Paul's first formal hearing before a high Roman official, the governor **Antonius Felix** (24:10–21), notice the issues Luke believes to be at stake. The High Priest's emissaries charge Paul with profaning the Jerusalem sanctuary and being a "ringleader of the **Nazarenes**," an early Jewish designation of the Christian "sect" (24:1–9). In his defense, Paul insists that he adheres to "the written Law" (an assertion contradicted in his letters), that he has done nothing to profane the Temple, and that the "real issue" is that of Jesus' resurrection from the dead (24:10–21).

CHRISTIANS' POLITICAL INNOCENCE

Addressing Luke-Acts to Theophilus, who may have been an influential Greco-Roman official, the author attaches great importance to showing that from its inception, Christianity is not incompatible with Roman law. Luke uses Paul's case to demonstrate his thesis and devotes approximately three chapters to Paul's two-year imprisonment in Caesarea, the Roman administrative capital of Palestine (chs. 23–26).

According to Luke, two Roman governors, Felix and his successor, **Porcius Festus,** personally absolve Paul of any illegal activity (25:25; 26:30–32). In one of Hellenistic literature's most dramatic courtroom scenes, Luke shows Paul facing not only the Roman emperor's personal representative, Festus, but also rulers of Herod's line. King Julius Agrippa II, son of Herod Agrippa I, who had beheaded the apostle James (12:1–2), appears with his sister (and mistress) Bernice. Because Festus is married to Drusilla, another of King Agrippa's sisters, the apostle confronts a ruling family in which the power of Rome and Jewish royalty is combined. In this confrontation, Luke shows Paul fulfilling Jesus' earlier prophecy that the apostle would testify "before kings" and the "people of Israel" (9:15).

Paul's long speech (26:1–29) is a vivid summary of his career as depicted in Acts, including a third account describing his "heavenly" vision of the risen Jesus. This discourse corresponds more closely to Paul's own account of his conversion (Gal. 1:1, 15–17) than do Acts' two earlier versions. But the author still represents Paul as operating under Jewish Law—asserting "nothing beyond what was foretold by the prophets and by Moses." In the author's view, Christianity is the logical and legitimate development of Judaism. Thus, Jews have no cause to condemn it as a perversion of their Mosaic heritage.

Luke's main emphasis, however, is that his hero is totally innocent. Echoing Pilate's opinion of Jesus, Governor Festus admits that Paul is guilty of "nothing that deserves death or imprisonment." Agrippa drives home the point: Paul could have been released a free man if "he had not appealed to the Emperor" (26:30–32). In Luke's presentation of the early church to Greco-Roman readers, the author makes clear that missionaries like Paul are prosecuted in Roman courts only through officials' misunderstanding or the malice of their false accusers.

Paul's Journey to Rome and His Preaching to Roman Jews

Luke begins his final section—Paul's sea journey to Rome—with an exciting account of a shipwreck (27:1–28:31). Told in the first person, this description of a Roman cargo ship disintegrating amid high winds and pounding waves reads like an eyewitness experience. (We do not know whether the author uses the diary of a participant in this passage or simply employs the first-person "we" as a literary device to heighten the immediacy of his narrative.) As always in Acts, the incident is included for its theological meaning. Although Paul is a prisoner

perhaps destined for conviction and death, he comforts his Roman captors during the storm, assuring them that Jesus destines him (and them) to arrive safely in Rome. As Paul had prophesied, all aboard—crew, military officers, and prisoner—survive the ordeal unscathed, swimming ashore on the island of Malta (27:6–44).

Luke concludes his history of the early church with Paul's arrival in Rome, where the apostle, although under house arrest, enjoys considerable freedom, receiving visitors and preaching openly. The author does not reveal Paul's ultimate fate. One tradition states that after remaining in the capital for two years, Paul was released and carried out his planned missionary trip to Spain (Rom. 15:24). Many historians, however, believe that Paul's first Roman imprisonment led to his execution, perhaps about 62 C.E., following the emperor Nero's order to impose the death penalty on anyone who spoke or behaved in a way that appeared to undermine his supreme authority. Other scholars date Paul's death at about 64 or 65 C.E., when Nero first persecuted Christians as a group. According to a brief reference in 1 Clement, a letter from the church overseer in Rome (about 96 C.E.), both Peter and Paul were martyred during Nero's persecution.

Some critics suggest that Luke, deeply concerned with Christianity's legal status in the Roman Empire, deliberately omits mentioning that Paul and Peter, like Jesus, were tried and executed for treason against Rome. This unfortunate outcome for the religion's two leading proponents runs counter to the author's insistence that Christianity is a lawful faith innocent of any sedition against the state.

Most scholars contend that Acts ends abruptly not because Luke wants to avoid political facts that do not fit his theme, but because he regards Paul's evangelizing in Rome as the fulfillment of his purpose in writing. Luke's conclusion well illustrates his principal historical-theological interest: Paul resolves to focus his message on receptive Gentiles, turning his primary attention from Jews to a Greco-Roman audience. Luke sees the church's future in the teeming millions of Gentiles throughout Rome's vast empire, a vision confirmed by later history.

As a believer who intuits religious meaning from historical events, Luke completes his picture of primitive Christianity with a sketch of Paul—representing the church's mission to all nations—vigorously proclaiming his vision of God ruling through Jesus. To Luke, Paul's activity symbolizes the divinely commanded business of the church that must continue into the distant future. Rather than end his account with a reaffirmation of Jesus' eschatological return (the Parousia), Luke looks to a future in which the "kingdom" can be preached "openly and without hindrance," attaining a recognized legal position in the world. Perhaps the least eschatologically oriented writer in the New Testament, Luke sees the world not as a wicked place to be destroyed, but as the arena in which God effects humanity's salvation.

Acts' ending thus echoes Jesus' departing words to the disciples recorded at the book's beginning. Believers are not "to know about dates or times" (eschatological speculations about the world's End) because such knowledge belongs exclusively to "the Father" and has been "set within his own control." Instead, Christians are to carry the "good news" of Jesus "to the ends of the earth" (1:7–8). With Paul's arrival in Rome, the work is well begun. Its completion Luke entrusts to his readers.

Summary

A continuation of Luke's Gospel, Acts is a theologically oriented history of the early Christian church. Focusing principally on two representative leaders of the faith, Peter and Paul, it traces the church's growth from exclusively Jewish origins in Jerusalem to its dissemination throughout the northeastern Roman Empire. The church's rapid expansion from a Jewish nucleus to an international community composed of many different ethnic groups brings major problems of adjustment, particularly the issue of requiring Gentiles to observe the Jewish Torah.

In many respects, the Book of Acts is an **apology** (*apologia,* an explanation or defense) for Christianity. Luke's history of Christian origins defends the *new* religion as the legitimate outgrowth of Judaism and a lawful faith intended for citizens of the Roman Empire. Luke stresses that there is no necessary or inherent conflict between Christianity and the Jewish religion that gave it birth or the Roman state in which it finds its natural environment. As in his Gospel, he minimizes early expectations of an imminent Parousia and emphasizes the church's objective to expand indefinitely into the distant future. Eager to find accommodation with the imperial government, the author makes no criticism of Roman officials but invariably pictures them as fair-minded and competent. He attributes Roman suspicion of the faith to the ill will of envious opponents. Historically, Luke-Acts paves the way for the adoption of Christianity as the empire's official religion, a triumph foreshadowed by Paul's preaching in Rome "without [legal] hindrance."

QUESTIONS FOR REVIEW

1. A sequel to Luke's Gospel, the Book of Acts continues the story of Christian origins. Which of the same themes that appear in the Gospel are also found in Acts? Compare the account of Jesus' trial before Pilate with that of Paul before Pilate's successors, Felix and Festus.

2. How does Luke organize his account of Christianity's birth and growth? Identify the leaders of the Jerusalem church and the missionaries who first helped carry "the new Way" into the large world beyond the Jewish capital.

3. In recording the events of Pentecost, how does Luke emphasize his theme that Christianity is a universal religion—led by the Holy Spirit and destined for peoples of all nations? In the author's view, what ancient Hebrew prophecy is fulfilled by the Spirit's descent upon the first disciples?

4. In what ways does the Jerusalem commune put into operation the social and economic principles enunciated in Luke's Gospel? How does the early church "equalize" wealth and poverty?

5. Summarize the events that led to the expansion of "the Way" from Jerusalem into Judea and Samaria. Describe the roles of Stephen and Philip in this process.

6. The conversions of an Ethiopian eunuch and a Roman centurion are milestones in Christianity's transformation from a Jewish sect into an international

religion dominated by Gentiles. Explain how this process of ethnic change led to problems in the early church. According to Acts 15, how is the problem resolved at the first church conference in Jerusalem?

7. Describe the roles played by Barnabas and his partner, Paul (formerly Saul) of Tarsus. Summarize the results of Paul's three missionary journeys into Gentile territories. What sequence of events leads to Paul's arrest and his imprisonment in Caesarea and Rome?

QUESTION FOR DISCUSSION AND REFLECTION

1. By adding a history of primitive Christianity to his Gospel narrative, how does Luke deemphasize apocalyptic hopes of Jesus' early return? What future does Paul's arrival in Rome forecast for church-state relations?

TERMS AND CONCEPTS TO REMEMBER

Ascension	Stephen
Jesus' postresurrection commission to the Apostles	Saul of Tarsus
	Philip
Matthias	Barnabas
Pentecost	Paul
Holy Spirit	the Jerusalem conference
glossolalia	Athens
Rabbi Gamaliel	Corinth
Hellenists	Luke's *apologia* (defense)
Hebrews	theodicy

RECOMMENDED READING

Bruce, F. F. *Commentary on the Book of Acts.* Grand Rapids, Mich.: Eerdmans, 1956.

Cadbury, H. J. "Acts of the Apostles." In *The Interpreter's Dictionary of the Bible,* Vol. 1, pp. 28–42. Nashville, Tenn.: Abingdon Press, 1962. A general introduction.

Dillon, Richard J. "Acts of the Apostles." In R. E. Brown et al., eds., *The New Jerome Biblical Commentary,* pp. 722–767. Englewood Cliffs, N.J.: Prentice-Hall, 1990. A thorough introductory study.

Haenchen, Ernst. *The Acts of the Apostles: A Commentary.* Philadelphia: Westminster Press, 1971. An excellent study.

Hanson, R. P. C. *The Acts.* New York: Oxford University Press, 1967.

Hengel, Martin. *Acts and the History of Earliest Christianity.* Philadelphia: Fortress Press, 1980.

Juel, Donald. *Luke-Acts: The Promise of History.* Atlanta: John Knox Press, 1984.

Talbert, C. H. *Acts.* Atlanta: John Knox Press, 1984.

For More Advanced Study

Arlandson, James M. *Women, Class, and Society in Early Christianity: Models from Luke-Acts.* Peabody, Mass.: Hendrickson, 1997. Applies social theory to the role of women in ancient society and the church.

Conzelmann, Hans. *The Theology of St. Luke.* Translated by G. Buswell. New York: Harper & Row, 1961. Scholarly and influential.

Dibelius, Martin. *Studies in the Acts of the Apostles.* Translated by M. Ling. Edited by H. Greeven. New York: Scribner, 1956. A standard reference.

Dunn, J. D. G. *Unity and Diversity in the New Testament.* Philadelphia: Westminster Press, 1977. A stimulating analysis of the several different forms of early Christianity; covers the conflicts between the Palestinian-Jewish Christians and the Hellenistic Gentile church.

Keck, L. E., and Martyn, J. L., eds. *Studies in Luke-Acts.* Nashville, Tenn.: Abingdon Press, 1966 (reprinted 1980). An important collection of scholarly essays on recent approaches to Luke's writings.

Lohse, Eduard. *The First Christians: Their Beginnings, Writings, and Beliefs.* Philadelphia: Fortress Press, 1983.

Malherbe, A. J. *Social Aspects of Early Christianity,* 2nd ed. Philadelphia: Fortress Press, 1983.

Markus, R. A. *Christianity in the Roman World.* New York: Scribner, 1974. Traces the growth of Christianity from outlawed sect to state religion of imperial Rome.

Talbert, C. H. *Luke-Acts: New Perspectives from the SBL Seminar.* Los Angeles: Crossroads, 1984.

Theissen, Gerd. *The Sociology of Early Palestinian Christianity.* Philadelphia: Fortress Press, 1978.

Tiede, D. L. *Prophecy and History in Luke-Acts.* Philadelphia: Fortress Press, 1980.

Wilken, R. L. *The Christians as the Romans Saw Them.* New Haven, Conn.: Yale University Press, 1984. A careful analysis of the social, religious, and political conflicts between early Christians and their Roman critics.

Williams, C. S. C. *A Commentary on the Acts of the Apostles.* New York: Harper & Row, 1957. Another helpful study.

CHAPTER 13

Paul

Apostle to the Nations

*I am a free man . . . but I have made myself every man's servant. . . .
To the Jews I became like a Jew, to win Jews. . . . To win
Gentiles . . . I made myself like one of them. Indeed, I have become
everything in turn to men of every sort, so that in one way or
another I may save some.*

Paul to the church at Corinth 1 Corinthians 9:19–22

Key Themes Paul is second only to Jesus in his contribution to the development of Christianity. Although Paul apparently never knew the living Jesus and once persecuted his disciples, he experienced an *apokalypsis* (revelation) of the risen Christ that transformed his life. Becoming a missionary to the Gentiles, Paul created and disseminated a view of Jesus' cosmic significance that profoundly shaped the future course of Christian thought. A former Pharisee rigorously educated in Torah interpretation, Paul reinterprets parts of the Hebrew Bible to defend his thesis that faith in Jesus' saving power replaced Torah obedience as the means of reconciling human beings to God.

Paul, former Pharisee and persecutor of the Church who later spearheaded Christianity's mission to the Gentiles, dominates the second half of Acts. To an incalculable extent, he also dominates the later history of Christian thought. His letters, which form the third unit of the New Testament, represent the new religion's first—and in important ways the most lasting—attempt to interpret the meaning of Jesus' sacrificial death and its significance to human salvation. Paul's startling view is that Jesus' crucifixion introduced a radically different relationship between God and all humanity—Gentiles as well as Jews. Paul's declaration that faith in Christ superseded Torah obedience as the means of reconciliation to God transformed Christianity from a Jewish sect into a new world religion. In his letters to the Romans and Galatians, Paul outlined a theology of redemption through faith that has become central to

Christianity's self-understanding. Later theologians as diverse as the Roman church father Augustine (354–430 C.E.) and Martin Luther (1483–1546), the German priest who sparked the Protestant Reformation, derived many of their doctrines from Paul's letters.

Many historians have remarked that there is perhaps more of Paul than Jesus in official Christianity. Even Mark, the earliest story of Jesus' life, bears the imprint of Pauline ideas in its bias toward Gentile believers, account of the Last Supper, and theology of the cross. Some commentators accuse Paul, who did not know the historical Jesus, of largely ignoring Christ's original proclamation—God's active rule in individual human lives—in favor of promulgating a mystery cult *about* Jesus. Certainly, Paul almost never cites Jesus' kingdom teaching and instead emphasizes his own personal experience of the risen Christ, which he interprets in cosmic and mystical terms.

In contrast to Jesus, who apparently wrote nothing, Paul speaks directly to us through his letters, permitting us to compare what he says about himself with what later writers, such as Luke, say about him. Paul's position in the canon is unique: He is the only historical personage who is both a major character in a New Testament book and the author of New Testament books himself. Church tradition ascribes no fewer than thirteen canonical letters to Paul, in total length nearly one-third of the New Testament. Most scholars regard only seven as genuinely Pauline, but the presence of other works attributed to him shows in what high esteem he was held. His ideas and personality so captured the imagination of later Christian authors that they paid tribute to the great apostle by writing in his name and perpetuating his teachings.

Seeking the Historical Paul

As a Christian thinker, Paul never forgets his Jewishness. Although he fights to free Christianity from the "bondage" of Torah observance, Paul consistently stresses the unbroken continuity between Judaism and the new religion. For him, as for Matthew, Christianity is revealed through Jesus' ministry but shaped and largely defined by the Hebrew Bible. Throughout his letters, Paul quotes selected parts of the Hebrew Scriptures to support the validity of his particular gospel. Despite Paul's ambivalent attitude toward the Mosaic Torah, much of the Hebrew biblical tradition retains its teaching authority for him.

Our most reliable source of Paul's biography is his letters, where he repeatedly stresses his Jewish heritage. Describing himself as a circumcised "Hebrew born and bred" from the Israelite tribe of Benjamin (Phil. 3:5–6), Paul states that as a "practicing Jew" he outstripped his Jewish contemporaries in strict observance of "the traditions of [his] ancestors" (Gal. 1:13–14). A member of the Pharisee sect, he obeyed the Torah completely. "In legal rectitude" — keeping the Torah commandments — Paul judges himself "faultless" (Phil. 3:6).

Figure 13.1 Ancient Christian mosaic portrait of Paul. Although no one knows what any New Testament figure looked like, later Christian artists commonly depicted Paul as physically unimpressive. In this mosaic, Paul stares directly at the viewer, the intensity of his gaze suggesting the apostle's passionate commitment to his calling. (© Alinari/Art Resource, NY)

Before his call to follow Jesus, Paul demonstrated his loyalty to Pharisaic Judaism by persecuting those who believed that Jesus was the Jewish Messiah. Whatever the nature of Paul's supernatural encounter with the risen Christ (Acts 9:1–9; 22:3–11; 16:12–19), it radically changed his attitude toward Christianity without modifying his essential personality. According to Acts and his own testimony, he displayed the same quality of religious zeal before Jesus appeared to him as he does afterward. Paul's experience seems less a conversion from one religion to another (he always stresses the connection between Judaism and the new faith) than a redirection of his abundant energies (see figure 13.1).

The Historical Reliability of Acts

Acts supplies much information about Paul not contained in his letters, but most scholars urge great caution about accepting Acts' data at face

Box 13.1
Some Differences Between Acts and Paul's Letters

ACTS	PAUL'S LETTERS
Is named Saul and raised in Tarsus	Is not mentioned (but was born to the tribe of Benjamin, whose first king was Saul [Phil. 3:5])
Studies under Rabbi Gamaliel	Is not mentioned
Belongs to the Pharisee party	Is confirmed in Philippians 3:6
Persecutes Christians	Is mentioned several times
Experiences a vision of Jesus on the road to Damascus	Receives a "revelation" of Jesus (Gal. 1:12, 16)
Following his call, goes immediately to Damascus, where he preaches in synagogues	Goes to "Arabia" for an unspecified period (Gal. 1:17)
At first is shunned by the Jerusalem disciples, is later introduced to the apostles (9:26–30)	Does not go to Jerusalem until three years after his return from "Arabia," and meets only Peter and James (Gal. 1:17–20)
Receives the Holy Spirit after **Ananias** baptizes and lays hands upon him	Asserts he owes his apostolic gospel and commission to no one; never refers to his baptism (Gal. 1:11–12, 16–17)
Attends an apostolic conference on his third Jerusalem visit	Attends the conference on his second Jerusalem visit (Gal. 2:1–10)
Agrees to impose Torah dietary restrictions on Gentile converts	Refuses to accept any legal restrictions (Gal. 2:5)
Agrees to forbid eating meat sacrificed to idols	Regards eating such meat as undefiling (1 Cor. 8; 10:27; Rom. 14:13–15:6)

value. A great deal of the material in the letters is difficult to reconcile with Acts' narrative sequence. Where discrepancies occur, scholars prefer Paul's firsthand version of events. The author of Acts investigated various sources to compile his account of Christianity's beginnings (Luke 1:1–4), but he appears to have worked with inadequate documentation in recording Paul's career. As noted in chapters 9 and 12, the author seems unaware of Paul's voluminous correspondence, his insistent claims to apostleship, and his distinctive teaching. Acts says virtually nothing about Paul's essential gospel— that people are saved not by obedience to Torah commands, but by faith in Christ. More to the point, the writer of Acts is concerned primarily with outlining a precise scheme of history into which he fits his characters as it seems appropriate.

In some cases, Acts provides biographical details that Paul never mentions, such as his birth in Tar-

sus, capital city of Cilicia (now included in southeastern Turkey), and the belief that Paul's family possessed Roman citizenship. These and similar traditions—such as Paul's originally being named Saul, his studying at the feet of Rabbi Gamaliel (the leading Pharisee scholar of his day), and his supporting himself by tent making—are never referred to in the Pauline letters, so we have no way of verifying their historical accuracy.

Other statements in Acts seem to contradict Paul's direct testimony (see box 13.1), particularly the chronological order of events following his decisive confrontation with the risen Jesus. With Acts' reliability in question and Paul's biographical disclosures so few, scholars are unable to reconstruct anything resembling a satisfactory life of Christianity's Apostle to the Gentiles. We do not know when he was born, how his family gained Roman citizenship (if Acts is correct on this point), whether he was once married, where or when he wrote many of his letters, and under what precise circumstances he died. These and other missing facts are more than compensated for, however, in the brilliant revelation of thought and personality that his letters impart.

Paul's Experience of the Risen Jesus

In both Acts and the letters, Paul's life can be divided into two contrasting parts. During his early career, he was a devout Pharisee who "savagely" persecuted the first Christians. During his later years, he was a Christian missionary who successfully implanted the new religion in non-Jewish territories and established the first churches of Europe. The event that changed Paul from a persecutor of Christians into an indomitable Christian evangelist was, in his words, "a revelation [*apokalypsis*] of Jesus Christ" (Gal. 1:12). Acts depicts the "revelation" as a blinding vision of the risen Messiah on the road to Damascus. The author stresses the importance of the event by narrating it fully three times (Acts 9:1–9; 22:3–11; 26:12–19). Paul's briefer allusions to the experience speak simply of being called by God's "grace" (Gal. 1:15) to an "abnormal birth" and of witnessing a postresurrection appearance of Jesus (1 Cor. 15:8–9). Paul does not state what form the apparition took, but he does imply that he maintained an ongoing communication with divine beings, experiencing a number of mystical visions (2 Cor. 12:1–10).

Paul's physical stamina—even today duplicating his travel itinerary would exhaust most people—is matched by the strength of his feelings. Paul's letters reveal their author's emotional intensity, ranging from paternal tenderness to biting sarcasm. In one letter, he insults his readers' intelligence and suggests that some of their advisers castrate themselves (Gal. 3:1; 5:12). In other letters, he reacts to criticism with threats, wild boasting, and wounding anger (2 Cor. 10–13). In still others, he expresses profound affection and gentle tact (1 Cor. 13; Phil. 1:3–9; 2:1–4; 4:2–3) (see figure 13.2).

Paul's conviction that Jesus had privately revealed to him the one true gospel (Gal. 1–2) isolated the apostle from many fellow believers. Acts and the letters agree that Paul quarreled with many of his intimate companions (Acts 15:37–39; Gal. 2:11–14), as well as with entire groups (Gal.; 2 Cor. 10–13). This sense of a unique vision, one not shared by most other Christians, may have shaped Paul's admitted preference for preaching in territories where no Christian had preceded him. The more distant his missionary field from competing evangelizers, the better it suited him. Paul's desire to impress his individual gospel on new converts may have influenced his ambition to work in areas as far removed from established churches as possible (Rom. 15:20–23).

Dating Paul's Career

In his letter to the Galatians, Paul briefly summarizes his career up to the time of writing, giving us a few clues on which to base a rough chronology of his life. After the decisive "revelation" of Jesus, "without going up to Jerusalem" to consult the Twelve, Paul went immediately to "Arabia" (probably an area east of the Jordan River), staying there for an unspecified time before returning to Damascus. Only after "three years" had passed did he travel to Jerusalem "to get to know Cephas" (Peter's Aramaic name). Staying precisely two weeks with Peter (Paul evidently counted the days), he visited no other "Apostle" except "James the Lord's brother." Paul insists on this point because he wants to stress his complete independence of the Jerusalem leadership: "What I write is plain truth; before God I am not lying" (Gal. 1:16–20).

After making Peter's acquaintance, Paul went north to Syria, allowing another fourteen years to elapse before he again visited Jerusalem. The occasion for this second visit is almost certainly the church conference described in Acts 15, a meeting of delegates from Antioch with the Jerusalem congregation to discuss whether Gentile Christians must become circumcised or follow other provisions of the Mosaic Law. Paul remembers the gath-

Figure 13.2 *The Apostle Paul* by Rembrandt (1606–1669). Rembrandt's somber portrait shows Paul in a deeply reflective mood and stresses the apostle's consciousness of the enormous burden he bears—the task of communicating his unique vision of Christ to the Gentiles. In his letters, Paul expresses a wide variety of emotions—joy, anger, bitter sarcasm—but Rembrandt captures here the sense of melancholy and isolation that typically characterize this great missionary. (Widener Collection, Photograph © 1998 Board of Trustees, National Gallery of Art, Washington)

ering as less formal than Acts depicts it, emphasizing his private conversations with the three "pillars" of the Jerusalem leadership—Peter, John, and Jesus' kinsman James (see box 12.2). Observing that **Titus,** a Greek youth accompanying him, was not required to become circumcised, Paul declares that the three Jerusalem "pillars" recognized the legitimacy of his peculiar "gospel" proclaiming freedom from the Torah's "bondage." The Jerusalem leaders shake hands on this agreement and endorse Paul as the recognized missionary to the Gentiles as Peter is to the Jews (Gal. 2:1–10).

Paul's account indicates that approximately seventeen years (or about fifteen, when calculated by the Hebrew method) passed between the time of his initial vision and the conference held in Jerusalem.

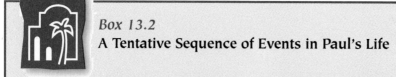

Box 13.2
A Tentative Sequence of Events in Paul's Life

Except for a few incidents, such as Paul's visit to Corinth when Gallio was proconsul in Achaea (Greece) (c. 51–53 C.E.), scholars do not agree on the dates of major events in Paul's life. From references in Paul's letters and a cautious use of material in Acts, however, it is possible to reconstruct a general outline of Paul's biography.

Paul is born a Hellenistic Jew (in Tarsus, first decade C.E.?). He is educated as a Pharisee (Phil. 3:5–6; 2 Cor. 11:22).

[Jesus is crucified (c. 30 C.E.?).]

Paul harasses members of the early Jesus movement (1 Cor. 15:9; Gal. 1:13–14).

Paul encounters the risen Jesus (c. 32–34 C.E.) (1 Cor. 15:9–10; Gal. 1:11–12, 16).

After his *revelation,* Paul travels to "Arabia" and then returns to Damascus (without visiting Jerusalem) (Gal. 1:16–17).

"After three years," he visits Jerusalem to meet Peter (Cephas) and James, "the Lord's brother" (Gal. 1:18–19).

He then travels to "Syria and Cilicia [southeast Turkey]," presumably as a missionary to Gentiles (and steering clear of Jewish churches) (Gal. 1:22).

"Fourteen years later," with Titus and Barnabas, Paul makes a second visit to Jerusalem (c. 49 C.E.), presumably to confer with Peter, John, James, and representatives from Antioch about admitting Gentiles as equal members of the church (Gal. 2:1–10; cf. Acts 15).

After the Jerusalem consultation, Paul returns to Antioch, where he opposes Peter over the issue of dining with Gentiles (Gal. 2:11–14).

Traveling from Antioch to Greece, Paul establishes the first Christian congregations of Europe (Philippi, Thessalonica, and Corinth), remains in Corinth for eighteen months (c. 49–51), and writes a letter to the Thessalonians (c. 50 C.E.) (see Acts 18:11–12).

Paul visits Ephesus (c. 52–55 C.E.) and writes 1 Corinthians (c. 54–55 C.E.).

Paul makes a (second?) tour of Macedonia and Greece (Acts 19:1, 10, 22) and writes various parts of 2 Corinthians (and Galatians?).

He makes a third and final visit to Corinth, writes Romans, and plans to revisit Jerusalem and then to stop by Rome en route to Spain (Rom. 15:23–29).

Paul makes a third visit to Jerusalem, where he is arrested and then imprisoned at Caesarea under Antonius Felix (procurator of Judea, c. 52–59 C.E.) and Felix's successor, Porcius Festus.

Under armed guard, Paul is transported to Rome, where he remains under house arrest for two years (c. 60–62 C.E.) (Acts 27–28).

Paul is executed in Rome under Nero (c. 62–64 C.E.).

If the Jerusalem conference took place about 49 C.E. as many historians believe, then Paul must have become a Christian about 32 or (possibly) 34 C.E., shortly after Jesus' crucifixion.

Two allusions to historical figures help us fix other dates in Paul's life. The first is a reference to King Aretas, whose commissioner forced Paul to escape from Damascus by being lowered down the city wall in a basket (2 Cor. 11:32–33). Aretas IV ruled the powerful Arab kingdom of Nabatea (located south and east of Palestine) between about 9 and 39 C.E. Fixing the time of Aretas's reign confirms the assumption that Paul was already an active Christian missionary during the same decade that witnessed Jesus' death.

The second historical reference (Acts 18:11) notes that Gallio was the Roman governor of Greece during the period of Paul's Corinthian visit. Because Gallio's administration took place between about 51 and 53 C.E. and because Paul had been in Corinth for about eighteen months when he was brought before the governor, Paul probably arrived in that city about 49 or 50 C.E. Additional evidence tends to confirm that date. Acts refers to the emperor Claudius's expulsion of Jews from Rome, a decree enacted about 49 C.E. Two Jewish Christians, Aquila and Priscilla, had recently moved from Rome to Corinth when Paul arrived in the city (Acts 18:1–2). Box 13.2 presents a summary of important events in Paul's life.

Box 13.3
Paul's Letters: Authentic, Disputed, and Pseudonymous

Paul's genuine letters, composed between about 50 and 62 C.E., form the oldest surviving Christian literature. In the decades after Paul's death, his influence became so great that different Christian groups apparently competed for the role of authoritative interpreter of his teaching. Following the Hellenistic-Jewish practice of pseudonymity (writing in the name of an honored religious authority of the past, such as Moses or one of the apostles), some Christian authors composed letters in Paul's name, using their understanding of the Pauline heritage to address problems of their own day. Whereas Paul's genuine letters invariably deal with specific problems besetting individual congregations (and presume a relatively informal church structure), pseudonymous letters such as 1 and 2 Timothy and Titus (the pastoral Epistles) typically deal with such issues as maintaining the doctrinal purity of apostolic traditions and presume a much more structured church administration.

LETTERS BY PAUL	LETTERS PROBABLY NOT BY PAUL	LETTERS DEFINITELY NOT BY PAUL
1 Thessalonians (c. 50 C.E.)	2 Thessalonians	Ephesians
1 and 2 Corinthians	Colossians	1 and 2 Timothy
Galatians		Titus
Romans		Hebrews (Even in early Christianity, most churchmen did not believe that Hebrews was by Paul.)
Philemon		
Philippians		

Paul's Letters

THE GENUINE LETTERS

New Testament historians generally agree that Paul became a Christian in the mid-30s C.E. and that he traveled extensively as a missionary during the 40s and 50s C.E., arriving in Rome about the year 60. Scholarly agreement disappears, however, in attempting to date Paul's letters or even establish the exact order in which he wrote them.

The majority of scholars accept seven letters as authentically Pauline. Virtually all scholars regard Romans, 1 and 2 Corinthians, Galatians, Philippians, 1 Thessalonians, and Philemon as Paul's own writing. Some also accept 2 Thessalonians and Colossians. By contrast, the majority doubt that Ephesians is genuine and are certain that three—Titus and 1 and 2 Timothy—were composed by a Pauline disciple after the apostle's death. Almost no reputable scholar believes that Hebrews, which is a sermon rather than a letter, is a Pauline composition (see box 13.3).

THE ORDER OF COMPOSITION

Although scholars debate the exact order in which Paul composed his letters, they generally agree that 1 Thessalonians was written first (about 50 C.E.) and is thus the oldest Christian writing in existence. If Paul also wrote 2 Thessalonians, it also dates from about 50 C.E. 1 and 2 Corinthians are usually placed in the mid-50s, and the more theologically mature letters, such as Romans and Philippians, are dated later. Four letters—Colossians, Philemon, Philippians, and possibly Ephesians—were reputedly composed while Paul was imprisoned and thus are known as the "captivity letters." Unfortunately, Paul does not reveal in the letters where he was jailed, so we do not know whether he wrote them from Ephesus, Caesarea, or Rome, all cities in which he presumably suffered imprisonment. The canonical letters (others have been lost) were probably all written during a relatively brief span of time, the decade between about 50 and 60 C.E.

PAUL'S USE OF THE LETTER FORM

Paul is aware that his letters are persuasive documents. He consciously uses letters as substitutes for his own presence, making them an effective means of influencing people and events from a distance. Although he gives directions on a wide variety of matters, his primary object is to correct his recipients' beliefs and to discipline their behavior. His letters are also potent weapons for shooting down opposition to his teaching.

Writing to the Corinthians, Paul states that his critics contrast his "weighty and powerful" letters with his unimpressive physical appearance and ineffectiveness as a speaker (2 Cor. 10:9–11). The apostle may exaggerate his defects for rhetorical effect, but he is right about his letters. From the time they were first written until now, they have exerted enormous influence on Christian thought and conduct.

Paul writes letters so effectively that he makes this literary category the standard medium of communication for many later Christian writers. The large majority of New Testament authors imitate Paul by conveying their ideas in letter form. Twenty-one of the twenty-seven canonical books are (at least theoretically) letters. Even the writer of Revelation uses this form to transmit Jesus' message to the seven churches of Asia Minor (Rev. 2–3).

HELLENISTIC LETTERS

In general, Paul follows the accepted Hellenistic literary form in his correspondence, modifying it somewhat to express his peculiarly Christian interests. Much Greco-Roman correspondence, both personal and business, has survived from early Christian times, allowing us to compare Paul's letters with those of other Hellenistic writers.

The Hellenistic letter writer typically begins with a prescript, identifying the writer and the reader, and a greeting, wishing good fortune to the reader and commonly invoking the blessing of a god. Paul varies this formula by mentioning the Christian allegiance of the writer and recipients, substituting "grace" and "peace" for the customary greetings, and frequently including an associate's name in the salutation. He also elaborates on the Hellenistic custom by giving praise, thanks, or prayers for the welfare of his recipients. A typical example of Paul's modification of the Hellenistic greeting appears in the opening of 1 Thessalonians:

> From Paul, Silvanus, and Timothy to the congregation of Thessalonians who belong to God the Father and the Lord Jesus Christ. Grace to you and peace. (1 Thess. 1:1)

Paul also modifies his letters' prescripts according to his attitude toward the church he is addressing. Paul's letter to his trusted friends at Philippi opens with an effusive outpouring of affection and praise for the Philippians (Phil. 1:1–11). By contrast, when he writes to the churches in Galatia, he is furious with the recipients and includes no warm or approving salutation (Gal. 1:1–5).

After stating the letter's principal message, the Hellenistic writer closes with additional greetings, typically including greetings from other people and sometimes adding a request that the recipient(s) convey the sender's greetings to mutual acquaintances. Paul often expands this custom to include a summary statement of faith and a benediction, as well as a list of fellow Christians to be greeted (Rom. 16; 1 Cor. 16:10–21; Col. 4:7–18).

THE ROLE OF DICTATION

As was customary in Greco-Roman correspondence, Paul apparently dictated all his letters to a secretary or scribe, occasionally adding a signature or a few other words in his own hand. In antiquity, secretaries ordinarily did not record the precise words of those dictating, but paraphrased the gist of what was said (Rom. 16:21–22; Gal. 6:11; Col. 4:18; Philem. 19; 2 Thess. 3:17), a practice that helps explain the spontaneous quality of Pauline letters.

THE CIRCUMSTANCES OF WRITING

Most of Paul's letters are composed under the pressure of meeting an emergency in a given church.

With the exception of Romans, which is addressed to a congregation that he had not yet visited, every Pauline letter is directed to a particular group, and most of the groups are personally known by the writer. In virtually every case, the recipients are experiencing some form of crisis, either of belief or behavior, which the author tries to resolve.

Paul's main concern is always pastoral; he deals with individual problems caused by church members' teaching or conduct. In counseling these small groups of infant Christians, Paul typically invokes theological arguments or examples to reinforce his advice. Because Paul's presentation of theological issues is secondary to his counseling, the letters do not represent a complete or systematic statement of Pauline belief. In addition, the reader will find Paul's thoughts changing and developing from one letter to another.

Paul's Major Assumptions and Concerns

Pauline thought is commonly subtle and complex, making it difficult even for scholars to achieve a consensus about the apostle's views on many important topics. In studying Paul's letters, it helps to keep in mind several of their author's basic beliefs about his relationship to God, Christ, and the spirit world. Based partly on the experience of divine intervention in his personal life, Paul's assumptions about God's intentions for humanity and the imminent End of history significantly shaped his theological views and motivated his behavior.

1. *Mysticism and eschatology.* Understanding Paul's writings means recognizing his sense of the spiritual power that inspired his apostolic career. Paul bases his authority as a Christian leader and the validity of his distinctive gospel on an *apokalypsis,* a private revelation of the postresurrection Jesus (Gal. 1:11–12, 15–17). This encounter with Christ, which he insists he received as a direct heavenly communication and not from any apostolic predecessor, informs Paul that the glorified Jesus now exists in two separate but related dimensions: the macrocosm (great world) of God's spiritual domain and the microcosm (little world) of human consciousness. This **dualism,** characteristic of apocalyptic thought (see chapter 19), expresses Paul's conviction that Christ possesses both an objective and a subjective reality. Christ is at once a cosmic figure who will soon return to judge the world and a being who also mysteriously dwells within the individual believer. The tension between the transcendent and the imminent Christ, one who is simultaneously universal and yet intimately experienced by the faithful, appears in almost every letter Paul wrote.

Paul's mysticism—his powerful sense of union with an unseen spiritual reality—is an important component of his worldview. In 2 Corinthians, he writes of being "caught up as far as the third heaven," "into paradise," where he "heard words so secret that human lips may not repeat them" (2 Cor. 12:1–4). These "visions and revelations granted by the Lord," which undoubtedly played their part in sustaining Paul through the many dangers and hardships he endured, may not have occurred as often as he would have liked. He adds that to prevent him "from being unduly elated by the magnificence of such revelations," he was given "a sharp physical pain," perhaps to remind him that even sporadic experiences of the infinite could not allow him to escape his finite humanity (2 Cor. 12:7–8).

Paul may have been familiar with the Book of 1 Enoch, which describes **Enoch's** visionary tour of seven (or ten) heavens—or at least tradition surrounding it—for he clearly shares its aspiration for mystical oneness with the divine. Paul also shares Enoch's apocalyptic viewpoint. His conviction that the Messiah's appearance has inaugurated the End of time permeates his thought and underlies much of his ethical teaching. Paul's advice on marriage, divorce, slavery, celibacy, and human behavior in general is largely shaped by his expectation of an imminent Final Judgment. In his oldest surviving letter, he states that he expects to witness the **Parousia:** "We who are left alive until the Lord comes . . . [will be] caught up in the clouds to meet the Lord in the air" (1 Thess. 4:15–17).

In 1 Corinthians, his expectation to live until the End is equally certain; hence, he advises his correspondents that "the time we live in will not last long. While it lasts, married men should be as if they had no wives; . . . buyers must not count on keeping what they buy, nor those who use the world's wealth. . . . For the whole frame of this world is passing away" (1 Cor. 7:29–31). Eagerly anticipating the *eschaton*, he also tells the Corinthians, "Listen! I will unfold a mystery [emphasis added]: we shall not all die, but we shall all be changed in a flash, in the twinkling of an eye, at the last trumpet-call. For the trumpet will sound, and the dead will rise immortal, and we shall be changed" (1 Cor. 15:51–52).

Like many Jewish apocalyptists of the first century, Paul sees human history as divided into two qualitatively different ages, or periods of time. The present evil age will soon be replaced by a New Age, a new creation, in which God will reign completely (Gal. 6:14; 1 Cor. 15; 20–28; 2 Cor. 5:17). Because the Messiah's arrival denotes the final consummation of history, Paul regards his generation as the last. His letters thus burn with special urgency because he believes that his day marks the crucial transition period between the two ages. Those about to be judged, especially members of his infant churches, must therefore prepare for the impending visitation, pursuing lives of unblemished virtue.

2. *The centrality and preeminence of Jesus.* Absolutely central to Paul's thought is his conviction that in Jesus, God accomplishes the world's salvation. Although Paul shows almost no interest in Jesus' earthly ministry or teachings (if he knew them in any detail), he sees the heavenly Christ in three roles: (1) as God's revealed Wisdom (1 Cor. 1–4), (2) as the divine Lord through whom God rules (Phil. 2:11; Rom.10:9; 1 Cor. 15:24–28), and (3) as the means by whom God's Spirit dwells in believers (Rom. 8; 14:17). The operation of the Spirit, God's active force denoting his presence and effecting his will in the world, characterizes all of Paul's churches.

3. *Christ and humanity.* In contrasting Christ with the symbol of earthly humanity, **Adam** (in Genesis, God's first human creation), Paul emphasizes the vast change Jesus' activity has effected for the human race. Prior to Jesus' coming, human beings existed in Adam's perishable image, victims of sin and death (Rom. 5:12–21). By contrast, believers now "in Christ" (living under his power) will also share in the glorified Christ's life-giving nature

(1 Cor. 15:21–24, 45–49). "As in Adam all men die, so in Christ all will be brought to life. . . ."

4. *The faithful as Christ's body.* Using a corporate image to identify the believing community as the earthly manifestation of the exalted Christ, Paul states that the faithful collectively are Christ's "body" (1 Cor. 10:16–18; 12:12–30; Rom. 12). As a people defined and influenced by the Spirit, the church functions in union with Christ so fully that it reveals his visible form.

5. *Christ as liberator from sin, Torah, and death.* In Paul's view, all human beings are negatively influenced by sin's power and hence alienated from the perfect God (Rom. 7). Sin's invariable consequence is death, a condition of the defective humanity we share with Adam (Rom. 5:12–21). By defining the nature as well as the punishment of sin, the Torah increased its power, revealing the universality of sin and condemning all sinners—the entire human race (Rom. 1–3).

Christ's total obedience to the Father and his selfless death on the cross, taking unto himself the Torah's penalty for sin, liberates those persons accepting him (living fully under his power) from sin, death, and the Torah's curses (Gal. 3–5; Rom. 3–7). For Paul, "freedom in Christ" means deliverance from the old order of sin and punishment, including the Torah's power to condemn.

6. *Christ's universal sufficiency.* To Paul, Jesus' sacrificial death and God's act in exalting Christ as the agent by whom God rules and imparts his Spirit constitute a total change in the relationship between God and humanity. Christ is the final and complete means of canceling the powers of sin and destruction. Because Christ is now all-sufficient in reconciling human beings to God, neither "angelic powers" nor the Torah any longer play a decisive role in achieving human salvation.

7. *Justification by faith.* Given his overwhelming sense of Christ's essential role in reconciling imperfect humanity to the perfect God, Paul wrestles with the question of the Deity's previous revelations to Israel—the Torah. In two of his most theologically important letters, Romans and Galatians, he concludes that spiritual union with Christ, who on the cross paid the penalty for human sin, is now God's

sole means of redemption. When believers become one with Christ, they share in the benefits of his sacrifice, receiving divine favor and eternal life, benefits that works of Torah cannot provide. To Paul, one is justified or "made right" before God only through placing faith—complete trust—in Jesus' power to save persons with whom he is spiritually united. (For a more detailed discussion of Paul's ideas about faith in Christ replacing works of Torah, see chapter 15.)

Summary

Reading Paul's Letters. In the New Testament canon, Paul's letters are listed roughly according to their length. Letters to churches, such as Romans, appear first, and those to individuals, such as Philemon, appear last. In this text, we discuss the letters in the general order of their composition, beginning with 1 Thessalonians and concluding with later works like Philippians and Philemon.

A sensitivity to Paul's eschatological hope and his mystical experience of Christ may make it easier for readers to appreciate Paul's ideas. Despite the difficulty of understanding some passages (2 Pet. 3:15–16), the rewards of entering the brilliant world of Pauline thought are well worth the effort.

QUESTIONS FOR REVIEW

1. Summarize Paul's biography, from his career as a zealous Pharisee to his work as a missionary among Gentile populations in Macedonia and Greece. In what respects does the biographical information contained in Acts differ from that found in Paul's letters?

2. How did Paul's experience of a revelation (*apokalypsis*) of the risen Jesus change his life and affect his religious outlook?

QUESTION FOR DISCUSSION AND REFLECTION

1. Discuss some of the topics and themes that dominate Paul's letters, including his apocalyptic outlook and his views on faith, righteousness, justification, and the saving power of Christ.

TERMS AND CONCEPTS TO REMEMBER

Apostle to the Gentiles
apokalypsis (the "revelation" that changed Paul's life)
Paul's use of the letter form

Paul's eschatology
Torah and faith
Christ's role in human redemption
justification by faith

RECOMMENDED READING

Baird, W. R. "Paul." In P. J. Achtemeier, ed., *Harper's Bible Dictionary*, pp. 757–765. San Francisco: Harper & Row, 1985. A basic introduction to Paul's life and thought.

Beker, J. C. *Paul the Apostle: The Triumph of God in Life and Thought.* Philadelphia: Fortress Press, 1980.

Betz, Hans D. "Paul." In D. N. Freedman, ed., *The Anchor Bible Dictionary*, Vol. 5, pp. 186–201. New York: Doubleday, 1992. Surveys Paul's life and theological views.

Bornkamm, Gunther. *Paul.* New York: Harper & Row, 1971. An analysis of Paul's life and thought in the context of his Jewish and Hellenistic environments.

Cousar, Charles B. *The Letters of Paul.* Nashville, Tenn.: Abingdon Press, 1996. Places the letters in their historical and theological context.

Dunn, James D. G. *Unity and Diversity Within the New Testament,* 2nd ed. Philadelphia: Trinity Press International, 1990. A careful study of the many different ways in which Jesus' significance was understood within the various groups that composed the first-century Christian community.

Fitzmyer, Joseph. *Paul and His Theology,* 2nd ed. Englewood Cliffs, N.J.: Prentice-Hall, 1989. A brief but careful introduction to Paul's central teachings.

———. "Paul." In Raymond E. Brown, Joseph A. Fitzmyer, and Roland E. Murphy, eds., *The New Jerome Biblical Commentary*, pp. 1329–1337. Englewood Cliffs, N.J.: Prentice-Hall, 1990. A helpful survey of Paul's contribution to Christian thought by an eminent Roman Catholic scholar.

Holmberg, B. *Paul and Power.* Philadelphia: Fortress Press, 1980. An incisive study of the social forces at work in the Pauline communities and of Paul's difficult relationships with other apostolic leaders.

Jewett, Robert. *A Chronology of Paul's Life.* Philadelphia: Fortress Press, 1979. Evaluates earlier systems of dating events in Paul's career and provides a new chronology.

Murphy-O'Connor, Jerome. *Paul: A Critical Life.* New York: Clarendon, 1996. Explores psychological motivation for Paul's persecution of Christians, his Pharisaic background, and his missionary tours.

Neyrey, Jerome H. *Paul, in Other Words: A Cultural Reading of His Letters.* Louisville, Ky.: Westminster Press/John Knox Press, 1990. An analysis of Paul's writings to discover the underlying cultural and social assumptions on which Paul bases his worldview and theology.

Sanders, E. P. *Paul, the Law, and the Jewish People.* Philadelphia: Fortress Press, 1983. An excellent exploration of Paul's Jewish heritage.

Segal, Alan F. *Paul the Convert: The Apostolate and Apostasy of Saul the Pharisee.* New Haven, Conn., and London: Yale University Press, 1990. Examines Paul's views of the Christ event in the light of his Jewish heritage.

Soards, Marion L. *The Apostle Paul: An Introduction to His Writings and Teaching.* Mahwah, N.J.: Paulist Press, 1987. A clearly written introduction to Paul's thought, emphasizing his eschatology.

Theissen, Gerd. *The Social Setting of Pauline Christianity.* Philadelphia: Fortress Press, 1982. A study of the social dynamics operating in the church at Corinth; one of the most illuminating studies of primitive Christianity.

CHAPTER 14

Unity, Freedom, and Christ's Return

Paul's Letters to Thessalonica and Corinth

The time we live in will not last long. . . . For the whole frame of this world is passing away.   1 Corinthians 7:29, 31

Key Themes The dominant theme of Paul's letters to Thessalonica and Corinth is that the *eschaton* is near: Paul expects to witness Jesus' return and the resurrection of the dead in his lifetime (1 Thess. 4:13–18). However, believers must not waste time speculating about the projected date of the Parousia (1 Thess. 5:1–3).

Paul's letters to Corinth are aimed at healing serious divisions in the newly founded church there. Paul urges members to give up their destructive competitiveness and work toward unity of belief and purpose. His most important topics include (1) differences between human and divinely revealed wisdom (1:10–3:23), (2) Christian ethics and responsibilities (5:1–11:1), (3) behavior at the Communion meal (11:17–34) and the handling of gifts of the Spirit (chs. 12–14), and (4) the resurrection of the dead (ch. 15).

A composite work composed of several letters or letter fragments, 2 Corinthians shows Paul defending his apostolic authority (2 Cor. 10–13); chapters 1–9, apparently written after chapters 10–13, describe his reconciliation with the church at Corinth.

Paul's early letters are dominated by his eschatology. Convinced that the Messiah's death and resurrection have inaugurated End time, Paul strives to achieve several related goals. Traveling from city to city, he establishes small cells of believers whom he calls to a "new life in Christ." He argues that Jesus' crucifixion has brought freedom from both Torah observance and the power of sin, and he stresses the necessity of leading an ethically pure life while awaiting Christ's return. In his letters to the young Greek churches at Thessalonica and Corinth, Paul emphasizes the nearness of the Parousia—the Second Coming—an event that he believes to be imminent. Much of Paul's advice to these congregations is based on his desire that they achieve unity and purity before Christ reappears.

While he is attempting to keep believers faithful to the high ideals of Christian practice, Paul also finds himself battling opponents who question the correctness of his teaching and/or his apostolic authority. In the first generation of Christians, an apostle was one whom Jesus had personally called to follow him and who had witnessed the Resurrection (Acts 1:21–22). Not only had Paul not known the earthly Jesus, he had cruelly persecuted the disciples. Paul's sole claim to apostolic status was his private revelation of the risen Lord, a claim others repeatedly challenged. To achieve the goal of guiding his

---

FIRST THESSALONIANS

Author: Paul, missionary Apostle to the Gentiles.

Date: About 50 C.E.

Place of Composition: Probably Corinth.

Audience: Mostly Gentile members of a newly founded congregation in Thessalonica, Greece.

---

flock through End time, Paul must ensure that his apostolic credentials are fully recognized (1 Cor. 15:9–10; 2 Cor. 11:1–13:10).

To appreciate the urgency of Paul's first letters, we must approach them from the writer's historical perspective: The Messiah's coming spelled an end to the old world. The New Age—entailing the Final Judgment on all nations, a universal resurrection of the dead, and the ultimate fulfillment of God's purpose—was then in the process of materializing. Paul writes as a parent anxious that those in his care survive the apocalyptic ordeal just ahead and attain the saints' reward of eternal life.

First Letter to the Thessalonians

The oldest surviving Christian document, 1 Thessalonians preserves our earliest glimpse of how the new religion was established in Gentile territory. Capital of the Roman province of Macedonia, Thessalonica (now called Thessaloniki) (see figure 14.1) was a bustling port city located on the Via Egnatia, the major highway linking Rome with the East. According to the Book of Acts, Paul spent only three weeks there, preaching mainly in the local synagogue to generally unreceptive Jews, who soon drove him out of town (17:1–18:5).

Paul's letter to the newly founded Thessalonian congregation, however, gives a different picture, making no reference to a synagogue ministry and implying that his converts were largely Gentile (1 Thess. 1:9). Probably written in Corinth about 50 C.E., a scant twenty years after the Crucifixion, 1 Thessalonians is remarkable in showing how quickly essential Christian ideas had developed and

how thoroughly apocalyptic Paul's message was. Referring to the Parousia in no fewer than six different passages, at least once in each of the letter's five brief chapters, Paul makes the imminence of Jesus' return his central message (1:10; 2:19; 3:13; 4:13–18; 5:1–11).

The Thessalonians, he says, have become a shining example to other Greek churches because they have

> turned from idols to be servants of the true and living God, . . . to wait expectantly for his Son from heaven, whom he raised from the dead, Jesus our deliverer from the retribution to come. (1:10)

This passage may, in fact, epitomize the principal themes of Paul's oral gospel, the *kerygma* he preached in urban marketplaces, shops, and private homes. In general content, it resembles the more elaborate proclamation that Luke placed on Paul's lips when he spoke to the Athenians (Acts 17:22–31). Urging the Greeks to forsake lifeless idols for the "living God" of Judaism, Paul presents Jesus' resurrection from the dead as introducing history's climactic moment: his soon-to-occur descent from heaven to rescue his followers from the catastrophe of divine judgment.

For Paul, the implications of the impending apocalypse are clear: The Thessalonians must reform their typically lenient Gentile attitudes toward sexual activity. They have already made progress in living "to please God," but they can do better, abstaining from "fornication," becoming "holy," living "quietly," and showing love to all (4:1–12).

Although the Thessalonians do not exhibit the kind of opposition Paul describes in letters to the Corinthians and Galatians, he devotes considerable space to self-justification, emphasizing how nurturing, altruistic, and hard-working he was when in their company (2:1–12). In particular, he stresses the fact that he remained financially independent of the people he taught, working "night and day" to be self-supporting (2:9). The passage concluding chapter 2, in which he suddenly departs from praising his healthy relationship with the Thessalonians to castigate his fellow Jews, referring to the "retribution" inflicted on them, may have been inserted

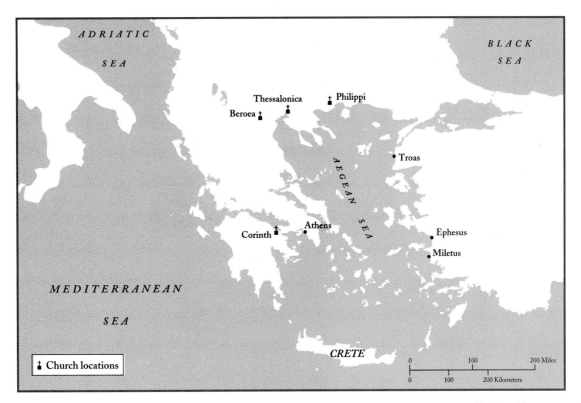

Figure 14.1 Paul established largely Gentile churches in the northeastern Mediterranean region at Philippi, Thessalonica, Beroea, and Corinth. Paul's teaching was also influential in the Asia Minor city of Ephesus, where he lived for at least two years.

by a later copyist after Rome's destruction of Jerusalem in 70 C.E. (2:13–16).

THE PAROUSIA AND THE RESURRECTION

After the long introductory section (1:1–4:12), Paul arrives at his principal reason for sending the letter—a clarification of his teaching about End time (4:13–5:11). Christians must cling firmly to their newfound faith and live ethically correct lives because Jesus will soon return to judge them. Apparently, some Thessalonians believed that the Parousia would occur so swiftly that all persons converted to Christ would live to see his Second Coming. That belief was shaken when some believers died before Jesus had reappeared. What would

become of them? Had the dead missed their opportunity to join Christ in ruling over the world?

Paul explains that the recently dead are not lost, but will share in the glory of Christ's return. Revealing his conviction that he would personally witness the Parousia, Paul states that "we who are left alive until the Lord comes" will have no advantage over the faithful dead. Using the traditional language of Jewish apocalyptic writing, Paul writes that when the trumpet call of Final Judgment sounds, the Christian dead will rise first. Simultaneously, Christians who are still alive—Paul and his fellow believers—will be lifted from earth into the air to join the resurrected saints on their journey to heaven. In both life and death, then, the believer remains with Jesus (4:13–18). (Compare 1 Thess.

with Paul's more elaborate discussion of the resurrection in 1 Cor. 15.)

ON NOT CALCULATING "DATES AND TIMES"

Although he eagerly expects Jesus' reappearance "soon," Paul has no patience with those who try to predict the exact date of the Parousia. He discourages speculation and notes that calculating "dates and times" is futile because the world's final day will come as quietly as a thief at midnight. Stressing the unexpectedness of the Parousia, Paul declares that it will occur while men proclaim "peace and security" (a common political theme in Roman times as well as the present). Disaster will strike the nations suddenly, as labor pains strike a woman without warning (5:1–3).

In the Hebrew Bible, the "Day of the Lord" was the time of Yahweh's intervention into human history, his visitation of earth to judge all nations and to impose his universal rule (Amos 5:18; Joel 2:14–15). In Paul's apocalyptic vision, Jesus serves as the divinely appointed agent of *eschaton*. As the eschatological Judge, Jesus serves a double function: He brings punishment to the disobedient ("the terrors of judgment") but vindication and deliverance to the faithful. Paul's cosmic Jesus is paradoxical: He dies to save believers from the negative judgment that his return imposes on unregenerate humanity. Returning to his main theme, Paul concludes that "we, awake [living] or asleep [dead]" live in permanent association with Christ (5:4–11).

ROLE OF THE SPIRIT

With anticipation of Jesus' speedy return a living reality, Paul reminds the Thessalonians that the Holy Spirit's visible activity among them is also evidence of the world's impending transformation. As noted in Acts, the Spirit motivating a believer to prophesy, heal, or speak in tongues was taken as evidence of the Deity's presence. Thus, Paul tells his readers not to "stifle inspiration" or otherwise discourage believers from prophesying. Christian prophets, inspired by the Spirit, play a major role in Pauline churches, but Paul is aware that enthusiastic visionaries can cause trouble. Believers are to

---

> **FIRST CORINTHIANS**
>
> **Author:** Paul.
> **Date:** Early 50s C.E.
> **Place of Composition:** Ephesus.
> **Audience:** Members of the newly established church at Corinth, Greece.

---

distinguish between "good" and "bad" inspirations, avoiding the latter, but they are not to inhibit charismatic behavior. Besides providing evidence that the End is near, the Spirit's presence also validates the Christian message (Joel 2:28–32; Acts 2:1–21; 1 Cor. 2:9–16; 12–14).

(A disputed letter, 2 Thessalonians, is discussed in chapter 17.)

First Letter to the Corinthians

According to Acts (17:1–18:17), after establishing churches at Philippi, Thessalonica, and Beroea (all in northern Greece), Paul briefly visited Athens and then journeyed to Corinth, where he remained for a year and a half (about 50–52 C.E.). Accompanied by Priscilla and Aquila, Jewish Christians exiled from Rome, he subsequently sailed to Ephesus, from which city he addressed several letters to the Corinthians. The first letter has been lost (1 Cor. 5:9), but the books presently numbered 1 and 2 Corinthians embody the most voluminous correspondence with any single church group in the New Testament. Whereas 1 Corinthians is a single document, scholars believe that 2 Corinthians is a patchwork of several Pauline letters or parts of letters written at different times and later combined by an editor.

Paul's correspondence with the Corinthian church was not a one-way affair, for the Corinthians also wrote to the apostle (1 Cor. 7:1). Delegations from Corinth also kept Paul in touch with the group (1:11; 16:15–18; 2 Cor. 7:5–7, 13). Preserving a comprehensive picture of the diversity of ideas and behavior of a youthful Jewish and Gentile

Figure 14.2 In this portrait uncovered at Pompeii (buried by the eruption of Mount Vesuvius in 79 C.E.), Terentius Neo and his wife proudly display the pen and wax tablets that advertise their literary skills. Similar young Roman couples of the professional classes undoubtedly were among the members of Paul's newly founded churches in Corinth and other Greco-Roman cities. (© Erich Lessing/PhotoEdit)

church, the Corinthian letters give us an unrivaled sociological study of primitive Christianity.

THE CITY AND ITS PEOPLE

The emperor Augustus made Corinth, the richest and most populous city in Greece, the Greek capital in 27 B.C.E. By Paul's day, Corinth had long been famous for its prosperity, trade, and materialism. As a busy seaport, it was also notorious for its legions of prostitutes, who entertained sailors from every part of the Greco-Roman world. With Aphrodite—supreme goddess of love and fertility—as its patron deity, Corinth enjoyed a reputation for luxury and licentiousness remarkable even in pagan society. Given this libertine environment, it is not surprising that Paul devotes more space to setting forth principles of sexual ethics to the Corinthians than he does in letters to any other churches (1 Cor. 5:1–13; 7:1–40).

Recent sociological studies of early Christianity indicate that the Corinthian group may have been typical of Gentile churches in many parts of the Roman Empire. In the past, many historians thought that the first Christians largely belonged to the lower social and economic ranks of Greco-Roman society. Recent analyses of Paul's Corinthian letters, however, suggest that early Christians came from many different social classes and represented a veritable cross-section of the Hellenistic world.

Paul's statement that "few" members of the Corinthian congregation were highborn, wealthy, or politically influential (1 Cor. 1:26–28) implies that some were. This inference is borne out by the fact that some Corinthian believers apparently held important positions in the city (see figure 14.2). Acts identifies the Crispus whom Paul baptized (1 Cor. 1:14) as the leader of a local synagogue, a function ordinarily given to persons rich enough to maintain the building. Erastus, who also seems to have belonged to the Corinthian church, was the civic treasurer (Rom. 16:23).

A diverse assortment of Jews and Gentiles, slaves and landowners, rich and poor, educated and unlettered, the Corinthian group was apparently divided by class distinctions and educational differences as well as by varieties of religious belief. Even in observing the Communion ritual, members' consciousness of differences in wealth and social status threatened to splinter the membership (1 Cor. 11:17–34).

From Paul's responses to their attitudes and conduct, the reader learns that the Corinthians individually promoted a wide range of ideas. Some advocated a spiritual marriage in which sexual union played no part; others visited prostitutes. Some defrauded their fellow believers, causing victims to seek restitution in the public courts. Some, believing that other gods did not exist, dined at banquets in Greco-Roman temples and attended their religious ceremonies. Still others claimed a superior understanding of spiritual matters, viewed themselves as already living in the kingdom, denied the necessity of a bodily resurrection, or questioned Paul's right to dictate their behavior.

As the Corinthian correspondence shows, Paul faced the almost impossible challenge of bringing this divisive and quarrelsome group into a working harmony of belief and purpose. In reading Paul's letters to Corinth, remember that he is struggling to communicate his vision of union with Christ to an infant church that has apparently only begun to grasp the basic principles of Christian life.

TOPICS OF CONCERN

Paul's first extant letter to the group is distinguished by some of his most memorable writing. Two passages in particular, chapter 13 (on love) and chapter 15 (on resurrection), are highlights of Pauline thought and feeling. His praise of love (ch. 13) uses the Greek term *agapē*, "selfless love," as opposed to *eros*, the word denoting the sexual passion associated with Aphrodite. This may be an appropriate hint to those Corinthians sexually involved with persons other than their legal mates. Paul's mystic vision of attaining immortality (ch. 15) is the most extensive commentary on life after death in the New Testament. It also contains the earliest record of Jesus' postresurrection appearances.

Organization   1 Corinthians divides into two main sections. In the first six chapters, Paul directly addresses his principal objective—helping the church, split by rivalries and factions, attain the unity befit-

ting a Christian congregation. Here, Paul shows the futility of false wisdom and human competitiveness and of attempts to demonstrate Christian freedom by violating the sexual conventions honored even by unbelievers. In the second half (chs. 7–15), he answers specific questions addressed to him by the Corinthians. These issues include marriage and divorce, the consumption of meat previously sacrificed to Greco-Roman gods, proper conduct during the **Lord's Supper,** and eschatology—the Final Judgment and resurrection of the dead.

Paul's Eschatological Urgency   As in his letters to the Thessalonians, Paul structures his advice to the Corinthian church according to his eschatological convictions. The Parousia is imminent: The Corinthians "wait expectantly for our Lord Jesus to reveal himself," for he will keep them "firm to the end . . . on the Day of our Lord Jesus" (1:7–8). Like the Thessalonians, the recipients of Paul's Corinthian letters expect to experience the **Day of Judgment** soon, a belief that affects their entire way of life. Paul advises single people to remain unmarried; neither slaves nor free citizens are to change their status because "the time we live in will not last long." All emotions—sorrow and joy—are only temporary, as are ordinary human pursuits. "Buyers must not count on keeping what they buy," because "the whole frame of this world is passing away" (7:29–31). Paul speaks here not of the philosopher's conventional wisdom—that the wise person shuns life's petty goals to pursue the superior values of eternity—but of the *eschaton*, the End of all the familiar world.

In anticipating the coming resurrection, Paul echoes his words in 1 Thessalonians 4: When judgment's trumpet sounds, "we [Christians then living] shall not all die, but we shall all be changed in a flash, in the twinkling of an eye" (15:51–55). Such passages reveal that Paul, along with his contemporaries, expects to be alive when Christ returns to raise the dead.

THE NECESSITY OF CHRISTIAN UNITY

Paul's first objective is to halt the rivalries that divide the Corinthians. Without imposing a dogmatic conformity, he asks his readers to work together cooperatively for their mutual benefit (1:8–10). Like all early Christian congregations, that at Corinth met in a private house large enough to accommodate the entire group. Although the membership was small, numbering perhaps 50 or 100 persons, it was broken into several opposing cliques. Some members placed undue importance on the particular leader who had converted or baptized them and competed with one another over the prestige of their respective mentors.

Avoiding Competitiveness and Cultivating Divine Wisdom A more serious cause of division may have sprung from the members' unequal social and educational backgrounds. As in any group, modern or ancient, some individuals believed they were demonstrably superior to their neighbors. Examining chapter 1 carefully, the reader will see that Paul's attack on false "wisdom" is really an attempt to discourage human competitiveness. In Paul's view, all believers are fundamentally equal: "For through faith you are all [children] of God in union with Christ Jesus. . . . There is no such thing as Jew and Greek, slave and freeman, male and female; for you are all one person in Christ Jesus" (Gal. 3:26, 28). This assumption underlies Paul's method of presenting the *kerygma*—the proclamation about Jesus. When he reminds the Corinthians that he taught them the message as simply as possible, he does so to show that the new faith is essentially incompatible with individual pride or competitiveness.

Paul's concurrent theme is that human "weakness" is the unexpected medium through which God reveals his strength. In contrast to the Roman soldiers who crucified him, Christ was weak. Paul is also weak in refusing to use the rhetorical embellishments with which Hellenistic teachers were expected to present their ideas. Thus, with almost brutal directness, he proclaims "Christ nailed to the cross" (1 Cor. 1:23 and 2:1). (Paul's relative lack of success debating philosophers in Athens just before coming to Corinth [Acts 17] may have influenced his decision to preach henceforth without any intellectual pretensions.)

Paul's weak and "foolish" proclamation of a crucified Messiah offends almost everyone. It is a major obstacle to Jews (who look for a victorious conqueror, not an executed criminal) and an absurdity to the Greeks (who seek rational explanations of the universe). To the believer, however, the paradox of a crucified Messiah represents God's omnipotent wisdom (1:22–24).

Paul's argument (1:17–2:5) is sometimes misused to justify an anti-intellectual approach to religion, in which reason and faith are treated as if they were mutually exclusive. The apostle's attack on "worldly wisdom" is not directed against human reason, however. It is aimed at individual Corinthians who boasted of special insights that gave them a "deeper" understanding than that granted their fellow Christians. Such elitism led some persons to cultivate a false sense of superiority that devalued less educated believers, fragmenting the congregation into groups of the "wise" and the "foolish."

Paul seeks to place all believers on an equal footing and allow them no cause for intellectual competition. He reminds the Corinthians that human reason by itself did not succeed in knowing God, but that God revealed his saving purpose through Christ as a free gift (1:21). No one merits or earns the Christian revelation, which comes through God's unforeseen grace, not through human effort. Because all are equally recipients of the divine benefits, no believer has the right to boast (1:21–31).

Paul does, however, teach a previously hidden wisdom to persons mature enough to appreciate it. This wisdom is God's revelation through the Spirit that now dwells in the Christian community. The hitherto unknown "mind" of God—the ultimate reality that philosophers make the object of their search—is unveiled through Christ (2:6–16). The divine mystery, although inaccessible to rational inquiry, is finally made clear in the weakness and obedient suffering of Christ, the means by which God reconciles humanity to himself.

The Limits of Christian Freedom Paul's doctrine of freedom from Torah restraints is easily abused by those who interpret it as an excuse to ignore all ethical principles. As a result of some Corinthians' misuse of Christian freedom, Paul finds it necessary to impose limits on believers' individual liberty. Exercising his apostolic authority, Paul orders the Corinthians to excommunicate a Christian living openly with his stepmother. Apparently, the

Corinthian church was proud of the man's bold use of freedom to live as he liked, though his incest scandalized even Greek society. Directing the congregation to evict the sinner from their midst, Paul establishes a policy that later becomes a powerful means of church control over individual members. In excommunication, the offender is denied all fellowship in the believing community and is left bereft of God as well. Although consigned "to Satan" (the devil-ruled world outside the church), the outcast remains a Christian destined for ultimate salvation on the Lord's Day (5:1–13).

Lawsuits Among Christians   Claiming freedom "to do anything," some Corinthians bring lawsuits against fellow Christians in civil courts, allowing the unbelieving public to witness the internal divisions and ill will existing in the church. Paul orders that such disputes be settled within the Christian community. He also commands men who frequent prostitutes to end this practice. Answering the Corinthians' claim that physical appetites can be satisfied without damaging faith, Paul argues that Christians' bodies are temples of the Holy Spirit and must not be defiled by intercourse with prostitutes (6:1–20).

ANSWERING QUESTIONS FROM THE CONGREGATION

Marriage, Divorce, and Celibacy   In chapters 7–15, Paul responds to a letter from the Corinthians, answering their questions on several crucial topics. The first item concerns human sexuality (7:1–40), a subject in which the writer takes a distant but practical interest. Paul clearly prefers a single life without any kind of sexual involvement. Notice that he begins this section by declaring that "it is a good thing for a man to have nothing to do with women," and he closes by observing that women whose husbands have died are "better off" if they do not remarry. In both these statements, Paul may be quoting some Corinthians who boasted of their superior self-control. Although he does not find marriage personally attractive, he is far from forbidding others to marry (7:2–9). He also stresses the mutual obligations of marriage,

stating that husbands and wives are equally entitled to each other's sexual love. Note, however, that he pragmatically describes marriage as an inevitably painful experience that can interfere with a believer's religious commitment (7:28, 32–34).

Paul's general principle is for everyone to remain in whatever state—single or married, slave or free—that the believer was in when first converted. Although aware of Jesus' command forbidding divorce, he concedes that a legal separation is acceptable when a non-Christian wishes to leave his or her Christian mate (7:10–24).

It is important to remember that Paul's advice, particularly on celibacy, is presented in the context of an imminent Parousia. The unmarried remain free "to wait upon the Lord without distraction." Freedom from sexual ties that bind one to the world is eminently practical because "the time we live in will not last long" (7:25–35). Paul regards singleness not as the prerequisite to a higher spiritual state, but as a practical response to the eschatological crisis.

A Problem of Conscience   In the next long section (8:1–11:1), Paul discusses a problem that ceased to be an issue over 1500 years ago—eating meat that had previously been sacrificed in Greco-Roman temples. (The meat was then commonly sold in meat markets or cooked and served in public dining halls, some of which the Corinthian Christians frequented.) Although the social conditions that created the issue have long since disappeared, the principle that Paul articulates in this matter remains relevant to many believers.

Paul argues that although Christians are completely free to do as they wish when their consciences are clear, they should remember that their behavior can be misinterpreted by other believers who do not think as they do. Some may interpret such actions as eating meat that had been given to "idols" as violating religious purity. Paul rules in favor of the "weak" who have trouble distinguishing between abstract convictions and visible practice. Respecting a fellow Christian's sensitive conscience, the mature believer will forfeit his or her right to eat sacrificed meat— or, presumably, to engage in any other action that troubles the "weak" (8:1–13; 10:23–11:1).

Notice that Paul interrupts his argument to insert a vigorous defense of his apostolic authority (9:1–27) and give examples of ways in which he has sacrificed his personal freedoms to benefit others. The rights Paul has voluntarily given up suggest some significant differences between his style of life and that practiced by leaders of the Jerusalem church. Unlike Peter, Jesus' brothers, and the other apostles, he forfeits the privilege of taking a wife or accepting money for his missionary services. He even sacrifices his own inclinations and individuality, becoming "everything in turn to men of every sort" to save them. Paul asks the "strong" Corinthians to imitate his selfless example (9:3–23; 10:33–11:1).

Paul's demand to live largely for other people's benefit and to accommodate one's conduct to others' consciences raises important issues. Some commentators observe that although Paul's argument protects the sensibilities of believers who are less free-thinking, it places the intellectually aware Christian at the mercy of the overscrupulous or the literal-minded believers. Followed explicitly, the apostle's counsel here seriously compromises his doctrine of Christian freedom.

REGULATING BEHAVIOR IN CHURCH

Chapters 11–14 contain Paul's advice regulating behavior in church. The issues he addresses include the participation of women, conduct during reenactments of the Last Supper, and the handling of charismatic "gifts," such as the Spirit-given ability to prophesy, heal, or speak in tongues.

The Importance of Women in the Church   In recent decades, Pauline regulations about women's roles in the church have been attacked as culture-bound and chauvinistic. Because we know so little of very early Christian practice, it is difficult to establish to what degree women originally shared in church leadership. Jesus numbered many women among his most loyal disciples, and Paul refers to several women as his "fellow workers" (Phil. 4:3). In the last chapter of Romans, in which Paul lists the missionary Prisca (Priscilla) ahead of her husband, Aquila, the apostle asks the recipients to support **Phoebe,** a presiding officer in the Cenchreae church, in discharging her administrative duties (Rom. 16:1–6).

In Corinthians, however, Paul seems to impose certain restrictions on women's participation in church services. His insistence that women cover their heads with veils (11:3–16) is open to a variety of interpretations. Is it the writer's concession to the existing Jewish and Greco-Roman custom of secluding women, an attempt to avoid offending patriarchal prejudices? If women unveil their physical attractiveness, does this distract male onlookers or even sexually tempt angels, such as those who "lusted" for mortal women before the Flood (Gen. 6:1–4)? Conversely, is the veil a symbol of women's religious authority, to be worn when prophesying before the congregation?

Paul's argument for relegating women to a subordinate position in church strikes many readers as labored and illogical. (Some scholars think that this passage [11:2–16] is the interpolation of a later editor, added to make Corinthians agree with the non-Pauline instruction in 1 Tim. 2:8–15.) Paul grants women an active role, praying and prophesying during worship, but at the same time he argues that the female is a secondary creation, made from man, who was created directly by God. The apostle uses the second version of human origins (Gen. 2) to support his view of a human sexual hierarchy, but he could as easily have cited the first creation account in which male and female are created simultaneously, both in the "image of God" (Gen. 1:27). Given Paul's revelation that Christian equality transcends all distinctions among believers, including those of sex, class, and nationality (Gal. 3:28), many commentators see the writer's choice in a Genesis precedent as decidedly arbitrary.

The Communion Meal (the Lord's Supper, or Eucharist)   Christianity's most solemn ritual, the reenactment of Jesus' last meal with his disciples, represents the mystic communion between the Lord and his followers. Meeting in a private home to commemorate the event, the Corinthians had turned the service into a riotous drinking party. Instead of a celebration of Christian unity, it had become another source of division. Wealthy participants came early and consumed all the delicacies of the Communion meal before the working poor arrived, thus relegating their social inferiors to hunger and public embarrassment (11:17–22).

Paul contrasts this misbehavior with the tradition coming directly from Jesus himself. Recording Jesus' sacramental distribution of bread and wine, he stresses that the ceremony is to be decorously repeated in memory of Christ's death until he returns. This allusion to the nearness of Jesus' reappearance reminds the Corinthians of the seriousness with which they must observe the Last Supper ceremony (11:23–34).

Regulating Gifts of the Spirit   Led by the Holy Spirit, the early Christian community was composed of many persons gifted with supernatural abilities. Some had the gift of prophecy; others were apostles, teachers, healers, miracle workers, or speakers in tongues. In Corinth, such individual gifts and rivalries among those possessing them were yet another cause of division. Reminding them that one indivisible Spirit grants all these different abilities, Paul employs a favorite metaphor in which he compares the church to the human body, with its many differently functioning parts. Each Christian gift is to be used to benefit the whole body, the church.

The Hymn to Love (Agapē)   In his most celebrated burst of inspiration, Paul interrupts his advice on the use of spiritual gifts to show the Corinthians "the best way of all" (13:1–13). Listing the most highly honored charismatic gifts—prophecy, knowledge, power, and self-sacrifice—Paul states that "without love" these gifts are meaningless. His description of love (in Greek, *agapē*, meaning "selfless giving") stresses its human application: Love is patient, kind, forgiving; it keeps no record of offenses. Its capacity for loyal devotion is infinite: "there is no limit to its faith, its hope, and its endurance." Love once given is never withdrawn. Whereas other spiritual gifts are only partial reflections of the divine reality and will be rendered obsolete in the perfect world to come, the supreme trio of Christian virtues—faith, hope, and love—endures forever.

Speaking in Tongues (Glossolalia)   Although he gives love top priority, Paul also acknowledges the value of other spiritual gifts, especially prophecy, which involves rational communication. "Ecstatic utterance"—speaking in tongues, or glossolalia—may be emotionally satisfying to the speaker, but it does not "build up" the congregation as do teaching and prophecy. Although he does not prohibit ecstatic utterance (Paul states that he is better at it than any Corinthian), the apostle ranks it as the least useful spiritual gift (14:1–40).

THE ESCHATOLOGICAL HOPE: RESURRECTION OF THE DEAD

Paul's last major topic—his eschatological vision of the resurrection (15:1–57)—is theologically the most important. It appears that some Corinthians challenged Paul's teaching about the afterlife. One group may have questioned the necessity of a future bodily resurrection because they believed that at baptism (and upon receiving the Spirit), they had already achieved eternal life. Others may have denied Paul's concept of resurrection because they shared the Greek philosophical view that a future existence is purely spiritual. According to Socrates, Plato, and numerous mystery religions, death occurs when the immortal soul escapes from the perishable body. The soul does not need a body when it enters the invisible spirit realm. To believers in the soul's inherent immortality, Paul's Hebrew belief in the physical body's resurrection was grotesque and irrelevant.

The Historical Reality of Jesus' Resurrection   To demonstrate that bodily resurrection is a reality, Paul calls on the Corinthians to remember that Jesus rose from the dead. Preserving our earliest tradition of Jesus' postresurrection appearances, Paul notes that the risen Lord appeared to as many as 500 believers at once, as well as to Paul (15:3–8). Paul uses his opponents' denial against them and argues that if there is no resurrection, then Christ was not raised and the Christian hope is vain. He trusts not in the Greek concept of innate human immortality, but in the Judeo-Christian faith in

God's ability to raise the faithful dead. Without Christ's resurrection, Paul states, there is no afterlife, and of all people Christians are most pitiable (15:12–19).

Paul now invokes two archetypal figures to illustrate the means by which human death and its opposite, eternal life, entered the world. Citing the Genesis creation account, Paul declares that the "first man," Adam (God's first earthly son), brought death to the human race, but Christ (Adam's "heavenly" counterpart, a new creation) brings life. The coming resurrection (perhaps salvation as well) is universal: "as in Adam all men die, so in Christ all will be brought to life." The first product of the resurrection harvest, Christ will return to raise the obedient dead and defeat all enemies, including death itself. Christ subjects the entire universe to his rule but himself remains subordinate to God, so that God is "all in all" (15:20–28). Noting that the Corinthians practice baptism of their dead (posthumously initiating them into the church), Paul argues that this ritual presupposes the resurrection's reality (15:29).

Paul next responds to the skeptics' demand to know what possible form bodily resurrection might take. Although he admits that "flesh and blood can never possess the [immaterial] kingdom of God," Paul retains his Hebraic conviction that human beings cannot exist without some kind of body. First, he uses analogies from the natural world, demonstrating that life grows from buried seeds and that existence takes different forms. As heavenly bodies surpass earthly objects in beauty, so the resurrection body will outshine the physical body: "Sown [dead and buried] . . . as a perishable thing [it] is raised imperishable." Paul describes here a supernatural transformation of the human essence, a process that creates a paradox, a contradiction in terms — a material body that is also spirit (15:35–44).

Paul gives his exposition immediacy by unveiling a divine mystery: When the last trumpet sounds, he and other living Christians will be instantly transformed and clothed with an imperishable, immortal existence. In the universal restoration, death itself will perish, consumed in Christ's life-giving victory (15:51–57).

SECOND CORINTHIANS

Author: Paul.

Date: Mid 50s C.E.

Place of Composition: The "severe letter" was probably sent from Ephesus, and the letter of reconciliation from Macedonia.

Audience: The congregation at Corinth, Greece.

Closing Remarks Returning abruptly from his cosmic vision of human destiny to take up earthly affairs again, Paul reminds the Corinthians of their previous agreement to help the Jerusalem church. They are to contribute money every Sunday, an obligation Paul had assumed when visiting the Jerusalem leadership (Gal. 2). The letter ends with Paul's invocation of Jesus' speedy return — "*Marana tha*" ("Come, O Lord") — an Aramaic prayer dating from the first generation of Palestinian Christians.

Second Letter to the Corinthians

Whereas 1 Corinthians is a unified document, 2 Corinthians seems to be a compendium of several letters or letter fragments written at different times and reflecting radically different situations in the Corinthian church. Even casual readers will note the contrast between the harsh, sarcastic tone of chapters 10–13 and the generally friendlier, more conciliatory tone of the earlier chapters. In the opinion of many scholars, chapters 10–13 represent the "painful letter" alluded to in 2 Corinthians 2:3–4, making this part necessarily older than chapters 1–9. Some authorities find as many as six or more remnants of different letters in 2 Corinthians, but for this discussion we concentrate on the work's two main divisions (chs. 10–13 and 1–9), taking them in the order in which scholars believe they were composed.

Behind the writing of 2 Corinthians lies a dramatic conflict between Paul and the church he had founded. After he had dispatched 1 Corinthians, several events took place that strained his relationship with the church almost to the breaking point. New opponents, whom Paul satirizes as "superlative apostles" (11:5), infiltrated the congregation and rapidly gained positions of influence. Paul then made a brief, "painful" visit to Corinth, only to suffer a public humiliation there (2:1–5; 7:12). His visit a failure, he returned to Ephesus, where he wrote the Corinthians a severe reprimand, part of which is preserved in chapters 10–13. Having carried the severe letter to Corinth, Titus then rejoins Paul in Macedonia, bringing the good news that the Corinthians are sorry for their behavior and now support the apostle (7:5–7). Paul subsequently writes a joyful letter of reconciliation, included in chapters 1–9. Although this reconstruction of events is speculative, it accounts for the sequence of alienation, hostility, and reconciliation found in this composite document.

THE "SEVERE" LETTER: PAUL'S DEFENSE OF HIS APOSTOLIC AUTHORITY

In the last three chapters of 2 Corinthians, Paul writes a passionate, almost brutal defense of his apostolic authority. A masterpiece of savage irony, chapters 10–13 show Paul boasting "as a fool," using every device of rhetoric to demolish his opponents' pretensions to superiority. We don't know the precise identity of these opponents, except that they were Jewish Christians whom Paul accuses of proclaiming "another Jesus" and imparting a "spirit" different from that introduced by his "gospel." The label "superlative apostles" suggests that these critics enjoyed considerable authority, perhaps as representatives from the Jerusalem church.

Whoever they were, the "superlative apostles" had succeeded in undermining many Corinthians' trust in Paul's individual teaching and personal integrity. Pointing to Paul's refusal to accept payment for his apostolic services (perhaps implying that he knew he was not entitled to it), his critics seriously questioned his credentials as a Christian leader. When he fights back, Paul is defending both himself (hence the many autobiographical references) and the truth of the gospel he proclaims. In some passages, Paul sounds almost desperately afraid that

the church for which he has labored so hard will be lost to him.

Although Paul's bitter sarcasm may offend some readers, we must realize that this unattractive quality is the reverse side of his intense emotional commitment to the Corinthians' welfare. Behind the writer's "bragging" and threats (10:2–6; 11:16–21; 13:3, 10) lies the sting of unrequited affection. The nature of love that Paul had so confidently defined in his earlier letter (1 Cor. 13) is now profoundly tested.

The Nature of Apostleship and the Christian Ministry Whereas in 1 Corinthians Paul deals with ethical and doctrinal issues, in 2 Corinthians he struggles to define the qualities and motives that distinguish the Christian ministry. His main purpose in boasting "as a fool" (11:1–12:13) is to demonstrate that true apostleship does not depend on external qualities like race or circumcision or the strength to browbeat other believers. Paradoxically, it depends on the leader's "weakness"—his complete dependence on God, who empowers him to endure all kinds of hardship to proclaim the saving message. Outwardly "weak" but inwardly strong, Paul willingly suffers dangers, discomforts, humiliations, and unceasing toil—daily proof of selfless devotion—for the sake of a church that now openly doubts his motives (11:16–33).

It is not certain that the "superlative apostles" (11:5) are the same opponents as the "sham apostles" (11:13) whom Paul accuses of being Satan's agents (11:12–15). Whatever their identity, they apparently based their authority at least in part on supernatural visions and revelations. Paul responds by telling of a believer, caught up to "the third heaven" (in Jewish belief, the spiritual Eden), who experienced divine secrets too sacred to reveal. Disclosing that the mystic is himself, Paul states that to keep from becoming over-elated by such mystical experiences, he was given a counterbalancing physical defect. This unspecified "thorn in the flesh" ties Paul firmly to his earthly frame and grounds him in the human "weakness" through which God reveals spiritual power (12:1–13; 13:3–4).

Paul implores the Corinthians to reform so that his planned third visit will be a joyous occasion rather than an exercise in harsh discipline. He closes the letter with a final appeal to the congregation to practice unity and "live in peace" (13:1–14).

THE LETTER OF RECONCILIATION

Although scholars discern as many as five separate letter fragments in this section, we discuss chapters 1–9 here as a single document. The opening chapters (1:1–2:13) contrast sharply with the angry defensiveness of chapters 10–13 and show a "happy" writer reconciled to the Corinthians. The unnamed opponent who had publicly humiliated Paul on his second visit has been punished and must now be forgiven (2:5–11). Titus's welcome news that the Corinthians are now on Paul's side (7:5–16) may belong to this section of the letter, misplaced in its present position by a later copyist.

Paul's Real Credentials Despite the reconciliation, the Corinthian church is still troubled by Paul's rivals, whom he denounces as mere "hawkers" (salespersons) of God's word (2:17). Although he is more controlled than in chapters 10–13, his exasperation is still evident when he asks if he must begin all over again proving his apostolic credentials (3:1). Placing the responsibility for recognizing true apostolic leadership squarely on the Corinthians, the writer reminds them that they are his living letters of recommendation. Echoing Jeremiah 31:31, Paul contrasts the Mosaic Covenant—inscribed on stone tablets—with the New Covenant written on human hearts. Inhabited by the Holy Spirit, the Christian reflects God's image with a splendor exceeding that of Moses (3:2–18).

Nurturing a Spiritual Body Paul pursues his theme of the indwelling Spirit and further develops ideas about the future life that he had previously outlined in discussing the resurrection (1 Cor. 15). In the earlier letter, Paul wrote that the believer will become instantly transformed—receive an incorruptible "spiritual body"—at Christ's return. He said nothing about the Christian's state of being or consciousness during the interim period between death and the future resurrection. In the present letter (4:16–5:10), Paul seems to imply that believ-

ers are already developing a spiritual body that will clothe them at the moment of death.

Paul appears to state that God has prepared for each Christian an eternal form, a "heavenly habitation," that endows the bearer with immortality. Yearning to avoid human death, he envisions receiving that heavenly form now, putting it on like a garment over the physical body, "so that our mortal part may be absorbed into life immortal." The presence of the Spirit, he concludes, is visible evidence that God intends this process of spiritual transformation to take place during the present lifetime (5:1–5). United with Christ, the believer thus becomes a new creation (5:11–17).

The spiritual renewal is God's plan for reconciling humankind to himself. As Christ's ambassador, Paul advances the work of reconciliation; his sufferings are an act of love for them (5:18–6:13). Imploring the Corinthians to return his affection, Paul ends his defense of the apostolic purpose with a not-altogether-convincing expression of confidence in their loyalty (7:2–16). (Many scholars believe that 6:14–7:1, which interrupts Paul's flow of thought, either belongs to a separate letter or is a non-Pauline fragment that somehow was interpolated into 2 Corinthians. Because of its striking resemblance to Essene literature, some critics suggest that this passage originated in Qumran.)

Chapters 8 and 9 seem to repeat each other and may once have been separate missives before an editor combined them at the end of Paul's reconciliation letter. Both concern the collections for the Jerusalem church, a duty that had been allowed to lapse during the hostilities between the apostle and his competitors. Highlighting Titus's key role, Paul stresses the generosity of Macedonia's churches, an example the Corinthians are expected to imitate. He reminds prospective donors that "God loves a cheerful giver" (9:7).

Summary

Paul's letters to the young Greek churches at Thessalonica and Corinth reveal that the first Christians held widely diverging opinions about the content and practice of their new religion. In 1 Thessalonians, Paul battles to correct misconceptions about the fate of believers who die before the Parousia. In 1 Corinthians, he urges the congregation to overcome rivalries and unite as a single body for the spiritual welfare of all believers. The passionate arguments with which Paul defends his right to lead and teach his churches (especially 2 Cor. 10–13) are reminders that God operates through human instruments who, like Paul, are "weak" and dependent on divine power. The key to understanding the urgency of Paul's plea for unity in belief and behavior is his assumption that his generation stands at the turning point between two ages. The history of Evil is nearly finished; Christ will soon return to establish the New Age, in which God rules all.

QUESTIONS FOR REVIEW

1. Which passages in 1 Thessalonians and 1 Corinthians indicate that Paul believed the End to be very near?

2. When Paul advises believers about choosing between marriage and a single life, to what extent does his expectation that ordinary history will soon end affect his counsel? What eschatological assumptions underlie his view of the world?

3. What kinds of wisdom does Paul discuss in 1 Corinthians 1–3?

4. Why do some Corinthians disagree with Paul's belief in the future resurrection of the body? Explain the difference between the notion of having an inherently immortal soul and the concept of receiving eternal life through resurrection. How does Paul link Jesus' resurrection to the Christian hope of an afterlife?

5. In 2 Corinthians 10–13, what arguments do Paul's Corinthian opponents use against him? Why does he respond by boasting "as a fool"? Why are his mystical experiences important to the Corinthians?

QUESTIONS FOR DISCUSSION AND REFLECTION

1. If Paul was wrong about the occurrence of the Parousia during his lifetime, to what extent does that mistaken view affect a reader's confidence in Paul's teachings?

2. After reading 1 Corinthians 7 and 11, discuss Paul's views on human sexuality and the relative status of men and women. On what tradition does Paul base his opinion of women's role in the church? How have Paul's attitudes influenced modern policies on the ordination of women for the ministry?

3. In 2 Corinthians 1–9, the Corinthian majority apparently decided to accept Paul and his individual gospel on the apostle's own terms. Which of Paul's threats or arguments do you think most influenced the church to become reconciled with its founder?

TERMS AND CONCEPTS TO REMEMBER

eschatology
the two ages
Paul's view of the Parousia
    (1 Thessalonians)
Aphrodite
causes of division in
    Corinth
roles of reason and faith
the "wise" and the
    "foolish"
sexual ethics
conscience
role of women
gifts of the Spirit
agapē (1 Corinthians 13)
ecstatic speech
    (glossolalia)
Greek doctrine of
    immortality
Hebrew belief in bodily
    resurrection
superlative apostles
Paul's apostolic
    credentials

RECOMMENDED READING

1 and 2 Thessalonians

Beker, J. C. *Paul's Apocalyptic Gospel: The Coming Triumph of God.* Philadelphia: Fortress Press, 1982.
Collins, R. F. "The First Letter to Thessalonians." In *The New Jerome Biblical Commentary,* pp. 772–779. Englewood Cliffs, N.J.: Prentice-Hall, 1990.
Keck, L. E., and Furnish, V. P. *The Pauline Letters.* Nashville, Tenn.: Abingdon Press, 1984.
Krentz, Edgar M. "Thessalonians, First and Second Epistles to the." In D. N. Freedman, ed., *The Anchor Bible Dictionary,* Vol. 6, pp. 515–523, New York: Doubleday, 1992.
Marshall, I. H. *1 and 2 Thessalonians.* Grand Rapids, Mich.: Eerdmans, 1983.
Orr, W. F., and Walther, J. A., eds. *1 and 2 Corinthians and 1 and 2 Thessalonians.* Vol. 32 of the Anchor Bible. Garden City, N.Y.: Doubleday, 1976.
Reese, J. M. *1 and 2 Thessalonians.* Wilmington, Del.: Michael Glazier, 1979.

1 and 2 Corinthians

Betz, H. D. "Corinthians, Second Epistle to the." In D. N. Freedman, ed., *The Anchor Bible Dictionary,* Vol. 1, pp. 1148–1154. New York: Doubleday, 1992.

Betz, H. D., and Mitchel, M. M. "Corinthians, First Epistle to the." In D. N. Freedman, ed., *The Anchor Bible Dictionary*, Vol. 1, pp. 1139–1148. New York: Doubleday, 1992.

Bruce, F. F. *1 and 2 Corinthians*. Grand Rapids, Mich.: Eerdmans, 1978.

Furnish, V. P. *Second Corinthians*. Anchor Bible Commentary, Vol. 32A. Garden City, N.Y.: Doubleday, 1984.

Georgi, Dieter. *The Opponents of Paul in Second Corinthians*. Philadelphia: Fortress Press, 1986.

Hays, Richard B. *Interpretation: First Corinthians*. Louisville, Ky.: Westminster/John Knox Press, 1997. Examines Paul's theological response to socioeconomic problems at Corinth.

Hooker, M. D. "Authority on Her Head: An Examination of 1 Cor. 11:10." *New Testament Studies* 10 (1963): 410–416.

Hurd, J. C. *The Origin of 1 Corinthians*. Macon, Ga.: Mercer University Press, 1983.

Meeks, Wayne. *The First Urban Christians: The Social World of the Apostle Paul*. New Haven, Conn.: Yale University Press, 1983. An insightful investigation into the cultural environment and socioeconomic background of the earliest Christians.

Murphy-O'Connor, Jerome. *St. Paul's Corinth: Text and Archaeology*. Wilmington, Del.: Michael Glazier, 1983. An archaeologist's illumination of the Corinthian life and customs in Paul's day.

Schmithals, Walter. *Gnosticism in Corinth: An Investigation of the Letters to the Corinthians*. Translated by J. Steely. Nashville, Tenn.: Abingdon Press, 1971.

Schütz, J. H., ed. *The Social Setting of Pauline Christianity*. Philadelphia: Fortress Press, 1982.

Scroggs, Robin. "Paul and the Eschatological Woman." *Journal of the American Academy of Religion* 40 (1972): 283–303; 42 (1974): 532–537.

Soards, Marian L. *The Apostle Paul: An Introduction to His Writing and Teaching*. New York: Paulist Press, 1987.

Talbert, C. H. *Reading Corinthians: A Literary and Theological Commentary on 1 and 2 Corinthians*. New York: Crossroad, 1987.

Theissen, Gerd. *The Social Setting of Pauline Christianity: Essays on Corinth*. Edited, translated, and with an introduction by J. H. Schütz. Philadelphia: Fortress Press, 1982.

CHAPTER 15

Freedom from Law and Justification by Faith

Galatians and Romans

> For through faith you are all [children] of God in union with Christ Jesus. . . . There is no such thing as Jew and Greek, slave and free-man, male and female; for you are all one person in Christ Jesus.
>
> Galatians 3:26, 28

Key Themes In his letters to the Galatians and the Romans, Paul defines Christianity's relationship to Judaism. He uses the Hebrew Bible to demonstrate that faith was always God's primary means of reconciling humanity to himself. God's revelation (*apokalypsis*) of Jesus frees believers from the "bondage" of Torah observance.

Paul argues in Romans that all humanity imitates Adam's disobedience and is therefore enslaved to sin and alienated from God. The "holy" and "just" Law of the Torah serves only to increase an awareness of human imperfection and to condemn the lawbreaker. Thus, obedience to the Torah cannot rescue people from sin's consequence—death—or unite them with the Deity. Only God's undeserved love expressed through Christ and accepted through faith can reconcile humanity with the Creator.

The Jewish lack of faith in Jesus as the divinely appointed agent of redemption is only temporary, a historical necessity that allows believing Gentiles also to become God's People.

Galatians and Romans are two of Paul's most important letters, for in these he spells out his distinctive vision of freedom from the Mosaic Torah and justification by faith in Christ. An angry declaration of Christianity's independence from Torah obligations, Galatians argues that obedience to Torah commandments cannot justify the believer before God. Only trust (faith) in God's gracious willingness to redeem humanity through Christ can now win divine approval and obtain salvation for the individual.

This uniquely Pauline gospel revolutionized the development of Christianity. By sweeping away all Torah requirements, including circumcision and dietary restrictions, Paul opened the church wide to Gentile converts. Uncircumcised former adherents of Greco-Roman religions were now granted full equality with Jewish Christians. Although the process was only beginning in Paul's day, the influx of Gentiles would soon overwhelm the originally Jewish church, making it an international community with members belonging to every known ethnic group. This swift transformation would not have been possible without Paul's radical insistence on the abandonment of all Mosaic observances, which for centuries had separated Jew from Gentile.

GALATIANS

Author: Paul.

Date: About 56 C.E.

Place of Composition: Perhaps Ephesus or Corinth.

Audience: The "churches of Galatia," perhaps southern Galatia, a Roman province containing the towns of Lystra, Iconium, and Derbe.

Occasion or Purpose: To refute opponents who advocated circumcision and to demonstrate that Jew and Gentile are equally saved by faith in Jesus' redemptive power.

An Angry Letter to the "Stupid" Galatians

Perhaps written at about the same time he was battling the "superlative apostles" of Corinth (2 Cor. 10–13), Paul's Galatian letter contains a similar impassioned defense of his apostolic authority and teaching. It seems that almost everywhere Paul founded new churches, troublemakers infiltrated the congregation, asserting that Christians must keep at least some provisions of the Mosaic Law. Influenced either by representatives from the Jerusalem church or by a wish to combine Jewish practices with elements of pre-Christian religions, the Galatians had abandoned Paul's gospel (1:6) and now required all male converts to undergo circumcision (5:2–3; 6:12–13), the physical sign of belonging to God's covenant community (Gen. 17).

THE RECIPIENTS

The identity of the Galatian churches Paul addresses is uncertain. In Paul's time, two different geographical areas could be designated "Galatia." The first was a territory in north-central Asia Minor inhabited by descendants of Celtic tribes that had invaded the region during the third to first centuries B.C.E. Brief references to Galatia in Acts (16:6; 18:23) suggest that Paul traveled there, but this is not certain.

The other possibility, as some historians suggest, is that Paul was writing to Christians in the Roman province of **Galatia.** The southern portion of this province included the cities of Iconium, Lystra, and Derbe, places where the apostle had established churches (Acts 14). If the "southern Galatia" theory is correct, it helps to explain the presence of "Judaizers" (those persons advocating circumcision), for the Roman province was much closer to Jewish-Christian centers at Antioch and at Jerusalem than was the northern, Celtic territory (see figure 15.1).

THE IDENTITY OF PAUL'S OPPONENTS

Some commentators identify Paul's opponents as emissaries of the Jerusalem church, such as those apparently sent by James to inspect the congregation at Antioch (2:12). It is unlikely, however, that Jewish Christians from Jerusalem would be unaware that requiring circumcision also means keeping the entire Torah (5:2–3). Paul's opponents appear to combine aspects of Greco-Roman cult worship, such as honoring cosmic spirits and observing religious festival days (4:9–10), with selected Torah requirements (6:12–14). This **syncretism** (mixing together aspects of two or more different religions to create a new doctrine) suggests that the opponents are Galatian Gentiles. In Paul's view, their attempt to infuse Jewish and pagan elements into Christianity misses the point of the Christ event.

PURPOSE AND CONTENTS

Writing from Corinth or Ephesus about 56 C.E., Paul has a twofold purpose: (1) to prove that he is a true apostle, possessing rights equal to those of the Jerusalem "pillars" (chs. 1–2) and (2) to demonstrate the validity of his gospel that Christian faith replaces works of Law, including circumcision. The letter can be divided into five parts:

1. A biographical defense of Paul's autonomy and his relationship with the Jerusalem leadership (1:1–2:14)
2. Paul's unique gospel: justification through faith (2:15–3:29)
3. The adoption of Christians as heirs of Abraham and children of God (4:1–31)

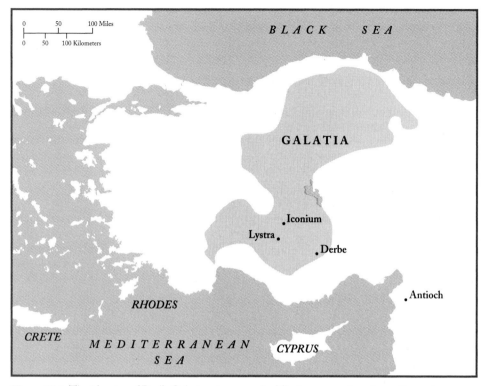

Figure 15.1 The identity of Paul's Galatians is uncertain. The letter may have been directed to churches in the north-central plateau region of Asia Minor (near present-day Ankara, Turkey) or to churches in the southern coastal area of east-central Asia Minor (also in modern Turkey). Many scholars believe that the Galatians were Christians living in Iconium, Lystra, Derbe, and other nearby cities that Paul had visited on his first missionary journey.

4. The consequences and obligations of Christian freedom from the Mosaic Law (5:1–6:10)
5. Final summary of Paul's argument (6:11–18)

PAUL'S FREEDOM
FROM INSTITUTIONAL AUTHORITY

Largely dispensing with his usual greetings and thanksgiving, Paul opens the letter with a vigorous defense of his personal autonomy. His apostolic rank derives not from ordination or "human appointment," but directly from the Deity (1:1–5). Similarly, his message does not depend on information learned from earlier Christians, but is a direct "revelation of Jesus Christ" (1:12). Because he regards his gospel of faith as a divine communication, Paul sees no need to consult other church leaders about the correctness of his policies (1:15–17).

In contrast to Acts, in Galatians Paul presents himself as essentially independent of the mother church at Jerusalem. Nevertheless, he apparently recognizes the desirability of having his work among the Gentiles endorsed by the Palestinian Christian leadership. His visit with the Jerusalem "pillars" — Peter (Cephas), John, and James — is probably the same conference described in Acts 15. According to Paul, the pillars (a term he uses somewhat ironically) agree to recognize the legitimacy of his Gentile mission. Imposing no Torah restrictions on Gentile converts, the Jerusalem trio ask only that Paul's congregations contribute financially to the mother church, a charitable project Paul gladly undertakes (2:1–10; cf. Paul's appeals for donations in 2 Cor. 8–9 and Rom. 15).

After the Jerusalem conference, Paul meets Peter again at Antioch, a meeting that shows how far the Jewish-Gentile issue is from being resolved. Paul charges that Jesus' premier disciple is still ambivalent about associating with uncircumcised believers. When James sends emissaries to see if Antiochean Christians are properly observing Mosaic dietary laws, Peter stops sharing in communal meals with Gentiles. Apparently, Peter fears James's disapproval. Although Paul denounces Peter's action as hypocrisy, claiming that Peter privately does not keep Torah regulations, we cannot be sure of Peter's motives. He may have wished not to offend more conservative Jewish believers and behaved as he did out of respect for others' consciences, a policy Paul himself advocates (1 Cor. 8:1–13).

JUSTIFICATION BY FAITH

Paul's strangely negative attitude toward the Mosaic Law has puzzled many Jewish scholars. Why does a Pharisee trained to regard the Torah as God's revelation of ultimate Wisdom so vehemently reject this divine guide to righteous living? Is it because of a personal consciousness that (for him) the Law no longer has power to justify his existence before God? In both Galatians and Romans, Paul closely examines his own psychological state, attempting to show how the experience of Christ achieves for him what the Law failed to do—assure him of God's love and acceptance.

Replacing Law with Faith   In Paul's interpretation of the Crucifixion, Jesus' voluntary death pays the Torah's penalty for all lawbreakers (3:13–14). Thus, Paul can say that "through the law I died to law." He escaped the punishments of the Torah through a mystical identification with the sacrificial Messiah. Vicariously experiencing Jesus' crucifixion, Paul now shares in Christ's new life, which enables him to receive God's grace as never before (2:17–21).

Paul also appeals to the Galatians' experience of Christ, reminding them that they received the Spirit only when they believed his gospel, not when they obeyed the Law (3:1–5). If they think that they can be judged righteous by obeying the Torah, then there was no purpose or meaning to Christ's death (2:21). Paul reinforces his argument in the rabbinic tradition by finding a precedent in the Hebrew Bible that anticipates his formula of "faith equals righteousness." Paul notes that Abraham's "faith" in God's call "was counted to him as righteousness" (Gen. 15:6). Therefore, Paul reasons, persons who exercise faith today are Abraham's spiritual children, heirs to the promise that God will "bless," or justify, pagan nations through faith (3:6–10). Faith, not obedience to Law, is the key to divine approval.

In support of his appeal to biblical authority, Paul finds only one additional relevant text, Habakkuk 2:4: "he shall gain life who is justified through faith." Paul interprets the Habakkuk text as prophetic of the messianic era and contrasts its emphasis on faith with the Law's stress on action (3:11–12). The faith Habakkuk promised comes to the lawless Gentiles because Christ, suffering a criminal's execution, accepted the Law's "curse" on unlawful people and allowed them to become reconciled to God (3:13–14).

Role of the Mosaic Torah in Human Salvation
If, as Paul repeatedly asserts, the Torah cannot really help anyone, why was it given? Paul's answer is that the Mosaic Torah is a temporary device intended to teach human beings that they are unavoidably lawbreakers, sinners whose most conscientious efforts cannot earn divine favor. Using an analogy from Roman society, Paul compares the Law to a tutor—a man appointed to guide and protect youths until they attain legal adulthood. Like a tutor imposing discipline, the Law makes its adherents aware of their moral inadequacy and their need for a power beyond themselves to achieve righteousness. That power is Christ. Having served its purpose of preparing Abraham's children for Christ, the Torah is now obsolete and irrelevant (3:19–25).

The Equality of All Believers   Paul abolishes the Law's power to condemn and separate Jew from Gentile and asserts the absolute equality of all believers, regardless of their nationality, social class, or sex. Among God's children "there is no such thing as Jew and Greek, slave and freeman, male and female," because all are "one person in Christ Jesus" (3:26–28).

All Believers as Heirs of Abraham   Because Jesus purchased Christians' freedom from slavery to the Torah's yoke, all are now God's adopted heirs. As such, they are entitled to claim the Deity as *Abba* ("father" or "daddy") and to receive the Abrahamic promises. Paul stresses the contrast between the church and Judaism by interpreting the Genesis story of Abraham's two wives as an allegory, a narrative in which the characters symbolize some higher truth. Hagar, Abraham's Egyptian slave girl, is earthly Jerusalem, controlled by Rome. Sarah, the patriarch's free wife, symbolizes the "heavenly Jerusalem," the spiritual church whose members are also free (4:21–31).

Responsibilities of Freedom   What does freedom from Torah regulations mean? Aware that some Galatians used their liberty as an excuse to indulge any desire or appetite (a practice called **antinomianism**), Paul interprets his doctrine as freedom to practice neighborly love without external restrictions. Quoting lists of vices and virtues typical of Stoic ethical teaching, the apostle notes that the Spirit will transcend believers' natural selfishness to produce generous actions (5:13–26).

Paul's exasperation with the Galatians' failure to understand that Jesus' death and resurrection are God's complete and all-sufficient means of human salvation inspires his most brutal insult. With savage irony, he suggests that persons who insist on circumcision finish the job by emasculating themselves (5:7–12). Paul's remark may refer to an infamous practice among adherents of the goddess Cybele, some of whose male adherents mutilated themselves in a religious frenzy. This oblique allusion to a pagan cult also implies that Paul's opponents were Galatian syncretists.

In closing his letter, Paul seizes the pen from his secretary to write a final appeal to the Galatians in his own hand. Accusing his opponents of practicing circumcision only to escape persecution, presumably from Torah-abiding Jews, Paul summarizes his position: Torah obedience is meaningless because it implies that God's revelation through Jesus is not sufficient. Contrary to his opponents' limited view, Paul asserts that Jesus alone makes possible the new creation that unites humanity with its Creator. Note that Paul's closing words are as abrupt and self-directed as his opening complaint (1:6): "In future let no one make trouble for me" (6:11–17).

Letter to the Romans

Galatians was dictated in the white heat of exasperation; Romans is a more calmly reasoned presentation of Paul's doctrine of salvation through faith. This letter is generally regarded as the apostle's most systematic expression of his theology. In it, Paul thoughtfully explores an issue central to all world religions: how to bridge the moral gap between God and humanity, to reconcile imperfect, sinful humanity to a pure and righteous Deity. As a Jew, Paul is painfully aware of the immense disparity between mortals and the immaculate holiness of the Supreme Being, whose justice cannot tolerate human error or wrongdoing. Yet Paul sees these irreconcilable differences between humanity and God as overcome in Christ, the Son who closes the gulf between perfect Father and imperfect children. In Paul's vision of reconciliation, God himself takes the initiative by re-creating a deeply flawed humanity in his own transcendent image.

PURPOSE, PLACE, AND TIME OF COMPOSITION

Unlike other Pauline letters, Romans is addressed to a congregation the writer has neither founded nor previously visited. In form, the work resembles a theological essay or sermon rather than an ordinary letter, lacking the kind of specific problem-solving advice that characterizes most of Paul's correspondence. Some commentators regard Romans as a circular letter, a document intended to explain Pauline teachings to various Christian groups who may at that time have held distorted views of the apostle's position on controversial subjects.

Most scholars view chapter 16, which contains greetings to twenty-six different persons, as a separate missive. It was probably a letter of recommendation for Phoebe, who was a **deacon** of the church at Cenchreae, the port of Corinth. Because Aquila and Prisca (Priscilla) are mentioned, chapter 16 may originally have been sent to Ephesus, where Paul had worked with the couple (1 Cor. 16:19; Acts 18:18, 26). According to this view, an editor later attached the Ephesian letter to Romans, making it an appendix to the longer work.

Although Paul may have intended the document we call Romans to circulate through many different churches, at the time of writing he has compelling personal reasons to open communications with Rome. As 2 Corinthians 10–13 and Galatians reveal, Paul's churches in the northeastern Mediterranean region were rife with divisions and rebellion against his authority. Perhaps in hope of leaving this strife behind, Paul intends to move westward to Spain. He frankly confesses that he prefers to work in territories where no Christian has preceded him (Rom. 15:19–24; 1 Cor. 3:10–15; 2 Cor. 10:15–16). Paul writes not only to enlist Roman support for his Spanish mission (15:24) but also to make sure that his doctrines are understood and endorsed by the prestigious church at Rome, center of the imperial government and capital of the civilized world. He assures the Romans that he intends only to pass through their city, lest they fear a long visit from so difficult and controversial a figure.

Before journeying to Rome, however, Paul plans to take the money collected from his churches in Greece to the Jerusalem headquarters. He feels some anxiety about the trip to Judea, stronghold of his Jewish and Jewish-Christian opponents, and may have composed Romans as a means of marshaling the most effective arguments for his stand on the relationship between Judaism and Christianity (15:26–32). Chapters 9–11 contain his most extensive analysis of the mother religion's role in the divine plan. As Acts indicates, Paul's premonition of future trouble was fully justified by his subsequent arrest in Jerusalem and imprisonment in Caesarea (Acts 21–26). The letter was probably sent from Corinth about 56–57 C.E.

ORGANIZATION

The longest and most complex of Paul's letters, Romans can be divided into nine thematically related parts:

1. Introduction (1:1–15)
2. Statement of theme (1:16–17) and exploration of the human predicament: God's wrath directed at all humanity because all people are guilty of deliberate error (1:18–3:31)
3. Abraham as the model of faith (4:1–25)
4. Faith in Christ ensuring deliverance from sin and death (5:1–7:25)
5. Renewed life in the Spirit (8:1–39)
6. The causes and results of Israel's disbelief (9:1–11:36)
7. Behavior in the church and the world (12:1–15:13)
8. Paul's future plans and greetings (15:14–33)
9. Appendix: A letter recommending Phoebe, a woman serving as deacon of the Cenchreae church (16:1–27)

INTRODUCTION

Paul opens the letter with an affirmation of his apostleship as the result of God's direct call (again implicitly denying that he owes his authority to any human ordination). He notes that Jesus became "Son of God" upon his resurrection, an echo of the early view of divine sonship ascribed to Peter in Acts 2:36. Similarly, Paul is chosen for a special role; he is divinely commissioned to achieve both faith and obedience among all people. As Apostle to the Gentiles, he now plans to bring his gospel to Rome (1:1–15).

Wrestling with the Human Predicament   Paul announces his main theme in terms of Habakkuk 2:4, the same verse proclaiming salvation "through faith" that he had quoted in his earlier letter to the Galatians (Gal. 3:11). The close relationship between Galatians and Romans is suggested by this repetition. Throughout this section of Romans (1:16–3:31), Paul attempts to demonstrate that faith in Christ is humanity's only way to escape God's just anger and its own deserved punishment. Because all human beings are guilty of willful error, whether Jew or Gentile, all stand condemned by God's justice.

The Gentiles' Error   Paul continues with a thorough indictment of the entire human race, using ammunition borrowed from the arsenal of Hellenistic Judaism. He echoes passages from the Wisdom of Solomon, a Greek-Jewish work included in the Old Testament Apocrypha, as well as the concepts of "natural" and "unnatural" from the philosophies of Aristotle and the Stoics to denounce everyone who fails to recognize and worship the one true God. God's qualities, he argues, can be deduced from the physical world of nature. The wisdom and power of God, as well as his grand design, are evident in the cosmic order, so that persons who worship idols have perverted natural law. They honor created things in human or animal form instead of the One who created them (1:18–23).

Turning their backs on the Creator, human beings fall into ethical and sexual errors as well (see Wisd. of Sol. 14:11–31). In this controversial passage, Paul attributes the homosexual love affairs that characterized Greek and Roman culture to the Gentile practice of idolatry. Notice that Paul describes homosexual acts as a deliberate or willful turning away from a person's natural state. He assumes that physical attraction to a member of the same sex is a matter of conscious moral choice (rather than culturally or genetically determined) and identifies it as a rebellion against the divine will. How this attitude relates to Paul's doctrine of human freedom and his principle of conscience he does not explain (1:24–2:16).

The Jews Are Equally Guilty   Although God provided the Jews with the Torah to guide them in righteousness, a fact that gives them an initial advantage over the pagans, they have not, Paul asserts, lived up to the Law's high standards. As a result, Jews have not achieved justification before God any more than Gentiles have. Paul reiterates his argument to the Galatians that the Torah fails to effect a right relationship between God and the law-keeper; it serves only to make one conscious of sin (2:17–3:20).

All humanity, then, both Jew and Gentile, is in the same sinking boat, incapable of saving itself. No one can earn through his or her own efforts the right to enjoy divine approval. Paul now goes on to show how God—whose just nature does not permit him to absolve the unjust sinner—works to rescue undeserving humanity (3:21–31).

ABRAHAM AS THE MODEL OF ONE "JUSTIFIED" BY FAITH

Paul realizes that if his doctrine is to convince Jewish Christians, it must find support in the Hebrew Bible. He therefore argues that God's plan of rescuing sinners through faith began with Abraham, foremost ancestor of the Jewish people. As in Galatians, he cites Genesis 15:5: Abraham's faith in God "was counted to him as righteousness." Long before Abraham was circumcised or the Mosaic Law was given, faith was made the means by which the just God, without compromising his impartiality, succeeds in justifying or declaring "righteous" his human creation. Thus is the way opened for believers to attain union with their Creator. As the example of one possessing faith even though uncircumcised, Abraham is the progenitor not only of Jews but of believing Gentiles as well. In his person, he foreshadows the equality of all who manifest a similar faith. As Abraham proved his faith by obediently responding to God's voice, so must the faithful now respond to God's new summons through Christ (4:1–25).

FAITH IN CHRIST ENSURES DELIVERANCE FROM SIN AND DEATH

The Roles of Adam and Christ   At the outset of his letter (1:5), Paul declares that he tried to bring the whole world to a state of obedient faith. In chapter 5, he outlines a theory of history in which God uses these two qualities—obedience and faith—to achieve human salvation. God's intervention into human affairs became necessary when the first human being, Adam (whose name means "humankind"), disobeyed the Creator. Through this act, Adam alienated not only himself but all his descendants from their Maker. Like other Jewish teachers of the first century, Paul interprets the Genesis story of Adam's disobedience as a tragic **Fall** from grace, a cosmic disaster that introduces sin and death into the world. (Paul's word for "sin"—*hamartia*—is a Greek archery term, that means "missing the mark," "falling short of a desired goal." Aristotle used the same term to denote the "fatal flaw" of the tragic hero in Greek drama. *Hamartia* commonly refers to an error of judgment rather than an act of inborn human wickedness.) In Paul's moral scheme, the entire race fails to hit the target of reunion with God, thus condemning itself to death—permanent separation from the Source of life.

Obedience to the Torah cannot save because the Law merely defines errors and assigns legal penalties. It is God himself who overcomes the hopelessness of the human predicament. He does this by sending his Son, whose perfect obedience and sacrificial death provide a saving counterweight to Adam's sin. As all Adam's children share his mortal punishment, so all will share the reward of Christ's resurrection to life. It is the believer's faith in the saving power of Christ that makes him or her "righteous," enabling the just Deity to accept persons trustfully responding to his call (5:12–21).

Some later theologians used Romans 5 to formulate a doctrine of **original sin,** a teaching that all human beings inherit an unavoidable tendency to do wrong and are innately corrupt. From Augustine to Calvin, such theologians took a deeply pessimistic view of human nature, in some cases regarding the majority of humanity as inherently depraved and justly damned.

Paul, however, stresses the joyful aspects of God's reconciliation to humanity. It is the Deity who initiates the process, making God's "grace"—

his gracious will to love and give life—far exceed the measure of human failings. So universally powerful is God's determination to redeem humanity that Paul implies he will ultimately save all people, a concept the writer also alludes to in 1 Corinthians (cf. Rom. 5:18–19; 1 Cor. 15:21–23).

A Distortion of Paul's Teaching on Freedom   In chapter 6, Paul seems to be refuting misconceptions of his doctrine on Christian freedom. As in Galatia, some persons were apparently acting as if liberty from the Law entitled them to behave irresponsibly. In some cases, they concluded that "sinning" was good because it allowed God's grace more opportunity to show itself. Paul reminds such dissidents that sin is a cruel tyrant who pays wages of death. By contrast, Christ treats his servants generously, bestowing the gift of everlasting life (6:1–23).

THE LAW'S HOLINESS AND HUMAN PERVERSITY

Paul makes one final attempt to place the Torah in the context of salvation history and to account for its failure to produce human righteousness. In Galatians, Paul describes the Law harshly, referring to it as slavery, bondage, and death. Writing more temperately in Romans, he judges the Law "holy and just and good" (7:12). If so, why does it not serve to justify its practitioners?

In this case, Paul answers that the fault lies not in the Torah but in human nature. The Torah is "spiritual," but human beings are "unspiritual," enslaved by sin. Throughout this long passage (7:7–25), Paul uses the first person as if he were analyzing his own nature and then projecting his self-admitted defects onto the rest of humanity. His "I," however, should probably read "we"—for he means to describe human nature collectively. Laws not only define crimes, he asserts, but create an awareness of lawbreaking that does not exist in their absence. Thus, the Torah makes sin come alive in the human consciousness (7:7–11).

Speaking as if sin were an animate force inside himself, Paul articulates the classic statement of ethical frustration—the opposition between the "good" he wishes to do and the "wrong" he actually performs. As he confronts the huge gap between his conscious will and his imperfect actions, Paul can only conclude that it is not the real "he" who produces the moral failure, but the "sin that lodges in me" (7:14–20).

With his reason delighting in the Torah but his lower nature fighting against it, he finds that he incurs the Law's punishment—death. He bursts with desire to attain God's approval but always "misses the mark." In agony over his fate, he seeks some power to rescue him from an unsatisfying existence that ends only in death (7:21–25). Paul may be accused of attributing his personal sense of moral imperfection to everyone else, but his despairing self-examination illustrates why he feels the Law is unable to deliver one from the lethal attributes of imperfect human nature (8:3).

RENEWED LIFE IN THE SPIRIT

Paul then tries to show how God accomplishes his rescue mission through Christ (8:1–39). By sharing humanity's imperfect nature and dying "as a sacrifice for sin," Christ transfers the Torah's penalties to sin itself, condemning it and not the human nature in which it exists (8:3–4). Because Christ's Spirit now dwells within the believer, sin no longer exerts its former control, and new life can flourish in the Christian's body. Thus, Christians escape their imperfection, having put it to death with Christ on the cross. No longer sin's slaves, they become God's children, joint heirs with Christ (8:5–17).

Universal Renewal   Paul uses mystical language to describe not only human nature but the physical Cosmos itself struggling to be set free from the chains of mortality. During this period of cosmic renewal, the whole universe wails as if in childbirth. Believers now hope for a saving rebirth, but the reality is still ahead. Then they will be fully reshaped in the Son's image, the pattern of a new humanity reconciled to God (8:18–30).

Doxology   Paul concludes this section of his letter with one of his most memorable **doxologies.** It is a

moving hymn of praise to the God who has lovingly provided the means for humanity to transcend its weakness and attain "the liberty and splendour" of God's children. In this brilliant credo, Paul declares his absolute confidence that no suffering or power, human or supernatural, can separate the believer from God's love (8:31–39).

THE CAUSES AND RESULTS OF ISRAEL'S DISBELIEF

Now that he has explained his position on the Law and the means by which God arranges human salvation, Paul explores the difficult question of Israel's rejection of its Messiah. How does it happen that the people to whom God granted his covenants, Torah, Temple, and promises failed to recognize Jesus as the Christ? First, Paul argues that God never intended all Israelites to receive his promises; they were meant for only a faithful remnant, represented in Paul's day by Jewish Christians (9:1–9). (Note that Paul's theory of a "faithful remnant" does not fully agree with other parts of his argument.)

Second, Paul tries to show that Israel's present unbelief is part of God's long-range plan to redeem all of humanity. In a long discourse sprinkled with loose paraphrases of passages from the Hebrew Bible, Paul makes several important assumptions about God's nature and the manner in which the Deity controls human destiny. He first assumes that because God's will is irresistible, human beings' freedom of choice is severely limited. Citing the Exodus story, Paul reminds his readers that Yahweh manipulated the Egyptian king in order to demonstrate his divine strength (Exod. 9:15–16). He argues that God's omnipotence entitles him to show favor or cruelty to whomever he pleases. Paul compares the Deity's arbitrariness to that of a potter who can assign one clay pot an honorable use and smash another if it displeases him. Implying that might makes right, Paul declares that no human being can justly challenge the supreme Potter's authority to favor one person and not another (9:10–21; 10:7–10).

Paul's assumption is that the Creator predetermines the human ability to believe or disbelieve, thus foreordaining an individual's eternal destiny. This assumption troubles many believers for its apparent repudiation of free will, although some have embraced it. Later theologians such as Augustine and Calvin formulated a doctrine of **predestination,** in which God—before the world's creation—decreed everyone's fate, selecting a few to enjoy heavenly bliss and relegating the majority to damnation.

Paul, however, emphasizes the positive aspect of God's apparent intervention into the human decision-making process. In God's long-range plan, Jewish refusal to recognize Jesus as the Messiah allows Gentiles to receive the Gospel; thus, nations previously ignorant of God can achieve redemption. In a famous analogy, Paul likens Gentile believers to branches from a wild olive tree that have been grafted onto the cultivated olive trunk, which is natural Israel. If some of the old branches from the domesticated tree had not been lopped off, there would have been no room for the new (11:16–18). For humanity's universal benefit, God has taken advantage of Israel's unresponsiveness to produce a greater good.

Paul also states that the creation of churches in which Greeks and Romans now worship Israel's God will incite a healthy envy among Jews, kindling a desire to share the churches' spiritual favor. Furthermore, Israel's disbelief is only temporary. When all Gentiles become believers, then the natural branches will be regrafted onto God's olive tree and "the whole of Israel will be saved" (11:19–27).

Paul does not explain why both Israelites and Gentiles could not have been saved simultaneously, but he remains absolutely certain that the Jews are still God's chosen people. Writing before Rome destroyed the Jewish state in 70 C.E., Paul does not predict divine vengeance upon Israel. He affirms instead that God's own integrity ensures that he will honor his promises to the covenant community. Some later Christian writers argue that God disowned Israel, replacing it with the Christian church. By contrast, Paul's witness confirms Israel's continuing role in the divinely ordered drama of human salvation (11:1–36).

BEHAVIOR IN THE CHURCH AND THE WORLD

Paul's ethical instruction (chs. 12–15) is again closely tied to his sense of apocalyptic urgency. Because the New Age is about to dawn, believers must conduct themselves with special care. Their rescue from the present evil age is extremely near—closer now than it was when they first believed (13:11). Paul apparently believed that the Parousia lay only a few years in the future.

Cooperation with Government Authority Paul's advice, written before his imprisonment and prosecution in Rome, extends to behavior outside the church and includes a program of obedience and cooperation with government authorities. Echoing the Stoic view that the state exists to maintain public order and punish wrongdoing, Paul argues that the Roman Empire is a "divine institution"—an opinion in contrast with his earlier view that the present world is ruled by demonic forces (2 Cor. 4:4).

Although he emphasizes the Christian's duty to pay taxes and submit to legally constituted authority, Paul does not consider the ethical problem of a citizen's duty to resist illegal or unethical acts by the state. He does not advise believers to expend energy trying to change the present social system (13:1–10), perhaps because he sees it as so near its end. (Compare his attitude toward the state-supported institution of slavery discussed in chapter 16.)

Rome as Anti-Christ Paul implies that voluntary cooperation with Rome will benefit Christians; he could not know that he soon would be among the first victims of a state-sponsored persecution of his faith (see figure 15.2). Following the emperor Nero's legal murder of many Roman believers (about 64–65 C.E.) and the threat of more persecution under Domitian (81–96 C.E.), some New Testament authors came to regard the state as Satan's earthly instrument to destroy God's people. After the Jerusalem Temple was razed in 70 C.E., Rome became the new Babylon in the eyes of many

Figure 15.2 Because early church traditions assert that both Peter and Paul were executed in Rome during Nero's reign, their images are commonly paired, as in this fourth-century Roman lime relief depicting the two apostles. Paul's letter to the Galatians indicates that their historical relationship was not so close (Gal. 2:11–13). (© Erich Lessing/PhotoEdit)

Christians. The author of Revelation pictures Rome as a beast and predicts its fall as a cause of universal rejoicing (Rev. 17–19). At the time Paul wrote, however, the adversarial relationship between church and state was still in the future.

Summary

Romans is the most comprehensive statement of Paul's teaching. In it, Paul wrestles with the problems of humanity's estrangement from God and God's response to human need. Arguing that Torah observance cannot justify one to the righteous God, Paul states that in Christ the Deity creates a new humanity, a new beginning. Through Christ, all persons with faith are able to become God's children and benefit from the promises made to Abraham.

God's ultimate plan is to defeat sin and reconcile all humanity—ironically, first Gentiles and then Jews—to himself. Because the time remaining is so short, believers must submit to existing governments and lead blameless lives.

QUESTIONS FOR REVIEW

1. As Paul describes it in Romans 1–3, how is all humanity trapped in a hopeless predicament? How has God acted to rescue people from the power of sin and death?

2. Define what Paul means by such terms as *righteousness, justification,* and *faith.* According to Paul's evaluation of the Torah in Galatians and Romans, why are Torah observances such as circumcision irrelevant to God's action through Christ?

3. In both Galatians and Romans, Paul cites excerpts from Genesis 15 and Habakkuk 2 to prove that God always intended faith to be the means by which humanity was to be "justified." Compare Paul's inter-

pretation of Abraham's example with that given by James (2:14–26). Does James agree with Paul's explanation of the Genesis text?

QUESTION FOR DISCUSSION AND REFLECTION

1. Some commentators have argued that Paul misunderstands the purpose of Torah obedience. They claim that most Jewish teachers of his day did not present Torah observance as a means of salvation and that Paul's contrast between "works" and "faith" misrepresents first-century Judaism. From your reading of Galatians and Romans, how would you explain Paul's position?

TERMS AND CONCEPTS TO REMEMBER

Galatia
Judaizers
circumcision
Torah obedience
Paul's apostolic authority
Paul's doctrine of salvation by faith
purpose of the Torah
social and sexual equality in Christ
children of Abraham
Rome
hamartia
nature of human error
Abraham's faith

righteousness (justification)
God's plan for human salvation
Adam and Christ connection between sin and death
original sin
Jesus' death and the "curse" of the Law
universal salvation
role of natural Israel
wild olive tree
government authority

RECOMMENDED READING

General

Beker, J. C. *Paul the Apostle: The Triumph of God in Life and Thought.* Philadelphia: Fortress Press, 1980.

Bornkamm, Gunther. *Paul.* New York: Harper & Row, 1971. Contains an incisive summary of Paul's thought in each of the genuine letters.

Keck, Leander, and Furnish, V. P. *The Pauline Letters.* Nashville, Tenn.: Abingdon Press, 1984. Contains a concise survey of Paul's major ideas.

Soards, M. L. *The Apostle Paul: An Introduction to His Writings and Teaching.* Mahwah, N.J.: Paulist Press, 1987. A valuable analysis of Paul's life, letters, and theology.

Ziesler, John. *Pauline Christianity.* New York: Oxford University Press, 1983. A relatively brief but careful and systematic analysis of key Pauline concepts.

Galatians

Betz, H. D. *Galatians.* Hermeneia Commentary. Philadelphia: Fortress Press, 1979. A scholarly analysis.

Cousar, C. B. *Galatians.* Interpretation. Commentary. Atlanta: John Knox Press, 1982.

Ebeling, Gerhard. *The Truth of the Gospel: An Exposition of Galatians.* Philadelphia: Fortress Press, 1985.

Martyn, J. Louis. *Galatians.* Anchor Bible Series. New York: Doubleday, 1997. A new translation and commentary.

Romans

Achtemeier, P. J. *Romans.* Interpretation. Commentary. Atlanta: John Knox Press, 1985.

Cranfield, C. E. B. *A Critical and Exegetical Commentary on the Epistle to the Romans.* International Critical Commentary. 2 Vols. Edinburgh: T. & T. Clark, 1975, 1979. A standard work incorporating the history of Pauline interpretation.

Fitzmyer, Joseph A. *Romans.* The Anchor Bible, Vol. 33. New York: Doubleday, 1993. A new translation with extensive commentary.

Käsemann, Ernst. *Commentary on Romans.* Grand Rapids, Mich.: Eerdmans, 1980. An intensely scholarly study for more serious readers.

Sanders, E. P. *Paul and Palestinian Judaism.* Philadelphia: Fortress Press, 1978. An important scholarly study of Paul's relationship to rabbinic Judaism.

——. *Paul, the Law and the Jewish People.* Philadelphia: Fortress Press, 1983.

CHAPTER 16

Letters from Prison

Philippians and Philemon

He [Jesus] did not think to snatch at equality with God, but made himself nothing, assuming the nature of a slave.   Philippians 2:6-7

Key Themes Although it contains some sharp criticism of his opponents, Paul's letter to the Philippian church reveals an unusual warmth and friendliness in general. Urging cooperation for the mutual benefit of all believers, Paul cites an early hymn that depicts Jesus as the opposite of Adam—a humbly obedient Son whose self-emptying leads to his heavenly exaltation.

The apostle's only surviving personal letter, Philemon shows Paul accepting the Greco-Roman institution of slavery while simultaneously stressing that Christians of all social classes are intimately related in love.

According to an early church tradition, Paul wrote four canonical letters while imprisoned in Rome—Ephesians, Philippians, Colossians, and Philemon. Known as the "captivity letters," they were long believed to represent the apostle's most mature reflections on such topics as the divine nature of Christ (Phil. 2:5–11; Col. 1:13–20; 2:9–15) and the mystic unity of the church (Eph. 1–5).

Rigorous scholarly analysis of the four works, however, has raised serious questions about the time and place of their composition, as well as the authorship of two of them. All leading scholars accept Philippians and Philemon as genuinely Pauline writings, but many (perhaps 60 percent) challenge Paul's authorship of Colossians. Even more deny that he wrote Ephesians, a work that differs in content, tone, and style from the apostle's accepted letters. Because so many scholars question Paul's responsibility for Colossians, we discuss them among the disputed letters in chapter 17. (For

scholarly arguments defending or denying Pauline authorship of these works, see the "Recommended Reading" at the end of this chapter.)

Place of Origin

Scholars pose various objections to the old belief that Paul wrote Philippians and the other letters while under house arrest in Rome (Acts 28). In the apostles' day, traveling the almost 800 miles between Rome and Philippi, located in northeastern Greece, took as long as ten months (see figure 16.1). Philippians implies that Paul's friends made four journeys between Philippi and his place of imprisonment and that a fifth trip was planned (Phil. 2:25–26). Some scholars consider the distance separating these two cities too great to travel so frequently. They propose Ephesus, a city where Paul

Figure 16.1 Paul may have written his "letters from prison" from Rome (in the far west on this map), from Ephesus (on the coast of present-day Turkey), or from Caesarea (in the far eastern Mediterranean). Note that Ephesus is much closer to Philippi than either of the other two cities.

spent three years (Acts 20:31) and which is only about ten days' travel time from Philippi, as the place of origin. Philippians' references to the Praetorian Guard, the Roman emperor's personal militia (1:13), and "the imperial establishment" (4:22) do not necessarily mean that the letter originated in Rome. Ancient inscriptions recently discovered in Ephesus show that members of the Praetorian Guard and other imperial officials were stationed in the Roman province of Asia, where Ephesus and Colossae are located.

Although many scholars support the "Ephesian theory," others suggest that Paul wrote from Caesarea, where he was imprisoned for two years (Acts 23–25). Still other critics point out that we lack proof that Paul was actually jailed in Ephesus; they also claim that the difficulties in traveling between Macedonia and Rome have been overstated. Where

Paul was imprisoned remains an open question, although many commentators still uphold the traditional view that Paul's prison letters emanate from the Roman capital (see figure 16.2).

Letter to the Philippians

Paul enjoyed an unusually warm and affectionate relationship with Christians at Philippi. He and Timothy had established the church during their first tour of Greece (Acts 16:11–40), and he maintained an intimate communication with the Philippians, who were the only group from whom he would accept financial support (4:15–16). In welcome contrast to the "boasting" and threats that characterize the letters to Corinth and Galatia,

Figure 16.2 St. Paul in Prison by Rembrandt (1606–1669). In his murky cell, Paul composes letters to inspire faith and hope in the membership of his tiny, scattered churches. Notice that the light from the cell's barred window seems to emanate from Paul himself, surrounding his head like a halo and glowing from the pages of the manuscripts he holds. (© Staatsgalerie, Stuttgart)

Philippians contains no impassioned defense of his authority (his friends in Philippi did not question it). The author instead exposes a more kindly and loving aspect of his personality.

Like all genuinely Pauline letters, Philippians reveals the author's quick changes of mood, ranging from a personal meditation on the meaning of his impending death to a brief but savage attack on his opponents. The letter features so many abrupt changes of subject and shifts of emotion that many analysts believe that, like 2 Corinthians, it is a composite work, containing parts of three or four different missives.

According to this theory, the note thanking the Philippians for their financial help (4:10–20 or 23) was composed first, followed by a letter warning the church about potential troublemakers (partially preserved in 1:1–3:1a and 4:2–9). A third letter bitterly attacks advocates of circumcision (3:1b–4:1). The letter may be a unity, however, for Paul commonly leaps from topic to topic, registering different emotional responses to different problems in the course of a single letter.

Philippians is important not only for the insight it permits into Paul's volatile character but also for the clues it gives to early Christian beliefs about Jesus' nature. The key passage appears in Philippians 2:5–11, in which Paul seems to quote a primitive hymn celebrating Jesus' humble obedience and subsequent exaltation.

ORGANIZATION

Philippians covers a variety of topics, but it can be divided into six relatively brief units:

1. Salutation and thanksgiving (1:1–11)
2. Paul's meditation on his imprisonment (1:12–30)
3. Exhortation to humility, in imitation of Christ's example (2:1–18)
4. Recommendation of Timothy and Epaphroditus (2:19–3:1a)
5. Attack on advocates of circumcision and exhortation to live harmoniously, in imitation of Paul (3:1b–4:9)
6. Note of thanks for financial help (4:10–23)

THE SIGNIFICANCE
OF PAUL'S IMPRISONMENT

After affectionately greeting the Philippians (1:1–11), Paul explores the significance of his prison experience and courageously stresses its positive results. Apparently widely talked about, his case gives other believers the opportunity to witness publicly for Christ. On the other hand, not all of Paul's fellow Christians support him; they use his imprisonment as a means of stirring up new troubles for the prisoner. Paul does not identify those Christians whose personal jealousies complicate his already difficult situation, but they may have been connected with the "advocates of circumcision" denounced in chapter 3. In Acts' narration of Paul's arrest, imprisonment in Caesarea, and transportation to Rome under armed guard, the Jerusalem church leadership

is conspicuously absent from his defense. Perhaps those who shared James's adherence to Torah obligations were in some degree pleased to see Paul and his heretical views under legal restraint.

Paul's attitude toward his troublesome rivals is far milder than it is in Galatians. Determined to find positive results even in his opponents' activities, he concludes that their motives, whether sincere or hypocritical, are finally irrelevant: They successfully proclaim the Christian message (1:12–18).

As he contemplates the possibility of his execution, Paul is torn between wishing to live for his friends' sake and wishing to "depart and be with Christ." He would thus attain a posthumous union with his Lord while awaiting resurrection (see 1 Cor. 15). Paul places himself on a par with his beloved Philippians when he states that they run the same race as he to win life's ultimate prize (1:19–30). Despite his ceaseless efforts, Paul remains aware of his imperfection and explicitly states that he is not yet certain of victory (3:10–14).

THE HYMN TO CHRIST

Chapter 2 contains the letter's most important theological concept. Urging the Philippians to place others' welfare before their own, Paul cites Jesus' behavior as the supreme example of humble services to others. To enable his readers to share the same attitude and experience as Christ, he recites a hymn that illustrates his intent. The rhythmic and poetic qualities of this work, as well as the absence of typically Pauline ideas and vocabulary, indicate that it is a pre-Pauline composition. The first stanza reads as follows:

> Who though he was in the form of God,
> Did not count equality with God
> A thing to be grasped,
>
> But emptied himself,
> Taking the form of a servant,
> Being born in the likeness of men.
>
> And being found in human form
> He humbled himself
> And became obedient unto death.
> (2:6–8, Revised Standard Version)

The hymn's second stanza (2:9–11) describes how God rewards Jesus' selfless obedience by granting him universal lordship. God elevates Jesus "to the glory of God, the Father."

In this famous passage, which has been translated in various ways to stress different theories about Christ's divinity, Jesus' relation to the Father is ambiguously stated. Since the fourth century C.E., when the church adopted the doctrine of the Trinity, it has commonly been assumed that the hymn refers to Jesus' prehuman existence and affirms the son's coeternity and coequality with the Father. (See box 2.3.)

Remembering Paul's explicit subordination of Jesus to God in 1 Corinthians (15:24–28), many readers will be cautious about attributing post-New Testament ideas to the apostle. A growing number of scholars believe that Paul employs the hymn in order implicitly to contrast two "sons" of God—Adam (Luke 3:38) and Jesus. (The Adam-Christ contrast figures prominently in 1 Cor. 15:21–23, 45–49, and Rom. 5:12–19.) The mention of "form" (Greek *morphe*) refers to the divine image that both Adam and Jesus reflect (Gen. 1:26–28). But whereas Adam tried to seize God-like status (Gen. 3:5), Jesus takes the form of a slave. Instead of rebelling against the Creator, he is submissively obedient unto death.

Finally, Adam's disobedience brings shame and death, but Jesus' total obedience brings glory and exaltation. Jesus' self-emptying earns him the fullness of God's reward, the bestowal of "the name above all names," to whom all creation submits. In accordance with his usual method of using theology to drive home behavioral instruction, Paul implicitly compares the reward given Jesus' humility with that in store for humbly obedient Christians. Now shining like "stars in a dark world," they will inherit a future life similar to that now enjoyed by Jesus (2:14–18).

RECOMMENDATIONS OF TIMOTHY AND EPAPHRODITUS

The references to Timothy and Epaphroditus, two of his favorite companions, suggest Paul's warm capacity for friendship. Timothy, whose name appears as courtesy coauthor of this letter (1:1), is one of Paul's most reliable associates. Unlike Barnabas and

John Mark, with whom Paul quarreled, Timothy (who is half Jewish and half Greek) shares Paul's positive attitude toward Gentile converts. In the apostle's absence, Paul trusts him to act as he would (2:19–24).

Epaphroditus, whom the Philippians had sent to assist Paul in prison, has apparently touched Paul by the depth of his personal devotion. Epaphroditus's dangerous illness, which delayed his return to Philippi, may have resulted from his helping the prisoner. Paul implies his gratitude when urging the Philippians to give Epaphroditus an appreciative welcome home (2:25–3:1a).

Paul's concern for individual believers in Philippi is also apparent in his personal message for two estranged women, Euodia and Syntyche. Pleading with sensitivity and tact for their reconciliation, he ranks the two women as co-workers who share his efforts to promote the Gospel (4:2–3).

ATTACKING ADVOCATES OF CIRCUMCISION

In chapter 3, flashes of Paul's old fire give his words a glowing edge. This section (3:1b–20), which is thought to have originated as a separate memorandum, attacks Judaizers who insist on circumcising Gentile converts. Denouncing circumcision as "mutilation," he contemptuously dismisses his opponents as "dogs"—the common Jewish tag for the uncircumcised. Paul provides valuable autobiographical information when he cites his ethnic qualifications—superior to those of his enemies—to evaluate the advantages of being a Jew. Despite his exemplary credentials—and his perfection in keeping the Jewish regulations—he discounts his Jewish heritage as "garbage." All human advantages are worthless when compared to the new life God gives in Christ (3:1–11).

Letter to Philemon

Philemon is Paul's only surviving personal letter, but it is not an entirely private communication. Besides **Philemon,** it is addressed to "Apphia our sister" and "Archippus our comrade in arms," perhaps the chief recipient's wife and son. The family may have been leaders in "the congregation at [their] house," before which the letter was probably intended to be read (vv. 1–2).

Although it is Paul's shortest letter, it deals with a big subject—the problem of human slavery among Christians. Paul writes to Philemon on behalf of the runaway slave **Onesimus,** who had apparently stolen money and illegally departed from Philemon's household. Onesimus's fate brought him from Colossae to Rome (or Ephesus, if that is where Paul's captivity letters originated), where the slave was converted to Christianity, perhaps by Paul himself.

Although Onesimus has made himself almost indispensable to the imprisoned apostle, Paul—compelled by Roman law—has no choice but to send the slave back to his master. Maintaining a fine balance between exercising his apostolic authority and appealing to the equality existing among all Christians, Paul asks Philemon to receive Onesimus back, treating him "no longer as a slave, but . . . as a dear brother" (v. 15). We do not know if Paul is thereby requesting the master to free Onesimus, granting him legal and social status to match his Christian freedom, but the writer clearly stresses the slave's human value. Paul writes that Onesimus is "a part of myself" and that Philemon should welcome him as he would the apostle himself (vv. 12, 17).

Paul also gives his guarantee that he will reimburse Philemon for any debt Onesimus may have incurred (or, perhaps, money he may have stolen) (vv. 18–20). Appealing to Philemon's love (v. 7) and duty (v. 8), he anticipates the master's generosity by predicting that Philemon will "do better than [he] asks" (v. 21). Some commentators observe that Paul is asking Philemon in not too subtle a way to free Onesimus in order for him to remain in Paul's service.

In a final request, Paul asks that Philemon have a guest room prepared for him, indicating that the apostle expects to be released from prison in the foreseeable future. The letter closes with greetings from, among others, Mark and Luke, traditional authors of the two Gospels bearing their respective names.

THE QUESTION OF SLAVERY

Readers may be disappointed that Paul does not denounce human slavery as an intolerable evil. Instead, he merely accepts its existence as a social fact, nowhere ordering Christians to free the human beings they owned as chattel. Paul's attitude is consistent with both the biblical tradition and the practices of Greco-Roman society.

The Hebrew Bible regulates slavery, distinguishing between Gentile slaves captured in battle and Hebrew slaves who sold themselves or their children to pay off financial debts. In a Torah passage known as the "Book of the Covenant," the Law decrees that after six years' servitude, a male Hebrew slave is to be set free. Any children born to him and one of his master's female slaves, however, are to remain the master's property. If at the end of six years' time the freed man wishes to remain with his wife and family, he must submit to a mutilation of the ear (the organ of obedience) and remain a slave for life (Ex. 21:2–6).

Following the Torah and the institutions of society at large, the New Testament writers neither condemn slavery nor predict its abolition. At the same time, the persistence of slavery was inconsistent with the ethical principles of Christian freedom and the human being's innate worth advocated in Paul's letters and the Gospels. In American history, both pro- and anti-slavery parties used the New Testament to support their conflicting views. Slavery's proponents argued that Bible writers, including Paul, implicitly accepted the institution as a "natural" condition. Those against slavery extrapolated from Paul's doctrine of freedom and Christian equality a corresponding social and legal freedom for all people.

Paul's Lasting Influence

During his lifetime, Paul fought constantly to win other Christians' recognition that his Gospel and claim to apostleship were legitimate. Even his own churches frequently challenged his authority and doubted his view that humans receive salvation through God's free gift, accepted in faith, rather

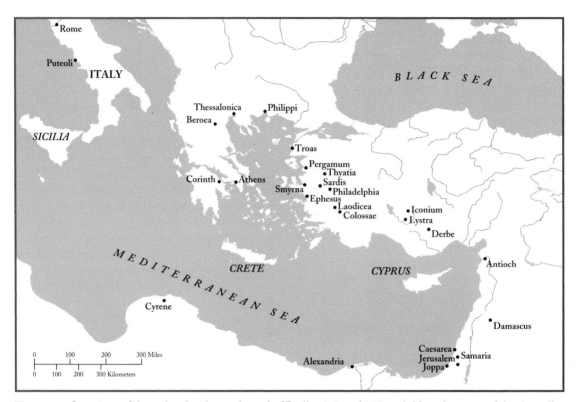

Figure 16.3 Locations of the major churches at the end of Paul's ministry (c. 62 C.E.). Note that most of the tiny cells of Christians are at the eastern end of the Mediterranean (Palestine and Syria) or in Asia Minor (present-day Turkey). Paul established most of the churches in western Asia Minor as well as the first churches in Greece (Philippi to Corinth). We do not know who founded the Italian churches, including the one in Rome. How or when Christianity was introduced to Egypt (Alexandria and Cyrene) is also unknown.

than through obedience to the biblical Torah. Ironically, in the decades following his death—as the church slowly changed from a mostly Jewish to a largely Gentile institution—Paul was recognized as chief among the missionary apostles, and his doctrine became the basis for much of the church's theology.

By the mid-second century, when the document known as 2 Peter was written, Paul's collected letters had assumed the authority of Scripture, at least in some Christian circles. At the same time, Paul's difficult ideas and sometimes obscure phrasing left his work open to a variety of interpretations. The author of 2 Peter denounces students of Paul who interpret Pauline thought in a way contrary to official church teaching:

[Paul] wrote to you with his inspired wisdom. And so he does in all his other letters, . . . though they contain some obscure passages, which the ignorant and unstable misinterpret to their own ruin, as they do the other scriptures. (2 Pet. 3:16)

Then, as now, not only the "ignorant and unstable" but also the well educated and relatively well balanced may disagree on Paul's intentions in many "obscure passages."

PAUL'S ACCOMPLISHMENTS

In a characteristic remark, Paul observes that he works harder than any other apostle to bring the Christian message to potential converts (2 Cor.

11:23). Even today the enormous distances he traveled, by sea and on foot, would challenge the physical stamina of the most dedicated missionary. He established Christian "colonies" throughout Syria, Asia Minor, Macedonia, and Greece and left behind an impressive network of churches (see figure 16.3). These were interconnected by itinerant missionaries (many trained by Paul himself) and at least partly united by memories of Paul's preaching and the written legacy of his voluminous correspondence. As the author of Acts realized, Paul also made himself a formidable model for later believers to emulate.

PAUL — CHRISTIANITY'S FIRST GREAT INTERPRETER OF CHRIST

In introducing Pauline thought (in chapter 13), we listed some of the assumptions and personal experiences, such as his mystical encounter with the risen Christ, that helped determine Paul's distinctive ideas about God's changed relationship to humanity, Jew and Gentile alike. In assessing his legacy, we can now briefly review several of Paul's most enduring contributions, teachings that have influenced the church for almost two millennia.

Although not a systematic thinker, he was the first to create a coherent theology about Jesus and is thus counted as Christianity's first theologian. Interpreting Jesus' career theologically—showing how God (*theos*) revealed his will through Jesus' death and resurrection—Paul laid the foundations on which later interpreters of the "Christ event" have built. We have space here to summarize only a few of Paul's main ideas. The ones we select illustrate the general trend of his views on the nature of God and his purpose in using Jesus to reconcile the previously alienated human and divine components of the universe.

God   As a "Hebrew born and bred" (Phil. 3:5), Paul is unquestionably a monotheist, recognizing the Jewish God as the entire world's Supreme Power and Judge. Steeped in the Hebrew Bible's composite portrait of Yahweh, Paul regards God as embodying human traits on a superhuman scale.

Both "severe" and "kind," he manifests his dual nature to human beings, alternately condemning or showing mercy according to an irresistible will. He is incomparably holy, just, and pure; his perfect justice does not allow full communion with imperfect, deliberately unjust, and otherwise sinful humanity. His infinite love, however, sets in motion a joyous process of reconciling an estranged human creation to himself.

The Role of Jesus   Paul realized that his fellow Jews expected an undefeated Messiah and that Jesus' crucifixion was a major "stumbling block" to Jewish acceptance. He therefore formulated a theology of the cross. In Romans and Galatians, he interprets the Crucifixion as a redemptive act in which human "weakness"—Jesus' "shameful" death—is the means by which God bridges the great moral gulf between himself and humanity. Demonstrating absolute obedience to the divine will, Jesus sacrifices his life to satisfy God's justice and obtain forgiveness for others.

Justification   By *justification* or *righteousness*, Paul means a right standing or relationship with God. Keeping the Mosaic Torah cannot justify people because the Torah only serves to make one aware of lawbreaking, of committing "sin" (*hamartia*), of falling short of ethical perfection. When he died voluntarily, Jesus not only took on himself the Law's penalty for all sinners but transferred just punishment to sin itself. He thus rid sin of its power to operate uncontrolled in what Paul calls our "fleshly" (physical) or "lower" nature (Rom. 1–4).

Adam and Christ   In Paul's view of human history, the earthly prototype—Adam—willfully disobeyed God, thus separating himself from life's source and bringing sin (error) and death to himself and all his descendants. In Jesus, God found Adam's moral opposite, a man of perfect obedience who achieved a right relationship with God and through his resurrection became God's Son (Rom. 1:4). Now the model of a renewed humanity reconciled to God, Jesus as Christ brings life to all who place their trust (faith) in him (Rom. 5; 1 Cor. 15).

Salvation Through Faith   The idea that human beings are saved by their faith is one of Paul's most distinctive and revolutionary ideas. By *faith*, Paul does not mean belief in a creed or a set of religious doctrines. Pauline faith denotes an individual's inner awareness of and trust in God's ability—and willingness—to draw believers to him in love. To Paul, faith is a dynamic force that motivates people to accept God's free gift of salvation; it is a voluntary response to divine grace. Because God gives his rewards freely, a person can neither earn nor deserve them. Hence, the works of the Torah—including circumcision and food purity laws—are irrelevant.

God and Christ   Although he calls the glorified Jesus "lord" (Greek, *kyrios*) and assigns him the highest possible status in God's plan for universal redemption, Paul remains a Jewish monotheist, always regarding the Son as subordinate to the Father (1 Cor. 15:24–28). Jesus refuses to attempt "equality with God" and is eternally the model of humble submission to the paternal will (Phil. 2:6–7). In some metaphysical sense, however, the Son is the agent by whom God created the universe, in whom "the complete being of the Godhead dwells embodied," and through whom the divine purpose is revealed (Col. 1–2). As human beings were originally created in God's "image" (Gen. 1:27), so Christ is that divine–human image perfected (Col. 1:15).

Eschatology   Because he believes that he is living at the very edge of the New Age introduced by Jesus' advent, Paul places much of his ethical instruction to the church in the context of End time. Jesus' resurrection and ascension to heaven now allow Christ's Spirit to dwell in each believer, giving him or her charismatic gifts of prophesying, healing, teaching, and speaking in or interpreting ecstatic language. Paul regards these spiritual gifts as further evidence of the "last days" and urges believers to produce the Spirit's good fruits—joyful virtues and a grateful awareness that in Christ they attain a new nature. Thus, they are prepared for the "splendor" of the resurrection body they will receive at the Parousia.

Summary

This brief survey, concentrating on Paul's vision of the Deity's gracious plan to redeem humanity through Christ, does scant justice to the range and profundity of Pauline thought. The apostle's views on free will and predestination, Christian ethics, the church, human sexuality, and related matters require fuller discussion than we can offer here.

Embattled in his own day, within two generations after his death Paul became a monument of orthodoxy (correct teaching) to many church leaders. The letters to Timothy and Titus, written in Paul's name by a later disciple, show in what high regard the apostle was held (see chapter 17). After another 1400 years had passed, Paul again became a center of controversy. During the Protestant Reformation, conflicting interpretations of the Pauline belief that human beings are saved by faith and not by works (including the performance of sacramental rituals) deeply divided Roman Catholics and Protestants. Today, Paul remains a stimulating, dynamic influence wherever the New Testament is read. Second only to Jesus in his lasting influence on Christendom, he is the prism through which Jesus' image is most commonly viewed.

QUESTIONS FOR REVIEW

1. Why is it difficult to know exactly where Paul was imprisoned when he wrote to Philemon and the church at Philippi?

2. Although the hymn Paul cites in Philippians 2 is commonly interpreted as describing Jesus' prehuman existence, many commentators believe that it contains instead an implied contrast between Adam's disobedience and Jesus' humble obedience. Summarize the arguments for and against these differing interpretations.

3. Identify Philemon and Onesimus and their connection to Paul. Why do you think Paul does not condemn human slavery as an evil institution?

4. Summarize Paul's major contributions to Christian thought, including his beliefs about the *eschaton*, his teachings about the nature and function of Christ (Christology), and his doctrine of justification by faith.

QUESTION FOR DISCUSSION AND REFLECTION

1. Like all historical figures, Paul is firmly linked to his particular time and place. On many issues, such as the restricted role of women and a hierarchical view of society, Paul reflects the accepted norms of his day. Writing as a former Pharisee who believed that the crucified Messiah would imminently return to judge the world, bringing human history to an end, Paul often fails to address such important issues as the evils of slavery, widespread poverty, and governmental injustice. Do you think that if Paul were alive today—and fully aware of the last 1900 years of human development—he would revise his opinions on such topics as master–slave relationships, celibacy, homosexuality, and unquestioning submission to governmental authorities? If they had followed Paul's advice in Romans 13, could the leaders of the American Revolution have framed the Declaration of Independence or broken free of British control?

TERMS AND CONCEPTS TO REMEMBER

Philippi

city at which the "prison letters" originated

Jesus' submission and exaltation (Phil. 2)

Timothy

Epaphroditus

Onesimus

Paul's attitude toward slavery

biblical view of slavery

Jesus as "image of God"

Jesus' nature and function

Jesus' cosmic role

Christology

initiation into Christ

Paul's achievements

Paul's most distinctive teachings

RECOMMENDED READING

Barth, M., ed. and trans. *Colossians and Philemon.* Vol. 34a of the Anchor Bible. Garden City, N.Y.: Doubleday, 1974. A scholarly translation and analysis.

Beare, F. W. *A Commentary on the Epistle to the Philippians.* Harper's New Testament Commentaries. New York: Harper & Row, 1959. Another new translation with solid, concise commentary.

Byrne, Brendan. "The Letter to the Philippians." In R. E. Brown et al., eds., *The New Jerome Biblical Commentary,* 2nd ed., pp. 791–797. Englewood Cliffs, N.J.: Prentice-Hall, 1990.

Duncan, G. S. "Letter to the Philippians." In G. A. Buttrick, ed., *The Interpreter's Dictionary of the Bible,* Vol. 3, pp. 787–791. New York and Nashville, Tenn.: Abingdon Press, 1962.

Knox, John. *Philemon Among the Letters of Paul,* rev. ed. New York: Abingdon Press, 1959. Develops Edgar Goodspeed's theory that about 90 C.E. a Paulinist—perhaps the former slave Onesimus, who may then have been bishop of Ephesus—collected Paul's letters and circulated them among the entire church.

Lohse, Eduard. *Colossians and Philemon.* Hermeneia. Philadelphia: Fortress Press, 1971. A scholarly analysis concluding that Colossians is by a Pauline disciple.

Martin, R. P. *Carmen Christi: Philippians 2:5–11 in Recent Interpretation and in the Setting of Early Christian Worship,* rev. ed. Grand Rapids, Mich.: Eerdmans, 1983.

———. *Philippians.* New Century Bible Commentary. Grand Rapids, Mich.: Eerdmans, 1983.

O'Brien, P. T. *Colossians, Philemon.* Word Biblical Commentary 44. Waco, Tex.: Word Books, 1982. Defends Pauline authorship of Colossians; includes author's translation.

Stendahl, K., ed. and trans. *Romans, Galatians, and Philippians.* Vol. 33 of the Anchor Bible. Garden City, N.Y.: Doubleday, 1978. A new translation with editorial commentary.

CHAPTER 17

Continuing the Pauline Tradition

2 Thessalonians, Colossians, Ephesians, and the Pastoral Epistles

Stand firm . . . and hold fast to the traditions which you have learned from us by word or letter.
2 Thessalonians 2:15

Keep before you an outline of the sound teaching which you heard from me. . . . Guard the treasure [apostolic tradition] put into our charge.
2 Timothy 1:13–14

Key Themes Paul's continuing influence on the church was so great after his death that various Pauline disciples composed letters in his name and spirit, claiming his authority to settle new issues besetting the Christian community. Whereas a minority of scholars defend Pauline authorship of 2 Thessalonians and Colossians, a large majority are certain that he did not write Ephesians, 1 or 2 Timothy, or Titus.

Repeating themes from Paul's genuine letter to the Thessalonians, 2 Thessalonians reinterprets Paul's original eschatology, asserting that a number of traditional apocalyptic "signs" must precede the eschaton.

In Colossians, a Pauline disciple emphasizes Jesus' identification with the cosmic power and wisdom by and for which the universe was created. The divine "secret" is revealed as Christ's Spirit dwelling in the believer. A deutero-Pauline composition, Ephesians contains ideas similar to those in Colossians, revising and updating Pauline concepts about God's universal plan of salvation for both Jews and Gentiles and about believers' spiritual warfare with supernatural evil.

Writing to Timothy and Titus as symbols of a new generation of Christians, an anonymous disciple (known as the Pastor) warns his readers against false teachings (heresy). He urges them to adhere strictly to the original apostolic traditions, supported by the Hebrew Bible and the church.

Six canonical letters in which the author explicitly identifies himself as Paul, Apostle to the Gentiles, contain discrepancies that cause scholars to question their Pauline authorship. Two of the letters—2 Thessalonians and Colossians—are still vigorously disputed, with a large minority championing their authenticity. By contrast, an overwhelming scholarly majority deny that Paul wrote the four others—Ephesians, 1 and 2 Timothy, and Titus. The latter three are called the **Pastoral Epistles** because the writer—as a pastor or shepherd—offers guidance and advice to his flock, the church.

According to tradition, Paul wrote 2 Thessalonians shortly after his first letter to believers at

Thessalonica, and Ephesians and Colossians while imprisoned in Rome. After being released, he traveled to Crete, only to be thrown in prison a second time (2 Tim.). During this second and final incarceration, the apostle supposedly composed these farewell letters to his trusted associates, Timothy and Titus, young men who represent a new generation of Christian leadership.

Since the eighteenth century, however, scholars have increasingly doubted Paul's responsibility for either Ephesians or the pastorals. More recently, they have also suspected that both 2 Thessalonians and Colossians are the work of later authors who adopted Paul's persona. Detailed analyses of these six documents, especially Ephesians and the pastorals, strongly indicate that they were composed long after Paul's time.

The Problem of Pseudonymity

The author of 2 Thessalonians tells his recipients not to become overly excited if they receive a letter falsely bearing Paul's name, indicating that the practice of circulating forged documents purportedly by apostolic writers had already begun (2 Thess. 2:1–3). To some modern readers, the notion that unknown Christians wrote in Paul's name is ethically unacceptable on the grounds that such "forgeries" could not be part of the New Testament. In the ancient world, however, twentieth-century ideas about authorship would have been irrelevant, for it was then common for disciples of great

thinkers to compose works perpetuating their masters' thoughts. They wrote about contemporary issues as they believed their leader would have if he were still alive.

This practice of creating new works under the identity of a well-known but deceased personage is called pseudonymity. Intending to honor an esteemed figure of the past rather than necessarily to deceive the reading public, both Jews and early Christians produced a large body of pseudonymous literature. In an attempt to apply the teachings of a dead prophet or spiritual mentor to current situations, Hellenistic-Jewish authors wrote books ascribed to such revered biblical figures as Daniel, Enoch, Noah, David, Isaiah, Ezra, and Moses. Some, such as the Book of Daniel, were accepted into the Hebrew Bible canon; others, such as 1 Enoch (quoted as scripture in the New Testament letter of Jude), were not. Still others, including the apocalyptic 2 Esdras (4 Ezra), became part of the Apocrypha.

The precise motives inspiring pseudonymous writers are unknown, but some may have wished to obtain a respectful hearing for their views that only a work purportedly by Paul, Peter, or another authority in the early church could command. During the first three centuries C.E., numerous works, including Gospels, apostolic Acts, letters, and apocalypses, appeared in the names of Peter, John, James, Barnabas, and Paul (see chapters 18 and 20). Some of these pseudonymous books conveyed a message persuasive enough to gain them a place in the New Testament.

Second Letter to the Thessalonians

An increasing number of scholars are skeptical about the genuineness of 2 Thessalonians. If Paul actually composed it, why does he repeat—almost verbatim—so much of what he had already just written to the same recipients? More seriously, why does the author present an eschatology so different from that presented in the first letter? In 1 Thessalonians, the Parousia will occur stealthily, "like a thief in the night." In 2 Thessalonians, a number of apocalyptic "signs" will first advertise its arrival. The interposing of these mysterious events between the writer's time and that of the Parousia has the effect of placing the *eschaton* further into the future—a contrast to 1 Thessalonians, in which the End is extremely close.

Scholars defending Pauline authorship advance several theories to explain the writer's apparent change of attitude toward the Parousia. In the first letter, Paul stresses the tension between the shortness of time the world has left and the necessity of believers' vigilance and ethical purity as they await the Second Coming. In the second missive, Paul writes to correct the Thessalonians' misconceptions about or abuses of his earlier emphasis on the nearness of End time.

If Paul is in fact the author, he probably wrote 2 Thessalonians within a few months of his earlier letter. Some converts, claiming that "the Day of the Lord is already here" (2:2), were upsetting others with their otherworldly enthusiasms. In their state of apocalyptic fervor, some even scorned everyday occupations and refused to work or support themselves. It is possible that the visionary Spirit of prophecy that Paul encouraged the Thessalonians to cultivate (1 Thess. 5:19–22) had come back to haunt him. Empowered by private revelations, a few Christian prophets may have interpreted the Spirit's presence—made possible by Jesus' resurrection and ascension to heaven—as a mystical fulfillment of the Parousia. According to this belief in presently realized eschatology, the Lord's Day is now. Paul, however, consistently stresses that Jesus' resurrection and the Spirit's coming are only the first stage in God's plan of cosmic renewal. God's purpose can be completed only at the apocalyptic End of history.

PLACING THE SECOND COMING IN PERSPECTIVE

In 2 Thessalonians, Paul (or some other writer building on his thought) takes on the difficult task of urging Christians to be ever alert and prepared for the Lord's return and at the same time to remember that certain events must take place before the Second Coming can occur. The writer achieves this delicate balance partly by insisting on a rational and practical approach to life during the unknown interim between his writing and the Parousia.

Notice that the author invokes a vivid picture of the Final Judgment to imprint its imminent reality on his readers' consciousness. He paraphrases images from the Hebrew prophets to imply that persons now persecuting Christians will soon suffer God's wrath. Christ will be revealed from heaven amid blazing fire, overthrowing those who disobey Jesus' gospel or fail to honor the one God (1:1–12).

Having assured the Thessalonians that their present opponents will be punished at Jesus' return, Paul now admonishes them not to assume that the punishment will happen immediately. Believers are not to run wild over some visionary's claim that the End is already here. Individual prophetic revelations declaring that Jesus is now invisibly present were apparently strengthened when a letter—supposedly from Paul—conveyed the same or a similar message. (This pseudo-Pauline letter reveals that the practice of composing letters in Paul's name began very early in Christian history.) Speculations founded on private revelations or forged letters, the apostle points out, are doomed to disappointment (2:1–3).

TRADITIONAL (NON-PAULINE?) SIGNS OF THE END

As mentioned above, one of the strongest arguments against Paul's authorship of 2 Thessalonians is the letter's presentation of apocalyptic events that presage the End. Although the writer maintains the Parousia's imminence (1:6–10), he also insists that the final day cannot arrive until certain developments characteristic of Jewish apocalyptic thought have occurred. At this point, 2 Thessalonians reverts to the cryptic and veiled language of apocalyptic discourse, referring to mysterious personages and events that may have been understood by the letter's recipients but that are largely incomprehensible to modern readers. The End cannot come before the final rebellion against God's rule, when evil is revealed in human form as a demonic enemy who desecrates the Temple and claims divinity for himself. In this passage, Paul's terminology resembles that contained in the Book of Daniel, an apocalyptic work denouncing Antiochus IV, a Greek-Syrian king who polluted the Jerusalem Temple and tried to destroy the Jewish religion.

Some commentators suggest that Paul regards the Roman emperor, whose near-absolute power gave him virtually unlimited potential for inflicting evil on humankind, as a latter-day counterpart of Antiochus. Paul's explicitly stated view of the Roman government, however, is positive (Rom. 13), so readers must look elsewhere to identify the doomed figure.

Reminding the Thessalonians that he had previously informed them orally of these apocalyptic developments, Paul states that the mysterious enemy's identity will not be disclosed until the appointed time. This is an allusion to the typically apocalyptic belief that all history is predestined: Events cannot occur before their divinely predetermined hour. Evil forces are already at work, however, secretly gathering strength until the unidentified "Restrainer" disappears, allowing the evil personage to reveal himself.

Apocalyptic Dualism   In this passage, the writer paints a typically apocalyptic worldview, a moral dualism in which the opposing powers of Good and Evil have their respective agents at work on earth. The enemy figure is Satan's agent; his opposite is Christ. As Jesus is God's representative working in human history, so the wicked rebel is the devil's tool. Operating on a cosmic scope, the conflict between Good and Evil culminates in Christ's victory over his enemy, who has deceived the mass of humanity into believing the "Lie." (This is, perhaps, the false belief that any being other than God is the source of humanity's ultimate welfare.) An evil parody of the Messiah, the unnamed Satanic dupe functions as an **anti-Christ** (2:3–12).

The writer's language is specific enough to arouse speculation about the identities of the enigmatic "wicked man" and the "Restrainer" who at the time of writing kept the anti-Christ in check. It is also vague enough to preclude connecting any known historical figures with these apocalyptic roles. In typical apocalyptic fashion, the figures are mythic archetypes that belong to a realm beyond the reach of historical investigation.

A Disputed Letter to the Colossians

If Paul is the author of Colossians, as a large minority of scholars believe, he had not yet visited the city when he wrote this theologically important letter. A small town in the Roman province of Asia, **Colossae** was located about 100 miles east of Ephesus, the provincial capital (see figure 16.1). **Epaphras,** one of Paul's missionary associates, had apparently founded the church a short time prior to Paul's writing (1:7).

If genuine, Colossians was probably composed at about the same time as Philemon, to which it is closely related. In both letters, Paul writes from prison, including his friend Timothy in the salutation (1:1) and adding greetings from many of the same persons — such as Onesimus, Archippus, Aristarchus, Epaphras, Mark, and Luke — cited in the earlier missive (4:9–18). If Philemon's was the house church at Colossae, it is strange that Paul does not mention him, but his absence from the letter does not discredit Pauline authorship.

PURPOSE AND ORGANIZATION

Although it was not one of his churches, Paul (or one of his later disciples) writes to the Colossae congregation to correct some false teachings prevalent there. These beliefs apparently involved cults that gave undue honor to angels or other invisible spirits inhabiting the universe. Some Colossians may have attempted to worship beings that the angels themselves worshiped. Paul refutes these "hollow and delusive" notions by emphasizing Christ's uniqueness and supremacy. Christ alone is the channel to spiritual reality; lesser spirit beings are merely his "captives."

Paul writes to make sure that the Colossians clearly recognize who Christ really is. The author emphasizes two principal themes: (1) Christ is supreme because God's power now manifested in him was the same power that created the entire universe, including those invisible entities the false teachers mistakenly worship; and (2) when they realize Christ's supremacy and experience his indwelling Spirit, the Colossians are initiated into his mystery cult, voluntarily harmonizing their lives with the cosmic unity he embodies.

CHRIST THE SOURCE OF COSMIC UNITY

In the opinion of some analysts, both the complex nature of the false teachings, which seem to blend pagan and marginally Jewish ideas into a Gnostic synthesis, and the Christology of Colossians seem too "advanced" for the letter to have originated in Paul's day. Other critics point out that if the letter was written late in Paul's career to meet a situation significantly different from others he had earlier encountered, it could well have stimulated the apostle to produce a more fully developed expression of his views about Christ's nature and function.

Jesus as the Mediator of Creation   As in the second chapter of Philippians, the author seems to adapt an older Christian hymn to illustrate his vision of the exalted Jesus' cosmic role:

> He is the image of the invisible god, the first-born of all creation;
> for in him all things were created, in heaven and on earth, visible and invisible, whether thrones or dominions or principalities or authorities,
> all things were created through him and for him.
>
> He is before all things,
>   and in him all things hold together.
> He is the head of the body, the church;
> He is the beginning, the first-born from the dead, that in everything he might be pre-eminent.
>
> For in him all the fullness of God was pleased to dwell,
> and through him to reconcile to himself all things, whether on earth or in heaven,
>   making peace by the blood of his cross.
>   (1:15–20, Revised Standard Version)

Like the prolog to John's Gospel, this beautiful poem is modeled on biblical and Hellenistic-Jewish concepts of divine Wisdom (Prov. 8:22–31; Ecclus. 24:1–22; see also the discussion of John's usage of Logos [Word] in chapter 10). Hellenistic Jews had created a rich lore of speculative thought in which God's chief attribute, his infinite Wisdom, is the source of all creation and the means by which he communicates his purpose to humanity. Many historians believe that early Christian thinkers adopted these ready-made wisdom traditions and applied them to Jesus.

Like Philippians 2, the Colossians hymn is traditionally seen as proclaiming Jesus' heavenly preexistence and his personal role as mediator in creation. More recently, many scholars—recognizing the hymn's use of wisdom language—view it as a declaration that the same divine Presence and Power that created the Cosmos now operates in the glorified Christ. The personified Wisdom whom God employed as his agent in fashioning the universe is now fully revealed in Christ, the agent through whom God redeems his human creation.

The phrase "image [*eikon*] of the invisible God" (1:15) may correspond to the phrase "form [*morphes*] of God" that Paul used in Philippians (2:6). In both cases, the term echoes the words of Genesis 1, in which God creates the first human beings in his own "image" (Gen. 1:26–27). (Notice that the writer describes the Colossians as also bearing the divine "image" [3:10].) Rather than asserting that the prehuman Jesus was literally present at creation, the hymn may affirm that he is the ultimate goal toward which God's world trends.

Whatever Christology he advances, the writer's main purpose is to demonstrate Christ's present superiority to all rival cosmic beings. The "thrones, sovereignties, authorities and powers" mentioned (1:16) probably represent the Jewish hierarchy of angels. Christ's perfect obedience, vindicating God's image in humanity, and his ascension to heaven have rendered these lesser beings irrelevant and powerless. By his triumph, Christ leads them captive as a Roman emperor leads a public procession of conquered enemies (2:9–15).

Moving from Christ's supremacy to his own role in the divine plan, Paul states that his task is to deliver God's message of reconciliation. He is the agent chosen to reveal the divine "secret hidden for long ages"—the glorified Christ dwelling in the believer, spiritually reuniting the Christian with God. Christians thus form Christ's visible body, here identified with the church (1:21–2:8).

The Mystical Initiation into Christ Employing the rather obscure language of Greek mystery religions (see chapter 3), Paul compares the Christian's baptism to a vicarious experience of Christ's death and resurrection (2:12, 20; 3:1). It is also the Christian equivalent of circumcision, the ritual sign that identifies one as belonging to God's people, and the rite of initiation into Christ's "body" (2:12–14). Raised to new life, initiated believers are liberated from religious obligations sponsored by those lesser spirits who transmitted the Torah revelation to Moses.

Empowered by Christ's Spirit, the Colossians should not be intimidated by self-styled authorities who mortify the body and piously forbid partaking of certain food and drink, for Christ's death ended all such legal discriminations. Although the author declares the equality of all believers, regardless of nationality or social class, notice that he omits the unity of the sexes that Paul included in Galatians 3:28 (2:20–3:11). As with many Greco-Roman mystery cults, initiation into Christ is a union of social and religious equality.

Obligations of Initiation Consistent with Paul's custom, the author concludes by stressing the ethical implications of his theology. Because Christians experience the indwelling Christ, they must live exceptionally pure and upright lives. The list of vices (3:5–9) and virtues (3:12–25) is typical of other Hellenistic teachers of ethics, but the writer adds a distinctively Christian note: Believers behave well because they are being re-created in Christ's nature and "image" (3:10).

Letter to the Ephesians

THE CASE OF EPHESIANS

Whereas Paul's authorship of Colossians is seriously doubted, the claim that he wrote Ephesians is almost universally repudiated. Although it closely resembles Colossians (the style and theology of which also seem untypical of Paul), Ephesians differs from the undisputed Pauline letters in (1) vocabulary (containing over ninety words not found elsewhere in Paul's writings), (2) literary style (written in extremely long, convoluted sentences, in contrast to Paul's usually direct, forceful statements), and (3) theology (lacking typically Pauline doctrines such as justification by faith and the nearness of Christ's return).

Despite its similarity to Colossians (75 of Ephesians' 155 verses parallel phrases in Colossians), it presents a different view of the sacred "secret" or "mystery" revealed in Christ. In Colossians, God's long-kept secret is Christ's mystical union with his followers (Col. 1:27), but in Ephesians, it is the union of Jew and Gentile in one church (Eph. 3:6).

More than any other disputed letter (except those to Timothy and Titus), Ephesians seems to reflect a time in church history significantly later than Paul's day. References to "Apostles and prophets" as the church's foundation imply that these figures belong to the past, not the author's generation (2:20; 3:5). The Gentiles' equality in Christian fellowship is no longer a controversial issue but an accomplished fact; this strongly suggests that the letter originated after the church membership had become largely non-Jewish (2:11–22). Judaizing interlopers no longer question Paul's stand on circumcision, again indicating that the work was composed after Jerusalem's destruction had largely eliminated the Jewish influence of the mother church.

When Paul uses the term *church (ekklesia),* he always refers to a single congregation (Gal. 1:2; 1 Cor. 11:16; 16:19, etc.). By contrast, Ephesians' author speaks of the "church" collectively, a universal institution encompassing all individual groups. This view of the church as a worldwide entity also points to a time after the apostolic period.

The accumulated evidence convinces most scholars that Ephesians is a deutero-Pauline document, a secondary work composed in Paul's name by an admirer thoroughly steeped in the apostle's thought and general theology. The close parallels to Colossians, as well as phrases taken from Romans, Philemon, and other letters, indicate that unlike the author of Acts, this unknown writer was familiar with the Pauline correspondence. Some scholars propose that Ephesians was written as a kind of "cover letter" or essay to accompany an early collection of Paul's letters. Ephesians, then, can be seen as a tribute to Paul, summarizing some of his ideas and updating others to fit the changing needs of a largely Gentile and cosmopolitan church.

The phrase "in Ephesus" (1:1), identifying the recipients, does not appear in any of the oldest manuscripts. That fact, plus the absence of any specific issue or problem being addressed, reinforces the notion that Ephesians was intended to circulate among several churches in Asia Minor.

DATE AND ORGANIZATION

If the letter to the Ephesians is by Paul, it probably originated from his Roman prison (60–64 C.E.). If it is by a later Pauline disciple, as almost all scholars believe, Ephesians was written about the time Paul's letters first circulated as a unit, perhaps about 90 C.E.

Ephesians' diverse contents can be subsumed under two major headings:

1. God's plan of salvation through the unified body of the church (1:3–3:21)
2. Instructions for living in the world while united to Christ (4:1–6:20)

Despite its long and sometimes awkward sentence structures (rephrased into shorter units in most English translations), Ephesians is a masterpiece of devotional literature. Unlike Paul's undisputed letters, it has a quiet and meditative tone, with no temperamental outbursts or attacks on the writer's enemies. Although it imitates the letter form by including a brief salutation (1:1–2) and a final greeting (6:21–24), Ephesians is really a highly sophisticated tract.

GOD'S PLAN OF SALVATION THROUGH THE UNITED BODY OF CHRIST

Ephesians' main theme is the union of all creation with Christ, manifested on earth by the church's international unity (1:10–14). Echoing Romans' concept of predestination, the author states that be-

fore the world's foundation, God selected Christ's future "children" (composing the church) to be redeemed by Jesus' blood, a sacrifice through which the chosen ones' sins are forgiven.

According to his preordained plan, God has placed Christ as head of the church, which is his body. The Spirit of Christ now fills the church as fully as God dwells in Christ (1:22–23). This mystical union of the human and divine is God's unforeseen gift, his grace that saves those who trust him (2:1–10).

The Sacred Secret — the Union of Jews and Gentiles in One Church God's long-hidden secret is that Gentiles, previously under divine condemnation, can now share in the biblical promises made to Israel. This divine purpose to unite Jew and Gentile in equal grace is the special message that Paul is commissioned to preach (3:1–21). (Note that the writer assumes a general acceptance of the Gentile-dominated church, a condition that did not obtain in Paul's day.)

INSTRUCTIONS FOR LIVING IN THE WORLD

Ephesians' last three chapters are devoted to instructions on living properly in the world while remaining united to Christ. Combining ideas from Philippians 2 and Colossians 1, the author reinterprets the concept of Jesus' descent from and reascension to the spirit realm whereby he made lesser spirits his prisoners and filled the universe with his presence. The author also alludes to Jesus' descent into the Underworld, a mythical exploit that appears in 1 Peter (3:19–20).

Advancing Paul's conviction that the Christian revelation requires the highest ethical conduct, Ephesians contrasts Greco-Roman vices with Christian virtues and urges believers to transform their personalities to fit God's new creation (4:17–5:20). Home life is to be as reverent and orderly as behavior in church. Although he insists on a domestic hierarchy — "man is the head of the woman, just as Christ . . . is head of the church" — the writer reminds husbands to love their wives and thus honor them as a treasured equivalent of the self (5:21–6:9). Ephesians endorses the rigid social and domestic hierarchy of the day but makes the system

Figure 17.1 The Book of Ephesians's famous description of a Christian's spiritual defenses against Evil is based on the armor and other military equipment used by Roman soldiers, depicted in this bas-relief (Eph. 6:13–17). (© Mansell Collection-Time Inc.)

more humane by insisting that Christian love apply to all public and private relationships.

Heavenly Armor   In Ephesians' most famous passage, the Pauline analogy of Christians armed like Roman soldiers is vividly elaborated (see figure 17.1). In 1 Thessalonians (5:8), Paul urges believers to imitate armed sentries who stay awake on guard duty, for Christians must remain similarly alert for Christ's sudden reappearance. Ephesians discards the eschatological context of Paul's metaphor, however, and instead presents an ongoing battle between Good and Evil with no end in sight. In the genuine Pauline letters, the apostle foresees Evil demolished at Christ's Second Coming. The Ephesian writer, on the other hand, paints a picture of cosmic conflict reminiscent of Zoroastrianism — the Persian religion in which the world is viewed as a battlefield between invisible forces of light and darkness, Good and Evil.

In Zoroastrian terms, the Ephesian Paul describes two levels of "cosmic powers" — earthly rulers of the present dark age and the invisible forces of evil in heaven (6:10–12). Like Mark, the author apparently senses the reality of an evil so powerful that mere human wickedness cannot explain it. Instead of despairing, however, he rejoices that God provides ammunition that successfully defeats even supernatural evil. According to the author, each article of God's armor is a Christian virtue; cultivated together, qualities like truth and faith offer full protection from even the devil's worst attacks (6:13–19).

Rich in spiritual insight, Ephesians is a creative summary of some major Pauline concepts. Even if not by Paul, it is nevertheless a significant celebration of Christian ideals, an achievement worthy of the great apostle himself.

The Pastorals: Letters to Timothy and Titus

In the opinion of most scholars, the case against Paul's connection with the pastorals is even stronger. Besides the fact that they do not appear in early lists of Paul's canonical works, the pastorals seem to reflect conditions that prevailed long after Paul's day, perhaps as late as the first half of the second century C.E. Lacking Paul's characteristic ideas about faith and the Spirit, they are also un-Pauline in their flat style and different vocabulary (containing 306 words not found in Paul's unquestioned letters). Furthermore, the pastorals assume a church organization far more developed than that current in the apostle's generation.

Known for convenience as "the Pastor," the same Pauline disciple is the author of all three pastoral letters. He views Paul's teaching as the norm or standard for all Christians and writes primarily to combat false teachings, urging the church to reject any deviations from the apostolic heritage. An examination of the Pastor's interpretation of Pauline thought shows that he does not always use terms in the same way as his master, nor is he as vigorous and creative a thinker. Writing to preserve an inherited tradition, he tends to view Christian faith as a set of static doctrines rather than as the ecstatic experience of Christ that Paul knew.

LETTERS TO TIMOTHY

The first two pastorals are addressed to Timothy, the son of a Jewish mother and a Greek father (Acts 16:1), who served as Paul's missionary companion and trusted friend (1 Cor. 4:17; 16:10). According to Acts and Paul's authentic letters, Timothy was an important contributor to Paul's evangelism in Greece and Asia Minor, a cofounder of churches in Macedonia, and later a diplomatic emissary to Philippi, Thessalonica, and Corinth. In listing him as coauthor of as many as six different letters, Paul affirms Timothy's vital role in the Christian mission (1 Thess. 1:1; 2 Thess. 1:1; 2 Cor. 1:1; Phil. 1:1; Philem. 1:1; Col. 1:1).

In the pastorals, however, Timothy is less a historical character than a literary symbol, representative of a new generation of believers to whom the task of preserving apostolic truths is entrusted. Youthful (postapostolic) Christians must take on the job of defending "wholesome doctrine" against devilish heresies (1 Tim. 4:2, 11–12).

I TIMOTHY

Organization   The first letter to Timothy does not present us with a smooth progression of thought, so it makes sense to examine it in terms of topics rather than consecutive sections:

1. Timothy's duty to repress false teachings
2. Church order: the qualifications of bishops, deacons, and elders
3. The roles of women and slaves

Attacking False Teachings (Heresies)   As inheritor of the true faith, Timothy is to combat church members' wrong ideas (1:3). Because the Pastor, unlike Paul, does not offer a rational criticism of his opponents' errors, we do not know the exact nature of the beliefs attacked. Some commentators suggest that the false teachers practiced an early form of Gnosticism, a cult of secret "knowledge" mentioned

in 6:20, but the letter reveals too little about the heresies involved to confirm this suggestion.

Because the author describes the deviants as teaching "the moral law" and being wrongly preoccupied with "interminable myths and genealogies" (1:3–4, 7–9), many critics suppose that some form of Hellenistic Judaism is under attack. Practicing an extreme asceticism (severe self-discipline of the physical appetites), these persons forbid marriage and abstain from various foods (4:1–3). Gnostic practice took many diverse forms, ranging from the kind of self-denial mentioned here to the libertine behavior Paul rebuked in Corinth, Galatia, and elsewhere. Timothy (and the pastorship he represents) must correct such misguided austerity by transmitting the correct Pauline teachings (4:11), thereby saving himself as well as those who obey his orders (4:16).

Qualifications for Church Offices   Invoking Paul's authority, the Pastor is eager to preserve sound doctrine through a stable church organization. His list of qualifications for "bishops" (overseers), "deacons" (assistants), and "elders" (the religiously mature leadership) implies a hierarchy of church offices much more rigidly stratified than was the case in Paul's day. Paul once used the terms *bishop* and *deacon* (Phil. 1:1), but presumably as designating areas of service rather than the specific ecclesiastical offices enumerated here. Although the author says that church officials must demonstrate all the virtues typical of Hellenistic ethical philosophy (3:2–23), he says nothing about their intellectual qualifications or possession of the Spirit. Rather than the spiritual gifts that Paul advocates, the Pastor's standards for church offices are merely hallmarks of middle-class respectability.

The Pastor regards the institution of the church—rather than the Spirit of Christ dwelling in the believer—as "the pillar and bulwark of the truth" (3:15). In the writer's time, an organization administered by right-thinking leaders replaces the dynamic and charismatic fellowship of the Pauline congregations.

Ranking the Church Membership   In 1 Timothy, the church membership reflects the social order of the larger Greco-Roman society external to it. Bishops, deacons, and elders govern a mixed group composed of different social classes, including heads of households, masters, slaves, wives, widows, and children (all of whom are commanded to submit to their respective superiors).

Women   Whereas Paul recognizes women as prophets and speakers (1 Cor. 11:5), the Pastor does not permit a woman to teach because the first woman, Eve, was weak-minded and tempted her husband to sin (2:8–15). The detailed instruction on women's dress and conduct in 1 Timothy probably applies to public worship and parallels the restricted position assigned women in some Hellenistic societies. A reflection of then-current social customs, it is not necessarily a timeless prescription limiting women's roles in Christian life.

In his discussion of the church's treatment of widows, the Pastor distinguishes between "true" widows who demonstrate their worth by good deeds and women unqualified for that status because of their youth or inappropriate conduct. Following Jewish law (Exod. 22:22; Deut. 24:17–24), the church early assumed responsibilities for supporting destitute widows (Acts 6:1), but the author stipulates that widows must be sixty years old before they can qualify for financial assistance. Relatives must support underage widows (5:3–16).

As Christians are to pray for government rulers (2:1–3), so slaves are to recognize their duties to masters and obey them (6:1–2). Yet the rich and powerful are reminded to share their wealth (6:17–19). Those ambitious to acquire riches are told that a passion for money is the cause of much evil, a source of grief and lost faith (6:9–10).

The letter ends with an admonishment to Timothy to guard the apostolic legacy given him. Anyone who disagrees with the Pastor's updated interpretation of Paul's doctrine is "a pompous ignoramus" (6:3).

2 TIMOTHY

Of the three pastorals, 2 Timothy most closely resembles Paul's genuine letters. Although the letter is similarly concerned with refuting false teachings, its tone is more intimate and personal. Especially poignant are several passages in which the author depicts himself as abandoned by former associates and languishing alone in prison except for the companionship of Luke (1:15; 4:9–11, 16). Although these and other flashes of Paul's characteristic vigor and emotional fire (see 4:6–8, 17–18) lead some scholars to speculate that the work contains fragments of otherwise lost Pauline letters, such theories are not widely accepted.

The part of 2 Timothy with the best claim to Pauline authorship is the section ending the letter (4:6–22), in which the writer emulates the fluctuations between lofty thoughts and mundane practicalities so typical of the apostle. In the first part, he compares himself to a runner winning the athlete's coveted prize—not the Greek competitor's laurel crown, but a "garland of righteousness" justifying him on God's Judgment Day (6:6–8). Switching abruptly to practical matters, the author asks the recipient to remember to bring his books when he comes. In another quick change of subject, he complains that during his court hearing nobody appeared in his defense and that the testimony of one "Alexander the coppersmith" seriously damaged his case. Then, in a seemingly contradictory about-face, the writer states that he has (metaphorically) escaped the "lion's jaws" and expects to be kept safe until the Parousia (6:13–18).

Although such rapid changes of subject and shifts from gloom to optimism characterize Paul's genuine correspondence, most scholars believe that the entire document is the Pastor's work. The more vivid passages are simply the writer's most successful homage to the apostle's memory.

In describing the false teachings within the church that he identifies as signs of the last days, the Pastor reveals that he is using Paul to predict conditions that characterize the writer's own time. During the world's last days (3:1), hypocrites insinuate their way into Christians' homes, corrupting their occupants. These pretenders typically prey upon women because, in the Pastor's insulting opinion, even when eager to learn, women lack the ability to understand true doctrine (3:6–8). Instead of the false teachings' being punished at the Second

Coming, the Pastor implies that the mere passage of time will expose their errors (3:9).

As in 1 Timothy, the Pastor does not refute the heretics with logical argument, but merely calls them names and lists their vices (3:1–6, 13; 4:3–4), duplicating the catalogs of misbehavior common in Hellenistic philosophical schools. Even believers do not adhere to healthy beliefs, but tolerate leaders who flatter them with what they want to hear.

Whereas the church is the stronghold of faith in 1 Timothy, in 2 Timothy the Hebrew Bible is the standard of religious orthodoxy (correct teaching), confounding error and directing the believer to salvation. Scripture also provides the mental discipline necessary to equip the believer for right action (3:15–17).

Concluding with his memorable picture of the apostle courageously facing martyrdom, the Pastor graciously includes all the faithful in Christ's promised deliverance. Not only Paul but all who trust in Jesus' imminent return will win victory's crown at the Parousia (6:6–8).

LETTER TO TITUS

Although it is the shortest of the pastorals, Titus has the longest salutation, a fulsome recapitulation of Paul's credentials and the recipient's significance (1:1–4). This highly formal introduction would be inappropriate in a personal letter from Paul to his friend but is understandable as the Pastor's way of officially transmitting Paul's authoritative instruction to an apostolic successor.

Titus The historical Titus, a Greek youth whom Paul refused to have circumcised (Gal. 2), accompanied the apostle on his missionary tours of Greece, acting as Paul's emissary to reconcile the rebellious Corinthians (Gal. 2:1, 3, 10; 2 Cor. 8:6, 16–23). Like the "Timothy" of the other pastorals, however, "Titus" also represents the postapostolic church leadership, the prototype of those preserving the Pauline traditions. Consequently, the commission of "Titus" is to establish an orthodox and qualified ministry. The letter's chief purpose is to outline the requirements and some of the duties of church elders and bishops.

Organization Titus can be divided into two main sections:

1. Qualifications for the Christian ministry
2. Christian behavior in an ungodly world

Qualifications for the Christian Ministry The writer states that he left "Titus" in Crete, an ancient island center of Greek civilization, to install church assistants (elders) in every town (1:5). Such persons must be socially respectable married men who keep their children under strict parental control (1:6). Besides possessing these domestic credentials, bishops (church supervisors) must also have a reputation for devotion, self-control, and hospitality (1:7–8). Again, the writer says nothing about the leaders' mental or charismatic gifts so highly valued in the Pauline churches (2 Cor. 11–14).

One of the bishop's primary functions is to guard the received religion, adhering to established beliefs and correcting dissenters (1:7–9). Titus is the only book in the New Testament that uses the term *heretic* (3:10), which at the time of writing (early-to-mid-second century) probably meant a person who held opinions of which the elders disapproved. Such dissenters are to be warned twice and then ignored (excluded from the church?) if they fail to change their ways (3:10–11).

Christian Behavior in an Ungodly World The Pastor reminds his readers that because they are Christians in a nonbelieving world, they must live exemplary lives of obedience and submission to government authorities (3:1). Men and women, old and young, slaves and masters—all are to behave in a way that publicly reflects well on their religion (2:1–10). Christians must preserve an ethically pure community while awaiting Christ's return (2:13–14).

In a moving passage, the author contrasts the negative personality traits that many believers had before their conversion with the grace and hope for eternal life that they now possess (3:3–8). In counsel similar to that in the letter of James, he urges believers to show their faith in admirable and useful deeds and to refrain from "foolish speculations, genealogies, quarrels, and controversies over the Law" (3:9–10).

The Pastor's Contribution

Although compared to Paul's the Pastor's style is generally weak and colorless (except for some passages in 2 Tim.), he successfully promotes Paul's continuing authority in the church. His insistence that Paul's teaching (as he understood it) be followed and that church leaders actively employ apostolic doctrines to refute false teachers helped to ensure that the international Christian community would build its future on an apostolic foundation.

Although the Pastor values continuity, he does not seem to show an equal regard for continuing the individual revelations and ecstatic experiences of Christ's Spirit that characterized the Pauline churches. (Regarding the "laying on of hands" as the correct means of conferring authority [2 Tim. 1:6], he would probably not welcome another like Paul who insisted that his private experience of Jesus—not ordination by his predecessors—validated his calling.) Using Scripture, inherited doctrines, and the institutional church as guarantors of orthodoxy, the Pastor sees the Christian revelation as already complete, a static legacy from the past. He ignores Paul's injunction not to "stifle inspiration" or prophetic speech (1 Thess. 5:19–20); his intense conservatism allows little room for future enlightenment.

Summary

Although it may shock modern sensibilities, innumerable ancient writers—Jewish, Greco-Roman and Christian—practiced pseudonymity, composing books under the names of famous dead authors. In the decades following Paul's demise, several groups of Christians apparently contended for the right to claim the Pauline legacy and to use his posthumous authority to settle later church problems. Two letters, 2 Thessalonians and Colossians, seem to be much closer to genuine Pauline thought than Ephesians or the Pastorals, which emphasize the kind of church offices and institutional structure that evolved after his day.

QUESTIONS FOR REVIEW

1. Define the term and explain the practice of pseudonymity among Hellenistic-Jewish and early Christian writers. Which books of the New Testament do many scholars think are pseudonymous?

2. In what specific ways concerning Jesus' return does 2 Thessalonians differ from Paul's first letter to the Thessalonians? What elements in the second letter make scholars suspect that it was written after Paul's day? Describe the conventional apocalyptic "signs" that the writer says must occur before the End.

3. Summarize the arguments for and against Paul's authorship of Colossians.

4. What factors cause scholars to doubt Paul's responsibility for Ephesians? In this document, how are Christ and the church related? What does their union imply for believers? What is the significance of the author's emphasizing warfare with unseen spirits rather than the Parousia?

5. Describe the evidence that persuades most scholars that the pastorals were written by a later churchman. In what specific concerns do the pastorals reflect church organization and administration that are different from those obtaining in Paul's time? Why are these letters so concerned about holding to tradition and combating "heresy"?

QUESTIONS FOR DISCUSSION AND REFLECTION

1. Analyze the similarities between the two Christian hymns quoted respectively in Philippians 2 and Colossians 1. Compare the view that humanity bears God's image (Gen. 1:27) with the similar language applied to Jesus (Col. 1:15). In what ways does the Colossians hymn apply the concepts of Israel's Wisdom tradition to Jesus?

2. Discuss the Pastor's views about women, children, and slaves. How does his prescription for internal church order reflect the hierarchical organization of the contemporary Greco-Roman society? What similarities and differences do you see between the character and behavior of Jesus and the Pastor's list of qualifications for church leaders? Would the historical

Jesus, an unmarried itinerant prophet, have met the Pastor's standards for qualifying for church leadership?

TERMS AND CONCEPTS TO REMEMBER

deutero-Pauline writings
authorship of
  2 Thessalonians,
  Colossians, Ephesians,
  and the Pastorals
pseudonymity
Ephesians' "sacred secret"
cosmic conflict
Christian armor
the Pastor
apocalyptic "signs"
the enemy (anti-Christ)
  (2 Thessalonians)
Timothy and Titus as
  representatives of a later
  Christianity

heresy
bishop
deacon
elder
social hierarchy
the Pastor's view of
  women
role of the institutional
  church
the Pastor's view of
  qualifications for the
  ministry
heretics
differences between Paul
  and the Pastor

RECOMMENDED READING

2 Thessalonians

Krentz, Edgar M. "Thessalonians, First and Second Epistles to the." In D. N. Freedman, ed., *The Anchor Bible Dictionary*, Vol. 6, pp. 515–523, New York: Doubleday, 1992.

Marshall, I. H. *1 and 2 Thessalonians*. Grand Rapids, Mich.: Eerdmans, 1983.

Colossians

Barth, M., ed. and trans. *Colossians and Philemon*. Vol. 34a of the Anchor Bible. Garden City, N.Y.: Doubleday, 1974. A scholarly translation and analysis.

Lohse, Eduard. *Colossians and Philemon*. Hermeneia. Philadelphia: Fortress Press, 1971. A scholarly analysis concluding that Colossians is by a Pauline disciple.

O'Brien, P. T. *Colossians, Philemon*. Word Biblical Commentary 44. Waco, Tex.: Word Books, 1982. Defends Pauline authorship of Colossians; includes author's translation.

Schweizer, Eduard. *The Letter to the Colossians: A Commentary*. Minneapolis: Augsburg, 1982. Less technical than works by Lohse and O'Brien; suggests that Timothy played a role in writing Colossians.

Ephesians

Barth, Markus, ed. and trans. *Ephesians*. Vols. 34 and 34a of the Anchor Bible. Garden City, N.Y.: Doubleday, 1974. This extensive commentary defends Pauline authorship.

Bruce, F. F. *The Epistles to the Colossians, to Philemon, and the Ephesians*. New International Commentary on the New Testament. Grand Rapids, Mich.: Eerdmans, 1984.

Furnish, V. P. "Ephesians, Epistle to the." In D. N. Freedman, ed., *The Anchor Bible Dictionary*, Vol. 2, pp. 535–542. New York: Doubleday, 1992.

Goodspeed, E. J. *The Meaning of Ephesians*. Chicago: University of Chicago Press, 1933. An older but perceptive study arguing that Ephesians was written as a cover letter for the first collected edition of Paul's correspondence.

Mitton, C. L. *Ephesians*. New Century Bible. Grand Rapids, Mich.: Eerdmans, 1981. A brief study of Ephesians as a work produced by one of Paul's disciples.

Taylor, W. F., and Rleumann, J. H. P. *Ephesians, Colossians*. Augsburg Commentary on the New Testament. Minneapolis: Augsburg, 1985.

The Pastorals

Dibelius, Martin, and Conzelmann, Hans. *The Pastoral Epistles*. Hermeneia Commentary. Philadelphia: Fortress Press, 1972. Conzelmann's updating of Dibelius's famous commentary, first published in German in 1913.

Hanson, A. T. *The Pastoral Epistles*. New Century Bible. Grand Rapids, Mich.: Eerdmans, 1982. A brief but helpful treatment.

MacDonald, D. R. *The Legend and the Apostle*. Philadelphia: Westminster Press, 1983.

Quinn, J. D., ed. and trans. *1 and 2 Timothy and Titus*. Vol. 35 of the Anchor Bible. Garden City, N.Y.: Doubleday, 1976. A recent translation with commentary.

——. "Timothy and Titus, Epistles to." In D. N. Freedman, ed., *The Anchor Bible Dictionary*, Vol. 6, pp. 560–571. New York: Doubleday, 1992.

CHAPTER 18

General Letters on Faith and Behavior

Hebrews and the Catholic Epistles

The kind of religion which is without stain or fault . . . is this: to go to the help of orphans and widows in their distress and keep oneself untarnished by the world.   James 1:27

The message you have heard from the beginning is this: that we should love one another.   1 John 3:11

Key Themes Addressed to believers scattered throughout the world, Hebrews and the other general epistles make the point that God's revelation through Jesus is final and complete. The very image of God's nature, Jesus now serves in heaven as an eternal High Priest and mediator for humanity (Hebrews). Believers must therefore adhere to a high standard of conduct, maintaining a true understanding of Jesus' Incarnation (1 John), practicing charitable acts (James), setting examples of ethical behavior for the world (1 Peter), and keeping alive their hope of the Second Coming (2 Peter).

As noted in chapter 17, Paul's extensive use of the letter form influenced many later New Testament writers. Besides authors like the Pastor, who wrote in Paul's name, other early Christians imitated the apostle by composing "letters" to instruct and encourage the faithful. Unlike Paul's genuine correspondence, these later documents commonly are not addressed to individual congregations, but are directed to the Christian community as a whole. This group of eight disparate writings, headed by the Book of Hebrews, forms a discrete unit between the collection of letters traditionally ascribed to Paul and the book of Revelation.

Because of their general nature, seven of these writings are known collectively as the catholic epistles (or universal epistles). The seven—James, 1 and 2 Peter, 1, 2, and 3 John, and Jude—are called epistles because most of them are formal communications intended for public reading in the church at large. In this respect, they differ from genuine letters like those of Paul, which were composed for specific recipients known to the author and are much less formal.

Even the term *epistle* does not adequately describe the diverse literary forms encompassed in these works. Of the three missives ascribed to John,

321

HEBREWS AND THE CATHOLIC EPISTLES

Although some scholars argue that 1 Peter was written by the historical Peter, and James and Jude by Jesus' kinsmen, most scholars believe that this entire section of the New Testament is pseudonymous. In general, we do not know when or where these documents originated, or, in most cases, to whom they were sent.

---

for example, the first is actually a sermon or tract, the second is a warning letter to a specific group, and the third is a private note. In this chapter, we show that although such works as James and 1 Peter superficially resemble letters, they in fact belong to different categories of religious literature.

Authors and Dates

Besides their dubious categorization as epistles, another significant factor links these seven writings. All are attributed to prominent leaders of the original Jerusalem church. Six are ascribed to the three Jerusalem "pillars"—Peter, James, and John (Gal. 2)—while the seventh, Jude, purportedly was written by James's brother.

With the exception of 1 Peter, most of the catholic writings are also linked by the fact that as a group, they are the last writings to be accepted into the New Testament canon. As late as the fourth century, Eusebius classified several as "doubtful" and noted that many churches did not accept them (*History* 3.39.6; 3.24.18; 3.25.4; 2.24.1; 2.3). Church writers do not even mention most of these epistles until almost 200 C.E., and Jude, James, 2 Peter, and 3 John are typically absent from early lists of canonical books.

Near the end of the second century, the church began to associate many previously anonymous works with Jesus' apostles and their companions. This seems to have been the case with the catholic epistles, which scholars believe to include the latest-written documents in the New Testament.

In our discussion of these general works on faith and behavior, we begin with two commonly associated with Jewish Christianity—Hebrews and James—followed by the epistles attributed to Peter, Jude, and John. Despite their heterogeneous character, these documents are thematically united by their authors' profound commitment to prescribing an ethical way of life appropriate for believers living at the End of time. 2 Peter, which is probably the last-written book in the canon, marks a fervent reaffirmation of primitive Christianity's apocalyptic hope. However long the Parousia is delayed, Christians must live as if Jesus will return at any moment to judge the world and the conduct of the faithful (2 Pet. 3:1–15).

The Book of Hebrews

The Book of Hebrews was written by an early Christian scholar who was equally well acquainted with the Hebrew Bible and with Greek philosophical concepts. The work challenges the reader as does no other New Testament book except Revelation. With the warning that he offers "much that is difficult to explain" (5:11), the writer presents a dualistic view of the universe in which earthly events and human institutions are seen as reflections of invisible heavenly realities. Employing a popular form of Platonic thought, he assumes the existence of two parallel worlds: the eternal and perfect realm of spirit above and the inferior, constantly changing world below. Alone among New Testament authors, he attempts to show how Christ's sacrificial death links the two opposing realms of perishable matter and eternal spirit. He is the only Bible writer to present Jesus as a heavenly priest who serves as an everlasting mediator between God and humanity.

AUTHORSHIP AND DATE

Hebrews is an elaborate sermon rather than a letter, but it ends with a postscript recalling one of Paul's missives (13:17–25). Although some early Christians attributed the work to Paul, many others recognized that the theology, language, and style of Hebrews were distinctly un-Pauline. (The ending comments and reference to Timothy [13:23] do not fit the rest of the work and may have been appended by a later copyist or editor.) Various commentators have speculated that the author may have been Barnabas, Priscilla, or Paul's eloquent coworker, Apollos of Alexandria.

Such attempts to link Hebrews with some well-known figure associated with first-generation Pauline Christianity have proven futile. Most scholars agree with Origen, a church scholar prominent during the early third century, who remarked that the writer's identity is known only to God. The book's date and place of composition are also unknown. Various critics suggest Alexandria, Rome, Antioch, Corinth, or some equally cosmopolitan center as the city of origin, with the time of writing estimated as between about 80 and 100 C.E.

THE WRITER'S METHODS OF INTERPRETATION

Whoever he was, the anonymous author was a master of rhetoric, the art of speaking or writing effectively. He uses excellent Greek and also shows familiarity with Hellenistic-Jewish methods of scriptural analysis and interpretation. This suggests to many scholars that the writer may have lived in Alexandria, a metropolis where Greek-educated Jews like Philo Judaeus developed highly sophisticated ways of making ancient biblical texts relevant to the demands of Greco-Roman culture. As expounded by Philo and other Alexandrine scholars, the Hebrew Bible became much more than a mere repository of legal commandments or a record of past events. To Philo and the author of Hebrews, it is an allegory in which earthly events symbolize heavenly realities.

Hebrews' thesis is that, through Jesus, God gives his ultimate revelation of spiritual reality. The author examines selected passages from the Hebrew Bible—principally Genesis 14:18–20 and Psalms 110:4—to demonstrate Christ's unique role in the universe. In his view, the biblical texts can be understood only in the light of Christ's death and ascension into heaven. He thus gives the Hebrew Bible a strictly christological interpretation (**typology**).

Of special importance to the author is the Genesis figure of **Melchizedek,** a mysterious king-priest of Canaanite Salem to whom the patriarch

Abraham gave a tenth of the goods he had captured in war (Gen. 14:18–20). Melchizedek becomes a type or prophetic symbol of Jesus, whom the author regards as both a king (Davidic Messiah) and a priest (like Melchizedek). In the author's interpretation, Melchizedek's story serves to prefigure Jesus' priesthood.

PURPOSE AND ORGANIZATION

The book's title—"To the Hebrews"—is not part of the original text; it may have been added by an editor who assumed that the writer's interest in Jewish ritual implied that he wrote for Jewish Christians. The term may apply equally well to Gentile recipients, however, and probably refers to "spiritual Israel," the Christian church at large. Whatever the intended audience, Hebrews' purpose is to urge believers to hold fast to their faith, remembering their former loyalty during persecution (10:32–34) and avoiding the pitfalls of apathy or indifference.

After an introduction (1:1–4), Hebrews is arranged in three main sections:

1. Christ, the image of God, is superior to all other human or heavenly beings (1:5–4:16).
2. The Torah's priestly regulations foreshadowed Jesus' role as a priest like Melchizedek (5:1–10:39).
3. Believers are exhorted to emulate biblical examples and act on faith in Jesus' supremacy (11:1–13:16).

CHRIST'S SUPERIORITY TO ALL OTHER BEINGS

Stressing his theme of Christ's superiority to all others, the author begins Hebrews by contrasting earlier biblical revelations with that made in the last days through the person of Jesus. Whereas God formerly conveyed his message in fragmentary form through the Hebrew prophets, in Jesus he discloses a complete revelation of his essential nature and purpose. As in Colossians and John's Gospel, Jesus is the agent (or goal) of God's creative purpose and a perfect reflection of the divine being (1:1–4).

Echoing Paul's assertion that Jesus attained heavenly glory through obedient humility (Phil. 2), the author states that Jesus was perfected through suffering. As a perfectly obedient Son, he is greater than Moses, leading his followers not to an earthly destination, but to God's celestial throne (3:1–4:16). Through him, God makes his complete and final revelation.

CHRIST — A PRIEST LIKE MELCHIZEDEK

Asking his hearers to move beyond basic ideas and to advance in understanding (5:11–6:3), the author introduces his unparalleled interpretation of Jesus as an eternal High Priest, one foreshadowed by Melchizedek. To show that Christ's priesthood is superior to that of Aaron, Israel's first High Priest, and the Levites who assisted him at the **Tabernacle,** Hebrews cites the narrative about Abraham paying **tithes** to Melchizedek (14:18–20). Because Melchizedek blessed Abraham and accepted offerings from him, the writer argues that the king-priest of Salem was Abraham's superior. Furthermore, Abraham's descendants, the Levitical and Aaronic priests, also shared in the patriarch's homage to Melchizedek. Present in his ancestor's "loins" when Abraham honored Melchizedek, Aaron and all his priestly offspring also confessed their inferiority to Melchizedek (7:1–10). Melchizedek is thus acknowledged as the superior of Israel's Levitical priests by virtue of his priority in time.

The author now adds Psalm 110 to his explication of Genesis 14. He notes that Yahweh swore that his king or "messiah" is both his son and an everlasting priest like Melchizedek (Ps. 110:4). Hebrews further argues that because Genesis does not mention either ancestors or descendants for Melchizedek, the absence of human roots or connections implies that the king-priest is without either beginning or end—an eternal priest. The symbolic everlastingness of Melchizedek's priesthood is thus the prototype of Christ, who similarly remains a priest for all time (7:3, 21–24).

In biblical times, a priest's main function was to offer animal sacrifices to atone for the people's sins and elicit God's forgiveness (**expiation**). According to Hebrews, Jesus is both the priest and the sacrifice. His offering fulfills the reality of the Torah's required sacrifices, but it is superior to the old system because his life was perfected through suffering (5:8–9). Unlike the sacrifices offered at Israel's Tabernacle or Temple, which must be repeated endlessly to ensure divine approval, Jesus' sacrifice is made only once. It remains eternally effective and brings forgiveness and salvation to those accepting its efficacy (7:26–28).

EARTHLY COPY AND HEAVENLY REALITY

Hebrews employs the view that the universe is composed of two levels, a lower physical realm and a higher, unseen spirit world. The author envisions Israel's earthly ceremonies of sacrifice and worship as reflections, or copies, that parallel invisible realities in heaven (8:5) (see figure 18.1). He then cites the solemn ritual of the Day of Atonement, the one time of the year that the High Priest was permitted to enter the Tabernacle's innermost room, the Holy of Holies, where God's glory was believed to dwell. Interpreting the atonement ritual allegorically, the author states that the priest's annual entry into God's presence foreshadowed Christ's ascension into heaven itself. There, his life stands as an eternally powerful sacrifice, making humanity forever "at one" with God (8:1–6; 9:1–14).

Because his sacrifice surpasses those decreed under the old Mosaic Covenant, Jesus inaugurates a New Covenant with his shed blood. He acts as a permanent mediator, always pleading for humanity's forgiveness (7:24–25; 9:15–22). The writer repeatedly emphasizes that neither the Mosaic Tabernacle nor Herod's Temple in Jerusalem was intended to be permanent. Both sanctuaries are only copies of heavenly realities (9:23), mere "shadows, and no true image" of Christ's supreme priestly sacrifice (10:1–25).

EXHORTATION TO REMAIN FAITHFUL

After reminding his audience that God's redemption through Christ is absolutely final, permitting no second chance at salvation (10:26–31), the writer urges Christians to imitate the many examples of faith found in the Hebrew Bible (11:4–40). The author is the only New Testament writer to define faith, and he does so in terms of his belief in

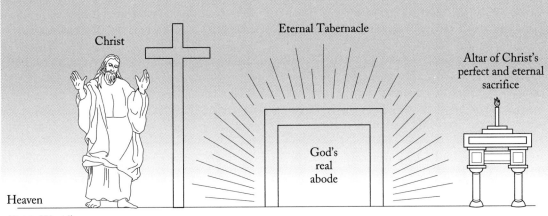

Figure 18.1 The Book of Hebrews expounds a theory of correspondences, the belief that reality exists in two separate but parallel dimensions—the spirit world (heaven) and the physical world (earth). Material objects and customs on earth are temporary replicas, or shadows, of eternal realities in heaven. The author's notion that Jesus' "perfect" sacrifice has rendered Jewish worship obsolete is clearly partisan and a claim that many scholars find highly unacceptable.

two parallel worlds. Hebrews 11 expresses Plato's classic view of an eternal realm superior to the world of physical matter. This passage defines *faith* as primarily a hopeful confidence that the unseen universe really exists and that it is the source of the physical Cosmos (11:1–3). Unlike Paul, who always associates faith with a living trust in Jesus' saving power, the author of Hebrews defines faith with no reference to Christ.

The faithful are thus armed with a conviction that invisible realities include an eternal High Priest whose perfect sacrifice provides a potentially cease-

less forgiveness and union with God. Christians must maintain their faith while awaiting the imminent Day of Judgment (10:36–39). Characters in the Hebrew Bible, such as Abel, Noah, Abraham, Moses, and Rahab (the Canaanite harlot), proved their loyalty when they had only a dim preview of heavenly realities. Believers now possess a complete vision of God's purpose and must behave accordingly. Just as God introduced the Mosaic Covenant amid blazing fire, earthquake, and other frightening signs, Jesus' New Covenant embodies even more awe-inspiring phenomena, not on earthly Mount

Sinai, but in heavenly Jerusalem. If the Israelites who disobeyed the Mosaic Law were punished by death, how much more severe will be the punishment of those who fail to keep faith in the new dispensation (12:1–29).

Urging believers to lead blameless lives of active good deeds, the author reminds them that Jesus Christ is "the same yesterday, today, and for ever." This is another powerful reason to regard this world, with its temptations and troubles, as a temporary trial resolved in the light of eternity (13:1–9). Christians have no permanent home on earth but seek the unseen and perfect city above as their life's goal (13:14).

James

AUTHORSHIP

Addressing his work to "the Twelve Tribes dispersed throughout the world" (presumably "spiritual Israel," the international church), the author calls himself "James, a servant of God and the Lord Jesus Christ." He does not claim apostolic rank or mention a kinship with Jesus, but church tradition identifies him as the person whom Paul calls "James the Lord's brother" (Gal. 1:19), the principal leader of Palestinian Jewish Christianity between about 50 and 62 C.E. He was a devout respecter of the Mosaic Torah and was known to his fellow Israelites as "James the Righteous." Despite his high reputation among both Jews and Christians, however, a violent mob killed him about 62 C.E.

If the author is Jesus' brother (or close relative), it is strange that he rarely mentions Christ and almost never refers to Jesus' teachings. As a man who had known Jesus all his life (Mark 6) and had seen the risen Lord (1 Cor. 15), he might be expected to use his personal acquaintance with Jesus to lend authority to his instructions. The fact that his writing contains virtually nothing about Jesus suggests the author did not personally know him and consequently could not have been a member of Jesus' family (see box 12.2).

Two qualities of this document offer general clues to its author's background. Besides being written in excellent Greek (not something a Galilean native was likely to be capable of), it repeatedly echoes Greek editions of the Hebrew Bible, especially the book of Proverbs and later Hellenistic wisdom books like Ecclesiasticus and the Wisdom of Solomon. Both James's subject matter and his language reflect a deep interest in Greek-Jewish wisdom literature. This fact suggests that the author is a Hellenistic-Jewish Christian concerned about applying the principles of Israel's later sages to problems in his Christian circle. The writer may have lived in any Greek-speaking Jewish community in Syria, Palestine, Egypt, or Italy.

FORM AND ORGANIZATION

Except for the brief opening salutation, the work bears no similarity to a letter. It is instead a collection of proverbs, commentaries, scriptural paraphrases, and moral advice. As a literary genre, James is the only New Testament document resembling the compilations of wise counsel found in the Hebrew Bible.

Lacking any principle of coherence, James leaps from topic to topic and then back again. The only unifying theme is the author's view of the purpose and function of religion (1:26–27), which he defines as typically Jewish good works, charitable practices that will save the soul and cancel a multitude of sins (5:19–20). Following the author's order, we examine several of his main interests:

1. The nature of trials and temptations (1:2–27)
2. Respect for the poor (2:1–13)
3. "Works," or good deeds, as the only measure of faith (2:14–26)
4. Controlling the tongue (3:1–12)
5. Warnings against violent ambition and exploitation of the poor (4:1–5:6)

THE RECIPIENTS AND THE DATE

From the topics covered, this book seems directed at Jewish-Christian groups that had existed long enough to have developed a sense of class distinction within the church. Wealthy Christians snub poorer ones (2:1–9), fail to share their material possessions (2:14–26), engage in worldly competition (4:1–10), and exploit fellow believers of the laboring class (4:13–5:6). These socially stratified and economically divided communities suggest a time long after that of the impoverished Jerusalem commune described in Acts 2. Most scholars date the work in the late first century, considerably after the historic James's martyrdom in the early 60s.

TRIALS AND TEMPTATIONS

In this introductory section (1:2–27), James articulates a philosophy of human experience that puts his ethical advice in perspective. Dealing with the twin problems of external suffering and internal temptations to do wrong, the author offers insight into God's reasons for permitting evil to afflict even the faithful. "Trials" (presumably including persecutions) are potentially beneficial experiences because they allow the believer the opportunity to demonstrate faith and fortitude under pressure, thus strengthening character. To help Christians endure such trials, God grants insight to persons who pray for it single-mindedly and never doubt that God will provide the understanding necessary to maintain faith.

Arguing that the Creator is not responsible for tests of faith or private temptations to sin, James declares that God, "untouched by evil," does not tempt anyone. Human temptation arises from within through the secret cultivation of forbidden desire that eventually inspires the act of "sin," which in turn breeds death (1:12–15). By contrast, God is the source of perfection (1:17) and the origin of life (1:12). In this miniature theodicy (defense of God's goodness despite the world's evil), the writer insists that God is not responsible for injustice or undeserved suffering. Society's evils result from purely human selfishness. If believers resist evil, God grants them the power to drive away even the devil (4:7–8).

Religion Defined   The only New Testament writer to define *religion*, James describes it as the active practice of good works, an imitation of the One who sets the example of generosity (1:16). The religion God approves is practical: helping "orphans and widows" and keeping "oneself untarnished by the world" (1:27). In James's two-part definition, the "orphans and widows" are Judaism's classic symbols of the defenseless who are God's special care, and "the world" represents a society that repudiates

Figure 18.2 *Mother of the Streets.* In painting this (homeless) black Madonna and Christ child, the artist Robert Lentz invites viewers to remember that the Judeo-Christian tradition emphasizes God's unceasing concern for the poor and powerless of society. In Matthew's parable of the Last Judgment, people are judged according to their generosity toward persons lacking adequate food, clothing, shelter, or medical care. (© Robert Lentz. Used with permission of Bridge Building Images, P.O. Box 1048, Burlington, VT 05402)

God. Thoroughly Jewish in its emphasis on merciful deeds, James's "true religion" cannot be formalized by doctrine, creed, or ritual (cf. Matt. 25:31–46).

RESPECT FOR THE POOR

Addressing a social problem that plagues virtually every social group, whether religious or secular, James denounces all social snobbery. Christians must make the poor feel as welcome in their midst as the rich and powerful (2:1–13). Noting that it is the wealthy who typically oppress the church, James reminds his audience that the poor will inherit "the kingdom" and that insulting them is an offense against God (see figure 18.2). Interestingly, the author does not use Jesus' teaching to drive home

God's gracious intent to reward those now poor, but instead quotes from the Hebrew Bible. If believers do not love their fellow human beings (Lev. 19:18), they break all of God's laws, for to fail to keep one legal point is to disobey the entire Torah (2:10).

FAITH LIVES ONLY THROUGH GOOD WORKS

In James's most famous passage (2:14−26), the author exposes the futility of persons who claim they have faith but do not follow the practical religion of good works. To James, belief that fails to inspire right action is dead. Only "deeds"—serving the "orphans and widows" and others suffering comparable need—can demonstrate the reality of faith.

Many interpreters see this section as an attack on Paul's doctrine of salvation through faith (the apostle's rejection of "works" of Torah obedience in favor of trust in God's saving purpose in Christ). Like Paul, James cites the Genesis example of Abraham to prove his point, but he gives it a strikingly different interpretation. James asserts that it was Abraham's action—his willingness to sacrifice his son Isaac—that justified him. The writer's conclusion is distinctly un-Pauline: "a man is justified by deeds and not by faith in itself" (2:24). With its implication that one earns divine approval through hard effort and service to others, this conclusion seems to contradict Paul's assertion that salvation comes only through God's grace, accepted on trust (faith) (see Gal. and Rom. 1−8).

James's conclusion that faith without actions is as dead as a corpse without breath (2:26) seems to many scholars an attack on Paul's viewpoint. Others regard it as a necessary corrective to a common misuse of Pauline doctrine. It must be remembered, however, that although Paul labored to the point of exhaustion serving others, he did not see his "works" as the means God provided for his "justification." Martin Luther doubted the validity of James's argument, describing the work as "strawlike" for its failure to recognize the primacy of divine grace.

CONTROLLING THE TONGUE

Like earlier writers in the Hebrew wisdom tradition, James stresses the importance of self-control

in speech (3:1−12; cf. Prov. 15:1−4, 26, 28; Ecclus. 5:11−6:1; 28:13−26). The tongue is a fire fed by the flames of hell (3:6), paradoxically both the instrument of divine praise and the organ of destructive gossip. Contrasting its abuses with spiritual wisdom, James emphasizes the constructive, peace-enhancing quality of the latter (3:13−18).

WARNINGS AGAINST AMBITION AND EXPLOITATION

True wisdom produces peace and harmony; James's recipients, on the other hand, are divided by envy, ambition, and conflict. Their ambitious pursuit of unworthy goals makes them God's enemy (4:3−4). Boastful of their financial successes, they forget that their continued existence depends on God's patience and mercy. Christian merchants and landowners are the author's prime target in the New Testament's most incisive attack on the rich (4:13−5:4). Those whose wealth gives them power over their economic inferiors have exploited it shamelessly. Without conscience, wealthy employers have defrauded their workers, delaying payment of wages on which the laboring poor depend to live. Such injustice outrages the Creator, who views the luxury-loving exploiters as overfed animals ripe for slaughter.

Reminding his audience that the Lord will return (5:7), presumably to judge those who economically murder the defenseless (5:6), James ends his sermon on a positive note for any who have strayed from the right path. Sinners and others who are "sick," perhaps spiritually as well as physically, can hope for recovery. God's healing grace operates through congregational prayer for the afflicted. A good person's prayer has power to rescue a sinner from death and to erase countless sins (5:13−20).

1 Peter

Like James, 1 Peter is ascribed to one of the three Jerusalem "pillars." The two works have other points in common as well, including similar convictions about proper Christian behavior and a shared belief that spiritual gifts like love and prayer can wipe out sin (James 5:20; 1 Pet. 4:8). Both also refer to social discrimination, and even persecution, against believers (James 1:2–8; 5:7–11; 1 Pet. 1:6–7; 4:12–19). A philosophy of peaceful submission and patience during trials and tests of faith characterizes both documents.

AUTHORSHIP AND DATE

Scholars are divided on the authorship of 1 Peter. Many accept the tradition that the apostle Peter composed it in Rome shortly before he was executed during Nero's persecution of Christians (about 64 or 65 c.e.). Other scholars point out that if the "ordeals" mentioned in the letter refer to Nero's Roman persecution, it is strange that the epistle is addressed to churches in Asia Minor (1:1). Historians find no evidence that Nero's attack on the faith extended beyond the imperial capital.

Those doubting Petrine authorship note that the fine Greek in which the epistle is written suggests that an unlettered Galilean fisherman was not the author. Advocates of Peter's responsibility for the letter retort that it was produced "through Sylvanus [Silas]" (5:12), a former companion of Paul (Acts 15:22) who acted as Peter's secretary, transforming his dictation into the epistle's smooth Greek.

Of all the catholic epistles identified with various members of the Jerusalem church, the best case for authenticity can perhaps be made for 1 Peter. Although the majority of scholars regard the work as pseudonymous, many eminent critics defend its traditional authorship and date it in the mid-60s c.e. Those assigning the work a postapostolic date—between about 90 and 115 c.e.—note that the author does not reveal personal knowledge of Jesus, as an apostle would be expected to do, and that the social conditions described in 1 Peter indicate a period later than Nero's reign.

According to some interpreters, the epistle's references to believers' troubles (1:6) may mean nothing more than the social discrimination and hostility Roman society accorded many early Christians. Other commentators explain the "fiery ordeals" (4:12–13) as official persecutions under the emperors Domitian (about 95 c.e.) or Trajan (about

Figure 18.3 Under Trajan (98–117 c.e.), the Roman Empire reached its greatest geographical extent, stretching from Britain in the northwest to Mesopotamia (Iraq) in the east. Pliny the Younger wrote to Trajan about the proper method of handling Christians. The emperor replied that he opposed anonymous accusations and ordered that accused persons who demonstrated their loyalty to the state by making traditional sacrifices should not be prosecuted. (© Foto Marburg-Art Resource, NY)

112 c.e.). 1 Peter indicates that believers are punished merely for bearing Christ's name (4:14–16), a situation that did not obtain during Nero's era but does fit the policies of his later successors. Letters exchanged between the emperor Trajan and Pliny the Younger, his appointed governor of Bithynia, one of the provinces of Asia Minor to which 1 Peter is addressed, seem to reflect the same conditions the epistle describes (Pliny, *Letters* 97) (see figure 18.3). For that reason, many scholars favor a date in the early second century for the epistle, though there is no scholarly consensus.

A date after 70 c.e. is indicated by the author's sending greetings from "her who dwells in Babylon"

(5:13). "Her" refers to the writer's church (2 John 1), and "Babylon" became the Christian code name for Rome after Titus destroyed Jerusalem, thus duplicating the Babylonian Empire's infamous desecration of the holy city (587 B.C.E.). As an archetype of the ungodly nation, "Babylon" is also Revelation's symbol of Rome (Rev. 14:8; 18:2). Most critics assume that 1 Peter originated in the capital, the traditional site of Peter's martyrdom.

PURPOSE AND ORGANIZATION

The author's purpose is to encourage believers to hold fast to their integrity (as Christians like Peter did in Nero's time) and to promote Christian ethics. He urges the faithful to live so blamelessly that outsiders can never accuse them of anything illegal or morally reprehensible. If one endures legal prosecution, it should be only "as a Christian" (4:14–16).

1 Peter often has been described as a baptismal sermon, and indeed the author structures his work to delineate both the privileges and the dangers involved in adopting the Christian way of life. As a basic summary of Christian ideals and ethics, it can be divided into the following three sections:

1. The privileges and values of the Christian calling (1:3–2:10)
2. The obligations and responsibilities of Christian life (2:11–4:11)
3. The ethical meaning of suffering as a Christian (4:12–5:11)

THE PRIVILEGES AND VALUES OF THE CHRISTIAN CALLING

Addressing an audience who had not known Jesus, Peter stresses the rarity and inestimable value of the faith recently transmitted to them. They must regard their present trials and difficulties as opportunities to display the depth of their commitment and the quality of their love (1:3–7). By remaining faithful, they will attain the salvation of which the Hebrew prophets spoke (1:9–12). Proper appreciation for Christ's sacrifice, which makes him the "living stone" of the heavenly temple, will also

make the believer a living part of the eternal sanctuary (2:4–8). Christians, including Gentiles, are the new "chosen race"—"a royal priesthood, a dedicated nation, and a people claimed by God for his own" (2:9–10).

THE OBLIGATIONS AND RESPONSIBILITIES OF CHRISTIAN LIFE

Many commentators have noted that 1 Peter contains many Pauline ideas, particularly on matters of Christian behavior and obedience to the Roman state. In the second section (2:11–4:11), the author focuses on the responsibilities and moral conduct of God's people, who should act in a way that even nonbelievers admire (2:12). Echoing Romans 13, 1 Peter advises peaceful submission to government authorities (3:13–15). In the writer's social and political hierarchy, slaves and servants are subject to their masters (2:18), and women to their husbands (3:1–2). Those who suffer unjustly must bear it as Jesus bore his sufferings (1:19–25; 3:13–18; 4:1–5).

In alluding to Christ's crucifixion, the author includes two fascinating references about Jesus' descent into the Underworld (Hades), presumably during the interval between his death and his resurrection (3:18–20; 4:6). Suggesting the existence of a rich early Christian lore surrounding Jesus' posthumous experiences, Peter's brief allusions inspired a later tradition that after his death Jesus entered hell and rescued the souls of faithful Israelites who had been imprisoned there before the way to heaven was open.

THE ETHICAL MEANING OF SUFFERING AS A CHRISTIAN

The third part (4:12–5:11) of 1 Peter examines the ethical meaning of suffering for the faith. Believers must not be surprised to experience difficulties because as followers of Christ they must expect to share his sufferings (4:12–16). Judgment has come, and it begins with the Christian community. If the righteous are but narrowly saved, what will happen to the wicked (4:17–19)? Elders must shepherd the flock with loving care; younger people must submit humbly to their rule (5:1–7). All must remain alert because the devil prowls the earth like a hungry lion, seeking to devour the unwary. The faithful who resist him will partake of Christ's reward (5:8–11).

Letter of Jude

Placed last among the general epistles, Jude is less a letter than a tract denouncing an unidentified group of heretics. Its primary intent is to persuade the (also unidentified) recipients to join the writer in defending orthodox Christian traditions (v. 3). Rather than specify his opponents' doctrinal errors or refute their arguments, the writer instead threatens the heretics with apocalyptic punishment drawn from both biblical and nonbiblical sources.

AUTHORSHIP AND DATE

The author refers to himself as Jude (Judas), a servant of Jesus Christ and brother of James (v. 1) — and presumably also a kinsman of Jesus (Matt. 13:55; Mark 6:3). According to Eusebius, Jude, whom he describes as "the brother, humanly speaking, of the Savior," left descendants who played an important role in the Jerusalem church, even after the Romans destroyed the city in 70 c.e. Eusebius quotes an older historian, Hegesippus, who reported that during Domitian's reign the emperor ordered Jude's two grandsons to appear before him. Worried that their Davidic ancestry might make them potential leaders of another Jewish revolt, Domitian released the two when they demonstrated that they were only hard-working peasants with no pretensions to royalty (*History* 3.20) (see box 12.2).

Scholars believe that Jude is not the work of Jesus' "brother," but rather is a pseudonymous work that entered the canon because of its presumed association with the Lord's family. Like James, the author shows no personal familiarity with Jesus and cites none of his characteristic teachings. He refers to Christianity as a fixed body of beliefs that the faithful already possess (v. 3) and to the apostles as prophets of a former age (vv. 17–18). This indicates

that the book was composed significantly after the historical Jude's time. Most scholars suggest a date between about 100 and 125 c.e.

STYLE AND CONTENT

The letter of Jude represents a kind of rhetoric known as *invective*—an argument characterized by verbal abuse and insult. Without describing the heretics' teachings, Jude calls them "brute beasts" (v. 10), "enemies of religion" who have wormed their way into the church to pervert it with their "licentiousness" (v. 4). A "blot on [Christian] love feasts" (v. 12), they are doomed to suffer divine wrath as did Cain, Balaam, Korah, and other villains of the Hebrew Bible. Because the author does not try to explain his reasons for disagreeing with his opponents, but merely calls them names, accuses them of immorality, and predicts their future destruction, Jude has been called the least theologically creative book in the New Testament.

APOCALYPTIC JUDGMENT

Jude views the heretics' misbehavior as fulfilling the apostles' predictions about End time (v. 18). Because their **apostasy** proves the nearness of the Last Judgment (an idea also expressed in 1 John 2:18), Jude reminds his audience of earlier punishments on the wicked, citing the plagues on Egypt (v. 5), the fallen angels of Genesis (v. 6), and the fiery punishment of Sodom and Gomorrah (vv. 6–7).

Use of Noncanonical Writings Jude is the only New Testament writer to go beyond the Hebrew Bible and quote directly from the Pseudepigrapha, Jewish religious works not included in the biblical canon. Citing the book of 1 Enoch (1:9) verbatim, Jude reproduces a passage describing the Lord's negative judgment on "the ungodly" (v. 15). From copies of Enoch preserved among the Dead Sea Scrolls, we know that the Essenes studied the work. Jude's quotation, as well as several other allusions to the work (1 Enoch 1:1–9; 5:4; 18:12, 14–16; 27:2; 60:8; 93:2), proves that certain early Christian groups also regarded Enoch as authoritative.

In addition, Jude's allusion to a postbiblical legend about the archangel Michael contending with the devil for Moses' body (v. 9) may be taken from the incompletely preserved Assumption of Moses, another late noncanonical work. (When a later writer incorporated much of Jude into chapter 2 of 2 Peter, he deleted all references to the noncanonical writings.)

Exhortation to the Faithful   Jude's advice to his orthodox recipients is as general as his denunciation of the false teachers. Counseling them to pray and live anticipating Jesus' return (vv. 20–21), he concedes that some involved with the heretics deserve pity and can be helped. Others are pitiable but corrupted by sensuality. The author's opinion that the clothing (or bodies) of such persons must be despised (v. 23) suggests that Jude advocates a strict asceticism—a self-discipline that denies physical appetites and desires.

To balance its largely vindictive tone, the work closes with a particularly lyric doxology praising "the only God our Savior" (vv. 24–25).

2 Peter

Like Jude, 2 Peter was written for the double purpose of condemning false teachers and warning of the imminent world judgment. Theologically, its importance lies in the author's attempt to explain why God allows evil to continue and to reassert the primitive Christian belief that Jesus' Second Coming is near (3:1–15). Offering a theory that human history is divided into three distinct chronological epochs, or "worlds," 2 Peter is the only New Testament book to argue that the present world will be entirely consumed by fire.

AUTHORSHIP AND DATE

Whereas many scholars defend Petrine authorship of 1 Peter, virtually none believe that 2 Peter was written by Jesus' chief disciple. The unknown author, however, takes pains to claim Peter's identity (1:1), asserting that he was present at Christ's transfiguration (1:17–18) and that he wrote an ear-

lier letter, presumably 1 Peter (3:1). Under the great fisherman's name, he writes to reaffirm his concept of the true apostolic teaching in the face of heretical misinterpretation of it. Picturing the church leader as about to face death, the writer offers this epistle as Peter's last will and testament, a final exposition of the apostolic faith (1:14–15).

The pseudonymous author's claims are not persuasive, however, because 2 Peter contains too many indications that it was written long after Peter's martyrdom in about 64 or 65 C.E. The letter's main intent—to reestablish the apostolic view of the Parousia—shows that the writer addresses a group that lived long enough after the original apostles' day to have given up believing that Christ would return soon. The author's opponents deny the Parousia doctrine because the promised Second Coming has not materialized even though the "fathers" (first-generation disciples) have long since passed away. In addition, the writer makes use of Jude, itself an early second-century document, incorporating most of it into his work.

The work also refers to Paul's letters as Scripture (3:16), a status they did not achieve until well into the second century. A late date is also indicated by the author's insistence on divinely inspired Scripture as the principal teaching authority (1:20–21). This tendency to substitute a fixed written text for the Spirit's operation or the "living voice" of the gospel also appears in the Pastor's letters (2 Tim. 3:15–16), which are similarly products of the second century.

Finally, many leaders of the early church doubted 2 Peter's apostolic origins, resulting in the epistle's absence from numerous lists of "approved" books. Not only was 2 Peter one of the last works to gain entrance into the New Testament, but scholars believe that it was also the last canonical book written. Composed at some point after 100 C.E., it may not have appeared until as late as about 150 C.E.

ORGANIZATION AND PURPOSE

2 Peter is a brief work and can be divided into three main sections:

1. The writer's apostolic authority and eschatological purpose (1:1–32)

2. Condemnations of false teachers (based on Jude) (2:1–22)
3. Defense of the Parousia doctrine, including a theodicy, and exhortation to behavior appropriate to End time (3:1–18)

THE DELAYED PAROUSIA

Chapter 2 is devoted to invective. It is a brutal attack on false teachers whom the author describes as "slaves of corruption" and compares to dogs that eat their own vomit (2:1–22). Like the authors of Jude and 1 John, the writer seems unaware of any incongruity between the teaching of Christian love on the one hand and the savage abuse of fellow believers who disagree with him on the other. To him, dissenters have no more claim to respect than wild animals that are born only to be trapped and slaughtered (2:12).

It is not clear whether the opponents castigated in chapter 2 are the same skeptics who deny the Parousia in 3:3–4. In any case, the author's primary goal is to reinstate the early Christian apocalyptic hope. To convince his hearers, he reminds them that one world has already perished under a divine judgment—the world destroyed in Noah's Flood (3:5–6). The present "heavens and earth" are reserved for burning, a divine act that will destroy unbelieving persons, presumably including the writer's opponents.

In his prediction of this world's coming devastation, the author apparently borrows the Stoic philosophers' theory that the Cosmos undergoes cycles of destruction and renewal. Employing Stoic images and vocabulary, 2 Peter foretells a cosmic conflagration in which heaven will be swept away in a roaring fire and the earth will disintegrate, exposing all its secrets (3:10).

Because the entire universe is destined to fall apart in a cosmic catastrophe, the author advises his recipients to prepare for an imminent judgment. They should work hard to hurry it along, the implication being that correct human behavior will influence God to accelerate his schedule for the End (3:11–12).

Citing either Revelation's vision (21:1–3) or the Isaiah passages on which it is based (Isa. 65:17; 66:22), the author states that a third world will re-

place the previous two destroyed, respectively, by water and fire. "New heavens and a new earth" will host true justice (3:13), the apocalyptic kingdom of God.

Peter's Theodicy   The author is aware that some Christians who doubt the Parousia may do so because God, despite the arrival, death, and ascension to heaven of the Messiah, has not acted to conquer evil. God's seeming delay, however, has a saving purpose. Holding back judgment, the Deity allows time for more people to repent and be spared the coming holocaust (3:9, 15). Although exercising his kindly patience in the realm of human time, God himself dwells in eternity where "a thousand years is like one day." From his vantage point, the Parousia is not delayed; his apparent slowness to act is really a manifestation of his will to save all people (3:8–9).

Paul's Letters   The author returns to criticizing his opponents in a famous reference to Paul's letters. Admitting that the Pauline correspondence contains unclear passages, he accuses immature Christians of twisting their meaning. Although he refers to Paul as a friend and brother, he clearly does not approve of the way in which some groups interpret Paul's teachings (3:15–16). Some critics suggest that if 2 Peter originated in Rome, the writer may be referring to Marcion or other Gnostic teachers who based their doctrines on a collected edition of Paul's letters. As in the case of Jude, the author does not give us enough information to identify his opponents with any certainty.

As the last-written New Testament book, 2 Peter affirms the primitive Christian hope that Jesus would soon return to establish his kingdom and eliminate evil from the universe. Although predicting that our world will disappear in a fiery holocaust, 2 Peter foresees a renewed creation in which righteousness prevails. While they await the Lord's return to bring about the promised new world, Christians must cling to the apostles' original teachings, avoiding heretical misinterpretations and by their good works shortening the time before the final day arrives (3:10–15). Although 2 Peter adopts the Stoic view that the present universe must perish in flames (an extreme belief that even

Revelation does not advocate), it also shares Revelation's ultimately optimistic vision of the final and complete triumph of absolute good.

Letters from the Johannine Community

Three documents produced by a Johannine Christian a decade or two after John's Gospel was published reveal that the community of the Beloved Disciple had become divided by internal dissension. In one of the great ironies of theological history, the community that was to be distinguished by the love its members showed to one another (John 13:34–35) disintegrated amid bitter controversy. According to the author of 1 John, the writer's former associates, who had recently withdrawn from the original group and apparently formed their own church, were anti-Christs (2:18–19). 1 John accuses them of both doctrinal and behavioral error: misrepresenting the nature of Christ and failing to love their one-time friends.

The opponents whom 1 John denounces were apparently proto-Gnostics who taught that Christ was pure spirit, uncontaminated by association with physical matter (presumably even during his earthly life). Many scholars suggest that the writer's adversaries espoused a form of Docetism, arguing that "the Christ" only *seemed* to be human; he was actually a celestial Revealer who temporarily *appeared* as Jesus but who escaped physical death by reascending to the spirit realm. In refuting this extreme position, 1 John's author decisively set the limits to which the Johannine Gospel's portrayal of Christ could be interpreted spiritually (or Gnostically). By insisting that "Jesus Christ has come *in the flesh*" (4:2, italics added), the writer affirms that the man of history who died on the cross and the exalted Christ are one and the same. The divine Logos, "the word of life," assumed physical humanity in the person of Jesus (1:1–4; 4:2). Many scholars believe that 1 John's unequivocal assertion of the Incarnation—the heavenly Logos becoming flesh—not only defined what eventually became the church's official view of Jesus' dual nature but also interpreted John's Gospel in a way that made it ac-

ceptable to mainstream Christianity (see chapter 10). Even though the secessionists from the Johannine group claimed the Fourth Gospel for the Gnostic community, the author's group also took the Gospel with them when they later merged with the larger apostolic church (see R. E. Brown, "Recommended Reading").

AUTHORSHIP AND DATE

Like the Fourth Gospel, the brief writings called 1, 2, and 3 John are traditionally ascribed to the apostle John. Whereas 1 John is anonymous, the author of 2 and 3 John identifies himself as "the Elder" (*presbyteros*) (2 John, v. 1; 3 John, v. 1). Most scholars believe that the same person wrote all three documents but that he is not to be identified with either the apostle John or the author of the Gospel. Although some critics link him with the editor who added chapter 21 to the Gospel, most commentators view the letter writer as a separate party, albeit an influential member of the Johannine family (John 21:23). The majority of scholars date the letters at about 100–110 C.E., a period when Gnostic Christianity began to be seen as a threat to orthodox church leaders.

1 JOHN

An important tract directed against proto-Gnostic secessionists from the Johannine church, 1 John establishes a set of criteria by which to distinguish true belief from error. Lacking a salutation or closing greeting, 1 John is more a sermon than a genuine letter. Addressed to persons who are devoted to the Son of God (5:13) (probably the author's supporters in his battle with the secessionists), it presents a more conventional view about events heralding the *eschaton* than the Fourth Gospel. 1 John states that the very fact of the "anti-Christ's" activity proves that the "last hour" has arrived (2:18; cf. John 21:22–23). (In the Johannine church, the Gospel's realized eschatology may have existed side-by-side with more traditional ideas about the Parousia.) Like most early Christian groups, the Elder's community relied on prophetic inspiration, an ongoing communication with the Holy Spirit (the Johannine Paraclete) that continued the process of interpreting Jesus' message and meaning (John 15:26–27; 16:12–14). Problems arose when Christian prophets contradicted each other, as the anti-Christ secessionists were then doing. How was the believer to determine which among many opposing "inspirations" was truly from God?

Writing to a charismatic group long before a central church authority existed to enforce official belief, the Elder is the first Christian writer to propose standards by which believers can distinguish "the spirit of error" from "the spirit of truth" (4:1–6). He echoes the apostle Paul, who experienced similar difficulties (1 Thess. 5:19–21), when he asks Christians to "test the spirits" (4:1) critically to evaluate the reliability of their message.

Because the Elder sets up his particular tests to refute the secessionists' errors, we can infer something about their teaching from the nature of his proposals. Basically, he offers two areas of testing— doctrinal and ethical. His document is accordingly divided into two parts, the first beginning with his affirmation of the community's pristine teaching: "Here is the message we heard from him and pass on to you: that God is light" (1:5). The light from God illuminates the doctrinal truth about Jesus. In his prolog (1:1–7), which strikingly resembles the Gospel's Hymn to the Logos, the Elder claims that his group possesses a direct, sensory experience of Jesus' humanity. The Word was visible and physical; he could be seen and touched. Yet those who abandoned the community apparently deny Christ's full humanity, causing the Elder to impose a christological test of the true faith: belief that the Incarnation of the Word is the historical Jesus. Those who deny this "light" now walk in "darkness."

Next to the Incarnation test, the Elder places a requirement expressing his community's cardinal rule. He begins the second part of his discourse with a declaration that parallels his first criterion: "For the message you have heard from the beginning is this: that we should love one another" (3:11). Like Cain, who murdered his brother, the secessionists fail to show love for the former associates whom they have abandoned. In his most quoted statement, the author declares that people who do not love cannot know God because "God is love" (4:8–9). Emphasizing the unity between di-

vine and human love, the Elder reminds us that to love God is also to cherish God's human creation (4:19–21).

Implying that the secessionists not only fail to love but also neglect Christian ethics, the author insists that loving God necessitates keeping his commandments (5:5). This means living as Jesus did, serving others' welfare (2:6). The author refers to "the old command" that his group has always possessed, apparently the single commandment that John's Gospel ascribes to Jesus—the instruction to love (John 13:34–35; 15:12, 17). The Elder can cite no other ethical injunction from his group's tradition.

2 JOHN

Although containing only thirteen verses, 2 John is a true letter. It is addressed to "the Lady chosen by God" (v. 1), a house church that belongs to the Johannine community. As in 1 John, the writer's purpose is to warn of the anti-Christ, the deceiver who falsely teaches that Jesus Christ did not live as a material human being (v. 7). He urges his recipients not to welcome such renegade Christians into the believers' houses or otherwise encourage them (vv. 10–11). As before, the author can prepare against the secessionists' attacks by citing only one cardinal rule, the love that is their community's sole guide (vv. 5–6).

Disclosing that he has more to say than he cares to spell out on paper, the Elder promises to visit the recipients soon, ending with greetings from the writer's home congregation.

3 JOHN

In a private note to his friend Gaius, the Elder asks his recipient to extend hospitality to some Johannine missionaries led by Demetrius (otherwise unknown). The writer asks Gaius to receive these travelers kindly, honoring their church's tradition of supporting those who labor to spread their version of "the truth" (v. 8).

By contrast, one Diotrephes, a rival leader, offends the elder by not only refusing his emissaries' hospitality but also expelling from the congregation any persons who attempt to aid them. We do not know if the spiteful charges Diotrephes brings against the Elder relate to the secessionists' false teaching denounced in 1 John. Although Diotrephes may not be one of the "anti-Christ" faction, his malice and lack of charity suggests that he does not practice the Johannine community's essential commandment.

Some scholars have noted that the Elder's disapproval of Diotrephes may stem from the latter's acting with undue authority. Whereas the Johannine community seems to have existed with little ecclesiastical structure, Diotrephes behaves as if he has the power, in effect, to excommunicate a member of the Elder's group. In exercising this prerogative, Diotrephes anticipates the actions of monarchical bishops in the hierarchically organized church of later centuries.

Summary

A diverse anthology of early Christian literature roughly comparable to the miscellaneous "writings" of the Hebrew Bible, this section of the New Testament reflects the variety of ideas and practices obtaining in different parts of the international Christian community during the late first and early second centuries C.E. The three documents traditionally ascribed to John, son of Zebedee, provide a window on the evolving Johannine community, which was apparently split between the writer's group and proto-Gnostic opponents. Writing in the names of the three apostolic "pillars"—Peter, James, and John—to whom Paul alluded in Galatians, pseudonymous writers dispatched letters and tracts to defend their positions on church order and belief. Probably the last-written book in the Judeo-Christian Bible, 2 Peter warns against "misinterpretations" of Paul's letters and defends traditional Christian eschatology—expectation of the Parousia.

QUESTIONS FOR REVIEW

1. Define the term *catholic epistle* and describe the general nature of these seven documents. According to tradition, to what specific group of authors are these works attributed? Why do many scholars believe that all seven are pseudonymous?

2. Identify and explain the major themes in Hebrews. How does the author's belief in a dualistic universe—an unseen spirit world that parallels the visible Cosmos—affect his teaching about Jesus as an eternal High Priest officiating in heaven?

3. Almost every book in this unit of the New Testament—Hebrews and the catholic epistles—contains a theme or concept not found in any other canonical document. For example, only Hebrews presents Jesus as a celestial High Priest foreshadowed by Melchizedek; it is also unique in being the only New Testament work to define faith (11.1).

Indicate which of the catholic epistles contains the following definitions or statements:

a. A definition of religion

b. A belief that Jesus descended into Hades (the Underworld) and preached to spirits imprisoned there

c. A definition of God's essential nature

d. A set of standards by which to determine the truth of a religious teaching

e. An argument that actions are more important than faith

f. A concept that human history is divided into three separate stages, or "worlds"

g. A defense of the primitive apocalyptic hope involving Jesus' Second Coming (the Parousia)

h. Citations from the noncanonical books of the Pseudepigrapha, including the Book of Enoch

i. The New Testament's most severe denunciation of the rich

QUESTION FOR DISCUSSION AND REFLECTION

1. Hebrews presents certain biblical characters like Melchizedek and Israel's High Priest as foreshadowing the later role of Jesus. Explain the author's methods of biblical interpretation, including his uses of typology, allegory, and symbolism. According to his view, what is the relation of Israel's sacrificial ritual to the death and Ascension of Jesus?

TERMS AND CONCEPTS TO REMEMBER

catholic epistles	definition of religion
epistle	relationship of rich and
dualism	poor
Platonism	salvation through faith
corresponding worlds	or through good
Hebrews' major theme	works
reasons for suffering	authorship of 1 Peter

privileges of Christian belief

obligations and risks of adopting Christianity

Jesus' descent into Hades

authorship of Jude

invective

Pseudepigrapha

Book of 1 Enoch

asceticism

date of 2 Peter

Melchizedek

Aaron

Jesus as both sacrifice and High Priest

definition of faith

authorship of James

wisdom literature

the delayed Parousia

cosmic fire

three "worlds"

new heavens and a new earth

Johannine community

the anti-Christ

Gnosticism

Docetism

the Incarnation

authorship of 1, 2, and 3 John

spirit of error and spirit of truth

tests of belief and behavior

chief rule of the Johannine community

definition of God's nature

RECOMMENDED READING

Hebrews

Attridge, Harold W. *The Epistle to the Hebrews*. Philadelphia: Fortress Press, 1989. An authoritative analysis of the book's origin and theology.

Bourke, Myles M. "The Epistle to the Hebrews." In R. E. Brown et al., eds., *The New Jerome Biblical Commentary*, 2nd ed., pp. 920–941. Englewood Cliffs, N.J.: Prentice-Hall, 1990. A helpful introduction.

Buchanan, G. W., ed. and trans. *Hebrews*. Vol. 36 of the Anchor Bible. Garden City, N.Y.: Doubleday, 1972. Provides editor's translation and commentary.

Dinker, E. "Hebrews, Letter to the." In *The Interpreter's Dictionary of the Bible*, Vol. 2, pp. 571–575. Nashville, Tenn.: Abingdon Press, 1962. A relatively brief but useful discussion.

Fuller, R. H. "The Letter to the Hebrews, James, Jude, Revelation, 1 and 2 Peter." In G. Krodel, ed., *Proclamation Commentaries*. Philadelphia: Fortress Press, 1977.

Kasemann, E. *The Wandering People of God: An Investigation of the Letter to the Hebrews*. Minneapolis: Augsburg, 1984.

Neil, W. *The Epistle to the Hebrews*. London: SCM Press, 1955. A more popular treatment interpreting Hebrews' message.

James

Barnett, A. E. "James, Letter of." In *The Interpreter's Dictionary of the Bible*, Vol. 2, pp. 794–799. Nashville, Tenn.: Abingdon Press, 1962. A useful introduction.

Dibelius, Martin, and Greeven, Heinrich. *A Commentary on the Epistle of James*. Hermeneia Commentary. Translated by M. A. Williams. Philadelphia: Fortress Press, 1976. An excellent study.

Laws, Sophie. *A Commentary on the Epistle of James*. Harper's New Testament Commentary. San Francisco: Harper & Row, 1980.

Leahy, Thomas W. "The Epistle of James." In R. E. Brown et al., eds., *The New Jerome Biblical Commentary*, 2nd ed., pp. 909–916. Englewood Cliffs, N.J.: Prentice-Hall, 1990.

Milton, C. L. *The Epistle of James*. Grand Rapids, Mich.: Eerdmans, 1966. A thorough analysis.

Reicke, Bo. *The Epistle of James, Peter, and Jude*. Vol. 37 of the Anchor Bible. Garden City, N.Y.: Doubleday, 1964. Recent translations with some provocative commentary.

1 and 2 Peter and Jude

Best, Ernest. *1 Peter*. London: Oliphants, 1971.

Brown, R. E.; Donfried, K.; and Reumann, J., eds. *Peter in the New Testament; A Collaborative Assessment by Protestant and Roman Catholic Scholars*. Minneapolis: Augsburg, 1973. A recommended study of Peter's role in the New Testament tradition and literature.

Dalton, William J. "The First Epistle of Peter." In R. E. Brown et al., eds., *The New Jerome Biblical Commentary*, 2nd ed., pp. 903–908. Englewood Cliffs, N.J.: Prentice-Hall, 1990.

Elliott, J. H. *A Home for the Homeless: A Sociological Exegesis of 1 Peter, Its Situation and Strategy*. Philadelphia: Fortress Press, 1981. A sociological analysis of historical conditions underlying the message and meaning of 1 Peter.

Neyrey, Jerome H. "The Epistle of Jude." In R. E. Brown et al., eds. *The New Jerome Biblical Commentary*, 2nd ed., pp. 917–919. Englewood Cliffs, N.J.: Prentice-Hall, 1990.

Neyrey, Jerome H. "The Second Epistle of Peter." In R. E. Brown et al., eds., *The New Jerome Biblical Commentary*, 2nd ed., pp. 1017–1022. Englewood Cliffs, N.J.: Prentice-Hall, 1990.

Reicke, Bo. *The Epistles of James, Peter, and Jude*. Vol. 37 of the Anchor Bible. Garden City, N.Y.: Doubleday, 1964.

van Unnik, W. C. "Peter, First Letter of." In *The Interpreter's Dictionary of the Bible*, Vol. 3, pp. 758–766. Nashville, Tenn.: Abingdon Press, 1962. A helpful introduction.

1, 2, and 3 John

Brown, R. E. *The Community of the Beloved Disciple*. New York: Paulist Press, 1979. An extraordinarily insightful analysis of the Johannine group that produced the Gospel and letters of John.

———. *The Epistles of John.* Vol. 30 of the Anchor Bible. Garden City, N.Y.: Doubleday, 1982. A scholarly translation and commentary on the letters of John.

———. *The Churches the Apostles Left Behind.* New York: Paulist Press, 1984. A wonderfully concise study of several different Christian communities at the end of the first century C.E.

Culpepper, R. A. *1 John, 2 John, 3 John.* Knox Preaching Guides. Atlanta: John Knox Press, 1985.

von Whalde, Urban C. *The Johannine Commandments: 1 John and the Struggle for the Johannine Tradition.* New York: Paulist Press, 1990. For advanced study.

CHAPTER 19

Continuing the Apocalyptic Hope
The Book of Revelation

Then I saw a new heaven and a new earth, for the first heaven and the first earth had vanished. . . . Now at last God has his dwelling among men!
                                                                  Revelation 21:1, 3

Key Themes Revelation affirms Christianity's original hope for an immediate transformation of the world and assures the faithful that God's pre-arranged plan, including the destruction of evil and the advent of Christ's universal reign, is about to be accomplished. The book presents an *apokalypsis* ("unveiling") of unseen realities, both in heaven as it is now and on earth as it will be in the future. Placing government tyranny and Christian suffering in a cosmic perspective, Revelation conveys its message of hope for believers in the cryptic language of metaphor and symbol.

Although Revelation was not the last New Testament book written, its position at the end of the canon is thematically appropriate. The first Christians believed that their generation would witness the end of the present wicked age and the beginning of God's direct rule over the earth. Revelation expresses that apocalyptic hope more powerfully than any other Christian writing. Looking forward to a "new heaven and a new earth" (21:1), it envisions the glorious completion of God's creative work begun in the first book of the Bible. In this sense, it provides the **omega** (the final letter of the Greek alphabet) to the alpha (the first letter) of Genesis.

Revelation's climactic placement is also fitting because it reintroduces Jesus as a major character. Its picture of an all-powerful heavenly Jesus provides a counterweight to the Gospels' portrait of the human Jesus' earthly career. In Revelation, Jesus is no longer Mark's suffering servant or John's embodiment of divine Wisdom. Revelation's Jesus is the Messiah of popular expectations, a conquering warrior-king who slays his enemies and proves beyond all doubt his right to universal rule. In striking contrast to the Gospel portraits, the Jesus of Revelation comes not to forgive sinners and instruct them in a higher righteousness, but to inflict a wrathful punishment upon his opponents (19:11–21).

Revelation's depiction of Jesus' character and function, qualitatively different from that presented in the Gospels, derives partly from the author's apocalyptic view of human history. Like the authors of Jude and 2 Peter, the writer perceives a sharp contrast between the present world, which he regards as hopelessly corrupt, and God's planned future world, a realm of ideal purity. In the author's opinion, the righteous new order can be realized only through God's direct intervention in human affairs, an event that requires Jesus to act as God's Judge and destroyer of the world as we know it. To

---

REVELATION

Author: John of Patmos.

Date: c. 95 C.E.

Place of Composition: Western Asia Minor.

Audience: Seven churches of Asia Minor.

---

understand Revelation's emphasis on violence and destruction, with its correspondingly harsher picture of Jesus' cosmic rule, we must remember that the author belongs to a particular branch of the Jewish and Christian apocalyptic movement.

Revelation and the Apocalyptic Tradition

THE APOCALYPSE

"Revelation" translates the Greek term *apokalypsis*, which means an uncovering, an unveiling, a stripping naked of what was formerly covered. An apocalypse is thus a disclosure of things previously hidden, particularly unseen realities of the spirit world (Heb. 11:1) and future events. Apocalyptic writers typically describe visions or dreams in which they encounter supernatural beings ranging from hideous monsters to angels who communicate God's future intentions (2 Esd. 3–9; Dan. 7–12). Sometimes, apocalyptists are carried out of their bodies to behold the Deity's heavenly throne or other celestial regions normally invisible to human eyes.

The apocalyptic tradition to which Revelation belongs is commonly regarded as a later outgrowth of the prophetic movement in ancient Israel. Israel's great prophets had delivered Yahweh's Word to the people during the period of the Davidic monarchy (about 1000–587 B.C.E.). Following the monarchy's end and the Babylonian captivity (587–538 B.C.E.), however, prophecy declined rapidly. Eventually, many Jews came to believe that authentic prophecy had ceased after the time of Ezra (about 400 B.C.E.). Priests took the place of prophets as Israel's spiritual leaders.

During the last two centuries before the Christian epoch, and for at least a century after, numerous Jewish writers attempted to fill the vacuum left by the prophets' disappearance. They composed innumerable books in the names of Israel's leaders who had lived before the time of Ezra. These pseudonymous works were attributed to figures like Enoch, Moses, Isaiah, David, Solomon, and Ezra. Many of them are apocalypses, containing visions of End time, such as Daniel (the only such work to become part of the Hebrew Bible), 1 and 2 Enoch, 4 Ezra (2 Esdras), 2 Baruch, and the Essene War Scroll from Qumran.

During the early centuries C.E., many Christian writers contributed to the apocalyptic genre. We have already discussed the apocalyptic elements in the Gospels, especially Mark 13 and its parallels in Matthew 24 and Luke 21, as well as Paul's eschatological concerns in his letters to the Thessalonians and the Corinthians. Besides these canonical works, other Christian authors composed apocalyptic books, typically attributing them to prominent apostles, including Peter, John, James, Thomas, and Paul. The canonical Revelation is unique in being ascribed not to a figure of the distant past, but to a contemporary member of the first-century church named John. The work is also unique in being the only surviving document by a Christian prophet (1:3), which was a common function or office in the early church (Acts 2:15–17; 1 Thess. 5:19–20; 1 Cor. 12:10; 14:22, 24–25, 31–33).

CHARACTERISTICS OF APOCALYPTIC WRITING

Besides the mystical, otherworldly quality of its content, apocalyptic literature is distinguished by the following characteristics:

Universality In contrast to prophetic oracles, which focus almost exclusively on Israel and its immediate neighbors, apocalyptic visions are universal in scope. Although the writers' religious communities (Israel or the church) stand at the center of their concern, their work encompasses the whole of human history and surveys events both in heaven and on earth. Apocalyptists view all spirit beings, as

Figure 19.1 *Christ over New York City.* In this painting on a steel door, an unknown Ukrainian-American artist projects the image of a cosmic Christ above the skyscrapers of Manhattan. Depicting two dimensions of reality, the painter contrasts New York's towers of cold steel and concrete—monuments to modern commerce and banking—with his vision of Jesus' unseen presence. Encompassing the largely unaware inhabitants of American's secular society in his spiritual embrace, Christ extends his arms in a gesture that is both protective and beseeching. In his apocalyptic visions, John of Patmos exhibited a similar, if somewhat less compassionate, view of Christ's relation to the Roman Empire. (© Boltin Picture Library)

well as all nations and peoples, as swept together in a conflict of cosmic proportions.

Cosmic Dualism   The apocalyptic worldview borrows much of its cosmology from Greek philosophical ideas about parallel worlds of matter and spirit (see figure 19.1). Postulating a dualistic "two-story universe" composed of visible earth and invisible heaven, apocalyptists see human society profoundly influenced by unseen forces, angels and demons, operating in a celestial realm. Events on earth, such

as persecution of the righteous, reflect the machinations of these heavenly beings.

Chronologic Dualism   Besides dividing the universe into two opposing domains of physical matter and viewless spirit, apocalyptists regard all history as separated into two mutually exclusive periods of time, a current wicked era and a future age of perfection. Seeing the present world situation as too thoroughly evil to reform, apocalyptists expect a sudden and violent change in which God or his

Messiah imposes divine rule by force. In the apocalyptic vision, there is no normal historical progression from one age to the next and no real continuity between them. Thus, the Book of Daniel depicts God's kingdom as abruptly interrupting the ordinary flow of time, shattering all worldly governments with the impact of a colossal meteorite (Dan. 2:31–45).

Ethical Dualism   In the apocalyptic view, there are only two kinds of human beings, just as there are only two epochs of world history and two levels of existence, material and spiritual. Apocalyptists see humanity divided into two opposing camps of intrinsically different ethical quality. The vast majority of people walk in spiritual darkness and are doomed victims of God's wrath. Only a tiny minority — the religious group to which the writers belong and direct their message — remain faithful and receive salvation. Deeply conscious of human imperfection and despairing of humanity's ability to meet God's standards, apocalyptists take a consistently pessimistic view of society's future.

Predestination   Whereas most biblical writers emphasize that historical events are the consequence of our moral choices (e.g., Deut. 28–29; Josh. 24; Ezek. 18), apocalyptists view history as running in a straight line toward a predetermined end. Just as the rise and fall of worldly empires occur according to God's plan (Dan. 2, 7–8), so will the End take place at a time God has already set. Human efforts, no matter how well intended, cannot avert the coming disaster or influence God to change his mind. The vast complexity of human experience means nothing when confronted with the divinely prearranged schedule.

Exclusivism   Many apocalypses, including Daniel and Revelation, were composed to encourage the faithful to maintain integrity and resist temptations to compromise with "worldly" values or customs. Apocalyptists typically equate religious fidelity with a total rejection of the ordinary goals, ambitions, social attachments, and other pursuits of unbelieving society. Regarding most people as condemned, apocalyptists commonly urge their audience to adopt a rigidly sectarian attitude, avoiding all association with unbelievers.

Limited Theology   Consistent with this strict division of history and people into divinely approved or disapproved units, apocalyptists usually show little sympathy for differing viewpoints or compassion for nonbelievers. All modes of life are either black or white, with no psychological or spiritual shades of gray in between. As a result of the authors' mindsets, the apocalyptic picture of God is ethically limited. The Deity is almost invariably portrayed as an enthroned monarch, an omnipotent authority who brings history to a violent conclusion in order to demonstrate his sovereignty, confound his enemies, and preserve his few worshipers. The notion that God might regard all people as his children or that he might establish his kingdom by less catastrophic means does not appeal to the apocalyptic temperament or satisfy the apocalyptic yearning.

Portrait of a Violent God   Assuming that the Deity achieves control over heaven and earth through a cataclysmic battle with a formidable opponent (the Dragon of Chaos, or, in the New Testament, Satan), apocalyptists imagine this transference of power by picturing God as a destroyer who exterminates much of his sentient creation. Using the Exodus story of the ten plagues Yahweh inflicted on Egypt as their model, apocalyptists typically show God angrily punishing disobedient humanity with a devastating series of natural disasters, famines, and loathsome diseases. That the use of evil to defeat evil is ethically questionable does not seem to trouble the apocalyptic mentality.

Eschatological Preoccupations   Along with uncovering the mysteries of the invisible world, apocalyptists reveal the posthumous fate of people during God's terrifying judgment. Because they were commonly written at a time when fidelity brought no earthly rewards but only the danger of imprisonment, torture, and death, apocalyptic works pioneered the way in popularizing new beliefs about compensatory blessings in the New Age. Apocalyptists were the first Bible writers to speculate about the nature of the afterlife, which they commonly pictured as resurrection of the body rather than as the survival of an immortal soul (Dan. 12:1–3). The apocalyptists' rejection of the old Hebrew belief that human souls were consigned to eternal oblivion in Sheol (the Underworld) and their insistence that God makes moral distinctions between virtuous and wicked lives marked a theological innovation that was adopted by several later Jewish groups, including the Pharisees, Essenes, and early Christians.

The Use of Symbols and Code Words   Perhaps because they are the work of sages immersed in arcane learning, almost all apocalypses contain deliberately obscure language that veils as well as expresses the authors' meaning. In addition, most were written during periods of crisis and persecution, a situation that encouraged apocalyptists to use terms and images that their original audiences could understand but that will bewilder outsiders. In Enoch, Daniel, Revelation, and other apocalypses, the authors employ symbols from a wide variety of sources, both pagan and biblical.

In its broadest sense, a **symbol** is a sign that represents something other than itself, typically an abstract quality or religious concept. Symbols take the form of persons, places, objects, or actions that suggest an association or connection with another dimension of meaning. Both Daniel and Revelation depict Gentile nations as animals because, to the authors, they resemble wild beasts in their savage and irrational behavior. Kings who demand worship are symbolized as idols, and paying homage to them is labeled idolatry. Using code words for a pagan opponent, such as "Babylon" or "the beast," helps shield the apocalyptist's seditious message.

AUTHORSHIP AND DATE

Who was the writer who created the bedazzling kaleidoscope of images in Revelation? According to some late second-century traditions, he is the apostle John and the same person who wrote the Gospel and letters of John. Other early Christian sources recognized that the immense differences in

thought, language, and theology between Revelation and the Fourth Gospel indicate that they could not have originated with the same author. Eusebius suggests that another John, known only as the "Elder," an official of the late first-century Ephesian church, may have written the Apocalypse (*History* 3.39.1–11).

Virtually all modern scholars agree that the Gospel and Revelation stem from different authors. A few accept Eusebius's theory about John the Elder of Ephesus, but the scholarly majority notes that we have no evidence to link the book with that obscure figure. Most scholars prefer to accept no more than the writer's own self-identification. He simply calls himself John, a "servant" of Jesus Christ (1:2). Because he does not claim apostolic authority and never refers to having known the earthly Jesus, most analysts conclude that he is not one of the Twelve, whom he categorizes as different from himself. In the author's day, the apostles had already become "cornerstones" of the heavenly Temple (21:14). Exiled to the island of **Patmos** in the eastern Aegean Sea where he received his visions (1:9), the author perhaps is best described as John of Patmos, a mystic who regarded himself as a Christian prophet and his book as a preview of future events (1:1–3; 22:7–10).

By studying the contents of his work, scholars can infer something of John's background. He is intimately familiar with internal conditions in the seven churches addressed (Rev. 2:1–3:23), even though he seems to belong to none of them (see figure 19.2). To some commentators, this indicates that John was an itinerant Christian prophet who traveled among widely scattered churches. Although he held no congregational office, his recognized stature as a mystic and visionary gave him considerable influence in the communities to which he directed his apocalypse.

Because he writes Greek as if it were a second language, phrasing idiosyncratically in a Semitic style, most scholars believe that John was a native of Palestine, or at least had spent much time there. A few critics suggest that he had some connection with the Johannine community, for, like the author of John's Gospel, he refers to Christ as Logos

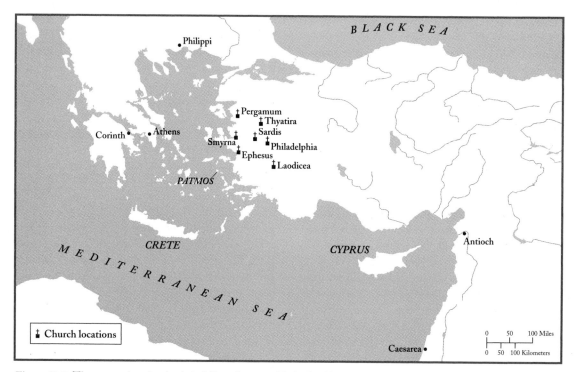

Figure 19.2 The seven churches in Asia Minor (western Turkey) addressed in Revelation 1–3 include Ephesus, one of the major seaports of the Roman Empire, and Sardis, once capital of the older Lydian Empire (sixth century B.C.E.). John pictures the heavenly Christ dictating letters to seven angels who act as invisible guardians of the individual churches. With this image, John reminds his audience that the tiny groups of Christians scattered throughout the Roman Empire do not stand alone. Although seemingly weak and insignificant, they are part of God's mighty empire of the spirit and are destined to triumph over their earthly oppressors.

(Word), Lamb, Witness, Shepherd, Judge, and Temple. Both Revelation and the Gospel express a duality of spirit and matter, Good and Evil, God and the Devil. Both regard Christ as present in the church's liturgy and view his death as a saving victory. Important differences range from the quality of the Greek—excellent in the Gospel and awkward in the Apocalypse—to the writers' respective theologies. Whereas the Gospel presents God's love as his primary motive in dealing with humanity (John 3:15–16), Revelation mentions divine love only once. The Johannine Jesus' pre-eminent command to love is conspicuously absent from Revelation.

Writing about 180 C.E., the churchman Irenaeus stated that Revelation was composed late in the reign of Domitian, who was emperor from 81 to 96 C.E. Internal references to government hostilities

toward Christians (1:9; 2:10, 13; 6:9–11; 14:12; 16:6; 21:4), policies then associated with Domitian's administration, support Irenaeus's assessment. Most scholars date the work about 95 or 96 C.E.

THE EMPEROR CULT

Domitian was the son of Vespasian and the younger brother of Titus, the general who had successfully crushed the Jewish revolt against Rome and destroyed the Jerusalem Temple (see figure 19.3). After Titus's brief reign (79–81 C.E.), Domitian inherited the imperial throne, accepting divine honors offered him and allowing himself to be worshiped as a god in various parts of the empire. We have no real evidence that Domitian personally enforced a universal observance of the emperor cult, but in certain

Figure 19.3 This bust of Julia, daughter of the emperor Titus, shows the elaborate hairstyles popular among aristocratic women of the late first century. Julia's contemporary, the author of Revelation, denounces Rome in the symbol of a vain and luxurious woman (Rev. 17). (© Erich Lessing/PhotoEdit)

Figure 19.4 Bust of Domitian, emperor of Rome from 81 to 96 C.E. Many historians believe that an overzealous cult of emperor worship in Asia Minor stimulated the attacks on Christians described in Revelation. To what extent Domitian personally encouraged his subjects to honor him as a god is uncertain. Most Greco-Roman historians thoroughly disliked Domitian's policies and presented him as a tyrant. This ancient prejudice makes it difficult for modern scholars to evaluate his reign objectively. (© Alinari/Art Resource, NY)

areas—especially in Asia Minor—some governors and other local officials demanded public participation in the cult as evidence of citizens' loyalty and patriotism (see figure 19.4). During this period, persecution of Christians for refusing to honor the national leader seems to have been local and sporadic. Despite the lack of a concentrated official assault on the faith, however, John clearly feels a growing tension between church and state, a sense of impending conflict that makes him regard Rome as a new Babylon, destroyer of God's people.

Because Rome had recognized their religion's monotheism, Jews were generally exempted from the emperor cult. Jewish and Gentile Christians, however, were not. To most Romans, their "stubborn" refusal to honor any of the many Greco-Roman gods or deified emperors was not only unpatriotic but also likely to bring the gods' wrath upon the whole community. Early Christians denied the existence of the Hellenistic deities and rejected offers to participate in Roman religious festivals and other communal events. They became known as unsocial "atheists" and "haters of humankind." Rumors spread that they met secretly to drink blood and perform cannibalistic rites (a distorted reference to the sacramental ingesting of Jesus' blood and body). Labeled as a seditious secret society dangerous to the general welfare, early Christian groups endured social ostracism and hostility. When they also refused to pledge their allegiance to the emperor as a symbol of the Roman state, many local governors and other magistrates had them arrested, imprisoned, tortured, and even executed.

Only a few decades after John composed Revelation, Pliny the Younger, a Roman governor of Bithynia (located in the same general region as Revelation's seven churches), wrote to the emperor Trajan inquiring about the government's official policy toward Christians. Pliny's description of the situation as it was about 112 C.E. may also apply to John's slightly earlier time.

Although a humane and sophisticated thinker, Pliny reports that he did not hesitate to torture two slave women, "deacons" of a local church, and execute other believers. If Christians hold Roman citizenship, he sends them to Rome for trial. Trajan replies that although his governors are not to hunt out Christians or accept anonymous accusations, self-confessed believers are to be punished. Both the emperor and Pliny clearly regard Christians as criminals threatening the empire's security (Pliny, *Letters* 10.96–97).

PURPOSE AND ORGANIZATION

The Christians for whom John writes were experiencing a real crisis. They were faced with Jewish hostility, public suspicion, and sporadic government persecution, imprisonment, and even execution. Many believers must have been tempted to renounce Christ, as Pliny asked his prisoners to do, and conform to the norms of Roman society. Recognizing that the costs of remaining Christian were overwhelmingly high, John recorded his visions of cosmic conflict to strengthen those whose faith wavered, assuring them that death is not defeat but victory. In the light of eternity, Rome's power was insignificant, but its victims, slaughtered for their fidelity, gained everlasting life and the power to judge the fates of their former persecutors.

Despite its many complexities, we can outline Revelation as follows:

1. Prolog: the author's self-identification and the basis for his authority—divine revelation (1:1–20)
2. Jesus' letters to the seven churches of Asia Minor (2:1–3:22)
3. Visions from heaven: a scroll with seven seals; seven trumpets (4:1–11:19)
4. Signs in heaven: visions of the woman, the Dragon, the beast, the Lamb, and the seven plagues (12:1–16:21)
5. Visions of the "great whore" and the fall of Babylon (Rome) (17:1–18:24)
6. Visions of heavenly rejoicing, the warrior Messiah, the imprisonment of the beast and Satan, judgment of the dead, and the final defeat of evil (19:1–20:15)
7. Visions of the "new heaven and new earth" and the establishment of a new Jerusalem on earth (21:1–22:5)
8. Epilog: authenticity of the author's prophetic visions and the nearness of their fulfillment (22:6–21)

From this outline, we observe that John begins his work in the real world of exile and suffering (1:1–10) and then takes his readers on a visionary tour of the spirit world—including a vivid dramatization of the imminent fall of satanic governments and the triumph of Christ. He returns at the end to earth and gives final instructions to his contemporary audience (22:6–21). The book's structure thus resembles a vast circle starting and ending in physical reality but encompassing a panorama of the unseen regions of heaven and the future.

Alone among New Testament writers, John claims divine inspiration for his work. He reports that on "the Lord's day"—Sunday—he "was caught up by the Spirit" to hear and see heaven's unimaginable splendors (1:9). His message derives from God's direct revelation to Jesus Christ, who in turn transmits it through an angel to him (1:1–2). John's visions generate an intense urgency, for they reveal the immediate future (1:1). Visionary previews of Jesus' impending return convince the author that what he sees is about to happen (1:3). This warning is repeated at the book's conclusion when Jesus proclaims that his arrival is imminent (22:7, 10, 12).

REVELATION'S USE OF SYMBOLS

John's Prophetic Style   Revelation's opening chapter gives a representative example of John's writing style. It shows how profoundly he was influenced by the Hebrew Bible and how he utilizes its vivid images to construct his fantastic symbols. Without ever citing specific biblical books, John typically fills his sentences with metaphors and phrases borrowed from all parts of the Hebrew Bible. Scholars have counted approximately 500 such verbal allusions. (The Jerusalem Bible helps the reader recognize John's biblical paraphrases by printing them in italics.)

In his first symbolic depiction of a heavenly being (1:12–16), John paints a male figure with snow-white hair, flaming eyes, incandescent brass feet, and a sharp sword protruding from his mouth. These images derive largely from Daniel (chs. 7 and 10). To universalize this figure more completely, John adds astronomical features to his biblical symbols. Like a Greek mythological hero transformed into a stellar constellation, the figure is described as holding seven stars in his hand and shining with the brilliance of the sun.

The next verses (1:17–19) reveal the figure's identity. As the "first and the last" who has died but now lives forever, he is the crucified and risen Christ. The author's purpose in combining biblical and nonbiblical imagery is now clear: In strength and splendor, the glorified Christ surpasses rival Greco-Roman deities like Mithras, Apollo, Helios, Amon-Ra, and other solar gods worshiped throughout the Roman Empire.

John further explains his symbols in 1:20. There, Christ identifies the stars as angels and the lampstands standing nearby as the seven churches of John's home territory. This identification reassures the author that his familiar earthly congregations do not exist solely on a material plane, but are part of a larger visible/invisible duality in which angelic spirits protectively oversee assembled Christians. The symbols also serve John's characteristic purpose in uncovering the spiritual reality behind physical appearance. To John, the seven churches are as precious as the golden candelabrum that once stood in the Jerusalem sanctuary. Like the eternal stars above, they shed Christ's light on a benighted world.

The Lamb and the Dragon

In asking us to view the universe as God sees it, John challenges his readers to respond emotionally and intuitively as well as intellectually to his symbols. Thus, he depicts invisible forces of Good or Evil in images that evoke an instinctively positive or negative reaction. Using a tradition also found in the Fourth Gospel, the author pictures Christ as the Lamb of God, whose death "takes away the sin of the world" (John 1:29, 36; Rev. 4:7–14; 5:6; 7:10, 14). Harmless and vulnerable, the Lamb is appealing; his polar opposite, the **Dragon,** elicits feelings of fear and revulsion. A reptilian monster with seven heads and ten horns, he is equated with "that serpent of old . . . whose name is Satan, or the Devil" (12:3, 9). (In the Eden story, the **serpent** that tempted Eve to disobey God is not described as evil. The Genesis serpent's identification with Satan is a much later development in Jewish thought [Wisd. of Sol. 2:23–24].)

In his vision of the Dragon waging war and being thrown down from heaven (12:1–12), John evokes one of the world's oldest conflict myths. Dating back to ancient Sumer and Babylon, the dragon image represents the forces of Chaos—darkness, disorder, and the original void—that preceded the world's creation. In the Babylonian creation story, the *Enuma Elish,* the young god Marduk must defeat and kill Tiamat, the Dragon of Chaos, before the orderly Cosmos can be brought into being. Echoes of these primordial creation **myths** appear in the Hebrew Bible, including the symbol of the dark, watery abyss (Gen. 1:2) and passages in which Yahweh defeats the chaotic monsters Rahab, Behemoth, and Leviathan (Ps. 74:13–17; 89:9–10; Job 26:1–14; Isa. 51:9). Consistent with the ancient Chaos myth, the defeat of the Dragon in Revelation returns him to the original abyss—the dark void that represents forces opposing God's light and creative purpose (20:1–3, 7).

To unspiritual eyes, the Lamb—tiny and vulnerable—might appear a ridiculously inadequate opponent of the Dragon, particularly because John views Satan as possessing immense power on earth as he wages war against the Lamb's people, the Church (12:13–17). Although nations that the Dragon controls, figuratively called Sodom and Egypt (11:8), have already slain the Lamb (when Rome crucified Jesus), God uses this apparent weakness to eliminate evil in both heaven and earth. John wishes his readers to draw comfort from this paradox: Christ's sacrificial death guarantees his ultimate victory over the Dragon and all he represents.

The Lamb's death and rebirth to immortal power also delivers his persecuted followers. The Church will overcome the seemingly invincible strength of its oppressors; the blood of its faithful martyrs confirm that God will preserve it (6:9–11; 7:13–17). Although politically and socially as weak as a lamb, the Christian community embodies a potential strength that is unrecognized by its enemies. John expresses this belief in the image of an angel carrying a golden censer, an incense burner used in Jewish and Christian worship services. He interprets the censer's symbolism very simply: Smoke rising upward from the burning incense represents Christians' prayers ascending to heaven, where they have an astonishing effect. In the next image, the angel throws the censer to earth, causing thunder and an earthquake. The meaning is that the prayers of the faithful can figuratively shake the world (8:3–5). The author gives many of his most obscure or grotesque symbols a comparably down-to-earth meaning.

Limited space permits us to discuss here only a few of John's most significant visions. We focus on those in which he pictures the cosmic tension between Good and Evil, Light and Darkness, Christ and Satan. In commenting on the notorious beast whose "human" number is 666 (13:1–18)—a favorite topic for many of today's apocalyptists—we also briefly review the author's use of numerology, the occult art of assigning arcane meanings to specific numbers.

Jesus' Letters to the Seven Churches

Having validated his prophetic authority through the divine source of his prophecy, John now surveys the disparate churches of Asia Minor, the seven lamps that contrast with the world's darkness. Like the contemporary author of 2 Esdras (14:22–48),

John presents himself as a secretary recording the dictation of a divine voice, conveying the instructions of a higher power (see figure 19.2).

Christ's letters to the seven communities all follow the same pattern. After he commands John to write, Jesus identifies himself as the sender and then employs the formula "I know," followed by a description of the church's spiritual condition. A second formula, "but I have it against you," then introduces a summary of the church's particular weaknesses. Each letter also includes a prophetic call for repentance, a promise that the Parousia will occur soon, an exhortation to maintain integrity, a directive to "hear," and then a final pledge to reward the victorious.

After reading Jesus' messages to Ephesus (2:1–7), **Smyrna** (2:8–11), **Pergamum** (2:12–17), **Thyatira** (2:18–29), **Sardis** (3:1–6), **Philadelphia** (3:7–13), and **Laodicea** (3:14–22), the student will have a good idea of John's method. Church conditions in each of these cities are rendered in images that represent the spiritual reality underlying those conditions. Thus, Pergamum is labeled the site of Satan's throne (2:13), probably because it was the first center of the emperor cult. (John sees any worldly ruler who claims divine honors as an agent of Satan and hence the opposite of Jesus, an anti-Christ.) The Balaam referred to here was a Canaanite prophet hired to curse Israel (Num. 22–24), and hence a false teacher, like those who advocate eating meat previously sacrificed to Greco-Roman gods (2:14). John's strict refusal to tolerate consuming animals slaughtered in non-Christian rituals (which included virtually all meats sold in most Roman cities) is typical of his exclusivism and contrasts with Paul's freer attitude on the same issue (1 Cor. 8:1–13).

Visions in Heaven

John's initial vision made visible and audible the invisible presence of Christ; his second (4:1–11:19) opens the way to heaven. After the Spirit carries him to God's throne, John is shown pictures of events about to occur (4:1–2). It is important to remember, however, that John's purpose is not merely to predict future happenings but to remove the material veil that shrouds heavenly truths and to allow his readers to see that God retains full control of the entire universe. The visions that follow are intended to reassure Christians that their sufferings are temporary and their deliverance is certain.

BREAKING THE SEVEN SEALS

John conveys this assurance in two series of seven visions involving seven seals and seven trumpets. Seen from the perspective of God's heavenly throne (depicted in terms of Isa. 6 and Ezek. 1 and 10), the opening of the seven seals reveals that the future course of events has already been determined, written down in advance on a heavenly scroll. In John's day, almost all writing was done on long narrow strips of paper that were then rolled up around a stick, forming a scroll. Important communications from kings or other officials were commonly sealed with hot wax, which was imprinted while still soft with the sender's identifying seal. Because the scroll could not be opened without breaking the seal, the wax imprint effectively prevented anyone from knowing the scroll's contents until the intended recipient opened it.

In John's vision, the Lamb opens each of the seven seals in sequence, disclosing either a predestined future event or the revelation of God's viewpoint on some important matter. (Breaking the seventh seal is an exception, producing only an ominous silence in heaven—the calm preceding the Lord's Final Judgment [8:1].) Unsealing the first four seals unleashes four horses and riders—the famous Four Horsemen of the Apocalypse—representing, respectively, conquest, war, food shortages (including monetary inflation), and death, the "sickly pale" rider, followed closely by Hades (the grave or Underworld) (6:1–8).

Breaking the fifth seal makes visible the souls of persons executed for their Christian faith. With their blood crying for divine vengeance, they are given white clothing and told to rest until the full number of predestined martyrs has been killed (6:9–11). In such scenes, John indicates that be-

lievers' willingness to die for their religion earns them the white garment of spiritual purity—and that God soon will act to avenge their deaths.

Showing how terrifying the great day of God's vengeance will be, John pictures it in terms of astronomical catastrophes. Apparently borrowing from the same apocalyptic tradition that the Synoptic Gospel writers used to predict Jesus' Second Coming (Mark 13; Matt. 24–25; Luke 21), the author says the sun will turn black, the moon will turn a bloody red, and the stars will fall to earth as the sky vanishes into nothingness (6:12–14). As he clothes Jesus in astronomical images, so John also paints the End in livid colors of cosmic dissolution.

As the earth's population hides in fear, angels appear with God's distinctive seal to mark believers on the forehead, an apocalyptic device borrowed from Ezekiel 9. The symbolic number of those marked for salvation is 144,000 (a multiple of 12), the number representing the traditional twelve tribes of Israel. This indicates that John sees his fellow Jews redeemed at End time (compare Paul's view in Rom. 9:25–27). In chapter 14, the 144,000 are designated the first ingathering of God's harvest (14:1–5). Accompanying this group is a huge crowd from every nation on earth, probably signifying the countless multitudes of Gentile Christians. Both groups wear white robes and stand before God's throne. (By contrast, see John's description of those marked by the demonic "beast" [13:16–17].)

The Seven Trumpets As if answering the churches' prayers (symbolized by the censer in 8:4–5), seven angels blow seven trumpets of doom. The first six announce catastrophes reminiscent of the ten plagues on Egypt. The initial trumpet blast triggers a hail of fire and blood, causing a third of the earth to burn (8:6–7). The second causes a fire-spewing mountain to be hurled into the sea, perhaps a reference to the volcanic island of Thera, which was visible from Patmos (8:8–9). Devastating volcanic eruptions like that of Vesuvius in 79 C.E. were commonly regarded as divine judgments.

The third and fourth trumpets introduce more astronomical disasters, including a blazing comet or meteorite called Wormwood (perhaps picturing

Satan's fall from heaven) and causing the sun, moon, and stars to lose a third of their light (8:10–12). After the fifth trumpet blast, the fallen star opens the abyss, releasing columns of smoke that produce a plague of locusts, similar to those described in Exodus (10:12–15) and Joel (1:4; 2:10). Persons not angelically marked are tormented with unbearable agonies but are unable to die to end their pain (9:1–6). These disasters, in which the locusts may represent barbarian soldiers invading the Roman Empire (9:7–11), are equivalent to the first disaster predicted (8:13; 9:12).

Despite the unleashing of further hordes as the sixth trumpet sounds (9:14–19), John does not believe that such afflictions will stop the world's bad behavior. People who survive the plagues will continue committing crimes and practicing false religion (9:20–21). In fact, John presents the world's suffering as gratuitous and essentially without moral purpose. Revelation's various plagues compound human misery, but they fail to enlighten their victims about the divine nature or produce a single act of regret or repentance.

Eating the Scroll As he had taken his device of marking the saved from Ezekiel 9, John now draws upon the same prophet to describe the symbolic eating of a little scroll that tastes like honey but turns bitter in the stomach (Ezek. 2:8–3:3). The scroll represents the dual nature of John's message: sweet to the faithful but sour to the disobedient (10:8–11).

In the next section, John is told to measure the Jerusalem Temple, which will continue under Gentile (pagan) domination for forty-two months. In the meantime, two witnesses are appointed to prophesy for 1260 days—the traditional period of persecution or tribulation established in Daniel (7:25; 9:27; 12:7). The witnesses are killed and, after three and a half days, resurrected and taken to heaven. (The executed prophets may refer to Moses and Elijah, Peter and Paul, or collectively, to all Christian martyrs whose testimony caused their deaths.) After the martyrs' ascension, an earthquake kills 7000 inhabitants of the great city whose ethical reality is represented by Sodom and Egypt. Sodom, guilty of violence and inhospitality, was consumed in fire from heaven. Egypt, which enslaved God's people, was devastated by ten plagues. So Rome, the tyrannical state that executed Christ and persecutes his disciples (11:1–13), suffers deserved punishment.

The seventh trumpet does not introduce a specific calamity, but proclaims God's sovereignty and the eternal reign of his Christ. With the Messiah invisibly reigning in the midst of his enemies (Ps. 2:1–12), God's heavenly sanctuary opens to view amid awesome phenomena recalling Yahweh's presence in Solomon's Temple (1 Kings 8:1–6).

Signs in Heaven: The Woman, the Dragon, the Beast, and the Seven Plagues

Chapter 12 introduces a series of unnumbered visions dramatizing the cosmic battle between the lamb and the Dragon. In this section (12:1–16:21), John parallels unseen events in heaven with their consequences experienced on earth. The opening war in the spirit realm (12:1–12) finds its earthly counterpart in the climactic battle of **Armageddon** (16:12–16). Between these two analogous conflicts, John mixes inspirational visions of the Lamb's domain with warnings about "the beast" and God's negative judgment upon disobedient humanity.

THE CELESTIAL WOMAN, THE DRAGON, AND THE BEAST FROM THE SEA

This section's first astronomical sign reveals a woman dressed in the sun, moon, and stars, a figure resembling Hellenistic portraits of the Egyptian goddess Isis. Despite its nonbiblical astrological features, however, John probably means the figure to symbolize Israel, historically the parent of Christ. Arrayed in "twelve stars" suggesting the traditional twelve tribes, the woman labors painfully giving birth to the Messiah. John's fellow first-century apocalyptist, the author of 2 Esdras, similarly depicted Israel's holy city, Jerusalem, the mother of all believers, as a persecuted woman (2 Esd.

9:38–10:54). Like most of John's symbols, this figure is capable of multiple interpretations, including the Roman Catholic view that it represents the Virgin.

The Dragon, whom the archangel **Michael** hurls from heaven, wages war against the woman's children, identified as the faithful who witness to Jesus' sovereignty (12:13–17). Lest they despair, however, John has already informed his hearers that this satanic attack on the Church is really a sign of the Dragon's last days. His expulsion from heaven and his wrath on earth signify that Christ has already begun to rule. Satan can no longer accuse the faithful to God as he did in Job's time (Job 1–2). In John's mystic vision, the Lamb's sacrificial death and believers' testimony about it have conquered the Dragon and overthrown evil (12:10–12).

His activities now limited to human society, the Dragon lifts his ugly head in the form of a monster sprouting ten horns and seven heads. The reversed number of heads and horns shows his kinship to the Dragon, who gives the beast his power (13:1–4). Most scholars believe that at the time of writing, John intended the beast as a symbol of Rome, a government he regarded as satanic in its persecution of the Church (13:3, 5–8).

The picture grows more complicated after the beast is slain, only to revive unexpectedly. A second beast emerges not from the sea, but from the earth, to work miracles and enforce public worship of the first beast. In a parody of the angelic sealing, the beast allows no one to conduct business unless he bears the beast's mark. John then adds a "key" to this bestial riddle: The beast's number is that of a "man's name," and the "numerical value of its letters is six hundred and sixty-six" (13:14–18).

JOHN'S NUMERICAL SYMBOLS

The reader is aware by this point that John's use of particular numbers is an important part of his symbolism. In this respect, John is typical of the Hellenistic age in which he lived. For centuries before his time, Greco-Roman thinkers regarded certain numbers as possessing a special kind of meaning. The Greek philosopher Pythagoras speculated that the universe was structured on a harmony of numerical relationships and that certain combinations of numbers held a mystical signification.

In the Jewish tradition, seven represented the days of creation, culminating in God's Sabbath ("seventh-day") rest (Gen. 1). Hence, seven stood for earthly completion or perfection. By contrast, six may represent that which is incomplete or imperfect. When John depicts divine activities affecting earth, as in the seven seals or seven trumpets, he signifies that God's actions are perfectly completed. When he wishes to represent a personification of human inadequacy or corruption, he applies the number six, tripling it for emphasis.

The Mystical Number of the Beast To calculate the beast's numerical symbol, we must remember that in the author's day, all numbers, whether in Hebrew, Aramaic, or Greek, were represented by letters of the alphabet. Thus, each letter in a person's name was also a number. By adding up the sum of all letters in a given name, we arrive at its "numerical value." (The awkward system of having letters double for numbers continued until the Arabs introduced their Arabic numerals to Europeans during the Middle Ages.)

John's hint that the beast's cryptic number could be identified with a specific person has inspired more irresponsible speculation than almost any other statement in his book. In virtually every generation from John's day until ours, apocalyptists have found men or institutions that they claimed fit the beast's description and thus filled the role of anti-Christ, whose appearance confirmed that the world was near its End.

By contrast, most New Testament scholars believe that John (or the source he employs) refers to a historical personage of his own time. Who that person might have been, however, is still hotly debated. Some historians believe the man who best fit John's description of the beast was Nero, the first Roman head of state to torture and execute Christians (see figure 19.5). Following Nero's suicide in 68 C.E., popular rumors swept the empire that he was not dead but in hiding and planned to reappear at the head of a barbarian army to reassert his sovereignty. (This view explains the beast's recovery from its "death-blow" and his putting to death

Figure 19.5 Coin portrait bust of Nero (54–68 C.E.). According to the Roman historian Tacitus, Nero was the first emperor to persecute Christians. Nero's violence toward believers made him seem to some the image of bestial attacks on God's people. In depicting the "beast" who demands his subjects' worship, John of Patmos may have had Nero—and other worldly rulers who imitated the emperor's methods—in mind. (Courtesy American Numismatic Society, Photographic Services)

those Christians who refused to acknowledge his divinity.) Proponents of this hypothesis point to the fact that in Aramaic the "numerical value" of the name Nero Caesar is 666.

Although it is widely accepted, the theory identifying John's beast with Nero leaves much unexplained. We have no evidence that the author intended us to use Aramaic letters in computing the name's mystical significance. Other historians suggest that John intended to imply that Nero was figuratively reborn in Domitian, his vicious spirit ascending "out of the abyss" (17:8) to torment Christians in a new human form. Still others observe that we do not have "the key" (13:18) necessary to understand John's meaning.

Historians' speculations about the beast's identity have been disappointingly inconclusive. Whatever contemporary figure the author had in mind, his achievement was to create a symbol of timeless significance. Every age has its beast, a distortion of the divine image in which God created humanity (Gen. 1:27), who somehow gains the power to per-

petrate evil on a large scale. In the universality of his symbols, John achieves a continuing relevance.

METHODS OF INTERPRETATION

First Method   Our brief scrutiny of John's mysterious beast illustrates the more general challenge of trying to find a reliable method of interpreting Revelation's complex system of symbols. In the tentative identifications mentioned previously, we have already touched on two possible methods. The first approach, favored by scholars, assumes that Revelation was composed for a first-century audience familiar with apocalyptic imagery and that its chief purpose was to give an eschatological interpretation of then-current events. Reasoning that the book could not have been written or understood well enough to have been preserved if it did not have considerable immediate significance to its original hearers, the scholar looks to contemporary Roman history to supply the primary meanings of John's symbols. According to this scholarly method, Babylon (18:2, 10) is Rome, the beast personifies the empire's blasphemous might (represented in human form by the emperors), and the various plagues described are metaphorically intensified versions of wars, invasions, famines, earthquakes, and other disasters experienced (or feared) during the late first century.

Second Method   A second view, favored by apocalyptists, sees Revelation as largely predictive. The visions may have had a contemporary application in Roman times, but John's main purpose was to prophesy about future events. Invariably, apocalyptist interpreters regard their own time as that predicted by John. During the last several centuries, such interpreters, comparing Daniel's use of "times," "years," and "days" with similar terms in Revelation (12:6, 14; 13:5; etc.), have tried to calculate the exact year of the End. In the United States alone, the years 1843, 1844, 1874, 1914, 1975, 1984, and 2000 have been announced by different apocalyptic groups as the year in which Christ will return to judge the earth, slaughter the wicked, or establish a new world. Thus far, all such groups have been wrong, probably because apocalypses like John's were not intended to be blueprints of the future. To try to construct a paradigm of End time from Daniel's or Revelation's chronological or numerical symbols is to miss their purpose, as well as to ignore Paul's advice about computing "dates and times" (1 Thess. 5:1). Given human nature, however, it is unlikely that their predecessors' repeated failures will deter future apocalyptists from publicizing their ingeniously revised schedules of the End.

Third Method   Although the historians' attempt to correlate Revelation's images and symbols with conditions in the first-century Roman Empire is helpful, it does not exhaust the book's potential meaning. A third method recognizes that John's visions have a vitality that transcends any particular time or place. John's lasting achievement lies in the universality of his symbols and parabolic dramas. His visions continue to appeal not because they apply explicitly to his or some future era, but because they reflect some of the deepest hopes and terrors of the human imagination. As long as dread of evil and longing for justice and peace motivate human beings, Revelation's promise of the ultimate triumph of good over Chaos will remain pertinent. John's visions speak directly to the human condition as thousands of generations experience it.

In surveying Revelation's last chapters (17–22), we focus on those aspects of the book that dramatize the ever-repeated struggle and make John's visions relevant not merely to his or End time but to ours as well. The reader may have noted that John's method in presenting his visions is to retell the same event in different terms, using different symbols to depict the same reality. Thus, to dramatize Christ's victory over evil, he does not proceed in a straight line from the opening battle to the devil's final defeat, but turns back to narrate the conflict again and again.

After the seventh trumpet blast, we are told that Jesus is victorious and now reigns as king over the world (11:15). However, another battle ensues in chapter 12, after which John declares that Christ has now achieved total sovereignty (12:10). Yet, still another conflict follows—the infamous battle of Armageddon (16:13–16)—after which the angel repeats, "'It is over!'" (16:18). But it is not finished, for Satan's earthly kingdom—Babylon—is yet to fall (chs. 17–18). When she does and a fourth victory is proclaimed (19:1–3), the empowered Christ must repeat his conquest again (19:11–21). In John's cyclic visions, evil does not stay defeated but must be fought time after time. Similarly, life is a continual battleground in which the contestants must struggle to defend previous victories and combat the same opponents in new guises.

VISIONS OF THE FINAL TRIUMPH

In contrast to the cyclic repetitions of earlier sections, after chapter 20 John apparently (we cannot be sure) pursues a linear narration, presenting a chronological sequence of events. In this final eschatological vision (20:1–22:5), events come thick and fast. An angel hurls the Dragon into the abyss, the primordial void that existed before God's creative light ordered the visible world (20:1–3). With the Dragon's temporary imprisonment, Christ's reign at last begins. Known as the **millennium** because it lasts 1000 years, even this triumph is impermanent because at its conclusion, Satan is again released to wage war on the faithful. The only New Testament writer to present a 1000-year prelude to Christ's kingdom, John states that during the millennium, the martyrs who resisted the beast's influence are resurrected to rule with Christ (20:4–6).

The Dragon's release and subsequent attack on the faithful (based on Ezekiel's prophetic drama involving the mythical **Gog** of Magog, symbols of Israel's enemies [Ezek. 38–39]) ends with fire from heaven destroying the attackers. A resurrection of all the dead ensues. Released from the control of death and Hades (the Underworld), they are judged according to their deeds (20:7–13).

The Lake of Fire   John's eschatology includes a place of punishment represented by a lake of fire, an image drawn from popular Jewish belief (see Josephus's *Discourse on Hades* in Whiston's edition). Defined as "the second death" (20:15), it receives a number of symbolic figures, including death, Hades, the beast, the false prophet, and persons or human qualities not listed in God's book of life (19:20; 20:14–15). Earlier, John implied that persons bearing the beast's fatal mark would be tormented permanently amid burning sulphur (14:9–11), a destiny similar to that described for the rich man in Luke (17:19–31).

John's fiery lake also parallels that depicted in 2 Esdras (written about 100 C.E.):

> Then the place of torment shall appear, and over against it the place of rest; the furnace of hell shall be displayed, and on the opposite side the paradise of delight . . . here are rest and delight, there fire and torments. (2 Esd. 7:36–38)

Although John uses his image of torture to encourage loyalty to Christ, his metaphor of hell incites many commentators to question the author's understanding of divine love.

The Wedding of the Lamb and the Holy City

John's primary purpose is to demonstrate the truth of a divine power great enough to vanquish evil for all time and create the new universe described in chapters 21–22. The author combines images from Isaiah and other Hebrew prophets to paint an oasis of peace contrasting with the violent and bloody battlefields of his previous visions. Borrowing again from ancient myth, in which epics of conflict are commonly ended with a union of supernatural entities, John describes a sacred marriage of the Lamb with the holy city that descends from heaven to earth.

The wedding of a city to the Lamb may strike the reader as a strange metaphor, but John attains great heights of poetic inspiration describing the brilliance of the heavenly Jerusalem. Rendered in terms of gold and precious stones, the jewel-like city is illuminated by the radiance of God himself. John draws again on Ezekiel's vision of a restored Jerusalem Temple to describe a crystal stream flowing from God's throne to water the tree of life. Growing in a new Eden, the tree's fruits restore humanity to full health. The renewed and purified faithful can now look directly upon God (21:1–22:5). With his dazzling view of the heavenly city, rendered in the earthy terms of the Hebrew prophets (Isa. 11, 65,

66), John completes his picture of a renewed and completed creation. God's will is finally done on earth as it is in heaven.

Warning that his visions represent the immediate future and that the scrolls on which they are written are not to be sealed (because their contents will soon be fulfilled), John adds a curse upon anyone who tampers with his manuscript (22:6, 10, 18–19). Despite his urgent affirmation of Jesus' imminent Parousia, the book's final address to the reader makes for an anticlimactic conclusion to the Bible's most puzzling book.

Summary

In Revelation, John asks his readers to see the course of human history from God's viewpoint. John's series of visions unveil the spiritual realities of the universe that are ordinarily hidden from human eyes. The visions disclose that events on earth are only part of a universal drama in which invisible forces of Good and Evil contend for control of human society. John shows that the battle between Good and Evil is an ongoing process by picturing the struggle as a cycle of repeated conflicts. God's forces win, only to find their evil opponents reappearing in a new guise. In combating spiritual and social evil, the faithful must be prepared to fight again and again.

Despite the cyclic nature of the struggle against chaotic powers, John assures his audience that through Christ's death God has already determined the outcome. The last part of Revelation shows the Dragon finally defeated and creation renewed. The Lamb's marriage to heavenly Jerusalem, descended to earth, reveals that the end purpose of history is the joyous union of humanity with the presence and image of God. In John's ultimate vision, the original goal and essential goodness of creation are realized.

QUESTIONS FOR REVIEW

1. Define the term *apocalypse* and explain how the Book of Revelation unveils realities of the unseen spirit world and previews future events.

2. Identify and discuss the characteristics of apocalyptic literature. When and where did this type of visionary writing originate, and what is its main purpose?

3. Connect John's visions with conditions prevailing in his own time. What events taking place during the late first century C.E. would cause Christians to despair of the present evil world and hope for divine intervention in the near future?

4. Identify and explain some of the myths of cosmic conflict that John incorporates into his vision of the universal struggle between Good and Evil. In the ancient view of the world, why is disorder commonly identified with Evil and an orderly creation synonymous with Good?

QUESTIONS FOR DISCUSSION AND REFLECTION

1. Discuss John's use of symbols and cryptic language. Do you think that the author deliberately made his mystical visions difficult to understand in order to confuse "outsiders" who might be hostile to his group?

2. Martin Luther thought that Revelation did not truly reveal the nature of God and Christ. Discuss the ethical strengths and religious limitations of John's view of the Deity and the divine purpose.

3. Revelation repeatedly shows God's kingdom triumphing only to be engaged again in further battles with evil, until the symbol and source of evil—the chaotic Dragon—is finally exterminated by fire. Do you think that Revelation's frequently repeated battles between Good and Evil indicate a continuing cycle in which divine rule (the kingdom) alternates with wicked influences on humanity—a cycle in which each nation and individual participates until the final judgment? Cite specific passages to support your answer.

TERMS AND CONCEPTS TO REMEMBER

apokalypsis (Greek term)
apocalypse (literary form)
apocalyptic literature
apocalyptic dualism
ethical qualities of
   apocalyptic writing
cryptic language
symbol
authorship of Revelation

Roman emperor cult
Domitian
position of Christians in
   Roman society
Lamb
Dragon
means by which the
   Lamb conquers the
   Dragon

seven churches of
   Asia Minor
seven seals
four horsemen
astrological images
seven trumpets
the celestial woman
Armageddon
Michael
war in heaven
the beast
numerology
Nero

methods of interpreting
   apocalyptic literature
Revelation's abiding
   significance
the abyss
millennium
lake of fire
descent of the heavenly
   city
wedding of the Lamb
a new heaven and a new
   earth

RECOMMENDED READING

Aune, David. *Prophecy in Early Christianity and the Ancient Mediterranean World.* Grand Rapids, Mich.: Eerdmans, 1983. Places Christian apocalypticism in historical perspective.

Batto, Bernard F. *Slaying the Dragon: Mythmaking in the Biblical Tradition.* Louisville, Ky.: Westminster Press/ John Knox Press, 1992. Devoted mainly to the Hebrew Bible; also shows how New Testament writers used archetypal myths to express their understanding of Christ and the cosmic battle between God and the primordial Dragon of Chaos.

Collins, A. Y. *The Apocalypse.* Wilmington, Del.: Glazier, 1979.

———. *Crisis & Catharsis: The Power of the Apocalypse.* Philadelphia: Westminster Press, 1984. A carefully researched, clearly written, and rational analysis of the sociopolitical and theological forces affecting the composition of John's visions.

———. *Early Christian Apocalypticism: Genre and Social Setting.* Semeia 36. Decatur, Ga.: Scholars Press, 1986.

———. "The Apocalypse (Revelation)." In R. E. Brown et al., eds., *The New Jerome Biblical Commentary,* 2nd ed., pp. 996–1016. Englewood Cliffs, N.J.: Prentice-Hall, 1990. A close reading of the text that places John's visions in their original Greco-Roman social and historical context.

Collins, J. J., ed. *Apocalypse: The Morphology of a Genre.* Semeia 14. Chico, Calif.: Scholars Press, 1979.

———, ed. *The Apocalyptic Imagination: An Introduction to the Jewish Matrix of Christianity.* Los Angeles: Crossroads, 1984.

Efird, J. M. *Daniel and Revelation: A Study of Two Extraordinary Visions.* Valley Forge, Pa.: Judson Press, 1978.

Fiorenza, Elizabeth Schussler. "Book of Revelation." In G. A. Buttrick, ed., *The Interpreter's Dictionary of the Bible: Supplementary Volume,* pp. 744–746. Nashville, Tenn.: Abingdon Press, 1976.

———. *Invitation to the Book of Revelation.* New York: Image Doubleday, 1981.

———. *The Book of Revelation: Justice and Judgment.* Philadelphia: Fortress Press, 1985.

Hanson, P. D. *The Dawn of Apocalyptic: The Historical and Sociological Roots of Jewish Apocalyptic Eschatology.* Philadelphia: Fortress Press, 1979.

Josephus, Flavius. "Josephus' Discourse to the Greeks Concerning Hades." In *Josephus: Complete Works.* Translated by William Whiston. Grand Rapids, Mich.: Kregel, 1960. Presents first-century Jewish views of the afterlife similar to those postulated in the Synoptic Gospels and Revelation.

Perkins, Pheme. *The Book of Revelation.* Collegeville, Minn.: Liturgical Press, 1983. A brief and readable introduction for Roman Catholic and other students.

Rist, Martin. "Introduction and Exegesis of the Revelation of St. John the Divine." In G. A. Buttrick, ed., *The Interpreter's Bible,* Vol. 12, pp. 345–613. New York and Nashville, Tenn.: Abingdon Press, 1957. An informative analysis for the student.

Russell, D. S. *The Method and Message of Jewish Apocalyptic: 200 B.C.–A.D. 100.* Philadelphia: Westminster Press, 1964. A useful review of apocalyptic literature of the Greco-Roman period.

Stone, M. E. *Scriptures, Sects, and Visions: A Profile of Judaism from Ezra to the Jewish Revolts.* Philadelphia: Fortress Press, 1980.

CHAPTER 20

Outside the Canon

Other Early Christian Writings

> *If [all that Jesus did] were to be recorded in detail, I suppose the whole world could not hold the books that would be written.*
>
> John 21:25

Key Themes Besides the twenty-seven books officially accepted into the New Testament canon, early Christianity produced a large number of other writings, including Gospels, letters, apocalypses, and "memoirs" of the apostles. Some of these works appear in early lists of New Testament books but were later denied canonical status and consigned to oblivion. Although many noncanonical writings are highly fanciful, some, such as the Gospel of Thomas and Secret Mark, may preserve authentic traditions about Jesus.

The early Christian community produced a large number of writings besides the twenty-seven books comprising the New Testament, and many of them significantly influenced later Christian thought. Some of these documents, once included in church lists of "recognized books" along with familiar New Testament titles, are as old as or older than many works eventually accepted into the canon. No one knows why particular works were accepted and others were not. Paul wrote letters besides those accorded canonical status (1 Cor. 5:9–11); we cannot be sure that their exclusion was the result of their being destroyed or otherwise lost. Specific works may have been accepted or rejected primarily because of their relative usefulness in supporting the traditional church teachings.

As noted in chapter 1, as late as the fourth century and even later, many individual churches rejected books like Hebrews, James, Jude, 2 Peter, and Revelation; others regarded them as possessing only "doubtful" authority. By contrast, 1 Clement (a letter from the Roman bishop to the Corinthian church, composed about 95–96 C.E.) was commonly included among the "recognized books" (Eusebius, *History* 3.16.24–26; 3.16.37; 6.13; etc.).

Works Included in Some Early Editions of the New Testament

The Codex Sinaiticus, an ancient Greek edition of the New Testament, contains several books that supplemented the central canon. These extracanonical works include the Shepherd of Hermas, a mystical apocalypse incorporating documents that may have been written in the late first century C.E.; and the Epistle of Barnabas, a moralistic commentary on the Hebrew Bible supposedly written by Paul's mentor and traveling companion.

Although these two works are contained in an appendix to the codex, they apparently achieved a quasi-authoritative position in the church's list of approved books. Other influential documents include the Didache, also called the Teaching of the Twelve Apostles. A two-part volume, the Didache's first section outlines the "Two Ways of Life and Death"; the second includes a primitive manual of church ritual and discipline, some of which may reflect practices of the very early Christian community. Several important church leaders held the work in high esteem. Clement of Alexandria, who also cites the Secret Gospel of Mark, refers to the Didache as "Scripture," and Bishop Athanasius recommends it for teaching Christian students. First Clement, a letter the bishop of Rome sent to the Corinthian church in the mid-90s C.E., was also apparently widely read. All these works are probably older, and therefore closer to the apostolic era, than many of the canonical catholic epistles.

Another early list of New Testament books, the Muratorian Canon (which may date as late as the fourth century C.E.) accepts the Apocalypse of Peter, a visionary tour of hell based largely on the eschatological terrors described in Mark 13 and Matthew 24. Existing now only in an Ethiopic translation, this apocalypse—unlike the eventually canonical Revelation—paints no eschatological picture of future history or Jesus' Second Coming.

Among other writings that remained influential for centuries are the seven epistles of Ignatius, including letters to the congregations at Ephesus, Rome, Philadelphia, and Smyrna, all cities associated with Paul or the author of Revelation. The letters date from about the year 107, when Ignatius, the bishop of Antioch, was traveling under armed escort to Rome, where he was martyred. A few decades later, in the second century, Polycarp, a bishop of Smyrna, wrote to Philippi, another important Pauline church. Polycarp, who was martyred about 155 C.E., possessed unusual authority because he was reputed to have been a disciple of the apostle John.

Works like the Didache, the Shepherd of Hermas, and the epistles of Clement, Ignatius, and Polycarp, as well as a few others, hovered for centuries on the fringe of the New Testament canon.

Although they did not win final acceptance, they became known collectively as the "Apostolic Fathers" and continued to play a role in shaping church belief and practice.

The New Testament Apocrypha

In addition to works that for a time enjoyed near-canonical status, early Christian writers composed a large body of writings known as the New Testament Apocrypha (see box 20.1). The term *apocrypha*, meaning "hidden" or "secret," may have been applied to these writings either because they were kept secret from the ordinary Christian or because they were believed to contain hidden meanings. Many, but not all, of the Christian Apocrypha derived from Gnostic circles, which helps to account for their ultimate exclusion from church usage.

OTHER GOSPELS

The Gospel of Thomas   Writers of the apocryphal books imitated the literary forms of canonical works—Gospels, apostolic histories, letters, and apocalypses. Many of the noncanonical Gospels are pseudonymous, ascribed to apostles like Thomas, Peter, and James, as well as to members of Jesus' family. Only fragments of these Gospels now exist—with one salient exception, the Gospel of Thomas. Found in 1945 among the documents buried in a Christian grave near Nag Hammadi, Egypt, the Gospel of Thomas survives complete in a Coptic translation. Originally composed in Greek and attributed to "Didymos [the twin] Judas Thomas" (according to some traditions, Jesus' twin brother), the Gospel is a compilation of 114 sayings, proverbs, parables, and prophecies that Jesus allegedly taught an inner circle of disciples. Containing almost no narrative material, it represents the kind of sayings collection that scholars imagine the hypothetical Q (source) document to have been.

Although some of the teachings ascribed to Jesus reflect Gnostic thought, many of the Thomas sayings parallel those in the canonical writings. According to many scholars, in some cases the Gospel

Box 20.1
Selected List of Early Christian Noncanonical Gospels, Apocalypses, and Other Writings

WORKS FORMERLY APPEARING IN SOME NEW TESTAMENT LISTS

The Epistle of Barnabas (attributed to Paul's Jewish-Christian mentor)

The Didache (supposedly a summary of the Twelve Apostles' teachings on the opposing ways leading to life or death)

1 Clement (a letter by the third bishop of Rome to the Corinthians)

Apocalypse of Peter (visions of heaven and hell ascribed to Peter)

The Shepherd of Hermas (a mystical apocalyptic work)

GOSPELS POSSIBLY PRESERVING SOME OF JESUS' TEACHINGS OR OTHER HISTORICAL INFORMATION ABOUT HIM

The Gospel of Thomas (a compilation of 114 sayings of Jesus found in the Nag Hammadi Library)

The Gospel of Peter (a primitive account of Jesus' crucifixion, burial, and resurrection ascribed to Peter)

The Secret Gospel of Mark (two excerpts from an early edition of Mark preserved in a letter from Clement of Alexandria)

The Egerton Papyrus 2 (a fragment of an unknown Gospel that may have provided a source for some of the Johannine discourses)

The Apocryphon of James (a private dialog between Jesus and two disciples, Peter and James)

OTHER GOSPELS, MOST SURVIVING ONLY IN FRAGMENTARY FORM

The Protoevangelium of James

The Dialogue of the Savior

The Gospel of the Egyptians

The Gospel of the Hebrews

The Gospel of the Nazoreans

The Gospel of the Ebionites

The Infancy Gospel of Thomas

Papyrus Oxyrhynchus 840

MISCELLANEOUS OTHER WORKS

The Acts of Pilate

The Acts of John

The Epistula Apostolorum

2 Clement

The Epistle to Diognetus

OTHER IMPORTANT EARLY CHRISTIAN WRITINGS

The Epistles of Ignatius:
　　To the Ephesians
　　To the Magnesians
　　To the Trallians
　　To the Romans
　　To the Philadelphians
　　To the Smyrnaeans
　　To Polycarp

The Epistle of Polycarp to the Philippians

The Martyrdom of Polycarp

---

of Thomas preserves an older (and perhaps closer to the original) form of Jesus' words, as well as genuine sayings not found in the canonical texts. Some historians believe that the Gospel of Thomas was compiled during the second half of the first century C.E., making it roughly contemporaneous with the Synoptic accounts.

The Gospel of Thomas promises that whoever finds the right "interpretation" of Jesus' "secret say-

ings" (i.e., understands the spiritual meaning of his metaphors) "will not experience death" (will not know what it is to die spiritually). This statement strikingly resembles the Johannine Jesus' declaration that people who believe in him will never die (John 11:25–26). Along with the "mysteries" and "secrets of the kingdom" in Mark and the concept of divine Wisdom in John, the Gospel of Thomas represents a distinctly metaphysical and otherworldly component of early Christianity, a tradition perhaps similar to but not necessarily identical to some Gnostic ideas. Future analysis of the text may reveal that Thomas contains essential aspects of Jesus' worldview that have long been ignored or neglected, particularly his views on the nature of reality, including the interpenetration of physical matter and spirit.

The Gospel of Peter Although only a fragment remains, an early Gospel incorrectly ascribed to Peter narrates a version of Jesus' trial, crucifixion, and resurrection that some scholars believe is independent of the canonical tradition. The only Gospel to depict Jesus' actual rising from the tomb, Peter's account has even more supernatural elements than Matthew's. Late Saturday night, as Roman soldiers guarding the tomb watch, the heavens open and two celestial figures descend, rolling away the stone sealing the entrance and entering the burial chamber. Three towering figures then emerge from the sepulcher, two whose heads reach the sky and a third even taller, followed by a cross that speaks. The text breaks off with Peter fishing the Sea of Galilee, apparently about to witness a postresurrection appearance (see box 20.2).

Whereas some critics regard this Gospel as a somewhat fantastic elaboration of Matthew, others believe that it contains a substratum preserving a more "primitive" (and thus older) "witness" to the Resurrection. A few scholars date it as early as the last third of the first century C.E. and suggest that in its earliest form, the Gospel of Peter was a major source for the Passion stories in Mark and Matthew.

Secret Mark A fragment of this Gospel was discovered in 1958, preserved in a letter by Clement of Alexandria (about 200 C.E.). The section of Secret Mark that Clement quotes narrates the resuscitation of a rich young man whom Jesus then initiates into "the mystery of the kingdom of God." According to Clement, the excerpt would appear in canonical Mark between verses 10:34 and 35.

A second and briefer excerpt refers to the resuscitated young man as "the youth whom Jesus loved." Secret Mark is important because it provides a link between the Synoptic Gospels and the Fourth Gospel's account of Lazarus's raising as well as the Johannine tradition that Jesus had a particularly Beloved Disciple. Whereas the canonical editions of the Synoptic Gospels are silent about the episode, Secret Mark reveals that a primitive version of John's resurrection story was once part of the Synoptic tradition (see box 10.7).

The Infancy Gospel of Thomas Early Christian curiosity about Jesus' boyhood inspired several narratives that attempted to fill in the "missing years" of his youth. (Except for Luke's brief reference to Jesus' Temple visit at age twelve, the canonical Gospels offer no information about what happened between his infancy and his appearance at the Baptist's revival campaign thirty years later.) The Infancy Gospel of Thomas, dating from the mid-second century C.E., is ascribed to the apostle Thomas. Unrelated to the Coptic Gospel of Thomas, which was written much earlier, this infancy account uncritically incorporates popular legends and speculations about Jesus' youthful character and activities.

The Infancy Gospel (Protoevangelium) of James Also called the Book of James, this work supplies background information on Jesus' parents and family, covering events that occurred up to and including his birth. Based partly on the infancy accounts in Matthew and Luke and partly on oral tradition, this prolog to Jesus' life story may contain a few historical facts among its legendary elements. The work implies that its author is James, Jesus' stepbrother and Joseph's son by a former marriage. The narrative focuses on the personal history of Mary, Jesus' future mother, who is born to a previously childless couple, Joachim and Anna. At age three, Mary is taken to the Jerusalem Temple, where she is raised by priests who later place her under the care of Joseph, a widower with children, who functions strictly as her guardian and respects her virginity.

The genealogies in Matthew and Luke both trace Jesus' Davidic ancestry through his presumed father, Joseph. By contrast, James states that Mary, too, descends from David. Thus, her virgin-born son inherits his messianic heritage directly from her. The Infancy Gospel of James provides the names of Mary's parents, the manner of her birth and

Box 20.2
Excerpts from Some Noncanonical Gospels (Scholars Version Translation)

THE GOSPEL OF THE NAZOREANS

Although written in Aramaic, probably during the first half of the second century C.E., the Gospel of the Nazoreans was based on the Greek text of canonical Matthew and apparently contained no independent traditions about the historical Jesus. It survives only in a few quotations from later Christian scholars, such as Jerome, Origin, and Eusebius. In the following excerpt, quoted by Origin early in the third century C.E., the Nazorean Gospel edits Matthew's version of Jesus' encounter with a rich young man (Matt. 19:16–30) to emphasize compassion and responsibility for the poor.

Gospel of the Nazoreans 6–8

The second rich man said to him, "Teacher, what good do I have to do to live?"

He said to him, "Mister, follow the Law and the Prophets."

He answered, "I've done that."

He said to him, "Go sell everything you own and give it away to the poor and then come follow me."

But the rich man didn't want to hear this and began to scratch his head. And the Lord said to him, "How can you say that you follow the Law and the Prophets? In the Law it says: 'Love your neighbor as yourself.' Look around you: many of your brothers and sisters, sons and daughters of Abraham, are living in filth and dying of hunger. Your house is full of good things and not a thing of yours manages to get out to them." Turning to his disciple Simon, who was sitting with him, he said, "Simon, son of Jonah, it's easier for a camel to squeeze through a needle's eye than for a wealthy person to get into heaven's domain."

THE GOSPEL OF PETER

Although known and used in some early churches, the Gospel of Peter, eventually condemned as heretical, disappeared entirely until 1886, when French archaeologists discovered part of it in the tomb of an Egyptian monk. The fragmentary Gospel, which begins and ends in mid-sentence, is a Passion narrative, recounting Jesus' trial, crucifixion, burial and resurrection. The only Gospel to portray directly Jesus' rising from the dead, it contains spectacularly supernatural,

even bizarre, phenomena. While Roman soldiers assigned to guard the tomb watch in awe, the predawn heavens part, and two supernatural figures descend in a blaze of light, causing the great stone that sealed the tomb entrance miraculously to roll away. Christ is shown emerging from the sepulcher, supported on each side by towering figures whose heads touch the sky, while his head "reached beyond the skies." When a celestial voice, reminiscent of that at the Transfiguration, asks if Christ has brought his message to the subterranean realm of the dead, a cross, the fourth figure in the procession, bears witness that he has. Traditions of a speaking cross, an animated vocalizer of the Christian *kerygma,* appear only in this account.

Although scholars agree that the historical Peter had nothing to do with the Gospel ascribed to him, they are sharply divided about the document's importance to the Jesus tradition. Whereas a majority see it as a secondary source, derived primarily from Matthew and the other canonical Gospels, others argue that in its earliest edition, it may represent the first written Passion story on which the canonical accounts, at least in part, are based. In its final, extant edition, the Gospel of Peter exhibits several Gnostic touches: Jesus' silence during the Crucifixion intimates that (as pure spirit) he does not feel physical pain; his death, moreover, is expressed euphemistically, for he is described as "taken up," implying a divine rescue or escape to the spirit world (2:1; 5:5). The cross's later testimony that Jesus devoted the period between his (apparent) death and resurrection to preaching in the netherworld (a similar tradition appears in the two canonical letters ascribed to Peter [1 Pet. 3:19; 4:6; cf. 2 Pet. 2:4]) also suggests that the Gospel of Peter's author saw Jesus' spiritual existence, in this life and the next, as a continuum.

[Following the Crucifixion, a Roman guard is stationed at Jesus' tomb.]

When the scholars and the Pharisees and the priests had gathered together, and when they heard that all the people were moaning and beating their breasts, and saying "If his death has produced these overwhelming signs, he must have been entirely innocent!", they became frightened and went to Pilate and begged him, "Give us soldiers so that [we] may guard his tomb for three [days], in case his disciples come and steal his

(continued)

Box 20.2 *(continued)*

body and the people assume that he is risen from the dead and do us harm." So Pilate gave them the centurion Petronius with soldiers to guard the tomb. And elders and scholars went with them to the tomb. And all who were there [with] the centurion and the soldiers helped roll a large stone against the entrance to the tomb. And they put seven seals on it. Then they pitched a tent there and kept watch.

Early, at first light on the sabbath, a crowd came from Jerusalem and the surrounding countryside to see the sealed tomb. But during the night before the Lord's day dawned, while the soldiers were on guard, two by two during each watch, a loud noise came from the sky, and they saw the skies open up and two men come down from there in a burst of light and approach the tomb. The stone that had been pushed against the entrance began to roll by itself and moved away to one side; then the tomb opened up and both young men went inside.

Now when these soldiers saw this, they roused the centurion from his sleep, along with the elders. (Remember, they were also there keeping watch.) While they were explaining what they had seen, again they see three men leaving the tomb, two supporting the third, and a cross was following them. The heads of the two reached up to the sky, while the head of the third, whom they led by the hand, reached beyond the skies. And they heard a voice from the skies that said, "Have you preached to those who sleep?" And an answer was heard from the cross: "Yes!"

These men then consulted with one another about going and reporting these things to Pilate. While they were still thinking about it, again the skies appeared to open and some sort of human being came down and entered the tomb. When those in the centurion's company saw this, they rushed out into the night to Pilate, having left the tomb which they were supposed to be guarding. . . .

THE INFANCY GOSPEL OF JAMES (THE PROTOEVANGELIUM OF JAMES)

Beginning in the second century C.E., Christian writers produced a body of literature to satisfy believers' curiosity about Jesus' childhood and family background. Two of these works, the Infancy Gospel of Thomas and the Infancy Gospel (Protoevangelium) of James, survive complete. The first narrative, ascribed to "Thomas the Israelite" (perhaps the Judas

[Thomas] listed as Jesus' "brother" in Mark 6:3), recounts entertaining anecdotes about Jesus' youthful pranks, suggesting that the divine child did not always use his supernatural powers responsibly. When five years old, Jesus violated Torah prohibitions against unnecessary work on the Sabbath by fashioning twelve sparrows out of soft clay. After a shocked resident of Nazareth threatens to report his misconduct to Joseph, his supposed father, Jesus gets rid of the incriminating evidence by commanding the sparrows to fly away, much to his neighbors' amazement. On other occasions, the young Jesus is shown arbitrarily manipulating his peers, severely punishing some for showing lack of respect and generously healing others.

One of the most popular—and probably the most influential—of the New Testament apocrypha, the Infancy Gospel of James takes a far more reverent approach to its subject, albeit with a few touches of genuine humor. Divided into three approximately equal parts, the Gospel is largely a prose hymn of praise to Jesus' mother, Mary, whose astonishing purity makes her the most divinely favored of all women. Going beyond canonical themes of Jesus' virginal conception, the first section relates the story of Mary's miraculous birth to a wealthy herdsman, Joachim, and his previously barren wife, Anna. Dedicated to holy service at age three, Mary is raised in the Jerusalem Temple, where she remains until she is twelve, when her sexual maturation renders her presence a pollution to the sanctuary.

In the Gospel's second part, Mary moves from the Temple to the protection of a Torah-abiding carpenter, Joseph, who is already a widower with grown children. Although the narrator emphasizes that Joseph is only Mary's guardian, not her husband, their situation becomes complicated after an angel visits Mary, announcing that she will bear a child by divine intervention. When Joseph returns home after a long absence at work to find that Mary is six months pregnant, he agonizes over his apparent failure to protect her virginity. Reproducing a lively conversation between the almost equally bewildered—and celibate—pair, the author creates a scene that combines sensitivity to the plight of a human couple caught up in forces beyond their control and the inescapable humor inherent in their strange predicament.

Interspersing elements from the infancy stories of Matthew and Luke with his own special material, the narrator devotes the final third of his Gospel to recounting Jesus' birth at Bethlehem, closing with Herod's murderous attempts to eliminate a future rival. To guarantee the historicity of this account, the author then reveals that he is James (whom Paul calls "the Lord's brother"), the son of Joseph by his deceased wife. By insisting that Mary was immaculately conceived and remained perpetually virginal even after giving birth to Jesus (two midwives testify that her virginity remained intact), the Infancy Gospel of James contributed significantly to the growing veneration of Mary that characterized many branches of early Christianity.

[Her prayers answered, Anna is informed that she will miraculously give birth to a child—Mary, the future mother of Jesus.]

Suddenly a messenger of the Lord appeared to her and said: "Anna, Anna, the Lord God has heard your prayer. You will conceive and give birth, and your child will be talked about all over the world."

And Anna said, "As the Lord God lives, whether I give birth to a boy or a girl, I'll offer it as a gift to the Lord my God, and it will serve him its whole life."

And right then two messengers reported to her: "Look, your husband Joachim is coming with his flocks." You see, a messenger of the Lord had come down to Joachim and said, "Joachim, Joachim, the Lord God has heard your prayer. Get down from there. Look, your wife Anna is pregnant."

And Joachim went down right away and summoned his shepherds with these instructions: "Bring me ten lambs without spot or blemish, and the ten lambs will be for the Lord God. Also, bring me twelve tender calves, and the twelve calves will be for the priests and the council of elders. Also, one hundred goats, and the one hundred goats will be for the whole people."

And so Joachim came with his flocks, while Anna stood at the gate. Then she spotted Joachim approaching with his flocks and rushed out and threw her arms around his neck: "Now I know that the Lord God has blessed me greatly. This widow is no longer a widow, and I, once childless, am now pregnant!"

And Joachim rested the first day at home.

But on the next day, as he was presenting his gifts, he thought to himself, "If the Lord God has really been merciful to me, the polished disc on the priest's headband will make it clear to me." And so Joachim was presenting his gifts and paying attention to the priest's headband until he

went up to the altar of the Lord. And he saw no sin in it. And Joachim said, "Now I know that the Lord God has been merciful to me and has forgiven me all my sins." And he came from the temple of the Lord acquitted and went back home.

And so her pregnancy came to term, and in the ninth month Anna gave birth. And she said to the midwife, "Is it a boy or a girl?"

And her midwife said, "A girl."

And Anna said, "I have been greatly honored this day." Then the midwife put the child to bed.

When, however, the prescribed days were completed, Anna cleansed herself of the flow of blood. And she offered her breast to the infant and gave her the name Mary. . . .

Mary rejoiced [after the angel's annunciation] and left to visit her relative Elizabeth. She knocked at the door. Elizabeth heard her, tossed aside the scarlet thread, ran to the door, and opened it for her. And she blessed her and said, "Who am I that the mother of my Lord should visit me? You see, the baby inside me has jumped for joy and blessed you."

But Mary forgot the mysteries which the heavenly messenger Gabriel had spoken, and she looked up to the sky and said, "Who am I that every generation on earth will congratulate me?"

She spent three months with Elizabeth. Day by day her womb kept swelling. And so Mary became frightened, returned home, and hid from the people of Israel. She was just sixteen years old when these mysterious things happened to her.

She was in her sixth month when one day Joseph came home from his building projects, entered his house, and found her pregnant. He struck himself in the face, threw himself to the ground on sackcloth, and began to cry bitterly: "What sort of face should I present to the Lord God? What prayer can I say on her behalf since I received her as a virgin from the temple of the Lord God and didn't protect her? Who has set this trap for me? Who has done this evil deed in my house? Who has lured this virgin away from me and violated her? The story of Adam has been repeated in my case, hasn't it? For just as Adam was praying when the serpent came and found Eve alone, deceived her, and corrupted her, so the same thing has happened to me."

So Joseph got up from the sackcloth and summoned Mary and said to her, "God has taken a special interest in you—how could you have done

(continued)

Box 20.2 *(continued)*

this? Have you forgotten the Lord your God? Why have you brought shame on yourself, you who were raised in the Holy of Holies and fed by a heavenly messenger?"

But she began to cry bitter tears: "I'm innocent. I haven't had sex with any man."

And Joseph said to her, "Then where did the child you're carrying come from?"

And she replied, "As the Lord my God lives, I don't know where it came from."

And Joseph became very frightened and no longer spoke with her as he pondered what he was going to do with her. And Joseph said to himself, "If I try to cover up her sin, I'll end up going against the law of the Lord. And if I disclose her

condition to the people of Israel, I'm afraid that the child inside her might be heaven-sent and I'll end up handing innocent blood over to a death sentence. So what should I do with her? [I know,] I'll divorce her quietly."

But when night came a messenger of the Lord suddenly appeared to him in a dream and said: "Don't be afraid of this girl, because the child in her is the holy spirit's doing. She will have a son and you will name him Jesus — the name means 'he will save his people from their sins.'" And Joseph got up from his sleep and praised the God of Israel, who had given him this favor. And so he began to protect the girl.

---

upbringing, and a doctrine of her perpetual virginity. These traditions greatly contributed to the later veneration of Mary in the Greek Orthodox and Roman Catholic Churches. The fact of its immense popularity in the church is reflected by the proto-Gospel's survival in over 130 Greek manuscripts. Although never officially listed in the New Testament canon, in some Christian groups the book has exerted as much influence as the canonical Gospels.

OTHER WRITINGS

Other pseudonymous works include the Apocryphon (secret book) of James, a Coptic-language edition of an originally Greek document that presents Jesus' teaching in the form of a conversation between the apostles Peter and James. The Dialogue of the Savior, found in the Nag Hammadi Coptic library, employs a similar device, rendering Jesus' message as a four-way discussion among Christ and the disciples Judas, Matthew, and Mariam, a woman follower. Similarly, the Gnostic Gospel of the Egyptians presents a brief dialog between Jesus and a female disciple named Salome.

Although the Apocryphon may well preserve some of Jesus' authentic sayings, most apocryphal Gospels appear to contain editions of Christ's mes-sage that have been tailored to fit Gnostic preconceptions. These include the Gospel of the Hebrews, the Gospel of the Nazoreans, the Gospel of the Ebionites, and the Acts of Pilate, a dramatization of Jesus' confrontation with the Roman procurator. Except for the last named, most of these Gospels survive only in small fragments. Others are known by their titles alone.

The proliferation of new Gospels continued for centuries, resulting in increasingly fanciful versions of Jesus' life and teachings. Exhausting the supply of "apostolic" writers, pseudonymous authors created Gospels attributed to the Virgin, Nicodemus, Gamaliel, and even Eve!

Spurious apostolic histories modeled on the Book of Acts also abounded. Besides "Acts" purportedly describing the adventures of Peter and Paul, there were fictional narratives about Andrew (Peter's brother), Thomas, and John. Apocryphal letters also circulated under the apostles' names, and Christian mystics and prophets added to a collection of futuristic visions called the Sibylline Oracles. This was originally a Jewish compilation written in imitation of Greco-Roman prophecies attributed to Apollo's inspired oracle, the Sibyl.

Students interested in reading noncanonical works dating from the New Testament period can find several modern editions in most libraries. Particularly recommended is R. J. Miller's *The Complete Gospels* (1994), which includes the complete texts of the Gospel of Thomas as well as the surviving parts of other Gospels compiled during the early centuries C.E. A new English edition of *The Nag Hammadi Library* (1988), edited by James Robinson, contains a wide variety of early Christian and Christian-Gnostic material, including the Apocryphon of James, the Gospel of Thomas, and the Apocalypse of Peter. For recent translations of the Didache, the Epistle of Barnabas, and the letters of Ignatius and Polycarp, see *Early Christian Writings* (1968), a Penguin paperback. The two-volume *New Testament Apocrypha*, edited by Wilhelm Schneemelcher (1990 and 1992), provides a scholarly anthology of the extracanonical texts. (For additional references, see "Recommended Reading.")

QUESTION FOR REVIEW

1. Describe some early Christian Gospels, such as the Gospel of Thomas, Secret Mark, and the Gospel of Peter, that were not included in the New Testament canon. Why do you think that these and other Gospels were not officially approved? In what ways do they differ from the canonical accounts of Jesus' life?

QUESTIONS FOR DISCUSSION AND REFLECTION

1. Discuss some early Christian documents, such as the Shepherd of Hermas, the Epistle of Barnabas, and 1 Clement, that were once apparently on the margins of the New Testament canon but that were eventually deleted from the church's list of authoritative works. Define the term *New Testament Apocrypha*, and evaluate some of the similarities between such accepted works as Revelation and the noncanonical Apocalypse of Peter.

2. Do you think that the New Testament canon is now irrevocably closed? What are the possibilities that existing noncanonical writings—or even books not yet written—will eventually be added to the church's approved list? Describe the effect on Christian doctrine if such works as the Gospel of Thomas, Secret Mark, or the Book of Mormon were officially approved to be read in church as examples of legitimate Christian thought and experience.

TERMS AND CONCEPTS TO REMEMBER

New Testament Apocrypha
Gospel of Thomas
Gospel of Peter
Infancy Gospel of Thomas

Protoevangelium of James
Epistle of Barnabas
The Didache
Apocalypse of Peter
Shepherd of Hermas

RECOMMENDED READING

Cameron, Ron, ed. *The Other Gospels: Non-Canonical Gospel Texts*. Philadelphia: Westminster Press, 1982. Scholarly translations of several early Christian Gospels, including those attributed to Peter, James, and Mark.

Crossan, John D. *The Cross That Spoke: The Origins of the Passion Narrative*. San Francisco: Harper & Row, 1988. Analyzes the Gospel of Peter as source for the canonical Gospels.

Ehrman, Bart D. *The New Testament and Other Early Christian Writings: A Reader*. New York: Oxford University Press, 1998. Anthologizes both canonical and noncanonical writings composed by the mid-second century C.E.

Eusebius. *The History of the Church from Christ to Constantine*. Translated with an introduction by G. A. Williamson. Baltimore: Penguin Books, 1965. Read with caution, provides excellent atmospheric background for the early church and fascinating traditions about the apostles and second-century church leaders.

Josephus, Flavius. *The Jewish War*. Translated by G. A. Williamson. Revised by E. M. Smallwood. Baltimore: Penguin Books, 1981. An eyewitness account of political events in Palestine that provided the background for the birth and growth of Christianity, including the Jewish revolt against Rome (66–73 C.E.), its causes and aftermath, and a few references to Jesus and the martyrdom of his "brother" James.

Koestler, Helmut. *Ancient Christian Gospels: Their History and Development*. Philadelphia: Trinity Press International, 1990. Provides technical analysis of all extant Gospels and fragments.

Miller, Robert J., ed. *The Complete Gospels*, 2nd ed. Annotated Scholars Version. San Francisco: HarperSanFrancisco, 1994. Includes complete texts of the Gospel of Thomas, Infancy Gospel of Thomas, Infancy Gospel of James, Gospel of Peter, Secret Gospel of Mark, and numerous fragmentary works.

Musurillo, Herbert A. *The Fathers of the Primitive Church.* New York: New American Library, 1966. A useful paperback collection of early Christian writings through the fourth century.

Pagels, Elaine. *The Gnostic Gospels.* New York: Random House, 1979. Argues that the church suppressed Gnostic Christianity on political grounds.

Robinson, James M., ed. *The Nag Hammadi Library,* rev. ed. San Francisco: Harper & Row, 1988.

Schneemelcher, Wilhelm, ed. *New Testament Apocrypha,* rev. ed. Vol. 1, *Gospels and Related Writings,* Philadelphia: Westminster Press, 1990; Vol. 2, *Writings Relating to the Apostles.* Philadelphia: Westminster, 1992.

Staniforth, Maxwell. *Early Christian Writings: The Apostolic Fathers,* rev. ed. New York: Penguin Books, 1987. A paperback anthology of the more important Christian Apocrypha, with helpful prefaces and notes.

CHAPTER 21

The Judeo-Christian Bible and Subsequent History

"Do you believe because you have seen me?" asks Jesus [of skeptical Thomas]. "Those who can believe without having to see are the ones to be congratulated."   John 20:29, Scholars Version

The "great tribulation" that marked Rome's destruction of the Jewish state (70 C.E.) — along with the original center of Palestinian Christianity — offers a chaotic background to the formation of the Judeo-Christian Bible. The loss of homeland, Temple, sacrifice, and priesthood was a terrible blow to Palestinian Jews and also a shock to infant Christianity, which lost its mother church and center of apostolic teaching. Jerusalem's devastation evoked a series of religious responses that influenced not only modern Judaism and Gentile Christianity but also the form and content of their Scriptures.

Of the twenty-seven New Testament documents, only Paul's letters, Q (a collection of Jesus' sayings), and the Gospel of Mark existed at that time. Most of the Christian Greek Scriptures were yet to be written, and it would be centuries before the church agreed on their exact contents. Although the Hebrew Bible was complete, the precise number of books to be included had not yet been agreed on.

The Evolution of the Hebrew Bible and the Christian Greek Scriptures

Throughout the wars, trials, and persecutions of the calamitous late first century C.E., the Hebrew Bible remained the primary authority for both Judaism and the fledgling church. Led by Rabbi Yohanan ben Zakkai, a small group of rabbinical scholars assembled at Jamnia (Yavneh) on the Palestinian coast to provide essential leadership in coping with the post-70 C.E. crisis, particularly in shaping the final contours of the Hebrew Bible canon. As noted in chapter 5, the rabbis at Jamnia did not formally close the biblical canon, but they seem to have applied several criteria that excluded numerous books used by Jewish congregations outside Palestine. Accepting the thesis that inspired prophecy had ceased shortly after the time of Ezra (about 400 B.C.E.), the Jamnia scholars apparently rejected books clearly composed after that period, such as Ecclesiasticus or 1 Maccabees. Only Daniel, of all the apocalypses, was accepted because its author plausibly claimed to write during the sixth century B.C.E. Books that contradicted the Torah or that were not originally written in Hebrew, such as the Wisdom of Solomon, were also excluded. The Christian community, however, which adopted the Septuagint as its preferred version of the Bible, generally recognized the deuterocanonical status of these disputed books — commonly known as the Apocrypha — and later included them in its official Latin Bible, the Vulgate.

Today's Hebrew and Christian Bibles differ not only in the number of accepted books but also in the order of their contents. Rabbinical scholars place the Books of Chronicles at the end of the canon, thus giving a climactic position to Cyrus the Great's order to repatriate Jewish exiles and rebuild the Jerusalem Temple (2 Chron. 36:22–23). This promise of national and cultic restoration, presented as Yahweh's intervention in Judah's history, may have voiced Jewish hopes that their God would again restore his people as he had done after the Babylonian captivity (587–538 B.C.E.).

By contrast, Christian editions of the Hebrew Bible follow the Septuagint order and place Chronicles, despite its late date, among the Former Prophets and conclude the Old Testament with the twelve Minor Prophets. The Christian Old Testament thus makes Malachi's prediction that "Elijah the prophet" will return to earth just before Yahweh's eschatological Day of Judgment (Mal. 3:22–24) the ultimate Old Testament message. (The Synoptic Gospel writers relate Malachi's prophecy to Christian origins, identifying John the Baptist, seen as Jesus' forerunner, as the predestined Elijah [Mark 6:14–15; Matt. 11:10–14; Luke 7:27–28].) The church's rearrangement of the Hebrew Bible expressed its Christological interests, an assumption that the Hebrew Scriptures serve largely to foretell and elucidate the Christ event.

When added to Greek translations of the Hebrew Bible canon, the twenty-seven New Testament books—all of which extensively quote from or allude to Israel's Scriptures—promulgate a Christological fulfillment of Old Testament covenant promises. In the Christian reinterpretation, virtually the entire Hebrew Bible becomes prophetic of Christ, giving startlingly innovative meanings to familiar scriptural passages. Jesus of Nazareth becomes Eve's "seed" (Gen. 3:15), his death and resurrection are foreshadowed in the Abraham-Isaac drama (Gen. 22), and his universal rulership is anticipated by the reigns of Davidic kings (2 Sam. 7; Pss. 2, 110; Isa. 7, 11; etc.).

Jesus is also the commanding figure who binds together the diverse collection of narratives, letters, sermons, and apocalyptic visions that form the New Testament. The order in which the canonical books are arranged reinforces his dominance. The New Testament opens with Matthew's genealogy, proclaiming "Jesus Christ, son of David, son of Abraham," at the outset as the embodiment of Israel's prophetic hopes. Matthew and other Gospels provide theological interpretations of Jesus' Jewish messiahship, and Acts and Paul's letters offer pro-found meditations on Jesus' meaning to the world at large. The pseudo-Pauline letters, Hebrews, and the catholic epistles further explore Jesus' continuing significance to the community developing in his name, typically distinguishing between correct and incorrect views about his being and nature.

The New Testament closes with John's dazzling revelation of the postresurrection Jesus as a cosmic divinity, empowered at last to establish the longed-for universal kingdom. As the First Gospel's opening verse roots Jesus in Israel's historical past, the "son" or heir of David and Abraham, so the last New Testament book concludes with a Christian mystic's passionate evocation of Jesus' return to finish the task he had begun on earth, echoing Malachi's fervent call for the reappearance of God's agent. Because Christianity emerged historically as an apocalyptic movement within first-century Judaism, it is fitting that its canonical text closes with the apocalyptic conviction that Christ is "coming soon," preserving as a final word the assurance of Jesus' imminent Parousia (Second Coming) (Rev. 22:17–21).

Before the end of the first century C.E., some Christians were keenly aware that expectations for a speedy Parousia had failed to materialize. Neither Christ nor the kingdom had rescued the church from Rome's intermittent persecutions. In 1 Clement, an epistle included in some editions of the New Testament, Clement, bishop of Rome, states:

> Let that Scripture be far from us which says: "Wretched are the double-minded, those who doubt in their soul and say, 'We have heard these things [predictions of the End] even in our fathers' times, and see, we have grown old and none of this has happened.'"
>
> (1 Clem. 23:3–5; about 96 C.E.)

Two generations after Clement, in a work attributed to the apostle Peter, the problem of the delayed Parousia was again raised. Skeptics complained that Jesus' promised coming had proved to be a nonevent; everything "continues exactly as it has always been since the world began" (2 Pet. 3:1–10). The writer responded to this criticism of an unconfirmed doctrine by asserting that a delayed world judgment allowed time and opportunity for sinners to repent and was thus an act of divine mercy.

Figure 21.1 The Arch of Constantine, standing near the Roman Forum and Flavian Amphitheater (Colosseum), commemorates the political and military achievements of Rome's first Christian emperor. After defeating his rival Maxentius at the Battle of Milvian Bridge (312 C.E.), Constantine (306–337 C.E.) issued the famous Edict of Milan, legitimizing the Christian church and ending centuries of intermittent persecution. (© Scala-Art Resource)

Nonetheless, Jesus' failure to return visibly may have provoked a crisis of belief among many second-century Christians. Yet, the church not only survived its initial disappointments but also prospered. Despite dashed hopes that the Parousia would follow any number of seemingly "final" events—the Jewish revolt, the destruction of Jerusalem, the deaths of the last apostles, or the first- and second-century Roman persecutions—the believing community continued to grow in stature, wealth, and influence. By the fourth century, Christianity had become the state religion of the Roman Empire.

Constantine the Great

Following his victory at the Milvian Bridge over Maxentius, his rival for the imperial throne (312 C.E.), the emperor Constantine effected one of the most unexpected reversals in human history. Having experienced a vision in which Jesus was revealed as the divine power that enabled him to defeat his enemies, Constantine began a slow process of conversion to the Christian faith. The emperor's ultimate championing of Christ as his chief god had immense repercussions throughout the empire, altering forever the relationship of church and state (see figure 21.1).

Shortly before Constantine began his long reign (306–337 C.E.), his predecessor, Diocletian (284–305 C.E.), had initiated the most thorough and devastating persecution that Christians had yet endured, an ordeal that ended only with Diocletian's abdication and death. When Constantine issued his celebrated decree of religious toleration, the Edict of Milan (313 C.E.), and subsequently began restoring confiscated church property, consulting

Figure 21.2 Only the head and other fragments of a colossal statue of Constantine remain, but they reflect the enormous power wielded by this remarkable general and administrator. Seeking the support of a unified church, Constantine summoned and presided over the Council of Nicaea (325 C.E.), which, amid intense theological controversy, formulated the Trinitarian creed affirming that the Son is coequal, consubstantial, and coeternal with the Father. (© AKG Photo)

Christian leaders about official affairs, and appointing bishops to high public office, it was as if a miraculous deliverance of the faithful had occurred—as if a new Cyrus had arrived to rescue God's chosen ones (see figure 21.2). To many who benefited from Constantine's policy, it seemed that Revelation's seventh angel had sounded his trumpet: "the sovereignty of the world has passed to our Lord and his Christ" (Rev. 11:15).

In a more modest metaphor, the churchman Eusebius, who later became Constantine's biographer, compared the emperor's enthusiastic support of the church to the dawn of a brilliant new day, opening up glorious possibilities for the Christian religion. With the exception of Julian (361–363 C.E.), who was known as the Apostate for trying to revive pagan cults, all of Constantine's successors were nominally Christians. For the last century and a half of its existence, the empire that had crucified Jesus was ruled by emperors who professed to be his servants.

The Church and the Secular World

Rome's belated emergence as a putatively Christian empire that supported and protected the church was sometimes viewed as a historical fulfillment of apocalyptic expectations, with Christ now ruling through his imperial representatives on earth. In fact, historical developments during the fourth and fifth centuries C.E. bore out Luke's nonapocalyptic vision of a church expanding in cooperation with the imperial power more than Revelation's picture of violent conflict between church and state resolved only when God intervened to destroy the latter. Officially muting sporadic revivals of apocalyptic fervor, the church espoused the Gospel of John's doctrine of realized eschatology—with Jesus invisibly present among the believing community—as theologically desirable.

In part, the church preserved eschatological principles by adapting and applying them to individual lives. Christianity originally borrowed most of its eschatological beliefs from Jewish sources, which emphasized the external and material triumph of Yahweh's sovereignty over Gentile nations. This general eschatology—the terrifying Day of Yahweh, cosmic battles between Good and Evil, divine judgment and the supernatural imposition of God's kingdom—was replaced by personal eschatology. Jewish eschatological literature, such as 2 Baruch, the Testament of Abraham, the Books of Enoch, and 2 Esdras, had stressed Yahweh's (or the coming Messiah's) universal rule, violently imposed, but they had also provided graphic images of the consequences of apocalyptic events on individual human beings.

After the two disastrous Jewish wars against Rome (66–73 C.E. and 132–135 C.E.) that may have been partly fueled by apocalyptic hopes, rabbinic Judaism rejected such visionary speculations as typically misleading. However, the church embraced their eschatological revelations of heaven, hell, and the afterlife. In later Roman Christianity, eschatological ideas retained their emotional impact on a personal, individual level. All believers were faced with inevitable death and the attendant dangers and terrors of the next world. Jewish and Christian apocalyptic writers had painted memorable scenes of the fates awaiting the righteous and the wicked. Anticipation of the world's End might fade, but to the believer, postmortem judgment involving permanent assignment to celestial joy or eternal torment seemed certain. The church defined and regulated these eschatological concerns. While normative Judaism abandoned virtually all its eschatological literature, with its ethically problematic views of divine justice, the Christian community effectively transferred its inherited doctrines of "last things" to the human microcosm, postponing its hopes for the Parousia to an unknowable time in the indefinite future.

Whereas John of Patmos had eagerly anticipated Rome's fall, many Christian leaders who lived through the Roman Empire's disintegration regarded it as an unmitigated catastrophe for society, including the church. Writing of Alaric the Goth's invasion of Rome in 410 C.E., Jerome—the scholar who created the Vulgate Bible—lamented the "great city's" humiliation.

Judaism and Christianity, originator and inheritor of the world's first ethical monotheism, endured the Roman Empire's slow collapse as they had survived the earlier destruction of Jerusalem, the crisis under Domitian that inspired the writing of Revelation, and far more intense attacks on the Judeo-Christian communities under later emperors. The church replaced the state's crumbling authority with its own spiritual leadership. Along with descendants of the people who had created them, the Hebrew and Christian Scriptures survived the empire's demise, providing a continuity with Israel's ancient prophets and early Christian visionaries, as well as a fixed standard of belief in a rapidly changing world.

During the sixteenth and seventeenth centuries, fierce religious conflicts divided Western Christendom. Debates between Roman Catholic and Protestant leaders over matters of belief and ritual brought the New Testament writings into renewed prominence. Martin Luther claimed that "only Scripture"—not custom or tradition—was the correct basis of Christian teaching. As a result, many European believers studied the New Testament documents with great fervor. In most Protestant circles, the biblical texts were thought to provide the sole means of defining Christian doctrine and practice. By contrast, Roman Catholicism continues to place the authority of Scripture within the broader context of the Church, emphasizing unwritten tradition and the sacraments along with the biblical texts.

Summary

The New Testament message retains its vitality in the modern world. Today, literally thousands of Christian groups, each claiming the Bible as its doctrinal authority, compete for believers' allegiance. Although some persons regret Christendom's lack of unity, the student who has carefully read the New Testament books possesses an important clue to Christianity's present diversity. The observation in 2 Peter that Paul's letters contain passages that are difficult and open to more than one interpretation applies equally well to the rest of the canonical writings. The multiplicity of contemporary Christian denominations results less from the breaking up of an originally monolithic religion than from the rich variety of thought embodied in early Christian literature itself.

The New Testament Gospels, letters, apocalypses, and other documents do not conform to a single doctrinaire vision; they instead reflect their individual writers' intensely personal response to Christ's impact on human life and history. Proclaiming the good news of God's loving care for humanity, the twenty-seven different books bear a dual testimony to Christian unity and diversity: the unifying power of Christ and the multifarious ways that different canonical authors were moved to interpret Christ's meaning and message.

QUESTION FOR REVIEW

1. Discuss the differences in attitude toward Rome expressed in Romans 13 (and 1 Peter) on the one hand and in Revelation on the other. What changing historical conditions can help account for the shift from the positive attitude of Paul to the negative judgment of John of Patmos?

QUESTIONS FOR DISCUSSION AND REFLECTION

1. After the ascension of Constantine to the imperial throne, Christianity's position in the Roman Empire changed dramatically. Describe and explain the church's role during the later empire. How did many leading Christians react to the barbarian invasions that eventually destroyed the Roman world?

2. What role did the New Testament play in formulating later church creeds and doctrines? In what ways did the Protestant Reformation during the sixteenth and seventeenth centuries increase the influence of the New Testament texts?

TERMS AND CONCEPTS TO REMEMBER

Constantine I
Edict of Milan
Diocletian
Eusebius

Rome and the church
Martin Luther and the
Reformation

RECOMMENDED READING

Brown, R. E. *The Churches the Apostles Left Behind.* New York: Paulist Press, 1984. A concise but extremely important analysis of the theological diversity present in early Christian communities.

Dunn, J. D. G. *Unity and Diversity in the New Testament.* Philadelphia: Westminster Press, 1977. A thoughtful study of the variety of belief found among different canonical authors; highly recommended.

Eusebius. *The History of the Church from Christ to Constantine.* Translated with an introduction by G. A. Williamson. Baltimore: Penguin Books, 1965. Our principal source for the study of the growth and development of early Christianity.

Fox, R. L. *Pagans and Christians.* New York: Knopf, 1986. A comprehensive study of the historical processes that resulted in Constantine's conversion and the religious transformation of the Roman Empire.

Gonzalez, J. L. *The Story of Christianity.* Vol. 1. *The Early Church to the Dawn of the Reformation.* San Francisco: Harper & Row, 1984.

MacMullen, Ramsay. *Christianizing the Roman Empire, A.D. 100–400.* New Haven, Conn.: Yale University Press, 1984. A historical investigation of the social, political, and religious conditions under which the Roman people were converted.

Meeks, W. A. *The Moral World of the First Christians.* Philadelphia: Westminster Press, 1986. Explores the pagan and Jewish ethical context in which Christianity developed.

Robinson, J. M., and Koester, Helmut. *Trajectories Through Early Christianity.* Philadelphia: Fortress Press, 1971.

Wilken, R. L. *The Christians as the Romans Saw Them.* New Haven, Conn.: Yale University Press, 1984. A careful analysis of the social, educational, religious, and political conflicts between early Christians and their Roman critics.

Glossary of New Testament Terms and Concepts

Aaron In the Hebrew Bible, the brother of Moses and first High Priest of Israel (Exod. 4:14; 6:20, 26; Lev. 8; Num. 3:1–3). In the Book of Hebrews, the High Priest's function is said to foreshadow that of Christ (Heb. 5:1–4; 8:1-10:18).

Abba The Aramaic word for "father," used by Jesus and other early Christians to address God (Mark 14:36; Rom. 8:15; Gal. 4:6).

Abraham The founder of the Hebrew nation. In Genesis 12–24, Abraham (at first called Abram, meaning "exalted father") is the supreme example of obedience to Yahweh. All Jews were believed to be Abraham's descendants through his son Isaac.

Abraham's bosom In Luke's parable about Lazarus and the rich man, a term used to denote a position of divine favor (Luke 16:19–31).

Adam In Genesis 2–3, the first human being. In Paul's letters, Adam is a symbol of all humanity (1 Cor. 15:21–49; Rom. 5:12–21).

Academy of Jamnia (see Jamnia, Academy of)

Alexander the Great Son of King Philip of Macedonia and conqueror of most of the known world. Alexander (356–323 B.C.E.) united Greece and the vast territories of the Persian Empire as far east as India. The period of cultural assimilation and synthesis inaugurated by his conquests is called Hellenistic.

Alexandria A major port city and cultural center founded by Alexander on the Egyptian coast. The home of a large Jewish colony during the Hellenistic period, Alexandria nourished a fusion of Jewish and Greek ideas, one result of which was the Greek Septuagint translation of the Hebrew Bible (begun about 250 B.C.E.).

allegory A literary narrative in which persons, places, and events are given a symbolic meaning. Some Hellenistic-Jewish scholars, like Philo of Alexandria, interpreted the Hebrew Bible allegorically, as Paul does the story of Abraham, Sarah, and Hagar (Gal. 4:21–31).

Ananias

1. The High Priest who presided over the full council (Sanhedrin) before which Paul was brought by Claudius Lycias for creating a "riot" in the Jerusalem Temple (Acts 22:22–23:22).

2. An early Christian who with his wife Sapphira attempted to defraud the Jerusalem church (Acts 5:1–10).

Andrew A disciple of Jesus and brother of Simon Peter, he was a Galilean fisherman (Mark 1:16–18) who may first have been a follower of John the Baptist (John 1:35–42).

angel A spirit being commonly regarded in biblical times as serving God by communicating his will to humanity (Luke 1–2; Matt. 1); from a Greek word meaning "messenger."

Annas A former High Priest before whom Jesus was brought for trial (John 18:13). Annas was father-in-law to Caiaphas, then the currently reigning High Priest (see also Luke 3:2 and Acts 4:6).

Annunciation The angel Gabriel's declaration to Mary of Nazareth that she was to bear a son, Jesus, who would inherit David's throne (Luke 1:28–32).

anthropomorphism The practice of attributing human qualities to something not human; in particular, ascribing human shape and form to a deity.

anti-Christ The ultimate enemy of Jesus Christ who, according to Christian apocalyptic traditions, will manifest himself at the End of time to corrupt many of the faithful, only to be vanquished at Christ's Second Coming. The term appears only in 2 and 3 John but is clearly referred to in 2 Thessalonians (2:1–2) and Revelation 13.

antinomianism The belief and practice of certain early Christian groups who argued that faith in

Christ absolves the believer from obeying moral laws; literally, "opponents of law." Paul attacks this libertarian attitude in Galatians (5:13–6:10; see also 1 and 2 John).

Antioch

1. In Syria, the capital of the Macedonian Seleucid kings and, under Roman rule, a province of the same name. According to Acts, the first predominantly Gentile church was founded in Antioch (Acts 11:20, 21), where followers of "the Way" were first called Christians (Acts 11:26). Paul began all three of his missionary tours from here.

2. Pisidian Antioch, a major city in Galatia (in Asia Minor), also the site of an important early church, founded by Paul and Barnabas (Acts 13:14–50).

Antiochus The name of several Syrian monarchs who inherited power from Seleucus I, a general and successor of Alexander the Great. The most famous were Antiochus III, who gained control of Palestine in 198–197 B.C.E., and Antiochus IV (Epiphanes, or "God Manifest") (175–163 B.C.E.), whose persecution of the Jews led to the Maccabean revolt.

antitheses The section of Matthew's Sermon on the Mount (Matt. 5:21–48) in which Jesus contrasts selected provisions of the Mosaic Torah with his own ethical directives. The term refers to a rhetorical structure in which contrasting ideas are presented in parallel arrangements of words, phrases, or sentences.

aphorism A terse, memorable statement that expresses a (commonly ignored) truth about human experience. Jesus frequently spoke in aphorisms, proverblike sayings that were typically concise, vivid, and paradoxical.

apocalypse A disclosure (vision) of spiritual realities or truths that are normally hidden—in the future or in the invisible world of spirit beings; from the Greek *apokalypsis,* meaning "to uncover," "to reveal."

apocalyptic An adjective derived from *apocalypse,* it typically refers to visions of the unseen world, such as God's heavenly throne, the habitation of angels, or the Underworld, as well as to the Deity's future plans for human history. See *eschatology.*

apocalyptic literature

1. A body of Hellenistic-Jewish writings produced between about 200 B.C.E. and 140 C.E., including canonical works such as Daniel and noncanonical books such as 1 and 2 Enoch and 2 and 3 Baruch.

These visionary books purport to reveal spiritual realities hidden from ordinary eyes, typically predicting future catastrophes heralding the defeat of God's enemies and the ultimate triumph of Israel.

2. Apocalyptic themes dominate much of early Christian literature, including Paul's letters, the Synoptic Gospels, 2 Peter, and Revelation, all of which emphasize Christ's role as God's eschatological agent.

apocalypticism A belief that God, through visions to chosen seers or prophets, reveals his hitherto hidden purpose toward humanity, particularly his plan to bring human history to a cataclysmic End in a final climactic battle between both material and spiritual forces of Good and Evil.

Apocrypha A body of Jewish religious writings dating from about 200 B.C.E. to 100 C.E. that were included in Greek editions of the Hebrew Bible but not in the official Hebrew Bible canon. The term *apocrypha,* meaning "hidden," was applied to these deuterocanonical works by Jerome, who included them in his famous Latin (Vulgate) translation of the Hebrew and Christian Scriptures.

apology A form of literature in which the author defends and explains his particular worldview and behavior.

Apollos A Hellenistic Jew of Alexandria, Egypt, noted for his eloquence. Originally a follower of John the Baptist, he later became a Christian associate of Paul (Acts 18:24–28; 1 Cor. 1:12; 3:4–6, 22–23; 4:6).

apostasy The act of abandoning or rejecting a previously held religious belief; from a Greek term meaning "to revolt." An apostate is one who has defected from or ceased to practice his or her religion.

apostle A person sent forth or commissioned as a messenger, such as (but not restricted to) the Twelve whom Jesus selected to follow him. According to Acts 1, in the early Jerusalem church an apostle was defined as one who had accompanied Jesus during his earthly ministry and had seen the resurrected Lord. Lists of the original Twelve differ from account to account (Matt. 10:2–5; Mark 3:16–19; Luke 6:13–16; Acts 1:13–14).

apothegm In biblical criticism, a brief saying or instructive proverb found in the Gospels. See also *pericope.*

Aquila A prominent early Christian (apparently) expelled from Rome with his wife, Priscilla, by Claudius's edict (about 49 C.E.). Aquila is often associated with Paul (Acts 18; Rom. 16:3–5; 1 Cor. 16:19).

Aramaic The language of the Arameans (ancient Syrians), a West Semitic tongue used in parts of Mesopotamia from about 1000 B.C.E. After the Babylonian captivity (538 B.C.E.), it became the common language of Palestinian Jews and was probably the language spoken by Jesus.

Areopagus The civic court in Athens and the location of an important legal council of the Athenian democracy where, according to Acts 17, Paul introduced Christianity to some Athenian intellectuals.

ark of the covenant According to Israelite tradition, the portable wooden chest built in Mosaic times to contain artifacts of the Mosaic faith, such as Aaron's staff and the stone tablets of the Decalogue (Exod. 25:10–22). Sometimes carried into battle (Josh. 6:4–11; 1 Sam. 4), the ark was eventually housed in Solomon's Temple. Its fate after the Temple's destruction (587 B.C.E.) is unknown.

Armageddon A Greek transliteration of the Hebrew place-name *Har-Megiddon,* or "Mountain of Megiddo," a famous battlefield in the Plain of Jezreel in ancient Israel (Judg. 5:19; 2 Kings 9:27; 23:29). In Revelation (16:16), it is the symbolic site of the ultimate war between Good and Evil.

Artemis Greek goddess of wildlife, the hunt, and childbirth, whose magnificent temple at Ephesus was one of the Seven Wonders of the Ancient World (see Acts 19). The Romans called her Diana and associated her with the moon.

Ascension, the The resurrected Jesus' ascent to heaven (Acts 1:6–11).

Asclepius The son of a mortal woman, Coronis, and Apollo, the Greek god of prophecy, health, disease, and purification, he was the first physician, the founder and patron of medicine. Posthumously deified, he allegedly effected miraculous cures at shrines throughout the Greco-Roman world.

Athens Greece's dominant city-state and cultural capital in the fifth century B.C.E. Athens remained a leading intellectual center during Hellenistic and Roman times. Acts 17 depicts Paul debating Stoic and Epicurean philosophers there.

Atonement, Day of (Yom Kippur) A solemn, annual Jewish observance in which Israel's High Priest offered blood sacrifices ("sin offerings") to effect a reconciliation between the Deity and his people (Lev. 16). The banishment of a "scapegoat" to which

the priest had symbolically transferred the people's collective guilt climaxed the atonement rites. This day marked the priest's once-yearly entrance into the Temple's Holy of Holies, a ceremony that the author of Hebrews says is a foreshadowing of Jesus' sacrificial death and ascension to the heavenly Temple (Heb. 9).

Augustus (Augustus Caesar) The first emperor of Rome 27 B.C.E.–14 C.E.) who brought peace to the Roman Empire after centuries of civil war. According to Luke 2, his decree ordering a census of "the whole world" was the device that brought about Jesus' birth in Bethlehem.

Babylon An ancient city on the middle Euphrates that was the capital of both the Old Babylonian and the Neo-Babylonian empires. In 587 B.C.E., Babylonian armies destroyed Jerusalem and its Temple. As the archetypal enemy of God's people, Babylon became the symbol of any earthly government that opposed the faithful (Rev. 14:8; 18:12).

baptism A religious ceremony first associated with John the Baptist (Mark 1:4; 11:30; Luke 7:29) and performed on converts in the infant Christian community (Acts 2:38–41; 19:3–5). Baptism may have derived from ritual cleansings with water practiced by the Essenes, from the use of it by some Pharisees as a conversion alternative to circumcision, or from initiation rites into Hellenistic mystery religions. In Christianity, it is the rite of initiation into the church (1 Pet.), in which one is either totally immersed in water or water is poured on one's head.

bar Aramaic word used in names, meaning "son of."

Barabbas A condemned murderer and possibly a revolutionary whom the Roman procurator Pontius Pilate released instead of Jesus (Mark 15:6–15; Matt. 27:15–18; Luke 23:16–25; John 18:39–49).

bar Kochba The name (meaning "son of the star") applied to the leader of the second Jewish revolt against Rome (132–135 C.E.).

Barnabas A prominent leader of the early churches in Jerusalem and Antioch, Paul's mentor and later his traveling companion (Acts 9:26–30; 11:22–30; 13:1–3, 44–52; 14:1–15:4; 15:22–40; Col. 4:10; 1 Cor. 9:6; Gal. 2:1–13).

Bartholomew One of Jesus' twelve chief disciples (Mark 3:16–19; Matt. 10:2–4; Luke 6:14–16; Acts 1:13), about whom virtually nothing is known. Because Bartholomew's name follows that of Philip in all three Synoptic apostolic lists and because Philip brings an otherwise unknown "Nathanael" to Jesus in the Fourth Gospel (which does not mention Bartholomew), some commentators speculate that Nathanael and Bartholomew are the same person.

Beatitudes The list of blessings or sources of happiness with which Jesus begins the Sermon on the Mount (Matt. 5:3–12). Luke gives a simpler version of these sayings (6:20–23).

ben Hebrew word used in names, meaning "son of."

Bethlehem A village about five miles south of Jerusalem, birthplace of David (1 Sam. 17:12) and the traditional site of the Messiah's birth (Micah 5:2; Matt. 2:5–6; Luke 2; John 7:42).

Bible A collection of Jewish and Christian sacred writings commonly divided into two main sections—the Hebrew Bible (Old Testament) and the later Christian Greek Scriptures (New Testament), from the Greek term *biblia*, meaning "little books."

bishop The supervisor or presiding officer of a church; from the Greek term *episcopos*, meaning "overseer."

Bithynia In New Testament times, a Roman province in northern Asia Minor (modern Turkey) along the Black Sea coast and the location of several Christian churches (Acts 16:7; 1 Pet. 1:1).

Boanerges "Sons of thunder," an epithet Jesus bestows upon the brothers James and John (Mark 3:17; Luke 9:52–56).

Caesar A hereditary name by which the Roman emperors commemorated Gaius Julius Caesar, great-uncle of Augustus, Rome's first emperor (Luke 2:1; 3:1; Mark 12:14; Acts 11:28; 25:11).

Caesarea An important Roman city, built by Herod the Great on the Palestinian coast about sixty-four miles northwest of Jerusalem and named in honor of Caesar Augustus. Caesarea was Pilate's administrative capital and later a Christian center (Acts 8:40; 10:1; 24; 18:22; 21:18). Paul was imprisoned there for two years (Acts 23–26).

Caesarea Philippi An inland city north of the Sea of Galilee built by Philip, son of Herod the Great, and named for the emperor Tiberius Caesar; the site of Peter's recognition that Jesus was the Messiah (Mark 8:27; Matt. 16:13).

Caiaphas Joseph Caiaphas, High Priest of Jerusalem during the reign of the emperor Tiberius (Matt. 26:3; 57–66; John 9:49; 18:13–28; Acts 4:6). Son-in-law to his immediate predecessor, Annas, he was appointed to the office by the procurator Valerius Gratus and presided over Jesus' hearing before the Sanhedrin.

Calvary The site outside Jerusalem's walls, exact location unknown, where Jesus was crucified (Luke 23:33). Calvary derives from the Latin word *calveria*, a translation of the Greek *kranion*, meaning "skull." Calvary was also called Golgotha, a name that comes from the Aramaic for "skull" (Matt. 27:33; John 19:17).

canon

1. A list of books that a religious community finds sacred and authoritative; from the Greek *kanon*.

2. A standard by which religious beliefs or documents are judged acceptable.

Capernaum A small port on the northwest shore of the Sea of Galilee that Jesus used as headquarters for his Galilean ministry (Matt. 9:1, 9–11; Mark 1:21–29; 2:3–11; Luke 7; John 4:46–54).

catholic epistles Seven short New Testament documents that were addressed to the church as a whole and thus are described as general, or "catholic" (universal).

centurion A low-ranking officer in the Roman army in charge of a "century" or division of 100 men.

Cephas A name meaning "stone," bestowed by Jesus upon Simon Peter (John 1:42).

Chaos In ancient Greco-Roman belief, the original Void (the formless darkness) that existed before the ordered world (Cosmos) came into being.

Christ The Messiah; from the Greek *Christos*, a translation of the Hebrew *Mashiah* (messiah), meaning "the anointed one." The term derives from Israel's practice of anointing (putting oil on the heads of) kings at their coronation.

Christology Theological interpretation of the nature and function of Jesus, including doctrines about his divinity, his prehuman existence, his role in creating the universe, and so on.

Church In New Testament usage, the community of believers in Jesus Christ (Matt. 16:18; 18:17; Eph. 5:27; 1 Tim. 3:15; 1 Cor. 12:12–27; Col. 1:18). The term translates the Greek *ekklesia*, meaning "assembly of ones called out."

circumcision An ancient Semitic operation in which the foreskin of an eight-day-old male is removed as a ceremony of initiation into the religion and community of Israel. Genesis represents the practice as beginning with Abraham (Gen. 17:10–14); Exodus implies that circumcision began with Moses (Exod. 4:24–46). The question of whether to circumcise Gentile converts to the early Christian church was an important source of dissension (Acts 15; Gal. 2).

Claudius The fourth Roman emperor (41–54 C.E.), who expelled the Jews from Rome (Acts 11:28; 18:2).

codex A manuscript book of an ancient biblical text, a form pioneered by Christians to replace the unwieldy scrolls on which the Scriptures were originally recorded.

Colossae An ancient Phrygian city situated on the south bank of the Lycus River in central Asia Minor, important for its position on the trade route between Ephesus and Mesopotamia (Col. 1:1–2; 4:13). Paul or a Pauline disciple composed a canonical letter to Christians there.

Coptic A term relating to the church or liturgical language of the Copts, a people reputedly descended from the ancient Egyptians who preserved an early form of Christianity. The Nag Hammadi library was written in Coptic.

Corinth A large and prosperous Greek city that the Romans first destroyed (146 B.C.E.) and later rebuilt, making it the capital of the Roman province called Achaia (Greece). About 50 C.E., Paul and his associates founded an important church there (Acts 18:24; 19:1; 1 and 2 Cor.).

Cornelius A Roman centurion associated with the synagogue in Caesarea who became the first Gentile convert to Christianity (Acts 10–11).

Cosmos The Greek term for the ordered universe, a world system characterized by structure, stability, and harmony.

covenant A vow, agreement, or contract between a deity and a group of people who regard themselves as the god's chosen community. In Exodus, Yahweh makes a covenant with Israel in which the people agree to obey all his laws and instruction (the Torah) and to worship him exclusively (Exod. 20–24; 34; see also Deut. 28; Josh. 24). In Christian tradition, Jesus introduced a "New Covenant" with his disciples, making them the true Israel (Mark 14:22–25; Matt. 26:26–29; 1 Cor. 11:25).

cult The formalized practices of a religious group, particularly its system of worship and public (or secret) rites.

Damascus The capital of Syria and the terminus of ancient caravan routes in the Fertile Crescent. Damascus was the site of Paul's earliest experiences as a Christian (Acts 9; Gal. 1:17).

David Popular king of Israel and second king of the united twelve-tribe monarchy (about 1010–970 B.C.E.). Son of Jesse (Ruth 4:18–22) and successor to Saul, David created an Israelite empire (1 Sam. 16; 2 Kings 2). After his short-lived kingdom disintegrated, later ages remembered his reign as a model of God's rule on earth and regarded David as a prototype of the Messiah, whom the prophets foresaw as an heir to the Davidic throne (Isa. 9:5–7; 11:1–16; Jer. 23:5; 30:9; Ezek. 34:23–31; Matt. 1–2; Rom. 1:3; etc.).

Day of Atonement (see Atonement, Day of (Yom Kippur)).

deacon A church officer in early Christianity; the term refers to one who serves or ministers.

Dead Sea Scrolls A collection of ancient documents found preserved in caves near Qumran on the northwest shore of the Dead Sea. The scrolls included copies (many in fragmental form) of all canonical books of the Hebrew Bible except Esther, works from the Apocrypha and the Pseudepigrapha, and commentaries and other writings of the Essene community.

Decalogue The Ten Commandments (Exod. 20: Deut. 5).

Dedication, Feast of An eight-day Jewish celebration (now known as Hanukkah) instituted in 165 B.C.E. by Judas Maccabeus and held annually on the twenty-fifth day of Kislev (November–December). The holiday commemorates the cleansing and rededication of the Jerusalem Temple, which Antiochus IV had polluted. Referred to in John (10:22–38), it is also known as the Festival of Lights.

deuterocanon The fourteen books of the Old Testament Apocrypha included in the Latin Vulgate but not in the Hebrew Bible. The Roman Catholic Church regards these works as deuterocanonical— that is, belonging to a second and later canon.

devil The English word commonly used to translate two Greek words with different meanings:

1. *diabolos,* "the accuser" (John 8:44).

2. *daimonion,* one of the many evil spirits inhabiting the world, who were thought to cause disease, madness, and other afflictions (see Matt. 10:25; Mark 3:22; Luke 8; 11:14–16). In Rev. 12:9, the devil is identified with the Hebrew Satan and the serpent of Genesis 3.

Diana of the Ephesians The Near Eastern form of the Greek goddess Artemis (identified by the Romans with Diana). She was worshipped in Ephesus, which in Paul's time was the capital of the Roman province of Asia (Acts 19).

Diaspora The distribution of Jews outside their Palestinian homeland, such as the many Jewish communities established throughout the Greco-Roman world; literally, a "scattering."

Dionysus The son of Zeus and the mortal Semele, princess of Thebes, he was the Greek god of wine, ecstasy, and emotional liberation. The only Olympian god to suffer death, a descent into the Underworld (Hades), resurrection, and ascension to heaven, he presided over mystery cults that apparently promised their adherents a future immortality.

disciple In the New Testament, a follower of a particular religious figure, such as Moses (John 9:28), John the Baptist (Luke 11:1; John 1:35), the Pharisees (Mark 2:18), or Jesus (Matt. 14:26; 20:17) from the Greek word meaning "learner."

Docetism The belief, commonly associated with Gnostic Christianity, that Jesus was pure spirit and only appeared to be physically human; from the Greek verb meaning "to seem."

doxology In a religious writing or service, the formal concluding expression of praise ascribing glory to God.

Dragon The image applied in Revelation 12 to Satan, the embodiment of evil forces opposing God. Derived from ancient Near Eastern mythology, the symbol of the giant reptile represents the powers of darkness and disorder (the original Chaos) that God first conquered in creating the ordered universe (Cosmos).

Dualism A philosophic or religious system that posits the existence of two parallel worlds, one of physical matter and the other of invisible spirit. Moral dualism views the universe as divided between powers of Good and Evil, Light and Dark, which contend for human allegiance.

Elijah The leader of Israel's prophetic movement during the ninth century B.C.E. Elijah fiercely championed the exclusive worship of Yahweh and opposed the Israelite cult of the Canaanite god Baal (1 Kings 17–19; 21; 2 Kings 1–2). Reportedly carried to heaven in a fiery chariot (2 Kings 2:1–13), he was expected to reappear shortly before the Day of Yahweh arrived (Mal. 4:5–6). Although some Christian writers identified John the Baptist with Elijah (Luke 1:17; Mark 9:12–13), some contemporaries viewed Jesus as Elijah returned (Mark 9:28; 16:14). Along with

Moses, Elijah appears at Jesus' transfiguration (Mark 9:4; Matt. 17:3; Luke 9:30).

Elizabeth The wife of the Levite priest Zechariah and mother of John the Baptist (Luke 1).

Emmaus A village (site unknown) near Jerusalem, along the road to which the resurrected Jesus appeared to two disciples (Luke 24:13–32).

Enoch A son of Cain (Gen. 4:17) or Jared (Gen. 5:18) and father of Methuselah (Gen. 5:21), taken by God (apparently to heaven). Legends surrounding Enoch's mysterious fate gave rise to a whole body of noncanonical literature in which Enoch returns to earth to describe his experiences in the spirit world and foretell events leading to the End.

Epaphras An early Christian of Colossae who reported on the Colossian church to the imprisoned Paul (Col. 1:7; 4:12; Philem. 23).

Epaphroditus A Macedonian Christian from Philippi who assisted Paul in prison (Phil. 2:25–27).

Ephesus A wealthy Hellenistic city, in New Testament times the capital of the Roman province of Asia, site of the famous temple of Artemis (Diana) (Acts 19–20). Mentioned frequently in Paul's correspondence (1 Cor. 16:19; 2 Cor. 12:14; 13:1; 1 Tim. 3:1; etc.), the Ephesian church receives the author's favorable judgment in Revelation 2:1–7.

epiphany An appearance or manifestation, particularly of a divine being.

epistle A formal communication intended to be read publicly.

eschatology Beliefs about the supernaturally directed destiny of humanity and the universe; from the Greek word meaning "study of last things." Associated with an apocalyptic worldview, eschatology has both personal and general applications:

  1. beliefs about the individual soul following death, including divine judgment, heaven, hell, and resurrection;

  2. larger concerns about the fate of the Cosmos, including convictions about a divinely guided renewal of the world and human society in the near future or in the present (realized eschatology).

eschaton From the Greek *eschatos*, meaning "last," term designating the end of history or human life.

Essenes According to Josephus, one of the three major sects of Judaism in the first century C.E. Characterized by apocalyptic beliefs in the world's imminent End, some of the group founded monastic communities in the Judean desert, such as the Qumran settlement that produced the library known as the Dead Sea Scrolls.

Eucharist The Christian ceremony of consecrated bread and wine that Jesus initiated at the Last Supper (Mark 14:22–25; Matt. 26:26–29; etc.); from the Greek word meaning "gratitude" or "thanksgiving."

Evangelist From the Greek *euangelion* (good news); the writer of a Gospel.

exegesis Close analysis and interpretation of a text to discover the original author's exact intent and meaning. Once the writer's primary intent has been established, other interpretations can be considered.

exorcism The act or practice of expelling a demon or evil spirit from a person or place (Tobit 8:1–3; Mark 1:23–27, 32–34; 5:1–20; Matt. 8:25–34; Acts 19:13–19; etc.).

expiation The act of making atonement for sin, usually by offering a sacrifice to appease divine wrath (Lev. 16; Heb. 9).

Fall, the Humanity's loss of innocence and divine favor through the first human beings' sin of disobedience (Gen. 3). According to some interpretations of Pauline thought (Rom. 5:12–21; 1 Cor. 15:45–49), the Fall resulted in the transmission of death and a proclivity toward wrongdoing to the entire human race. As a medieval rhyme expressed it, "In Adam's fall, we sinned all."

Feast of Dedication (see **Dedication, Feast of**).

Felix, Antonius The Roman procurator of Judea before whom Paul was tried at Caesarea (Acts 23:23–24:27).

Festus, Porcius The procurator of Judea whom Nero appointed to succeed Felix and through whom Paul appealed to be tried by Caesar's court in Rome (Acts 24:27–26:32).

Flavius Josephus (see **Josephus, Flavius**)

form criticism A method of biblical analysis that attempts to isolate, classify, and analyze individual units or characteristic forms contained in a literary text and to identify the probable preliterary form of these units before their incorporation into the written text; the term is an English rendition of the German *Formsgeschichte*. Form criticism also attempts to discover the setting in life (*Sitz-im-Leben*) of each unit — that is, the historical, social, religious, and cultural environment from which it developed — and to trace or reconstruct the process by which various traditions evolved from their original oral state to their final literary form.

Fourth Gospel The Gospel of John, last-written of the four canonical Gospels, it differs strikingly in form, order, and content from the three Synoptics.

Gabriel In the Hebrew angelic hierarchy, one of the seven archangels whose duty it was to convey the Deity's messages. Gabriel explained Daniel's visions to him (Dan. 8:15–26; 9:20–27) and, in the New Testament, announced the births of John the Baptist and Jesus (Luke 1:15–17, 26–38). The name may mean "person of God" or "God has shown himself mighty."

Galatia A region in the interior of Asia Minor (Turkey) settled by Gauls; in New Testament times, a Roman province visited by Paul and his associates (Acts 16:6; 18:23; 1 Cor. 16:1; Gal. 1:2; 1 Pet. 1:1).

Galilee The region of northern Palestine lying west of the Jordan River, where Jesus grew up and carried out much of his public ministry (Mark 1–9; Matt. 2:23; Luke 4); from the Hebrew term *Ghil-ha-goyim*, meaning "circle of Gentiles." In Jesus' day, Herod Antipas administered this region for the Romans (Luke 23:5–7).

Galilee, Sea of The major body of fresh water in northern Palestine, source of livelihood to many Galilean fisherman, such as Peter, Andrew, James, and John (Matt. 4:18–22).

Gallio A proconsul of Achaia (the Roman province of Greece) who dismissed charges brought against Paul by Corinthian Jews (Acts 18:12–17). Gallio was a brother of Seneca, the Stoic philosopher.

Gamaliel A leading Pharisee and scholar, a member of the Sanhedrin, the reputed teacher of Paul (Acts 5:34–40; 22:3), and an exponent of the liberal wing of the Pharisaic party developed by his grandfather, Hillel.

Gehenna The New Testament name for the "Valley of the Son [or Children] of Hinnom," a depression in the earth that bordered Jerusalem on the south and west and that had been the site of human sacrifices to Molech and other Canaanite gods (Jer. 7:32; Lev. 18:21; 1 Kings 11:7; 2 Chron. 28:3; 33:6). Later used as a dump in which garbage was burned, the valley became a symbol of punishment in the afterlife and is cited as such by Jesus (Matt. 5:22; 10:28–29; 18:8; 25:30, 46; etc.). *Gehenna* is commonly translated as "hell" in the Gospels.

Gemara The second part of the Talmud, an extensive commentary, in Aramaic, on the Hebrew Mishnah.

Gentile A non-Jewish person, a member of "the nations" that are not in a covenant relationship with Yahweh. Jewish writers commonly refer to Gentiles as "the uncircumcised," persons not bearing the ritual mark of the covenant people.

Gethsemane The site of a garden or orchard on the Mount of Olives where Jesus took his disciples after the Last Supper; the place where he was arrested (Matt. 26:36–56; Mark 14:32–52; Luke 22:39–53; John 18:1–14).

gnosis The Greek word for "knowledge."

Gnosticism A widespread and extremely diverse movement in early Christianity. Followers of Gnosticism believed that salvation is gained through a special knowledge (*gnosis*) revealed through a spiritual Savior (presumably Jesus) and is the property of an elite few who have been initiated into its mysteries. In its various forms, Gnosticism became a major heresy in the primitive church, though little is known about its precise tenets.

Gog In Ezekiel, a future leader of Israel's enemies (Ezek. 38) whose attack on the Jerusalem sanctuary will precipitate Yahweh's intervention and the ultimate destruction of the wicked (Rev. 20:8).

Gospel

1. The Christian message, literally meaning "good news."

2. The literary form of Christian narratives about Jesus.

Gospel, Fourth The Gospel attributed to John.

Gospels, apocryphal Christian Gospels, such as those attributed to Peter, Thomas, James, or others, that were not admitted to the New Testament canon.

Gospels, canonical The Gospels of Matthew, Mark, Luke, and John.

Gospels, Synoptic The three canonical Gospels — Matthew, Mark, and Luke — that present Jesus' public life from a strikingly similar viewpoint, structuring their respective narratives so that the contents can be arranged in parallel columns.

Hades In Greek religion, the name of the god of the Underworld, a mythic region that also came to be known by that name. In translating the Hebrew Bible into Greek, the Septuagint translators rendered *Sheol* (the Hebrew term for the subterranean abode of all the dead) as *Hades* (Gen. 42:38; 1 Sam. 2:6; Job 7:9; Prov. 27:20; Eccles. 9:10). New Testament writers also refer to the place of the dead as Hades (Rev. 1:18, 20:14). See also *Gehenna*.

Haggadah The imaginative interpretation of the nonlegal (historical and religious) passages of the Hebrew Bible. A collection of Haggadah, dating from the first centuries C.E., appears in the Palestinian Talmud. See *Halakah*.

Hagiographa The third major division of the Hebrew Bible, a miscellaneous collection of poetry, wisdom literature, history, and an apocalypse (Daniel); from the Greek term meaning "sacred writings."

Halakah The interpretation of the legal sections of the Mosaic Torah. The term derives from a Hebrew word meaning "to follow"; Halakah deals with rules that guide a person's life. Collections of halakic interpretations dating from the first centuries C.E. are incorporated into the Talmud. See *Haggadah*.

Hanukkah The Feast of Dedication celebrating the Maccabees' restoration of the Jerusalem Temple about 165 B.C.E.

Hasidim Devout Jews who refused to forsake their religion during the persecution inflicted by Antiochus IV (second century B.C.E.). The Jewish religious parties of the New Testament period are descended from the Hasidim.

Hasmoneans The Jewish royal dynasty founded by the Maccabees and named for Hasmon, an ancestor of Mattathias.

Hebrew Bible A collection of Jewish sacred writings originally written in the Hebrew language (although some later books are in Aramaic); also known as the Old Testament. The Hebrew Bible is traditionally divided into three main parts: the Torah or Law (Genesis through Deuteronomy); the Prophets (Joshua through the twelve minor prophets); and the Writings (Psalms through Chronicles).

Hellenism The influence and adoption of Greek thought, language, values, and customs that began with the conquest of the eastern Mediterranean world by Alexander the Great and intensified under his Hellenistic successors and various Roman emperors.

Hellenistic Greek-like; pertaining to the historical period following Alexander's death in 323 B.C.E. during which Greek language, ideas, and customs permeated the eastern Mediterranean and Near Eastern worlds.

Hellenists Jews living outside Palestine who adopted the Greek language and, to varying degrees, Greek customs and ideas (Acts 6:1; 9:29).

Hellenization The diffusion of Greek language and culture (Hellenism) throughout the Mediterranean region, beginning with the conquests of Alexander of Macedonia in the fourth century B.C.E. Enforced Hellenization of the Jews by Antiochus IV sparked the Maccabean Revolt.

heresy A religious opinion contrary to that officially endorsed by the religion to which one belongs. Applied to early Christianity by its detractors (Acts 24:14), the term was not generally used in its modern sense during New Testament times except in the pastoral epistles (1 Tim. 1:3; Titus 3:10).

Herod The name of seven Palestinian rulers:

1. Herod I (the Great), the Idumean Roman-appointed ruler when Jesus was born (Matt. 2:1). An able administrator who lavishly reconstructed the Jerusalem Temple, he was notorious for reputed cruelty and was almost universally hated by the Jews.

2. Herod Antipas, son of Herod I, tetrarch of Galilee (Luke 3:1) and Perea (4 B.C.E.–39 C.E.), frequently mentioned in the New Testament. Jesus, who called him "that fox" (Luke 13:31–32) and regarded him as a malign influence (Mark 8:15), was tried before him (Luke 9:7, 9; 23:7–15). Antipas was also responsible for executing John the Baptist (Matt. 14:1–12).

3. Herod Archelaus, ethnarch of Judea, Samaria, who so misruled his territory that he was recalled to Rome, an event to which Jesus apparently refers in Luke 19:12–27. Archelaus's evil reputation caused Joseph and Mary to avoid Judea and settle in Nazareth (Matt. 2:22–23).

4. Herod, a son of Herod the Great and half-brother to Herod Antipas (Matt. 14:3; Mark 6:17).

5. Herod Philip II, son of Herod the Great and half-brother of Herod Antipas, who ruled portions of northeastern Palestine and rebuilt the city of Caesarea Philippi near Mount Hermon (Luke 3:1).

6. Herod Agrippa I, son of Aristobulus and grandson of Herod the Great, who ingratiated himself at the imperial court in Rome and, under Claudius, was made king over most of Palestine (41–44 C.E.). A persecutor of Christians, he reportedly died a horrible death immediately after accepting divine honors (Acts 12:1–23).

7. Herod Agrippa II, son of Herod Agrippa I and great-grandson of Herod the Great, first king of Chalcis (50 C.E.) and then of the territory formerly ruled by Philip the Tetrarch, as well as of the adjoining area east of Galilee and the Upper Jordan. This was the Herod, together with his sister Bernice, before whom Paul appeared at Caesarea (Acts 25:13–26:32).

Herodians The name applied to members of an influential political movement in first-century C.E. Judaism who supported Herod's dynasty, particularly that of Herod Antipas. Opposing messianic hopes (Mark 3:6), they conspired with some Pharisees to implicate Jesus in disloyalty to Rome (Mark 12:13; Matt. 22:16).

Herodias Granddaughter of Herod the Great, daughter of Aristobulus, and half-sister of Herod Agrippa I. Herodias was criticized by John the Baptist for having deserted her first husband for her second, Herod Antipas, who divorced his wife to marry her. In revenge, she demanded the head of John the Baptist (Mark 6:17–29; Matt. 14:1–12; Luke 3:19–20).

Hinnom, Valley of A depression in the earth lying south and west of Jerusalem; also called the "Valley of the Son (or Children) of Hinnom" (Jer. 7:32; 2 Kings 23:10). Called Gehenna in the New Testament, it is a symbol of the place of posthumous torment. See *Gehenna.*

historical criticism A critical method involving the analysis of a document to determine its relative historical accuracy and plausibility, including such matters as the author's purpose (or bias) and the sociohistorical context in which it emerged.

Holy of Holies The innermost and most sacred room of the Jerusalem Temple, where Yahweh was believed to be invisibly enthroned.

Holy Spirit The presence of God active in human life, a concept most explicitly set forth in John 14:16–26 and in the Pentecost miracle depicted in Acts 2. In post–New Testament times, the Holy Spirit was defined as the Third Person in the Trinity (see Matt. 28:19–20).

Idumea The name (meaning "pertaining to Edom") that the Greeks and Romans applied to the country of Edom, Judah's southern neighbor; the homeland of Herod the Great (Mark 3:8).

Immanuel The name (meaning "God is with us") that Isaiah gave to a child whose birth he predicted as a sign to King Ahaz during the late eighth century

B.C.E. Although not originally presented as a messianic prophecy, it was later interpreted as such (Micah 5:3; Matt. 1:22–23).

Incarnation The Christian doctrine that the prehuman Son of God became flesh, the man Jesus of Nazareth—a concept based largely on the Logos hymn that opens John's Gospel (John 1:1–18, especially 1:14).

Isaac The son of Abraham and Sarah (Gen. 21:1–7), child of the covenant promise by which Abraham's descendants would bring a blessing to all the earth's families (Gen. 17:15–22; 18:1–15) but whom Yahweh commanded to be sacrificed to him (Gen. 18:1–18). Reprieved by an angel, Isaac marries Rebekah (Gen. 24:1–67), who bears him twin sons, Esau and Jacob (Gen. 25:19–26), the latter of whom tricks his dying father into bestowing the firstborn's birthright on him (Gen. 27:1–45). Paul interprets the near-sacrifice of Isaac as an allegory of Christ (Gal. 4:21–31).

Isis Egyptian mother goddess who was worshiped in mystery cults throughout the Roman Empire. Images in which she nurses her infant son Horus anticipate later Christian renditions of the Madonna.

Jairus The head of a synagogue in Galilee who asked Jesus to heal his dying child, for which act of faith he was rewarded with the girl's miraculous cure (Luke 8:41–42, 49–56; Mark 5:35–43; Matt. 9:18–20, 23–26).

James

1. Son of Zebedee, brother of John, and one of the Twelve Apostles (Mark 1:19–20; 3:17; Matt. 4:21–22; 10:2; Luke 5:10; 6:14). A Galilean fisherman, he left his trade to follow Jesus and, with John and Peter, became a member of his inner circle. He was among the three disciples present at the Transfiguration (Mark 9:2–10; Matt. 17:1–9; Luke 9:28–36) and was at Jesus' side during the last hours before his arrest (Mark 14:32–42; Matt. 26:36–45). James and John used their intimacy to request a favored place in the messianic kingdom, thus arousing the other apostles' indignation (Mark 10:35–45). James was beheaded when Herod Agrippa I persecuted the Jerusalem church (41–44 C.E.) (Acts 12:2).

2. James, son of Alphaeus and Mary (Acts 1:13; Mark 16:1), one of the Twelve (Matt. 10:3–4), called "the less" or "the younger" (Mark 15:40).

3. James, the eldest of Jesus' three "brothers" (or close male relatives) named in the Gospels (Mark 6:3; Matt. 13:55). He first opposed Jesus' work (Matt. 12:46–50; Mark 3:31–35; Luke 8:19–21; John 7:3–5) but was apparently converted by one of Jesus' postresurrection appearances (1 Cor. 15:7) and became a leader in the Jerusalem church (Acts 15:13–34; 21:18–26). According to legend, a Nazirite and upholder of the Mosaic law, he apparently clashed with Paul over the latter's policy of absolving Gentile converts from circumcision and other legalistic requirements (Gal. 1:18–2:12). The reputed author of the New Testament epistle of James, he was martyred at Jerusalem in the early 60s C.E.

Jamnia, Academy of An assembly of eminent Palestinian rabbis and Pharisees held about 90 C.E. in the coastal village of Jamnia (Yabneh) to define and guide Judaism following the Roman destruction of Jerusalem and its Temple. According to tradition, a leading Pharisee named Yohanan ben Zakkai had escaped from the besieged city by simulating death and being carried out in a coffin by his disciples. Yohanan, who had argued that saving human lives was more important than success in the national rebellion against Rome, was given Roman support to set up an academy to study the Mosaic Law. Under his direction, the Pharisees not only preserved the Torah traditions but apparently formulated what was to become the official biblical canon of Palestinian Judaism. Out of the deliberations at Jamnia came the authoritative list of books in the Writings, the third major division of the Hebrew Bible.

Jesus The English form of a Latin name derived from the Greek *Iesous,* which translated the Hebrew *Jeshua,* a later version of *Jehoshua* or *Joshua,* meaning "Yahweh is salvation." The name was borne by several biblical figures, including Joshua, leader of the conquest of Canaan; an ancestor of Jesus (Luke 3:29); and a Jewish Christian also called Justus (Col. 4:11). It was also the name of the author of Ecclesiasticus, Jesus ben Sirach.

Jesus Christ The name and title given the firstborn of Mary and Joseph (the child's legal father), the one whom Christians regard as the Spirit-begotten Son of God and Savior of the world (Matt. 1:21; Luke 1:31). The term *Christ* is not a proper name but the English version of the Greek *Christos,* a translation of the Aramaic *meshiha* and the Hebrew *mashiah* (messiah, meaning "the anointed one").

Jew Originally, a member of the tribe or kingdom of Judah (2 Kings 16:6; 25:25). The term later included any Hebrew who returned from the Babylonian captivity (538 B.C.E.), and it finally encompassed Hebrews scattered throughout the world (Matt. 2:2) during the Second Temple period (c. 515 B.C.E.–70 C.E.).

Jewish Bible See *Hebrew Bible*.

Joanna Wife of Chuza, an administrator in Herod Antipas's Jerusalem household, who became a disciple of Jesus (Luke 8:3) and was among the women who discovered his empty tomb (Luke 23:55–24:11).

John the apostle A Galilean fisherman, son of Zebedee and brother of the apostle James, called by Jesus to be among his twelve most intimate followers (Mark 1:19–20; Matt. 4:21–22). Jesus called James and John Boanerges (sons of thunder), possibly because of their impetuous temperaments (Mark 3:17; 9:38; Luke 9:52–56). Always among the first four in the Gospel lists of the Twelve (Mark 3:14–17; Matt. 10:2; Luke 6:3–14), John was present at the Transfiguration (Matt. 17:1; Mark 9:2; Luke 9:28) and at Gethsemane (Matt. 26:37; Mark 14:33). Tradition identifies him with the Beloved Disciple (John 13:23; 21:20) and as the author of the Gospel of John, a premise that most scholars believe is impossible to prove. Along with Peter and James, he was one of the triple "pillars" of the Jerusalem church (Acts 1:13; 3:1–4:22; 8:14–17; Gal. 2:9). He may have been martyred under Herod Agrippa, although a late second-century tradition states that he lived to old age in Ephesus.

John the Baptist The son of Zechariah, a priest, and Elizabeth (Luke 1:5–24, 56–80), John was an ascetic who preached the imminence of judgment and baptized converts in the Jordan River as a symbol of their repentance from sin (Matt. 3:1–12; Mark 1:2–8; Luke 3:1–18). The Gospel writers viewed him as an Elijah figure and forerunner of the Messiah (Luke 1:17; Matt. 11:12–14; John 1:15, 9–34; 3:22–36) who baptized Jesus but also recognized his superiority (Matt. 3:13–17; Mark 1:9–11; Luke 3:21–22). When imprisoned by Herod Antipas, he inquired whether Jesus was the expected "one who is to come." Jesus' answer was equivocal, but he praised John's work as fulfilling prophecy (Matt. 11:2–19; Luke 7:24–35). At his stepdaughter Salome's request, Herod had John beheaded (Matt. 14:6–12; Mark 6:17–29). Some of John's disciples later became Christians (John 1:37; Acts 18:25).

Joseph

1. The husband of Mary and legal father of Jesus, a descendant of the Bethlehemite David (Matt. 1:20) but resident of Nazareth (Luke 2:4), where he was a carpenter (Matt. 13:55). Little is known of him except for his piety (Luke 2:21–24, 41–42) and his wish to protect his betrothed wife from scandal (Luke 2:1–5). Because he does not appear among Jesus' family members during his (supposed) son's public ministry, it is assumed that he died before Jesus began his preaching career (Matt. 1:18–2:23; 13:55–56).

2. Joseph of Arimathea, a wealthy member of the Sanhedrin and, according to John 19:38, a secret follower of Jesus who claimed Jesus' crucified body from Pilate for burial in his private garden tomb (Matt. 27:57–60; Mark 15:42–46; Luke 23:50–53; John 19:38–42).

Josephus, Flavius An important Jewish historian (about 37–100 C.E.) whose two major works—*Antiquities of the Jews* and *The Jewish War* (covering the revolt against Rome, 66–73 C.E.)—provide valuable background material for first-century Judaism and the early Christian period.

Judaeus, Philo (see **Philo Judaeus**).

Judaism The name applied to the religion of the people of Judah ("the Jews") after the northern kingdom of Israel fell (721 B.C.E.) and particularly after the Babylonian exile (587–538 B.C.E.).

Judas A late form of the name Judah, popular after the time of Judas ("the Jew") Maccabeus and borne by several New Testament figures:

1. The brother (or son) of James, one of the Twelve Apostles (Luke 6:16), who is sometimes identified with the Thaddeus of Matthew 10:3 or the Judas of John 14:22.

2. The "brother" or kinsman of Jesus (Mark 6:3; Matt. 13:55).

3. Judas Iscariot ("Judas the man of Kerioth"), son of Simon Iscariot (John 6:71; 13:26), the apostle who betrayed Jesus to the priests and Romans for thirty pieces of silver (Mark 3:19; 14:10; Luke 6:16; Matt. 26:14–16, 47; John 18:3) but later returned the blood money and committed suicide (Matt. 27:3–5; Acts 1:18–20). The Gospel writers little understood Judas's motives, attributing them to simple greed or to the influence of Satan (Luke 22:3; John 6:71; 12:1–8; 13:11, 27–29).

Judas the Galilean A Jewish patriot from Galilee who led an unsuccessful insurrection against Rome in 6 C.E. (Acts 5:37).

Judas Maccabeus The third of five sons of the Judean priest Mattathias, leader of the successful Jewish uprising (c. 167–160 B.C.E.) against the Syrian king Antiochus IV. The epithet *Maccabeus* is believed to mean "the hammer," referring to Judas's effectiveness in striking blows for Jewish freedom. His story is told in 1 Maccabees.

Jude An Anglicized form of the name Judah or Judas; one of Jesus' "brothers" (or a close male relative) (Mark 6:3; Matt. 13:55), perhaps a son born to Joseph before his marriage to Mary. Jude is less prominent in the early Christian community than his brother James (Jude 1:1) and is the traditional author of the Epistle of Jude, though most scholars doubt this claim.

Judea The Greco-Roman designation for territory comprising the old kingdom of Judah. The name first occurs in Ezra 5:8, a reference to the "province of Judea." In the time of Jesus, Judea was the southernmost of the three divisions of the Roman province of western Palestine, the other two of which were Samaria and Galilee (Neh. 2:7, Luke 1:39; John 3:22; 11:7; Acts 1:1; Gal. 1:22).

Judgment, Day of A theological concept deriving from the ancient Hebrew belief that the Day of Yahweh would see Israel's triumph and the destruction of its enemies, a confidence the prophet Amos shattered by proclaiming that it would mean calamity for Israel, as for all who broke Yahweh's laws (Amos 5:18–20). This view prevails in Zephaniah 1:1–2; 3 and Malachi 3:1–6; 4:1–6. Isaiah also refers to "that day" of coming retribution (Isa. 11:10–16; 13:9, 13), and it is given an apocalyptic setting in Daniel 7:9–14, an idea developed in several apocryphal and pseudepigraphal books as well as in the New Testament (Matt. 25; Rev. 20).

Jupiter Latin name of the chief Roman deity, counterpart of the Greek Zeus, king of the Olympian gods for whom some ignorant men of Lycaonia mistook Paul's companion Barnabas (Acts 14:12–18).

kavod Yahweh's presence in the Jerusalem Temple; a Hebrew term commonly translated as "glory" or "splendor."

kerygma The act of publicly preaching the Christian message; a Greek term meaning "proclamation."

kingdom of God The rule of dominion of God in human affairs; the translation of the Greek *basileia tou theou.*

koinē The common Greek in which the New Testament is written. *Koinē* Greek was a later form of classical Greek and was the everyday language of the Hellenistic world.

L Abbreviation for special Lucan material, the scholarly term designating passages that appear only in the Gospel of Luke.

Laodicea A commercial city on the Lycus River in Asia Minor and one of the seven churches of Asia (Col. 4:15–16; Rev. 3:14–22).

Last Supper Jesus' final meal with his disciples. Depicted as a Passover observance in the Synoptic Gospels, it was the occasion at which Jesus instituted a "New Covenant" with his followers and inaugurated the ceremony of bread and wine (Holy Communion, or the Eucharist) (Mark 14:12–26; Matt. 26:20–29; Luke 22:14–23; 1 Cor. 11:23–26).

latter prophets The books of Isaiah, Jeremiah, Ezekiel, and the twelve minor prophets; also known as the "writing prophets."

Law The Torah ("teaching," "instruction"), or Pentateuch, the first five books of the Bible containing the legal material traditionally ascribed to Moses.

Lazarus

 1. The brother of Mary and Martha, a resident of Bethany whom Jesus resurrected (John 11:1–12:10).

 2. The beggar in Jesus' parable of rewards and punishments in the afterlife (Luke 16:20–25).

legend An unverifiable story or narrative cycle about a celebrated person or place of the past. Legends grow as the popular oral literature of a people. Their purpose is to provide not historical accuracy, but entertainment; they illustrate cherished beliefs, expectations, and moral principles. Scholars consider much of the material associated with the stories of the patriarchs, Moses, and prophets as legendary.

Levites The Israelite tribe descended from Levi, son of Jacob (Num. 3; 1 Chron. 5:27–6:81) that was given priestly duties in lieu of land holdings when Israel conquered Canaan (Deut. 18:1–8). According to a priestly writer, only descendants of Aaron were to be priests (Exod. 28:1; Num. 18:7); the Levites were regarded as their assistants and servants (Num. 18:2–7; 20–32). They served as priests of secondary rank and as temple functionaries during the postexilic period, which was dominated by a priestly hierarchy (1 Chron. 24–26). Other stories involving Levites appear in Judges 19–21 and Luke 10:32.

literary criticism A form of literary analysis that attempts to categorize or define literary types, the stages of composition from oral to written form, a text's characteristic rhetorical features, and the stages and degree of redaction (editing) of a text.

Logos A Greek term meaning both "word" and "reason," used by Greek philosophers to denote the rational principle that creates and informs the universe. Amplified by Philo Judaeus of Alexandria, Egypt, to represent the mediator between God and his material creation, as Wisdom had been in Proverbs 8:22–31, the term found its most famous expression in the prolog to the Fourth Gospel to denote the prehuman Jesus — "the Word became flesh and dwelt among us" (John 1:14).

Lord's Supper, the The ritual meal that Jesus held with his closest disciples the night before his death. Here he introduced the New Covenant and shared the bread and wine that symbolized his body and blood about to be sacrificed on behalf of humanity (Mark 14:22–25; Matt. 26:26–29; Luke 22:14–20). Paul first calls the Christian "love feast" (*agapē*), or Communion, by this name in 1 Corinthians 11:20, in which he describes the ceremony of the Eucharist (1 Cor. 11:23–26). John's version of the event (John 13:1–35) differs strikingly from that in the Synoptics.

Lucifer An epithet applied to the king of Babylon and later mistakenly taken as a name for Satan before his expulsion from heaven. The term means "light bearer" and refers to the planet Venus when it is the morning star; the English name *Lucifer* translates the Hebrew word for "shining one" (Isa. 14:12).

Luke A physician and traveling companion of Paul (Col. 4:14; Philem. 24; 2 Tim. 4:11) to whom a late second-century tradition ascribes the Gospel of Luke and the Book of Acts.

LXX A common abbreviation for the Septuagint, the Greek translation of the Hebrew Bible made in Alexandria, Egypt, during the last three centuries B.C.E.

Lycaonia A district in Asia Minor added to the Roman Empire around 25 B.C.E., where Paul endured persecution (Acts 13:50; 14:6–19).

Lycia A small province in southwestern Asia Minor, bordering the Mediterranean, which Paul visited on his missionary travels (Acts 21:1; 27:5–7).

Lystra A city in the Roman province of Galatia where Paul and Barnabas performed such successful healings that they were identified as Hermes and Zeus (Mercury and Jupiter) (Acts 14:6–19; 16:1; 18:23).

M Abbreviation for special Matthean material, the scholarly term designating passages found only in Matthew's Gospel.

Maccabees A name bestowed upon the family that won religious and political independence for the Jews from their Greek-Syrian oppressors. Judas, called Maccabeus ("the hammer"), son of the aged priest Mattathias, led his brothers and other faithful Jews against the armies of Antiochus IV (Epiphanes) (175–163 B.C.E.). The dynasty his brothers established was called Hasmonean (after an ancestor named Hasmon) and ruled Judea until 63 B.C.E., when the Romans occupied Palestine.

Macedonia The large mountainous district in northern Greece ruled by Philip of Macedon (359–336 B.C.E.). Philp's son Alexander the Great (356–323 B.C.E.) extended the Macedonian Empire over the entire ancient Near East as far as western India, incorporating all of the earlier Persian Empire. Conquered by Rome (168 B.C.E.) and annexed as a province (146 B.C.E.), Macedonia was the first part of Europe to be Christianized (Acts 16:10–17:9; 18:5; 19:29; 20:1–3).

Magdala A town on the northwest shore of the Sea of Galilee, home of Mary Magdalene ("of Magdala") (Matt. 15:39).

Magnificat Mary's beautiful hymn of praise, recorded in Luke 1:46–55.

Marcion An early Gnostic Christian who attempted to establish a Christian Scripture distinct from the Hebrew Bible, which he rejected. Marcion's canon included only Luke's Gospel and the Pauline letters, the only documents he believed to reflect true belief. The church at Rome expelled him as a heretic about 140 C.E.

Mark (John Mark) Son of Mary, a Jerusalem Jew who accompanied Barnabas (his cousin) and Paul on an early missionary journey (Acts 12:12–25; 13:5, 13; 15:37). For reasons unstated, he left them at Perga (Acts 13:13), which so angered Paul that he refused to allow Mark to join a later preaching campaign (Acts 15:38), though he and the apostle were later reconciled (Col. 4:10; Philem. 24). Some identify Mark with the youth who ran away naked at the time of Jesus' arrest (Mark 14:51–52). An early tradition ascribes authorship of the Gospel of Mark to him, as Papias and Eusebius (*History* 3.39.15) testify.

Martha The sister of Mary and Lazarus of Bethany (Luke 10:38–42; John 11:1–12:2), whose home Jesus frequently visited.

martyr A "witness" for Christ who prefers to die rather than relinquish his faith. Stephen, at whose stoning Saul of Tarsus assisted, is known as the first Christian martyr (Acts 22:20; Rev. 2:13; 17:6).

Mary From the Latin and Greek *Maria*, from the Hebrew *Miryam* (Miriam), a name borne by six women in the New Testament:

1. Mary the Virgin, wife of Joseph and mother of Jesus, who, the angel Gabriel informed her, was conceived by the Holy Spirit (Matt. 1:18–25; Luke 1:26–56; 2:21). From her home in Nazareth, Mary traveled to Bethlehem, where her first son was born (Luke 2:1–18), and thence into Egypt to escape Herod's persecution (Matt 2:1–18), returning to Nazareth in Galilee after Herod's death (4 B.C.E.) (Matt 2:19–23). She had one sister (John 18:25), probably Salome, wife of Zebedee, mother of James and John (Matt. 27:56), and was also related to Elizabeth, mother of John the Baptist (Luke 1:36). Gabriel's Annunciation of the Messiah's birth occurs in Luke 1:26–36; the Magnificat, in Luke 1:46–55. Mary visited Jerusalem annually for the Passover (Luke 2:41) and reprimanded the twelve-year-old Jesus for lingering behind at the Temple (Luke 2:46–50). She may have been among family members convinced that Jesus' early preaching showed mental instability (Mark 3:21) and apparently humored his requests during the wedding celebration at Cana (John 2:1–12). Although Jesus showed his mother little deference during his ministry (Mark 3:31–35; Luke 11:27–28; John 2:4), on the cross he entrusted her care to his Beloved Disciple (John 19:25–27). Mary last appears in the upper room praying with the disciples just before Pentecost (Acts 1:13–14).

2. Mary Magdalene, a woman from Magdala, from whom Jesus cast out seven demons (Luke 8:1–2) and who became his follower. A common tradition asserts that she had been a prostitute whom Jesus had rescued from her former life (Mark 16:9; Luke 7:37–50), but this is by no means certain. She was present at the Crucifixion (Mark 15:40; Matt. 15:47), visited Jesus' tomb early Sunday morning (Matt. 28:1; Mark 16:1; Luke 24:10; John 20:1), and was one of the first to see the risen Jesus (Matt. 28:9; Mark 16:9; John 20:11–18), although the male disciples refused to believe her (Luke 24:9–11).

3. Mary, sister of Lazarus and Martha, whose home at Bethany Jesus frequented (Luke 10:38–42; John 11:1–12:8).

4. Mary, wife of Cleophas, mother of James the Less and Joseph (Joses), was a witness to Jesus' crucifixion, burial, and resurrection (Matt. 27:56–61; 28:1; Mark 15:40, 47; 16:1; Luke 24:10; John 19:25).

5. Mary, sister of Barnabas and mother of John Mark, provided her Jerusalem home as a meeting place for the disciples (Acts 12:12; Col. 4:10).

6. An otherwise anonymous Mary mentioned in Romans 16:6.

Masada A stronghold built by Herod the Great on a fortified plateau 800 feet above the Dead Sea. Masada was captured by Zealots during the revolt against Rome (66 C.E.). When the attacking Romans finally entered Masada (73 C.E.), they found only 7 women and children alive, 953 others having died in a suicide pact.

Masoretes Medieval Jewish scholars who copied, annotated, and added vowels to the text of the Hebrew Bible; from a Hebrew term meaning "tradition."

Masoretic Text (MT) The standard text of the Hebrew Bible as given final form by the Masoretes in the seventh through eleventh centuries C.E.

Mattathias A Jewish priest who, with his sons John, Simon, Judas, Eleazar, and Jonathan, led a revolt against the oppressions of Antiochus IV (about 168–167 B.C.E.) (1 Macc. 2:1–70).

Matthew A Jewish tax collector working for Rome whom Jesus called to be one of the Twelve Apostles (Matt. 9:9; 10:3; Mark 2:13–17; 3:18; Luke 5:27–32; 6:15; Acts 1:13). Matthew (also called Levi) is the traditional author of the Gospel of Matthew, an attribution contested by most scholars.

Matthias The early Christian elected to replace Judas among the Twelve (Acts 1:23–26). The name means "gift of Yahweh."

Megiddo An old Palestinian city overlooking the Valley of Jezreel (Plain of Esdraelon), the site of numerous decisive battles in biblical history (Josh. 12:21; 2 Kings 9:27; 23:29–30; 2 Chron. 35:20–24; Zech. 12:11) and symbolic location of the climactic War of Armageddon (Rev. 16:16).

Melchizedek The king-priest of Canaanite Salem (probably the site of Jerusalem) to whom Abraham paid a tenth of his spoils of war (Gen. 14:17–20); cited by the author of Hebrews as foreshadowing Jesus Christ (Ps. 110:4; Heb. 5:6–10; 7:1–25).

Mercury Roman name for Hermes, Greek god of persuasion, business, and trade and messenger of Zeus, for whom Paul was mistaken in Lystra (Acts 14:12).

Mesopotamia The territory between the Euphrates and Tigris rivers at the head of the Persian Gulf (modern Iraq); cradle of the Sumerian, Akkadian, Assyrian, and Neo-Babylonian civilizations (Gen. 24:10; Judg. 3:8–10; 1 Chron. 19:6; Acts 2:9; 7:2).

messiah A Hebrew term meaning "anointed one," designating a king or priest of ancient Israel who had been consecrated by having his head smeared with holy oil, marking him as set apart for a special role. King David is the model of Yahweh's anointed ruler; all his descendants who ruled over Judah were Yahweh's messiahs (2 Sam. 7:1–29; Ps. 89:3–45). After the end of the Davidic monarchy (587 B.C.E.), various Hebrew prophets applied the promises made to the Davidic dynasty to a future heir who would eventually restore the kingdom of David (Pss. 2; 110; Dan. 9:25–26). Christians believe that Jesus of Nazareth was the promised Messiah (Christ) as expressed in Peter's "confession" (Matt. 16:13–20; Mark 8:27–30; Luke 9:18–22; etc.).

messianic secret The phrase that the German scholar William Wrede used to describe a major theme in Mark's Gospel—Jesus' "hidden messiahship," particularly his oft-repeated injunction to persons he heals to keep quiet about his miraculous actions.

Michael The angel whom the Book of Daniel represents as being the spirit prince, guardian, and protector of Israel (Dan. 10:13, 21; 12:1). Jude 9 depicts him as an archangel fighting with Satan for Moses' body. In Revelation 12:7, he leads the war against the Dragon (Satan) and casts him from heaven. His name means "who is like God?"

midrash A commentary on or interpretation of Hebrew Scripture. Collections of such haggadic or halakic expositions of the significance of the biblical text are called midrashim; from a Hebrew word meaning "to search out."

millennium A 1000-year epoch, particularly the period of Christ's universal reign (Rev. 20:1–8) during which Satan will be chained and the dead resurrected.

Mishnah A collection of Pharisaic oral interpretations (Halakah) of the Torah compiled and edited by Rabbi Judah ha-Nasi about 200 C.E.; from the Hebrew verb "to repeat."

Mithras Persian savior god who killed a celestial bull and was worshiped in mystery cults throughout the Roman Empire. A serious rival to early Christianity, Mithraism was limited by the fact that only men were initiated into the religion.

money An imprinted metal generally accepted as a medium of exchange. In early biblical times, before coins were first minted, value in business transactions was determined by weighing quantities of precious metals. In the early period, the term *shekel* refers not to a coin, but to a certain weight of silver. The use of

coinage was first introduced in Palestine during the Persian era when the daric or dram, named for Darius I (521–486 B.C.E.), appeared. After Alexander's conquest of Persia, Greek coinage became the standard. The silver drachma (Luke 15:8), a coin of small value, was equivalent to the Roman denarius. The lepton was a small copper coin (Luke 12:59; 21:2), the least valuable in circulation, and one of the denominations coined by the Jews for use in the Temple. This was the "widow's mite" (Mark 12:42). The talent (Matt. 18:24) was not a coin, but money of account; it was divided into smaller units—60 minas or 6000 drachmas—and was worth at least $2000. The denarius (Matt. 18:28), the basic unit in the New Testament, was a silver coin, the day's wage of a rural laborer (Matt. 20:20).

monotheism Belief in the existence of one God, a major theme of Second Isaiah (Isa. 40–46).

Mosaic Covenant In the Hebrew Bible, the pact between Yahweh and Israel mediated by Moses (Exod. 19–24). According to the terms of the Mosaic concept, Yahweh's support of Israel was dependent on the people's obedience to his will, expressed in the laws and principles of the Torah (Deut. 28–29).

Moses The great Hebrew lawgiver, religious reformer, founder of the Israelite nation, and central figure of the Pentateuch. Moses was the son of Amram (a Levite) and Jochebed and brother to Aaron and Miriam (Exod. 2:1–4). Adopted by pharaoh's daughter and raised at the Egyptian royal court (Exod. 2:5–10; Acts 7:22), he fled Egypt after killing an Egyptian bully and settled in Midian among the Kenites, where he married Jethro's daughter Zipporah (Exod. 2:11–22). After an encounter with Yahweh at the burning bush (Exod. 3:1–4:17), he returned to Egypt (Exod. 4:18–31), interceded with pharaoh during the ten plagues (Exod. 5–11), and led the Israelites across the Red Sea (Exod. 14–15) to Sinai. There, he mediated the Law covenant between Yahweh and Israel (Exod. 19–31) and pleaded for his people (Exod. 33–34; Num. 14) and directed their migration through the Sinai wilderness (Num. 11–14; 20–25). He appointed Joshua as his successor (Num. 27:18–23) and died in Moab (Deut. 34:1–7; Acts 7:20–44). He is also credited with building the Tabernacle (Exod. 35–40), organizing Israel (Exod. 18:13–26), restating Israel's Law code shortly before his death (Deut. 1–31), and composing several hymns (Deut. 32–33; Ps. 90). Although Moses' name became synonymous with the covenant concept and Israel's traditions (Pss. 77:20; 103:7; 105:26; 106:23; Isa. 63:12; Mic. 6:4; Matt. 17:3; Luke 16:29; John 1:17; 3:14; 5:46; 7:19; 9:29; Acts 3:22; 21:21), modern scholars have concluded that much of the material in the Pentateuch dates from post-Mosaic times. Moses also figured prominently in Paul's theology (Rom. 5:14; 10:5; 1 Cor. 10:2; 2 Cor. 3:7; 3:15) and that of the author of Hebrews (Heb. 3:2; 7:14; 9:19; 11:23). Jude preserves an old tradition, probably derived from the pseudepigraphal Assumption of Moses, that Satan disputed the angel Michael for Moses' body (Jude 9; Rev. 15:3).

mystery Derived from a Greek work meaning "to initiate" or "to shut the eyes or mouth," probably referring to the secrets of Hellenistic "mystery religions," and used variously in the New Testament. Jesus speaks at least once of the "mystery" of the kingdom (Matt. 13:11; Mark 4:11; Luke 8:10), but Paul employs the term frequently as if the profounder aspects of Christianity were a religious secret into which the Spirit-directed believer becomes initiated (Rom. 11:5; 16:25; 1 Cor. 2:7; 4:1; 13:2; 14:2; 15:51; Col. 1:26; 2:2; 4:3; 2 Thess. 2:7, 1 Tim. 3:9; 3:16; see also Rev. 1:20; 10:7; 17:5–7).

myth A narrative expressing a profound psychological or religious truth that cannot be verified by historical inquiry or other scientific means; from the Greek *mythos,* meaning a "story." When scholars speak of the "myth of Eden," for example, it is not to denigrate the tale's historicity, but to emphasize the Eden story's archetypal expression of humanity's sense of alienation from the spirit world. Myths typically feature stories about gods and goddesses who represent natural or psychological forces that deeply influence humans but that they cannot control. The psychologist Carl Jung interpreted myth as humanity's inherited concept of a primeval event that persists in the unconscious mind and finds expression through repeated reenactments in ritual worship and other cultic practices. Israel's covenant renewal ceremonies and retellings of Yahweh's saving acts during the Exodus are examples of such cultic myths.

mythology A system or cycle of myths, such as those featuring the deities of ancient Greece or Rome. Once the embodiment of living religious beliefs, Greco-Roman and other mythologies are now seen as archetypal symbols that give philosophic meaning to universal human experiences. Mythologies are thus "falsehoods" only in the narrowest literal sense. They are probably akin to dreams in revealing persistent images and attitudes hidden in the human subconscious.

Nag Hammadi The Egyptian village where a collection of early Christian and Gnostic books, including the Gospel of Thomas, was discovered in 1945.

narrative criticism A critical methodology applied to analyzing a literary narrative, including its structure, the point of view from which it is told, the author's implied attitude toward his characters, and the work's assumed audience.

Nazarenes A name applied to early Christians (Acts 24:5).

Nazareth A town in Lower Galilee above the Plain of Esdraelon (Megiddo) where Jesus spent his youth and began his ministry (Matt. 2:23; Luke 1:26; 4:16; John 1:46).

Nero (Nero Claudius Caesar Augustus Germanicus) Emperor of Rome (54–68 C.E.), the Caesar by whom Paul wished to be tried in Acts 25:11 and under whose persecution Paul was probably beheaded (64–65 C.E.). A first-century superstition held that Nero, slain during a palace revolt, would return at the head of an army. Regarded by some Christians as the anti-Christ, Nero's reappearance is apparently suggested in Revelation 13:4–18.

Nicodemus A leading Pharisee and member of the Sanhedrin (John 3:1; 7:50; 19:39) who discussed spiritual rebirth with Jesus (John 3:1–21), visited him by night and defended him against other Pharisees (John 7:45–52), and, with Joseph of Arimathea, helped entomb his body (John 19:38–42).

Olives, Mount of (Olivet) A mile-long limestone ridge with several distinct summits paralleling the eastern section of Jerusalem, from which it is separated by the narrow Kidron Valley. Here David fled during Absalom's rebellion (2 Sam. 15:30–32), and according to Zechariah 14:3–5, here Yahweh will stand at the final eschatological battle, when the mountain will be torn asunder from east to west. From its summit, with its panoramic view of Jerusalem, Jesus delivered his eschatological judgment on the city that had rejected him (Matt. 24–25). He often retreated to its shady groves in the evening (John 7:53; 8:1), including the night before his death (Matt. 26:30–56; Mark 14:26; Luke 22:39; see also Matt. 21:1; Mark 11:1; Luke 19:29; Acts 1:12).

omega The last letter in the Greek alphabet, used with alpha (the first letter) as a symbol of the eternity of God (Rev. 1:8; 21:6) and Jesus (Rev. 1:17; 22:13), probably echoing Isaiah's description of Yahweh as "the first and the last" (Isa. 44:6; 48:12).

Onesimus The runaway slave of Philemon of Colossae whom Paul converted to Christianity and reconciled to his master (Philem. 8–21; Col. 4: 7–9).

oracle

1. A divine message or utterance (Rom. 3:2; Heb. 5:12; 1 Pet. 4:11) or the person through whom it is conveyed (Acts 7:38).

2. An authoritative communication, such as that from a wise person (Prov. 31:1; 2 Sam. 16:23).

3. The inner sanctum of the Jerusalem Temple (1 Kings 6:5–6; 7:49; 8:6–8; Ps. 28:2).

4. The supposedly inspired words of a priest or priestess at such shrines as Delphi in ancient Greece and Cumae in Italy.

oral tradition Material passed from generation to generation by word of mouth before finding written form. Scholars believe that much of Israel's early history, customs, and beliefs about its origins, such as the stories about the patriarchs and Moses in the Pentateuch, were so transmitted before an anonymous writer first committed them to writing about 950 B.C.E.

original sin The concept that the entire human race has inherited from the first man (Adam) a tendency to sin. Some theologians, such as Augustine and Calvin, argued that humanity is born totally corrupt. The doctrine is based partly on an extremist interpretation of Romans 5:12.

Palestine A strip of land bordering the eastern Mediterranean Sea, lying south of Syria, north of the Sinai Peninsula, and west of the Arabian Desert. During the patriarchal period, it was known as Canaan (Gen. 12:6–7; 15:18–21). Named for the Philistines, it was first called Palestine by the Greek historian Herodotus about 450 B.C.E.

parable A short fictional narrative that compares something familiar to an unexpected spiritual value; from the Greek *parabole,* meaning "a placing beside," "a comparison." In the Synoptic Gospels, Jesus typically uses a commonplace object or action to illustrate a religious principle (Matt. 13:3–53; 22:1; 24:32; Mark 4:2–3; 13:28; Luke 8:4–18; 13:18–21; 21:29). A recurrent tradition held that Jesus used parables to prevent most of his hearers from understanding his message (Matt. 13:10–15; Mark 4:10–12; Luke 8:9–10). Famous Hebrew Bible parables or fables include Nathan's (2 Sam. 12:1–14), Isaiah's (Isa. 5:1–7), Jotham's (Judg. 9:7–21), Jehoash's (2 Kings 14:8–10), and Ezekiel's (Ezek. 17:22–24; 24:1–14), the last two of which are allegories.

Paraclete A Greek term meaning "an advocate" or "intercessor summoned to aid," used to denote the Holy Spirit in the Gospel of John. *Paraclete* is variously translated as "Comforter," "Helper," "Advocate," or "Spirit or Truth" (John 7:39; 14:12, 16–18; 15:26; 16:7; see also 1 John 2:1).

paradise Literally, a "park" or walled garden, the name applied to Eden (Gen. 2:8–17) and in post–Hebrew Bible times to the abode of the righteous dead, of which the lower part housed souls awaiting resurrection and the higher was the permanent home of the just. It is possible that Jesus referred to the lower paradise in his words to the thief on the cross (Luke 23:43), Paul's reference to being "caught up" into paradise may refer to the third of the seven heavens postulated in later Jewish eschatology (as in the books of Enoch) (2 Cor. 12:2–5). John's vision of the tree of life in "the garden of God" (Rev. 2:7; 22:1–3) depicts an earthlike heaven.

Parousia The Second Coming or appearance of Christ, commonly regarded as his return to judge the world, punish the wicked, and redeem the saved. The term is Greek and means "being by" or "being near." The Parousia is a major concept in apocalyptic Christianity (Matt. 24–25; Mark 13; Luke 21; 1 and 2 Thess.; 2 Pet. 2–3; Rev.); but see also John 14:25–29, which emphasizes Jesus' continued spiritual presence rather than an eschatological apparition.

Passion The term commonly used to denote Jesus' suffering and death (Acts 1:3).

Passover An annual Jewish observance commemorating Israel's last night of bondage in Egypt when the Angel of Death "passed over" Israelite homes marked with the blood of a sacrificial lamb to destroy the firstborn of every Egyptian household (Exod. 12:1–51). Beginning the seven-day Feast of Unleavened Bread, it is a ritual meal eaten on Nisan 14 (March–April) and includes roast lamb, unleavened bread, and bitter herbs (Exod. 12:15–20; 13:3–10; Lev. 23:5; Num. 9:5; 28:16; Deut. 16:1). Passover was scrupulously observed by Israel's great leaders, including Joshua (Josh. 5:10), Hezekiah (2 Chron. 30:1), Josiah (2 Kings 23:21–23, 2 Chron. 35:1–18), and the returned exiles (Ezra 6:19), as well as by Jesus and his disciples (Matt. 26:2, 17–29; Mark 14:1–16; Luke 22:1–13; John 13:1; 18:39). According to the Synoptics, Jesus' Last Supper with the Twelve was a Passover celebration (Matt. 26; Mark 14; Luke 22) and the model for Christian Communion (the Eucharist) (1 Cor. 11:17–27).

Pastoral Epistles The New Testament books of 1 and 2 Timothy and Titus, presumably written by the apostle Paul to two of his fellow ministers (pastors) but believed by modern scholars to have been composed by an anonymous disciple of Pauline thought living in the mid-second century C.E.

Patmos A small Aegean island off the coast of western Asia Minor (Turkey) where John, author of Revelation, was exiled by the emperor Domitian about 95 C.E. (Rev. 1:9).

Paul The most influential apostle and missionary of the mid-first-century church and author of seven or nine New Testament letters. Saul of Tarsus was born in the capital of the Asia Minor province of Cilicia (Acts 9:11; 21:39; 22:3) into a family of Pharisees (Acts 23:6) of the tribe of Benjamin (Phil 3:5) and had both Roman and Taurean citizenship (Acts 22:28). Suddenly converted to Christianity after persecuting early Christians (Acts 7:55–8:3; 9:1–30; 22:1–21; 26:1–23; 1 Cor. 9:1; 15:8; Gal. 1:11–24; Eph. 3:3; Phil. 3:12), he undertook at least three international missionary tours, presenting defenses of the new faith before Jewish and Gentile authorities (Acts 13:1–28:31). His emphasis on the insufficiency of the Mosaic Law for salvation (Gal. 3–5; Rom. 4–11) and the superiority of faith to Law (Rom. 4–11) and his insistence that Gentiles be admitted to the church without observing Jewish legal restrictions (Gal. 2; 5; Rom. 7–8) were decisive in determining the future development of the new religion. He was probably martyred in Rome about 64–65 C.E.

Pella A Gentile city in Palestine east of the Jordan River, to which tradition says that Jesus' family and other Jewish Christians fled during the Jewish revolt against Rome (66–70 C.E.). Before this time, Jerusalem had been the center of the Palestinian-Jewish Christian church. References in Acts and Paul's letters indicate that Palestinian Christian teachings differed significantly from those Paul stressed in the churches of Gentile Christianity. No writings from the Palestinian Christians survive, so the fate of the Pella community is not known.

Pentateuch The first five books of the Hebrew Bible, the Torah; from a Greek work meaning "five scrolls."

Pentecost

1. Also known as the Feast of Weeks (Exod. 34:22; Deut. 16:10), the Feast of Harvest (Exod. 23:16), and the Day of the First Fruits (Num. 28:26), a one-day celebration held fifty days after Passover at the juncture of May and June.

2. The occasion of the outpouring of the Holy Spirit on early Christians assembled in Jerusalem (Acts 2:1–41), regarded as the spiritual baptism of the church.

Pergamum A major Hellenistic city in western Asia Minor (modern Bergama in west Anatolian Turkey), site of a magnificent temple of Zeus, which some commentators believe is referred to as "Satan's Throne" in Revelation 2:13. Pergamum is one of the seven churches addressed by the Revelator (Rev. 1:11; 2:12–17).

pericope In form criticism, a literary unit (a saying, anecdote, parable, or brief narrative) that forms a complete entity in itself and is attached to its context by later editorial commentary. Many of Jesus' pronouncements probably circulated independently as pericopes before they were incorporated into the written Gospel records.

pesher In Hebrew, an analysis or interpretation of Scripture. The term is applied to the commentaries (*persherim*) found among the Dead Sea Scrolls.

Peter The most prominent of Jesus' twelve chief disciples, also known as Simon (probably his surname), Simeon (Symeon), and Cephas (the Aramaic equivalent of *petros,* meaning "rock" or "stone") (John 1:40–42). The son of Jonas or John (Matt. 16:17; John 1:42; 21:15–17), brother of the apostle Andrew, and a native of Bethsaida, a fishing village on the Sea of Galilee (John 1:44), he was called by Jesus to be "a fisher of men" (Matt. 4:18–20; Mark 1:16–18; Luke 5:1–11). The first to recognize Jesus as the Messiah (Matt. 16:13–20; Mark 8:27–30; Luke 9:18–22), Peter later denied him three times (Matt. 26:69–75; Mark 14:66–72; Luke 22:54–62; John 18:15–18). Commanded to "feed [the resurrected Jesus'] sheep" (John 21:15–19), Peter became a leader of the Jerusalem church (Acts 1:15–26; 2:14–42; 15:6–12) and miracle worker (Acts 3:1–10). He was instrumental in bringing the first Gentiles into the church (Acts 10–11), although Paul regarded him as a conservative obstacle to this movement (Gal. 2:11–14). He appeared before the Sanhedrin (Acts 4:1–12) and was miraculously rescued from at least one imprisonment (Acts 5:17–42; 12:1–19). A married man (Matt. 8:14; Mark 1:30; Luke 4:8; 1 Cor. 9:5), Peter was to be the "rock" on which Jesus' church was built (Matt. 16:16–20). Although some scholars regard him as the source of 1 Peter, virtually all experts deny Petrine authorship to the second epistle bearing his name. He was martyred under Nero about 64–65 C.E.

Pharisees A leading religious movement or sect in Judaism during the last two centuries B.C.E. and the first two centuries C.E. The Pharisees were probably descendants of the Hasidim who opposed Antiochus IV's attempts to destroy the Mosaic faith. Their name may derive from the Hebrew *perisha* (separated) because their rigorous observance of the Law bred a separatist view toward common life. Although the New Testament typically presents them as Jesus' opponents, their views on resurrection and the afterlife anticipated Christian teachings. The "seven woes" against the Pharisees appear in Matthew 23:13–32. Paul was a Pharisee (Acts 23:6; 26:5; Phil. 3:5).

Philadelphia A city in Lydia (modern Turkey) about twenty-eight miles from Sardis, one of the seven churches addressed in Revelation 3:7–13.

Philemon A citizen of Colossae whose runaway slave, Onesimus, Paul converted to Christianity (Philem. 5, 10, 16, 19).

Philip

1. King of Macedonia (359–336 B.C.E.), father of Alexander the Great (1 Macc. 1:1; 6:2).

2. One of the Twelve, a man of Bethsaida in Galilee (Matt. 10:3; Mark 3:18; Luke 6:14; John 1:43–49; 12:21–22; 14:8–9; Acts 1:12–14).

3. An evangelist of the Jerusalem church who was an administrator (Acts 6:1–6) and preacher (Acts 8:4–8), the converter of Simon the sorcerer (Acts 8:9–13) and of an Ethiopian eunuch (Acts 8:26–39). Paul visited him at Caesarea (Acts 21:8–15).

4. A son of Herod the Great and Palestinian tetrarch (4 B.C.E.–34 C.E.) (Luke 3:1).

Philippi A city of eastern Macedonia, the first European center to receive the Christian message (Acts 16:10–40). Philippi became the apostle Paul's favorite church (Acts 20:6; Phil. 4:16; 2 Cor. 11:9); it is the one to which his letter to the Philippians is addressed.

Philo Judaeus The most influential philosopher of Hellenistic Judaism. Philo was a Greek-educated Jew living in Alexandria, Egypt (about 20 B.C.E.–50 C.E.), who promoted a method of interpreting the Hebrew Bible allegorically (which may have influenced Paul in such passages as 1 Corinthians 10:4 and Galatians 4:24, as well as the authors of the Fourth Gospel and Hebrews). His doctrine of the Logos (the divine creative Word) shaped the prolog to the Gospel of John.

Phoebe A servant or deacon of the church at Cenchrae, a port of Corinth, whose good works Paul commends in Romans 16:1–2.

phylacteries One of two small leather pouches containing copies of four scriptural passages (Exod. 13:1–10, 11–16; Deut. 6:4–9; 11:13–21), worn on the left arm and forehead by Jewish men during weekday prayers (Exod. 13:9, 16; Deut. 6:8; 11:18; Matt. 23:5).

Pilate, Pontius The Roman prefect (also called a procurator) of Judea (26–36 C.E.) who presided at Jesus' trial for sedition against Rome and sentenced him to be crucified (Matt. 27:1–26; Mark 15:1–15; Luke 3:1; 13:1; 23:1–25; John 18:28–19:22; Acts 3:13; 13:28; 1 Tim. 6:13).

polytheism Belief in more than one god, the most common form of religion in the ancient world.

Pontius Pilate (see **Pilate, Pontius**).

predestination The act of foreordaining or predetermining by divine decree the ultimate destiny of an individual or a people, a theological doctrine asserting the absolute, irresistible power and control of God. In the biblical tradition, particularly in apocalyptic literature, both divine predetermination of events and the individual's freedom of choice seem to operate simultaneously.

Prisca (Priscilla) The wife of Aquila and a leading member of the early church (Acts 18:18; Rom. 16:3; 2 Tim. 4:19).

proconsul A Roman governor or administrator of a province or territory, such as Gallio, proconsul of Achaia, before whom Paul appeared (Acts 18:12).

procurator The Roman title of the governor of a region before it became an administrative province. During the reigns of Augustus and Tiberius, Judea was governed by a prefect, the most famous of whom was Pontius Pilate. The office was upgraded to the level of procurator under Claudius.

prophet One who preaches or proclaims the word or will of his or her deity (Amos 3:7–8; Deut. 18:9–22). A true prophet in Israel was regarded as divinely inspired.

Prophets The second major division of the Hebrew Bible, from Joshua through the twelve minor prophets and including the books of Samuel and Kings, Isaiah, Jeremiah, and Ezekiel.

proverb A brief saying that memorably expresses a familiar or useful bit of folk wisdom, usually of a practical or prudential nature.

providence The quasireligious concept of God as a force sustaining and guiding human destiny. It assumes that events occur as part of a divine plan or purpose working for the ultimate triumph of good.

psalm A sacred song or poem used in praise or worship of the Deity, particularly those in the book of Psalms.

Pseudepigrapha

1. Literally, books falsely ascribed to eminent biblical figures of the past, such as Enoch, Noah, Moses, or Isaiah.

2. A collection of religious books outside the Hebrew Bible canon or Apocrypha that were composed in Hebrew, Aramaic, or Greek from about 200 B.C.E. to 200 C.E.

pseudonymity A literary practice, common among Hellenistic-Jewish and early Christian writers of writing or publishing a book in the name of a famous religious figure of the past. Thus, an anonymous author of about 168 B.C.E. ascribed his work to Daniel, who supposedly lived during the 500s B.C.E. The pastoral Epistles, 2 Peter, James, and Jude are thought to be pseudonymous books written in the mid-second century C.E. but attributed to eminent disciples connected with the first-century Jerusalem church.

Ptolemaic dynasty The royal dynasty that was established by Alexander's general Ptolemy I and that ruled Egypt from about 323 to 30 B.C.E. Ptolemaic Egypt controlled Palestine until about 200 B.C.E.

Ptolemy

1. Ptolemy I (323–285 B.C.E.), a Macedonian general who assumed rulership of Egypt after the death of Alexander the Great. The Ptolemaic dynasty controlled Egypt and its dominions until 30 B.C.E., when the Romans came to power.

2. Ptolemy II (285–246 B.C.E.), who supposedly authorized the translation of the Hebrew Bible into Greek (the Septuagint).

publican In the New Testament, petty-tax collectors for Rome, despised by the Jews from whom they typically extorted money (Matt. 9:10–13; 18:17; 21:31). Jesus dined with these "sinners" (Matt. 9:9–13 and called one, Levi (Matthew), to apostleship (Matt. 9:(9–13; Luke 5:27–31). He also painted a publican as more religiously acceptable than a Pharisee (Luke 18:9–14).

Q An abbreviation for *Quelle*, the German term for "source," a hypothetical document that many scholars believe contained a collection of Jesus' sayings (*logia*). The theory of its existence was formed to explain material common to both Matthew and Luke but absent from Mark's Gospel. It is assumed that Matthew and Luke drew on a single source (Q), assembled about 50–70 C.E., for this shared material.

Qumran Ruins of a community (probably of Essenes) near the northwest corner of the Dead Sea, where the Dead Sea Scrolls were produced.

rabbi A Jewish title (meaning "master" or "teacher") given to scholars learned in the Torah. Jesus was frequently addressed by this title (Matt. 23:8; 26:25, 49; Mark 8:5; 10:51; 11:21; 14:45; John 1:38, 49; 3:2; 4:31; 6:25; 9:2; 11:8 ; 20:16), as was John the Baptist (John 3:26), although Jesus supposedly forbade his followers to be so called (Matt. 23:7–8).

redaction criticism A method of analyzing written texts to define the purpose and literary procedures of editors (redactors) who compile and edit older documents, transforming shorter works into longer ones, as did the redactors who collected and ordered independent traditions about Jesus to compose the present Gospels.

resurrection The returning of the dead to life, a late Hebrew Bible concept (Isa. 26:19; Dan. 12:2–3, 13) that first became prevalent in Judaism during the time of the Maccabees (after 168 B.C.E.) and became a part of the Pharisees' doctrine. Like the prophets Elijah and Elisha (1 Kings 17:17–24; 2 Kings 4:18–37), Jesus performed several temporal resuscitations: of the widow of Nain's son (Luke 7:11–17), the daughter of Jairus (Mark 5:21–43), and Lazarus (John 11:1–44). Unlike these personages, however, Jesus ascended to heaven after his own resurrection (Acts 1:7–8). Paul gives the fullest discussion of the Resurrection in the New Testament (1 Thess. 4; 1 Cor. 15), although he leaves many questions unanswered (see also Rev. 20:11–15).

Roman Empire The international, interracial government centered in Rome, Italy, that conquered and administered the entire Mediterranean region from Gaul (France and southern Germany) in the northwest to Egypt in the southeast. The empire ruled the Jewish state in Palestine from 63 B.C.E. until Hadrian's destruction of Jerusalem during the second Jewish War (132–135 C.E.).

Sabbath The seventh day of the Jewish week, sacred to Yahweh and dedicated to rest and worship. Enjoined upon Israel as a sign of Yahweh's covenant (Exod. 20:8–11; 23:12; 31:12–17; Lev. 23:3; 24:1–9; Deut. 5:12–15) and a memorial of Yahweh's repose after six days of creation, the Sabbath was strictly observed by leaders of the returned exiles (Neh. 13:15–22; Isa. 56:2–6; Ezek. 46:1–7). Jesus was frequently criticized for his liberal attitude toward the Sabbath, which he contended was made for humanity's benefit (Matt. 12:1–12; Mark 2:23–28; Luke 6:1–9; John 5:18).

sacrifice In ancient religion, something precious—usually an unblemished animal, fruit, or grain—offered to a god and thereby made sacred. The Mosaic Law required the regular ritual slaughter of sacrificial animals and birds (Lev. 1:1–7:38; 16:1–17:14; Deut. 15:19–23; etc.).

Sadducees An ultraconservative Jewish sect of the first century B.C.E. and first century C.E. composed largely of wealthy and politically influential landowners. Unlike the Pharisees, the Sadducees recognized only the Torah as binding and rejected the Prophets and the Writings, denying both resurrection and a judgment in the afterlife. An aristocracy controlling the priesthood and Temple, they cooperated with Roman rule of Palestine, a collusion that made them unpopular with the common people (Matt. 3:7; 16:1; 22:23; Mark 12:18; Luke 20:27; Acts 4:1; 5:17; 23:6).

saints Holy ones, persons of exceptional virtue and sanctity, believers outstandingly faithful despite persecution (Dan. 7:18–21; 8:13; Matt. 27:52; Acts 9:13; 26:10; Rom. 8:27; 1 Cor. 6:2; 1 Thess. 3:13; 2 Thess. 1:10; Heb. 13:24; Rev. 5:8; 13:7–10; 17:6; 20:9).

Salome

1. Daughter of Herodias and Herod (son of Herod the Great) and niece of Herod Antipas, before whom she danced to secure the head of John the Baptist (Matt. 14:3–11; Mark 6:17–28). Anonymous in the New Testament, her name is given by Josephus (*Antiquities* 18.5.4).

2. A woman present at Jesus' crucifixion (Matt. 27:56; Mark 15:40) and at the empty tomb (Mark 16:1).

Samaria Capital of the northern kingdom (Israel), Samaria was founded by Omri (c. 876–869 B.C.E.) (1 Kings 16:24–25) and included a temple and altar of Baal (1 Kings 16:32). The Assyrians destroyed it in 721 B.C.E. (2 Kings 17), a fate the prophets warned awaited Jerusalem (Isa. 8:4; 10:9–11; Mic. 1:1–7).

Samaritans Inhabitants of the city or territory of Samaria, the central region of Palestine lying west of the Jordan River. According to a probably biased southern account in 2 Kings 17, the Samaritans were regarded by orthodox Jews as descendants of foreigners who had intermarried with survivors of the north-

ern kingdom's fall to Assyria (721 B.C.E.). Separated from the rest of Judaism after about 400 B.C.E., they had a Bible consisting of their own edition of the Pentateuch (Torah) and a temple on Mount Gerizim, which was later destroyed by John Hyrcanus (128 B.C.E.) (Matt. 10:5; Luke 9:52; John 4:20–21). Jesus discussed correct worship with a woman at Jacob's well in Samaria (John 4:5–42) and made a "good Samaritan" the hero of a famous parable (Luke 10:29–37).

sanctuary A holy place dedicated to the worship of a god and believed to confer personal security to those who took refuge in it. Solomon's Temple on Mount Zion in Jerusalem was such a sacred edifice, although Jeremiah denounced those who trusted in its power to save a disobedient people from punishment (Jer. 7, 26).

Sanhedrin The supreme judicial council of the Jews from about the third century B.C.E. until the Romans destroyed Jerusalem in 70 C.E. Its deliberations were led by the High Priest (2 Chron. 19:5–11). Jesus was tried before the Sanhedrin and condemned on charges of blasphemy (Matt. 26:59; Mark 14:55; 15:1; Luke 22:66; John 11:47). Stephen was stoned as a result of its verdict (Acts 6:12–15). Peter, John, and other disciples were hailed before its court (Acts 4:5–21; 5:17–41), and Paul was charged there with violating the Mosaic Torah (Acts 22).

Sarah The wife and half-sister of Abraham (Gen. 11:29; 16:1; 20:12). Sarah traveled with Abraham from Ur to Haran and ultimately to Canaan and after a long period of barrenness bore him a single son, Isaac (Gen. 18:9–15; 21:1–21). She died in Hebron (Gen. 23:2) and was buried at Machpelah in Canaan (Gen. 23:19; see also Rom. 4:9; Heb. 11:11; 1 Pet. 3:6).

Sardis Capital of the kingdom of Lydia (modern Turkey), captured by Cyrus the Great (546 B.C.E.); later part of the Roman province of Asia and the site of a cult of Cybele, a pagan fertility goddess (Rev. 3:1–6).

Satan In the Hebrew Bible, "the satan" appears as a prosecutor in the heavenly court among "the sons of God" (Job 1–2; Zech. 3:1–3) and only later as a tempter (1 Chron. 21:1; cf. 2 Sam. 24:1). Although the Hebrew Bible says virtually nothing about Satan's origin, the pseudepigraphal writings contain much legendary material about his fall from heaven and the establishment of a hierarchy of demons and devils. By the time the New Testament was written, he was believed to head a kingdom of evil and to seek the corruption of all people, including the Messiah (Matt.

4:1–11; Luke 4:1–13). Satan ("the opposer" or the "adversary") is also "the evil one" (Matt. 6:13; 13:19; Eph. 6:16; 1 John 2:13; 5:18–19), "the devil" (Matt. 4:1; 13:39; 25:41; John 8:44; Eph. 4:27), and the primordial serpent who tempted Eve (Rev. 12:9).

Saul Son of Kish, a Benjaminite, and the first king of Israel (c. 1020–1000 B.C.E.). Saul was anointed by Samuel to meet the Philistine crisis, which demanded a strong centralized leadership (1 Sam. 9:1–10:27). He defeated the Ammonites (1 Sam. 11:1–11) and Philistines at Geba and Michmash but rapidly lost support after antagonizing Samuel (1 Sam. 13:8–15) and refusing to kill the Amalekite king (1 Sam. 15:7–35). He was also upstaged by David, of whom he became intensely jealous (1 Sam. 18:6–24; 23). Saul and his son Jonathan were killed by the Philistines at the Battle of Gilboa (1 Sam. 31) and commemorated by one of David's most beautiful psalms (2 Sam. 1:17–27).

Savior One who saves from danger or destruction, a term applied to Yahweh in the Hebrew Bible (Ps. 106:21; Isa. 43:1–13; 63:7–9; Hos. 13:4) and to Jesus in the New Testament (Luke 2:11; John 4:42; Acts 5:31; 13:23; Phil. 3:20; 1 Tim. 4:10; 2 Tim. 1:10; 1 John 4:14).

scapegoat According to Leviticus 16, a sacrificial goat upon whose head Israel's high priest placed the people's collective sins on the Day of Atonement, after which the goat was sent out into the desert to Azazel (possibly a demon). The term has come to signify anyone who bears the blame for others (see Isa. 53).

scribes Professional copyists who recorded commercial, royal, and religious texts and served as clerks, secretaries and archivists at Israel's royal court and temple (2 Kings 12:10; 19:2; Ezra 4:8; 2 Chron. 34:8; Jer. 36:18). After the Jews' return from exile, professional teachers or "wise men" preserved and interpreted the Mosaic Torah (Ezra 7:6; Neh. 7:73–8:18). In the New Testament, scribes are often linked with Pharisees as Jesus' opponents (Matt. 7:29; 23:2, 13; Luke 11:44) who conspired to kill him (Mark 14:43; 15:1; Luke 22:2; 23:10), although some became his followers (Matt. 8:19; see also Acts 6:12; 23:9; 1 Cor. 1:20).

scripture A writing or collection of documents that a religion holds to be sacred and binding upon its adherents. The Hebrew Bible (Old Testament) is Scripture to both Jews and Christians; only Christians accord the status of Scripture to the New Testament.

scroll A roll of papyrus, leather, or parchment such as those on which the Hebrew Bible and New Testament

were written. The rolls were made of sheets about nine to eleven inches high and five or six inches wide, sewed together to make a strip up to twenty-five or thirty feet long, which was wound around a stick and unrolled when read (Isa. 34:4; Rev. 6:14; Jer. 36).

Scythians A fierce nomadic people from north and east of the Black Sea who swept southward toward Egypt and Judah about 626 B.C.E. Jeremiah prophesied that Judah would be devastated (Jer. 4:5–31; 5:15–17; 6:1–8, 22–26), and Zephaniah saw the invasion as a sign that the Day of Yahweh had arrived (Zeph. 1:7–8, 14–18); but the Scythians were bribed by Pharaoh Psammetichus I (664–610 B.C.E.) and returned north by the coastal route without attacking Palestine.

Second Coming The return of the risen Jesus to earth; also called the Parousia, from the Greek *Parousia* (a standing by). The Synoptic authors use this term to denote Jesus' supernatural reappearance to establish the kingdom of God (Matt. 24; Mark 13; Luke 21).

Seleucids The Macedonian Greek dynasty founded by Alexander's general Seleucus (ruled 312–280 B.C.E.), centered in Syria with Antioch as its capital. After defeating the Ptolemies of Egypt, it controlled Palestine from 198 to 165 B.C.E., after which the Maccabean revolt defeated the forces of Antiochus IV and eventually drove the Syrians from Judea (142 B.C.E.) (1 and 2 Macc.)

Semites According to Genesis 10:21–31, peoples descended from Noah's son Shem, whose progeny included Elam, Asshur, Arpacshad (Hebrews and Arabs), Lud (Lydians), and Aram (Syrians) (Gen. 10:22). In modern usage, the term applies to linguistic rather than to racial groups, such as those who employ one of a common family of inflectional languages, including Akkadian, Aramaic, Hebrew, and Arabic.

Septuagint (LXX) A Greek translation of the Hebrew Bible traditionally attributed to seventy or seventy-two Palestinian scholars during the reign of Ptolemy II (285–246 B.C.E.), but actually the work of several generations of Alexandrine translators, begun about 250 B.C.E. and not completed until the first century C.E. The later additions to the Septuagint were deleted from the standard Hebrew Bible (Masoretic Text) but included in the Christian Scriptures as the Apocrypha.

serpent A common symbol in Near Eastern fertility cults, the original tempter of humanity (Gen. 3–4), and a symbol of Assyria, Babylon (Isa. 27:1), and the Israelite tribe of Dan (Gen. 49:17). A bronze image of a snake that was used to heal the Israelites during a plague of snakes in the wilderness (Num. 21:4–9) was later destroyed by King Hezekiah (2 Kings 18:4). Revelation 12:9 identifies the serpent with the devil and Satan (the primordial Dragon).

Shema Judaism's supreme declaration of monotheistic faith, expressed in the words of Deuteronomy 6:4–9 beginning "Listen (Hebrew *shema*, "hear"), Israel, Yahweh our God is the one Yahweh." The complete Shema also includes Deuteronomy 11:13–21 and Numbers 14:37–41 (cf. Mark 12:29–34).

Sheol According to the Hebrew Bible, the subterranean region to which the "shades" of all the dead descended, a place of intense gloom, hopelessness, and virtual unconsciousness for its inhabitants. The term was translated *Hades* in the Greek Septuagint. In later Hellenistic times, it was regarded as an abode of the dead awaiting resurrection (Gen. 42:38; 1 Sam. 2:6; Job. 7:9; 14:13–14; 26:6; Pss. 6:5; 16:10; 55:15; 139:8; Prov. 27:20; Eccles. 9:10; Isa. 14:15; 28:15; 38:10, 18; Hos. 13:14; Jon. 2:2; cf. references to Hades in Matt. 16:18; Luke 10:15; Acts 2:31; Rev. 1:18; 20:15). It is *not* the same theological concept as hell or Gehenna (Matt. 10:28; 23:33; Mark 9:43; Luke 12:5).

Signs Gospel A hypothetical early Christian document describing seven of Jesus' miraculous acts; according to one theory, it forms the principal source for John's Gospel.

Silas The Semitic, perhaps Aramean, name of an early Christian prophet (Acts 15:32), otherwise called Silvanus, who accompanied Barnabas and Paul to Antioch with decrees from the Jerusalem council (Acts 15:1–35) and who joined Paul on his second missionary journey (Acts 16–18; 1 Thess. 1:1, 2 Thess. 1:1). He may have been the author of 1 Peter (1 Pet. 5:12).

Simeon

1. Another name for Simon Peter (Acts 15:14; 2 Pet. 1:1).

2. The devout old man who recognized the infant Jesus as the promised Messiah (Luke 2:22–34).

simile A comparison using "like" or "as," usually to illustrate an unexpected resemblance between a familiar object and novel idea. Jesus' parables about the kingdom of God are typically cast as similes (Matt. 13:31–35, 44–50; Mark 4:26–32; Luke 13:18–19).

Simon The name of several New Testament figures:

1. Simon Peter (Matt. 4:18; 10:2).

2. One of the Twelve Apostles, Simon the Canaanite (Matt. 10:4; Mark 3:18), perhaps a nationalist Zealot (Luke 6:15; Acts 1:13).

3. One of Jesus' "brothers" (Matt. 13:55; Mark 6:3).

4. A leper whom Jesus cured (Mark 14:3–9).

5. The man from Cyrene in North Africa who was forced to carry Jesus' cross (Mark 15:21).

6. A Pharisee who entertained Jesus in his home (Luke 7:36–50).

7. Simon Iscariot, father of Judas the traitor (John 6:71; 13:26).

8. A leather tanner of Joppa with whom Peter stayed (Acts 9:43; 10).

Simon Magus A Samaritan sorcerer ("magus") who tried to buy the power of the Holy Spirit from Peter (Acts 8:9–24); thought by some to be the forerunner of the Faust figure. The sale of church offices is known as *simony*, after Simon Magus.

Sitz-im-Leben In form criticism, the social and cultural environment out of which a particular biblical unit grew and developed; German, "setting in life."

Smyrna An Aegean port city of western Asia Minor (Turkey), site of an early Christian church that the author of Revelation praises for its poverty and faithfulness (Rev. 1:11; 2:8–10).

Sodom Along with Gomorrah, Admah, Zebolim, and Zoar (Gen. 13:10–12; 14:2; Deut. 29:23), one of the "five cities of the plain" (near the south shore of the Dead Sea) destroyed by a great cataclysm attributed to Yahweh (Gen. 19:1–29). Abraham, who had been royally welcomed by Sodom's king (Gen. 14:13–24), pleaded for it to be spared (Gen. 18:16–32). Contrary to legend, its sins were regarded as violence and inhospitality to strangers rather than homosexuality. Later Bible writers cite it as a symbol of divine judgment upon wickedness (Isa. 3:9; Lam. 4:6; Matt. 10:15; 2 Pet. 2:6; Jude 7; Rev. 11:8).

Solomon Son of David and Bathsheba and Israel's third king (c. 961–922 B.C.E.) (2 Sam. 12:24–25), who inherited the throne through David's fondness and the intrigues of his mother and the prophet Nathan (1 Kings 1:9–2:25). He became famous for his wisdom (1 Kings 3:5–28) but left his people financially exhausted and politically discontented (1 Kings 11:41–12:25). An idealized account of his reign is given in 2 Chronicles 1–9.

Solomon's Porch A magnificent covered colonnade built along the east side of Herod's Temple in Jerusalem in which Jesus walked (John 10:23); the site of several apostolic miracles (Acts 3:11; 5:12).

Son of Man

1. A Hebrew Bible phrase used to denote a human being (Pss. 8:4; 80:17; 144:3; 146:3; Isa. 56:2; Jer. 51:43), including a plural usage (Pss. 31:19; 33:13; Prov. 8:4; Eccles. 3:18–19; 8:11; 9:12). The phrase is characteristic of the Book of Ezekiel, where it is commonly used to indicate the prophet himself (Ezek. 2:1).

2. In Daniel 7:12–14, a reference—"one like a [son of] man"—to Israel itself or to a divinely appointed future ruler of Israel, although this figure is not given specific messianic significance.

3. In certain pseudepigraphal writings, particularly the Similitudes of the Book of Enoch, he who serves as Yahweh's agent in the coming Day of Judgment, variously called "the Elect One," "the Anointed One," and "the Son of Man."

4. In the Gospels, a phrase always spoken by Jesus and in most cases applied to himself (Matt. 8:20; 9:6; 11:19; 12:8; 16:27–28; 19:28; 24:30; 28:31; Mark 2:28; 8:38; 9:31; 10:45; 13:26; Luke 12:8–10; 18:8; 21:27; 22:22; John 3:14). Outside the Gospels, it is used only once (Acts 7:56), although the author of Revelation echoes Daniel 7:13 (Rev. 14:14).

sons of thunder (see **thunder, sons of**)

soul In Hebrew, *nephesh* (breath), meaning the quality of being a living creature, applied to both humans and animals (Gen. 1:20; 2:7; 2:19; 9:4; Exod. 1:5; 1 Chron. 5:21). Nephesh was translated *psyche* in the Greek Septuagint, the same term used (commonly for "life" rather than the immortal personality) in the New Testament (Matt. 10:28; 16:26; Acts 2:27; 3:23; Phil. 1:27; Rev. 20:4).

source criticism The analysis of a document to discover its written sources. See *form criticism*.

Stephen A Hellenistic Jew of Jerusalem who was stoned for his Christian heresy (Acts 6:8–60), thus becoming the first martyr of the early church. The name means "royal" or "crown."

Stoicism A Greek philosophy that became popular among the upper classes in Roman times. Stoicism emphasized duty, endurance, self-control, and service to the gods, the family, and the state. Its adherents believed in the soul's immortality, rewards and punishments after death, and a divine force (providence) that directs human destiny. Paul encountered Stoics when

preaching in Athens (Acts 17:18–34), and Stoic ideas appear in Ecclesiastes, the Wisdom of Solomon, Proverbs, John 4:23 and 5:30, James 1:10, and 1 Peter 2:17.

symbol In its broadest usage, anything that stands for something else; from the Greek *symbolon*, a "token" or "sign," and *symballein*, to "throw together" or "compare." For example, the star of David is a symbol of Judaism, and the cross is a symbol of Christianity. The use of symbols characterizes prophetic and apocalyptic writing. In Daniel, for example, wild beasts symbolize pagan nations; in Ezekiel, Yahweh's presence is symbolized by his radiant "glory."

synagogue In Judaism, a gathering of no fewer than ten adult males assembled for worship, scriptural instruction, and administration of local Jewish affairs. Synagogues probably began forming during the Babylonian exile when the Jerusalem Temple no longer existed. Organization of such religious centers throughout the Diaspora played an important role in the faith's transmission and survival. The synagogue liturgy included lessons from the Torah, the Prophets, the Shema, Psalms, and eighteen prayers.

syncretism The blending of different religions, a term Bible scholars typically apply to the mingling of Canaanite rites and customs (Baalism) with the Israelites' Mosaic faith. Although the practice was repeatedly denounced by the prophets (Judg. 2:13; 3:7; 6:31; 8:33; 1 Kings 16:31; 18:26; 2 Kings 10:18; Jer. 2:8; 7:9; 19:5; 23:13; Hos. 2:8), Judaism borrowed many of its characteristic forms, psalms, concepts, and religious rituals from earlier Canaanite models.

Synoptic Problem A term referring to scholars' attempts to discover the literary relationship among the three strikingly similar Synoptic Gospels: Mark, Matthew, and Luke.

Synoptics The first three Gospels, so named because they share a large quantity of material in common, allowing their texts to be viewed together "with one eye."

Syro-Phoenician A woman living near the Phoenician cities of Tyre and Sidon whose daughter Jesus healed (Matt. 15:21–28; Mark 7:24–30).

Tabernacle The portable tent-shrine, elaborately decorated, that housed the ark of the covenant (Exod. 25–31; 35–40; Num. 7–9) from the Exodus to the building of Solomon's Temple (1 Kings 6–8); used in both the Hebrew and Christian Bibles as a symbol of

God's presence with humanity (Num. 9:5; Deut. 31:15; Pss. 15:1; 43:3; 61:4; 132:7; Isa. 4:6; 33:20; Hos. 12:9; Acts 7:46; Heb. 8:2; 9:11; 2 Pet. 1:14; Rev. 21:3).

Talmud A huge collection of Jewish religious traditions consisting of two parts: (1) the Mishnah (written editions of ancient oral interpretations of the Torah), published in Palestine by Judah ha-Nasi (died about 220 C.E.) and his disciples; (2) the Gemara, extensive commentaries on the Mishnah. The Palestinian version of the Talmud, which is incomplete, was produced about 450 C.E.; the Babylonian Talmud, nearly four times as long, was finished about 500 C.E. Both Talmuds contain Mishnah and Gemara.

Tanak A term designating the three divisions of the Hebrew Bible: *T* for Torah (Law, or Instruction), *N* for Nevi'im (Prophets), and *K* for Kethuvim (Writings).

Targum Interpretative translations of the Hebrew Bible into Aramaic, such as that made by Ezra after the Jews' return from the Babylonian exile (Neh. 8:1–18). The practice may have begun in the postexilic synagogues, where Hebrew passages were read aloud and then translated into Aramaic with interpretative comments added.

Tarsus Capital of the Roman province of Cilicia (southeastern Turkey) and birthplace of Paul (Saul) (Acts 9:11; 11:25; 21:39; 22:3); a thriving commercial center in New Testament times.

Temple

1. The imposing structure built by King Solomon (using Phoenician architects and craftsmen) on Mount Zion in Jerusalem to house the ark of the covenant in its innermost room (the Holy of Holies) (1 Kings 5:15–9:25). Later recognized as the only authorized center for sacrifice and worship of Yahweh, it was destroyed by Nebuchadnezzar's troops in 587 B.C.E. (2 Kings 25:8–17; 2 Chron. 36: 18–19).

2. The Second Temple, rebuilt by Jews returned from the Babylonian exile under Governor Zerubbabel, dedicated about 515 B.C.E. (Ezra 1:1–11; 3:1–13; 4:24–6:22; Hag. 1–2; Zech. 1:1–8:13).

3. Herod's splendid Temple replaced the inferior edifice of Zerubbabel's time and took nearly a half-century to complete (John 2:20). Jesus, who visited the Temple as a child (Luke 2:22–38, 41–50) and often taught there (Matt. 21:23–24:1; Luke 20:1; John 7:14–52; 10:22–39), assaulted its moneychangers (Matt. 21:12–17; Mark 11:15–19; Luke 19:45–46; John 2:13–22) and prophesied its destruction (Matt. 24:1–2; Mark 13:1–4; Luke 21:5–7),

which was fulfilled when the Romans sacked Jerusalem in 70 C.E. Until that event, the apostles continued to preach and worship there (Acts 3:1–26; 5:42; 21:26–22:29).

testament Either of the two main divisions of the Bible—the Old Testament (canonical Hebrew Scriptures) and the New Testament (Christian Greek Scriptures); from the Latin for "covenant."

tetragrammaton The four consonants (YHWH) comprising the sacred name Yahweh, the God of Israel. Although the name appears nearly 7000 times in the canonical Hebrew Bible, some modern Bible translations continue the Jewish practice of inaccurately rendering it as "the Lord."

textual criticism Comparison and analysis of ancient manuscripts to discover copyists' errors and, if possible, to reconstruct the true or original form of the document; also known as "lower criticism."

Thaddeus One of the most obscure of Jesus' apostles, listed among the Twelve in Matthew 10:3 and Mark 3:18 but not in Luke 7:16 or Acts 1:13.

theodicy A literary work that attempts to explain how an all-good, all-powerful god can permit the existence of evil and undeserved suffering; from a Greek term combining "god" and "justice." Job, 2 Peter, and 2 Esdras contain notable theodicies.

theology The study and interpretation of concepts about God's nature, will, and intentions toward humanity; from the Greek *theos*, meaning "god," and *logos*, reason.

theophany An appearance of a god to a person, as when El wrestled with Jacob (Gen. 32:26–32), Yahweh appeared to Moses (Exod. 3:1–4:17; 6:2–13) and the elders of Israel (Exod. 24:9–11), or the resurrected Jesus revealed himself to Thomas (John 20:24–29) and Paul (Acts 9:3–9).

Theophilus The otherwise unknown man to whom the Gospel of Luke and the Book of Acts are addressed. He may have been a Roman official who became a Christian.

Thessalonica A major Macedonian city (modern Thessaloniki) where Paul and Silas converted "some" Jews, "many" Greeks and "Godfearers," and numerous "rich women" to Christianity (Acts 17:1–9). Paul later revisited it (1 Cor. 16:5) and wrote his earliest surviving letter to its congregation (1 Thess.).

Thomas One of the Twelve Apostles (Matt. 10:3; Mark 3:18; Luke 6:15; Acts 1:13) seldom mentioned in the Synoptics but relatively prominent in the Fourth Gospel, where he is called Didymus ("twin") (John 11:16; 20:24; 21:2). Thomas doubted the other disciples' report of Jesus' resurrection, but when suddenly confronted with the risen Jesus, he pronounces the strongest confession of faith in the Gospel (John 20:24–29). He is the reputed author of the apocryphal Gospel of Thomas.

thunder, sons of An epithet (Boanerges) applied to the apostles James and John (Mark 3:17), possibly because of their impulsive temperaments (Luke 9:52–56).

Thyatira A city of ancient Lydia in Asia Minor (modern Turkey), original home of Lydia, Paul's first European convert (Acts 16:14) and one of the seven churches of Asia in Revelation 2:18–19.

Tiberias A city on the western shore of the Sea of Galilee founded by Herod Antipas and named after the Emperor Tiberius; a well-known spa in Jesus' day.

Tiberius (Tiberius Claudius Nero) Stepson of Augustus and second emperor of Rome (14–37 C.E.). According to Luke 3:1, Jesus came to John for baptism in the fifteenth year of Tiberius's reign. Except for Luke 2:1, he is the Caesar referred to in the Gospels (Matt. 22:17; Mark 12:14; Luke 20:22; John 19:12).

Timothy Younger friend and fellow missionary of Paul, who called him "beloved son" (1 Cor. 4:17; 1 Tim. 1:2–28; 1 Tim. 1:2), Timothy was the son of a Greek father and a devout Jewish mother (Acts 16:1; 2 Tim. 1:5). To please the Jews, Paul circumcised Timothy before taking him on his second evangelical tour (Acts 16:1–4; 20:1–4). Paul later sent him to Macedonia (1 Thess. 3:6) and thence to Corinth to quiet the dissension there (Acts 19:22; 1 Cor. 4:17; 16:11), which he failed to do (2 Cor. 7:6, 13–14; 8:6, 16, 23; 12:18). The picture of Timothy in the pastoral Epistles seems irreconcilable with what is known of him from Acts and Paul's genuine letters.

tithe A tenth of one's income paid in money, crops, or animals to support a government (1 Sam. 8:15–17) or religion (Lev. 27:30–33; Num. 18:24–28; Deut. 12:17–19; 14:22–29; Neh. 10:36–38); also, to pay such a part. In Israel, the High Priest, the Levites, and Temple upkeep were supported by required levies. Abraham is reported to have paid Melchizedek tithes (Gen. 14:20; see also Heb. 7:2–6), Jesus regarded tithing as an obligation of his people (Luke 11:42; 12:13–21; 18:12).

Titus A Greek whom Paul converted and who became a companion on his missionary journeys (2 Cor. 8:23; Gal. 2:1–3; Titus 1:4). Titus effected a reconciliation between Paul and the Corinthians (2 Cor. 7:5–7; 8:16–24; 12:18). A post-Pauline writer makes him the type of the Christian pastor (Titus 1–3).

Titus, Flavius Sabinius Vespasianus Son and successor of Vespasian and emperor of Rome (79–81 C.E.); he directed the siege of Jerusalem, which culminated in the destruction of the city and Herodian Temple in 70 C.E. His carrying of the Temple treasures to Rome is commemorated in the triumphal Arch of Titus that still stands in the Roman Forum.

tongues, speaking in An ecstatic phenomenon of the early church (Acts 2:1–45), presented at first as a miraculous and intelligible speaking and understanding of foreign languages by those who did not know these tongues (Acts 2:5–12) but later criticized by Paul as an inferior spiritual gift (1 Cor. 12–14); also called *glossolalia*.

Torah The Pentateuch (the first five books of the Hebrew Bible) and in a general sense all the Hebrew canonical writings, which are traditionally regarded as a direct oracle, or revelation, from Yahweh. *Torah* is a Hebrew term usually translated "law," "instruction," or "teaching."

tradition

1. Collections of stories and interpretations transmitted orally from generation to generation and embodying the religious history and beliefs of a people or community. Traditions of the patriarchs were eventually compiled in narratives by Israel's earliest historians and finally incorporated into the first book of the Torah.

2. Oral explanations, interpretations, and applications of the written Torah (1 Chron. 4:22; Mark 7:5, 9; Matt. 15:2; Gal. 1:15), many of which were eventually compiled in the Mishnah.

3. Recollections and interpretations concerning Jesus that circulated orally through various early Christian churches and some of which were included in the Gospel narratives (1 Cor. 15:1–8; 2 Thess. 2:15).

tradition criticism Analysis of the origin and development of specific biblical themes—such as the Exodus motif in the Tanak and the eschatology of the kingdom of God in the New Testament—as presented by different Bible writers. In some cases, tradition criticism emphasizes the early and oral stages of development.

Trajan (Marcus Ulpius Nerva Trajanus) Emperor of Rome (98–117 C.E.) who was born in Spain about 53 C.E., became a successful military leader, and brought the Roman Empire to its greatest extent, annexing Dacia, Armenia, Mesopotamia, Assyria, and Arabia. Probably following the policies of Vespasian (69–79 C.E.), he conducted a persecution of Christians, although he wrote to Pliny the Younger, governor of Bithynia, that Christians were not to be sought out or denounced anonymously.

Transfiguration According to the Synoptic Gospels, a supernatural transformation of Jesus into a being of light, witnessed by Jesus' three closest disciples—Peter, James, and John—on an isolated mountaintop. In this awesome revelation of Jesus' divinity, the Hebrew Bible figures Elijah and Moses also appear (Matt. 17:1–13; Mark 9:2–13; Luke 9:28–36).

Trinity The post–New Testament doctrine that God exists as three divine Persons in One—Father, Son, and Holy Spirit. After heated ecclesiastical debate on the subject had seriously divided the church, Constantine, the first Christian emperor of Rome but then unbaptized, called a council of church leaders in Nicaea to define the doctrine (325 C.E.). The council decreed the orthodoxy of the trinitarian formula, so that the mystery of Trinity in unity (although still opposed by Arian Christians) eventually became central to the Christian faith (Matt. 28:19–20; 2 Cor. 13:14; Gal. 1:1–5).

Twelve, the The Twelve Apostles whom Jesus specifically chose to follow him. Different names appear on different New Testament lists of the Twelve (Matt. 10:1–5; Mark 3:16–19; Luke 6:12–16; Acts 1:13–14).

Tychicus A loyal helper and companion of Paul who accompanied him through the Roman province of Asia on his third missionary journey (Acts 20:4). Tychicus delivered letters to the Colossians (Col. 4:7–9) and Ephesians (Eph. 6:21).

typology A form of biblical interpretation in which the narratives and teachings of the Hebrew Bible (Old Testament) and viewed as prophetic types or patterns for what Jesus was later to say and do.

Tyre An ancient Phoenician seaport famous for its commerce and wealth, originally built on a small offshore island about twenty-five miles south of Sidon. King Solomon made an alliance with its ruler, Hiram, the skills of whose architects and craftsmen he utilized in constructing the Jerusalem Temple (1 Kings 5:15–32; 7:13–51). Its power and luxury were later denounced by the prophets (Isa. 23; Ezek. 26–28; Amos 1:19–20; Zech. 9:3–4). Alexander the Great sacked the city in 332 B.C.E., although it had been rebuilt by Jesus' day (Mark 7:24–31; Luke 3:8).

veil, the The elaborately decorated curtain separating the Holy Place from the Most Holy Place in the Tabernacle and Jerusalem Temple (Exod. 26:31–37, which was reputedly rent in two at Jesus' crucifixion (Matt. 27:51; Heb. 6:19; 9–10).

Vespasian Emperor of Rome (69–79 C.E.) who led Roman legions into Judea during the Jewish Revolt (66–73 C.E.), the siege of Jerusalem passing to his son Titus when Vespasian became emperor.

Vulgate Jerome's Latin translation of the Bible (late fourth century C.E.), including the Apocrypha, which became the official version of Roman Catholicism.

Weeks, Feast of See *Pentecost*.

wisdom literature Biblical works dealing primarily with practical and ethical behavior and ultimate religious questions, such as the problem of evil. The books include Proverbs, Job, Ecclesiastes, Ecclesiasticus, and the Wisdom of Solomon. Habakkuk, 2 Esdras, and the New Testament Book of James also have characteristics of Wisdom writing.

woes, seven messianic The series of seven condemnations of scribes and Pharisees attributed to Jesus when he was rejected by official Judaism (Matt. 23:13–32).

Word

1. The "word" or "oracle" of Yahweh, a phrase characteristic of the Hebrew prophets, typically referring to a divine pronouncement, judgment, or statement of purpose that the prophet delivers in his God's name.

2. The preincarnate Jesus (John 1:1–3). See *Logos*.

Yahweh A translation of the sacred name of Israel's God, represented almost 7000 times in the canonical Hebrew Bible by the four consonants of the tetragrammaton (YHWH). According to Exodus 6:2–4, it was revealed for the first time to Moses at the burning bush; according to another account, it was used from the time of Enosh before the Flood (Gen. 4:26). Scholars have offered various interpretations of the origin and meaning of the divine name. According to a widely accepted theory, it is derived from the Hebrew verb "to be" and means "He is" or "He causes to be," implying that Yahweh is the maker of events and shaper of history.

Yom Kippur See *Atonement, Day of*.

Zealots An extremely nationalistic Jewish party dedicated to freeing Judea from foreign domination that coalesced about 67–68 C.E. during the great rebellion against Rome (66–73 C.E.). According to Josephus's possibly biased account, their intransigence led to the destruction of Jerusalem and the Temple. The Simon of Luke 6:15 and Acts 1:13 is called a "Zealot."

Zebedee A Galilean fisherman, husband of Salome, and father of the apostles James and John (Matt. 27:56; Mark 1:19–20; 3:17; 14:33; 15:40).

Zechariah

1. A Judean priest married to Elizabeth, a descendant of Aaron, whose long childless marriage was blessed in old age by the birth of the future John the Baptist (Luke 1:5–25, 57–80; 3:2). A vision foretelling the birth rendered Zechariah temporarily paralyzed, but he recovered his speech in time to name the child and to utter a prayer of thanksgiving—the Benedictus (Luke 1:67–79).

2. A Jewish martyr mentioned in Jesus' phrase "from Abel to Zecharias" (Matt. 23:35; Luke 11:51), usually identified with Zechariah, son of Jehoiada in 2 Chronicles 24:20–24.

Zeus In Greek mythology, the son of Cronus and Rhea, king of the Olympian gods, and patron of civic order. A personification of storm and other heavenly powers, he ruled by wielding the lightning bolt. The Romans identified him with Jupiter (Jove). Some people of Lystra compared Barnabas to Zeus and Paul to Hermes (Acts 14:12). The erection of a statue of Zeus in the Jerusalem Temple courts helped spark the Maccabean revolt (c. 168 B.C.E.).

Zion The name, probably meaning "citadel," for a rocky hill in old Jerusalem, originally a Jebusite acropolis that David captured and upon which he built his palace and housed the ark of the covenant (Judg. 19:11–12; 2 Sam. 5:6–12; 6:12–17; 1 Chron. 11:5–8).

Zoroastrianism A dualistic religion established by the east Iranian prophet Zoroaster in about the late sixth century B.C.E. Zoroaster saw the universe as a duality of Spirit and Matter, Light and Darkness, Good and Evil. The present age witnesses the conflict between Ahura-Mazda, a deity of light, and his evil spirit opponents. This conflict eventually will culminate in a cosmic battle in which good finally triumphs. Zoroastrian ideas about angels, demons, and the end of the present world appear to have influenced both Jewish and Christian writers, particularly in the realm of apocalyptic thought.

Selected Bibliography

Bibliographic references for specific topics covered in this text are listed at the ends of individual chapters. The list below includes readily accessible reference works that will help you continue your research on the New Testament.

Dictionaries and Commentaries

Achtemeir, Paul J., ed. *Harper's Bible Dictionary,* San Francisco: Harper & Row, 1985. One of the best and most accessible of recently published Bible dictionaries.

Ackroyd, P. R., et al., eds. *The Cambridge Bible Commentary.* Cambridge: Cambridge University Press, 1972. A series of brief commentaries by British scholars.

Albright, W. F., and Freedman, D. N., eds. *The Anchor Bible.* New York: Doubleday, 1964 –. A multivolume series containing new translations of individual books of the Bible, with extensive commentary by Jewish, Roman Catholic, Protestant, and other scholars.

Brown, R. E.; Fitzmeyer, J. A.; and Murphy, R. E. *The New Jerome Biblical Commentary.* Englewood Cliffs, N.J.: Prentice-Hall, 1990. Provides theological discussions of all books in the biblical canon by leading Roman Catholic scholars.

Buttrick, George A., ed. *The Interpreter's Dictionary of the Bible,* Vols. 1 – 4 and supplementary vol. Nashville, Tenn.: Abingdon Press, 1962, 1976. Both scholarly and readable; the standard work for general readers.

Freedman, David Noel, ed. *The Anchor Bible Dictionary,* Vols. 1 – 6. New York: Doubleday, 1992. An indispensable resource.

Harvey, A. E. *The New English Bible: Companion to the New Testament.* Oxford and Cambridge: Oxford University Press and Cambridge University Press, 1979. A line-by-line commentary on the NEB translation of the New Testament.

Mays, James L., ed. *Harper's Bible Commentary.* San Francisco: Harper & Row, 1988. A scholarly, book-by-book analysis of both the Tanak and the New Testament, including the Apocrypha.

Metzger, Bruce M., ed. *The Oxford Companion to the Bible.* New York: Oxford University Press, 1993.

Interpretive commentary on biblical topics by a group of mainly British scholars.

Atlases

Aharoni, Y., and Avi-Yonah, M. *The Macmillan Bible Atlas.* New York: Macmillan, 1977. Uses numerous maps to illustrate major events in biblical history.

Rogerson, John. *Atlas of the Bible.* New York: Facts on File, 1985. A well-illustrated source of geographical and historical background on both the Hebrew Bible and the New Testament.

General Introductions

Brown, Raymond E. *An Introduction to the New Testament.* New York: Doubleday, 1997. A wonderfully thorough and scholarly approach.

Kee, Howard C. *Understanding the New Testament,* 5th ed. Englewood Cliffs, N.J.: Prentice-Hall, 1993. A scholarly, analytical approach to New Testament study.

Koester, Helmut. *Introduction to the New Testament,* Vol. 1, *History, Culture and Religion of the Hellenistic Age,* 2nd ed., 1995. Vol. 2, *History and Literature of Early Christianity.* Philadelphia: Fortress Press, 1982. An English translation of an authoritative German study; provides superb historical and cultural backgrounds to the New Testament books.

Pregeant, Russell. *Engaging the New Testament: An Interdisciplinary Introduction.* Minneapolis: Fortress Press, 1997. Applies historical, literary, and sociological theories to New Testament literature.

Parallel Gospels and Concordances

Funk, Robert W. *New Gospel Parallels,* Vols. 1 and 2. Philadelphia: Fortress Press, 1985. The first volume presents textual parallels of the Synoptics, and the second volume includes John and apocryphal Gospels.

Index

Aaron, 69, 324
Abba, 122, 220, 225, 226
abbreviations, 27
Abel, 325
abomination, 52, 122, 123, 151, 160, 181
Abraham, 49, 158, 192, 198, 247
  in Catholic Epistles, 328
  in Hebrews, 323, 324, 325
  in Paul's letters, 289, 290, 292
Abraham, Testament of, 370
Abraham's bosom, 205
Academy of Jamnia, 66, 71, 241, 367
Acts, Book of, 237–257
  Antioch in, 136
  and Apocrypha, 364
  apostles in, 114, 237–239, 240–241, 271
  ascension in, 240
  attitudes toward Roman Empire, 9, 57, 255
  and canon formation, 12
  and canon organization, 15
  Christ as fulfilling prophecy in, 238–239, 241, 242
  Christianity as continuation of Judaism in, 159, 170, 238, 239, 243, 256
  Christianity as lawful in, 166, 181, 249, 250, 252, 255–256
  Claudius' expulsion in, 215, 264
  commune in, 175, 242–243
  composition circumstances, 93, 160, 238, 241
  Cornelius episode in, 245–246, 247
  dedication of, 159–160
  discrepancies with Paul's letters, 160, 246, 247, 249, 260–262
  divine plan in, 238–239, 240, 243, 256–257
  and First Thessalonians, 274
  Greek philosophy in, 35, 251, 277
  James in, 102
  Jerusalem church founding in, 95, 105, 159, 240–243
  Jerusalem Temple in, 54, 239
  Jesus as Son of God in, 225
  John Mark in, 102

John (son of Zebedee) in, 188
John the Baptist sect in, 189
journey motif in, 159, 161
literary form/style, 8
miracles in, 238, 243, 246, 253
organization of, 237–238, 239, 240
parables in, 114
Parousia in, 180, 181, 272
and Passion, 182
Paul's conversion in, 241, 245, 255, 256, 260, 262
Paul's imprisonment in, 255–256, 291, 298, 301
Paul's independence in, 262
Paul's missionary travels in, 159, 161, 244, 246, 247, 249–255, 277, 287, 291, 299
Paul's relationship to Jerusalem church in, 249, 291
Pentecost in, 164, 175, 239, 241–242
persecution of early Christians in, 243–244, 246
Pharisees in, 66, 243, 255
and political involvement theories, 72
and postresurrection appearances, 183, 240
prayer in, 164
Sadducees in, 64, 243, 244, 246, 255
Samaritans in, 67, 172–173, 244–245
service in, 181
Stoicism in, 37
Temple destruction in, 180, 181
temptation of Jesus in, 29
Thessalonica in, 272
on Torah role in Christianity, 49, 133, 169, 246–247, 249
Zealots in, 72
Adam, 207, 268, 281, 293, 302, 305
Adonai, 48
Advocate. *See* Paraclete
Aeneid, The (Virgil), 34
afterlife
  and apocalypticism, 343, 358
  Gehenna, 95, 144, 145, 148
  in Greco-Roman religion, 36, 40, 42–43, 145
  in Greek philosophy, 34, 145, 280

in Luke, 175
in Revelation, 36, 145, 349
See also Hades; resurrection
Akiba, Rabbi, 75
Alaric the Goth, 371
alert householder parable, 152–153
Alexander the Great, 6, 29–30, 31, 34, 58
Alexandria, 12, 323
allegory, 113
Amos, Book of, 274
Ananias, 246
Andrew (apostle), 96, 97, 104, 114, 193
Andrew, Acts of, 12
angels, 98, 115, 138, 140, 153, 311
Anglican church, 22–23. *See also* King James Version
Anna, 96, 167, 169
Anna (mother of Mary), 360
Annals (Tacitus), 215
Annas, 98, 193, 208, 243
Annunciation, 168–169
anointing story, 97, 172, 206
anti-Christ, 311, 334, 335, 348, 351
Antigonus, 31
antinomianism, 290
Antioch (Pisidian), 246
Antioch (Syria), 246, 287
  and canon formation, 12, 98
  and Matthew, 9, 10, 133, 136
  and oral tradition, 87
Antiochus IV, 52–53, 123, 311
Antiquities of the Jews (Josephus), 60, 74, 102, 115, 124, 215
anti-Semitism, 95, 150
Antisthenes, 35
antitheses, 143, 150
Antonius Felix, 255
aphorisms, 9, 219, 220
Aphrodite, 36, 275
Apocalypse, Four Horsemen of the, 349
Apocalypse of Peter. *See* Peter, Apocalypse of
apocalypticism
  in Catholic Epistles, 322
  in Luke, 179, 180, 181
  in Mark, 110–111, 114, 181, 340
  in Matthew, 144, 181, 340